THE

RAIL ROAD BOOK

OF

ENGLAND.

THE

RAIL ROAD BOOK

OF

ENGLAND:

HISTORICAL, TOPOGRAPHICAL, AND PICTURESQUE;

DESCRIPTIVE

OF THE CITIES, TOWNS, COUNTRY SEATS, AND OTHER SUBJECTS
OF LOCAL INTEREST.

With a brief Sketch of the Lines in

SCOTLAND AND WALES.
VOLUME I
All Routes from London

BY

EDWARD CHURTON.

SIDGWICK & JACKSON
LONDON

Originally published in 1851 by
Edward Churton Publisher, 26, Holles Street, Cavendish Square.
Reprinted in 1973 by Sidgwick and Jackson Limited

ISBN 0 283 97944 5

Printed in Great Britain by
Lewis Reprints Ltd
member of Brown Knight & Truscott Group
London and Tonbridge
for Sidgwick and Jackson Limited
1 Tavistock Chambers, Bloomsbury Way
London, WC1A 2SG

ADVERTISEMENT.

THE first prospectus of this work was issued five years ago: it was then proposed to include every Railroad for which a Bill had passed the Legislature; but whilst the manuscript was preparing, so many new "Lines" were projected, and so many doubts entertained of the ultimate fate of several, that it was thought unadvisable to **produce** a book that in a few months might become out of date. At the **present** time no such objections exist, nearly all the main "Lines" are completed, and the branches yet unfinished are so few as to render further delay unnecessary.

The work contains every Railroad now open, and in one instance, that of the Great Northern from Peterborough to Retford, a "Line" which will not be ready for traffic for some few months.

In a literary point of view I claim for my undertaking little more than the merit of compilation. For many of my statements I am indebted to the researches of previous topographical and historical writers, a list of whose works, to obviate the necessity of incumbering my pages with references, is appended on the other side. In addition to the details thus derived, I have been much aided by the valuable information supplied by the landed proprietors in the neighbourhood of the various "Lines," in reply to upwards of four thousand applications I made at the commencement of my undertaking. For that kind and considerate assistance, I beg to return my respectful and grateful thanks; nor must I omit to acknowledge my obligations to more than one hundred and fifty of the principal country booksellers, who favoured me with local particulars of a very valuable character.

E. C.

AUGUST, 1851.

AUTHORITIES.

"Beauties of England and Wales," "Lewis's Topographical Dictionary," "John-ston's General Gazetteer," "Clarendon's History of the Rebellion," "Macaulay's History of England," "Burke's Peerage," "Landed Gentry," and other genealogical works; "Manning's Lives of the Speakers," "Lyson's Magna Britannia," "Roscoe's London and North-Western Railway," "Howitt's Visits to Remarkable Places," and "Homes and Haunts of British Poets," "White's History of Suffolk and Yorkshire," "Granville's Spas of England," "The Post-Office County Directories," "Patterson's Road Book," "Neale's Views of Gentlemen's Seats," "Ordnance Survey Maps," "Philosophical Transactions," "Aubrey's MSS.," "Grose's Antiquities," "Blore's Monumental Remains," "Camden's Britannia," "Dugdale's Monasticon," "Nash's Mansions," "Pennant's Works," "Pugin's Works," "Stothard's Monumental Effigies," "The Cyclopædias," "Manning and Bray's Surrey."

EXPLANATION OF THE ARRANGEMENT.

In the arrangement of the "Lines," it has been endeavoured to denote as clearly as possible the situation of the cities, towns, &c. The reader is in all cases supposed to be sitting with his face towards the engine, the inside marginal columns repre-senting the "Line," the left page showing the objects found to the left, the right page those to the right of the road. The bearings of the compass, N., S., E., W., &c., at the beginning of a paragraph indicate the position of the places from the station, but when different bearings are given in the same paragraph they are to be considered (unless the context reads otherwise) as from the last-mentioned in that paragraph.

PUBLISHERS' ADVERTISEMENT

~~~~~~~~~~~

VIGOROUSLY conscious of the earnest desire on the part of their valued readers to be fully acquainted with the circumstances, both bibliographical and historical, under which any book, but in particular those of a practical and informative utility, come into existence, the publishers of this present volume hasten to advise and notify purchasers and those who contemplate the purchase of Volume I of Edward Churton's *The Rail Road Book of England* that a subsequent and companion volume will be made available with all conceivable celerity which will comprise those "Lines" connecting the provincial stations and will exactly follow the formulation of Volume I by denoting all historical, topographical and picturesque aspects as well as being descriptive of cities, towns, country seats and other subjects of local interest. It is with this imminent volume in mind that the publishers, after much debate and extensive recourse to learned opinion, have decided to comprehend within this first volume the index in its entirety for both volumes. The publishers therefore humbly entreat their readers charitably to suppress any accusation with reference to illogicality of arrangement and to believe the publishers to be sincere in their attempt to allocate the components of this unique and original compendium in as lucid and practicable manner as possible. Finally, the publishers beg permission to trespass still further on their readers' good will by exhorting them to furnish their local booksellers with their esteemed orders for Volume II.

EDITOR

APRIL, 1973.

TABLE OF ROUTES

FROM LONDON TO ALL THE STATIONS

IN

ENGLAND, SCOTLAND, AND WALES.

ABBREVIATIONS.

E., Euston Square Station, page 20; F., Fenchurch Street Station, page 516; K. C., King's Cross Station, page 60; L., London Bridge Station, page 158; P., Paddington Station, page 193; S., Shoreditch Station, page 110; W., Waterloo Bridge Station, page 138.

The letters at the end of the lines refer to the station at the beginning of the line.

EXAMPLE.—Alloa. E. to Carlisle 56, thence 521 to Glasgow, thence 522 to Stirling, thence 526 to A. Should read thus: Alloa. *From* E., *Euston Station, page 20*, to Carlisle *page* 56, *from* thence *at page* 521 to Glasgow, *from* thence *at page* 522 to Stirling, *from* thence *at page* 526 to *Alloa*. The words in italics being left out to save space.

Abbey Wood. L. to, 252.

Aber. E. to Wolverhampton 40, thence 548 to Chester, thence 529 to A.

Aberdare. P. to Bristol 220, thence 531 to Cardiff, thence 532 to A.

Aberdeen. E. to Carlisle 56, thence 521 to Glasgow, thence 522 to A.

Abergele. E. to Wolverhampton 40, thence 348 to Chester, thence 529 to A.

Abernethy. To Edinburgh xvii, thence 527 to Perth, thence 526 to A.

Abingdon. P. to Didcot 210, thence 288 to A.

Abington. E. to, 58.

Accrington. E. to Newton 46, thence 396 to Manchester, thence 417 to A.

—— E. to Farrington 46, thence from Lostock Junction 400 to A.

Acklington. K. C. to, 94.

Acton. E. to, 44.

Addlestone. W. to Weybridge 142, thence 272 to A.

Adlington. E. to Rugby 32, thence 334 to Colwick, thence 374 to A.

——, Lancaster. E. to Wigan 46, thence 404 to Bolton, thence 410 to A.

Admaston. E. to Wolverhampton 40, thence 360 to A.

Ainsdale. E. to Newton 46, thence 396 to Liverpool, thence 398 to A.

Aintree. E. to Newton 46, thence 396 to Liverpool, thence 400 to A.

Alderley. E. to Crewe 42, thence 392 to A.

Aldermaston. P. to Reading 204, thence 284 to A.

Alexandria. E. to Carlisle 56, thence 521 to Glasgow, thence 520 to A.

Alford. K. C. to Peterborough 72, thence 104 to Boston, thence 510 to A.

Algerkirk. K. C. to Peterborough 72, thence 102 to A.

Allerton. K. C. to York 82, thence 442 to A.

Allesley Gate. E. to, 34.

Alloa. E. to Carlisle 56, thence 521 to Glasgow, thence 522 to Stirling, thence 526 to A.

Alne. K. C. to, 84.

Alnwick. K. C. to, 96.

Alrewas. E. to Bescott 38, thence 370 to A.

Alsagar. E. to Rugby 32, thence 336 to Colwick, thence 374 to A.

Alton. E. to Birmingham 36, thence 346 to Burton, thence 382 to Uttoxeter, thence 384 to A.

Altringham. E. to Crewe 42, thence 392 to Manchester, thence 420 to A.

Ambergate. E. to Birmingham 36, thence 346 to A.

—— E. to Rugby 32, thence 328 to Derby, thence 348 to A.

Ampthill. E. to Bletchley 28, thence 316 to A.

Andover Road. W. to, 144.

Anerley. L. to, 160.

Angmering. L. to, 168.

Annan. E. to Carlisle 56, thence 521 to A.

Apperley. E. to Rugby 32, thence 328 to Derby, thence 348 to Leeds, thence 432 to A.

Arbroath. E. to Carlisle 56, thence 521 to Glasgow, thence 522 to Guthrie Junction and A.

Arbroath. To Edinburgh xvii, thence 527 to
Perth, thence 526 to A.
Ardleigh. S. to, 134.
Ardler. E. to Carlisle, 56, thence 521 to
Glasgow, thence 522 to A.
Ardrossan. E. to Carlisle 56, thence 521 to
Glasgow, thence 520 to A.
Ardwick. E. to Newton 46, thence 396 to
Manchester, thence 420 to A.
—— E. to Crewe 42, thence 392 to Man-
chester, thence 420 to A.
Arkleley. E. to Carlisle 56, thence 476 to A.
Arksey. K. C. to, 68.
Arlsey. K. C. to, 69
Armitage. E. to Rugby 32, thence 334 to A.
Armley. E. to Rugby 32, thence 328 to
Derby, thence 348 to Leeds, thence 482 to A.
Arundel. L. to, 168.
Ash. P. to Reading 204, thence 282 to A.
—— W. to Woking 164, thence 262 to
Guildford, thence 264 to A.
Ashby-de-la-Zouch. E. to Rugby 32, thence
328 to Leicester, thence 332 to A.
Ashchurch. E. to Birmingham 36, thence
308 back to A.
—— P. to Bristol 220, thence 294 to A.
Ashford. W. to, 278.
——, Kent. L. to Reigate 164, thence 176
to A.
Ashton. E. to Crewe 62, thence 392 to
Manchester, thence 416 to A.
Ashwell. K. C. to Hitchin 68, thence 492 to A.
——, North. K. C. to Peterborough 72,
thence 478 to A.
Askern. K. C. to, 80.
Aslockton. K. C. to Grantham 74, thence
492 to A.
Aspatria. E. to Carlisle 56, thence 476 to A.
Astley. E. to Newton Junc. 46, thence 396
to A.
Atherstone. E. to Rugby 32, thence 334 to A.
Atherton. E. to Newton Junction 46, thence
396 to Kenyon, thence 406 to A.
Attleborough. S. to, 122.
Auchengray. E. to, 60.
Auchinleck. E. to Carlisle 56, thence 521
to A.
Auchterarder. E. to Carlisle 56, thence 521
to Glasgow, thence 522 to A.
Auchterhouse. E. to Carlisle 56, thence 521
to Glasgow, thence 522 to Meigle and A.
Audley End. S. to, 116.
Auldbar. E. to Carlisle 56, thence 521 to
Glasgow, thence 524 to A.
Auldgirth. E. to Carlisle 56, thence 521 to A.
Authorpe. K. C. to Peterborough 72, thence
104 to Boston, thence 512 to A.
Aycliffe. K. C. to, 88.
Aylesbury. E. to Cheddington 26, thence
312 to A.

Aynho. P. to Didcot 210, thence 288 to A.
Ayr. E. to Carlisle 56, thence 521 to
Glasgow, thence 520 to A.
Ayton. K. C. to, 100.
Bagitts. E. to Wolverhampton 40, thence
348 to Chester, thence 529 to B.
Bagworth. E. to Rugby 32, thence 378 to
Leicester, thence 332 to B.
Balbeuchly. E. to Carlisle 56, thence 521
to Glasgow, thence 522 to B.
Balcombe. L. to, 164.
Baldersby. E. to Rugby 32, thence 328 to
Derby, thence 348 to Leeds, thence 356
to B.
Baldock. K. C. to Hitchin, 68, thence 492
to B.
Baldovan. E. to Carlisle 56, thence 521 to
Glasgow, thence 524 to Meigle, thence
524 to B.
Baldragon. E. to Carlisle 56, thence 521
to Glasgow, thence 522 to Meigle and B.
Ballock. E. to Carlisle 56, thence 522 to
Glasgow, thence 519 to B.
Balsham Road. S. to Chesterford 118,
thence 496 to B. R.
Bamber Bridge. E. to Farrington 46, thence
from Lostock Hall Junction 400 to B. B.
Banbury. P. to Didcot 210, thence 288 to B.
—— E. to Bletchley 28, thence 314 to B.
Bangor. E. to Wolverhampton 40, thence
348 to Chester, thence 529 to B.
Bannockburn. E. to Carlisle 56, thence 521
to Glasgow, thence 522 to B.
Banwell. P. to, 224.
Barlaston. E. to Rugby 32, thence 334 to
Colwick, thence 374 to B.
Bardney. K. C. to Peterborough 72, thence
102 to B.
Bardon Mill. E. to Carlisle 56, thence 470
to B. M.
—— Hill. E. to Rugby 32, thence 328 to
Leicester, thence 352 to B. H.
Barford. E. to, 42.
Barnes. W. to, 276.
Barnet. K. C. to, 64.
Barnetby. K. C. to Retford, thence 424 to B.
Barnsley. E. to Birmingham 36, thence 346
to B.
—— E. to Rugby 32, thence 328 to
Derby, thence 348 to B.
Barnt Green. E. to Birmingham 36, thence
308 back to B. G.
Barnwell. E. to Blisworth 30, thence 320
to B.
Barrassie. E. to Carlisle 56, thence 521 to
Glasgow, thence 520 to B.
Barrow, Furness. E. to Preston 48, thence
412 to Fleetwood, thence by boat to Piel
472, and on to B.
—— Ash. E. to Rugby 32, thence 328 to B.

Barton Hall. K. C. to York 82, thence 444 to B.

—— Moss. E. to Newton Junction 46, thence 396 to B. M.

—— under Needham. E. to Birmingham 36, thence 346 to B.

Baschurch. E. to Wolverhampton 40, thence 360 to B.

Basford. K. C. to Grantham 74, thence 492 to Nottingham, thence 490 to B.

Basingstoke. P. to Reading 204, thence 284 to B.

—— W. to, 144.

Bath. P. to, 216.

Bathgate. To Edinburgh xvii, thence 519 to B.

Batley. E. to Crewe, 42, thence 392 to Manchester, thence 416 to B.

Bawtry. K. C. to 78.

Baxenden. E. to Newton 46, thence 396 to Manchester, thence 412 to B.

Bay Horse. E. to, 48.

Beal. K. C. to, 98.

Beattock. E. to, 58.

Beaulieu. W. to, 152.

Bebbington. E. to Crewe 42, thence 388 to B.

Bedale. K. C. to Northallerton, 86, thence 454 to B.

Bedford. E. to Bletchley 28, thence 316 to B.

Bedworth. E. to Coventry 34, thence 344 to B.

Beeston. E. to Crewe 42, thence 388 to B.

—— E. to Rugby 32, thence 378 to Kegworth, and 480 to B.

Beith. E. to Carlisle 56, thence 521 to Glasgow, thence 510 to B.

Belford. K. C. to, 98.

Bell Bush. E. to Farrington 46, thence from Lostock 400 to Skipton, and thence 434 to B.

Belmont. K. C. to, 90.

Belper. E. to Rugby 32, thence 328 to Derby, thence 348 to B.

Bempton. K. C. to Milford 82, thence 436 to Hull, thence 448 to B.

Bentley. S. to, 134.

—— E. to Lancaster, 48, thence 434 to B.

Berkeley Road. P. to Bristol 220, thence 294 to B. R.

Berkhampstead. E. to, 26.

Berwick. K. C. to, 100.

—— Sussex. L. to Hayward's Heath 164, thence 242 to B.

——, York. K. C. to Darlington 86, thence 460 to Witton, thence 462 and 456 to B.

Bescott. E. to, 38.

Betchworth. L. to Reigate 164, thence 260 to B.

Beverley. K. C. to Milford 82, thence 456 to Hull, thence 448 to B.

Bexhill. L. to Hayward's Heath 164, thence 242 to B.

Bicester. E. to Bletchley 28, thence 314 to B.

Biggleswade. K. C. to, 68.

Billing Road. E. to Blisworth 30, thence 320 to B. R.

Billingtoun. K. C. to Aycliffe 88, thence 462 to B.

Bilney. S. to Wymondham 122, thence 506 to Deerham, thence 512 to B.

Bingham. K. C. to Grantham 74, thence 492 to B.

Bingley. E. to Newton 46, thence 396 to Manchester, thence 412 to B.

—— E. to Rugby 32, thence 328 to Derby, thence 348 to Leeds, thence 432 to B.

Birkdale. E. to Newton 46, thence 396 to Liverpool, thence 398 to B.

Birkenhead. E. to Crewe 42, thence 388 to B.

Birmingham. E. to, 36.

—— P. to Bristol 220, thence 294 to B.

Bishop Briggs. E. to Carlisle 56, thence 521 to Glasgow, thence 519 to B. B.

Bishops Auckland. K. C. to Aycliffe, 88, thence 460 to B. A.

—— Stortford. S. to, 114.

Bishopstoke. W. to, 148.

Black Lane. E. to Wigan 46, thence 404 to B. L.

Blackburn. E. to Farrington 46, thence from Lostock 400 to B.

Blackford. E. to Carlisle 56, thence to Glasgow 521, thence 522 to B.

Blackheath. L. to, 252.

Blackwall. F. to, 516.

Blackwater. P. to Reading 204, thence 282 to B.

Blackwell. E. to Birmingham 36, thence 308 back to B.

—— P. to Bristol 220, thence 294 to B.

Blaydon. K. C. to Newcastle, thence 466 to B.

Blechynden. W. to, 150.

Bletchley. E. to, 28.

Blisworth. E. to, 30.

Blythe. E. to Birmingham 36, thence 346 to Burton, thence 382 to B.

Blue Pits. E. to Crewe 42, thence 392 to Manchester, thence 414 to B. P.

—— E. to Wigan 46, thence 406 to B. P.

Blyth. K. C. to Newcastle 92, thence 476 to B.

Brocklesby. K. C. to Retford 78, thence 424 to B.

Brockley Whins. K. C. to, 92.

Bromborough. E. to Crewe 42, thence 388 to B.

Bromley Cross. E. to Newton Junction 46, thence 396 to Kenyon, thence 406 to B. C.

Bromsgrove. E. to Birmingham 36, thence 308 back to B.

—— P. to Bristol 220, thence 294 to B.

Brooksby. K. C. to Peterborough 72, thence 472 to B.

Brotte. E. to Preston 48, thence 412 to Fleetwood, thence by boat to Piel 472 to B.

Brough. K. C. to Milford 82, thence 436 to B.

Broughton Astle. E. to Rugby 31, thence 328 to B. A.

——, Furness. E. to Preston 48, thence 412 to Fleetwood, thence by boat to Piel 472 to B.

——, Chester. E. to Wolverhampton 40, thence 348 to Chester, thence 530 to B.

——, Lancaster. E. to, 48.

Broughty. To Edinburgh xvii, thence 527 to Perth, thence 526 to B.

Brownhills. E. to Bescott 38, thence 370 to B. H.

Broxbourne. S. to, 112.

Broxburn. To Edinburgh xvii, thence 519 to B.

Brundall. S. to, 126.

Bubwith. K. C. to Milford 82, thence 436 to Selby, thence 440 to B.

Buckenham. S. to, 126.

Buckingham. E. to Bletchley 28, thence 314 to B.

Bulkington. E. to Rugby 32, thence 334 to B.

Bull Gill. E. to Carlisle 56, thence 476 to B. G.

Bullwell. K. C. to Grantham 74, thence 492 to Nottingham, thence 492 to B.

Burgess Hill. L. to, 166.

Burgh. K. C. to Peterborough 72, thence 104 to Boston, thence 510 to B.

Burnley. E. to Farrington 46, thence to Lostock Junction 400 to B.

——, York. K. C. to Milford 82, thence 436 to Selby, thence 440 to Market Weighton and to B.

Burnmouth. K. C. to, 100.

Burnt Mill. S. to, 114.

Burntisland. E. to Carlisle 56, thence 521 to Glasgow, thence 522 to Stirling, thence 527 to B.

—— To Edinburgh xvii, thence 527 to B.

Burrough. E. to Newton 46, thence 396 to Liverpool, thence 400 to B.

Burslem. E. to Rugby 32, thence 334 to Colwick, thence 374 to B.

Burston. S. to, 138.

Burton, Westmoreland. E. to, 50.

——, Stafford. E. to Rugby 32, thence 328 to Leicester, thence 332 to B.

—— E. to Birmingham 56, thence 346 to B.

—— Agnes. K. C. to Milford 82, thence 436 to Hull, thence 448 to B. A.

—— Salmon. K. C. to, 82.

—— Joyce. K. C. to Grantham 74, thence 492 to Nottingham, thence 480 to B. J.

Bury, Lancaster. E. to Wigan 46, thence 406 to B.

—— E. to Newton 46, thence 396 to Manchester, thence 412 to B.

—— Lane. E. to Newton Junction 46, thence 396 to B. L.

—— St. Edmund's. S. to Haughley 136, thence 504 to B.

Burybrough. E. to Newton 46, thence 396 to Manchester, thence 422 to Penistone, thence 438 to B.

Bushey. E. to, 22.

Byers' Green. K. C. to Ferry Hill 88, thence 464 to B. G.

Calveley. E. to Crewe 42, thence 388 to C.

Calverley. E. to Rugby 32, thence 328 to Derby, thence 348 to Leeds, thence 432 to C.

Camberslang. E. to Carstairs 50, thence 519 to Motherwell, thence 519 to C.

Camborne. P. to Plymouth 240, thence by coach to Redruth, thence 508 to C.

Cambridge. S. to, 118.

Camden Town, 516.

Camp Hill. P. to Bristol 220, thence 294 to C. H.

—— E. to Birmingham 36, thence 308 to C. H.

Campsie. E. to Carlisle 56, thence 521, to Glasgow, thence 519 to C.

—— To Edinburgh xvii, thence 518 to C.

Candlersford. W. to Bishopstoke 148, thence 270 to C.

Canterbury. L. to Reigate 164, thence 176 to Ashford, thence 184 to C.

Capel. S. to Bentley 134, thence 504 to C.

Cardiff. P. to Bristol 220, thence by coach and ferry to Chepstow, thence 530 to C.

Cargill. E. to Carlisle 56, thence 521 to Glasgow, thence 522 to C.

Carham. K. C. to Berwick 100, thence 476 to C.

Carlisle. E. to, 56.

Carlton, Lincoln. K. C. to, 78.

——, York. K. C. to Aycliffe 88, thence 462 to C.

Carlton. K. C. to Grantham 74, thence 492 to Nottingham, thence 482 to C.

Carluke. E. to Carstairs 60, thence 519 to C.

Carnaby. K. C. to Milford 82, thence 436 to Hull, thence 448 to C.

Carnforth. E. to, 50.

Carnoustie. To Edinburgh xvii, thence 527 to Perth, thence 526 to, C.

Carnworth. E. to, 60.

Carshalton. L. to Croydon 160, thence 258 to C.

Carstairs. E. to, 60.

Castle Ashby. E. to Blisworth 50, thence 320 to C. A.

—— Bromwich. E. to Birmingham 36, thence 346 to C. B.

—— Carey. To Edinburgh xvii, thence 518 to C. C.

—— Eden. K. C. to Aycliffe 88, thence 462 to Hartlepool, thence 464 to C. E.

—— Howard. K. C. to York 82, thence 444 to C.

Castor. E. to Blisworth 30, thence 320 to C.

Caton. E. to Lancaster 48, thence 434 to C.

Cattal. K. C. to York 82, thence 442 to C.

Catterick Bridge. K. C. to Dalton 86, thence 456 to C.

Cayton. K. C. to Milford 82, thence 436 to Hull, thence 441 to C.

Cefn. E. to Wolverhampton 40, thence 360 to C.

Chapel. S. to Marks' Tey 132, thence 500 to C.

—— Town. E. to Newton Junction 46, thence 396 to Kenyon, thence 406 to C.T.

Charfield. P. to Bristol 220, thence 294 to C.

Charlton. L. to, 262.

Chatham. L. to, 256.

Chathill. K. C. to, 98.

Chatteris. S. to Cambridge 118, thence 498 to St. Ives, thence 498 to C.

Cheadle. E. to Crewe 42, thence 392 to C.

——, Stafford. E. to Rugby 32, thence 334 to Colwick, thence 374 to C.

Cheam. L. to Croydon 160, thence 258 to C.

Checquerbent. E. to Newton Junction 46, thence 396 to Kenyon, thence 406 to C.

Cheddington. E. to, 26.

Cheddleton. E. to Birmingham 36, thence 346 to Burton, thence 382 to Uttoxeter, thence 384 to C.

Chelford. E. to Crewe 42, thence 392 to C.

Chelmsford. S. to, 130.

Cheltenham. P. to Swindon 212, thence 308 to Gloucester, and thence 296 to C.

—— P. to Bristol 220, thence 294 to C.

Chepstow. P. to Bristol 220 thence by coach and ferry to Chepstow 530.

Cherry Tree. E. to Farrington 46, thence from Lostock Junction 400 to C. T.

Chertsey. W. to Weybridge 142, thence 272 to C.

Cheshunt. S. to, 112.

Chester. E. to Crewe 42, thence 388 to C.

—— E. to Wolverhampton 40, thence 360 to C.

Chesterfield. E. to Birmingham 36, thence 346 to C.

—— E. to Rugby 32, thence 328 to Derby, thence 348 to C.

Chesterford. S. to, 118.

Chester-le-Street. K. C. to Painshaw 90, thence 456 to C.

Chettisham. S. to Ely 118, thence 502 to C.

Chichester. L. to, 170.

Chilham. L. to Reigate 164, thence 176 to Ashford, thence 184 to C.

Chilvers Coten. E. to Coventry 34, thence 344 to C. C.

Chilworth. L. to Reigate 164, thence 260 to C.

Chippenham. P. to, 214.

Chirk. E. to Wolverhampton 40, thence 366 to C.

Chiswick. W. to Barnes 276, thence 280 to C.

Chorley. E. to Wigan 46, thence 404 to Bolton, thence 410 to C.

Christchurch Road. W. to, 152.

Christon Bank. K. C. to, 98.

Church. E. to Farrington 46, thence from Lostock Junction 400 to C.

—— Fenton. K. C. to, 82.

Churwell. E. to Crewe 42, thence 392 to Manchester, thence 416 to C.

Cirencester. P. to Swindon 212, thence 308 to Tetbury, thence 509 to C.

Clackmannan. E. to Carlisle 56, thence 521 to Glasgow, thence 521 to Stirling, thence 526 to C.

Clapham Common. W. to, 140.

——, York. E. to Farrington 46, thence to Lostock 400, thence 434 to C.

Claremont. W. to, 160.

Claycross. E. to Birmingham 36, thence 346 to C.

—— E. to Rugby 32, thence 378 to Derby, thence 341 to C.

Claydon, Bucks. E. to Bletchley 28, thence 314 to C.

——, Suffolk. S. to, 134.

Claypole. K. C. to, 76.

Claythorpe. K. C. to Peterborough 72, thence 104 to Boston, thence 510 to C.

Clayton Bridge. E. to Crewe 42, thence 392 to Manchester, thence 416 to C. B.

Cleckheaton. E. to Newton 46, thence 396 to Manchester, thence 414 to North Dean, thence 426 to C.

Cleeve. P. to Bristol 220, thence 294 to C.

Clevedon. P. to, 223.

Cleveland Port. K. C. to Darlington 36, thence 452 to C. P.

Cliff. K. C. to Milford 82, thence 436 to C.

Clifton, Lancaster. E. to Newton 46, thence 396 to Manchester, thence 408 to C.

——, Cumberland. E. to, 52.

Clitheroe. E. to Newton Juncton 46, thence to Kenyon, thence 408 to C.

Clocksbriggs. E. to Carlisle 56, thence 521 to Glasgow, thence 522 to C.

Closeburn. E. to Carlisle 56, thence 521 to C.

Coalbridge. E. to Carstairs 60, thence 519 to C.

Coalville. E. to Rugby 32, thence 328 to Leicester, thence 332 to C.

Cockburn's Path. K. C. to, 100.

Codnor Park. E. to Rugby 32, thence 328 to Kegworth and 420 Long Eaton, thence 488 to C. P.

Codsall. E. to Wolverhampton 40, thence 360 to C.

Colchester. S. to, 132.

Cold Roley. K. C. to Darlington 86, thence 460 to Witton, thence 462 to C. R. 456

Coldstream. K. C. to Berwick 100, thence 476 to C.

Coleshill. E. to Birmingham 36, thence 346 to C.

Colewick. K. C. to Grantham 74, thence 492 to C.

Collepsie. To Edinburgh xvii, thence 527 to Perth, thence 526 to C.

Collingham. K. C. to Newark 76, thence 484 to C.

Collin's Green. E. to Newton Junction 46, thence 396 to C. G.

Colliston. E. to Carlisle 56, thence 521 to Glasgow, thence 522 to Guthrie Junction and C.

Collumpton. P. to, 230.

Colne. E. to Farrington 46, thence from Lostock Junction 400 to C.

—— Onley. E. to Rugby 32, thence 328 to Derby, thence 348 to Leeds, thence 432 to C.

Colney Hatch. K. C. to, 64.

Colwick. E. to Rugby 32, thence 334 to C.

Colwin. E. to Crewe 42, thence 385 to C.

Colwyn. E. to Wolverhampton 40, thence 348 to Chester, thence 529 to C.

Coningsborough. K. C. to Doncaster 80, thence 458 to C.

Congleton. E. to Rugby 32, thence 334 to Colwick, thence 374 to C.

Corbridge. K. C. to Newcastle 92, thence 466 to C.

Corrway. E. to Wolverhampton 40, thence 368 to Chester, thence 529 to C.

Cooper Bridge. E. to Crewe 46, thence 392 to Manchester, thence 414 to C. B.

Cook's Bridge. L. to Hayward's Heath 164, thence 242 to C. B.

Costerphine. To Edinburgh xvii, thence 518 to C.

Coppul. E. to, 46.

Copmanthorpe. K. C. to, 82.

Corbey. K. C. to, 74.

Corsham. P. to, 216.

Cosham. W. to Bishopstoke 148, thence 268 to Fareham, thence 270 to C.

Cottingham. K. C. to Milford 82, thence 436 to Hull, thence 448 to C.

Counden Road. E. to Coventry 34, thence 344 to C.

Countesthorpe. E. to Rugby 32, thence 328 to C.

Cove. E. to Carlisle 56, thence 521 to Glasgow, thence 525 to C.

Coventry. E. to, 34.

Cowbridge. P. to Bristol 220, thence by coach and ferry to Chepstow, thence 530 to C.

Cowton. K. C. to, 86.

Coxhoe. K. C. to Aycliffe 88, thence 46 to C.

Cramlington. K. C. to, 92.

Cranwick. K. C. to Milford 82, thence 436 to Hull, thence 448 to C.

Craigo. E. to Carlisle 56, thence 521 to Glasgow, thence 522 to C.

Crawley. L. to Three Bridges 164, thence 266 to C.

Cresswell. E. to Birmingham 36, thence 346 to Burton, thence 382 to C.

Crewe. E. to, 42.

Crofthead. To Edinburgh xvii, thence 519 to C.

Criggleston. E. to Newton 46, thence 396 to Manchester, thence 414 to North Dean, thence 426 to Wakefield, thence 426 to C.

Crick. E. to, 32.

Crook. K. C. to Darlington 86, thence 460 to Witton, thence 458 to C.

Croft. K. C. to, 86.

Cromford. E. to Birmingham 36, thence 346 to Ambergate, thence 488 to C.

Crosby. E. to Newton 46, thence 396 to Liverpool, thence 398 to C.

Crossgates. E. to Carlisle 56, thence 521 to Glasgow, thence 521 to Stirling, thence 526 to C.

Cross Lane. E. to Crewe 42, thence 392 to C. L.

—— K. C. to Milford 82, thence 436 to C. L.

Cross Roads. E. to Carlisle 56, thence 521 to Glasgow, thence 524 to Meigle, thence 524 to C. R.

Crowland. K. C. to Peterborough, 72, thence 102 to C.

Croydon. L. to, 160.

Cummertrees. E. to Carlisle 56, thence 521 to C.

Cupar. To Edinburgh xvii, thence 527 to Perth, thence 526 to C.

—— E. to Carlisle 56, thence 521 to Glasgow, thence 522 to Stirling, thence 527 to C.

—— Angus. E. to Carlisle 56, thence 521 to Glasgow, thence 522 to C.

Currie. E. to, 60.

Curthwaite. E. to Carlisle 56, thence 476 to C.

Dairsie. To Edinburgh xvii, thence 527 to Perth, thence 526 to D.

Dalhousie. To Edinburgh xvii, thence 528 to D.

Dalkeith. To Edinburgh xvii, thence 528 to D.

Dalry. E. to Carlisle 56, thence 521 to Glasgow, thence 520 to D.

Dalston. E. to Carlisle 56, thence 476 to D.

Dalton. K. C. to, 86.

—— in-Furness. E. to Preston 48, thence 412 to Fleetwood, thence by boat to Piel 472, and on to D.

Darcey Lever. E. to Wigan 46, thence 404 to D. L.

Darfield. E. to Birmingham 36, thence 346 to D.

—— E. to Rugby 32, thence 328 to Rugby, thence 348 to D.

Darlington. K. C. to, 86.

Darnal. E. to Crewe 42, thence 392 to Manchester, thence 422 to D.

—— K. C. to Retford 76, thence 424 back to D.

Dartford. L. to, 254.

Darley. E. to Birmingham 36, thence 346 to Ambergate, thence 488 to D.

Darton. E. to Newton, 46, thence 396 to Manchester, thence 414 to North Dean, thence 426 to Wakefield, thence 428 to D.

Datchet. W. to, 280.

Daubhill. E. to Newton Junction 46, thence 396 to Kenyon, thence 406 to D.

Dawlish. P. to, 237.

Deal. L. to Reigate 164, thence 176 to Ashford, thence 184 to Minster, thence 190 to D.

Dean. W. to Bishopstoke 148, thence 270 to D.

Dearham. E. to Carlisle 56, thence 476 to D.

Deepcar. E. to Crewe 42, thence 392 to Manchester, thence 422 to D.

Deeping. K. C. to Peterborough 72, thence 102.

Defford. E. to Birmingham 36, thence 308 back to D.

—— P. to Bristol 220, thence 294 to D.

Denver. S. to Ely 118, thence 500 to D.

Deptford. L. to 248.

Derby. E. to Rugby 32, thence 328 to D.

—— E. to Birmingham 36, thence 346 to D.

Dereham. S. to Wymondham 122, thence 506 to D.

Derford. E. to Rugby 32, thence 328 to Leicester, thence 337 to D.

Dewsbury. E. to Crewe 42, thence 392 to Manchester, thence 414 to D.

Dialls Bridge. K. C. to Milford 82, thence 436 to D. B.

Didcot. P. to, 210.

Diggle. E. to Crewe 42, thence 392 to Manchester, thence 416 to D.

Dinting. E. to Crewe 42, thence 392 to Manchester, thence 420 to D.

Diss. S. to, 138.

Ditchford. E. to Blisworth 30, thence 320 to D.

Dixon Fold. E. to Newton 46, thence 396 to Manchester, thence 408 to D. F.

Dockers' Lane. E. to, 34.

Dogdyke. K. C. to Peterborough 72, thence 102 to D.

Doncaster. K. C. to, 80.

Donnington. E. to Stafford 41, thence 372 to D.

Dorchester. W. to, 156.

Dorking. L. to Reigate 164, thence 260 to D.

Dornock. E. to Carlisle 56, thence 521 to D.

Dover. L. to Reigate 164, thence 176 to D.

Downham. S. to Ely 118, thence 500 to D.

Drayton. L. to, 170.

Drem. K. C. to, 100.

Driffield. K. C. to Milford 82, thence 436 to Hull, thence 448 to D.

Drig. E. to Preston 48, thence 412 to Fleetwood, thence by boat to Piel 472 to D.

Droitwich. E. to Birmingham 36, thence 308 back to D.

—— P. to Bristol 220, thence 294 to D.

Drumlithie. E. to Carlisle 56, thence 521 to Glasgow, thence 522 to D.

Dubton Junction. E. to Carlisle 56, thence 521 to Glasgow, thence 522 to D.

Durlsden. E. to Crewe 46, thence 392 to Manchester, thence 416 to D.

Dudley. E. to Bescott Junction 38, and 370 to D.

Duffield. E. to Rugby 32, thence 328 to Derby, thence 348 to D.

Dullingham. S. to Chesterford 118, thence 496 to D.

Dumblane. E. to Carlisle, 56, thence 521 to Glasgow, thence 522 to D.

Dumbarton. E. to Carlisle 56, thence 521 to Glasgow, thence 520 to D.

Dumfermline. E. to Carlisle 56, thence 321 to Glasgow, thence 222 to Stirling, thence 526 to D.

Dumfries. E. to Carlisle 56, thence 521 to D.

Dunbar. K. C. to, 100.

Dunbridge. W. to Bishopstoke 148, thence 270 to D.

Dundee. E. to Carlisle 56, thence 521 to Glasgow, thence 522 to D.

—— To Edinburgh xvii, thence 527 to Perth, thence 525 to D.

Dunham. E. to Crewe 42, thence 388 to Chester, thence 390 to D.

Dunhampstead. E. to Birmingham 36, thence 306 back to D.

—— P. to Bristol 220, thence 294 to D.

Dunning. E. to Carlisle 56, thence 521 to Glasgow, thence 521 to D.

Dunkeld Road. E. to Carlisle 56, thence 521 to Glasgow, and 522 to D. R.

Dunstable. E. to Leighton 28, thence 312 to D.

Durham. K. C. to 88.

Dysart. E. to Carlisle 56, thence 521 to Glasgow, thence 521 to Stirling, thence 527 to D.

—— To Edinburgh xvii, thence 527 to D.

Ealing. P. to, 194.

Earby. E. to Farrington 46, thence from Lostock Junction 400 to E.

East Farleigh. L. to Reigate 164, thence 176 to Paddock Wood, thence 246 to E. F.

—— Fortune. K. C. to, 100.

—— Haven. To Edinburgh xvii, thence 527 to Perth, thence 525 to E. N.

—— Ville. K. C. to Peterborough 72, thence 104 to Boston, thence 510 to E. V.

—— Winch. S. to Wymondham 122, thence 506 to Dereham, thence 512 to E. W.

Eastbourne. L. to Haywards Heath 164, thence 242 to E.

Eastringdon. K. C. to Milford 82, thence 436 to E.

Eastrea. S. to Ely 118, thence 502 to E.

Eastwood. E. to Crewe 46, thence 392 to Manchester, thence 414 to E.

Eassie. E. to Carlisle 56, thence to Glasgow 521, thence 522 to E.

Ecclefechan. E. to, 58.

Eccles. E. to Newton Junction 46, thence 396 to E.

—— Road. S. to, 122.

Eckington, Worcester. E. to Birmingham 36, thence 308 back to E.

—— P. to Bristol 220, thence 294 to E.

—— , Derby. E. to Birmingham 36, thence 346 to E.

—— E. to Rugby 32, thence 328 to Derby, thence 348 to E.

Edenbridge. L. to Reigate 164, thence 176 to E.

Edinburgh. E. to, 60.

—— K. C. to, 102.

Edmonton. S. to Water Lane 112, thence 496 to E.

Elland. E. to Crewe 42, thence 392 to Manchester, thence 414 to E.

Elmswell. S. to Haighley 136, thence 504 to E.

Elmsworth. L. to, 172.

Elsenham. S. to, 116.

Elslack. E. to Farrington 46, thence from Lostock Junction 400 to E.

Elton. E. to Blisworth 30, thence 320 to E.

—— K. C. to Grantham 74, thence 492 to E.

Elvanfoot. E. to, 58.

Ely. S. to, 118.

—— , S. Wales. P. to Bristol 220, thence by coach and ferry to Chepstow, thence 530 to E.

Enfield. S. to Water Lane 112, thence 496 to E.

Entwistle. E. to Newton Junction 46, thence 396 to Kenyon, thence 406 to E.

Epsom. L. to Croydon 160, thence 258 to E.

Erith. L. to, 254.

Errol. To Edinburgh xvii, thence 527 to Perth, thence 525 to E.

Esher. W. to, 140.

Esk Bank. To Edinburgh xvii, thence 528 to E. B.

Eskmeals. E. to Preston 48, thence 412 to Fleetwood, thence by boat to Piel 471 to E.

Essendine. K. C. to, 72.

Etruria. E. to Rugby 32, thence 334 to Colwick, thence 374 to E.

Euxton. E. to, 46.

Ewell. L. to Croydon 160, thence 258 to E.

Exeter. P. to, 232.

Exthorpe. K. C. to Doncaster 80, thence 438 to E.

Fairfield. E. to Crewe 42, thence 392 to Manchester, thence 422 to F.

Fakenham. S. to Wymondham 122, thence 508 to F.

Falkland. E. to Carlisle 56, thence 521 to Glasgow, thence 522 to Stirling, thence 527 to F.

Falkirk. To Edinburgh xvii, thence 518 to F.

Falmer. L. to Brighton 166, thence 192 to F.

Fangloss. K. C. to Milford 82, thence 436 to Selby, thence 440 to Market Weighton and F.

Fareham. W. to Bishopstoke 148, thence 266 to F.

Faringdon. P. to, 210.

Farnborough. W. to, 144.

—— P. to Reading 204, thence 282 to F.

Farnell Road. E. to Carlisle 56, thence 521 to Glasgow, thence 522 to F. R.

Farnham. W. to Woking 144, thence 262 to Guildford, thence 264 to F.

Farringdon. P. to, 211.

Farrington. E. to, 46.

Fay Gate. L. to Three Bridges 164, thence 266 to F. G.

Fazeley. E. to Birmingham 36, thence 346 to F.

Featherstone. E. to Newton 46, thence 396 to Manchester, thence 414 to North Dean, thence 426 to Dewsbury, thence 430 to F.

Feltham. W. to, 278.

Fence Houses. K. C. to, 90.

Fenny Stratford. E. to Bletchley 28, thence 316 to F. S.

Ferriby. K. C. to Milford 82, thence 436 to F.

Ferry Port on Craig. To Edinburgh xvii, thence 527 to Perth, thence 526 to F.P. on C.

Ferryhill. K. C. to 88.

Filey. K. C. to Milford 82, thence 436 to Hull, thence 448 to F.

Finningham. S. to, 136.

Firsby. K. C. to Peterbro 72, thence 104 to Boston, thence 510 to F.

Fiskerton. K. C. to Grantham 74, thence 492 to Nottingham, thence 480 to F.

Five Mile House. K. C. to Peterborough 72, thence 102 to F.

Flaxden. K. C. to York 82, thence 444 to F.

Fleetpond. W. to, 145.

Fleetwood. E. to Preston 48, thence 412 to F.

—— Surrey. W. to, 144.

Flint. E. to Wolverhampton 40, thence 348 to Chester, thence 529 to F.

Flordon. S. to, 138.

Foleshill. E. to Coventry 34, thence 344 to F.

Folkestone. L. to Reigate 164, thence 176 to F.

Forcester. P. to Bristol 220, thence 294 to F.

Fordoun. E. to Carlisle 56, thence 521 to Glasgow, thence 525 to F.

Forest Hill. L. to, 160.

Forfar. E. to Carlisle 56, thence 521 to Glasgow, thence 522 to F.

Forgardenny. E. to Carlisle 56, thence 521 to Glasgow, thence 522 to F.

Forge Mills. E. to Birmingham 36, thence 346 to F. M.

Formby. E. to Newton 46, thence 396 to Liverpool, thence 398 to F.

Forncett. S. to, 138.

Foulbridge. E. to Farrington 46, thence from Lostock Junction 400 to F.

Fountain Hall. To Edinburgh xvii, thence 528 to F.

Four Ashes. E. to, 40.

Four Stories. K. C. to Newcastle 92, thence 466 to F. S.

Fransham. S. to Wymondham 122, thence 506 to Dereham, thence 512 to F.

Frisby. K. C. to Peterborough 72, thence 478 to F.

Frodsham. E. to Crewe 42, thence 388 to Chester, thence 390 to F.

Froghall. E. to Birmingham 36, thence 346 to Burton, thence 382 to Uttoxeter, thence 382 to F.

Froickheim. E. to Carlisle 56, thence 521 to Glasgow, thence 522 to F.

Frome. P. to Chippenham 214, thence 514 to F.

Frosterley. K. C. to Aycliffe 88, thence 462 to F.

Furness Abbey. E. to Preston 48, thence 412 to Fleetwood, thence by boat to Piel 472, and on to F.

Furtriebridge. To Edinburgh xvii, thence 528 to F.

Gaerwen. E. to Wolverhampton 40, thence 388 to Chester, thence 529 to G.

Galashiels. To Edinburgh xvii, thence 528 to G.

Galgate. E. to, 48.

Galston. E. to Carlisle 56, thence 521 to G.

Ganton. K. C. to York 82, thence 444 to G.

Gainsborough. K. C. to Peterborough 72, thence 102 to G.

Garforth. K. C. to Milford 82, thence 436 to G.

Gargrave. E. to Farrington 46, thence from Lostock 400, to Skipton, thence 454 to G.

Garnkirk. E. to Carstairs 60, thence 519 to G.

Garstang. E. to, 48.

Gartcosh. E. to Carstairs 60, thence 519 to G.

Garton. E. to Crewe 42, thence 392 to Manchester, thence 420 to G.

Gartsherrie. E. to Carstairs 60, thence 519 to G.

Harburn. E. to, 60.

Hardingham. S. to Wymondham 122, thence 506 to H.

Harecastle. E. to Rugby 38, thence 334 to Colwich, thence 374 to H.

Harling Road. S. to, 122.

Harlow. S. to, 114.

Harrow. E. to, 20.

Harrowgate. E. to Rugby 32, thence 328 to Derby, thence 348 to Leeds, thence 356 to H.

—— K. C. to Church Fenton 82, thence 442 to H.

Hartford. E. to, 44.

Hartlepool. K. C. to Aycliffe 88, thence 462 and 464 to H.

Haseby. K. C. to York 82, thence 444 to H.

Haselor. E. to Birmingham 36, thence 346 to H.

Haslingden. E. to Newton 46, thence 396 to Manchester, thence 412 to H.

Hassendean. To Edinburgh xvii, thence 528 to H.

Hassocks Gate. L. to, 166.

Hastings. L. to Haywards Heath 164, thence 242 to H.

Haswell. K. C. to Aycliffe 88, thence 462 to Hartlepool, thence 464 to H.

Hatfield. K. C. to, 64.

Hatton. E. to Carlisle 56, thence 521 to Glasgow, thence 522 to Meigle and H.

Haughley. S. to, 136.

Haughton. E. to Stafford 40, thence 371 to H.

Havant. L. to, 172.

Hawkesbury Lane. E. to Coventry 34, thence 344 to H. L.

Hawick. To Edinburgh xvii, thence 528 to H.

Hay. E. to Newton 46, thence 396 to Manchester, thence 414 to North Dean, thence 426 to Wakefield, thence 428 to H.

Hayle. P. to Plymouth 240, thence per coach to Redruth, thence 508 to H.

Haywards Heath. L. to, 164.

Hazelhead. E. to Newton 46, thence 396 to Manchester, thence 422 to H.

Headcorn. L. to Reigate 164, thence 176 to H.

Headingley. E. to Rugby 32, thence 328 to Derby, thence 348 to Leeds, thence 356 to H.

Headland Cross. To Edinburgh xvii, thence 519 to H. C.

Heaton Lodge. E. to Crewe 42, thence 392 to Manchester, thence 416 to H. L.

—— Norris. E. to Rugby 32, thence 334 to Colwich, thence 374 to H. N.

—— E. to Crewe 42, thence 392 to H. N.

Hebden Bridge. E. to Crewe 42, thence 392, to Manchester, thence 414 to H. B.

—— E. to Newton 46, thence 396 to Manchester, thence 414 to H. B.

Heckmandike. E. to Newton 46, thence 396 to Manchester, thence 414 to North Dean, thence 426 to H.

Hele. P. to, 232.

Helmshore. E. to Newton 46, thence 396 to Manchester, thence 412 to H.

Helpstone. K. C. to Peterborough 72, thence 478 to H.

Hensall. K. C. to Knothingley 82, thence 430 to H.

Herford. P. to Didcot 210, thence 288 to H.

Heriot. To Edinburgh xvii, thence 528 to H.

Herne Bay. L. to Reigate 164, thence 176 to Ashford, thence 184 to H. B.

Hersham. W. to, 142.

Hertford. S. to Broxbourne 112, thence 494 to H.

Hesk Bank. E. to, 50.

Heslerton. K. C. to York 82, thence 444 to H.

Hessay. K. C. to York 82, thence 442 to H.

Hessle. K. C. to Milford 82, thence 436 to H.

Hetton. K. C. to Shincliffe 88, thence 470 to H.

Hexham. K. C. to Newcastle 92, thence 466 to H.

Heywood. E. to Wigan 46, thence 404 to H.

Higham. L. to, 256.

—— Ferrers. E. to Blisworth 30, thence 320 to H. F.

Highbridge. P. to, 224.

Highbury. Camden Town to, 516.

Hightown. E. to Newton 46, thence 396 to Liverpool, thence 400 to H.

Hilgay Fen. S. to Ely 118, thence 500 to H. F.

Hindley. E. to Wigan 46, thence 404 to H.

Hipperholme. E. to Newton 46, thence 396 to Manchester, thence 424 to North Dean, thence 426 to H.

Histon. S. to Cambridge 118, thence 498 to H.

Hitchin. K. C. to, 68.

Hoghton. E. to Newton 46, thence 396 to Liverpool, thence 400 to H.

Holborn. E. to Preston 48, thence 412 to Fleetwood, thence by boat to Piel, thence 472 to H.

Holme. K. C. to, 72.

—— S. to Ely 118, thence 500 to H.

—— Lancas. E. to, 50.

Holmes. K. C. to Milford 82, thence 436 to Selby, thence 440 to H.

—— Church. E. to Crewe 42, thence 392 to H. C.

Leicester. E. to Rugby 32, thence 328 to L.

Leigh. E. to Newton Junction 46, thence 396 to Kenyon, thence 406 to L.

Leighton. E. to 28.

Leith. To Edinburgh xvii, thence 527 to L.

Leland. E. to, 46.

Lenchars. To Edinburgh xvii, thence 527 to Perth, thence 526 to L.

Lenox Town. E. to Carlisle, 56, thence 522 to Glasgow, thence 519 to L.

Lentham. K. C. to Grantham 74, thence 492 to Nottingham, thence 490 to L.

Levenshulme. E. to Rugby 32, thence 334 to Colwick, thence 374 to L.

Levisham. K. C. to York 82, thence 444 to Rillington, thence 450 to L.

Lewes. L. to Hayward's Heath 164, thence 242 to L.

—— L. to Brighton 166, thence 192 to L.

Lewisham. L. to, 250.

Leysmill E. to Carlisle 56, thence 521 to Glasgow, thence 522 to Guthrie Junction and L.

Lichfield. E. to Rugby 32, thence 334 to L.

—— E. to Bescott 38, thence 370 to L.

Lidlington. E. to Bletchley 28, thence 316 to L.

Lightcliffe. E. to Newton 46, thence to Manchester 396, thence 414 to North Dean, thence 426 to L.

Limehouse. L. to, 516.

Limekiln Lane. E. to Crewe 42, thence 388 to L. L.

Linby. K. C. to Grantham 74, thence 492 to Nottingham, thence 490 to L.

Lincoln. K. C. to Peterborough 72, thence 102 to L.

—— K. C. to Newark 76, thence 484 to L.

Linlithgow. Edinburgh xvii, thence 518.

Linton. K. C. to 100.

Little Bytham. K. C. to, 72.

—— Dunham. S. to Wymondham 122, thence 506 to Deerham, thence 512 to L. D.

—— Hampton. L. to, 168.

—— Steeping. K. C. to Peterborough 72, thence 104 to Boston, thence 510 to L. S.

Littleborough. E. to Crewe 42, thence 392 to Manchester, thence 414 to L.

Littleport. S. to Ely 118, thence 500 to L.

Littleworth. K. C. to Peterborough 72, thence 102 to L.

Liverpool. E. to Newton Junction 46, thence 396, to L. 394.

Liversedge. E. to Newton 46, thence 396 to Manchester, thence 414 to North Dean, thence 426 to L.

Livington. To Edinburgh xvii, thence 519 to L.

Llandaff. P. to Bristol 220, thence to Cardiff 531, thence 532 to L.

Llanfair. E. to Wolverhampton 40, thence 348 to Chester, thence 529 to L.

Llangollen. E. to Wolverhampton 40, thence 360 to L.

Llantripant. P. to Bristol 220, thence by coach and ferry to Chepstow, thence 530 to L.

Llong. E. to Wolverhampton 40, thence 348 to Chester, thence 530 to L.

Lochwinnoch. E. to Carlisle 56, thence 521 to Glasgow, thence 520 to L.

Lockerbie. E. to, 58.

Lockington. K. C. to Milford 82, thence 436 to Hull, thence 448 to L.

Lockwood. E. to Newport 46, thence 396 to Manchester, thence 422 to Peniston, thence 438 to L.

Long Eaton. E. to Rugby 32, thence 328 to Kegworth, and 480 to L. E.

—— Forgan. To Edinburgh xvii, thence 527 to Perth, thence 525 to L. F.

—— Houghton. K. C. to, 98.

—— Preston. E. to Farrington 46, thence to Lostock 40, thence 434 to L. P.

—— Niddry K. C. to, 100.

—— Stanton. S. to Cambridge 118, thence 498 to L. S.

Longbridge. To Edinburgh xvii, thence 519 to L.

Longford. E. to Coventry 34, thence 344 to L.

Longhurst, Northumberland. K. C. to, 94.

Longsight. E. to Rugby, 32, thence 334 to Colwick, thence 374 to L.

Longton. E. to Birmingham 36, thence 346 to Burton, thence 382 to L.

Longwood. E. to Crewe 42, thence 392 to Manchester, thence 416 to L.

Lostock. E. to Newton 46, thence 396 to Liverpool, thence 400 to L.

—— Lane. E. to Wigan 46, thence 404 to Bolton, thence 410 to L. L.

Loughborough. E. to Rugby 32, thence 320 to L.

Louth. K. C. to Peterborough 72, thence 104 to Boston, thence 512 to L.

Low Gill. E. to, 50.

—— Moor. E. to Newton 46, thence 396 to Manchester, thence 414 to North Dean, thence 426 to L. M.

Lowdham. K. C. to Grantham 74, thence 492 to Nottingham, thence 480 to L.

Lower Darwen. E. to Newton Junction 46, thence 396 to Kenyon, thence 406 to L. D.

Lowestoft. S. to Reedham 126, thence 506 to L.

Lowthorpe. K. C. to Milford 82, thence 436 to Hull, thence 448 to L.

Ludborough. K. C. to Peterborough 72, thence 104 to Boston, thence 512 to L.

Luddenden Foot. E. to Crewe 42, thence 392 to Manchester, thence 414 to L. F.

Luffenham. K. C. to Peterborough 100, thence 476 to L.

Luncarty. E. to Carlisle 56, thence 521 to Glasgow, thence 522 to L.

Lyndhurst Road. W. to, 150.

Lynn. S. to Ely 118, thence 500 to L.

—— S. to Wymondham 122, thence 506 to Dereham, thence 512 to L.

Macclesfield. E. to Rugby 32, thence 334 to Colwick, thence 376 to M.

Madeley. E. to, 42.

Maghull. E. to Newton 46, thence 376 to Liverpool, thence 400 to M.

Maidenhead. P. to, 200.

Maidstone. L. to Reigate 164, thence 176 to Paddocks Wood, thence 246 to M.

Maldon. W. to, 140.

——, Essex. S. to Witham 132, thence 502 to M.

Malton. K. C. to York 82, thence 444 to M.

—— K. C. to Dalton 82, thence 456 to M.

Manchester. E. to Newton Junction 46, thence 396 to M.

—— E. to Crewe 42, thence 392 to M.

—— E. to Rugby 32, thence 334 to Colwick, thence 376 to M.

Manea. S. to Ely 118, thence 502 to M.

Mangotsfield. P. to Bristol 220, thence 294 to M.

Manningtree. S. to, 134.

Mansfield. K. C. to Grantham 74, thence 492 to Nottingham, thence 490 to M.

Manton. K. C. to Peterborough 100, thence 476 to M.

March. S. to Ely 118, thence 502 to M.

Marden. L. to Reigate 164, thence 176 to M.

Margate. L. to Reigate 164, thence 176 to Ashford, thence 184 to M.

Market Harborough. E. to Rugby 32, thence 326 to M. H.

—— Rasen. K. C. to Newark 76, thence 484 to M. R.

—— Weighton. K. C. to Milford 82, thence 436 to Selby, thence 440 to M. W.

Markinch. E. to Carlisle 56, thence 521 to Glasgow, thence 522 to Stirling, thence 526 to M.

Marks' Tey. S. to, 132.

Marrishes. K. C. to York 82, thence 444 to Rillington, thence 450 to M.

Marsden. E. to Crewe 42, thence 392 to Manchester, thence 416 to M.

—— E. to Farrington 46, thence from Lostock Junction 400 to M.

Marsh Lane. S. to, 112.

—— see Leeds.

——, Lancaster. E. to Newton 46, thence 396 to Liverpool, thence 398 to M.

Marshfield. P. to Bristol 220, thence by coach and ferry to Chepstow, thence 530 to M.

Marston. K. C. to York 82, thence 442 to M.

—— Green, E. to, 34.

Marton. K. C. to Milford 82, thence 436 to Hull, thence 448 to M.

Marykirk. E. to Carlisle 56, thence 521 to Glasgow, thence 525 to M.

Maryport. E. to Carlisle 56, thence 476 to M.

Masborough. E. to Birmingham 36, thence 346 to M.

—— E. to Rugby 32, thence 328 to Derby, thence 348 to M.

Maston. K. C. to Peterborough 72, thence 102 to M.

Matlock Bath. E. to Birmingham 36, thence 346 to Ambergate, thence 488 to M.

—— Bridge. E. to Birmingham 36, thence 346 to Ambergate, thence 488 to M.

Mauchline. E. to Carlisle 56, thence 521 to M.

Medbourne. E. to Rugby 32, thence 326 to M.

Meigle. E. to Carlisle 56, thence 521 to Glasgow, thence 522 to M.

Melksham. P. to Chippenham 214, thence 514 to M.

Mellis. S. to, 136.

Melrose. To Edinburgh xvii, thence 528 to M.

Melton Mowbray. K. C. to Peterborough 72, thence 478 to M.

Merstham. L. to Reigate 164, thence 176 to M.

Merthyr Tydvil. P. to Bristol 220, thence 531 to Cardiff, thence 532 to M. T.

Merton, Durham. K. C. to Shincliffe 88, thence 470 to M.

——, Surrey. W. to, 140.

Methley. E. to Rugby 32, thence 328 to Derby, thence 348 to M.

—— E. to Birmingham 36, thence 346 to M.

Mexborough. K. C. to Doncaster 80, thence 438 to M.

Micklefield. K. C. to Milford 82, thence 436 to M.

Midcalder. E. to, 60.

Middlesborough. K. C. to Darlington 86, thence 452 to M.

Middleton. S. to Wymondham 122, thence 506 to Dereham, thence 512 to M.

——, Durham. K. C. to Darlington 86, thence 452 to M.

Newton, Cheshire.   E. to Crewe 42, thence
  392 to Manchester, thence 420 to N.
——, Devon.   P. to, 236.
——, Lancashire.   E. to, 46.
——, Warwick.   E. to, 38.
——, York.   K. C. to Church Fenton 82,
  thence 442 to N.
Newtown St. Boswells.   To Edinburgh xvii,
  thence 528 to N.
Newtownhill.   E. to Carlisle 56, thence 521
  to Glasgow, thence 522 to N.
Newtyle.   E. to Carlisle 56, thence 521 to
  Glasgow, thence 522 to Meigle, thence
  524 to N.
Norham.   K. C. to Berwick 100, thence 476
  to N.
North Dean.   E. to Crewe 42, thence 392 to
  Manchester, thence 414 to N. D.
—— Kelsey.   K. C. to Newark 76, thence
  488 to N. K.
—— Rode.   E. to Rugby 32, thence 334
  to Colwick, thence 374 to N. R.
—— Shields.   K. C. to Newcastle 92, thence
  476 to N. S.
—— Thoresby.   K. C. to Peterborough 72,
  thence 104 to Boston, thence 512 to
  N. T.
Northallerton.   K. C. to, 86.
Northampton.   E. to Blisworth 30, thence
  320 to N.
Northfleet.   L. to, 254.
Northorpe.   K. C. to Retford 78, thence
  424 to N.
Normanton.   E. to Birmingham 36, thence
  346 to N.
——   E. to Rugby 32,   thence 328 to
  Derby, thence 348 to N.
Norton.   K. C. to Aycliffe 88, thence 462 to N.
—— Bridge.   E. to, 40.
Norwich.   S. to, 112 and 138.
Norwood.   L. to, 162.
Nottingham.   K. C. to Grantham 74, thence
  492 to N.
Notton.   E. to Birmingham 36, thence 346
  to N.
——   E. to Rugby 32, thence 328 to Derby,
  thence 348 to N.
Nuneaton.   E. to Coventry 34, thence 344
  to N.
——   E. to Crewe 42, thence 334 to N.
Oakenshaw.   E. to Birmingham 36, thence
  346 to O.
——   E. to Rugby 32, thence 320 to Derby,
  thence 348 to O.
Oakham.   K. C. to Peterborough 72, thence
  478 to O.
Oakington.   S. to Cambridge 118, thence
  498 to O.
Oakley.   E. to Birmingham 36, thence 346
  to O.

Oakley, N. B.   E. to Carlisle 56, thence 521
  to Glasgow, and 522 to Stirling, thence
  527 to O.
Oaks (The).   E. to Newton Junction 46,
  thence 396 to Kenyon, thence 406 to The O.
Oatamoor.   E. to Birmingham 36, thence
  346 to Burton, thence 382 to Uttoxeter,
  thence 384 to O.
Oatengates.   E. to Wolverhampton 40,
  thence 360 to O.
Oddington.   E. to Bletchley 28, thence 314
  to O.
Old Leake.   K. C. to Peterborough 72,
  thence 102 to Boston, thence 510 to O. L.
—— Cumnock.   E. to Carlisle 56, thence
  522 to O. C.
—— Trafford.   E. to Crewe 42, thence
  396 to Manchester, thence 420 to O. T.
Ormskirk.   E. to Newton 46, thence 376 to
  Liverpool, thence 400 to O.
Orrel.   E. to Newton 46, thence 396 to
  Liverpool, thence 404 to O.
Oswestry.   E. to Wolverhampton 40, thence
  360 to O.
Otterington.   K. C. to, 86.
Oughty Bridge.   E. to Crewe 42, thence
  392 to Manchester, thence 420 to O. B.
Oundle.   E. to Blisworth 30, thence 320 to O.
Overdarwen.   E. to Newton Junction 46,
  thence 396 to Kenyon, thence 406 to O.
Overton.   E. to Blisworth 30, thence 320 to O.
Overtoun.   E. to Carstairs 60, thence 519
  to O.
Oxford.   P. to Didcot 210, thence 288 to O.
—— Road.   E. to Bletchley 28, thence 314
  to O. R.
Paddock Wood.   L. to Reigate 164, thence
  176 to P. W.
Paeswood.   E. to Crewe 42, thence 388 to
  Chester, thence 530 to P.
Painshaw.   K. C. to 90.
Paisley.   E. to Carlisle 56, thence 521 to
  Glasgow, thence 520 to P.
Pangbourne.   P. to, 106.
Pannel.   E. to Rugby 32, thence 328 to
  Derby, thence 348 to Leeds, thence 356
  to P.
Park.   E. to Crewe 42, thence 392 to Man-
  chester, thence 416 to P.
Parkside.   E. to Newton Junction 46, thence
  396 to P.
Patricroft.   E. to Newton Junction 46,
  thence 396 to P.
Pavensey.   L. to Hayward's Heath 164,
  thence 242 to P.
Peakirk.   K. C. to Peterborough 72, thence
  102 to P.
Pelsall.   E. to Bescott 38, thence 370 to P.
Pemberton.   E. to Newton 46, thence 396
  to Liverpool, thence 404 to P.

Pencoed. P. to Bristol 220, thence by coach and ferry to Chepstow, then 530 to P.

Pendleton. E. to Newton 46, thence 396 to Manchester, thence 408 to P.

Penistone. E. to Crewe 42, thence 392 to Manchester, thence 420 to P.

Penkridge. E. to, 40.

Penmaenmawr. E. to Wolverhampton 40, thence 348 to Chester, thence 529 to P.

Penrith. E. to, 54.

Penshurst. L. to Reigate 114, thence 176 to P.

Pentyrch. P. to Bristol 220, thence 531 to Cardiff, thence 531 to P.

Perry Bar. E. to, 38.

Perth. E. to Carlisle 56, thence 521 to Glasgow, thence 522 to P.

—— To Edinburgh xvii, thence 527 to P.

Peterborough. K. C. to, 72.

—— E. to Blisworth 30, thence 320 to P.

—— S. to Ely 118, thence 502 to P.

Pevensey. L. to Hayward's Heath 164, thence 242 to P.

Pickering. K. C. to York 82, thence 444 to P.

Pickle Bridge. E. to Newton 46, thence 396 to Manchester, thence 414 to North Dean, thence 426 to P. B.

Piel. E. to Preston 48, thence 412 to Fleet-wood, thence by boat 472 to P.

Pillmore. K. C. to, 84.

Pimbo Land. E. to Newton 46, thence 396 to Liverpool, thence 404 to P. L.

Pinner. E. to, 22.

Pittingdon. K. C. to Shincliffe 88, thence 470 to P.

Pleasington. E. to Farrington 46, thence from Lostock Junction 400 to P.

Pluckley. L. to Reigate 164, thence 176 to P.

Plumpton. E. to, 56.

Plymouth. P. to, 240.

Plympton. P. to, 240.

Pocklington. K. C. to Milford 82, thence 436 to Selby, thence 440 to Market Weighton and to P.

Polegate. L. to Hayward's Heath 164, thence 242 to P.

Poleworth. E. to Rugby 32, thence 334 to P.

Polmont. To Edinburgh xvii, thence 518 to P.

Ponder's End. S. to, 112.

Pontefract. K. C. to Knottingley 82, thence 430 to P.

Pontypool. P. to Bristol 220, thence by coach and ferry to Chepstow 530 to P.

Poole. W. to, 154.

——, York. E. to Rugby 32, thence 328 to Derby, thence 346 to Leeds, thence 356 to P.

Poplar. Camden Town to, 516.

—— F. to, 516.

Poppleton. K. C. to York 82, thence 442 to P.

Porchester. W. to Bishopstoke 148, thence 286 to Fareham, thence 270 to P.

Port Clarence. K. C. to Darlington 86, thence 452 to P. C.

—— Talbot. P. to Bristol 220, thence by coach and ferry to Chepstow, thence 530 to P. T.

Portlethen. E. to Carlisle 56, thence 521 to Glasgow, thence 525 to P.

Portobello. K. C. to, 102.

Portskewett. P. to Bristol 220, thence by coach and ferry to Chepstow and on to P. 530.

Portsmouth. L. to, 174.

—— W. to Bishopstoke 168, thence 268 to Fareham, thence 270 to P.

Potter's Bar. K. C. to, 64.

Poulton. E. to Preston 48, thence 412 to P.

Poynton. E. to Rugby 32, thence 334 to Colwick, thence 374 to P.

Prestatyn. E. to Wolverhampton 40, thence 348 to Chester, thence 529 to P.

Prestbury. E. to Rugby 32, thence 374 to Colwick, thence 374 to P.

Preston. E. to, 48.

—— Brook. E. to, 44.

—— Roads. E. to Newton 46, thence 396 to Liverpool, thence 404 to P. R.

Prestwick. E. to Carlisle 56, thence 521 to Glasgow, thence 520 to P.

Prudhoe. K. C. to Newcastle 92, thence 466 to P.

Pulford. E. to Wolverhampton 40, thence 360 to P.

Purtgwyn. E. to Wolverhampton 40, thence 360 to P.

Purton. P. to Swindon 212, thence 308 to P.

Putney. W. to, 276.

Pyle. P. to Bristol 220, thence by coach and ferry to Chepstow, thence 530 to P.

Queen's Ferry. E. to Wolverhampton 40, thence 348 to Chester, thence 529 to Q. F.

Radcliffe. K. C. to Grantham 74, thence 492 to R.

—— Bridge. E. to Newton 46, thence 396 to Manchester, thence 412 to R. B.

Radford. K. C. to Grantham 74, thence 492 to Nottingham, thence 490 to R.

Radway Green. E. to Rugby 32, thence 336 to Colwick, thence 374 to R. G.

Rainford. E. to Newton Junction 46, thence 396 to Liverpool, thence 404 to R.

Rainhill. E. to Newton Junction 46, thence 396 to R.

Ramsbottom. E. to Newton Junction 46, thence 396 to Manchester, thence 412 to R.

Ramsgate. L. to Reigate 164, thence 176 to Ashford, thence 184 to R.

Rampside. E. to Preston 48, thence 412 to Fleetwood, thence by boat to Piel 472 on to R.

Raskelf. K. C. to, 84.

Ranskell. K. C. to, 78,

Ratho. To Edinburgh xvii, thence 518 to R.

Ravenglass. E. to Preston 48, thence 412 to Fleetwood, thence by boat to Piel 472 to R.

Rawcliffe. K. C. to Knottingley 82, thence 430 to R.

Raydon. S. to Bentley 134, thence 504 to R.

Reading. P. to, 204.

Rearsby. K. C. to Peterborough 72, thence 478 to R.

Redbridge. W. to, 150.

Redcar. K. C. to Darlington 86, thence 452 to R.

Rednal. E. to Wolverhampton 40, thence 360 to R.

Redruth. P. to Plymouth 240, thence by coach 508 to R.

Reedham. S. to, 126.

Reepham. K. C. to Newark 76, thence 484 to R.

Reigate. L. to, 164.

Renfrew. E. to Carlisle 56, thence 521 to Glasgow, thence 520 to R.

Renton. E. to Carlisle 56, thence 521 to Glasgow, thence 520 to R.

Reston. K. C. to, 100.

Retford. K. C. to, 78.

——— E. to Crewe 42, thence 392 to Manchester, thence 424 to R.

Rhos. E. to Wolverhampton 40, thence 360 to R.

Rhyl. E. to Wolverhampton 40, thence 348 to Chester, thence 529 to R.

Richmond, Surrey. W. 274 to 276.

———, York. K. C. to Dalton 86, thence 456 to R.

Ridgemount. E. to Bletchley 28, thence 316 to R.

Riding Mill. K. C. to Newcastle 92, thence 466 to R. M.

Rillington. K. C. to York 82, thence 444 to R.

Ringwood. W. to, 150.

Ringstead. E. to Blisworth 30, thence 320 to R.

Ripley. E. to Rugby 32, thence 328 to Derby, thence 348 to Leeds, thence 356 to R.

Ripon. E. to Rugby 32, thence 328 to Derby, thence 348 to Leeds, thence 356 to R.

Roade. E. to, 30.

Roby. E. to Newton Junction 46, thence 396 to R.

Rocester. E. to Birmingham 36, thence 346 to Burton, thence 382 to Uttoxeter, thence 384 to R.

Rochdale. E. to Newton 46, thence 396 to Manchester, thence 414 to R.

——— E. to Crewe 42, thence 382 to Manchester, thence 414 to R.

Rochester. L. to, 256.

Rock Lane. E. to Crewe 42, thence 388 to R. L.

Rockingham. E. to Rugby 32, thence 326 to R.

Rockliffe. E. to, 58.

Romford. S. to, 128.

Romsey. W. to Bishopstoke 148, thence 270 to R.

Rose Hill. E. to Carlisle 56, thence 470 to R. H.

Rosegrove. E. to Farrington 36, thence to Lostock Junction 400 to R.

Rossett. E. to Wolverhampton 40, thence 360 to E.

Rossington. K. C. to, 80.

Rotherham. E. to Crewe 42, thence 392 to Manchester, thence 422 to R.

Rousley. E. to Birmingham 36, thence 346 to Ambergate, thence 488 to R.

Royston. K. C. to Hitchin 68, thence 492 to R.

———, York. E. to Birmingham 36, thence 346 to R.

———, ——— E. to Rugby 32, thence 328 to Derby, thence 348 to R.

Ruabon. E. to Wolverhampton 40, thence 360 to R.

Rudyard. E. to Birmingham 36, thence 346 to Burton, thence 382 to Uttoxeter, thence 384 to R.

Rufford. E. to Newton 46, thence 376 to Liverpool, thence 400 to R.

Rugby. E. to, 32.

Rugeley. E. to Rugby 32, thence 334

Rushton. E. to Birmingham 36, thence to R. 346 to Burton, thence 382 to Uttoxeter, thence 384 to R.

Ruswark. K. C. to York 82, thence 444 to Rillington, thence 450 to R.

Rutherglen. E. to Carstairs 60, thence 79 to Motherwell, thence 519 to R.

Ruthwell. E. to Carlisle 56, thence 521 to R.

Rye House. S. to Broxbourne 112, thence 494 to R. H.

Ryton. K. C. to Newcastle 92, thence 466 to R.

Saddleworth. E. to Crewe 42, thence 392 to Manchester, thence 416 to S.

Sale Moor. E. to Crewe 42, thence 392 to Manchester, thence 420 to S. M.

Salford, Manchester. E. to Newton 46, thence 396 to S.

Salisbury. W. to Bishopstoke 148, thence 270 to S.

Saltford. P. to, 220.

Saltney. E. to Wolverhampton 40, thence 360 to S.

Salwick. E. to Preston 48, thence 410 to S.

Sandacre. E. to Rugby 32, thence 328 to Kegworth, and Long Eaton 480, thence 488 to S.

Sandbach. E. to Crewe 42, thence 392 to S.

Sandon. E. to Rugby 32, thence 334 to Colwick, thence 374 to S.

Sandwich. S. to Reigate 164, thence to Ashford 176, thence 184 to Minster, thence 190 to S.

Sandy. K. C. to, 68.

Sanquhar. E. to Carlisle 56, thence 521 to S.

Sawbridgeworth. S. to, 114.

Sawby. E. to Rugby 32, thence 328 to S.

Saxby. K. C. to Peterborough 72, thence 478 to S.

Saxilby. K. C. to Peterborough 72, thence 102 to S.

Scarborough. K. C. to York 82, thence 464 to S.

Scorton. E. to, 48.

——, York. K. C. to Dalton 86, thence 456 to S.

Scotby. E. to Carlisle 56, thence 470 to S.

Scotch Central. To Edinburgh xvii, thence 518 to S. C.

Scotswood. K. C. to Newcastle 92, thence 466 to S.

Scowby. K. C. to Retford 78, thence 424 to S.

Scremerston. K. C. to, 98.

Scrooby. K. C. to, 78.

Scropton. E. to Birmingham 36, thence 346 to Burton, thence 382 to S.

Seaforth. E. to Newton 46, thence 389 to Liverpool, thence 398 to S.

Seamer. K. C. to York 82, thence 444 to S.

Seascale. E. to Preston 48, thence 417 to Fleetwood, thence by boat to Piel, 472 to S.

Seaton. K. C. to Aycliffe 88, thence 462 to S.

Sedgebrook. K. C. to Grantham 74, thence 492 to S.

Selby. K. C. to Milford 82, thence 436 to S.

Sellefield. E. to Preston 48, thence 412 to Fleetwood, thence by boat to Piel 472 to S.

Sessay. K. C. to, 84.

Settle. E. to Farrington 46, thence 400 to Lostock, then 434 to S.

Shadwell. F. to, 516.

Shalford. L. to Reigate 164, thence 260 to S.

Shap. E. to, 52.

Sheffield. K. C. to Retford 78, thence 424 back to S.

—— E. to Crewe 42, thence 392 to Manchester, thence 422 to S.

Shefford Road. K. C. to, 68.

Sheldon. K. C. to Aycliffe 88, thence 460 to S.

Shelford. S. to, 118.

Sherburn, York. K. C. to, 82 and 446.

——, Durham. K. C. to, 88.

Shiffnal. E. to Wolverhampton 40, thence 360 to S.

Shilton. S. to Rugby 32, thence 334 to S.

Shincliffe. K. C. to, 88.

Shipley. E. to Newton 46, thence 396 to Manchester, thence 422 to Penistone, thence 438 to S.

—— E. to Rugby 32, thence 328 to Derby, thence 348 to Leeds, thence 432 to S.

Shipton. E. to Rugby 32, thence 328 to Derby, thence 348 to Leeds, thence 432 to S.

—— K. C. to, 84.

—— K. C. to Milford 82, thence 436 to Selby, thence 440 to Market Weighton and to S.

Shireoaks. E. to Crewe 42, thence 392 to Manchester, thence 424 to S.

—— K. C. to Retford 78, thence 424 to S.

Shoreham. L. to, 168.

Shrewsbury. E. to Wolverhampton 40, thence 360 to S.

Shrivenham. P. to, 212.

Sibsey. K. C. to Peterborough 72, thence 102 to Boston, thence 510 to S.

Sileby. E. to Rugby 32, thence 328 to S.

Sillycroft. E. to Preston 48, thence 412 to Fleetwood, thence by boat to Piel 472 to S.

Sinclair Town. E. to Carlisle 56, thence 521 to Glasgow, thence 522 to Stirling, thence 526 to S. T.

—— To Edinburgh xvii, thence 527 to S.

Six Mile Bottom. S. to Chesterford 118, thence 496 to S. M. B.

Skipton.   E. to Farrington 46, thence from Lostock Junction 400 to S.
Slateford.   E. to, 60.
Sleights.   K. C. to York 82, thence 404 to Pillington, thence 450 to S.
Slough.   P. to, 198.
Snaith.   K. C. to Knottingley 82, thence 430 to S.
Snelland.   K. C. to Newark 76, thence 484 to S.
Somerley.   E. to Reedham 126, thence 506 to S.
Somersham.   S. to Cambridge 118, thence 498 to St. Ives, thence 498 to S.
Sough.   E. to Newton Junction 46, thence 396 to Kenyon, thence 406 to S.
South Shields.   K. C. to Painshaw 90, thence 456 to S. S.
——— K. C. to Aycliffe 88, thence 462 to Hartlepool, thence 464 to S. S.
Southall.   P. to, 196.
Southampton.   W. to, 148.
Southgate.   K. C. to, 64.
Southport.   E. to Newton 46, thence 396 to Liverpool, thence 398 to S.
Southrow.   K. C. to Peterborough 72, thence 102 to S.
Southwaite.   E. to, 56.
Southwick.   L. to, 168.
Sowerby Bridge.   E. to Crewe 42, thence 392 to Manchester, thence 414 to S. B.
Spalding.   K. C. to Peterborough 72, thence 102 to S.
Speeton.   K. C. to Milford 82, thence 436 to Hull, thence 448 to S.
Spetchley.   E. to Birmingham 36, thence 308 back to S.
——— P. to Bristol 220, thence 302 to S.
Spilsby.   K. C. to Boston 104, thence 510 to S.
Spital.   E. to Crewe 42, thence 388 to S.
Spondon.   E. to Rugby 32, thence 328 to S.
Spotsborough.   K. C. to Doncaster 80, thence 438 to S.
Spread Eagle.   E. to, 40.
Springfield, N. B.   To Edinburgh xvii, thence 527 to Perth, thence 526 to S.
St. Bees.   E. to Preston 48, thence 412 to Fleetwood, thence by boat to Piel 472 to St. B.
——.Germans.   S. to Cambridge 118, thence 498 to St. Ives, thence to St. G.
— Helens.   E. to Newton Junction 46, thence 396 to St. H.
— Ives.   S. to Cambridge 118, thence 498 to St. I.
— James Deeping.   K. C. to Peterborough 72, thence 102 to St. J. D.
— Leonards.   L. to Hayward's Heath 164, thence 262 to St. L.

St. Margarets.   S. to Broxbourne 112, thence 494 to St. M.
— Neots.   K. C. to, 70.
Staddlethorpe.   K. C. to Milford 82, thence 436 to S.
Stafford.   E. to, 40.
——— E. to Rugby 32, thence 534 to S.
——— Road.   E. to Wolverhampton 40, thence 360 to S. R.
Staines.   W. to, 278.
Staithwaite.   E. to Crewe 42, thence 392 to Manchester, thence 418 to S.
Staleybridge.   E. to Crewe 42, thence 392 to Manchester, thence 416 to S.
Stallingborough.   K. C. to Retford 76, thence 424 to S.
Stamford.   K. C. to Peterborough 72, thence 478 to S.
——— Bridge.   K. C. to Milford 82, thence 436 to Selby, thence 440 to Market Weighton and S. B.
Standish.   E. to, 46.
Standon Bridge.   E. to, 46.
Stanford Hall.   E. to Rugby 32, thence 326 to S.
Stanhope.   K. C. to Darlington 86, thence 460 to Witton, thence 462 to S.
Stanley.   E. to Carlisle 56, thence 521 to Glasgow, thence 522 to S.
Stanstead.   S. to, 114.
Stapleford.   E. to Rugby 32, thence 328 to Kegsworth, thence 480 to Long Eaton, thence 488 to S.
Staplehurst.   L. to Reigate 164, thence 176 to S.
Starcross.   P. to, 234.
Staveley.   E. to Birmingham 36, thence 346 to S.
——— E. to Rugby 32, thence 328 to Derby, thence 340 to S.
Steeton.   E. to Farrington 46, thence from Lostock 400 to Shipton, thence 434 to S.
Stepney.   F. to, 516.
Steps Road.   E. to Carstairs 60, thence 519 to S. R.
Stetchford.   E. to, 34.
Stevenage.   K. C. to, 66.
Steventon.   P. to, 210.
Stewarton.   E. to Carlisle 56, thence 521 to S.
Stillington.   K. C. to Aycliffe 88, thence 462 to S.
Stirling.   E. to Carlisle 56, thence 521 to Glasgow, thence 522 to S.
Stixwold.   K. C. to Peterborough 72, thence 102 to S.
Stoat's Nest.   L. to, 162.
Stockbridge.   K. C. to, 80.
Stockfield.   K. C. to Newcastle 92, thence 466 to S.

Stockmoor. E. to Newton 46, thence 396 to Manchester, thence 422 to Penistone, thence 438 to S.

Stockport. E. to Rugby 32, thence 334 to Colwick, thence 374 to S.

Stockton. K. C. to Milford 82, thence 436 to Selby, thence 440 to Market Weighton and S.

—— K. C. to Darlington 86, thence 452 to S.

Stofford. K. C. to Church Fenton 82, thence 442 to S.

Stoke. K. C. to Rugby 32, thence to Colwick 334, thence 374 to S.

—— E. to Birmingham 36, thence 346 to Burton, thence 382 to S.

—— Works. E. to Birmingham 36, thence 308 back to S. W.

—— —— P. to Bristol 220, thence 294 to S. W.

Stone. E. to Rugby 32, thence 334 to Colwick, thence 374 to S.

Stonecleugh. E. to Newton 46, thence 396 to Manchester, thence 408 to S.

Stonehaven. E. to Carlisle 56, thence 521 to Glasgow, thence 525 to S.

Stonehouse. P. to Bristol 220, thence 294 to S.

—— P. to Swindon 212, thence 308 to S.

Stow. S. to Ely 118, thence 500 to S.

—— To Edinburgh xvii, thence 528 to S.

Stowmarket. S. to, 136.

Straithwait. E. to Crewe 42, thence 392 to Manchester, thence 416 to S.

Stratford. S. to, 111.

Strenshall. K. C. to York 82, thence 444 to S.

Stretford. E. to Crewe 42, thence 392 to Manchester, thence 420 to S.

Stretton. E. to Rugby 32, thence 334 to S.

—— E. to Birmingham 36, thence 346 to S.

—— E. to Rugby 32, thence 328 to Derby, thence 348·to S.

Stroud. L.·to, 256.

—— P. to Swindon 212, thence 308 to S.

Sturton. K. C. to Retford 78, thence 424 to S.

Sturry. L. to Reigate 164, thence 176 to Ashford, thence 184 to S.

Suchar. K. C. to, 98.

Sudbury. E. to, 20.

——, Suffolk. S. to Mark's Tey 132, thence 500 to S.

——, Notts. K. C. to Grantham 74, thence 492 to Nottingham, thence 490 to S.

——, Stafford. E. to Birmingham 36, thence 346 to Burton, thence 382 to S.

Summerseat. E. to Newton 46, thence 396 to Manchester, thence 412 to S.

Sunderland. K. C. to Aycliffe 88, thence 462 to Hartlepool, thence 464 to S. ·

Sunfleet. K. C. to Peterborough 72, thence 102 to S.

Sutton, York. K. C. to, 78 and 442.

——, Cheshire. E.·to Crewe 42, thence 388 to S.

——, Surrey. L. to Croydon 160, thence 258 to S.

Swaffham. S. to Wymondham 122, thence 506 to Dereham, thence 512 to S.

Swansea. P. to Bristol 220, thence by coach and ferry to Chepstow, 530 to S.

Swanington. E. to Rugby 32, thence 328 to Leicester, thence 332 to S.

Swansthorpe. S. to, 158.

Swavesy. S. to Cambridge 118, thence 498 to S.

Swinderby. K. C. to Newark 76, thence 484 to S.

Swindon. P. to, 212.

Swinton. E. to Birmingham 36, thence 346 to S.

—— E. to Rugby 32, thence 328 to Derby, thence 348 to S.

Sydenham. L. to, 160.

Syston. E. to Rugby 32, thence 328 to S.

—— K. C. to Peterborough 72, thence 478 to S.

Tadcaster. K. C. to Church Fenton 82, thence 442 to T.

Tallington. K. C. to, 72.

Taffowell. P. to Bristol 220, thence 530 to Cardiff, thence 532 to T.

Tamworth. E. to Rugby 32, thence 334 to T.

—— E. to Birmingham 36, thence 346 to T.

Tarporley. E. to Crewe 42, thence 388 to T.

Tattenhall. E. to Crewe 42, thence 388 to T.

Tattershall. K. C. to Peterborough 72, thence 102 to T.

Taunton. P. to, 226.

Tebay. E. to, 52.

Teignmouth. P. to, 236.

Tetbury. P. to Swindon 212, thence 308 to T.

Tewkesbury. P. to Bristol 220, thence 294 to T.

Thankerton. E. to, 58.

Thatcham. P. to Reading 204, thence 284 to T.

Theale. P. to Reading 204, thence 284 to T.

Thedingworth. E. to Rugby 32, thence 326 to T.

Thetford. S. to, 110.

Thirsk. K. C. to, 84.

—— E. to Rugby 32, thence 328 to Derby, thence 348 to Leeds, thence 356 to T.

Thornhill. E. to Newton 46, thence 396 to Manchester, thence 414 to North Dean, thence 426 to Dewsbury, thence 428 to T.

——, N. B. E. to Carlisle 56, thence 521 to T.

Thornton (Scotland). E. to Carlisle 56, thence 521 to Glasgow, thence 522 to Stirling, thence 526 to T.

—— E. to Farrington 46, thence from Lostock Junction 400 to T.

Thorpe. E. to Blisworth 30, thence 320 to T.

—— K. C. to Newark 76, thence 484 to T.

—— Arch. K. C. to Church Fenton 82, thence 442 to T. A.

Thrapston. E. to Blisworth 30, thence 320 to T.

Thredyrhlen. P. to Bristol 220, thence 531 to Cardiff, thence 532 to T.

Three Bridges. L. to, 164.

Thurgarton. K. C. to Grantham 74, thence 492 to Nottingham, thence 480 to T.

Thurston. S. to Haughley 136, thence 504 to T.

Timperley. E. to Crewe 42, thence 392 to Manchester, thence 420 to T.

Tiverton. P. to, 130.

Tivetshall. S. to, 138.

Todmorden. E. to Crewe 42, thence 392 to Manchester, thence 414 to T.

Tollerton. K. C. to, 84.

Topcliffe. E. to Rugby 32, thence 328 to Derby, thence 348 to Leeds, thence 356 to T.

Torquay. P. to, 226.

Totness. P. to, 238.

Tottenham. S. to, 112.

Tow Law. K. C. to Darlington 86, thence 460 to Witton, thence 458 to T. L.

Town Green. E. to Newton 46, thence 396 to Liverpool, thence 400 to T. G.

Tranent. K. C. to, 100.

Trefnest. P. to Bristol 220, thence 531 to Cardiff, thence 532 to T.

Trentham. E. to Rugby 32, thence 334 to Colwick, thence 374 to T.

Tring. E. to, 26.

Troon. E. to Carlisle 56, thence 521 to T.

Trowbridge. P. to Chippenham 214, thence 514 to T.

Tunbridge Wells. L. to Reigate 164, thence 176 to T. W.

Tutbury. E. to Birmingham 36, thence 346 to Burton, thence 382 to T.

Tuxford. K. C. to, 78.

Tweedmouth. K. C. to, 98.

Twerton. P. to, 220.

Twickenham. W. 276 to 278.

Twyford. P. to, 204.

Ty Croes. E. to Wolverhampton 40, thence 348 to Chester, thence 530 to T.

Tynehead. To Edinburgh xvii, thence 528 to T.

Tynemouth. K. C. to Newcastle 92, thence 470 to T.

Uddringston. E. to Carstairs 60, thence 519, to Motherwell, thence 519, to U.

Uffington. K. C. to Peterborough 72, thence 478 to U.

Ulceby. K. C. to Retford 78, thence 424 to U.

Ulleshelfe. K. C. to, 82.

Ullesthorpe. E. to Rugby 32, thence 328 to U.

Underhill. E. to Burton 48, thence 402 to Fleetwood, thence by boat to Piel 472 to U.

Upholland. E. to Newton 46, thence 396 to Liverpool, thence 404 to U.

Upton Magna. E. to Wolverhampton 40, thence 360 to W.

Usselby. K. C. to Newark 76, thence 484 to U.

Uttoxeter. E. to Birmingham 36, thence 346 to Burton, thence 382 to U.

Valley. E. to Wolverhampton 40, thence 348 to Chester, thence 529 to V.

Vauxhall. W. to, 140.

Victoria Park. S. to, 110.

Wadborough. E. to Birmingham 36, then 308 back to W.

—— P. to Bristol 220, thence 294 to W.

Wainfleet. K. C. to Boston 104, thence 510 to W.

Wakefield. E. to Newton 46, thence 396 to Manchester, thence 414 to North Dean, then 426 to W.

Walcot. E. to Wolverhampton 40, thence 360 to W.

Wallingford. P. to, 208.

Walsall. E. to Bescott 38, thence 370 to W.

Walsden. E. to Crewe 42, thence 392 to Manchester, thence 414 to W.

Waltham. S. to, 112.

——, Lincoln. K. C. to Peterborough 72, thence 104 to Boston, thence 512 to W.

Walthamstow. S. to, 112.

Walton. W. to, 142.

—— K. C. to Peterborough 72, thence 478 to W.

——, Stafford. E. to Birmingham 36, thence 346 to W.

Wamphray. E. to, 58.

Wandsworth. W. to, 274.

Wansford. E. to Blisworth 36, thence 320 to W.

Wantage. P. to, 210.

Ware. S. to Broxbourne 112, thence 494 to W.

Wareham. W. to, 154.

Warkworth. K. C. to, 96.

Warrington. E. to, 44.

Warwick. See Leamington.

Washerley. K. C. to Darlington 86, thence 460 to Witton, thence 458 to W.

Washingborough. K. C. to Peterborough 72, thence 102 to W.

Washington. K. C. to, 90.

Water Lane. S. to, 112.

—— Orton. E. to Birmingham 36, thence 346 to W. O.

Waterbeach. S. to, 118.

Wateringbury. L. to Reigate 164, thence 176 to Paddock Wood, thence 246 to W.

Waterloo. E. to Newton 46, thence 396 to Liverpool, thence 398 to W.

Watford. E. to, 22.

Wath, North Riding. E. to Rugby 32, thence 321 to Derby, thence 348 to Leeds, thence 356 to W.

——, West Riding. E. to Birmingham 36, thence 346 to W.

—— E. to Rugby 32, thence 320 to Derby, thence 348 to W.

Watlington. S. to Ely 118, thence 500 to W.

—— S. to Cambridge 118, thence 498 to St. Ives, thence 498 to W.

Waverton. E. to Crewe 42, thence 388 to W.

Weaste Lane. E. to Newton Junction 46, thence 396 to W. L.

Wednesbury. E. to Bescott 38, thence 370 to W.

——, Salop. E. to Stafford 41, thence 372 to W.

——, — E. to Wolverhampton 40, thence 360 to W.

Weedon. E. to, 30.

Weeton. E. to Rugby 32, thence 328 to Derby, thence 348 to Leeds, thence 356 to W.

Welford. E. to Rugby 32, thence 376 to W.

Wellingborough. E. to Blisworth 30, thence 320 to W.

Wellington, Somerset. P. to, 228.

——, Salop. E. to Stafford 40, thence 372 to W.

Welwyn. K. C. to, 66.

Wemmington. E. to Lancaster 48, thence 434 to W.

Wendling. S. to Wymondham 122, thence 506 to Dereham, thence 512 to W.

West Auckland. K. C. to Aycliffe 88, thence 460 to W. A.

—— Drayton. P. to, 166.

West India Docks. F. to, 516.

Westbury. P. to Chippenham 214, thence 514 to W.

Westhoughton. E. to Wigan 46, thence 404 to W.

Weston. E. to Rugby 32, thence 334 to Colwick, thence 574 to W.

Westonhanger. L. to Reigate 164, thence 176 to W.

Weston-super-Mare. P. to, 224.

Wetherley. K. C. to Church Fenton 82, thence 442 to W.

Wetheral. E. to Carlisle 56, thence 470 to W.

Weybridge. W. to, 142.

Whalley. E. to Newton Junction 46, thence 396 to Kenyon, thence 408 to W.

Whifflet. E. to Carstairs 60, thence 519 to P.

Whitacre. E. to Birmingham 36, thence 346 to W.

Whitehaven. E. to Preston 48, thence 412 to Fleetwood, thence by boat to Piel, and 477 to W.

Whilburn. To Edinburgh xvii, thence 519 to W.

Whitby. E. to York 82, thence 444 to Rillington, thence 450 to W.

Whitley Bridge. K. C. to Knottingley 82, thence 430 to W. B.

Whitmore. E. to, 42.

Whitstable. L. to Reigate 164, thence 176 to Ashford, thence 184 to W.

Whittington. E. to Wolverhampton 40, thence 360 to W.

Whittlesea. S. to Ely 118, thence 502 to W.

Whittlesford. S. to, 119.

Wickenby. K. C. to Newark 76, thence 484 to W.

Wickwar. P. to Bristol 220, thence 294 to W.

Widdrington. K. C. to, 94.

Wigan. E. to, 46.

Wigstowe. E. to Rugby 32, thence 328 to W.

Wigton. E. to Carlisle 56, thence 476 to W.

Willenhall. E. to, 38.

Willesden. E. to, 20.

Willington. E. to Birmingham 36, thence 346 to W.

Wilmslow. E. Crewe 42, thence 392 to W.

Willoughby. K. C. to Peterborough 72, thence 104 to Boston, thence 510 to W.

Wilncote. E. to Birmingham 86, thence 346 to W.

Wimbledon. W. to, 140.

Wimblington. S. to Cambridge 118, thence 498 to St. Ives, thence 498 to W.

Wimborne. W. to, 152.

Winchburgh. To Edinburgh xvii, thence 518 to W.

THE RAIL ROAD BOOK.

LONDON.

In a work especially intended as a guide to the Railroads of Great Britain, with the cities, towns, country-seats, and picturesque scenery through, or in the vicinity of which they pass, it will naturally be expected that we should say something of the capital from whence issue the main lines: we therefore offer the following brief account of the wonders of the metropolis to the general reader, referring those who are desirous to obtain more ample details upon points connected with its history, to Mr. Cunningham's admirable and deservedly popular "Hand Book for London."

> "Where has commerce such a mart,
> So rich, so throng'd, so drain'd, and so supplied
> As London? opulent, enlarged, and still
> Increasing London!"—THE TASK.

The author of these lines died in the eighteenth century, but who can say they are not now a perfect portraiture? or at what distant period they will be inapplicable to the state of this vast, colossal metropolis? More opulent than ever, enlarged threefold since Cowper's truthful lyre was mute; still, still it is increasing London; and the busy note, as well of preparation as of actual operation at all the cardinal points, defies the calculation of man as to the ultimate boundaries of this lateral Babylon.

London, the great capital of the freest and (despite occasional clouds and crises of misfortune, which, under the ordination of Providence, afflict the people of every land) the happiest nation of the earth, is situated on the banks of the Thames, the most wealthy and important, though not the largest, river in the universe; and extends its gigantic limbs over wide tracts of the four counties of Middlesex, Essex, Surrey, and Kent. The extent of this leviathan city, as defined by Act of Parliament for postal purposes, would give but a very inadequate idea of the enormous space occupied by this one town, comprised within London proper, the city and liberty of Westminster, with the boroughs of Marylebone, Finsbury, the Tower Hamlets, Southwark and Lambeth, the whole of which are, however, at present bounded by Fulham, Hammersmith, Acton and Willesden, on the West; by Limehouse, Greenwich and Blackwall on the East; by Kilburn, Hampstead and Highgate on the North; and Norwood, Dulwich and Camberwell on the South. The best idea of the extent of this city, although comprehending but a very small portion of its immediate suburbs, may be conceived from the following table of the number of acres occupied by each of its parliamentary subdivisions, to which is added the population of each borough, with the number of registered electors at the period therein indicated returning the sixteen metropolitan members of the House of Commons.

	Acres.	Population.	Parliamentary Electors, 1842—1843.
Finsbury Borough	4,670	265,043	14,038
Lambeth ditto...	8,840	197,412	9,083
London City	600	120,702	20,030
Southwark Borough	590	142,620	5,353
Marylebone ditto	5,310	287,465	13,361
Tower Hamlets	8,988	419,730	16,246
Westminster City and Liberty	2,500	219,930	14,801
Total average	31,498	1,652,902	92,912

The numbers of houses, 265,558, those inhabited producing an annual rent of about from 8 to £10,000,000.

The very large parishes of Chelsea, Camberwell, Wandsworth, Clapham, Greenwich and Lewisham, which have been added to the bills of mortality, but are not included in the foregoing table, augment the population by nearly half a million; which, with the proportional increase since 1841 (the period of the last census), brings the population at this time (1851) to 2,240,000.

Of the antiquity of London as a city, there is no question, but the accounts are very conflicting. It is said that Trinobantum, or New Troy, which stood on the site of the present city was built by Brute, a descendant of Æneas, some centuries before the Christian Era, and that a lineal succession of upwards of fifty Kings, ruled Britain, down to King Lud, who first surrounded the city with walls. Cornelius, Tacitus, and Amminianus Marcellinus mention this place as well as the Venerable Bede; and many of the coins of King Alfred, have inscribed upon them the monogram *London*. But that London was a Roman station, the excavations made from time to time, for the foundations of new buildings most satisfactorily attest, of which we may mention one of a very interesting character, discovered in 1848, when preparing the ground for the formation of the New Coal Exchange, in Thames Street, consisting of a hypocaust with all the flues, &c., in as perfect a state as at the period of their erection. Those who are curious in such matters will be amply rewarded by inspecting the tesselated pavements, urns, household utensils, coins, &c., which have been dug up within the boundaries of the ancient walls of the City of London during the last century, the finest specimens of which are in the British Museum, the Museums at the Guildhall Library, and the India House, and in the collections of Mr. Gwitt, F.S.A., Union Street, Borough; and of Mr. C. Roach Smith, F.S.A., Liverpool Street, City. London Stone which still remains in Cannon Street, is said to be the identical stone, or central milliarium (milestone), whence radiated the Roman high roads, of which Watling Street was the chief, and upon which the distances were inscribed.

In former times, when it was the policy of the rulers of this land to impress foreign ambassadors with the highest possible idea of England's wealth, strength, and power, a certain route was prescribed upon their landing at Dover, which, after exhibiting the cathedral and other ecclesiastical monuments of the rich city of Canterbury, and the imposing Castle of Rochester on the broad and noble waters of the Medway, brought them to Gravesend, where they took water, were rowed in the royal barge to London, and landed in great state at the Tower. All the commerce of London was thus brought under their view; for the Pool even then presented a forest of masts, each ship being an evidence of England's power, her commercial prosperity. How strange it is, that, amidst the changes effected by time, all observant writers admit, (and it is well that our country friends should receive the information,) that the only spot still capable of impressing the stranger with any just conception of the grandeur and magnificence of the metropolis, is that most splendid of all river roads, in the vicinity of the very Tower to which we have alluded, New London Bridge! It is from thence he will perceive those forests of masts, which have excited the astonishment of all foreigners, issuing from the decks of thousands of ships, from all parts of the world; so thickly covering the surface of the water, that two alleys, or lines of passage, of sufficient width to allow a passage for the outward and inward-bound vessels, can alone be spared to navigation. Here, too, the waters are in a constant state of boiling ferment, from the incessant motion of the sea-going and river steamers: the quays, too, are lined with busy workmen, loading and unloading, by countless cranes, the vessels alongside; while immediately below, on either side of the bridge, may be seen, at all hours of the day, thousands of passengers hurrying on board some steamer, in search of pleasure or for dispatch of business.

Turning from the contemplation of these proceedings in the inferior regions, the eye is astonished at the multitude and the rush of coaches, carts, omnibuses, and carriages of every description, from the humble donkey-cart of the costermonger to the gilded chariots of the Sheriffs; from the neat tax-cart of the retailer, with his broken bit of blood, to a succession of five, six, or seven of Barclay and Perkins's drays, each drawn by three or four of the proudest, the fattest, and the noblest-looking animals in Christendom; while, cutting in here and there, tearing away at a frightful pace, which vies almost with the railway trains to which they are hastening, are innumerable cabs and hackney vehicles of every denomination. If the stranger but turn his gaze from the moving scenes below and around him, what hundreds of steeples, churches, monuments and public buildings, are spread before the eye. Here then is the spot to which the traveller should first

devote his attention upon arriving in London, and as the task is easy of accomplishment, he should follow up his scenery of the interior of the metropolis by passing over, in succession, each of the seven bridges which cross this noble river, which have claims to his consideration.

A periodical of 1843, gives the following account of this great metropolis, which we insert, because, although it may not be perfectly accurate in all its details, it seems to our own long experience by no means overcharged, and is calculated to impress the traveller with a just idea of what he may expect :—"London occupies a surface of 32 square miles, thickly planted with houses, mostly three, four and five stories high. It contains 300 churches and chapels of the establishment; 364 Dissenters' chapels, 22 foreign chapels, 250 public schools, 1,500 private schools, 150 hospitals, 156 almshouses, besides 205 other institutions, 550 public offices, 14 prisons, 22 theatres, 24 markets; consumes annually 110,000 bullocks, 776,000 sheep, 250,000 lambs, 250,000 calves, and 270,000 pigs; 11,000 tons of butter, 13,000 tons of cheese, 10,000,000 gallons of milk, 1,000,000 quarters of wheat, or 64,000,000 of quartern loaves, 65,000 pipes of wine, 2,000,000 gallons of spirits, and 2,000,000, barrels of porter and ale; employs 16,502 shoemakers, 14,552 tailors, 2,391 blacksmiths, 2,013 whitesmiths, 5,030 house-painters, 1,076 fish-dealers, 2,062 hatters and hosiers, 13,208 carpenters, 6,822 bricklayers, &c., 5,416 cabinet-makers, 1,005 wheelwrights, 2,180 sawyers, 2,807 jewellers, 1,172 old-clothes men (chiefly Jews), 4,328 printers (viz. 3,628 compositors and 700 pressmen), 1,393 stationers, 2,633 watch and clock makers, 4,227 grocers, 1,430 milkmen, 5,655 bakers, 2,091 barbers, 1,040 brokers, 4,322 butchers, 1,586 cheesemongers, 1,082 chemists, 4,199 clothiers and linen drapers, 2,167 coachmakers, 1,367 coal merchants, 2,133 coopers, 1,381 dyers, 2,319 plumbers, 907 pastrycooks, 868 saddlers, 1,246 tinmen, 803 tobacconists, 1,470 turners, 556 undertakers, (the above are all males above 20 years of age). 10,000 private families of fashion, &c. About 77,000 establishments of trade and industry, 4,400 public houses, 330 hotels, 470 beer shops, 960 spirit and wine shops."

We will make but one addition to these curious statistics as illustrative of the ignorance of the Frenchman who asked an English traveller, "Connaissez-vous Monsieur Smith, de Londres ?" Of this patronymic, independently of gentlemen unconnected with commerce, the "Commercial Directory" gives eleven columns and a half, of eighty-three in each column, making the total number of Smiths carrying on business in London amount to nine hundred and fifty-seven.

With the foregoing general outline, we shall proceed to describe, as briefly as possible, such of the principal public buildings, ecclesiastical and other monuments, great public institutions, &c., as are most worthy of notice, beginning with the bridges.

BRIDGES.

London boasts seven bridges, all of which have claims upon the attention of the stranger; we shall take them in their regular succession.

1. LONDON BRIDGE.

This splendid specimen of architectural genius, was built from the design of Mr. John Rennie and his sons, Sir John and Mr. George Rennie; the first stone of which was laid in 1825, and the bridge opened to the public on the 1st of August, 1831, William IV. and Queen Adelaide being present on the occasion. It has five semi-elliptical arches over the river, the centre of which has one hundred and fifty-two feet span, with a rise above high-water mark of twenty-nine feet six inches; the arches next the centre are one hundred and forty feet in span, with a proportionate rise, and the abutment arches are of one hundred and thirty feet span, with a rise of twenty-four feet six inches. Architects in general assign the palm of beauty, strength and durability to this bridge above all others. The approaches to this noble structure are magnificent, both on the London and Surrey sides of the river.

2. SOUTHWARK BRIDGE,

erected from the design of Mr. John Rennie, was commenced in 1815, and opened to the public in 1819. It consists of three cast-iron arches, the centre one having a span of two hundred and forty feet, resting on stone piers. The iron work weighed five thousand seven hundred and eighty tons. The approach to this fine bridge on the City side is very bad; Queen Street being narrow and on a steep declivity; but it is now undergoing great alterations.

3. BLACKFRIARS BRIDGE

was considered a handsome structure until its repairs, in 1840, when the original character of its architecture was lost sight of entirely by the City architect, and the open balustraded parapets, essential to the harmony of the whole, were replaced by a plain stone wall, altogether out of character and keeping with the rest of the structure. It was built after the design and under the direction of Robert Mylne, a Scotchman, who died in 1811. The first stone was laid in 1760, and the bridge was opened generally to the public in 1769. It has nine elliptical arches, and is nine hundred and ninety-five feet in length. The approaches from the City by Bridge Street on the one side, and the Blackfriars Road on the other, are very noble.

4. WATERLOO BRIDGE.

The first stone of this truly magnificent structure, which has involved thousands in ruin, was laid in 1811, and it was opened to the public in 1817. During the progress of construction, that glorious event transpired which determined its proprietors to bestow upon it the name of Wellington's last and crowning victory. One of the most distinguished foreign senators (M. Dupin), pays the following brilliant compliment to the genius of its engineer, Mr. John Rennie. Speaking of this bridge he says: "It is a colossal monument worthy of Sesostris and the Cæsars." It consists of nine elliptical arches, each of one hundred and twenty feet span, supported on piers of twenty feet wide at the springing of the arches. The entire length of the bridge is two thousand four hundred and fifty-six feet, the river arches being one thousand three hundred and eighty feet in length, the remaining distance being borne by the land arches, three hundred and ten feet of noble approach from the Strand, and seven hundred and sixty-six feet on the Surrey side, or Bridge Road. The road in its whole distance is perfectly level.

5. HUNGERFORD SUSPENSION BRIDGE

For foot passengers only, is one of the lighest and most elegant of its kind in the empire. It crosses the Thames from Hungerford Market, near *Charing Cross* (under which denomination the bridge is also known), to Belvidere Road, Lambeth. It was erected under the superintendence and direction of Sir Isambert Brunel; the first stone was laid in 1841, and it was opened to the public in 1845. It consists of three arches, or more properly speaking of three divisions, the central being six hundred and seventy-six feet six inches in length, or one hundred and sixteen feet six inches longer than that of the Menai Bridge, and the other two three hundred and thirty-three feet each. The towers which carry the chains are in the Italian style, similar to the market buildings. It is, in fact, surpassed only in length by the bridge at Fribourg, in Switzerland, the span of which, from pier to pier, is about nine hundred feet.

6. WESTMINSTER BRIDGE

was built by Charles Labelye, a Swiss; the first stone was laid in 1738-9, and opened to the public in 1750. It is one thousand two hundred and twenty-three feet long by forty-five feet wide, and consists of fourteen arches of different dimensions, the centre being of seventy-six feet span. A few years ago this bridge was considered to be in a dangerous state, and its high parapets and heavy balustrades, which the French wits declared had been erected as a precaution against the English propensity to suicide, were taken down to relieve the foundations; but this has not cured the defect, and it is now allowed to remain only until another can be substituted.

7. VAUXHALL BRIDGE.

This light and pleasing bridge is from the designs of Mr. James Walker, and consists of nine arches of equal dimensions, of iron, reposing on stone piers, connecting Pimlico and Millbank with Vauxhall. It was begun in 1811, and opened in 1816. The exterior parapets of this bridge are leased to the London Gas Light Company, whose mains thus carried across the Thames, are of sufficient diameter to enable them to supply the distant parishes of St. Pancras and Marylebone, while they add considerably to the embellishment of the bridge. The approaches to Vauxhall Bridge from Westminster, as well as from Pimlico, are broad and handsome; and although it is only lately that speculators upon a grand scale have turned their attention to this latter spot, bordering upon the river, as an eligible site for building, almost a new town has already sprung up, whose streets, squares, and crescents, with their spacious houses, will soon vie with any other portion of the metropolis in elegance and architectural taste.

RIVER SCENERY.

The stranger having now visited each of London's splendid bridges, would probably desire to become better acquainted with the banks of the noble river over which they are thrown; let him, therefore, descend the steps near the centre of Vauxhall Bridge by the Steam Pier, and he will be re-conveyed to the point from whence he started, London Bridge, in an elegant steam-boat, for the small sum of two-pence. The satisfaction he will derive from his trip, will depend greatly upon his own temperament and habits of thought; but, under any circumstances, the feeling excited would probably be more that of wonderment than unqualified delight. Leaving Vauxhall Bridge, behind a splendid quay, a huge brick fortress, with pointed towers like the old Temple at Paris, is the only solitary building which presents itself for a long distance on the Middlesex side, called the Millbank Penitentiary; while on the Surrey, or opposite side of the river, with the exception of the fine and extensive works of the London Gas Company, near the bridge, an unbroken series of warehouses, wharfs, dilapidated sheds and boat-houses meet his view until he arrives at the venerable church of Lambeth, and the Archiepiscopal Palace of Canterbury, opposite to which, above the houses in Millbank, are seen the curious towers of St. John's, and Westminster's far-famed Abbey; while washed by the waters of the Thames, now appears the noble quay, on which stands the new Houses of Parliament, extending their highly elaborated *façade* for a length of nine hundred feet to the very abutment of Westminster Bridge. Passing under which, on the right, a constant succession of coal and timber wharfs, relieved by no important building, marks the Surrey banks as exclusively commercial, while on the left, though almost still in the midst of coal lighters, may be seen the Transport Office just beyond the bridge. Whitehall Gardens, where the late venerated statesman, Sir Robert Peel, resided, Privy Gardens, the abode of wealth and aristocracy, and Whitehall. Hungerford Bridge and Market now arrest the stranger's attention; immediately to the left of which, on the route eastward, is a narrow-walled quay, planted with trees, called Villiers' Walk, fronting the residence of the great Duke of Buckingham, who was assassinated by Felton, at Portsmouth, in the centre of which is still the handsome stone water-gate, adorned with the armorial ensigns of the potent Duke, built by Inigo Jones, to surprise him on his return to England.

A little further on is the Adelphi, built by the brothers Adams. It has been greatly admired by the scientific world; and although the wonders of engineering and architectural daring lately achieved, throw a shade over the pigmy efforts of the last century, great praise is due to the brothers for their bold design, and its admirable execution. This range of building, with its noble terrace overlooking the river, reaches to the backs of the houses in the Strand, and is raised from the level of high-water mark upon a series of dark arches, used as stables for the horses employed in the extensive coal trade here carried on. The entrances to these singular subterranean vaults are like those of a mine; but latterly they have been lighted by gas, and are well worthy of inspection. Beyond the Adelphi, just before arriving at Waterloo Bridge, although not now very conspicuous, lies the Savoy Church, or St. Mary-le-Savoy, for the particulars of which, and the ancient

palace which stood here, and wherein John, King of France, was so long imprisoned, and afterwards died, while on a visit to this country, the reader must refer to Cunningham's "Hand Book of London." On the opposite side of the river, the succession of wharfs before described is only broken by the huge shafts of the shot manufacturers, and the splendid establishment of Messrs. Goding, the Lion Brewery. Passing under Waterloo Bridge, the stranger's attention cannot fail to be arrested by the magnificent building which now opens to his view—Somerset House. This noble pile, the only one worthy the name of a palace in London, is perfect in all its architectural proportions, and whether regarded from the river, or from its grand interior court, at its principal entrance from the Strand, it must strike every beholder with astonishment that it is not the residence of royalty. Were the windows of this truly splendid edifice in a proportionate scale of grandeur with the rest of the elevation, few capitals of Europe could boast a nobler or more kingly residence. It is exclusively devoted to offices of government, and for the convenience of the Queen's stationery, &c. The traveller will see, that beneath the arches of its foundation on the river, barges can enter at high-water or half-tide, into the interior of the building, and unload the government stores. The east wing of this building on the river, with an entrance in the Strand forms the King's College and School. Going a-head, as brother Jonathan says, and passing the extremities of several respectable and tolerably neat streets, issuing at right angles from the Strand, the next objects which attract attention are the pretty gardens and buildings of the Temples, the two ancient Inns of Court, formerly the abode of the Knights' Templars, many of whom lie buried in the magnificent church of the Inner Temple. Beyond this spot little arrests the stranger's attention, or interrupts the general line of warehouses on either side of the river; but these have now become more important and more spacious as approaching nearer to the centre of commerce. We must, however, except from this remark the purest and best, we might almost say the only view of London's splendid Cathedral, St. Paul's, which will be described more fully hereafter, and the hundreds of steeples which meet the eye on every side. Just before reaching London Bridge, on the Surrey side, the extensive river-side premises of Messrs. Barclay and Perkins, the eminent brewers, a perfect town of itself, must excite both wonder and surprise ; to which, however, on Bankside, just beyond South-wark Bridge, will be seen (for some time to come, perhaps for centuries, in order to commemorate a popular but most lawless proceeding, which may be regarded in its only palliative light, as a proof of British hatred to woman's oppressors), the sign of the George, which is now inscribed in large letters, legible from the opposite side of the Thames, "Haynau's Refuge," to indicate where this unfortunate Austrian General found shelter from the brewers of Barclay and Perkins' establishment. With the exception of a slight view of the top of the venerable, but lately-restored church of St. Mary Olave's, in the Borough of Southwark, and the magnificent modern hall of the Fishmongers' Company on the opposite side at the foot of London Bridge, no other remarkable buildings present themselves to our recollection until after passing the bridge. For this purpose, in order to inspect the wonders of *below bridge*, as it is termed, it will be necessary to land and re-embark from the same place for a twopenny, fourpenny, or sixpenny ride, according to the distances of the objects required to be visited, in the Greenwich or Blackwall steamers. From this spot the stranger to London will pass through those forests of masts he witnessed from the bridge above, before which, as he glides by Billingsgate Market, we may invite his attention to a very elegant and conspicuous building, lately erected in Thames Street, for the Coal Exchange, beyond which, on a noble quay, with a magnificent broad terrace-walk fronting the Thames, and visible from the bridge, stands the Custom House. It is a building of immense dimensions, and well adapted to the object for which it was intended, although it cannot be said that its elevation betrays any great architectural beauty or embellish-ment. While upon this subject we may observe, that although the exports from London are not now to be compared with those of Liverpool, its import trade exceeds not only all the other parts of the empire, but that of any in the world, Mr. McCulloch having estimated it at the enormous annual amount of £80,000,000 sterling..

Beyond the Custom House we approach, but without trembling, that once dread fortress, the celebrated Tower of London, so full of great historical associations, so intimately connected with all those tales of blood and sorrow which have affected the youthful student even to tears while perusing the dark pages of history. It now inspires no horror on our minds, no thrill passes through our souls when inspecting its deepest dungeons, we shudder only for the crimes of our forefathers; for the emancipation of the mind from the thraldom of ignorance, has thus changed our sentiments from the fear of power to

humiliating pity for the misguided oppressors. Stow's description of this famous fortress was until within the two last centuries perfectly applicable, he says:

" This Tower is a citadel to defend or command the city; a royal palace for assemblies or treaties; a prison of state for the most dangerous offenders; the only place of coinage for all England at this time; the armoury for warlike provisions; the treasury of the ornaments and goods of the Crown; and general conserver of the most valuable records of the King's Courts of Justice at Westminster."—p. 23.

Shakspeare and earlier writers assign the erection of this stronghold to Julius Cæsar; but the account is unconfirmed, although for many centuries one part of the building was called "The Tower of Julius." It is generally supposed to have been built by William the Conqueror, and Stow confirms the fact of the great White Tower, the oldest portion of the whole structure, having been erected in 1078, under the superintendence of Gundolph, Bishop of Rochester, who was also the architect of Rochester Castle. A history of the Tower would be no small history of England, a close inspection of its many curiosities will amply repay the visitor. But as the steamer glides onwards towards the Pool, the stranger may detect the terrible "Traitor's Gate," a small postern, with a drawbridge, which Stow says, is "seldom let down but for the receipt of some great persons prisoners."

" On through that gate misnamed, through which before
Went Sidney, Russell, Raleigh, Cranmer, Moore."—ROGERS' HUMAN LIFE.

Now steaming through the narrow channels of the river literally choked with shipping, and in which a free passage is only preserved by the strict regulations of the Thames' Police, the stranger will be astonished at the enormous warehouses, granaries, ship-building yards, manufactories, wet and dry docks, &c., which line both banks of the Thames. The great docks we shall presently describe as structures of too much import-ance in a national point of view to be passed over without special notice; but we must first conduct our visitors to the principal object for which he has probably made this little excursion.

THE THAMES TUNNEL.

This wonderful undertaking of the genius, skill, and enterprise of Sir Isambert Brunel, was commenced in March, 1825, and opened to the public in March, 1843: seven years' cessation of labour having occurred in consequence of an inundation, which filled the tunnel with water, in 1828; the works were not recommenced until 1835, so that the period of actual operations, until entire completion, was eleven years. This tunnel, which connects Wapping with Rotherhithe, or Redriff, is twelve hundred feet in length beneath the bed of the river. It is a wonderful undertaking, but no good has yet been derived from it by those who invested their capital in the scheme, as the toll, one penny for each passenger, barely covers the expenditure. The descent and ascent are by cylindrical shafts, of one hundred steps each, but the trouble is amply repaid.

Our feeble description of the riches of the Thames—the greatest commercial river in the world—must here end, as the various interesting places below this point, will form subjects for the general body of the work; but not so those celebrated havens for ship-ping, and the rich produce of foreign trade, which are the glory of this essentially commercial country, they all lie in this immediate vicinity.

THE DOCKS.

1. THE EAST INDIA DOCKS, BLACKWALL,

which locality is reached, in ten minutes by the Blackwall Railway, from the principal station in Fenchurch Street, City, or by the innumerable omnibuses from the West End, and steam-boats from Hungerford Bridge, stopping to take in passengers at all the inter-vening piers, and plying from morning till night. These splendid basins were originally erected for the East India Company's shipping; but since the opening of the trade to India, they have become the property of the West India Dock Company. They were opened for the reception of shipping in 1806. The Import Dock has an area of nineteen acres, the Export Docks, ten acres, and the basin, three. It is here that the stranger,

after feasting his eyes with a view of the stout bulwarks of England's commercial marine, may satisfy his appetite upon the delicacies of a white-bait repast, for which Blackwall, and particularly the Brunswick Hotel, are so justly celebrated.

2. THE WEST INDIA DOCKS.

These immense shelters, erected originally for the ships employed in the once luxuriant West India trade, were opened in 1802, the first stone having been laid by the illustrious William Pitt in 1800. They are situate between Limehouse and Blackwall, and have an area of two hundred and ninety-five acres; Import Dock, one hundred and seventy yards long by one hundred and sixty-six broad; Export Dock, one hundred and seventy yards by one hundred and thirty-five. A canal, three-quarters of a mile long, cuts off a bend of the river, connecting Limehouse Reach with Blackwall Reach, and forming the northern boundary of the Isle of Dogs. The Import and Export Docks, with their spacious warehouses, are enclosed within lofty walls five feet thick. These docks, which now belong to the East and West India Dock Company (whose office is in Billiter Square), are open to every kind of shipping. The Blackwall Railway also affords the readiest access to them.

3. THE COMMERCIAL DOCKS,

belonging to the company of that name, consist of five spacious and commodious basins, entered from the Thames between Randall's Rents and Dog and Duck Stairs, nearly opposite King's Arms' Stairs, in the Isle of Dogs. They were opened in 1807, and were originally called the Greenland Docks.

4. THE LONDON DOCKS,

comprise an area of ninety acres; thirty-six acres of water, and twelve thousand nine hundred and eighty feet of quay and jetty frontage, with three entrances from the Thames—the Hermitage, Wapping, and Shadwell. The Western Dock has an area of twenty acres; the Eastern, seven; and the Wapping Basin, three acres. That portion of the dock which is completely walled in, possesses accommodation for three hundred and two vessels, exclusive of small craft, with warehouse room for two hundred and twenty thousand tons of goods, and cellarage for eight thousand pipes of wine or spirits. The tobacco warehouses, which cover five acres of ground, are rented by Government at £14,000 per annum. The basins and shipping are open to the public; but to inspect the vaults, &c., an order must be obtained from the Secretary at the London Dock House, in New Bank Buildings. Ladies are not admitted after 1 P.M.

5. ST. KATHARINE'S DOCKS,

situated near the Tower of London, derive their name from, and are built on the site of St. Katharine's Hospital, founded by Matilda, wife of King Stephen, about 1148, which hospital was removed to the Regent's Park. No less than twelve hundred and fifty other houses were purchased and pulled down to make room for this great undertaking, which was commenced in 1827, under Mr. Telford as engineer, and Mr. Hardwick as architect, and opened for the reception of shipping 25th October, 1828. Area of docks twenty-four acres, of which eleven and a half acres are the wet docks. Ships of seven hundred tons can enter at any time of the tide. The warehouses, vaults, &c., can hold one hundred and ten thousand tons of goods. The average profits exceed £100,000 per annum.

Independently of those we have enumerated, there are many private docks for ship-building purposes.

ECCLESIASTICAL BUILDINGS.

ST. PAUL'S CATHEDRAL.

At the head of this subject must be ranked the Cathedral of St. Paul's, built on the site of the old metropolitan church of London, began 1675, and finished 1710. It is one of the grandest pieces of architecture in the world. It matters not that St. Peter's, at

Rome, is infinitely larger, or that it contains priceless riches in statuary, in gold, in silver, and in precious stones, St. Paul's stands alone and unmasked, as a whole and uniform structure, although both the composite and Corinthian styles were adopted in the design of the single architect, Sir Christopher Wren, who began and completed it in thirty-five years; and it is related as somewhat singular, that during that period there was but one master mason, Mr. Thomas Strong, and that one Bishop, Dr. Henry Compton, presided all the time over the diocese. St. Paul's is built in the form of a Latin cross, with projections at the west-end of the nave, to give an imposing width to the great west entrance. Length from east to west, five hundred feet; breadth of the body of the church, one hundred feet; the towers at the west end are two hundred and twenty-two feet high; and the height of the whole building from the street to the top of the cross, is four hundred and four feet. No description can do justice to this splendid temple of religion, its monuments, its whispering gallery, its dome, its colossal grandeur, can only be properly appreciated by those who have ocular demonstration of the sublime and beautiful proportions of this noble metropolitan church.

WESTMINSTER ABBEY,

of a perfectly different style of architecture to its eastern rival, venerable and venerated for its historical associations, teeming with the ashes of kings, princes, warriors, statesmen, and poets, is one of the noblest specimens of the early English style of architecture extant (Wren's unsightly towers excepted), while some portions of this sacred edifice, particularly the Chapel of Henry VII., are of a highly-elaborated and florid Gothic. It was originally a Benedictine monastery, the "Minster west of St. Paul's," from which its vicinity derived the name of Westminster, founded by Sebert, King of the East Saxons, A.D. 616. It was afterwards considerably enlarged by Edward the Confessor and other kings, and rebuilt during the reigns of Henry II. and Edward I. It is the place of coronation for the kings and queens of England. Access to the Abbey can be had at all reasonable times, by the small entrance in Poet's Corner, and during the daily service a general view of this truly magnificent ecclesiastical structure may be obtained gratuitously; but the rich and resplendent chapels of Henry VII. and Edward the Confessor, with the royal tombs, the monuments of England's greatest nobles and most remarkable persons, with relics and curiosities of the most profound interest, can be viewed for a trifling fee to the verger; and it would be accounted almost heresy for a stranger to quit the metropolis without visiting this beautiful monument of antiquity.

CITY CHURCHES.

Of the City parochial churches most worthy of attention, we may cite St. Bride's, Fleet Street, styled one of Wren's "architectural glories;" St. Stephen's, Walbrook, the interior of which is grand and imposing; St. Mary-at-Hill, near Billingsgate; ditto Abchurch, in Abchurch Lane; ditto Aldermanbury, in Cripplegate Ward; ditto Le Bow, in Cheapside, all persons born within the sound of whose bells are accounted cockneys. This church was built upon the arches of the old one, which was destroyed in the fire of London, the most ancient church in the City of human construction, the crypt of which is now perfect. All the foregoing are by Wren, as well as St. Mary Magdalen, Old Fish Street; Christ Church, Newgate Street; and St. Mary, Somerset, in the Ward of Queenhithe; and St. Sepulchre, whose fatal bell has rung the knell of many a doomed malefactor in the adjacent cells of Newgate; St. Giles', Cripplegate, an ancient and interesting church, in which repose the ashes of John Milton and his father (to the former of whom there is a monument); Sir Martin Frobisher, the intrepid mariner; and John Speed, the topographer, to whom there is a monument similar to the frontispiece in his Survey of London. Many others have claim to notice, but it would be impossible to particularize them unless in a work devoted to this subject alone. At the West End we may cite St. Margaret's, adjacent to Westminster Abbey; St. John's; St. Martin's-in-the-Fields, Trafalgar Square, with its noble façade; St. Giles-in-the-Fields, with the well-executed tablet of the Last Judgment, in relief, over the gateway-entrance to the church-yard; St. George's, Hanover Square; St. Marylebone; St. Pancras New Church; and St. Luke's, Chelsea, besides many other ancient, and an infinity of modern, structures of different styles of architecture, but chiefly Gothic, which have sprung up almost like magic since the acts passed for the extension of church accommodation.

PALACES.

Of palatial residences, few cities can boast more than London; but of royal palaces, strictly so speaking, there are but two, neither of which, exteriorly, are worthy the dignity of the Crown, or the much-boasted majesty of the people.   St. James's, the most ancient, a miserable brick building, formerly a hospital for lepers, was rebuilt, and enclosed within the Park by Henry VIII., of which the gateway at the bottom of St. James's Street, and the Presence Chamber, the chimney-piece of which bears his initials, with those of Queen Anne Boleyn, are the only remaining portions.   The present unsightly mass of bricks, however, contains some fine reception rooms; and upon relieving guard at eleven o'clock each morning, the bands of the Foot Guards play pieces from the best operas in the best style, in the old quadrangle within the gateway.

BUCKINGHAM PALACE,

the enormous amount of expenditure upon which, might under judicious management have produced a palace worthy the vast empire of England and her dominions, and consequently one of the noblest proportions, is nevertheless, though a most extensive building, which has lately been greatly augmented, far, very far, from commanding respect as a proper residence of the Sovereign of these realms; and if Englishmen are generally of this opinion, what must be the feelings of foreigners as to our want of taste when comparing this palace with the really splendid architectural triumphs of almost all the Courts of Europe?   It was built on the site of Queen Charlotte's residence, at the Pimlico end of St. James's Park, by his late Majesty George IV., forming, upon its completion, three sides of a square; but not affording sufficient accommodation, a front has been added to it, which now encloses a perfect quadrangle, shut out from public gaze, which, until a recent but unpopular plan for enclosing a very slight portion of the Park, so as to form a sort of fore-court, would have been approached by all the idle boys who frequent that portion of St. James's Park.   That Buckingham Palace has now assumed a grander appearance it cannot be doubted, but it still exhibits a want of that noble and refined taste we could have desired for the permanent town residence of Her Majesty and her successors, and which no patching can ever bestow upon it.

KENSINGTON.

Another palace in name, but so little does this cumbrous red brick pile offer in the nature of attraction to the public taste, that visitors to the capital, and the residents in the Metropolis, are rarely tempted to lead their steps towards it.   Its gardens however, planted with rose-shrubs and the choicest flowers; its pleasure-grounds (considered by Frenchmen superior to the gardens of the Tuilleries), ornamented with noble elms, oaks, venerable chestnuts and stately beeches; and its broad terraces, and beautifully-kept gravel-walks, are the most attractive resort of the fashionable world during the summer months of the London season preceding the rising of Parliament.   On Tuesdays and Fridays, in July and August, between the hours of three and six, the promenade is enlivened by music, the bands of the Life or Horse Guards being in attendance, and playing selections from all the favourite operas.   Without incurring the imputation of national vanity, it may be said that no capital in Europe can produce such an assemblage of rank, fashion, and loveliness as are here congregated on these occasions.   These gardens are situated at the west end of Hyde Park, from which they are entered, as well as from the palace precincts in Kensington.

PALACES OF THE NOBILITY AND GENTRY.

While upon the subject of palaces, we may observe, that although the houses of the nobility and gentry in the principal squares and streets at the West End, are sumptuous within, they present but little evidence of grandeur externally; we may, however, except from this rule the following handsome, and in some instances noble, elevations:

Apsley House, Duke of Wellington; Gloucester House, Park Lane, H.R.H. the Duchess of Gloucester; Mr. Hope's splendid mansion, corner of Down Street; the Marquis of Hertford's new mansion; Cambridge House, H.R.H. the Duke of Cambridge; Bath House, Lord Ashburton; Devonshire House, Duke of Devonshire; Burlington House, Earl of Burlington : the above are all in Piccadilly. Stafford House, Stable Yard, Duke of Sutherland; the Earl of Ellesmere's splendid mansion in Cleveland Square; Earl Spencer's noble residence in St. James's Place; and the Duke of Northumberland's, at Charing Cross, are the most conspicuous and the finest in London. To these may be added, Lansdowne House, Berkeley Square; Marquis of Lansdowne; Chesterfield House, Great Stanhope Street; Uxbridge House, Burlington Street, the Marquis of Anglesey; Lord Rokeby's mansion, Upper Berkeley Street, Portman Square; Montague House, Whitehall Gardens, the Duke of Buccleugh; Harcourt House, the Duke of Portland; Grosvenor House, Upper Grosvenor Street, the Marquis of Westminster; Lambeth Palace, Archbishop of Canterbury; and Marlborough House, Pall Mall, the residence of the late Queen Adelaide, now devoted to the Vernon Gallery of pictures. Almost all these noble residences have considerable gardens; few of them however are superior in their internal accommodation to the general run of houses of the nobility and gentry in Belgrave, Grosvenor, and Portman Squares, Park Lane, Carlton Gardens, &c.

THE PARKS.

London has five parks, three ancient and two modern. Hyde Park is on the site of the ancient Manor of Hide, belonging formerly to the Abbey of Westminster. It was once celebrated as a hunting-ground of royalty, subsequently for horse races and duels, and is now exclusively used as a promenade for the nobility and gentry, and a place of recreation for the people in general. It contains an area enclosed within iron rails, of about two hundred and fifty acres, and is bounded and surrounded by Knightsbridge and Kensington Gore on the south, Kensington Gardens on the west, Connaught Place, the Bayswater Road, with the splendid residences of Hyde Park Gardens (behind which a new city of palaces has sprung up within the last few years) on the north, and Park Lane on the east. It is beautifully laid out in walks and drives, and is ornamented with a noble sheet of water, called the Serpentine River, which is crossed at the upper, or Kensington Garden end, by an elegant stone bridge of five arches. Rotten Row, on the south side of this beautiful park, is devoted exclusively to equestrians, a healthful exercise that has lately taken such extension amongst the fair sex, that many hundreds of beautiful amazons may be seen here at all hours of the day during the season. The Life Guards cavalry barracks are situated on this side of the park, in front of which the colossal building for the Exhibition of 1851, is erected. No carriages can pass up Rotten Row, except those of Her Majesty and the Duke of St. Alban's, as Hereditary Grand Falconer of England. Near the Piccadilly entrance to this park (a handsome screen from the designs of Decimus Burton), is a colossal statue of Achilles, by Westmacott, raised to commemorate the martial exploits of the Duke of Wellington, by the ladies of England. Opposite to the gate in question, is the splendid arch (also by Decimus Burton) which forms the entrance to

ST. JAMES'S PARK.

This triumphal arch, at the top of Constitution Hill, is surmounted by an equestrian statue of the hero of Waterloo, of colossal size, by Matthew Coles Wyatt, erected in 1846. Constitution Hill leads directly into St. James's Park and to Buckingham Palace; being bounded on the west by Grosvenor Place and the high wall of Her Majesty's private gardens, and on the east by the Green Park, from which it is separated only by an open iron railing. This park is in the form of a kite; the narrow, or Pimlico end, being terminated by Buckingham Palace, while the opposite, or Westminster end, is occupied by a noble parade at the back of the Horse Guards; to the right and left of which building, stand the Admiralty and the Treasury. The centre of St. James's Park

is enclosed by iron railings, and the grounds, which are beautifully laid out, are open to the public. The ornamental water, extending from the Palace to the parade, and running through these delightful pleasure-grounds, contains a wonderful collection of water-fowl from all parts of the world. The Bird Cage Walk, leading in a direct line to Westminster Bridge, and in which are the Wellington Infantry Barracks, forms the southern boundary of this park, while the Green Park, St. James's Palace, the Stable Yard, the gardens of Marlborough House, and the houses in Pall Mall and Carlton Gardens, form its northern boundary; at the east end of which is a noble flight of steps, immediately under the Duke of York's column, leading into Waterloo Place and Regent Street.

THE GREEN PARK.

This park which, as we before observed, is only divided from St. James's by an iron railing, extends from the Mall in St. James's Park, near the Palace of that name, at right angles, to about the centre of Piccadilly, of which it forms one side, from opposite Devonshire House to the triumphal arch at the top of Constitution Hill, already described. Here are some very pretty undulations and inequalities of surface; and when the newly-planted trees and shrubs come to maturity, it will be a very pleasing promenade. On the Piccadilly side there are many noble and venerable elms, and it is surrounded and intersected by gravel walks. On the highest ground by Piccadilly, there is a reservoir belonging to one of the great water companies.

REGENT'S PARK.

So called, in compliment to his late Majesty George IV., when Regent, was formerly known as Marylebone Fields. It contains an area of about three hundred and fifty acres, and is situated beyond the New Road, on the north side of London, under Primrose Hill. A great portion of this park is open to the public, and is intersected by broad gravel-walks, on which benches and seats are placed for their accommodation at convenient distances. Certain parts, however, are enclosed, and contain many beautiful villas of the nobility, &c., one of which, St. Dunstan's, was built by the late Marquis of Hertford, and contains the giants of St. Dunstan's old church, which were purchased by his Lordship when that venerable edifice was pulled down for the improvement of Fleet Street. The park is surrounded by handsome terraces of a superior order of architecture, and the interior contains a fine piece of water and several beautiful plantations. Here are also the Zoological Gardens and other institutions, which will be named under the head of Public Sights and Amusements. On the east side of the park is the Hospital of St. Katherine, which was removed to this spot when its original site was sold for the formation of the St. Katherine's Dock. Taken as a whole, it may be truly said that no capital in Europe, or the world, possesses so splendid an assemblage of houses and villas as the Regent's Park.

VICTORIA PARK.

Lying entirely out of our beat, we shall give Mr. Cunningham's brief account of this open space which was granted by the Crown for the recreation of the people of a densely-crowded neighbourhood: "It is a plot of pleasure-ground, a little larger than St. James's Park, planted and laid out in the reign of the Sovereign whose name it bears. It is bounded on the south by Sir George Ducket's Canal (sometimes called the Lea Union Canal); on the west, by the Regent's Canal; on the east, by Old Ford Lane, leading from Old Ford to Hackney Wick; and on the north, by an irregular line of fields. It serves as a lung for the north-east part of London, and has already added to the health of the inhabitants of Spitalfields and Bethnal Green."

PUBLIC BUILDINGS AND MONUMENTS.

Of the public buildings of London, the City, unquestionably, bears the palm, for it can boast at least half a dozen which surpass the general run of national edifices in the West End. Of these, we may cite the

NEW ROYAL EXCHANGE,

which, with all its faults, is a noble structure, which cannot fail to impress the stranger with the highest idea of the commerce of a country requiring such a space for the business of its merchants. The burning of the old, and the erection of this grand building, are too well known to require any detail. In front of the Exchange is an equestrian statue of the Duke of Wellington, and opposite is

THE BANK OF ENGLAND,

a vast and very fine building; the interior arrangements of which are truly wonderful, and are well worthy of inspection. Near this lies

THE MANSION HOUSE,

the official residence of the Lord Mayor of London. It is one of the handsomest buildings, as a residence, in the metropolis; built of stone, in 1739, at a cost of £71,000. The principal room is called the "Egyptian Hall," and it is here that the great dinners and balls are given.

THE POST OFFICE,

in St. Martin's-le-Grand, built from the designs of Sir Robert Smirke, R.A. (who is said to have adopted one by Inigo Jones) between the years 1825 and 1829. It is a noble pile—the *façade* elegant and stately, and the whole admirably adapted to the enormous amount of business there transacted. At the back of this building stands

GOLDSMITHS HALL,

a magnificent stone structure, highly elaborated, worthy the riches of this great and ancient Company. On Fish Street Hill is the celebrated

MONUMENT OF LONDON,

erected to commemorate the Great Fire in 1666. From the top of this column a splendid view is obtained of London and the adjacent country, for many miles round, with the sinuosities of the Thames. An iron cage erected over the flaming corn, its crowning ornament, effectually prevents the recurrence of those suicides which so shocked the feelings of the inhabitants a few years ago. The Monument is two hundred and two feet high, and is ascended by three hundred and forty-five steps. Admittance from nine till dark, sixpence each.

THE HALL OF COMMERCE,

in Threadneedle Street, built on the site of the French Church, 1830, by the private speculation of Mr. Edward Moxhay, is a splendid structure. Its principal room is a truly noble saloon. A fine Roman pavement (now in the British Museum) was discovered in for digging the foundations.

GUILDHALL,

originally built in 1411 (12th Henry IV.), was greatly injured by the Fire of London; the reparations are in barbarous taste; the new front was erected by Daun, the City architect, in 1789. The monuments of Chatham, Pitt, Nelson, Beckford, &c., are worthy inspection. In the various Courts of Law and Common Council, &c., are seen interesting

busts and pictures. It is in this Hall that the Lord Mayor gives his inauguration dinner on the 9th of November, after his grand procession by land and water to and from Westminster. Before quitting the City, we may mention Crosby Hall, in Bishopsgate Street, and many of the Halls of the City Companies, the South Sea House, and particularly the East India House, in Leadenhall Street, as worthy of inspection. Many other places demand attention, but their detail would fill a volume. On leaving the City, we may first call attention to the New Hall of Lincoln's Inn; and a little to the north,

THE BRITISH MUSEUM,

the riches, the wonder of which surpass imagination—and wherein may be found the rarest antiquities from all parts of the world; the most splendid library in the universe; the most wonderful collection of fossils and of natural history. A whole life passed within its walls would not suffice to learn even the catalogue of its contents. The building itself is the handsomest and most classical in the metropolis. Passing onwards to the West, the neighbourhood of Charing Cross possesses the greatest attractions. Here, in Trafalgar Square, stands

THE NATIONAL GALLERY.

It is not such a gallery of paintings as England should possess, but it contains many noble works of the greatest masters, deserving a better shelter than the singularly ungainly building which protects them from the weather. Nevertheless, Correggio, Guido, Titian, Raphael, Sebastian del Rainto, Michael Angelo, Leonardo da Vinci, Caracci, Velasquez, Murillo, Claude, Rubens, Vandyke, &c. The building occupies the whole north side of Trafalgar Square, and is built on the site of the Old King's Mews. The columns of the portico, the best part of the whole elevation, were taken from Carlton House. The noble column to Nelson is the grand ornament of this Square, which contains also an equestrian statue to George IV., and two machines, like dumb waiters, yclept fountains.

THE ADMIRALTY,

a little further on, is a large square building, extending to St. James's Park. The screen in front is from the design of the brothers Adams, the architects of the Adelphi. Beyond this is

THE HORSE GUARDS,

a plain stone building, with an excellent clock (now it goes again), and a couple of stone watch-boxes, which are tenanted during the day by two troopers of the Life or Horse Guards, on horseback. Opposite to this building is

THE BANQUETING HOUSE,

at Whitehall. This is a noble piece of architecture, by Inigo Jones, and had it been continued, would have proved a really splendid palace, of which England ought to have been justly proud. It was from a first-floor window of this building that Charles I. stepped on to the scaffold, erected before it, and met his fate in that Christian and right royal spirit which indicated, in spite of some kingly errors, the native dignity of his soul, and the purity and sincerity of his faith in the King of kings. The ceiling of the Banqueting House was painted on canvas, by Rubens, abroad, in 1635, for which he was paid £3000, and represents the apotheosis of James I. Divine service is performed in the Banqueting Hall every Sunday. Nearly opposite to this magnificent building stands

THE TREASURY,

between Downing Street and the Horse Guards. It is an old building with a new face, from the designs of Barry, R.A. The *façade* is handsome, and, coupled with the magnitude of the building, has an imposing appearance. Every inch of the ground, as we approach the precincts of the venerable Abbey of Westminster, becomes more interesting. Here,

WESTMINSTER HALL,

the finest chamber in the world, must strike the beholder with astonishment and respect for the works of our ancestors, while the historical associations connected with this vast Hall must increase his feelings of veneration. Much of the pristine dignity of the grand saloon is however lost, from the flooring having been raised from time to time, which, in a great measure, destroys its symmetrical proportions. We need scarcely observe, that the roof of Irish chestnut is esteemed a wonderful piece of architecture. Here are the Law Courts, which, by the way, are neither grand nor over convenient. A statue of Canning stands on the opposite side, in the gardens adjoining St. Margaret's Church.

THE HOUSES OF PARLIAMENT.

This splendid pile, though perhaps inappropriate for the situation in which it is placed, and the purpose for which it is intended, is, without doubt, the most splendid building in England. The style is highly-ornamented Gothic, and in this lies its great fault; for even now, ere the whole is completed, parts are so begrimed with London soot and smoke as to render some of the beautiful and elaborate ornaments almost indistinct. Whilst referring to these ornaments, we cannot refrain from drawing attention to the utter want of heraldic knowledge displayed in the coats-of-arms, supporters being given to the arms of all the kings, although they were never used before the time of Richard III. We have referred to the front in the part of this article on River Scenery. The north side, abutting on Westminster Bridge, contains the Speaker's residence, and has, at its north-western corner, the Clock Tower. It is forty feet square, and when finished, will be three hundred and twenty feet high. At the south end are the apartments of the Usher of the Black Rod and the Lords' Libraries. At the south-west corner is the Victoria Tower, a most stupendous work, containing the royal entrance. It is seventy-five feet square, and will rise to the height of three hundred and forty feet, only sixty-four feet less than the height of the cross of St. Paul's. The entrance is by an archway sixty-five feet high, and is most beautifully and elaborately worked. Inside are statues of St. George, St. Andrew, St. Patrick, and Her Majesty, supported by figures emblematical of Justice and Mercy. It will be some years ere this tower is finished, as, on account of its great height, the architect does not consider it safe to proceed with more than thirty feet each year. A great part of the west side is hid by Westminster Hall and the Law Courts; that open to inspection is well worthy of a minute examination, and when the new *façade*, which is to be substituted for that of the Law Courts, is erected the *tout ensemble*, will be most perfect. In the centre of the building is the Grand Central Octagonal Hall, sixty feet square, with a tower rising three hundred feet.

STATUES.

We have, no doubt, omitted to mention many public buildings of importance, but the foregoing are the most prominent. Independently of the public monuments and columns to which we have referred, we may cite the equestrian statue of Charles I., by Herbert Le Sœur, pupil of John of Bologna, at Charing Cross; and that of George III., at Pall Mall East; the Duke of York's Column, in Waterloo Place; the statue of James II., at the back of the Banqueting Hall, Whitehall; of William Pitt, by Chantrey, in Hanover Square; Charles James Fox, in Bloomsbury Square; Francis, Duke of Bedford, by Westmacott, in Russell Square; William IV., in King William Street, London Bridge, and many others in the various squares and public places of London, too numerous for insertion.

SQUARES.

The principal squares, for which elegant description of building London is remarkable, while Paris contains but one, *La Place Royale*, seldom visited, and indeed scarcely known to English visitors, are Bedford, Belgrave, Berkeley, Bloomsbury, Bryanston, Brunswick, Cavendish, Chester, Dorset, Eaton, Grosvenor, Hanover, Manchester, Montague, Portman, Tavistock, Russell, St. James's, Fitzroy, and Finsbury; but there are many others of less importance.

STREETS.

Of the streets, we shall merely observe that the principal for traffic and commerce are from Whitechapel, through Aldgate and Leadenhall Streets to Gracechurch Street, where it forms a junction with the end of Bishopsgate Street (which is a continuation of Shoreditch), and under the names of the Poultry and Cheapside, is continued in a straight line as far as St. Paul's, where there are two branches; one through Newgate Street, Holborn, New Oxford Street and Oxford Street, to the north or Edgware Road side of Hyde Park; and the other, rounding St. Paul's, by Ludgate Hill, Fleet Street, the Strand, and by a slight turning to the right into Piccadilly, to Park Corner, and Knightsbridge, on the south side of the Park. These two principal thoroughfares being parallel to each other from their junction at St. Paul's, and as near as possible equi-distant from Whitechapel Gate, are about six miles in length, presenting an almost uninterrupted display of elegant shops, tastefully decorated, and teeming with the productions of industry and art. We have named these great thoroughfares, because of their extent; but during all this immense distance, branching off or intersecting them are innumerable streets of nearly equal importance on both sides of the river, which it would require a thick volume to enumerate. We shall therefore conclude by drawing the stranger's attention to Regent Street, in the new part of the metropolis, which commences from the noble flight of steps to which we have before adverted, under the Duke of York's Column, in St. James's Park, by Waterloo Place, and passing through Piccadilly, the Quadrant, and Oxford Street, terminates by Portland Place, in the Regent's Park, which is its northern limit. Almost all the houses in that portion of this magnificent line, called Regent Street, are devoted to business; the shops surpassing in richness all that the mind could imagine.

Waterloo Place contains Club Houses and Insurance Offices. One word of the Club Houses: It may with truth be affirmed, that these are mostly of palatial grandeur and magnificence. The Conservative, in St. James's Street; Reform, Carlton, University, Athenæum, United Service, and the Army and Navy in Pall Mall and St. James's Square, are splendid mansions, while many others have a strong claim upon the stranger's attention.

To the lovers of antiquity, we may point out St. John's Gate, Clerkenwell, in an out-of-the-way part of the metropolis, but curious, as the only one existing of all the gates of London. It formed the great south entrance to the Hospital or Priory of St. John of Jerusalem, and was restored by public subscription in 1846. A part of the ancient priory still exists in the crypt of St. John's, Clerkenwell.

PLACES OF PUBLIC AMUSEMENT.

London and its environs possess twenty-two theatres; the principal of which are, Her Majesty's Theatre, Haymarket, and Covent Garden, both for Italian opera; Drury Lane; the Princess', in Oxford Street; and Sadler's Wells, for the legitimate drama of tragedy and comedy; the Haymarket, Lyceum, Strand, and Olympic, for comedy, farce, and melodrama; the Adelphi, for nondescript pieces peculiar to itself, but of singular attraction and popularity; Astley's, over Westminster Bridge, for equestrian spectacles and scenes in the ring; and the remainder consisting of the Victoria, Tottenham, or Queen's, Marylebone, Miss Kelly's, the City, the Grecian Saloon, &c., are for melodrama, farce, and miscellaneous pieces.

In the summer season the following gardens, in some of which, among other amusements, theatrical representations are given, are open to the public every evening, at the moderate admission price of one shilling: Vauxhall, Cremorne, Royal Surrey Zoological. The Zoological Gardens in the Regent's Park are open to the public from nine in the morning till sunset. Admission one shilling, except on Monday, when it is only sixpence. In this Park are also the Royal Botanical Gardens; the Colosseum, admittance two shillings; the Diorama, one shilling; and the Cyclorama (the entrance of which is in Albany Street), one shilling.

Independently of the above-named, we may cite as one of the most interesting, useful, and instructive exhibitions of London, the Polytechnic Institution, 309, Regent Street, where there is much to delight the eye of childhood, and improve the mind of the adult. Admirable lectures are here delivered by eminent chemists and men of scientific acquirements every day, after which dissolving views of the most interesting scenery of the whole continent of Europe are graphically described, by one who seems well acquainted with the localities, during the progress of Exhibition. The Adelaide Gallery, at Charing Cross, has lately been re-opened as a place of amusement; and Madame Tussaud's wonderful Wax Work Exhibition, in Baker Street, must not be forgotten. To the lovers of the arts, the British Artists' Institution, the Exhibition of Water-Colours, and the School of Design at Somerset House, will afford much pleasure.

To the foregoing we may add, that in, and within an easy ride of London, are the following—

EXHIBITIONS AND OTHER PLACES OPEN GRATUITOUSLY.

THE BRITISH MUSEUM—Monday, Wednesday, and Friday, May 8 to August 31, from 10 till 7. September 8 to April 30 (the 1st to 7th January excepted) 10 till 4.

NATIONAL GALLERY—Four first days of the week throughout the year, from 10 till 5. Closed from Saturday before middle of September for six weeks.

ST. PAUL'S—Each week-day from 9 to 11, and from 3 to 4; and on Sunday during the time of divine service. At other times twopence.

EAST INDIA HOUSE MUSEUM—Saturday, from 11 to 3; all the year except in September.

SOANE MUSEUM, 13, Lincoln's Inn Fields—Thursday and Friday during April, May, and June, from 10 to 4. Tickets must be applied for previously, and will be sent by post.

LONDON MISSIONARY MUSEUM, Bloomfield Street, Finsbury—Tuesday, Thursday, and Saturday, with orders from a director.

UNITED SERVICE MUSEUM, Middle Scotland Yard—Daily, with orders from members.

ENTOMOLOGICAL SOCIETY'S MUSEUM, 17, Old Bond Street—Every Tuesday from 3 to 8.

COLLEGE OF SURGEONS' MUSEUM—Monday, Wednesday, and Friday, with orders from members.

MUSEUM OF ECONOMIC GEOLOGY (Removed to Piccadilly)—Daily from 10 to 4.

WINDSOR CASTLE—By command of Her Majesty the Queen, the State Apartments at Windsor Castle will in future be open for inspection of visitors without any fee. Tickets of admission to be obtained *gratis* of Messrs. Ackerman, 96, Strand. The days of admission are Mondays, Tuesdays, Thursdays, and Fridays, from 10 to 4.

HAMPTON COURT PALACE—Every day except Friday, from 10 till 4.

KEW BOTANICAL GARDENS—Every day except Sunday, from 1 to 6.

WOOLWICH MODEL AND ROCKET ROOMS—Daily.

DULWICH GALLERY—Each week-day, except Friday, from 10 to 5 in summer, and from 11 to 3 in winter. Tickets to be had *gratis* of most of the respectable printsellers in London.

London and Birmingham Railway.

This important line of communication was commenced and completed under the immediate superintendence and direction of Robert Stephenson, one of the most distinguished engineers of the age, whose eminent skill and talent displayed in this gigantic undertaking alone, without reference to the numerous other public works executed by him, are sufficient to perpetuate his fame, and transmit his name with the greatest honour to posterity.

At the period when the London and Birmingham Railway was contemplated, the only experience the public had gleaned of the system of locomotion, was that which they derived from the experiment of the Manchester and Liverpool line, a distance of thirty miles; but its unquestionable success left no doubt on the public mind as to the desirableness of extending the system; and, after some opposition in Parliament, arising from prejudice, the fear of innovations, as well as the natural aversion of landed proprietors to any encroachment upon their estates, Acts were obtained, under which the Company was incorporated, and enabled in the course of a few years to put London and the north-western coasts of England within a few hours communication of each other.

Although the first Act of Parliament for the construction of the London and Birmingham Railway received the royal assent on the 6th of May, 1833, the works were not commenced until the 21st of April, 1834. Various portions of the line were opened at different periods, commencing in 1837, and the whole was completed and opened for the public service on the 17th of September, 1838—the distance of one hundred and twelve miles having been achieved in little more than four years. In estimating the wonderful celerity with which this first grand railway was executed, it must be borne in mind that there is scarcely any portion of the line that is not either carried by embankments above the general surface of the country, or much below it by means of excavations, that there are about two hundred and fifty bridges, independently of the viaducts, the principal of which are those over the Sowe, Coln, Brent, the Regent's Canal, at Camden Town, and Lawley Street, Birmingham; that there are also nine tunnels, and that each side of the line, throughout its whole extent, is fenced with posts and rails, and planted with quick, except where it was deemed expedient (as at the Camden depôt, as far as the crossing of the Edgeware Road), to resort to a fencing of substantial brick-wall with stone copings; such protection being necessary in a crowded locality near the metropolis. Of the tunnels, some of which are of great length, we cannot omit a slight description:

1. PRIMROSE HILL TUNNEL, which is entered at a depth of forty-five feet below the surface. It has an extremely handsome stone front, from the design of Mr. Budden, then secretary of Mr. Stephenson; it is upwards of eleven hundred yards in length, and about twenty-two feet in height and width; ventilated by a shaft fifty feet high before it reaches the summit; the whole of this extraordinary work is three bricks in thickness.

2. KENSAL GREEN TUNNEL. Three hundred and twenty yards in length, is similar in its construction.

3. WATFORD TUNNEL, the entrance to which is a nearly semicircular arch, twenty-five feet high, and twenty-four feet wide, with retaining walls on either side, extending to the slopes of the cutting; a blocking and cornice runs through the whole length of the front, and the arch is surmounted by a pediment. This tunnel is one thousand eight hundred yards, or about one mile and a tenth, in length. In consequence of the nature of the chalk and loose gravel, this work was one of considerable difficulty, and was attended with a considerable loss of life during the sinking of one of the shafts—ten men being buried under the falling earth; and it was to this accident that the enormous ventilating shaft, which the traveller cannot fail to notice, owes its origin, as the work of filling up the opening would have been more expensive, and less advantageous for the purpose for which it was required.

4. NORTH CHURCH TUNNEL is situated at about the centre of the Dudwell excavation, beyond Berkhampstead; its length is a fifth of a mile. It has two handsome stone fronts, and is of the same proportions as the Watford Tunnel.

5. LINSLADE TUNNEL, near Leighton Buzzard, is stated to be the only curved tunnel on this line; it is two hundred and eighty-five yards in length. The south entrance displays a rusticated stone front; the face of the arch is battered, and is surmounted by battlements forty feet high; the side walls, terminating with similar piers, being also in

London and Birmingham Railway.

the castellated style, and, coupled with the bold manner in which the cutting beyond it is executed, produces a very picturesque effect.

7. STOWE HILL (OR WEEDON) TUNNEL is four hundred and eighty-four yards in length; it is similar in its construction to the others; but the entrances are again of different styles of architecture; the south entrance, consisting of two piers, projecting boldly from the side walls with a cornice through the whole length, while the north is somewhat similar to that of the Linslade Tunnel, castellated, with a machioalated parapet, and the copings continued through its whole length, without being broken into embrasures. The whole is most pleasing to the eye of the traveller, but he loses the beautiful views of the country, which are so extensive and diversified on the summit.

7. KILSBY TUNNEL (near the Crick station), universally declared to be a mighty effort of the engineer's skill and ingenuity, is about two thousand four hundred and twenty-three yards long; the brickwork, generally, twenty-seven inches thick, and the whole built in Roman, or metallic cement. The entrances to this truly gigantic work are castellated, and similar in design, consisting of an immense tower, with battering sides, and a bold plinth; the side, or wing walls, are thrown back, making the tower a very prominent and conspicuous object, the effect of which is highly pleasing. The large ventilating shafts, one hundred and thirty-two feet deep, and sixty feet in diameter, are esteemed master-pieces of brickwork. When the water broke into this shaft, the men worked on rafts, which were floated into the excavation, a difficult and dangerous, but perfectly successful operation. This tunnel cost £300,000, although the contractor's original estimate was £99,000; but he gave up the contract, and the work was executed by the Company.

8. THE BEECHWOOD TUNNEL, near Berkswell, is two hundred and ninety-two yards in length, and has also a large ventilating shaft near the centre. The entrances are of stone, with chamfered joints, radiating from the arch, the face of which stands forth prominently from the wing walls.

Many of the cuttings on this line are scarcely inferior in point of the labour and engineering skill they display to the tunnels, and as they are visible to the traveller, we call his attention specially to those of Blisworth, Coventry (two miles and three-quarters long, and in some parts fifty feet high), and Dudwell.

Of the viaducts, the one which carries the railway across the Coln Valley, and that of Wolverton, are especially worthy of notice. The former is eight hundred and twelve feet long, and fifty feet high, and when viewed from the meadows below, has a remarkably lofty, yet light and elegant appearance. Wolverton viaduct stands near the centre of the great embankment, one mile and a half long, and forty-eight feet high, which crosses the valley of the Ouse. Beneath the viaduct, which is built of a peculiar brick, flow the rivers Ouse and Tow. It consists of six elliptical arches, each of sixty feet span, rising twenty feet; the height to the soffit being forty-six feet. At each end are two massive pilasters, with stone cornice and blockings, and beyond are three smaller arches, which pierce the retaining walls, built on the slope of the embankment, the cornice is continued throughout the whole length of the viaduct, and is surmounted by a parapet wall, the top of which is fifty-seven feet from the surface of the ground; the length of the viaduct six hundred and sixty feet, one-eighth of a mile, and the cost of its erection was £28,000. It is a magnificent structure, and the elegance of its proportions, together with the masterly manner in which the work is executed, reflect the highest credit upon both architect and builders.

Of the vast amount of capital invested in the grand project of the London and Birmingham Railway, and the expenses incurred in the various works to which we have adverted, it is not my province to speak, suffice it to say, that several millions have been sunk in bringing this magnificent achievement to its present state of perfection, and that the praises of the public are largely due to the distinguished engineer from whose designs, and under whose superintendence, this colossal work was executed. To the directors thanks are also due for their unwearied exertions, as well as to the original shareholders, who, whether from motives of pecuniary interest alone, or from nobler and more patriotic views, entered with so much public spirit into a scheme which has been attended with the most prosperous results to the country at large.

EUSTON STATION.

The grand entrance to the London and Birmingham Railway, in Drummond Street, Euston Square, consists of a Doric portico, similar to the propylea of the Greek cities, and was erected by Messrs. Cubitt, after the design of Mr. Hardwick, the celebrated architect. It is said to be the largest portico in the world, but majestic and truly elegant as are its proportions, it cannot be compared in point of grandeur with the "Arc de Triomphe," at the Barrière de l'Etoile, at Paris. The diameter of each column is eight feet six inches; their height, forty-two feet; the intercolumniation, twenty-eight feet, forming the carriage entrance; and the total height, to the apex of the pediment, seventy-two feet. It is built of Bramley Fall stone, of which, in this erection alone, above seventy-five thousand cubic feet were consumed; some of the blocks weighed thirteen tons; and, according to the authority from which we derive this account of its proportions, the building cost £35,000.

The grand entrance hall of the Euston Station is, perhaps, the most magnificent saloon in Europe. It is about one hundred and forty feet in length by sixty broad, and between seventy and eighty feet in height. The east and west walls are plain, of a greyish stone, and on three sides are surrounded by a light and elegant gallery, guarded by bronze railings, about fifteen feet above the floor, on a level with the Board Room, which is ascended by a noble flight of thirty steps, surmounted by a range of double columns of

---

Left of Railway from London.

The lines from the Euston station, through Camden Town to Park Street, are carried about nineteen feet beneath the street level, for upwards of two thousand two hundred yards, which distance is intersected by seven bridges and archways over the railway; and from Park Street to the Regent's Canal, at Camden Town, the rails are near the general surface of the ground. The Camden depôt, which is raised on an embankment of clay, the produce of the Primrose Hill tunnels and contiguous cuttings, occupies an area of twenty-seven acres, and is situated between Chalk Farm and the Hampstead Road.

1 m. s. Twyford Abbey, — Willan, Esq. Close to the Abbey stands the pretty little church of Twyford, which displays many tasteful ornaments in the Gothic style. 1½ m. further, PERRIVALE, which has a small ancient church.

3 m. s. w. GREENFORD; area, 2,070 A.; population, 588; there is a free school, with an annual revenue of £200. In the church are many monuments and brasses. At Greenford are, Greenford Hall, R. Rigg, Esq., F.R.S.; Greenford Cottage, W. Clarkson, Esq.; Greenford Lodge. F. T. Gibbs, Esq.

1 m. s. HARROW-ON-THE-HILL. A very pretty village and parish in the county of Middlesex, situated on a lofty eminence, containing an area of 9,870 A., with a population of 4,627, which includes the hamlet of Harrow Weald. It is famous for its public school, founded by a private gentleman, John Lyon, of Preston, in 1571, the structure of which, and the chapel in the Elizabethan style of architecture, are very handsome. Amongst the many learned and distinguished men who received the rudiments of education at this celebrated school, it will suffice to name the learned Dr. Parr, Sir William Jones, Richard B. Sheridan, the Marquis of Hastings, Byron, and the late truly-lamented statesman, Sir Robert Peel. The village is ornamented with many handsome houses, and the views on all sides are beautiful and

EUSTON STATION.

Camden Depôt.

Primrose Hill Tunnel.

3 m. Bridge under Edgeware Road.

4 m. Kensal Green Tunnel.

6 m. WILLESDEN STATION.

7 m. Bridge across river Brent.

Cross Harrow Road.

8 m. SUDBURY STATION.

11 m. HARROW STATION.

beautifully polished red granite, ornamented with Doric capitals, the angles being finished with three pilasters of the same material on either side. In the centre over the door leading into the Board Room, is a fine group of figures representing Britannia cultivating commerce and the arts. On the opposite, or south side of the hall, rising from the gallery, is another range of columns precisely similar to the before-mentioned, except that instead of being double, they are backed by pilasters, in the centre of which is a clock. At the height of about fifty feet from the floor, are ranges of windows, and on a line with them in the angles of the building are allegorical figures in bold relief, representing the counties traversed by the several railways, of which this splendid station is the terminus. The highly-ornamented roof, cornices, &c., are in strict keeping with the other parts of this majestic hall. On the east and west side are sixteen double doors, leading to the various offices and waiting-rooms of the establishment. The saloon, which is used also as a refreshment room, having an elegant counter, supplied with every delicacy, in the centre, is lighted at night by about fifty gas globes, tastefully arranged on light bronze standards, fixed in the railings of the gallery, two above, and two below the gallery, at given distances. In our account of this saloon, we have no intention of comparing it with Westminster Hall, which stands alone in all Europe, but we know no other chamber which presents so truly magnificent and imposing an appearance. On the right and left are the great booking-offices, the former for the Liverpool line, the latter for the Midland Railway. These rooms alone are of sufficient grandeur and magnificence to excite the admiration of the traveller; but they almost sink into insignificance when compared with the gigantic proportions of the grand saloon.

EUSTON STATION.	**Right of Railway from London.**
Camden Depôt.	There is a branch line from Camden Town to Blackwall, for the conveyance of heavy goods to the docks.
Primrose Hill Tunnel.	
3 m. Bridge under Edgeware Road.	At a village named Kingsbury, 6 miles down the Edgeware Road, resided Oliver Goldsmith during the time he was writing "The Vicar of Wakefield" and "History of Animated Nature."
4 m. Kensal Green Tunnel.	
6 m. WILLESDEN STATION.	WILLESDEN, the first station on this great and important railway is a parish, in the county of Middlesex, four miles north-west of Paddington, containing an area of 4,190 acres, with a population of 2,930. The village is picturesque, and has a very primitive appearance. The church is an interesting structure of great antiquity, in the churchyard of which repose the ashes of the notorious Jack Sheppard, who was a native of the place. Brandsferry House, C. Hambro, Esq.; Harlesden Green, Lord Decies.
7 m. Bridge across river Brent.	
Cross Harrow Road.	
8 m. SUDBURY STATION.	½ m. E. At WEMBLEY GREEN, Wembley Park, Rev. J Gray. This property in the year 1543 belonged to the family of Page, and was purchased by John Gray, Esq., in 1802, who erected the present very elegant mansion, which is surrounded by a well wooded park, containing 250 A. ½ m. further E. is Kingsbury; area, 1,700 A.; population, 536. The parish church is situated on the site of an ancient encampment. Hill House, Rev. H. Atchison; Grove House, W. A. Greatorex, Esq.
11 m. HARROW STATION.	1 m. N. HARROW WEALD. 3 m. E. WHITCHURCH, and ¼ m. further EDGEWARE, a town; area, 1,990 A.; population, 659. At Edgeware are, South Lodge, T. Hall Plumer, Esq.; North Lodge, Joseph Sladen, Esq.; St. Alban's Lodge, J. Bailey Haynes, Esq.; Red Hill, E. Hull, Esq.; Cannons Park, Lady Plumer. The Cannons was formerly the seat of the great Duke of Chandos, who built a magnificent palace there at a cost of £250,000. Nothing however now remains of it except the chapel, of which Handel was the chapel-master. On the north side of Cavendish Square, London, now stand two noble stone houses, which were erected as lodge gates to a road which was intended by the Duke to lead from that spot to The Cannons. The

extensive. The original church was built by Archbishop Lanfranc, temp. Conqueror, some part of which still exists. Its lofty spire is a conspicuous object throughout this and the adjoining counties. During the reign of Henry VIII. Harrow was inundated with superstitious cockneys, who flocked to the high ground to avoid the consequences of a stupid prediction that London was to be destroyed by a deluge. Near Harrow are Sudbury Grove, J. Hinkman, Esq.; Sudbury Hill House, John Browne, Esq.; The Mount, T. Sanctuary, Esq.; Butt House, Mrs. Spencer Webb; Sudbury Priory, G. Webster, Esq.; Lowlands, Benjamin Rotch, Esq., a structure in the modern Italian villa style.

1 m. w. PINNER, containing an area of 3,720 A., with a population of 1,331. Pinner Grove, Sir William George Milman, Bart.; The Hall, Major William Abbs. The mansion, which is of great antiquity, was formerly in possession of the noble family of St. Alban's. It stands on elevated ground, commanding pretty views of Harrow and the surrounding neighbourhood, and at the foot of the ascent runs a branch of the river Coln. The park, which is embellished by very fine old oak and other forest trees, considered to be coeval with the celebrated Middlesex Chase, was the spot chosen by Oliver Cromwell for the encampment of his troops during the civil wars. Eastcott High Grove, Lady Fuller; Eastcott Minor, Mrs. S. R. Maitland; South Hill Cot, Mrs. Thompson. 5 m. w. RUISLIP. Area, 6,260 A.; population, 1,413. The village has a very picturesque and antique church; Ruislip Lodge, Mrs. Parker.

2 m. s. w. EASTBOROUGH; C. A. March, Esq. 3 m. w. Moor Park, Lord Robert Grosvenor. This splendid mansion was originally built by James, the unfortunate Duke of Monmouth, and was allowed to be the best piece of brickwork in England. The present mansion is built of stone (the carriage of which, from London alone, is said to have cost £15,800) from the designs of the celebrated architect, Giacomo Leoni and Sir J. Thornhill. The principal or southern front has a very elegant and grand portico, the pediment being supported on four noble columns, each 37 feet high, independent of the base and the capital, the former of which is six feet in height, and the latter form a very rich cornice; a balustrade above goes round the house. The internal parts of this structure are uncommonly rich, and have an air of grandeur at once interesting and dignified. The hall is a spacious square apartment, splendidly ornamented with paintings, marble door-ways, military trophies, &c., the latter formed of a composition resembling stone. The park is about five miles round, having its surface finely diversified. It is well wooded, and includes almost every description of forest timber.

¼ m. WATFORD. This town derives its name from the Watling Street of the Romans, having been built on that highway near the ford, which crosses the river Coln. It was a long irregular place, and very dirty in winter, but it is much improved since the establishment of the railway station. The air is salubrious. The population 5,980, within an area of 10,980 A. The church stands a short distance from the town. It is a very ancient edifice, has side aisles, two chapels, and a square tower. Watford has a charity school, several alms-houses and free schools, with other charities; a weekly market on Tuesday, and a fair on Trinity Monday. By the old road it is 14 miles from London. The railway here passes through a tunnel upwards of one mile in length. On the west side of the town is the Grand Junction Canal. The matting trade is brisk, and many

---

13 m. PINNER STATION.

Enter Herts.

16 m. BUSHEY STATION.

Watford Viaduct.

Coln Viaduct.

17½ m. WATFORD STATION.

18¼ m. Watford Tunnel.

remains of the celebrated horse Eclipse are interred in a paddock in front of the present mansion.

THE MANOR HOUSE, BUSHEY.

13 m. PINNER STATION.

Enter Herts.

16 m. BUSHEY STATION.

Watford Viaduct.

Coln Viaduct.

BUSHEY, a parish, county of Hertfordshire, contains 3,130 A., with a population of 2,675. Adjoining is a spacious heath, which rises to a considerable eminence, and affords a delightful prospect.

The Manor House, Bushey, Lieut.-General Sir Frederick Walker, K.C.B., is situated adjacent to the Bushey Hall property, formerly the residence of the ancient family of Walker, knights and baronets. Lieut.-General Walker is lord of the manor of Bushy.

Bentley Priory, The Marquis of Abercorn. The mansion stands on the site of an old priory, the history of which is little known. It existed at the suppression of the monasteries in the time of Henry VIII. The property came into the possession of the Earls of Aberdeen in the year 1788, since which the mansion has been much enlarged and improved. It was built of brick, and has a very irregular outline, owing to the elevated situation of the ground. A most extensive and beautiful view is obtained of the surrounding country. The grounds contain more than 200 acres, and are laid out in a very ornamental manner.

3 m. N.E. STANMORE, GREAT. Population, 1,777. The Hill, H. Ashley, Esq.; The Cottage, H. G. Hooper, Esq.; The Grove, Sir R. Howard, Bart.; The Manor House, C. Otway Monro, Esq.; The Hall, J. M. Rhodes, Esq.; Bynnocks, Colonel Tovey Tamont; The Lymes, T. Whieldon, Esq.; Stanmore Park, Earl of Wicklow.

17½ m. WATFORD STATION.

N.E. Bushey Hall, D. L. Burton, Esq.; Bushey Grove, Stewart Majoribanks, Esq.; Otters' Pool, Mrs. Thellusson; Dellrow, Sir A. J. Dalrymple, Bt.

18¼ m. Watford Tunnel.

3 m. E. ALDENHAM, a parish, county of Herts, containing, with Theobald's Street, a population of 1,662. In the 31st of Elizabeth, Richard Platt founded and endowed fourteen alms-houses, also a free grammar school for sixty children, to be chosen from the poor of Aldenham, and the families of the freemen of the Brewers' Company of London; and in default of the full number of scholars from the children of Aldenham, the choice to be extended to the adjoining parishes; the children of the founder's name and kin to have the preference. The yearly income is now £1,032. Aldenham Abbey, W. Stuart, Esq; a little further, Munden House, Nathaniel Hibbert, Esq.; and The Wilds, R. Smith, Esq.

of the inhabitants are employed in the manufacture of straw plait. Kyte's Farm, W. Capel, Esq.; Nascall House, R. Clutterbuck, Esq.; Gorton House, J. Falcon, Esq.; Nascot Cottage, Mrs. Goodison; The Elms, T. Holt, Esq.; Watford Place, J. King, Esq.

N.W. Cassiobury, Earl of Essex. The house, built in the form of a Roman H, has a castellated appearance; there is also an ancient church, with a fine tower; the grounds abound with picturesque scenery, and were planted by the celebrated Le Notto, in the reign of Charles II. Grove Park, Earl of Clarendon. The mansion is a handsome brick building, standing on the west side of the river Gade, which flows through the grounds. Little Cassiobury, Sir T. B. Capel.

2 m. w. RICKMANSWORTH; market town and parish; area, 9,740 A.; population, 5,026. The town is neat and clean; the population chiefly employed in manufacture of straw and plait. Rickmansworth Park, J. Arden, Esq.; Scots' Hill, T. Ayers, Esq.; Horley Wood, J. Barnes, Esq.; Croxby Grove, Miss Kently; Scots' Bridge, Colonel C. Lester.

8 m. w. AMERSHAM consists of a long street, crossed by a shorter one, and has a very neat Gothic church, and contains a window of elegant glass, and several monuments of great beauty. The Challoner's school, founded in 1620, has three exhibitions to Corpus Christi College, Oxford. The poet, Waller, who sat twice for this borough in Parliament, was born at Cole's Hill, in this parish, in 1605. Shardeloes, formerly the property of William Tothill, Esq., and one of the places where Queen Elizabeth stopped during a royal progress. The mansion is a very elegant structure; its front is supported by a portico and four fluted Corinthian columns; it is beautifully situated on a hill,, overlooking the noble lake, 35 acres in extent; the gardens are most beautiful, and were originally formed out of a morass, by Sir William Drake, Kt. Shardeloes is now the residence of Sir William's representative, Thomas Tyrwhitt Drake. Esq.

KING'S LANGLEY is a large village in Hertfordshire, once celebrated for being the seat of Edward III., who here built a fine palace, some remains of which are said to be traceable at this time. Edmund, his son, commonly called Edmund of Langley, was born at this place; and with his wife, Isabel, daughter of Don Pedro of Castile, is interred in the parish church, which is a venerable Gothic structure. King James I. gave the manor to his son, Prince Henry, but afterwards it fell into different hands. It is 19¾ miles from London by the old coach road. Its population by the last census was 1,629; and the area of the parish, 3,400 A. King's Langley once possessed a priory, within whose walls Piers Gaveston, the favourite of Edward III., was buried. Chipperfield House, J. Parsley, Esq.; Barns' Lodge, Mrs. J. Lafont. *[21 m. KING'S LANGLEY STA.]*

[Cross Grand Junction Canal.]

Close to the station is Box Moor Hall, J. Mead, Esq. 1½ m. N.W. Westbrook Hay, the Hon. Granville Dudley Ryder. The house was built of brick at the close of the seventeenth century, by Thomas Lomax, Esq., whose only child married Richard Ryder, Esq., eldest brother of Sir Dudley Ryder, ancestor of the Earl of Harrowby. It was enlarged by the late Right Hon. R. Ryder, in 1813. It was further added to, and an Italian front put to it in 1841, by the Hon. Granville D. Ryder, the present possessor. The parterres near the house are laid out in the Italian style. It commands extensive and beautiful views. The richly wooded grounds are seen to great advantage from the railway between Boxmoor and Berkhampstead to the south-west. Bevington, Charles Henry Moore, Esq.; AshPark, Sir R. A. F. G. Colleton, Bart.; Latimers, Hon. Charles Compton Cavendish, M.P. *[24½ m. BOX MOOR STATION.]*

6½ m. N.E. St. Alban's. The town is built on the site of the ancient town of Verulam. It sends two members to Parliament. The market-days are Wednesday and Saturday. In the year 795, Offa, King of the Mercians, erected a monastery in the place where John Alban suffered martyrdom, and near to which the town was afterwards built. The abbot was reputed, by favour of Pope Adrian IV., who was born near Verulam, the first in dignity of all the abbots. The church of this monastery is still in being, and much admired for its size, beauty, and antiquity. (See also Great Northern.)

A few score yards before reaching the King's Langley Station, is

THE BOOKSELLERS' PROVIDENT RETREAT,

consisting of seven houses and a lodge, for the occupation of decayed members of the Booksellers' Provident Institution of London.

12 m. KING'S LANGLEY STA.

ABBOTTS LANGLEY, a parish, containing a population of 2,015. The church is partly in the Norman and partly in the English style of architecture; it has a square tower, surmounted by a short spire, and contains some handsome monuments and other sepulchral memorials. Nicholas Breakspeare, who first introduced Christianity amongst the Norwegians, and the only Englishman raised to the Popedom, was born in this parish, though the place from which he took his name is situated in the adjoining parish of St. Michael's. He assumed the title of Adrian IV., and was poisoned by a citizen of Rome, whose son he refused to consecrate bishop. Hill Side House, J. Currie, Esq.; Abbots' Hill, John Dickinson, Esq.; Nash Mills, C. Longman, Esq.; Rose Hill, Captain J. Fosket.

Cross Grand Junction Canal.

24⅓ m. BOX MOOR STATION.

1½ m. N.E. lies HEMEL HEMPSTEAD, pleasantly situated near the river Gade. It is a well-built market-town and parish, containing an area of 12,440 A., with a population of 7,268. The church, which is cruciform, is of Norman origin, and has an embattled tower surmounted by a lofty octagonal spire. The interior is richly ornamented, and contains a tomb of great antiquity. It has a union workhouse and an infirmary. Manufactures: straw plait and paper. Market granted by Henry VIII. Thursday. It is one of the largest corn markets in the county. Gadesbridge House, Sir A. Cooper, Bart.; Marchmont House, Dowager Lady Cooper; Felden House, B. Bruntnall, Esq.; Highfield, H. N. Neale, Esq.

6 m. N.E. REDBURNE. Redburne House, Lady Glamis and J. A. Slack, Esq.; Bylands, John Hawkins, Esq.; Elm Cottage Rev. T. Pugh. 2½ m. N.N.W. FLAMSTEAD. Flamstead Villa, W. Freeman, Esq. 3 m. further N.E. HARPENDEN. Rothamstead Park, Capt. C. D. Alexander. 3 m. E. Gorhambury, Earl of Verulam. The mansion was erected at the close of

BERKHAMPSTEAD, county Herts, the birth-place of the poet Cowper, is a place of great antiquity, supposed to have been a Roman station, from the coins and other relics so frequently found near the ruins of an ancient castle, which was in great repute during the Heptarchy, having served as a residence to the Mercian kings. The inhabitants of this place, assisted by the Abbot of St. Alban's, refused obedience to William the Conqueror until he had sworn to maintain the laws of Edward the Confessor. Prince Henry, Charles I., and Elizabeth of Bohemia, were sent to be nursed in this town, in consequence of the salubrity of the air. The town is built on the side of an eminence which rises from the bottom of a valley, and has a very tolerable street. There are traces of the moat which once encompassed it, and encloses about four acres. The church, an ancient Gothic structure, contains the remains of several chapels or oratories. It has a free grammar and charity schools, and Sayer's almshouse. Market, Saturday; annual fairs, Shrove-Monday, Whitsun-Monday, and 25th of July; area of parish, 4,250 A.; population, 2,978, many of whom are employed in the manufacture of straw plait. It is 26¼ m. from London by the old coach-road.

28 m. BERKHAMP-STEAD STATION.

LITTLE MISSENDEN. Population, 1,011. 1½ N.W. GREAT MISSENDEN. Population, 2,325. Sidewood Lodge; Rossway, Robert Sutton, Esq.; Norcott Court, Thomas A. Lochsley, Esq.—a small comfortable residence, of as ancient date as the 15th century, said to have been a court-house in the time of the wars of York and Lancaster.; the outer walls were re-built in 1767. Ashlyn's Hall, Augustus Smith, Esq.; Haresfoot, R. A. Smith Dorrien, Esq.

North Church Tunnel.

CHESHAM. Area, 11,880 A.; population, 5,593 The Bury, W. Lowndes, Esq. 1½ N.N.E. CHESHAM BORES; area, 810 A.; population, 218. 3¼ m. N. of Chesham is the small parish of STORRIDGE. Population, 233. LITTLE MILLHALL.

TRING, county Herts, is a neat market-town and parish, with an area of 7,390 A., and a population of 4,260. It has several small charitable institutions, a market-house, and a Lancasterian school. Manufactures—silk, canvas, and straw plait. The church is an elegant structure, with a massive tower at the west end, and the whole is embattled. It contains some beautiful monuments. Tring Park, in the neighbourhood, was built by Charles II. for Nell Gwynne. The ancient Roman way, Icknild Street, and the Grand Junction Canal, intersect the town. Market-day, Friday. At a short distance from this station lies the disfranchised borough and market-town of WENDOVER, which had the honour of being represented in five successive parliaments by the patriot Hampden. Near this small and meanly built town is a resorvoir of the Grand Junction Canal. It has some trade in lace-making. Area of parish, 6,250 A.; population, 1,877. The Hall, T. S. Collett, Esq.; Wendover Lodge, R. Fox, Esq.; Great House, Gen. Sir James Watson, K.C.B.; Chiltern House, Colonel Jacob Watson.

31¾ m. TRING · STATION.

33 m. enter Buck-ingham.

1¼ m. s. w. of Tring, WIGGINGTON. R. Powell, Esq. 1¾ m. N.N.E. from Wendover, is ALTON. Alton House, Sir John Dashwood King, Bart.

CHEDDINGTON; a small parish, county Bucks. Area, 1,170 A.; population, 439. It is an intermediate station, 4 m. N. of Tring, but contains nothing of note beyond being the locality from whence issues the short branch to Aylesbury—*vide* Branch Lines.

36¼ Cheddington Junction Station.

Aylesbury Br.

2 m. s.w. from Cheddington, SOUTH MARSTON.

5 m. w. WINGRAVE.

the eighteenth century, and consists of spacious centre and wings. The park and grounds are stocked with fine timber, and contain 600 acres.

28 m. BERKHAMP-STEAD STATION.

4 m. N.N.E. GREAT GADDESDEN. Area, 4,000 A.; population, 1,109. Gaddesden drew its name from the river Gade, on which it is situated. It anciently belonged to the Earls of Salisbury, and afterwards passed to the Zouches, and from thence by an heir female to the Hollands, afterwards Earls of Huntingdon. On the death of the last Earl, who died from a wound received at the battle of Barnet, whilst fighting on the side of the Earl of Warwick, it was seized by the Crown, and granted by Henry VII. to Thomas Lord Stanley, Earl of Derby. In the forty-third of Elizabeth, the daughters and co-heiresses of Ferdinando, Earl of Derby, conveyed it to Sir Robert Cecil, who granted it to Sir Adolphus Carey, of Berkhampstead, in the following year, and by his heirs it was sold to Lord Chancellor Ellesmere, from whom it has descended to the heir of the late Earl of Bridgewater. In the church are many monuments of the Halseys. Gaddesden Park, an elegant building, erected 1773, Rev. J. Fitz More Halsey; Friethsden, Francis Goodman, Esq.; Gaddesden Row, Admiral Gage; Hoo House, George Proctor, Esq.; Sedgemore, T. Proctor, Esq.

North Church Tunnel.

31¾ m. TRING STATION.

1 m. E. of Tring, ALDBURY. In the church, which is dedicated to St. John the Baptist, are several ancient monuments in commemoration of the Verneys and Andersons, of Pedley, and of the Hodes, the former lords of the manor. One of the Dukes of Leeds was also buried here, but neither inscription nor any other memorial has been consecrated to his memory. 2 m. Ashridge Park, the magnificent seat of the late Countess

33 m. enter Buckingham.

of Bridgewater, and more recently of Viscount Alford. It appears that a monastery was erected here about the year 1203, which after the dissolution, was frequently the seat of the Princess Elizabeth. It has lately been pulled down, and in its place a splendid mansion, in the Gothic style, has been built. The park is five miles in circumference. 2 m. further, Beechwood Park, Sir. T. Gage Saunders Sebright, Bart., formerly the site of a Benedictine nunnery, and called Woodchurch, or St. Giles'-in-the-Wood. The mansion is a handsome edifice, surrounded by a well-wooded park abounding in beech, from which it takes its name.

36¼ Cheddington Junction Station.

1 m. N. MONTMOOR, Baron Meyer Amschell Rothschild. 1 m. s. SLAPTON, Mrs. Turner. 3 m. s.s.w. is IVINGHOE. The town is situated on a declivity of chalk hills, and has an ancient Gothic church, in which are monuments of the Duncombe family, and the tomb of Henry of Blois, Bishop of Winchester, and brother of King Stephen. Near it are the ruins of a nunnery founded by this bishop. Delaford Park, C. Clowes, Esq.; Iver Lodge, John Bowles, Esq.; Heath Lodge, A. Edwards, Esq.; Broad Moor, R. Ellis, Esq.; Iver Grove, H. T. England, Esq.; Sandstone Castle, H. P. Lodington, Esq.; Mansfield House, William Medley, Esq.; Huntsmoor Park, Christopher Tower, Esq. M.P.; Thorney House, W. Tennant, Esq.

3 m. E.; the parish of EDDELSBOROUGH. 3½ m. W.S.W. EATON BRAY.

2 m. N.W. Liscombe House, the seat of the ancient family of Lovett, in whose possession it has remained nearly 600 years, and is said to obtain its name from a fortification raised in the adjoining woods, and the " combe," or valley, which runs from the front of the house.   It is a quadrangular building; one side of it is occupied by a chapel, part of which appears to have been built in the middle of the 14th century.   The house, however, appears to have been built about the time of Elizabeth, but has since been modernized.   The front of the house measures 166 feet, and is ornamented with five circular and two square turrets, rising from the ground and projecting before the building.   The whole is embattled, and assumes a castellated appearance.   In the parish church are some monuments of the Lovatts.   1 m. N. from Liscombe Park, SOULBURY.   Stoke Grove, Luke Hopkinson, Esq.   2 m. W. STEWKELEY, a large village, rendered interesting to the antiquary by its very ancient church, which is of Saxon workmanship, and is mentioned by Dr. Stukeley as the oldest and most entire he ever saw. Its shape is parallelogram, 90 feet by 24.   Half the length is allotted to the nave, and one-fourth to the chancel, which is vaulted with stone.   The remaining space is occupied with two round arches, supporting a square tower, the upper part of which is surrounded with 22 small intersecting circular arches attached to the wall.   The windows are all small, and the mouldings ornamented with zigzag sculpture.   The principal entrance is on the west side, which is more embellished than any other part.   On this side are the arches.   The centre one forms the doorway, and is supported by two pillars on each side, with square capitals and mouldings, the same as the windows.   The era of its erection is not known; but some workmen repairing the chancel after it had been damaged by a storm fifty years ago, are reported to have observed the date, 1006, inscribed on a stone. 3 m. S.W. of Leighton Buzzard, WING.   2 m. W. CUBLINGTON.   ASTON ABBOTS.   1 m. S. Aston House, Captain Sir J. Clark Ross.

40½ m. LEIGHTON BUZZARD JUNCTION STA.

42 m. Linslade Tunnel.

½ m. BLETCHLEY, county Bucks.   Area of parish, 3,150 A.; population, 685.   1 m. S. NEWTON LONGVILLE.   1½ m. W. TATTENHOWE.   1 m. further, Whaddon Hall, William Selby Lowndes, Esq.

4½ m. W. STONEY STRATFORD, built on the ancient Watling Street; it is chiefly built of freestone, and has a bridge over the river Ouse.   Though there is a neat market-place, but little business is done; the principal trade being carried on mostly by samples displayed by farmers at public-houses.   Population, 1,757, agricultural, but a few hands are employed in lace manufacture.   4 m. N.W. from station, Cosgrove Hall, J. C. Mansel, Esq.   2 m. further, POTTERS' BURY, a parish.   Area, 2,820 A.; population, 1,561.   David Wilkinson, Esq.   1 m. distant, situate in the royal forest of Whittlebury, is Wakefield Lodge, the seat of the Duke of Grafton; the

46¾ m. BLETCH-LEY STATION.
Banbury Br.
48 m. cross Holy-head Road.
52¼ m. WOLVER-TON STATION.

40½ m. LEIGHTON BUZZARD JUNCTION STA.

Dunstable Br. ☞

1 m. LEIGHTON BUZZARD, county of Beds, a market-town and parish, containing a population of 6,053 within an area of 8,990 A. It is situated on the Grand Junction Canal, at a short distance from the river Ouse. It is a place of great antiquity, and from the position of the Roman camp within half a mile, and other facts, is thought to have been the Saxon Sygeanburg that was captured by Cuthwolf from the Britons. The church, which is cruciform, is a venerable and spacious edifice, with a square tower, surmounted by a spire; the whole is ornamented with grotesque figures. The cross, a structure of great elegance, is supposed to be 500 years old. It stands near the market-house, and is thirty-eight feet high. Like all the neighbouring places, it has manufactures of straw plait and lace; market, Tuesday. Claremont Cottage, Mrs. Wheeler. 1½ m. N. LINCHLADE.

2½ m. E. EGGINGTON HALL. Great House, Rev. John Cumberlege.

4 m. N. GREAT BRICKHILL. The Cottage, David Harmer, Esq.

BRICKHILL MANOR, PHILIP DUNCOMBE PAUNCEFORT DUNCOMBE, ESQ.

42 m. Linslade Tunnel.

3 m. E. HOCHCLIFFE. Stockgrove, Col. W. H. Hanmer, K.H.; Houghton House, Humphrey Brandreth, Esq.; Hockliffe Grange, Lieut.-Col. Richard Thomas Gilpin, M.P.; The Lodge, Mrs. Gilpin. 2 m. N.W. Battlesden Park, Sir Edward Henry Page Turner, Bart. 2½ N. Milton Bryan, Sir Robert Harry Inglis, Bart., M.P. 2 m. N.E. Toddington Park, William Dodge Cooper Cooper, Esq. 2 m. further, HARLINGTON. Harlington House, George Pearse, Esq.

46¾ m. BLETCHLEY STATION. Bedford Br. ☞ 48 m. cross Holyhead Road. 52½ m. WOLVERTON STATION.

N. of Bletchley, SYMPSON. Staple Hall, John Richards, Esq. WALTON. Manor House, William Lipstocke, Esq. WAUGHTON-ON-THE-GREEN. MILTON KEYNES. GREAT WOOLSTON. LITTLE WOOLSTON.

WOLVERTON, county of Bucks. Area of parish, 2,260 A.; population, 1,261, which owes its increase to the establishment of the Company's factory and depôt at this central station, where the comforts of their officers and servants have been carefully provided for by the erection of streets of small dwelling-houses, a church, school, library, and market-house. Wolverton House, Richard Harrison Esq.

N. are HAVERSHAM, STANTON, GREAT LINFORD, LITTLE LINFORD. Mansion House, H. Athwatt, Esq. 2 m. S. BRADWELL. Bradwell House, Joseph Bailey, Esq.

lodge is delightfully placed on a gentle eminence sloping gradually to the margin of the lake; the opposite bank is an undulating lawn, nearly a mile in extent, beautifully contrasted by the bold and abrupt aspect of a dense woodland scene terminating the view. Delightful rides branch off in almost every direction from the house. The original lodge was built by Claypole, son-in-law to Oliver Cromwell. The present mansion has been lately much improved by the present Duke, who resides there during the greater part of the sporting season. 1 m. N.W. Whittlebury Lodge, Lord Southampton; Shelbrook Lawn, Hon. General Fitzroy. ½ m. s. Stoke Park, Levison F. Vernon Wentworth, Esq. The mansion is a very elegant structure, commenced in the year 1663, from an Italian design; the front has recently been cased with handsome white stone. 2 m. W. SILVERSTONE.

Enter
Northampton.

4 m. S.W. at TOWCESTER, Easton Neston, Earl Pomfret. Towcester is built on the banks of the river Tow, and is composed of one long street. A college and chantry were founded here by William Spooner, temp. Henry VI., to whose memory there is an elegant monument standing in the church. The town was probably founded by the Romans. It was surrounded with walls by Edward the Elder in 921. Numerous coins and other remains of the Romans have been found in the neighbourhood at different periods. Population, 2,749; manufacture, silk and bobbin lace; market-day, Tuesday. 1 m. GREEN'S NORTON. 3 m. BRADDEN. Bradden House, Rev. Cornelius Heves. 1½ m. further, BLAKESLEY. Blakesley Hall, supposed to have been a possession of the Knights of St. John. 3 m. further, Cannons Ashby, Sir Henry Edward Leigh Dryden, Bart.; Morton Pinkney, Edward Candler, Esq. PLUMPTON.

60 m. ROADE STA.

BLISWORTH, county of Northampton. Area of parish, 1,980 A.; population, 882 (vide Northampton and Peterborough Branch). 2 m. S.W TIFFIELD. Area, 2,530 A.; population, 146.

62½ m. BLIS-
WORTH STATION.

The great military depôt of WEEDON, one of the most extensive and complete establishments of its kind in the kingdom, is situated on the left-hand side of the railway; it consists of residence for the officers, store-houses for 2,000 stand of arms, artillery and ammunition, workshops for artisans, an hospital, and several magazines for gunpowder, capable of containing about 5,000 barrels each.

Stow Hill Tunnel.
Weedon Viaduct.
69¾ m. WEEDON
STATION.

3 m. W. Everdon Hall, — Doveton, Esq. 1½ m. further, Fawsley Park, Sir Charles Knightley, Bart. Some parts of the mansion are very ancient, and offer a curious display of the baronial customs of our ancestors. The kitchen, containing two fire-places, one 15, and the other 12½ feet wide; these are placed back to back, that the operations of either may not be interrupted. The hall is 52 feet long, with a beautiful carved oak ceiling; the windows are enriched with the armorial bearings of the families connected by marriage with the ancient lords of the domain. To preserve the uniformity of the hall as to windows, the fire-place is placed under one of them. The park is well stocked with deer, abounds with ornamental trees, and contains some noble sheets of water.

2 m. s. STOWE NINECHURCHES. In the church is a monument to the daughter of Lord Latimer; and 2 m. further, PATTISHALL. Cornhill, Thomas Drayson, Esq.; and COLD HIGHAM.

4 m. N.E. NEWPORT PAGNEL, a market-town and parish, county of Bucks, on the river Ouse, which is here crossed by two stone bridges. Area, 3,220 A.; population, 3,569; chiefly employed in manufacture of lace. 2 m. N.W. Gayhurst Park, Right Hon. H. Pierrepont. The mansion was originally built at the close of the 16th century, and though it has undergone great alterations, the principal front remains as of old, and is a venerable specimen of the then prevailing style. The grounds are extensive, and contain some spacious lawns and noble woods. Tichford Abbey, W. Powell, Esq.; Tichford End, Mrs. S. Ayres; Marsh End, Mrs. L. Stephens. 1 m. w. Hanslope Park, the seat of the Watts family. 5. m. N. OLNEY, a small but neat town, chiefly built of stone, and celebrated as the residence of Cowper. The house occupied by the poet stands near the eastern corner of the market-place. Cowper's summer-house still stands in the centre of the garden.

ROADE, a small parish, county of Northampton. Courteen Hall, Sir Charles Wake, Bart. 1 m. N.E. QUINTON. 1 m. further, PRESTON DEANERY. Preston Park, Langham Christie, Esq.; and still further, PIDDINGTON and HORTON LANE. Horton House, Sir Robert Henry Gunning, Bart. The house is a large handsome structure, with fine front towards the east, is seated in a park, which abounds with noble forest trees, and is enlivened with a broad piece of water.

4 M. N.W. MIDDLETON MALSO, W. Montgomery, Esq. 1 m. further, COLLINGTREE.

WEEDON (Weedon-Beck, or Weedon-on-the-Street), from its position on the ancient Watling Street of the Romans, is a parish, county of Northampton, containing an area of 1,710 A., and a population of 2,195. It is a place of great antiquity. Wulfhere, King of Mercia, had a palace here. 2 m. N. Brock Hall, Thomas Reeve Thornton, Esq. 1 m. further, WHILTON. From Weedon to the E. 1 m. FLOOXE. 3 m. further, parishes of HARPOLE, John Mannering, Esq.; and KISLINGBURY, Thomas Litchfield, Esq.

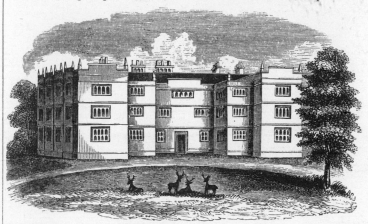

BROCK HALL, THOMAS REEVE THORNTON, ESQ.

Enter Northampton.

60 m. ROADE STA.

62¼ m. BLISWORTH STATION.
Northampton and Peterboro' Br.
Stow Hill Tunnel.
Weedon Viaduct.
69¾ m. WEEDON STATION.

About 5 m. N.W. lies the very ancient municipal borough town of DAVENTRY, through which also runs a branch of the Watling Street. The town, which is clean and well-built, is situated on the Nene, and has a modern church, a grammar school founded in 1576, a union workhouse, and branch bank. Manufactures, shoes, whips, &c. Its interesting monuments are the remains of a priory founded in 1090, now inhabited by poor people, and Dane's Hill, in the neighbourhood, the largest Roman encampment in the empire. Market, Wednesday. It has several fairs, chiefly for horses, for which it is celebrated as the principal mart in the Midland counties. Area of parish, 4,090 A.; population, 4,565. Hill Lodge, H. Arnold, Esq.; Badby House, Mrs. Watkins; The Lodge, Mrs. C. Watson. 2 m. E. Norton Hall, Beriah Botfield, Esq. The hall, which was enlarged and embellished by the present Mr. Botfield, is both handsome and commodious; the principal fronts are pinnacled and embattled; and the chief entrance on the east is through a cloister of five pointed arches; the house contains a valuable library, and a collection of pictures and armour. 1 m. N.W. Drayton Grange. 5 m. s.w. CATESBY ABBEY, a parish; area, 1,990 A.; population, 105. A priory was founded here in the reign of Richard I., from which it derives its name.

2 m. w. ASHBY ST. LEGER'S. The church has a richly-ornamented screen and roodloft, and contains the tombs of the Catesby family. Ashley Lodge, Mrs. S. Arnold; Manor House, Lady Mary Senhouse. 2 m. s.w. Welton Place, Richard Trevor Clarke, Esq.	75½ m. CRICK STATION. Kilsby Tunnel. Enter Warwickshire.
RUGBY, county of Warwick; a market-town, situated on an eminence south of the river Avon, is irregularly built, but contains some good modern brick, amongst many old timber buildings. The remains of an old castle erected by, or temp. King Stephen, are still traceable. The church is a very ancient edifice; but the principal attraction is its public school, founded by Lawrence, Sheriff temp. Queen Elizabeth, formerly of a humble character, but which, owing to the increase of its resources (principally from its possessions in Middlesex), has been rebuilt (1808) in the Tudor style, and now forms one of the great ornaments of the county. It has about 300 scholars, 50 of whom are on the foundation, the revenue of which exceeds £5000 per annum, 14 exhibitions to the two universities, and an almshouse appertaining to the foundation. Area of parish, 2,190 A.; population, 4,008. The rivers Swift and Dove, as well as the Oxford Canal, are near the town. ½ m. w. Dunchurch Road, Harry Scott Gibbs, Esq., J.P.; West Leyes, Rev. J. Hinton; Rugby Lodge, Thomas Caldecott, Esq.; Adelaide Villa, General S. Smith; Rugby Fields, John Watts, Esq. 1¾ m. s.w. BILTON. Here Addison resided after his marriage with the Countess of Warwick. Bilton Grange, Nathaniel Sutton, Esq. 3 m. s.w. DUNCHURCH. Bilton Grange, Captain Washington Hibbert. 7 m. s.w. at Dunsmore Heath, Birdingbury Hall, Sir Theophilus Biddulph, Bart.	83¾ m. RUGBY STATION. Valley of the Avon. Brandon Embankment. Avon Viaduct.
¼ m. s. of which is the parish of LEAMINGTON HASTANGS. The Hall, Sir Trevor W. Wheler, Bart. 2½ m. s.e. HILL MARTON. Manor House, T. Townsend, Esq.; Hill Marton House, J. T. Coote, Esq. ½ m. WOLSTON. Wolston Heath, W. Rose Rose, Esq. 2 m. s.w. RYTON ON DUNSMORE. Stephen Freeman, Esq.; Wolverhill Hall, Richard Warner, Esq.; Granary, Mrs. Warner. 1 m. further s. STRETTON ON DUNSMORE. Manor House, John Fullerton, Esq.; 1⅓ m. further, FRAMPTON, Samuel Heath, Esq.	89¼ BRANDON STATION.

2 m. s. NETHER HEYFORD; and 2 m. further, BUGBROOK.

5 m. N.E. Althorp, the seat of Earl Spencer. The house is a large pile of building, occupying three sides of a quadrangle. It stands low; and in the approach you go through and across those straight avenues of trees which, at one time, by a strange perverseness or deficiency of taste, were considered the line of beauty. The present edifice was built by the Earl of Sunderland, in the year 1688, and the estate has belonged to the Spencers ever since the reign of Henry VII.

It is remarked of Althorp House, by Dr. Dibdin: "There is neither colonnade nor vestibule, nor terrace, nor fountain, nor lake, as you approach the mansion; nor studied grandeur of architectural decoration as you enter it; but comfort, order, peace, unanimity, good management, choice society and splendid order, Gobelin tapestries, gilt balustrades, and all the pomp and circumstance of elaborate and overwhelming furniture."

With all due deference to the learned Doctor, we would venture to remark, that the inference implied in the last instance is anything but legitimate. Althorp, with its magnificent library and splendid collection of pictures, may well dispense with the adventitious and luxurious embellishments referred to; but for the life of us we cannot see that " silken hangings" are inconsistent with "comfort;" how "Gobelin tapestry," should be intolerant of " order and peace;" and why "good management" should be interdicted by the "pomp and circumstance of elaborate furniture!"

75½ m. CRICK STATION.
Kilsby Tunnel.
Enter Warwickshire.
Rugby and Stamford Line. ☞

CRICK, county of Northampton; the parish contains an area of 3,930 A.; with a population of 1,006. 1 m. N. Watford Park, Lord Henley. 5 m. N.E. WEST HADDON. The Hall, Mrs. Dembley. Warwick. E. EAST HADDON. Henry Barne Sawbridge, Esq.

83¾ m. RUGBY STATION.
Midland Counties. ☞
Trent Valley. ☞
Valley of the Avon.
Brandon Embankment.
Avon Viaduct

1½ N.E. NEWBOLD-UPON-AVON. Newbold Fields, Joseph Dand, Esq.; Newbold Grange, Thomas Walter, Esq. 2 m. w. Oldbrook Grange. 2 m. further, HARBOROUGH MAGNA. Ewershall, Miss Ann Barnes. 4 m. N. CHURCHOVER. Eaton House, The Dowager Marchioness of Queensberry. 8 m. N.N.E. LUTTERWORTH, a market-town and parish; area, 1,890 A.; population, 2,531. This place was formerly noted for the peculiar vassalage of the tenants of the manor, who were obliged to grind their corn at one particular mill of their lord, and their meal at another, so late as the year 1758, when they obtained a decision at the Leicester assizes empowering them to erect mills, and to grind where they pleased. The town is situated on the Swift, a tributary of the Avon, and has a handsome church, containing a part of the pulpit and a portrait of the Reformer, Wickliffe, who was its Rector, and who died in the year 1387, and was interred in the church; but in the year 1420, his bones were disinterred by a mandate from the Pope, and publicly burnt, and the ashes thrown into the river. The population is chiefly employed in the manufacture of hosiery and ribbons. 1 m. S.E. Misterton Hall, Mrs. Pochin.

89¼ BRANDON STATION.

BRANDON, a hamlet, county of Warwick, is an intermediate station. 6½ m. w. of Rugby. Brandon Lodge, James Beech, Esq.

2 m. N.E. BINLEY.

Sow Viaduct.

Sherbourn Viaduct.

Styvichall Hall, Arthur Francis Gregory, Esq. A substantial stone mansion, built about 1760. In the time of Henry VI. an anchorite fixed his melancholy abode at Styvichall. 1 m. Whitley Abbey, Lord Hood. A spacious stone structure, recently altered from the designs of the late Sir John Soane. It is supposed to have been the place from which Charles I. unsuccessfully summoned the city of Chester in 1642. 1 m. further, Baginton Hall, Right Hon. William Yates Peel. 1 m. further, BUBENHALL. A parish on the Avon, which is here crossed a bridge. Joseph Williamson, Esq. A little to the west is Stoneleigh Abbey, Lord Leigh. In olden times a Cistercian monastery stood upon the site of this abbey, and a large fragment of the structure, raised upon the expulsion of the monks, is still to be seen, and even some portions belonging to a yet remoter period, amongst which the most prominent feature is a gateway of the old abbey, which has in the outer front a large escutcheon of stone in memory of Henry II., the founder of the original structure. Through the grounds, rendered yet more picturesque by venerable woods, flows the river Avon, but so much increased beyond its usual width, as to deserve the epithet of magnificent. The park, adorned by some of the finest trees in England, extends to a considerable distance.

94 m. COVENTRY STATION.

Leominster and Warwick.

97 ½m. ALLESLEY STATION.

Dockers' Lane, a small station 1½ miles beyond Allesley Gate. 1½ m. w. BARSTON. E. Burton, Esq.; John Greene, Esq. 1½ m. s., at TEMPLE BASALL, is Barston House, the late General Northey Hopkins.

99 m. DOCKERS' LANE STA.

Cross the river Blythe.

HAMPTON (in Arden), a large parish, county of Warwick, containing 12,910 A., with a population of 2,036, 9½ m. E.S.E. of Birmingham. This is also a station for the West Branch of the Midland Railway. T. Hensman, Esq. 2 m. N.W. ELMDON. Mansion House, C. W. Alston, Esq.; Elmdon Hall, Spooner Lillingston, Esq.

103¼ m. HAMPTON STATION.

3 m. w. SOLIHALL. Has a good church, town-hall, and schools. Revenue of charities, £510 per annum. Shirley Heath, William Anderton, Esq.; Maids' Cross, Mrs. Bushell; Olton Cottage, T. Harlowe, Esq.; Malvern Hall, Henry Greswolde, Esq. 2 m. S.E. KNOWLE. Knowle Hall, William Henry Jordan Wilson, Esq.; Springfield Hall, Joseph Boultbee, Esq.; Springfield House, G. Whieldon, Esq.

1 m. w. SHELDEN. The church a handsome cruciform building is well worthy the attention of the tourist. Shelden Field House, Thomas Colmore, Esq.; William Harding, Esq.

106¼ m. MARSTON GREEN STA.

½ m. s., at YARDLEY, is Spark Hill, C. H. Coke, Esq., and Blakeley House.

109 m. STETCHFORD STA.

Sow Viaduct.

Sherbourn
Viaduct.

94 m. COVENTRY
STATION.

Coventry & Nun-
eaton Junc.

97½ m. ALLESLEY
STATION.

99 m DOCKERS'
LANE STA.
Cross the river
Blythe.

103¼ m. HAMPTON
STATION.

Midland, West
Branch.

106¼ m. MARSTON
GREEN STA.

109 m. STETCH-
FORD STA.

2 m. N. Coombe Abbey, Earl Craven. This noble mansion stands on the site of an ancient religious house of the Cistercian order of monks; it was chiefly erected in the reign of James I., but has been considerably added to since that time; sufficient of the monastery still remains to enable the observer to trace the ancient structure. The park and grounds contain 500 A. tastefully laid out, and adorned with wood and water. 2 m. E CHURCH LAWFORD.

COVENTRY, county of Warwick, on the Sherbourn, an afflux of the Avon, one of the most ancient and curiously picturesque cities in England, is a county within itself, and a municipal and parliamentary borough, returning two members to Parliament. Area of the city, 4,920 A; population, 30,743. Many of the houses in this city are of the 15th century, and have projecting upper stories; and the cross beams, which appear externally, being frequently painted black, contrast strangely with the white-wash of the body of the buildings. In those which have received coatings of plaster, or have otherwise been externally modernized, the antiquary will find little interior desecration, for there the carved work, denoting the prosperity of the owners in the days of the Plantagenets, is still abundant. No city in the empire contains more monuments of interest to the antiquarian. Independently of these curiosities, Coventry possesses some fine public buildings, amongst which, a noble Gothic structure, St. Michael's Church, is surmounted by one of the most elegant spires in Europe, 303 feet high. St. Mary's Hall, belonging to the corporation. At the time of Edward the Confessor, the city received its first charter from Earl Leofric, at the instance of his wife, the Lady Godiva, to commemorate which well known story an annual festival takes place. Two parliaments were held here in the 15th century. The remains of its ancient walls of circumvallation, Eheylesmore Castle, a monastery of White Friars, and its once celebrated cathedral and episcopal palace, are all traceable. It was a bishopric with Lichfield until 1836, when it was transferred to the see of Worcester. Markets, Wednesday and Saturday.

ALLESLEY, county of Warwick, 2 m. N. of Coventry. Hollebury End, John Dalton Lant, Esq. 2 m. N. Allesley Park, Rev. Edward Neale.

1½ m. N.W. Berkswell Hall, Sir John Eardley Eardley Wilmot, Bart. ½ m. further, Meriden Hall.

2 m. N. GREAT PACKINGTON. Packington Hall, Earl Aylesford. The hall is a very spacious and convenient mansion, but has nothing peculiarly ornamental in its structure; it is surrounded with grounds laid out to exhibit all the beautiful varieties of nature. 3 m. further, COLESHILL. The church, a handsome and attractive specimen of the decorated Gothic, or English style of architecture, contains many monuments of the Digby family.

4 m. Blythe Hall, William Stratford Dugdale, Esq., formerly the residence of his ancestor, Sir William Dugdale, the great historian.

4 m. Maxstoke Castle, William Dilke, Esq. The castle is built in the form of a parallelogram, and is encompassed with a moat. At each corner is an hexagonal tower with embattled parapets. The entrance is by a gateway, protected on each side by a tower.

2 m. N. Coleshill Park, Earl Digby.

BIRMINGHAM, county of Warwick, a very ancient town, which is supposed to have been the spot where arms were manufactured in the time of the ancient Britons, is one of the principal and most important manufacturing towns in England.   The details respecting the size of this great focus of industry, are curiously interesting, but too voluminous for the nature of this work.   It is a parliamentary and municipal borough, the area of which, including the townships of Aston, Edgbaston, and other places adjacent, is 18,700 A., and the population, 182,922, although only a century and a half ago it did not exceed 4,000.   It is situated on the river Rea, and the lower part of the town presents nothing to the eye of the traveller but a mass of brick factories and gigantic chimneys, almost as lofty as the church spires with which they are intermixed.   In the upper portion of the town, which is built on rising ground, are many broad streets, handsome edifices, and noble public buildings, which do honour to the taste of the inhabitants, of which we may cite particularly the Town Hall, St. George's and St. Philip's Churches, Queen's College, the grammar school founded by Edward VI., and the theatre.   The town hall, which is fronted with marble, is certainly one of the grandest edifices in the kingdom; its saloon is 145 feet in length, 65 feet broad, and 65 feet high, and is capable of holding conveniently 4,000 persons seated, or double that number standing.   It is here that the great musical festivals are held, and it is said that the organ is remarkable both for size and tone. All these public buildings we have enumerated, with the exception of some of the churches, are of modern erection, and mark the superior taste of

112½ m. BIRMING-
HAM STA.

Birmingham, Lancaster, and Carlisle Railway.

BIRMINGHAM TO CARLISLE.

This important line throughout the whole of the distance alternates in cuttings and embankments, and there are no less than one hundred and six bridges over, and sixty-three under the line, independently of seventeen level crossings.   The Birmingham Viaduct is the most important and stupendous work, challenging comparison with almost any of ancient or modern art.   It is built of brick, with stone groins and dressings, from the design of Mr. Locke, a very eminent engineer, and consists of twenty-eight segmental arches of upwards of thirty feet span, twenty feet high, and thirty-two feet wide, the length extending to about one thousand feet, the whole built on a curve of three-quarters of a mile radius.   The next object of beauty connected with the labours of the company which will occupy the traveller's attention, is the Aston Viaduct, one of the great ornaments of this line, which, with the embankment and the general aspect of the country of this locality, presents the most beautiful and picturesque scenery, heightened by the presence of a reservoir or inland lake, and a belt of noble elms, from which emerges the elegant spire of Aston church.   Proceeding onwards, the traveller passes through the Newton Excavation, which is sometimes eighty feet below the surface of the open country, and a splendid view opens to him at Penkridge, where the river accompanies the line for a considerable distance.   The Whitmore statue, which stands three hundred and ninety feet above low-water mark at Liverpool, cannot fail to excite interest, the abrupt cuttings in this locality producing a most romantic appearance.

Vale Royal Viaduct, which crosses the Weever, is a magnificent structure of five arches of sixty-three feet span each, twenty feet high.   It is impossible to imagine anything more lovely than the view from this noble bridge over the flowering meadows beneath, watered by the clear and sparkling stream of the Weever, as it glides through this enchanting valley, bounded on the West by Delamere Forest, and surmounted by distant heights covered with venerable woods.   The bridge near the Hartford Station is a structure of great elegance, and forms a picturesque object on this line.   The Dutton Viaduct over the Weever is a stupendous work of art, consisting of twenty arches, each of sixty feet span, and an equal height from the level of the water, crossing the entire valley of the Weever, a distance of nearly eighteen hundred feet.   The arches are cycloidal in their shape, and the piers, light and tapering, are, with the facing of the

112½ m. BIRMING-
HAM STA.

the age. Birmingham was formerly one parish, and its church, St. Martin, in which there is a very ancient and curious monument, dates from the 8th century. It is now divided into four—St. Martin, St. Philip, St. George, and St. Thomas, all of which are now (since 1836) included in the see of Worcester. Independently of these ecclesiastical buildings, there are chapels for every denomination of religious sectarian, hospitals, dispensaries, Athenæum, market-house, barracks, society of arts, mechanics' institution, and in fact every description of institution similar to that of the metropolis, but of a number and size commensurate with the population, together with public gardens and places of amusement. Its manufactures comprise every description of metal wares, and plated and japanned goods, steam-engines and machinery; indeed it would be difficult to name an article made by men's handicraft that is not here produced in perfection. It owes its great prosperity to the mines of coal and iron by which it is surrounded, and the canals communicating with the Thames, Severn, Mersey, Humber, &c., as well as the railways, of which its station forms a general point of junction from London, Liverpool, Derby, Worcester, &c. Birmingham sends two members to Parliament. Registered electors (1845), 6,129. Market-days, Monday, Thursday, and Saturday. Under the charter of incorporation of 1838, it is divided into sixteen wards, and is governed by a mayor, recorder, aldermen and common councilmen, and has a borough court of quarter sessions, and a court of requests. It has also two fairs in Whitsun-week and September.

Birmingham, Lancaster, and Carlisle Railway.

BIRMINGHAM TO CARLISLE.

bridge, of rusticated stone, the whole length being ornamented by a beautiful cornice and a stone coping. It is universally acknowledged that this magnificent structure is one of the most extraordinary specimens of the architectural art ever displayed since the days of the Romans. It cost upwards of £60,000, and took three years in its construction. We have not space to enlarge upon the scenic beauties of this locality, indeed they almost as much surpass description as they certainly do all other spots, however lovely and enchanting, along the course of this line; and the wildest imagination of the poet could scarcely exaggerate the beautifully fair and almost fairy vision which bursts upon the traveller as he emerges from Dutton Wood into this peaceful valley. Not far from this noble viaduct is the Preston Brook Cutting of one mile and a quarter, with a tunnel of about one hundred yards in length, over which passes the Northank and Runcorn turnpike road. At the end of this cutting is Preston Brook Station, which lies exactly 25 miles from Liverpool, and 72½ from Birmingham; and beside the line for some miles runs the Trent and Mersey Canal, which, near the station, forms a junction with the Bridgewater Canal, and by its traffic, adds importance to the busy little village of Preston Brook. Beyond this station the most important object is the Warrington Viaduct, which is inferior only to that which spans the valley of the Weever. This noble bridge consists of twelve arches of different dimensions, as well as purposes, two magnificent arches, each of seventy-five feet span, cross the broad stream of the Mersey, one of forty feet stretches across the canal, and the remaining land arches; three in the centre between the river and the canal; and three on each side complete this elegant structure. It is thirty feet above the river at low-water mark, and nineteen feet above the level of the canal. The Warrington Station, with its splendid embankment, and beautiful bridge across the Mersey, is well worthy of attention; the station itself is one of great importance. From the Winwick Station the train reaches the Newton Junction, where the Manchester and Liverpool Railway (which turns off to the right for the former town), receives the Grand Junction Line, and here the train proceeds on to the Sandymain Embankment, which is planted on either side with firs and shrubs, giving it the appearance of an approach to some noble mansion, while the various openings in the trees display the beauties of the fertile country it traverses. On the left is the turnpike road to Wigan, skirting Haydock Park

and the small town of Newton; on the right Winwick Church, its tapering spire, and the lofty hills of Staffordshire in the distance. At the Newton Bridge Station, where the train stops for a few minutes, is an excellent hotel on the right, and on the left the County Club Room, a handsome elevation, with Doric pillars and a terrace walk. At this part of the line the embankment is forty feet above the level of the road, and contains a handsome viaduct of four arches, each of thirty feet span, which crosses the valley below, and the road from Newton to Warrington—this is a remarkably picturesque spot. At a distance of half a mile is Park Side Station, memorable as the place where that enlightened statesman, Mr. Huskisson, met his untimely fate. On the left is the Wigan Junction, or, as it was formerly called, The North Union Railway, between Park Side and Preston, a distance of little more than 22 miles.

On account of the rugged nature of the country, the earth-works on this short line were of a very heavy nature, the largest embankment being at Wigan, the centre of the three principal stations. The bridges are twenty-eight over, and twenty-one under the railway, thirteen level road, and thirty-eight level field crossings. The bridge carrying the railway over Walgate, Wigan, is forty-six feet in length, and thirty-six feet in width, and is built on the level-beam principle; the iron beams or girders being supported intermediately by two rows of cast-iron fluted Doric columns, six on each side, which separate the footway from the carriageway. The greatest architectural work on this line is the bridge over the river Ribble, chiefly constructed of millstone-grit, from Longridge. It consists of five semi-elliptical arches, each of one hundred and twenty feet span, and rising thirty-three feet. The piers are twenty feet each in thickness, and the height from the surface of the water to the level of the rails, fourty-four feet. When this magnificent bridge is viewed from the river or its banks, it presents an extremely bold appearance. The only tunnel upon this line is a short and curved one, seventy-seven yards in length under Fishergate, Preston, near the junction with the Lancaster and Preston Railway. It is constructed of brick and stone, the arch of semi-elliptical form, and thirty feet in span. The Preston Station is approached from Fishergate by a carriage-road and footway of ample width, with sufficient space for road carriages in waiting. It is a plain building, but the offices of the Company are convenient and commodious.

The traveller now proceeds on his journey to Carlisle by the Preston, Lancaster Kendal, and Carlisle Railway.

### Left of Railway from Birmingham.	*Distance from London.*
Aston Hall, James Watt, Esq., consists of a large and handsome centre, with large projecting wings. Dugdale, in his "History of Warwickshire," speaks of it as a noble fabric, which for beauty and state much exceeded any in these parts.	116 m. PERRY BAR STATION.
Aston New Town, a parish partly in the borough of Birmingham. Population, 45,718, chiefly employed in the manufacture of Birmingham articles. Lea Hall, G. F. Muntz, Esq.	
1 m. N. Charleymount Hall, H. Dawes, Esq.	119½ m. NEWTON ROAD STA.
2 m. S.W. WEST BROMWICH. Oakwood House, William Bagnall, Esq.; Black Lake Hall, James Belson, Esq.; Sandwell Hall, Earl of Dartmouth; Island House, M. H. Dawes, Esq.; Hollies, Joseph Hatfield, Esq.; The Poplars, B. Haynes, Esq.; Highfield, T. Hood, Esq.; Elm Trees, J. Silvester, Esq.; Spur House, T. W. Vernon, Esq.; Highfield House, S. Wagstaff, Esq.; Summerfield House, William Carter, Esq.	
1 m. WEDNESBURY, a parish, county of Stafford; market-town; population, 11,625. Employed in coal and iron-mines, and various descriptions of hardware. In the church are some curious old monuments. Church Hill, J. Addersbrook, Esq.; Oakwell End, J. Crowther, Esq.; Wood Grove, S. Lloyd, Esq.	122 m. BESCOTT STATION. Bescott Junction, Dudley Br.
1 m. W. PORTOBELLO, built since the opening of the railway, W. Doody, Esq.	124½ m. WILLEN-HALL STA.

PRESTON, LANCASTER, KENDAL, AND CARLISLE RAILWAY.

It was well observed of that portion of this line which was first opened under the title of the Lancaster and Preston Railway, that it formed a direct and easy link in one of the great chains of railway communication between the metropolis and Scotland. Its course between the Preston and Lancaster termini is very direct, crossing the Preston turnpike-road near Barton Lodge, and passing between Garstang and Cleughton Hall, by Galgate and Scotforth, to Lancaster, the distance between the above-named important towns being slightly under 21 miles.

On this short line there are forty-eight bridges and viaducts, none of which however require any special notice, except the bridge which crosses the Wyre, and the Galgate Viaduct. The former consists of six semi-elliptical arches, each of thirty feet span, and two hundred and sixty-two feet in length; and the latter of the same number of semi-circular arches, the height of the viaduct from the level of the land being forty feet, and its whole length two hundred and sixty-five. Both these viaducts are built of brick, and faced with sandstone. The Lancaster Station occupies an area of about six acres, and is situated at the divergence of the Preston and Cockerham roads. The elevation is neat, and the offices commodious. After leaving Lancaster, the railway is carried over the river Lune by a handsome viaduct of nine arches—six of stone, and three of wood. Another viaduct of six arches, each of fifty feet span, crosses the river Mint near the Kendal Junction.

The embankments and cuttings in the solid granite rock near Tebay and Orton Street vary in depth from fifty to sixty feet. The viaduct which crosses the river Eamont, near Penrith, consists of five arches, each of fifty feet span, and seventy feet in height from the surface of the water, and has a very imposing appearance in the landscape. There are no other remarkable features on this line in reference to the undertaking itself, but the country it traverses is proverbial for the beauty of the scenery, its mountains, sea views, lakes, rivers, picturesque valleys and glens, all of which will be described in their several localities.

Distance from London.	𝕽𝖎𝖌𝖍𝖙 𝖔𝖋 𝕽𝖆𝖎𝖑𝖜𝖆𝖞 𝖋𝖗𝖔𝖒 𝕭𝖎𝖗𝖒𝖎𝖓𝖌𝖍𝖆𝖒.
116 m. PERRY BAR STATION.	PERRY BAR is a hamlet in the parish of Handsworth, county of Stafford. Population, 933. It has a very handsome modern church. 1 m. N. Perry Hall, Hon. F. Gough Gough; Bloomfield House, Joseph Cuttler, Esq.; Perry Park, H. W. Osborne, Esq.; New Tree Cottage, John Perkins, Esq. ½ m. further, Hampstead Hall.
119½ m. NEWTON ROAD STA.	½ m. Fairy Hall. 1 m. further, BARR MOGNA. Great Barr Hall, a spacious and handsome Gothic brick building, situated in a finely wooded park, Sir Edward Dolman Scott, Bart.; Aldridge Lodge, Rev. T. Adams; Red House, Thomas Bagnall, Esq.
122 m. BESCOTT STATION. Bescott Junction, Derby and Walsall. ☞	Bescott Hall, Horatio Barnett, Esq.; Gowry House, John James, Esq.; Myfield House, H. C. Windle, Esq. 1½ m. N. Betley Hall, Geo. Tollett, Esq.
124¾ m. WILLENHALL STA.	WILLENHALL is a chapel, county of Stafford, parish of Wolverhampton. Population, 8,695 1½ m. W. WEDNESFIELD. Edward the Elder here obtained a decisive victory over the Danes in 910. 1½ m. N. Perry Hall.

WOLVERHAMPTON, county of Stafford, is a parliamentary and municipal borough. Area of parish, comprising Bilston, Willenhall, &c., 16,630 A., with a population of 70,370. It returns two members to Parliament. Registered electors (1848), 2,692. It is a large, smoky, manufacturing town, principally celebrated for its locks, brass, tin, and japanned wares, tools, nails, &c. It has a vast trade, which is facilitated by several canals, as well as the railway, and the whole neighbourhood is glowing with forges, rolling-mills, foundries, coal-mines, and iron-stone pits. It has four churches, of which the collegiate church of St. Peter is the most considerable, independently of the Town Hall, hospital, dispensary, and Union Mill. It has all sorts of assembly and reading-rooms, and a theatre. Its grammar school has a revenue of £1,200 per annum; here Sir William Congreve and Abernethey were educated. It has also a blue-coat school. Markets, Wednesday and Saturday. Seats, Cleveland Hall, John Bushen, Esq.; Merridale, James Bradshaw, Esq.; Oriel Cottage, C. F. Farrell, Esq.; Slade Hill House, J. Peck, Esq. 2 m. N. Dunstall Hall, Marcus Annesley, Esq.; 3 m. W. Tettenhall Wood, Miss Hinckes; and 1 m. further, Wrottesley, Lord Wrottesley.

½ m. Somerford Hall, General Monckton. ½ m. further, BREWOOD.

4. m. W. The village of STRETTON. ½ m. N.W. LAPLEY. Stretton Hall, Lady Roos. 3. m. further, WHEATON ASTON. 1 m. further, Weston-under-Lizard, Earl Bradford. The hall is an extensive building, consisting of two stories, situated in a well-timbered park; the principal apartments occupy the centre of the mansion, and are tastefully furnished and elegantly ornamented; the grounds comprise a large tract of land in a very picturesque part of the country.

PENKRIDGE, county of Stafford, situated on the Penk, a branch of the Trent. This town is supposed to have been the Roman Pennocrucium, and has a large church, formerly collegiate. 2 m. W. Whiston Hall.

Close to the station, CASTLE CHURCH. 3 m. further, RANTON. Ranton Hall; Ranton Abbey, Earl of Lichfield; about 3 m. from which, is the village of HIGH OFFLEY. 1 m. further, Hill Hall.

At NORBURY, 8 m., Cob Hall; Knightley Hall; Norbury Park. At NEWPORT, 12 m. Aqualate Hall, Sir Thomas Fenton Fletcher Boughey, Bart.

2 m. W. Sleaford Hall, F. West, Esq.

3 m. W. ECCLESHALL, a market-town, county of Stafford. It is neatly built. Its church afforded a sanctuary to Margaret of Anjou. The bishops of Lichfield owned the manor temp. Conquest, and have inhabited the Castle here since the 13th century. Market, Friday. Eccleshall Castle, Bishop of Lichfield.

2 m. N.W. of which, Sugenhall. 3 m. further, Blore Park. ½ m. S. Johnson Hall, John Crochell, Esq. 1 m. S.W. Wharton Villa.

STANDON, a small village, with a population of 367. 4 m. W. Broughton Hall, Rev. Sir Harry Delves Broughton, Bart. An ancient mansion in the Elizabethan style of architecture.

126¾ m. WOLVER-HAMPTON STA.

132¼ m. FOUR ASHES STA.

134¼ m. SPREAD EAGLE STA.

Cross Watling Street.

136½ m. PENK-RIDGE STA.

141½ m. STAFFORD STATION.

Wellington Branch.

147½ m. NORTON BRIDGE STA.

151 m. STANDON BRIDGE STA.

East of Wolverhampton, are Albrighton Hall, Miss Parry; Wyrley, P. Fowke Hussey, Esq. 1 m N. LAWHILL. ½ m. further, village of BUSHBURY. A little further, Moseley Court, Henry Whitgreave, Esq.; Moseley Hall, T. Bickford, Esq. Moseley Hall is celebrated as the retreat of Charles II. after the battle of Worcester. Here the fugitive Prince was received and protected by the head of the ancient family of Whitgreave, whose descendant, the present George Thomas Whitgreave, Esq., has been granted an honourable augmentation of his arms, commemorative of his ancestor's devoted loyalty. 1 m. E. is Hilton Park, General Vernon.

132¼ m. FOUR ASHES STA.	1½ m. S.E. SHARESHILL.
134¼ m. SPREAD EAGLE STA. Cross Watling Street.	4 m. E. The village of HATHERTON. Hatherton Hall, Hon. Edward R. Littleton, M.P. 2 m. further, CANNOCK. Population, 2,852, partly employed in coal and tin mines. On Castle Hill are traces of a British encampment. Cannock Chase, a bleak tract of land of about 25,000 A., stretches N.W. to the river Trent.
136½ m. PENKRIDGE STA.	3 m. N.E. Teddesley Park, Lord Hatherton. 1 m. further, N. ACTON TRUSSEL. Bedenhall. 3 m. N. DUNSTON.
141½ m. STAFFORD STATION. Trent Valley Line. ☞	STAFFORD, a parliamentary and municipal borough town, capital of county, situated on the north bank of the river Sow. Area of borough, 2,510 A.; population, 9,149. The market and county halls are in the centre of the main street, near to which are the two parish churches. The castle is a very striking and remarkable object, on a singular hill. The keep, the principal portion of what now remains, contains three rooms with their ancient fireplaces. It is the third castle supposed to have been erected on the same site, and dates from shortly after the Conquest. Stafford has also a gaol, lunatic asylum, and general infirmary, with a grammar school, founded by Edward VI. The celebrated Isaac Walton was a native of Stafford. 2 m. N. Tillington House, John Locker, Esq; and Cresswell Hall, Rev. Edward Whitby.
147½ m. NORTON BRIDGE STA. Norton Bridge Junction. ☞	3 m. N.E. STONE, which takes its name from a monumental heap of stones, which according to the custom of the Saxons, were placed over the bodies of the Princes Wulford and Rufinus, who were here slain by their father Wulfhere, King of Mercia, on account of their conversion to Christianity. Stonefield House, James Beech, Esq.; Mansion House, Charles Bromley, Esq.; Park Lodge, Leigh Colman, Esq.; The Brooms, W. Bewley Taylor, Esq.; Brooms' Villa, T. Plant, Esq.
151 m. STANDON BRIDGE STA.	1½ m. W., at SWINNERTON, Swinnerton Park, Thomas Fitz-Herbert, Esq. The hall is a handsome edifice, erected in the time of Queen Anne; it is of stone, and has a centre with four pilasters and two wings, the whole surmounted by vases. From the roof of the house a very extensive prospect, extending over the north-west parts of Staffordshire and three adjoining counties of Shropshire, Cheshire, and Worcestershire, is obtained.

8 m. w. MARKET DRAYTON, a market-town and parish. Area, 6,880 A.;
population, 4,680; market-day, Wednesday. The charities, which comprise
a grammar school, &c., have an annual revenue of about £270.   Near
Market Drayton, Tunstall Hall, P. Broughton, Esq.; Oakley Hall, Sir
John Chetwode, Bart.; Betton Hall, W. Church Norcop, Esq.; Hales' Hall,
Richard Corbet, Esq.; Shavington Hall, Earl Kilmorey; Styche Hall, Messrs.
Clive; Buntingsdale Hall, John Taylor, Esq.; Hinstock, Henry Justice,
Esq.; Old Springs, Egerton Harding, Esq.; Goldstone Hall, William
Varden, Esq.; Peat's Wood, Thomas Twemlow, Esq.

155¾ m. WHIT-
MORE STA.

8 m. w. of Drayton, Sandford Hall, Thomas Hugh Sandford, Esq.   The
Manor of Sandford has descended, in an unbroken line, from father to son,
to the present proprietor, who is 27th in descent from Thomas de Sandford,
who fought under the banner of the Conqueror, and who obtained the lands
of Sandford as part of the spoliation.   About 9 m. N.W. of Drayton is Combermere Abbey, Viscount Combermere.   The Abbey stands in a delightful
park, abounding with fine trees of great age and size.   It was founded in
the 12th century as a Benedictine monastery, and some of the walls of the
old abbey form a part of the present mansion; it contains a handsome
library and collection of paintings.   In the park, and near the Abbey, is a
fine sheet of water, extending over 130 acres.   The banks are beautifully
undulated and well-wooded, and in a conspicuous part of the park is the
Wellington Oak, planted by his Grace the Duke of Wellington.

1 m. w. WORRE. 4 m. further w. AUDLEIN. Adderley Hall, Sir Andrew
Vincent Corbet, Bart.   4 m. further, Combermere Abbey, Viscount
Combermere.   (See above.)

158½ m. MADELEY
STATION.

Enter Cheshire.

2 m. N. of Worre, Doddington Hall, Rev. Sir Henry Delves Broughton,
Bart.   The mansion is a large fabric of stone; the south front overlooks a
fine sheet of water, and a short distance from the north are the venerable
and picturesque remains of the fortified mansion, erected by Sir John Delves
about the middle of the 14th century.

4 m. w. Nantwich, Charles Wickstead, Esq.; Hatherton House, John
Twemlow, Esq.; Dawford House, H. Tomkinson, Esq.

164 m. BASFORD
STATION.

3 m. S.W. NANTWICH, a market-town, county of Chester, situated on the
river Weever, which is crossed by a very fine bridge, and on the Birmingham
and Liverpool Canal.   Area of parish, 3,490 A.; population, 5,921.   It is
an irregularly built town, and consists chiefly of old houses.   At the time of
the Norman invasion, Nantwich was defended by a line of earthworks constructed along the banks of the river, but the opposition made to the progress
of the invaders was terminated by a battle, fought here in 1069.   The inhabitants then became subject to incursions from the Welsh, who are said to
have destroyed the town, 1133. The town hall was built in 1720, by George,

166½ m. CREWE
STATION.

Chester Rail-
way.

155¾ m. WHIT-
MORE STA.

1 m. N.E. WHITMORE, a village; population, 367.

WHITMORE HALL, CAPTAIN ROWLAND MAINWARING, R.N.,

is situated in a beautiful and fertile valley, from whence springs the source of the river Sow, which wends its silent course close to, and parallel with the railway for many miles through the county of Stafford, and falls into the Trent below Shugborough. The mansion is encompassed with magnificent oak and other timber, and the grounds are tastefully laid out. In fact, Nature has been the principal artist in this home domain, from the graceful undulations of the surrounding ground, which, with the happy position of the "Hall," the wood-walks and lakes, combine to give a pleasing diversity to the scenery, and (though small compared with the noble possessions in its immediate neighbourhood) claim for it its full share of general attraction.

158½ m. MADELEY
STATION.

Enter Cheshire.

MADELEY, a village, situate on the borders of Cheshire and Shropshire, consisting chiefly of cottages and farm-houses in the Elizabethan style. Madeley Manor, Weston Young, Esq. 1½ m. N. Betley Hall, George Tollett, Esq. 2 m. E. Keel Hall, Ralph Sneyd, Esq.

164 m. BASFORD
STATION.

1½ m. E. Doddlespool, J. Rasbottom, Esq. 2½ m. Betley Hall, G. Tollet, Esq. 3 m. Betley Court, F. Twemlow, Esq. 4 m. E. AUDLEY, a village abounding in mines of excellent coal. On the summit of a steep rock on the western boundary of the parish, are the remains of Hayley Castle, built by the Barons Audley.

166½ m. CREWE
STATION.

North Stafford
Railway. ☞

Manchester Line.
☞

CREWE Station is a very handsome building in the Elizabethan style, and a great railway depôt. It is situated in the parish of Barthomley. The population is chiefly employed in the stations and foundries of the several railways which centre in this locality, to which circumstance Crewe owes its origin and prosperity. The town consists of very neat houses appropriate to the wants and comforts of the officers and servants of the railway companies. A handsome church, a Roman Catholic chapel, schools, lecture-room, library, mechanics' institute, baths, and many good shops. Market, Saturday.

Prince of Wales and Earl of Chester, afterwards George II.; but in 1737 a portion of it fell down, and some persons were killed. It was rebuilt; but not many years afterwards a similar accident being apprehended from a certain crash during the holding of the sessions, it was taken down, and the present modern edifice erected on its site. It was once celebrated for its salt works, there being no less than 300 in operation temp. Henry VIII. One alone is now worked. The inhabitants are chiefly employed in the manufacture of silks, cottons, shoes, &c.

1 m. s.w. MINSHULL VERNON, a township, containing 349 inhabitants. ½ m. w. CHURCH MINSHULL.

171½ m. MIN-SHULL VERNON STATION.

1½ m. w. At OVER, Marten Hall. 3 m. further, Oulton Hall, Sir Philip De Malpas Grey Egerton, Bart. The Hall, standing in a park containing 350 acres, is supposed to have been erected from designs by Sir John Vanbrugh. It has undergone many alterations, and is now one of the most stately mansions in the county. 2 m. s.w. Darnhall Hall, Thomas George Corbett, Esq.

173¾ m. WINS-FORD STA.

1 m. w. Vale Royal, the truly magnificent seat of Lord Delamere. This is the site of an ancient monastery, which owed its origin to the piety of Edward, eldest son of Henry III. Tradition asserts that the Prince, on his return from an expedition to the Holy Land, was on the point of suffering shipwreck in a dreadful storm, when he made a vow to the Virgin, that if she interposed her aid for the preservation of himself and crew, he would found a convent for one hundred monks of the Cistercian Order. The vow, continues the chronicle of Vale Royal, was instantaneously accepted; the vessel righted itself, and was miraculously brought into port; the sailors disembarked, and the Prince landed last of all; the Divine protection then terminated, and every fragment of the wreck vanished under the waters. Without further reference to this traditionary superstitious tale, certain it is that Edward, shortly after his accession to the throne, planted a colony of the Dernhall monks at Vale Royal, and himself laid the first stone of the monastery. At the desolation of the monasteries, Vale Royal shared the fate of the other religious houses. The present mansion is built of red stone, and consists of a centre, with two projecting wings. Some portion, however, of the old Abbey may yet be traced. 1 m. N.W. CUDDINGTON. 1 m. further, Norley Hall, S. Woodhouse, Esq. 1 m. s.w. The Grange, Lady Brooke. 1½ m. further, Delamere House, George Wilbraham, Esq.

178 m. HARTFORD STATION.

1 m. w. Aston Park, Arthur Aston, Esq.

180¾ m. ACTON STATION.

Norton Priory, Sir Richard Brooke, Bart. The present mansion stands on the site of the old religious house of that name. It is a handsome spacious building, and has a delightful view of the river Mersey. The castle and rocks of Alton constitute a very striking feature on the other side of the prospect. Norton Priory was besieged by a party of Royalists in the year 1643, who were beaten off by the family with considerable loss. The grounds are laid out with much taste.

185 m. PRESTON BROOK STA.

〰 Chester Railway.

187 m. MOORE STATION. Cross the River Mersey.

4 m. w. GREAT SANKEY. The first canal navigation in modern times originated here in 1755. Bold Hall, H. Hoghton, Esq.; Old Hall, John Baskeville Glegg, Esq. 2½ m. s.w. Grappenhall Heyes, T. Parr, Esq. 5 m. Darnbury Hall, S. B. Chadwick, Esq. 2 m. N. Winwich Hall, Rev. J. S. Hornby.

190¾ m. WAR-RINGTON STA.

Liverpool and Manchester 〰 Railway.

½ m. E Crewe Hall, Lord Crewe. This mansion was commenced in 1615, and finished 1636. Fuller observes respecting it: "nor must it be forgotten that Sir John Randal first brought the model of this excellent building in these remote parts. Yea, brought London into Cheshire in the loftiness, lightness, and pleasantness of their structures." Crewe Hall still retains the peculiar character of the age in which it was built. The bricks of which it is constructed are dispersed diagonally, chequering the whole front; the quoins and ornamental decorations are of stone; the large windows have stone mullions and casings.

171½ m. MIN-SHULL VERNON STATION.

WARMINGHAM.

173¾ m. WINS-FORD STA.

2 m. E. MIDDLEWICH, where it is most probable the Romans had a station, as there are traces of a Roman road; and in the township of KENDERTON, 2 m. further E., is an intrenched camp, supposed to be the site of the Roman station called "Condate." 1 m. N. Wharton Lodge. 1 m. further, Bostock Hall, I. France France, Esq.

178 m. HARTFORD STATION.

1½ m. N.E. NORTHWICH, a market-town; population, 1,368, principally employed in salt-works, the quantity of which exported in the year 1840 was 230,000 tons. At and near Northwich, Hartford Lodge, Thomas Firth, Esq., a substantial, well-built house of Grecian style of architecture. Winnington Hall, Lord Stanley; Marbury Hall, James Smith Barry, Esq.; Belmont, Joseph Leigh, Esq.; Cog's Hall; Arley Hall, Rowland Eyles Egerton Warburton, Esq. Arley, built by "Wise Piers," has been the family mansion of the Warburtons since the time of Henry VII. The original structure, a timber house, surrounded by a moat, was modernized by the late Sir Peter Warburton's father, in the year 1758. A chapel, in the style of the 14th century, is now attached to the mansion, which has been almost entirely rebuilt by the present proprietor.

6 m. N.E. Over Tabley Hall, Lord De Tabley. The mansion stands on a slight elevation, and is built of stone, from the designs of Mr. Carr, of York. The Park is very extensive, and contains a magnificent lake, on an island, in the upper circuit of which stands the old Hall of Tabley, the ancient residence of the celebrated Sir Peter Leicester, author of the "Antiquities of Cheshire;" the eastern side is all that now remains. There is another object on this island worthy of notice—on the south-east part is a domestic chapel with large bay windows, and a turret with a bell at the west end.

180¾ m. ACTON STATION.

185 m. PRESTON BROOK STA.

PRESTON-ON-THE-HILL. Daresbury Hall, Rev. G. W. Horne; Newton Bank.

187 m. MOORE STATION. Cross the River Mersey.

The Elms; Hill Cliff Hall.

190¾ m. WAR-RINGTON STA.

WARRINGTON, a parliamentary and municipal borough. Area, 12,260 A.; population, 21,901: This town is unquestionably of great antiquity, and from the vestiges of a Castrum Foss, and the discovery of some Roman relics, no doubt exists that it had been a Roman station. The principal edifices are a church of Saxon architecture, a town hall, sessions house, assembly rooms, theatre, and infirmary. Its grammar school has an annual revenue of between £700 and £800, and is free to natives of Lancashire or Cheshire. The blue-coat school has an annual revenue of £450. The first newspaper in Lancashire, and first stage coach in England, were started here.

Liverpool and Manchester Railway ☞

¼ m. E. Bank Hall, J. Wilson Patten, Esq., M.P. 3 m. S.E. Appleton Hall, Thomas Lyon, Esq.; Walton Hall, Gilbert Greenall, Esq.; Grappenhall Hall, Mrs. Greenall. 3 m. N.E. Mydelton Hall, Mrs. Greenall.

There is an old hall at this place, said to have been formerly the residence of royalty; it is constructed with wood, and stands on a rock, having its windows decorated with painted glass, close to which is Ashton New Hall; Garswood Hall; Garswood Park, Sir John Gerard, Bart.; Goulbourne Park, Thomas Claughton, Esq.; Haydock Park, Thomas Leigh, Esq.

196¼ m. NEWTON BRIDGE STA.
Newton Junction.

3 m. Winstanley, Meyrick Bankes, Esq.

198¼ m. GOULBURNE STA.
Liverpool, Wigan, and Bolton Br.

2 m. Beech Hill, Ralph Anthony Thicknesse, Esq. 2 m. N.W. Standish Hall, Charles Standish, Esq. The Hall is an irregular brick building, and contains that invariable appendage to the mansions of ancient date, a private chapel.

204½ m. WIGAN SATION.
Manchester and Southport Br.

STANDISH. Two of the twelve ancient castles of Lancashire, Standish and Pentwortham stood here, but their sites only can now be distinguished.

207¼ m. STANDISH STA.

1 m. w. COPPULL, a chapelry in Standish parish. The township of Coppull is situated on an eminence, and was originally skirted by a copse, from which probably its name was derived. In the reign of Charles I., Edward Rigbye held the manor of Coppull, which was subsequently purchased by the late John Hodgson, Esq., M.P. for Wigan, of Ellerbert House, and is now occupied by his nephew and heir, Richard Cardwell, Esq. Chisnall Hall, Coppull, now a farm-house, was held in the time of Charles I. by Edward Chisnall, Esq. This was the residence of the Chisnalls, the representative of which family, Colonel Edward Chisnall, fought under the command of the Earl of Derby in the great Civil War, and was one of the defenders of Lathom House, when Charlotte Tremouille, Countess of Derby, held it out so strongly against the Roundheads. Wrightinton Hall, the seat of the Dicconson family, an old stone house, situated in a small but beautiful park, and is noted for having the first sash-windows of any house in the county, or in any part of the kingdom north of the Trent.

209¾ m. COPPULL STATION.

EUXTON, a chapelry in the parish of Leyland, county of Lancaster; population, 1,562. 1 m. w. Worden, Miss Ffarington. 1 m. s. Euxton Hall, William Ince Anderton, Esq.

213¼ m. EUXTON STATION.

LEYLAND, county of Lancaster. Area of parish, 17,950 A.; population, 14,032, employed principally in the manufacture of cotton. It has a fine old church, in which are monuments to the family of Farrington. Clayton Hall, John Lomax, Esq.

214¼ m. LEYLAND STATION.

FARRINGTON, a township in the parish of Penwortham, county of Lancaster; population, 1,719. Cuerden Park, Robert Townley Parker, Esq. 1½ m. N. Penwortham Lodge, Mrs. Rawstorne; Penwortham Priory, Colonel L. Rawstorne. 1½ m. E. Hutton Hall, Peter Horrocks, Esq.

215¼ m. FARRINGTON STA.
Liverpool and Blackburn.
Cross the Ribble

196¼ m. NEWTON
BRIDGE STA.

Newton Junction.

1 m. N.N.E. at LOWTON, Lowton Hall,

198¾ m. GOUL-
BURNE STA.

Liverpool, Wigan,
and Bolton Br.

GOULBURNE, where there is a small foundation, called Street's Charity, for the education of children.

204½ m. WIGAN
STATION.

Manchester and
Southport Br.

WIGAN, a parliamentary and municipal borough.   Population, 25,517. During the great Civil War several battles were fought here by the contending parties, it being the principal station of the King's troops, commanded by the Earl of Derby.   The church is a stately old edifice, containing several fine monuments.   The population are extensively engaged in the manufacture of wool and cotton goods, and hardware.   1 m. E., Bradshawe Hall, Thomas Bradshawe Isherwood, Esq.

207¼ m. STAND-
ISH STA.

HAIGH.   Haigh Hall, Earl of Crawford and Balcarres.   The mansion, a venerable structure, was evidently erected at various periods.   It is entirely constructed of Cannel Coal, and has a beautiful appearance, owing to the jet-black colour of the article, and its capability of receiving the highest polish.

209¾ m. COPPULL
STATION.

Adlington Hall, Richard Clayton Browne Clayton, Esq.

DUXBOROUGH HALL, WILLIAM STANDISH STANDISH, ESQ.

213¼ m. EUXTON
STATION.
Preston & Bolton
Branch.

Astley Hall   Sir Henry Bold Hoghton, Bart.; Gillebrand Hall, H. Fazakerly, Esq.

214¼ m. LEYLAND
STATION.

WHITTLEWOODS.   Here are several valuable millstone quaries, and a lead mine was formerly worked with great success.

215¼ m. FARRING-
TON STA.

Liverpool and
Blackburn.

Cross the Ribble.

2 m. N.W. ASHTON, a township in the parish of Preston. 3 m. further, CLIFTON. 2 m. further, HICKLAM, a parish in the hundred of Amoundurness. The town, which may be considered the capital of the surrounding district, called the "Foeld Country," though small, is neatly built, and the houses respectable.   The manufacture of sailcloth, sacking, and cordage, originally formed the principal source of employment, and is still carried on to a considerable extent.   The manufacture of cotton has been recently introduced, and a number of hand-looms are employed in the town and neighbourhood. Market-day, Thursday. Fairs, Feb. 4th and 5th, April 29th, and October 18th.   There is a free grammar school, originally founded by Isabella Wilbinge, which was endowed in 1605, by the Drapers' Company, by a portion of the proceeds of the rectory of Kirkham. It was further endowed in 1670, by Dr. Grimbaldson and the Rev. James Barker. Its income now being about £550 per annum. The masters are appointed by the Drapers' Company.   It is open to all the boys of the parish, and has an exhibition of about £100 per annum to either of the Universities. ½ m. w. Ribby Hall, Hugh Hornby, Esq.

218¼ m. PRESTON STATION.
Wyre & Preston.

½ m. w. WOODPLUMPTON.

222¾ m. BROUGH-TON STA.

MIERSCROFT. Mierscroft House.

225½ m. BROCK STATION.

GARSTANG, a market-town and parish, county of Lancaster, on the river Wyre and the Lancaster Canal.   Area of parish, 26,580 A.; population, 7,659, employed in cotton and worsted mills, and calico print works.   Here are also the ruins of Greenhalgh Castle, supposed by some to have been built in the time of the Saxon Heptarchy; by others, that it owes its origin to Thomas Stanley, first Earl of Derby. The structure appears originally to have consisted of seven or eight towers of great height and strength, but there is only one now in existence, and that in a very dilapidated condition. ½ m. s.w. Kirkland Hall, Butler Cole, Esq.

227⅜ m. GARS-TANG STA.

1m. w. CABUS, a township in the parish of Garstang.

230¾ m. SCORTON STATION.

2 m. w. COCKERHAM. Cockerham Hall, J. Dent Esq.

233¼ m. BAY HORSE STA.

2 m. w. Ellel Grange, G. Gillow, Esq. ½ m. further, Thurnham Hall, Miss Dalton.

236½ m. GALGATE STATION.

2 m. further N. Ashton Hall, Duke of Hamilton. Owing to the judicious nature of the various alterations that have from time to time been made in Ashton Hall, it presents a fine specimen of a baronial castle with its noble embattled towers.   The surrounding park is diversified with hill and dale, and adorned with an abundance of venerable timber.

At SCOTFORTH, Stoddy Lodge, Rev. S. Jameson; and at ALDCLIFFE, Aldcliffe Hall, E. Dawson, Esq.

2¼ m. Melling Hall, William Gillison Bell, Esq. From Lancaster there is a short branch, about three miles long, to Pulton, a favourite watering-place, and much resorted to by the inhabitants of Lancashire. It commands

238¼ m. LANCAS-TER STA.

218¼ m. PRESTON
STATION.
Preston and West
Riding Junction.
☞

PRESTON, a parliamentary and municipal borough, town and parish, county of Lancaster, in the hundred of Amounderness, on the Ribble. Area of borough, 2,650 A.; population, 50,332. It sends two members to Parliament. Registered electors (1848), 3,046. Preston is supposed to have been built on the site of Rebchester, the ancient Regigonium, and derived the name of Preston from the number of religious houses it formerly possessed, vestiges of which are now traceable. The town is well-built, consisting principally of a broad main street, a large market-place, and good public walks. It is well-drained and lighted. Its public buildings consist of exchange, town hall, court house, theatre, assembly rooms, county gaol, custom house, county infirmary, almshouses, house of recovery, and numerous places of worship. Its educational establishments comprise a grammar, blue-coat, national, and other schools. It has also a Provident Society, savings' bank, workhouse, and three public libraries, a museum, an agricultural society, and an institution for diffusing useful knowledge, with a considerable library. The population is employed in linen weaving and cotton spinning; and in 1838 the borough possessed thirty-five cotton and six flax mills, tanneries, iron works, fisheries in the Ribble, &c. Registered shipping, 8,205 tons; customs' revenue (1848), £83,960. Preston communicates by the Lancaster Canal and by railways with Wyre, on Morecombe Bay, and Bolton and Manchester. Corporation revenue (1848), £7,928. A jubilee, called Preston Guild, is celebrated here every 20th year. Markets, Wednesday, Friday, and Saturday.

222¾ m. BROUGH-
TON STA.

BROUGHTON, a chapelry, in the parish of Preston. ½ m. N. Banester Hall. 2 m. N. Barton Lodge, Charles Roger Jacson, Esq. A modern mansion, on a slight eminence, surrounded with wood, and backed by the Bleasdale Fells. The park, situated on the south and west of the house, is skirted by the railway.

225¼ m. BROCK
STATION.

1 m. N. CLAUGHTON, a small parish, the inhabitants of which are employed in quarrying flag-stones. Claughton Hall, Thomas Fitzherbert Brockholes, Esq. 2 m. E. BILSBOROUGH. Bilsborough Hall. ½ m. S. of Bilsborough, is Inglewhite Hall.

227½ m. GARS-
TANG STA.

8 m. E. Browsholme Hall, Edward Parker, Esq. The mansion stands on a commanding elevation, formerly forming part of the forest of Rowland. It is a large pile of building, with centre and two wings; the centre front is an ornamental façade, with pilasters of different orders of architecture, according to the fashion of the reigns of Elizabeth and James.

230¾ m. SCORTON
STATION.

At SCORTON is a spring, called St. Cuthbert's Well, the water of which is efficacious in cutaneous and rheumatic disorders.

233¼ m. BAY
HORSE STA.

At CLEVELEY. Wyre Side.

236¼ m. GALGATE
STATION.

2 m. N.E. QUERNMORE. Quernmore Park, William Garnett, Esq. Quernmore Park is a large, handsome mansion, constructed of white polished freestone, situate in a spacious and well-wooded park. It was built by the late Charles Gibson, Esq., of Myerscough House, upon part of the Quernmore estate, purchased from Lord Clifford, and commands rich and extensive views of the vale of the Lune. It is about four miles from Lancaster. Springfield Hall, the late Richard Godson, Esq., Q.C., M.P.

238¼ m. LANCAS-
TER STA.

LANCASTER, a parliamentary and municipal borough, sea-port town and parish, capital of same county, situated on the river Lune. Area of parish, 66,100 A.; population, 24,149; ditto of borough, 14,389. Returns two

fine views of Morecombe Bay, and the Westmoreland, Cumberland, and Yorkshire mountains. It is a chapelry, containing 700 inhabitants. There is a foundation free school, endowed by Francis Bowes, in 1732, in which sixty children are instructed.

From Lancaster, about 4¼ m. w. HEYSHAM, situated on a peninsula between the Bay of Morecombe and the mouth of the Lune. On the hill near the church are the remains of an ancient oratory, dedicated to St. Patrick. In the churchyard are several curious excavations in the solid rock, resembling the shape of the human body. 2 m. s. is MIDDLETON. That portion of the county of Lancaster, west of Morecomb Bay, is called Furness. It extends twenty-eight miles from north to south, by thirteen from east to west, and has the county of Northumberland for its northern boundary; whilst that of Westmoreland skirts it to the north and east, and the irregular outline of its southern side is washed by the Irish Sea. This district consists of an irregular and romantic mixture of high craggy hills, narrow vales, lakes, rivers, and brooks; and on the Cumberland border are some mountains of a wild, lofty, and ornamental character. The southern extremity, which projects into the sea, and is called Lower Furness, to distinguish it from the northern part, called High Furness, contains a considerable tract of level fertile land, fronted by the singular, bow-shaped Isle of Walney, which is of the same nature. Besides the mainland, it comprehends the islands of Foulney and Walney, Roe, Sheep Pile, Old Barrow, &c.

Here is also a short branch to Poulton.   241¼ m. HEST BANK STA.

Dunehall Mill Hole, a large cavern extending nearly 660 feet into the hill. From the roof at its mouth hang immense fragments of rock, which appear ready to fall on the spectator. The interior consists of several chambers, and the roof is hung with various stalactites, giving it altogether the most romantic appearance.   243 m. BOLTON STATION.

CARNFORTH, between Over and Nether Kellett, two adjoining townships, in the parish of Bolton-le-Sands, with a joint population of 737; and the parish of WARTON, county of Lancaster, which has an area of 10,470 A., with a population of 2,209. 2 m. N. Leighton Park.   245½ m. CARN-FORTH STA.

Enter Westmoreland.

2 m. N.W. BEETHAM. Population, 1,656. At a short distance from Beetham are the ruins of Helslach and Arnside Towers, which appear to have been erected to guard the Bay of Morecombe. Beetham Hall, William Hutton, Esq.   249¾ m. BURTON AND HOLME STA.

MILNTHORPE, or MILTHORPE, a market-town in the parish of Haversham, county of Westmoreland. Population, 1,159; manufactures, sheeting. It has also some trade with Lancaster, &c., by means of the river Ken, the coasting vessels coming within a short distance of the town. Dalham Tower, George Wilson, Esq.   252½ m. MILN-THORPE STA.

1½ m. N. EVERSHAM. The birthplace of the learned Dr. Richard Watson, Bishop of Llandaff. Eversham Hall, H. Eversham, Esq. ½ m. further, Levens' Hall, Hon. Colonel Howard. 1 m. further, Heaves' Lodge; and 1 m. further, Syzergh Park, Walter Strickland, Esq.   257 m. Kendal Junction.

OXENHOLME, and 1 m. W. HELSINGTON.   259½ m. KENDAL STATION.

Kendal and Windermere.

3 m. w. Over Greyrigg Forest is Winfield Beacon, 1,500 feet high. 2 m. further, HOLLOGATE, a narrow and picturesque vale, running for six miles between steep and rocky declivities, through which the Sprent flows.   268 m. LOW GILL STATION.

members to Parliament. Registered electors (1848), 1,313. It is a polling-place, and a place of election for the north division of the county. Lancaster owes its early importance to its castle, formerly a strong fortress of Norman origin, although the gateway and other portions were erected in the 14th century, by John of Gaunt. It stands on an eminence, and contains the county courts, gaol, and penitentiary, which are of modern date. The parish church, on the same eminence, is a spacious structure, with a handsome tower, and the interior contains many ancient monuments, &c., worthy of attention. The noble aqueduct of Rennie's construction, which carries the canal across the river, and the stone bridge of five equal arches, erected by the county at a cost of £12,000, are fine specimens of architectural taste and science. The town itself is well-built, and the houses generally of stone, but the streets are narrow. Lancaster has a grammar, national, and other schools, very ancient almshouses, a town hall, ornamented with a handsome portico, custom-house, market-house, county lunatic asylum, theatre, assembly rooms, mechanics' institute, and one for promoting the fine arts. Its manufactures consist of cotton, silk, linen, furniture, sail-cloth, most of which is exported. Its coasting trade increases, but the foreign trade is now almost monopolized by Liverpool. Although the navigation will be improved by the works now going on and deepening the river, the sands offer considerable impediments to large ships, which cannot approach the town within a distance of six miles. Registered shipping in 1847, 5,989 tons; customs' duties at the same period, £30,774; corporate revenue, £2,649. Market, Wednesday and Saturday.

241¼ m. HEST BANK STA.

243 m. BOLTON STATION.

BOLTON-LE-SANDS, county of Lancaster. Area of parish, 7,630 A.; population, 1,774; annual charities, £125. Near this place, at Styre, the Bay of Morecombe is forded at low water to the opposite coast, at Wreys-holme.

245½ m. CARN-FORTH STA.

3 m. N.E. BORWICK. 3½ m. E. at CAPERNWRAY, is Capernwray Hall, George Marton, Esq.

Enter Westmoreland.

249¾ m. BURTON AND HOLME STA.

¾ m. E. BURTON, a well-built market-town, in the counties of Lancaster and Westmoreland. It has a large market-place, several good inns, and an ancient church. Area of parish, 9,170 A.; population, 2,387; market, Tuesday; fair, Easter Monday. ½ m. S.E. Dalton Hall, Edward Hornby, Esq. Here is a castle erected in the reign of Edward III., and supposed to occupy a portion of a fort built by Agricola. 6 m. Whittington Hall. Thomas Greene, Esq., M.P., formerly a border tower, now a mansion of Tudor architecture; Clawthorpe Hall.

252¼ m. MILN-THORPE STA.

6 m. S.E. KIRBY LONSDALE, a market-town and parish. Population, 5,463. It is situated on the river Lune, here crossed by a beautiful old stone bridge; it lies in a picturesque valley, and has several handsome streets, a fine old church, a curious antique corn market, and a grammar school, founded in 1591, and endowed with several exhibitions to the Universities, ½ m. S.E. Summerfield House, T. Tatham, Esq.; High Casterton, W. W. Wilson, Esq.; Carfitt Hall; Underley Park, Alderman Thompson, M.P.;

257 m. Kendal Junction.

Beachside Hall. About 4 m. Barwick Hall. 1 m. further, Rigmaden Park; Heyham Hall.

259½ m. KENDAL STATION.

MIDDLESHAM, HILLHOLME, ESKRIGGE.

268 m. LOW GILL STATION.

5 m. S.E. JEDBURGH. Population, 4,486, employed in manufacture of cotton goods. Ingmire Hall, Thomas Upton, Esq. 3 m. E. The Calf, 2,188 feet high.

BORROWBRIDGE. About one hundred yards south of which, near the confluence of the river Lune, is a Roman burgh, or fortified camp, at present called Castlehows. It unquestionably gives name to the stream that washes it, and which, in ancient records, is written "Burrough Beche." This encampment is 135 yards long, and 104 yards broad; has been surrounded by a wall nine feet thick. On the north it has a fosse, with a vallum of earth on its south side. It occupies a strong position in the pass through the mountains, between the baronies of Kendal and Westmoreland. 272½ m. TEBAY STATION.

On this side the road the greater part of the country consists of what we may safely call mountains. Among these we have Wastlake Fells, Wasdale Pike, Harrow Pike, Highhouse Fell, and Banesdale Fell; in fact, with the exception of a tolerable tract of level ground on the eastern side of the county, the rest may be said to consist wholly of hill and dale. It contains but few mansions of any importance. The farm-houses are seated about the bases of the hills, with small, irregular fields spreading up the sides of the mountains, and almost universally divided by stone walls. This last circumstance gives the country a naked appearance, but the numerous tracts of woodland interspersed tend to enliven the scene. Every dell or hollow has its little brook, and the smallest of these are plentifully supplied with fish—of these the most important is the Lune, through the valley of which the line has passed from Low Gill to Tebay Station.

SHAP, county of Westmoreland. Area of parish, 27,000 A.; population, 995. Shap·is a long and straggling village; has a weekly market on Monday, and a fair May 4th. Its church was built shortly after the Conquest, but has undergone many repairs and modern alterations, which have not, however, entirely destroyed its original character. In the vicinity are the remains of a Druidical temple, and at a distance of about one mile, stand the venerable ruins of Shap Abbey. The tower and various portions of the abbey church, composed of a very durable white freestone, still remain; and the foundations of cloisters, and other conventual buildings, are traceable for a considerable distance around. The Hoggerd or Hogarth family, from whom the celebrated painter of that name derived, were tenants of the abbey at the dissolution of monastic institutions, and some of their descendants still reside in the neighbourhood. 279 m. SHAP STA.

5 m. W Haweswater, one of the lakes of Westmoreland, three miles long, half-mile broad, the property of the Earl of Westmoreland. Here are many pretty and romantic views, which well repay the trouble of visiting it. About 1 m. from the head of the water is Thornwaite Hall.

3 m. N.W. BAMPTON, a small village on the river Lowther. Bampton Park. 6 m. further to Ulleswater. This lake, which has been compared with the Swiss Lucerne, is nine miles in length, by three-quarters broad, and is divided into three reaches: the first reach, commencing at the foot, is terminated at the left by Shellen Fell, which stretches forward to a promontory on the opposite side, called Shelley Neb; the middle and longest reach is closed in by Bern Fell on the left, and on the right by Styborough Crag; the highest reach is the smallest and narrowest, but the grandeur and beauty which surround it are beyond the liveliest imagination to depict. Four or five diminutive islands dimple the surface, contrasting strangely with the vastness of the hills which tower above them, whilst Styborough Crag on one side, Burke Fell and Place Fell on the other, bind the view of this earthly paradise. In the neighbourhood, on the north-west shore, are Gowbarrow, Henry Howard, Esq.; Hallsteads, John Marshall, Esq., M.P. WATERMILLOCK. Waterfoot, James Salmond Esq.; Ramsbeck Lodge; Glenriddich House, Rev. M. Askew; and on the S.E. Patterdale Hall,

About 1 m. S.W. Lowther Castle, Earl of Lonsdale. A castle has stood on the spot of the present one for many ·centuries. The first stone of the present mansion was laid in 1808, after a design by Robert Smirke, Jun., Esq. The principal approach from the north is through a handsome arched 286¼ m. CLIFTON STATION.

272½ m. TEBAY STATION.

2½ m. N. ORTON. This parish was in ancient times of greater importance than it is now, as many Roman remains have been discovered in the neighbourhood. The whole parish was formerly encompassed by a rampart and ditch, and at one part is an intrenchment for the defence of the road, across which an iron chain was fixed, to guard against the moss-troopers during the border war. Orton Hall, John Bunn, Esq. 2 m. further, Hoddendale, John Gibson, Esq. 6 m. E. Ravenstone Dale, near which, at a place called Rasate, there are two tumuli, which on being opened, human bones were found; and near Rother Bridge there is a circle of stone, supposed to have been a place of worship. 2 m. further, Wharton Hall. 2 m. further, KIRBY STEPHEN. Population, 1,345, employed in silk and woollen manufactures, lead and coal mines. It is pleasantly situated on the Eden, and has a spacious old church, and a grammar school with two exhibitions to either University. Near it are the ruins of Hartley Castle. 3 m. N. of Kirby Stephen, is BROUGH. This town occupies the site of the ancient Verteroe, or Viteris, where towards the decline of the Roman Empire in Britain, a prefect with a band of *directores* was stationed. It was partly built with the ruins of that fort, and is distinguished from other places of the same name by its vicinity to a ridge of rocky mountains which separate this county from Yorkshire. It is the property of the Earl of Thanet. Hilbeck Hall.

79 m. SHAP STA.

4 m. E. at MOULDS, Meaburn Hall. 1½ m. S. is CROSBY-UPON-EDEN. The military road from Newcastle to Carlisle passes through this parish, and a portion of the site of the Picts' Wall is also discerned in it. RAVENSWORTH, where are extensive remains of a castle, built by Boyden, ancestor of the Fitzhughs. 12 m. E. APPLEBY, a municipal borough and market-town. Population, 2,509. It is built on the slope of a hill, and nearly surrounded by the river Eden, which is crossed by an old stone bridge, leading to that part of the parish called Bendgate, where is a fine old castle. Appleby Castle, said to have been in existence at the period of the Conquest, was rebuilt shortly after that period; it suffered greatly during the civil wars of the 17th century, when it was fortified for King Charles I. by the Lady Anne Clifford, and held out under the government of Sir Philip Musgrave against the parliamentary forces, until after the battle of Marston Moor. The principal portions of the present fabric were reconstructed from the ruins of the old castle, by Thomas, Earl of Thanet (to whom the property devolved by inheritance from the Cliffords), in 1806. Cæsar's Tower, as it is called, although most probably of Norman origin, is almost the only portion of the old fabric which is in its original state. The castle contains some noble apartments, adorned with fine paintings and a splendid collection of family portraits. The armour worn by George Clifford, in the tiltyard, as Champion to Queen Elizabeth, ornamented with *fleur-de-lis* and richly gilt, is here preserved. This fine castle is still the property of the noble family of Tufton, Earl of Thanet.

286¼ m. CLIFTON STATION.

1 m. N. Brougham Hall, Lord Brougham and Vaux. 1 m. further, Brougham Castle. The ancient city of Burgham was above a quarter of a mile to the south-west of the castle. Nothing is left of it except a few foundations, and one or two old stones, now built into a comparatively

gateway, with lodge, &c., which leads to the entrance court,—a smooth green lawn, rising to the terrace; which is 500 feet long, and 100 feet wide,

LOWTHER CASTLE, EARL OF LONSDALE.

and is enclosed by a high embattled wall, with towers at intervals; the north front is 420 feet, and contains eight lofty turrets; the south front is 280 feet in extent; the park and pleasure-grounds are very extensive; the great terrace is near one mile in length, and runs along the brink of a deep lime-stone cliff, which overlooks a part of the park; the prospects from the castle and park are most romantic. Close to the castle, Askam Hall, Earl of Lonsdale. 3 m. w. Dalemain, Edward Williams Hassell, Esq.

Enter Cumberland.

2 m. w. at NEWBIGGIN, Newbiggin Hall, Miss Clarke. 2 m. further, Greystock Castle, Henry Howard, Esq. This noble structure exhibits some remains of an ancient fortified castle. It is situated on an eminence, being principally erected in the 17th century, but has since received considerable additions; the grounds are extensive, and contain several fine plantations and ornamental bridges; they are much enlivened by a branch of the river Eamont that flows near the castle walls, and has been made to contribute to the beauty of the scenery, by being collected in reservoirs, and caused to descend in artificial cascades; the upper part forms a considerable lake, and contains several small but picturesque islands. Blencowe Hall, H. P. Blencowe, Esq. 2½ m. STAINTON. 4 m. further, PENRUDDOCK, Hutton, John Andrew Huddlestone, Esq. 7 m. further, TRELKELD. 4 m. further, KESWICK, a market-town between the foot of Skiddaw Down and Derwentwater. Among the interesting seats in this neighbourhood, we must first place Greta Hall, the residence of the late Dr. Southey, Poet Laureate; it is situated on a slight eminence, about half a mile north-west of the town. The other seats are Greta Bank, Thomas Spedding, Esq.; Brough Top, Hon. J. H. R. Curzon; Barrow House, J. Pocklington Senhouse, Esq.; Water End, Major-General Sir John Woodford; Mire-house, John Spedding, Esq.; Oakfield, James Spedding, Esq.; The Hollies, Misses Dunlop; Derwent Lodge, Misses Heathcote; Derwent Hill, Mrs. Turner; Southwaite, James Stanger, Esq.; Field Side, Joshua Stanger, Esq.; Syzzick Hall, Rev. J. Monkhouse; Derwent Isle, H. C. Marshall, Esq.

291 m. PENRITH STATION.

modern house. The original castle, which was built by the Normans, was demolished by the Scotch in 1412. It was rebuilt, and King James I. was entertained there in 1617; it sustained much damage during the parliamentary war, was restored in 1651, but has again fallen into decay. The ruins, which are extensive, are pleasingly situated on a woody eminence at the confluence of two streams. On the side next the river there still remains the old Norman tower, built about 1080. The shattered turrets which form the angles, and the hanging galleries, are overgrown with shrubs. The lower apartment in the principal tower was a square of twenty feet, covered with a vaulted roof of stone, consisting of light and excellent workmanship. The groins were ornamented with various grotesque heads, and supported in the centre with an octagon pillar, about four feet in circumference. All that may now be seen of this centre Norman pillar is four stones, six inches thick, octagonal, and even these are no longer in the tower, but lying about in the court-yard. When this groined room existed, it must have been either the hall or kitchen, from the great size of the circular-topped windows, and of the fire-place flue, that still remains, although all traces of the chimney-piece are gone.

Enter
Cumberland

291 m. PENRITH
STATION.

PENRITH, a market-town and parish, county of Cumberland. Area of parish, including part of Inglewood Forest, 6,640 a.: population, 6,429. The town, although irregularly built, contains many well-built houses, and is beautifully situated in the vale of the Eamont and Lowther. The church is a large plain structure of red stone, rebuilt in the 18th century; and in the churchyard is that curious monument of antiquity, the "Giants' Grave," upon the origin of which antiquarians have differed so much. It consists of two stone pillars, eleven feet six inches high, and five feet in circumference at the bottom, situated at each end of the grave, fifteen feet apart. The chief public buildings and institutions are the grammar school, founded by Queen Elizabeth, the county court house, house of correction, assembly room, library, and union workhouse. Here are also the remains of a castle, built in the 15th century, inhabited by Richard III. when Duke of Gloucester, and demolished by order of the Commonwealth. In the neighbourhood of Penrith are many interesting remains of castles, &c., and the scenery is strikingly picturesque. To the north of Penrith, on an eminence, stands a square stone building, called the Beacon, from which the most delightful and extensive views are presented to the eye, comprising the highest mountains and the most beautiful vale scenery in England. 3 m. E. Eden Hall, Sir G. Musgrove, Bart. At Eden Hall is preserved an old drinking-glass, called "The Luck of Eden Hall." It is traditionally said to have been taken from a party of fairies who were sporting near a spring in the garden, called St. Cuthbert's Well; and they observed, after an inefficient struggle to recover it,

" If that glass should break or fall,
Farewell the luck of Eden Hall."

3 m. further, Scowith Abbey, F. Yates, Esq. 3 m. N.E. Nunwick Hall, R. H. Allgood, Esq.; Chipchase Castle, John Reed, Esq.

2 m. s.w. Hutton Hall, Sir Ralph Fletcher Vane, Bart; Hutton Park, J. Huddleston, Esq. | 295¼ m. PLUMP-TON STA.

8 m. w. HESKET NEWMARKET, a small and neat, compact market-town, situated in a secluded and romantic district, on the western side of the river Calder. The surrounding country is mountainous, and contains mines of lead, copper, and manganese. Near the town is a petrifying spring, issuing from a rock on the margin of the river. 2 m. N. at SEBURGHAM, Warnell Hall, Earl of Lonsdale. 2 m. further, Clay Hall, Sir H. Fletcher, Bart.

4 m. w. Rose Castle, Bishop of Carlisle, delightfully situated on a gentle elevation, commanding a number of fine views; to the south-east, the remains of a gateway and two towers; the north side shows that at one time it must have had a fine castellated appearance. King Edward I. held his court here, while engaged in an expedition against the Scots, before it was burnt by Robert Bruce, temp. Edward II. It was again fortified in the following reign; and in the year 1400 Bishop Strickland rebuilt one of the principal towers, and almost every succeeding bishop has contributed, in a more or less degree, towards restoring it to its former beauty. About 3 m. further, Crofton Hall, Sir Wastell Brisco, Bart. | 301¼ m. SOUTH-WAITE STA.

Near Brisco Station are, Woodside, Miss Lock; Woodhall, — Fisher, Esq.; Red House. | 305¼ m. BRISCO STATION.
Maryport and Carlisle.

CARLISLE, the capital of the county of Cumberland, is a city, parliamentary borough, and river port, situated on a slight eminence, near the confluence of the rivers Eden, Calder, and Peteri, at the termination of the London and North-Western Railway, 300 miles N.N.W. of London. Area of parliamentary borough, 6,740 A.; population, 23,012. It is connected by railway with Edinburgh on the north, on the east with Newcastle, from which it is distant 60 miles, and with Windermere, Kendal, &c., on the south. A canal, twelve miles long, for vessels of 100 tons, connects it with Solway Firth, and it communicates by steamers with Liverpool, Belfast, &c. It sends two members to Parliament. Registered electors (1848), 990; corporate revenue (1847), £2,377; customs' revenue (1846), £48,122; registered shipping of port (1847), 2,942 tons. Carlisle is also a bishopric, the see having been founded by Henry I., and comprises 93 parishes in Cumberland and Westmoreland. Revenue (1843), £1,585; revenue of Dean and Chapter (1831), £5,318. Carlisle is the seat of county assizes and quarter sessions. City sessions twice every week. Its principal streets are broad, handsome and well paved, and diverge from an old-fashioned market-place. The cathedral stands on high ground, has a lofty tower and a beautiful east window . Its nave suffered great dilapidations during the civil wars of the 17th century. It now serves for the parish church of St. Mary. There are five other churches. The castle, now used as barracks, was built by William Rufus, and stands on an eminence above the Eden, across which river is a handsome bridge of ten arches, besides three others in the city. The town hall, gaol, council-chamber, news rooms, and the East Cumberland Infirmary, are the principal public buildings. The grammar school, founded by Henry VIII., has an annual revenue of £190. Carlisle has also literary, philosophical, and mechanics' institutes, an academy of arts, theatre, assembly rooms, public libraries, banks, and considerable manufactures of cotton goods, which are exported to the West Indies; print and dye-works, iron foundries, tanneries, &c. Carlisle is governed by a mayor, aldermen, and councillors. Markets, Wednesday and Saturday; fairs, | 308½ m. CARLISLE STATION.

295½ m. PLUMP-
TON STA.

PLUMPTON WALL. This is the ancient Veridæ, where a Roman altar has been found, and at a castle in the neighbourhood is an inscribed stone with a bust thereon. 4 m. E. KIRK OSWALD. This place, which derives its name from St. Oswald, the canonized king of Northumberland, belonged in the reign of John to Hugh Demoville, one of the murderers of Thomas à Beckett, It was burnt by the Scots in 1314, since which period it has not been distinguished by any events of historical importance. About 3 m. S. of Kirk Oswald are some curious relics of antiquity, called Long Meg and her Daughters; they consist of a circle 350 yards in circumference, formed of 67 stones, called the Daughters; and about 16 yards from the southern side is a square unhewn column of freestone, 15 feet in circumference, and 18 feet high, called Long Meg. 3 m. N.E. The Nunnery, H. A. Aglionby, Esq., M.P.

301½ m. SOUTH-
WAITE STA.

Situated on a wooded eminence overlooking the beautiful vale of the river Petteril, is Barrack Lodge, William James, Esq., M.P., A little further, Armathwaite Castle, Robert Milborne, Esq. The mansion, which is a modern erection, faced with stone, is situated in a deep vale close to the river Eden, which here spreading itself into a broad lake, is hemmed in at the southern extremity by Barrow Wood and Cat Glen. At a short distance another branch of the Eden forms a furious cataract on this side. The prospect terminates with a handsome little stone bridge, which harmonizes well with the other features of the landscape. 1¼ m. further, Ruins of Castle Lewin, and Pettrell Bank, J. Fawcett, Esq.

305½ m. BRISCO
STATION.
Carlisle and New-
castle. ☞

About 4 m. E., strictly speaking on the Newcastle and Carlisle line, is Corby Castle, the seat of Philip Henry Howard, Esq. Corby occupies the

308½ m. CARLISLE
STATION.

CORBY CASTLE, PHILIP HENRY HOWARD, ESQ.

site, but no longer possesses the character of an ancient castle. It consists, however, in part of the very walls of a large square tower, such as was not an unfrequent object upon the Marches in early times. Its present appearance on the summit of a precipitous cliff overhanging the east side of the river Eden, with the richly-wooded plantations below, attracts the admiration of every beholder. Hume, the historian, when on a tour through Cumberland, wrote on a pane of glass these lines:

"Here chicks in eggs for breakfast sprawl,
Here godless boys, God's glories squall,
While Scotsmen's heads adorn the wall;
But Corby's walks atone for all."

August 26, September 19, and second Saturday after October 10, principally for cattle.

ROCKLIFFE, a parish, county of Cumberland, 4½ m. N.W. Carlisle. Area of parish, 3,880 A.; population, 824. At CASTLE TOWN, Castle Town, G. F. Mounsey, Esq.

312½ m. ROCK-
LIFFE STA.

Cross the Border.

◁ Glasgow, Dumfries, and Carlisle.

Distance from London.

Carlisle to Edinburgh.

GRETNA, a parish and village of Scotland, county of Dumfries, on the Sark. Area of parish, 18 square miles; population, 1,761, partly employed as cotton weavers. The village of Gretna Green, on the boundary line between Scotland and England, has been long renowned as the resort of the votaries of Hymen, bent on the accomplishment of their wishes in opposition to that of their parents and guardians. It would be curious as a statistic, to know how many clandestine marriages had here taken place, and the amount of happiness they had produced.

317 m. GRETNA
STATION.

KIRKPATRICK.

321½ m. KIRKPA-
TRICK STA.

KIRTLEBRIDGE.

323½ m. KIRTLE-
BRIDGE STA.

4 m. W. Castlemilk. Originally a fortress, built by the Bruces, now a modernized residence.

326½ m. ECCLE-
FECHAN STA.

5 m. W. LOCHMABEN, a parliamentary borough, beautifully situated on a rising ground, surrounded by a chain of eight small lakes. In it are the magnificent ruins of the castle of Robert Bruce.

332½ m. LOCKER-
BIE STA.

NETHERCLEUGH.

335½ m. NETHER-
CLEUGH STA.

WAMPHRAY, a parish of Scotland, county of Dumfries, on the Wamphray, an afflux of the Annan. Area about 12,000 A.; population, 509.

341 m. WAMPHRAY
STATION.

346 m. BEATTOCK
STATION.

ELVANFOOT.

359½ m. ELVAN-
FOOT STA.

10 m. W. in the parish of MORTON, are the ruins of the ancient castle of that name.

364½ m. ABING-
TON STA.

10 m. W. Douglas, which gives the title of Baron to its almost sole proprietor, the heir-at-law of the Douglas family, and that of Marquis to the Duke of Hamilton. The ruins of St. Bride's Church is full of family tombs, including one of the "good Lord James," the friend of Bruce, and hero of Sir Walter Scott's "Castle Dangerous." The remains of that fortress still stand near the princely though incomplete modern seat of Lord Douglas, in a part stretching to Carra Table Mountain.

369½ m. LAMING-
TON STA.

SYMINGTON.

373 m. SYMING-
TON STA.

THANKERTON, a parish on the Clyde, county of Lanark. Population, 523, of which 113 belong to the village of Thankerton, in which this station is situated. Here are traces of ancient encampments.

375 m. THANKER-
TON STA.

◁ Caledonian
Railway.

The mansion was made uniform, and entirely cased with stone after the Grecian Doric order, in 1813. The picture gallery is rich in family portraits, and possesses beside some valuable specimens of the old masters. There are at Corby two curiosities worthy of notice: a square tablet in the hall, dug out of the ruins of Hyde Abbey, near Winchester, inscribed "Alfredus Rex, 881," and the claymore of Major Macdonald, the Fergus M'Ivor of "Waverley."

E. of the station, Harker Lodge, Richard Ferguson, Esq.; Houghton House, William Hodgson, Esq.; Houghton Hall, P. S. Dixon, Esq.; Scaleby Castle, James Fawcett, Esq.; Scaleby Hall, H. Farrer, Esq.

312½ m. ROCK-LIFFE STA.
Cross the Border.

4 m. N.W. Kirklington Hall, Joseph Dacre, Esq.

Distance from London.

Carlisle to Edinburgh.

317 m. GRETNA STATION.

3 m. E. LONGTOWN. 3 m. N.E. Netherby, Sir James Graham, Bart. The house is pleasantly situated on an elevation, near the Eske, and enjoys several extensive prospects. It was erected about the year 1760, but many additions have since been made. The pleasure-grounds and gardens are arranged with considerable taste.

321¼ m. KIRKPA-TRICK STA.

323¼ m. KIRTLE-BRIDGE STA.

326¼ m. ECCLE-FECHAN STA.

ECCLEFECHAN, a village, county of Dumfries, on the river Hoddam. Population, 768, employed in the manufacture of ginghams.

332¼ m. LOCKER-BIE STA.

LOCKERBIE, a market-town, county of Dumfries, in the parish of Dyfesdale. 10 m. N.N.W. Annan. Population, 1,315. It is well-built, has good schools, and is celebrated for its lamb fair.

335½ m. NETHER-CLEUGH STA.

341 m. WAMPHRAY STATION.

5 m. W. The mountain of Queensberry, 2,140 feet above the sea. It formerly gave title of Earl, Marquis, and Duke, to the Douglas family.

346 m. BEATTOCK STATION.

BEATTOCK.

359½ m. ELVAN-FOOT STA.

364¼ m. ABING-TON STA.

ABINGTON, a village, county of Lanark, near which some gold mines were wrought in the reign of James VI.

369½ m. LAMING-TON STA.

LAMINGTON, a parish, county of Lanark. Area, 11,000 A.; population, including Wandell, 358. The manor held by the Baillie family since the reign of David II.

373 m. SYMING-TON STA.

375 m. THANKER-TON STA.

4 m. E. RIGGAR, where some tumuli mark the scene of a battle fought between the Scots and English, in the time of Edward II.

I 2

380 m. CARSTAIRS
STATION.

381½ m. CARN-
WORTH STA.

386½ m. AUCHEN-
GRAY STA.

392½ m. HARBURN
STATION.

397½ m. MID-
CALDER STA.

402 m. CURRIE
STATION.

405½ m. SLATE-
FORD STA.

407½ m. EDIN-
BURGH STA.

HARBURN, the nearest station to West Calder, which has a population of 166. Here is an old castle and the traces of a Roman camp.

EDINBURGH, a city, parliamentary borough, and the capital of Scotland, is situated on the south bank of the estuary of the Forth, 392 miles north from London. In 1841 the population of the city and suburbs amounted to 138,182. The number of houses, including flats, 22,898. It returns two members to Parliament. Registered electors (in 1848), 6,462. Annual revenue of city, about £25,000. Edinburgh, or the Modern Athens, is one of the most beautiful and, in conjunction with the old town, the most picturesque of all the cities in the British empire. The old and new towns differ materially in every point. In the former, tall antique houses and narrow wynds, or closes, present themselves to view in the whole course of the High Street in one long and continuous line, from the Castle Heights to the Palace of Holyrood, at the bottom of the Canongate. In this street, or line of streets, are the High Church of St. Giles's, with a beautiful tower in the form of an imperial crown; the Tron Church; the assembly hall, with a spire 238 feet 6 inches high; the Parliament house and hall, with its curious oaken roof; the different courts of justice, the libraries of the advocates, and the writers to the signet. At the bottom of the Canongate, in the valley beneath Arthur's Seat and Carlton Hill, stands Holyrood Palace, and by its side the roofless ruins of the choir of its venerable abbey, the walls of which appear quite strong enough to endure another roof for ages and ages yet to come. The modern exterior of the Palace, built after the Restoration, has not that interest to the antiquary which the still remaining original tower at the north-west corner of the building possesses. Here are the private apartments of the beautiful but ill-fated Queen Mary, in which the furniture actually used by her Majesty is religiously preserved, and the blood of Rizzio carefully pointed out to the visitor in the stained flooring of her boudoir. The Castle, which crowns the top of the High Street, is a most picturesque and beautiful object at a distance, but it loses greatly upon closer inspection. Its position is, however, very grand, and it must have been regarded as an impregnable fortress before the novel tactics of war were understood. It is built on a precipitous rock of basaltic green stone, and contains several ancient chambers, in which are the crown and regalia of Scotland, an armoury and barracks for troops. In the old town is also the celebrated University of Edinburgh, founded in 1580, with a library of nearly 100,000 volumes, and many MSS., Museum and class-rooms. There are thirty-one professors, and the average annual number of students is 1,636. Here is also a theological college of united Presbyterians, and a Free Church college; a college of physicians and surgeons, with a fine hall and museum; the Royal, Highland, and Agricultural Societies, besides those of arts and antiquities, and a royal society of painting, a botanic garden, &c., with every description of literary, scientific, and

380 m. CARSTAIRS STATION.

CARSTAIRS, a parish, county of Lanark. Area about 12,000 A.; population, 950. Roman antiquities have been found here.

381½ m. CARNWORTH STA.

CARNWATH, a parish, county of Lanark, with a village seven miles E.N.E. of Lanark. Area of parish, 25,193 Scotch acres, with a population of 3,550. There is also a village here called after its founders, WILSONTOWN, which has extensive iron-works.

386½ m. AUCHENGRAY STA.

AUCHENGRAY.

392½ m. HARBURN STATION.

397¼ m. MIDCALDER STA.

MID CALDER, a parish, with a population of 1,456. It adjoins the preceding parish of West Calder.

402 m. CURRIE STATION.

CURRIE, from Coria. Population, 2,000, of whom 297 are in the village Here are some remains of a Roman camp, and of some baronial strongholds

405½ m. SLATEFORD STA.

SLATEFORD. a village, in the parish of Colinton, county of Edinburgh Population, 221.

407½ m. EDINBURGH STA.

mechanics' institutions, worthy the capital of a sober, sedate, and learned people. The New Town is perfect in all its plans, and mathematically true and formal in all its bearings. The streets are noble and spacious; the squares and crescents handsome; the monuments dignified and classical; Queen Street and gardens are remarkably handsome. Running parallel with it is George Street—a noble street which discharges itself into St. George's Square at one end, and St. Andrew's Square at the other, while Princes' Street has an uninterrupted run of the old town, to which access is obtained by a curious bridge over the market-place. The Royal Institution is a fine building, adorned with the statue of Queen Victoria; the register office, the post-office, and stamp-office, are handsome buildings; St. George's and St. Andrew's churches are also fine structures; George Heriot's, Trinity, Watson's, Gillespie's, the Merchant, Maiden, Trades, Maiden and Orphans' Hospitals, are most magnificent institutions. Here are also Donaldson's and Stewart's Hospitals, an asylum for the blind, a deaf and dumb institution, a royal infirmary, several public dispensaries, a night asylum for the houseless poor, and a house of refuge. Edinburgh has several banking establishments, and a savings' bank. On Carlton Hill is an astronomical observatory, the national monument, the High School, Sir Walter Scott's monument; and in St. Andrew's square is a monument to Lord Melville, 139 feet high. Edinburgh is divided in 17 parishes, and 13 *quod sacra* parishes. Independently of which there are 23 Free Church congregations, 14 United Presbyterians, 9 Episcopalian, 2 Roman Catholic chapels and nunnery, 3 Independent, with Methodists, Quakers, Baptists, and other sects. Ten newspapers are published in the city, with every description of periodical. Edinburgh is governed by a Lord Provost, 4 Bailies, a Dean of Guild, treasurer and council, amounting in the whole to 33. The advocates' library is very extensive, and contains 148,000 printed volumes, and 2,000 MSS. The police of the city is admirably effective; the prisons of the city and county, south of the Carlton Hill, are handsome castellated buildings. The trade of Edinburgh is almost entirely retail; but the Port of Leith, which adjoins, has long been celebrated for its extensive shipping. The chief manufactures of Leith are glass making, coach building, and strong ale brewing; printing, &c., in all its branches, is carried on very actively. Edinburgh is the central point where the great lines of railway meet, and a part of the New Town is traversed by an extensive tunnel of the Northern Railway. The views from various parts of the city over the Firth of Forth into Fife, the Islands of Inchkeith, with its lighthouse, and the distant hills of Perthshire, the Pentland Hills again on the opposite side of the city, and the whole surrounding scenery are truly beautiful; but its climate in the spring of the year is very trying to strangers.

The Great Northern Railway.

It cannot be doubted that this is one of the greatest undertakings in point of colossal labour, as well as public utility and national importance, to which the energetic mind of man has hitherto been applied, if we consider the obstacles which nature had sown in the path of science, and how skilfully they have been surmounted by the engineer, as well as the grand object contemplated by the construction of a railway which should form a direct line of communication between London and the metropolis of Scotland, passing through the largest agricultural, manufacturing, and commercial counties of England. It is pleasant to contemplate the benefits and the blessings which millions of the industrious classes will derive from this new impetus to their manufacturing energies; while it cannot fail to make an ample return to the holders of the stock, by means of which its gigantic labours have been effected. The admirably efficient manner in which the stupendous works of this Company have hitherto been achieved, offers earnest evidence of the perfection which may be anticipated when the whole is completed. The talent and genius of Cubitt, the eminently distinguished engineer under whose superintendence the whole works have been constructed, will be stamped on every portion of the line, while the line itself will form the best monument to his fame—one indeed that will perpetuate his name with honour to posterity.

In our necessarily brief notice of the principal works constructed on this line, we shall confine ourselves to those descriptions and features which are intelligible and visible to travellers in general, eschewing all professional and purely technical or scientific terms, as well as details.

We must observe, that the station at King's Cross is merely a temporary building, the plan and elevation of the permanent grand terminus not yet having been decided upon. The number of ordinary bridges between London and Peterborough, to which city the direct line only extends at present, is 104, of which, exactly one moiety are over, and the other moiety under the line.

Of the larger bridges and viaducts, we may cite the following :—

1. HOLLOWAY ROAD BRIDGE, which crosses the turnpike-road about one and a half mile from the London terminus, consisting of ten arches or openings of different spaces, varying from forty-five to twenty feet each.

2. HORNSEY BRIDGE, over the river, seventy-seven yards long, and three openings of twenty-five feet span—two square and one on the skew.

3. HARRINGHAY BRIDGE, sixty-five yards in length, consisting of five arches, of twenty-six feet span each.

4. EAST BARNET BRIDGE, over the coach-road, almost similar to the last

5. A VIADUCT over the river Lea, nineteen miles from London, consisting of five arches of thirty feet span each, forty feet six inches in height from the surface of the water.

6. THE DIGSWELL VIADUCT, twenty-one and a half miles from London, before arriving at the Welwyn Station. This magnificent structure carries the line over a valley, through which flows the river Mimsam. It is built of brick, is five hundred and twenty yards in length, and consists of forty arches, each of thirty feet span, rising to the height of ninety-eight feet from the lowest part of the valley. It is truly a gigantic construction, and coupled with the grand embankment with which it is connected, forms a highly picturesque object in the hilly and richly-wooded country by which it is surrounded, adding great beauty to the landscape.

7. At Robbery Wood, twenty-three and a half miles from London, and two miles from Digswell, is a bridge or viaduct of seven arches over the river, fifty-seven feet six inches in height from the surface of the water.

8. At Green Mill is a small viaduct of three openings, each of thirty feet span.

9. Over the river Ouse, fifty-eight miles from London, is a viaduct one hundred and two yards in length, consisting of three openings, each of seventy-five feet span, thirty-one feet in height, the piers of which are composed of sunk cylinders, on the principle of Dr. Potts, a gentleman of great scientific attainments.

The Great Northern Railway.

10. Monkslode, about sixty-seven miles from London, is another viaduct of seven openings, varying from fifty-four to eight feet, thirty feet high to the top of the parapet.

11. At Huntingdon, is a bridge over the railway, consisting of five openings, four of from fifteen to sixteen feet span on the square, and one of twenty-eight on the skew.

12. Over the river Nene, just beyond Peterborough, is a bridge two hundred and ninety-two yards in length, consisting of nineteen arches of brick, and three openings, composed of cast-iron girders, the whole being twenty-two feet in height.

The above are the principle viaducts on the Peterborough line.

Of tunnels, we may enumerate seven completed, and one in process of formation.

1. From the goods to the passengers' station, at King's Cross, passing under Maiden Lane and the Regent's Canal, of about one hundred yards in length.

2. At Tottenham, five hundred and ninety-four yards in length.

3. At East Barnet, six hundred and five yards in length.

4. At South Enfield, three hundred and seventy-four yards in length.

5. At North Enfield, two hundred and thirty-one yards in length.

6. At South Mimms, one thousand two hundred and ten yards in length.

7. At Locksley's Hill, four hundred and fifty yards in length.

9. At Harmer Green, one thousand and thirty-nine yards in length, making a total of four thousand five hundred and three yards.

Of the cuttings and embankments we have the following details :—

At about one and a half mile from London, near the Caledonian Road, is a cutting five hundred and seventeen yards in length, and nearly fifty feet in its greatest depth.

At Hornsey, one of six hundred and forty yards of the same depth.

Near Southgate the cutting is one thousand nine hundred and forty yards long, through blue clay, fifty-six feet deep.

The Digswell embankment connected with the splendid viaduct, which we have already described, is eight hundred and fourteen yards long, being fifty feet above the surface of the country at one end, and sixty feet at the other side of the viaduct. Its greatest height in any part being ninety-eight feet.

At Robbery Wood, by the Viaduct, is an embankment four hundred and forty yards long, and fifty-five feet in height.

Beyond this spot, the country becoming more level, the cuttings and embankments lose their picturesque appearance by their diminished height, but increase tenfold in distance. At Langford, near Biggleswade, is an embankment eight feet only in height, but two thousand three hundred yards in length ; just beyond the termination of which, commences a cutting two thousand yards long, and eighteen feet deep. At Sandy, near that station, is an embankment six thousand yards long, and about thirteen feet in greatest depth ; and a little further on, near St. Neot's, Hunts, is another, two thousand one hundred yards in length, and twenty-three feet deep. At Offerd D'Arcy, in the same county, is an embankment two thousand two hundred yards long, and about eight feet high ; and just beyond Huntingdon, a cutting, three thousand yards long, and thirty-nine feet at its greatest depth. But the most extraordinary and stupendous works of this nature, are those which cross the fenny lands near the Mere, by Cunnington, Sawtrey, and Wood-Walton. The embankment at this spot is eight thousand three hundred and thirty-eight yards in length, and forty feet in height, consisting of 1,218,000 cubic yards ; and the embankment at the Holm and Yaxley Fens, five thousand seven hundred yards, and nineteen feet at its greatest height. Just beyond Peterborough is a cutting four thousand two hundred and twenty-two yards in length, and thirteen feet deep. Before we go to press, we expect to be favoured with the nature of the works in progress of formation between Peterborough and East Retford ; but we have here shown sufficient to testify to the gigantic labours which have already been achieved—such indeed as are unsurpassed by the prodigies of the Romans or the Egyptians.

Left of Railway from London.

1 m. w. At Muswell Hill, The Grove, William Block, Esq., remarkable as having been visited by Dr. Johnson. The grounds were laid out by his favourite companion, Topham Beauclerck, and to this day one of the walks retains the name of Dr. Johnson's Walk. At and near Hornsey are Crouch Hall, Gilliatt John Booth, Esq.; Oakfield Park, George Buckton, Esq.; Priory Lodge, Francis Danvers, Esq.

Close to the station is the new County Lunatic Asylum. 1 m. N.W. FRYERN BARNET, and COLNEY HATCH. They form a small village in the parish of the former. The church is a low building of Roman architecture, with some old tombs. Woodhouse, William Lambert, Esq.; Colney Hatch, Charles Macfarlane, Esq. 1½ w. Moss Hall, J. Andrews, Esq. 1 m. s.w. FINCHLEY, at which are Brent Lodge, James Block, Esq.; Coburg Villa, Dr. James Bryant; Cromwell Hall, R. E. Butler, Esq.; Park Hall, J. S. Cooper, Esq.; Coney House, Captain Dunn, R.N.; Hope Lodge, R. Dixon, Esq.; Springcroft Lodge, James Ewart, Esq.; Wentworth Lodge, Henry Hammond, Esq.; Newstead House, Mrs. Hodgkinson; Finchley Lodge, R. W. Musson, Esq.; Elmshurst, Anthony Southern, Esq. 1½ m. further s.w. HENDON. The abbots of Westminster had anciently a palace here, and Hendon Palace was a retreat of Queen Elizabeth. Hendon Place, Lord Tenterden.

BARNET. Chipping Barnet is memorable as the field on which the great battle between the houses of York and Lancaster was fought in 1471, which resulted in the death of the great Earl of Warwick, an event which is commemorated by an obelisk erected near the town. The church, built in 1400, a grammar school founded by Queen Elizabeth, and some well-endowed almshouses, are the principal buildings of the town, which stands on a height, and has one of the greatest horse and cattle fairs in England. Area of parish, 1,040 A.; population, 2,485.

CHIPPING BARNET. Greenhill Grove, Samuel Block, Esq.; Lyonsdown, John Cattley, Esq. 2 m. s. TOTTERIDGE. R. S. Scrimgeour, Esq.; Totteridge Park, His Excellency Chevalier Bunsen; Mill Hill, Matthew Powers, Esq.; Highwood House.

Wrotham Park, Mrs. Byng; Dyrham Park, Captain and the Hon. Mrs. Trotter; Clare Hall, Mrs. Sharpe. 2 m. w. SOUTH MIMMS. Bridgefoot House, Captain Thomas Larkins; Mimms Hall, Thomas White, Esq.; 2 m. N. NORTH MIMMS. Pottrills, W. C. Cassamajor, Esq.; Abdale Place, Algernon Greville, Esq.; North Mimms Place, S. Fulke Greville, Esq.; Leggatts, Thomas Kemble, Esq. North Mimms Park, formerly one of the seats of the Duke of Leeds, from whom it passed to Henry Brown, Esq. The mansion is a handsome building, and its situation and the surrounding scenery extremely fine. A little to the w. LENDON CONEY. Tittenhanger Park, Dowager-Countess of Hardwicke; Colney House, Mrs. Oddie; Bridge House, Joseph Linett, Esq.

3 m. N. Brocket Hall, Viscount Melbourne. The mansion occupies the site of a more ancient structure, which formerly belonged to the family of the Brockets. It was completed by the first Lord Melbourne, having been commenced by his father, Sir Matthew Lamb. The park is of noble dimensions, and possesses great picturesque beauty. It is enriched by a spacious sheet of water, formed from the river Lea, which flows through the grounds. For several years George IV., when Prince of Wales, was here entertained with horse-racing.

6 m. w. ST. ALBAN'S (see London and Birmingham Railway). Childwick Hall, Rev. James Brogden; Abbey Cottage, James Addersly Dorant, Esq.; Dalton House, Samuel Jones, Esq.; Childwick Bury, R. P. H. Joddrell, Esq.; Waterside, Alfred Perkins, Esq.; Abbey Orchard House, William

Distance from London.	**Right of Railway from London.**

HORNSEY, county of Middlesex, on the New River. Area of parish, 2,960 A.; population, 5,937. A considerable portion of Highgate and Finchley Common lie in this parish. The village is finely situated, and possesses many spacious mansions, a church of the 16th century, and a grammar school at Highgate. Campsbourne, William Eady, Esq.; River Bridge, James Shaddock, Esq.; The Priory, George Warner, Esq.

1 m. N.E. SOUTHGATE. The church was founded 1615, by Sir John Weld, of Lulworth Castle, who was buried here. Minchendon, Duke of Buckingham; Collins Grove, Thomas Curtis, Esq.; Bowes Farm, Thomas Coster, Esq; Southgate House, Isaac Walker, Esq.; Broomfield House, Alexander Dalrymple, Esq.; Beevor Hall, John Schneider, Esq.; Woodlands, D. Taylor, Esq.; Grove House, Mrs. A. Walker; Bowes Manor, Lord Truro. 1 m. N.E. WINCHMORE HILL. It consists principally of villa residences, occupied by mercantile men from the metropolis. Bush Hill, William Brackenridge, Esq.; Palmer's Green, Thomas Cooper, Esq.

EAST BARNET, a small village, beautifully situated in a valley. Oak Hill, Sir Simon Clark, Bart., is delightfully situated on an eminence, and may be seen at a long distance. Belmont, David Bevan, Esq.; Rose Cottage, G. W. Hardisty, Esq.; Cockfosters, J. M. Venning, Esq.; Willenhall House, Mrs. Moore; Beech Hill Park, A. Paris, Esq.; Trent Park, J. Cummings, Esq.; Little Grove, Frederick Cass, Esq. It is situated on the brow of a hill, about 1¼ m. from the village of East Barnet. Its grounds abound in pleasant views over the adjoining country, particularly towards the south, where they are terminated by the high ground of Highgate and Hampstead.

POTTER'S BAR. Carpenter's Park, C. Marriott, Esq.; Barbins, R. G. Welford, Esq.; and at NORTHAUGH, ½ m. E. The Hook, Benjamin Cherry, Esq.; Northaugh, Charles Le Blanc, Esq.; Cooper's Lane, Rev. Henry George Watson. 2 m. N. of Potter's Bar, is Brookmans, North Mimms, R. W. Gaussen, Esq. The house is a respectable building, standing in a pleasant park. 3 m. E. Ponsburn Park. Wynne Ellis, Esq.; Epping House, Sir William Horne, Q.C.

HATFIELD, a market-town, county of Herts. Area of parish, 12,700 A.; population, 3,646. It is a polling-place for the county, and the head of a poor-law union. Hatfield is a very neatly built town, with a remarkably handsome church, in which is the mausoleum of the noble family of Cecil. Hatfield House, the seat of the Marquis of Salisbury, is a large brick edifice, with stone copings and decorations, consisting of a centre and projecting wings, with four turrets at the angles, and immediately in front surmounted by cupolas and vanes. In the centre is a colonnade of nine arches, and a lofty tower, adorned with three stories of columns of the Tuscan, Doric, and Composite orders. Between the second are the arms of the noble family of Cecil, with the date of 1611. The hall is a magnificent chamber, the roof of which is supported from the sides by lions, each holding a shield of the Cecil arms; and on the ceiling, in compartments, are

Roberts, Esq.; Sirge Hall, S. R. Solly, Esq.; Holywell Hill, George Sturt, Esq.; Gorhambury, Earl Verulam; New Barnes, Arthur Timperon, Esq.; The Præ, H. M. Baillie, Esq. M.P.   2 m. N.E. is SANDRIDGE.

WELWYN, county of Herts.   Area of parish, 3,100 A.; population, 1,395. The most interesting circumstance connected with this parish is the fact of its having been spiritually presided over for many years by Dr. Young, author of " Night Thoughts," who here founded and endowed a school with an annual revenue of about £60.   Codicote Lodge, Frederick Cavendish, Esq.; The Hoo, Lord Dacre; Bendish, Robert Hill, Esq.; Frith House, William Wiltshire, Esq.   About 2 m. further w. Ayot St. Peter, J. Peacock, Esq.; Ayot St. Lawrence, Cholmeley Dering, Esq.; Lamer, C. B. Drake-Garrard, Esq.   The mansion·is a handsome structure, situated on an eminence.   Sandridge Bury, John Kender, Esq.   About 1 m. s. of Welwyn, is DIGSWELL.   Digswell House, H. Pearce, Esq.; Digswell Hill, Henry Headland, Esq.

21¾ m. WELWYN STATION.

Elwood House, Mrs. Lucas; Clay Hall, J. J. Pryor, Esq.; Weston, Marlborough Pryor, Esq.; Stagenhoe House, Henry Rogers, Esq.   A handsome building, standing in a small park.   It was built by Sir John Hall, in 1650.   2 m. s. of STEVENAGE,

28½ m. STEVENAGE STA.

KNEBWORTH HALL, SIR E. L. BULWER LYTTON, BART.

profiles of the Cæsars. The grand staircase is elaborately carved. This estate belonged formerly to the see of Ely. It was rebuilt by Cardinal Merton in the reign of Henry VII., and was alienated from the see of Ely by Queen Elizabeth, who had previously resided there for many years, as well as other royal princes. Woodside, John Church, Esq.; Woodhill, William Franks, Esq.; Hill House, William Hall, Esq.; Tolmers, Thomas Mills, Esq.; Riddles, John Parnther, Esq.; Warren Wood, Earl Roseberry; Woodside, Hon. Mrs. York; Marshall's Wick, George Robert Marten, Esq.; Frogmore, F. Wigg, Esq.; St. Michael's, T. F. Gage, Esq.

21¾ m. WELWYN STATION. Tewing, or Tewin Water, Earl of Uxbridge, formerly parcel of the lands belonging to the Abbey of St. Alban's, and subsequently to the canons of St. Bartholomew, London, after having been granted at the dissolution to John Cock, Esq., of Broxbourne, in this county, came into the possession of Sir John Fleet, Lord Mayor of London, whose widow re-married General Sabine, who rebuilt the house on the site of the ancient mansion in a magnificent style, and embellished it with paintings of the great battles of the Duke of Marlborough, under whom he served, and was slain shortly after. His widow married thirdly, Charles, eighth Lord Carteret, in 1739, who died in the following year; and fourthly, to Colonel Hugh Macguire, who confined her with great cruelty in a remote and obscure part of Ireland until his death. She survived her cruel husband many years, and died in 1789, aged 98, and was buried in Tewin Church. At the age of 80, this lady was in the habit of dancing with all the sprightliness of youth. Tewin House is a very elegant structure, and its grounds are embellished with a beautiful serpentine water, which sweeps gracefully past its principal front. Water End, Thomas Oakley, Esq. A little further, Panshanger Park, Earl Cowper; Cole Green Captain Bailey. 2 m. N.E. from the station, DATCH-WORTH and WHALTON. Frogmore Lodge, William Hudson, Esq.; Wood Hall, Abel Smith, Esq., M.P.

28½ m. STEVEN-AGE STA. STEVENAGE, county of Herts. This is now only a village, but in former days it was a market-town. The manor was given by Edward the Confessor to the Abbey of Westminster, and it continued annexed to that foundation till Henry VIII. converted the Abbey into a bishopric. This being dissolved by Edward VI., Stevenage, with Ashwell and other manors in Herts that had formed part of its estates, were granted to the see of London, to which they have ever since belonged, excepting for a short period in the reign of Queen Mary. Monteine, Bishop of London in the time of James I., procured from that King the grant of a market and three fairs annually. Near Stevenage are six large barrows, lying in a row, some of which have been opened, but not anything of consequence found therein. They are supposed to be of Danish origin, the names of Danes' Field, Mundane, &c., having been conferred on different places in this part of the county. The church is a small structure, dedicated to St. Nicholas, and consists of a nave, chancel, and aisles, with a small chapel on each side the chancel, and a tower at the west end. Bragbury End, John Green, Esq.; Sheep Hall, Samuel Hugh Heathcote, Esq. and Unwin Heathcote, Esq.

This ancient baronial residence was reconstructed from the earlier fortress which had existed since the Conquest, by Sir Robert de Lytton (temp. Henry VII.), Knight of the Bath, Privy Councillor, Keeper of the Great Wardrobe, and Treasurer to Henry VII. In the time of his great grandson, Sir Rowland Lytton, Lieutenant of the counties of Essex and Herts, Commander of the forces of those counties at Tilbury Fort, and Captain of the Band of Gentlemen Pensioners, it was frequently honoured by the visits of Queen Elizabeth; Sir Rowland having, indeed, married a cousin to that Queen, viz., Anne, daughter of Lord St. John of Bletsoe, and fourth in descent from Margaret Beauchamp, Duchess of Somerset, grandmother to Henry VII. The present possessor is Sir Edward Bulwer Lytton, Bart., who derives the Knebworth estates from his mother, sole heiress and representative of the families of Lytton, and Robinson, or Norreys, de Guersylt, in Denbighshire.

HITCHIN, a market-town, county of Herts. It is a very ancient and well-built town, prettily situated at the base of a hill. Its church, erected in the reign of Henry VI., is spacious, and richly ornamented. The altar-piece, by Rubens, is a fine specimen of that great master; and there are also some interesting and curious monuments. In the neighbourhood of Hitchin are Hitchin Priory, F. P. Delmé Ratcliffe, Esq.; Offley Place, Lady Salisbury, is a large and interesting building, of the time of Elizabeth, it having been built by Sir Richard Spencer, about the year 1600. Welbury House, Mrs. Burroughs; Ippolitts, Mrs. Hale; Ickleford House, Hon. C. T. Ryder and Thomas Cockayne, Esq. 31¼ m. HITCHIN STATION.

Enter Bedfordshire.

4½ m. w. of Hitchin, is HEXTON. Hexton House, Madame de Lautour. On the s.w. side of Hexton is a complete intrenchment, called Ravensburg Castle, occupying a site of about twelve acres. Springs of water, slightly chalybeate, constantly descend from a hill here, so as to form a river in Hexton Park, and turn a mill.

¾ m. w. HENLOW. Henlow Grange, T. A. Raynsford, Esq. About 1 m. further, CLIFTON. Clifton Manor House, Henry Palmer, Esq.; and 2 m. further, SHEFFORD, near which is South Hill Park, William H. Whitbread, Esq.; Chicksand Abbey, Sir George Osborn, Bart. About 3 m. further, Hawnes Park, Rev. Lord John Thynne. About 4 m. s.w. from Shefford, Wrest Park, Earl de Grey. 36¾ m. ARLSEY AND SHEFFORD STATION.

Cross the Ivel.

BIGGLESWADE, a market-town, on the navigable river Ivel, county of Beds, 9½ m. from Bedford. Area of parish, 4,220 A.; population, 3,807. It is a neatly built town, has an ancient church, which was collegiate, erected A.D. 1230, two endowed parochial schools and an union workhouse. It is also a polling-place for the county. Its corn market is one of the most considerable in England; and vast quantities of vegetables are grown here for the London market. Here is also a manufacture of thread lace. Market, Wednesday, and five fairs. Shortmeade House, John Brightshew, Esq. 3 m. w. Ickwell Bury, John Harvey, Esq. Old Warden House, Lord Ongley. About ½ m. w. are the ruins of Warden Abbey. In the year 1217, Fulke de Brent, a powerful baron, treated the monks of this convent with much cruelty, and carrried thirty of them prisoners to Bedford Castle. Yet such was the ascendancy of the Church at that period, that though he set the civil power at defiance, he was glad to make his peace by submitting to receive manual discipline from the monks at the chapter-house at Warden, at the same time confirming to them the wood about which the dispute had arisen, and promised them protection hereafter. 41¾ m. BIGGLES-WADE STA.

SANDY. This is the site of the ancient Roman station, called Salanœ, which commanded another at Chesterfield, a piece of ground so called, near the village. The ramparts enclosed near thirty acres, and are surrounded by a deep fosse. In the centre is a mound, probably thrown up for the pretorium. At some distance on the other side of the valley, are the remains of Cæsar's camp. Owing to the sandy nature of the soil, cucumbers 43¾ m. SANDY STATION.

5 m. E. Bennington Place, William Wigram, Esq. BENNINGTON. At this place was a seat of the Mercian sovereigns, and in the year 850 a great council of nobility and prelates assembled under King Bertulph, but of which, the artificial mound of the keep, with the surrounding ditch, are now only discernible. On or near the site, a little westward from the church, is a small mansion, the residence of the present proprietor, John Cheshire, Esq. The church is a small fabric, dedicated to St. Peter, consisting of a nave and chancel, with a tower at the west end, and a chapel connected with the chancel on the north. It contains some ancient monuments of the family of Benstede, who resided here in the time of Edward I., and it is supposed they built the church, as their arms are displayed both upon the roof and on the tower. In a niche over the south porch is a statue of St. Michael and the dragon. 4 m. N.E. Yardley Place, Sir Robert Murray, Bart; Chesfield Lodge, Edward Parkins, Esq.

31¾ m. HITCHIN STATION.

Near HITCHIN are St. Ibbs, Andrew Amos, Esq.; Whitwell, Thomas Butler, Esq.; Cosmore, John Curling, Esq.; Paulswaldenbury, Mrs. Drake; Temple Dinsley, Thomas P. Halsey, Esq. 4 m. N.E. BALDOCK. The church is a handsome building of the 14th century, erected on the site of the Knights Templars', built in the reign of Stephen. At the west end is a tower of curious composition. The nave has a fine timber roof, and in the chancel are carved stalls, and stained glass windows, and some ancient tombs. The Elms, Mrs. Hagan. A little to the N.E. Bygrave, James Smythe, Esq. About 2 m. E. Wallington, James Franklin, Esq. 1½ m. E. is Rushden, A. Meetkirk, Esq.

Enter Bedfordshire.

8 m. N.E. of Baldock is ROYSTON. A house was built here by James I., who made it his occasional residence for enjoying hunting and hawking; and it was here that his favourite, the Earl of Somerset, was arrested in his presence for the murder of Sir Thomas Overbury. Melburn Bury, John Edward Fordham, Esq.; Kneesworth House, John Bendyshe, Esq.

36¾ m. ARLSEY AND SHEFFORD STATION.

ARLSEY, J. B. Edwards, Esq. 2 m. N.E. ASTWICK. 2 m. further, EDWORTH.

Cross the Ivel.

1½ m. E. STOTFORD. 1 m. further, RADWELL. Radwellbury, Samuel Mills, Esq.

41¾ m. BIGGLES-WADE STA.

1 m. S.E. Stratton Park, Charles Barnett, Esq. The valuable Cottonian Library, at that time the property of Sir John Cotton, was during the civil wars of Charles I. preserved at Stratton, whither it had been removed, for greater security, from Connington, the seat of the Cottons. A little further is DUNTON. EYWORTH. RESLINGWORTH.

2 m. N.E. Sutton Park, Sir John Montagu Burgoyne, Bart. There is a tradition current that Sutton belonged to John of Gaunt, Duke of Lancaster, who gave it in the following rhyming grant to an ancestor of the present proprietor:

> I, John of Gaunt,
> Do give and do graunt,
> Unto Roger Burgoyne,
> And the heirs of his loin,
> Both Sutton and Potten,
> Until the world's rotten.

About ½ m. further, POTTEN; and about 2 m. E. from Potten, COCKAYNE HATTLEY.

43¾ m. SANDY STATION.

1 m. E. The Hasells, Francis Pym, Esq.; close to which, at EVERTON, Everton Hall, William Astell, Esq. 3 m. from which, Waresley Park, Hon. Octavius Duncombe, M.P.; near which is GAMBLING GAY. Woodbury, Williamson Booth, Esq. and William Wilkinson, Esq. 3 m. further E. Bourne Hall, Earl Delawarr. 2 m. S. of which, is Wimpole, Earl Hardwicke. This, without doubt, the most splendid private residence in the

are cultivated in the open air in such abundance, that London is almost wholly supplied with that vegetable from this place. 2 m. w. Mogger-hanger Park, S. Thornton, Esq.

1½ m. w. from the station, Bluham Park, Sir Charles Payne, Bart. 1½ m. further, BARFORD. ½ m. further, Stowbury, C. Polhill, Esq.

2 m. N.N.W. Tempsford Hall, unoccupied. 1 m. further, Roxton House, Charles James Metcalfe, Esq. 1 m. further, LITTLE BARFORD.

Enter
Huntingdon.

MANOR HOUSE, REV. J. ALLINGTON.

ST. NEOT'S, a market-town, county of Huntingdon, situated on the river Ouse, over which here is a handsome stone bridge. Area of parish, 4,750 A. The town is neatly built, and has several good streets. Its trade is princi-pally retail. Market, Thursday. 8 m. N.W. A little north of STANGTON, Gaines Hall, James Duberley, Esq. 2 m. further, KIMBOLTON, a market-town and parish. Population, 1,634, partly employed in lace-making. Close to the town is Kimbolton Castle, the magnificent residence of the Duke of Manchester. It is a stone edifice of considerable antiquity, and was the residence of Catherine of Aragon, first wife of Henry VIII., subsequently to her divorce, where she also died. 1 m. N. Paxton Place, H. P. Stanley, Esq. 2 m. further, Diddington House, George Thornhill, Esq. A little further, Stirtlowe, John Linton, Esq. ½ m. further, Buckden Palace, the episcopal residence of the Bishops of Lincoln.

51½ m. ST. NEOT'S STATION.

Cross the Ouse.

Hinchinbrooke House, Earl Sandwich. This mansion occupies the site of a Benedictine nunnery, said to have been founded by William the Conqueror. In August, 1564, Queen Elizabeth, after a visit to the University of Cambridge, honoured the mansion with her presence. King James also several times visited the then proprietor, Sir Oliver Cromwell. Hinchinbrooke was sold by Sir Oliver to Sir Sidney Montague, ancestor of the present noble proprietor in 1627. The mansion is pleasantly situated on an elevation, commanding some pleasing views over the neighbouring country, watered by the river Ouse. It is an irregular structure, and contains some remains of the original Benedictine nunnery. A little further, Brampton Park, Lady Olivia Sparrow.

58½ m. HUNTING-DON STA.

About 2 m. N.W. Stukely Hall, James Torkington, Esq.

county, consists of a spacious mansion and wings; that towards the east connected with the offices, and that towards the west with a large green-house. The entrance to the hall is by a double flight of steps, and the interior of the structure contains many rooms of noble dimensions. The grounds near the mansion, though, like a great portion of this county, remarkably flat, possess every embellishment which fine timber, well-disposed sheets of water, ornamental bridges, and the river Cam can afford. From some parts of the park the views are extensive and delightful. Opposite the south front of the mansion is an avenue of fine trees, about two miles and a half in length. This is crossed by a branch of the Cam, which flows through this part of the grounds. On the north side of the house are three pieces of water, which greatly contribute to the interest excited by the surrounding scenery, and on a rising ground is an artificial ruin, denominated a Gothic Tower. WIMPOLE Church stands near the east end of this mansion. Four of the windows are of plated glass, containing the arms of the different families to whom the Yorkes are allied by marriage, and a very beautiful figure of David playing on the harp. There are several splendid monuments—one in particular, that to the memory of Lord Chancellor Hardwicke. On the upper part is a medallion of the Earl, and beneath it a sarcophagus, with the figure of Wisdom leaning over it in a mourning position. In the enclosure a few neat cottages have been built, with a small piece of ground attached to each for the use of the labourers.

Enter Huntingdon. [margin note]

51¼ m. ST. NEOT'S STATION. [margin note]

4 m. E. Croxton Park, Samuel Newton, Esq.; and 1 m. further, ELTISLEY. The church is dedicated to St. Pandionia, the daughter of a Scotch King, who in her flight from some persons who attempted her chastity, is said to have taken refuge in a nunnery at Eltisley, the prioress of which was her relative. 4 m. further is CAXTON. Mathew Paris, the historian, was born in this town, which is reported to be the birth-place of the celebrated William Caxton, who introduced the art of printing into this country. This however is erroneous, as we have Caxton's own authority for affirming that he was born in Kent instead of Cambridgeshire.

Cross the Ouse. [margin note]

58½ m. HUNTINGDON STA. [margin note]

GODMANCHESTER, the "Durolipons" of the Romans, is a suburb of Huntingdon, separated only by the river. It is a poor and meanly built town, included within that of Huntingdon. Area of parish, 5,590 A.; population, 2,152. It has, however, an endowed grammar school and other charities.

HUNTINGDON, the capital of the county, is a parliamentary and municipal borough, and market-town, on the Ouse, here crossed by three bridges, which connect it with Godmanchester. Area of its four parishes, 1,230 A.; population of parliamentary borough, 5,500. It sends two members to Parliament. Registered electors (1848), 374. Huntingdon has one principal street, of great length. Its two venerable churches are highly interesting; and it has an ancient grammar school, at which Oliver Cromwell, a native of the town, was partly educated, and a green-coat school, the two producing an annual revenue of about £600. The principal

2 m. s.w. Conington Castle, John Meyer Heathcote, Esq. 2 m. w. is STILTON; and 1 m. further, Washingley Hall, near which is Norman Cross. At this place, during the late war with France, extensive barracks and prisons stood, covering an immense area. From the extent and number of buildings, probably more Frenchmen were confined here than at any, or all other barracks in the kingdom. A few years back they were taken down and the materials sold.

69 m. HOLME STATION.

Enter Northampton.

Northampton and Peterborough Railway.

1 m. s.w. of station, Woodstone, Colonel Wright Vaughan. 1½ m. further, OVERTON LONGUEVILLE. Orton Hall, Earl of Aboyne. The mansion is pleasantly situated amongst clumps of trees and fruitful meadows. 1 m. N.W. Thorp Hall. 1 m. further, Milton Park, both the property of Earl Fitzwilliam. The latter mansion is a large irregular structure, part appearing to be of the age of Queen Elizabeth. In the windows are several pieces of stained glass, which were removed from Fotheringay Castle when that building was demolished. The mansion is also decorated with several paintings, amongst which is a portrait of Mary Queen of Scots, and another of James I. when a boy, the latter bearing an inscription, stating that it was given by Mary Queen of Scots, on the morning of her execution, to Sir William Fitzwilliam, for his humane treatment of her during her confinement at Fotheringay, of which place he was then governor. 4 m. N.E. from which, Walcot Park, — Nevile, Esq.; and 3 m. further, Burghley House, Marquis of Exeter. This magnificent and truly splendid pile was built by the Lord Treasurer Burleigh, in the reign of Queen Elizabeth, on the site of a very ancient minster, called Burghe, and is a brilliant specimen of the Elizabethan style of architecture; the principal front, which looks to the north, is nearly 200 feet in extent. At each corner are turrets, mounted by triangular cupolas, and terminating with their vanes. A parapet goes round the whole building in a series of open work, consisting of arches supported by balustrades and obelisks, interspersed with armorial ensigns of the family. To the general antiquarian however, the most interesting parts are the glimpses of the old minster, which show themselves in divers fragments in the hall, chapel, and kitchen, upon the eastern side of the edifice.

76¾ m. PETERBOROUGH STA.

Syston and Peterborough Railway.

TALLINGTON, a parish, county of Lincoln. 3 m. w.s.w. MARKET DEEPING. Area, 690 A.; population, 1,246.

3 m. w. STAMFORD (see Syston and Peterborough). 1½ N.W. Casewick, Sir John Trollope, Bart., M.P.

TALLINGTON STATION.*

Enter Lincolnshire.

ESSENDINE, parish, county of Rutland. Area, 1,440 A. 3 m. s.w. Tolthorpe Hall, Everson Harrison, Esq. 2 m. w of which, is Tickencote Hall, S. R. Fydell, Esq.

ESSENDINE STA.

Pass through about 2 miles of Rutlandshire.

LITTLE BYTHAM, county of Lincoln, parts of Kesteven. Area of parish, 1,110 A.; population, 311. It adjoins the parish of Castle Bytham. 5 m. s.s.w. CORBY. 2 m. s. Holywell, General Reynardson; and 2 m. w. of which, is Stocken Hall, Gilbert John Heathcote, Esq.

LITTLE BYTHAM STATION.

Viaduct 101 yards long.

* The direct line between Peterborough and East Retford not being finished, the trains now run by the way of Boston and Lincoln. Having, however, been favoured by the Secretary of the Great Northern Railway with the probable stations on this part of the line, we have thought it bette to make it as complete as possible, by continuing our line to Retford. The stations, however,

buildings of the town are the town hall, county gaol, borough gaol, theatre, assembly rooms, baths, and the traces of an ancient castle, built by Edward the Elder in 917. Trade in corn, coals, wool, and timber, carried on by the Ouse; and several large breweries. Market, Saturday.

69 m. HOLME
STATION.

Enter
Northampton.

March and Ely
Railway. ☞

6 m. S.E. at RAMSEY, Ramsey Abbey, Edward E. Fellowes, Esq, M.P. On the site of this mansion stood an abbey of Benedictine monks, of great wealth and magnificence, founded in 969 by Hale Ailwyne, Alderman of all England, and Duke or Earl of the East Angles, the revenue of which at the dissolution was valued at £1,983 15s. 3d. The present mansion consists partly of the ancient fabric, exhibiting the gateway in a fine state of preservation. About 2 m. E. of Holme, till lately, was a large expanse of water, called Whittlesea Mere, or the White Sea. It has recently been drained and turned to agricultural purposes.

76¼ m. PETERBO-
ROUGH STA.

PETERBOROUGH, a city, an episcopal see, parliamentary borough and parish, county of Northampton, is situated on the river Nene, which is here crossed by a wooden bridge. The streets of this small city are regular, and the buildings neat. In the time of the Anglo-Saxons it was celebrated for its magnificent monastery, founded in the 8th century. It was erected into a bishopric in 1541, by Henry VIII., when the fine abbey church was converted into a cathedral. Catherine, the first wife of Henry VIII., and Mary Queen of Scots were buried here, but the body of the latter Princess was afterwards removed to Westminster Abbey. St. John's Church, near the centre of the city, has an altar-piece, presented by Sir R. K. Porter, and a tablet with figures, executed by Flaxman; both of which are highly and abundantly esteemed. The Cathedral Close is deeply interesting to the antiquary, owing to the remains of cloisters and many other impressive vestiges of monastic buildings by which it is surrounded. The grammar school has five scholarships, and a fellowship to St. John's College, Cambridge. The principal public buildings and institutions are the town hall, market-place, infirmary, union workhouse, prison, house of correction, and a theatre. Peterborough, which is under the jurisdiction of the Dean and Chapter, is a polling-place for the northern division of the county, and sends two members to Parliament. Registered electors (1848), 553. Area of parish, 1,430 A.; population, 5,920; area of liberty, 51,430 A.; population, 1,125; population of parliamentary borough, 6,991. The see comprises 305 benefices, and extends over Northampton, Leicester, and Rutland. Average annual revenue of Dean and Chapter, £5,000. Peterborough was the birth-place of Dr. Paley. One m. E. are FLETTON and STANDGROUND. 4 m. further, WHITTLESEA. Manor House, Thomas Bowker, Esq.; Grove House, Henry Haines, Esq.; Mansion House, Charles Smith, Esq.

TALLINGTON
STATION.

Enter
Lincolnshire.

ESSENDINE STA.

Pass through
about 2 miles of
Rutlandshire.

3 m. N. Witham-on-the-Hill, General W. A. Johnson. 3 m. further, BOURNE. Supposed from the discovery of Roman coins and tesselated pavement, to have been anciently a place of importance. The great Lord Burghley was born here, 1520, and Dr. Dodd, in 1729. Red Hall, Mrs. Pochin.

LITTLE BYTHAM
STATION.

Viaduct 101 yards
long.

3 m. N.E. Grimsthorpe Castle, Lord Willoughby De Eresby. Some parts of the castle appear to have been erected in the time of Henry III.; but the principal part, called by Fuller an "extempore structure," was raised suddenly by Charles Brandon, Duke of Suffolk, to entertain Henry VIII. during his progress through this part of the kingdom.

not being fixed for certainty, we could not add the distances; and it must be remembered, that when the line is open throughout, about fifteen miles will have to be deducted from the distances as put down between East Retford and Edinburgh.

CORBY STATION.

6 m. w. Buckminster Park, Earl of Dysart. 4 m. N.W. Easton House, Sir Montague J. Cholmeley, Bart.; Stoke Rochford, Christopher Turnor, Esq. This park is prettily varied with wooded banks and water. The house, lately erected by the present proprietor, is a large handsome stone building, in the Elizabethan style of architecture, with gardens and terraces. Beyond is seen the obelisk erected to the memory of Sir Isaac Newton, that great philosopher having been born at Wolsthorpe, in a house belonging to Mr. Turnor, and having for some years attended the school at Stoke Rochford.

GREAT PENTON STATION.

GREAT PONTON, a parish, county of Lincoln. Area, 2,930 A.; population, 469. In the vicinity, about 2½ m. S.S.E. of Grantham, lies the parish of LITTLE PONTON, which has an area of 1,490 A., and a population of 212. 4 m. Hungerton Hall. 6 m. S.W. Croxton Park. 2 m. further, Goady Hall.

BELVOIR CASTLE, DUKE OF RUTLAND.

GRANTHAM STA.

5 m. w. Belvoir Castle, the Duke of Rutland, is considered the most splendid seat in the county of Leicester; it was founded by Robert de Todeni, called afterwards Robert de Belevedire, a noble Norman, and standard-bearer to William the Conqueror. It was probably at first a part of the adjoining township of Wolsthorpe, which is particularly noticed in "Domesday Book," as containing two manors, and having in one of these a church and presbyter, till becoming, in consequence of the owner choosing it as his residence, the head of the lordship, the whole was distinguished by the title of "Manerium de Belvoir, cum membris de Wollesthorpe." The great design in raising Belvoir Castle was to oppose a barrier to the Saxons.

In 1520, the first Earl Rutland restored and rebuilt the castle, which had remained in ruins since the time of the wars of the White and Red Roses, when it was attacked and destroyed by William Lord Hastings. It remained a noble and princely residence till the unhappy war between the King and the Parliament, during which time it was successively occupied by both parties, and by each attacked and defended.

After the Restoration the castle was again repaired and restored, and in the early part of the present century upwards of two hundred thousand pounds were expended on various additions, when in 1816 a most calamitous fire destroyed a great part of this beauteous pile, and totally consumed the celebrated picture gallery, containing, besides the family pictures, a large

CORBY STATION.

1 m. E. CORBY, a market-town and parish, county of Lincoln. Area, 3,790 A.; population, 714. Market, Thursday. Fairs, 26th August, and Monday before October 11th. 1 m. N.E. Irnham Hall, Lord Arundel of Wardour.

GREAT PENTON STATION.

10 m. E. on the road from Stamford to Lincoln, is FOLKINGHAM, supposed to have originated from a baronial castle in the vicinity, which having been garrisoned by the Royalists in the time of Charles I., was subsequently demolished by order of Oliver Cromwell. It occupies an extensive elevation, which commands a good view over the fens. The manor of Folkingham was given by William the Conqueror to Gilbert de Gaunt, who came over with him from Normandy, and eminently distinguished himself at the decisive battle of Hastings, for which service William amply rewarded him. At this place he resided, but no traces of the ancient baronial residence remains. A descendant of his, who died without issue, in 1274, appointed Edward I. heir to the manor and lands of this barony. Subsequently the manor was given by that monarch to Henry de Bellamotte, in whose family it continued till the time of Henry VII. After that period it passed to the family of the Duke of Norfolk; but being forfeited by attainder, it was granted by King Edward VI. in exchange for other lands, to the family of Clinton. Here was formerly a castle built by Henry de Bellamotte, but the ruins have disappeared, and the only remains to mark where once the castle stood, are the moats and mounds on the east side of the town. South-east of the town is a large encampment, with a deep fosse and vallum. Within the area is a square keep of raised earth, defended also by a fosse capable of being filled with water from the adjoining brook. Without the area, at the north-east corner, is a small fortified enclosure, intended as an advanced work to secure the water for the use of the garrison. The church is a handsome structure, principally in the later style of English architecture; the chancel is of earlier date, and exhibits some fine decorated windows, and the tower has a rich battlement and light pinnacles.

GRANTHAM STA.

GRANTHAM, a parliamentary and municipal borough, market-town and parish, county of Lincoln, parts of Kesteven, on the river Witham. Area of parish, 5,560 A.; population, 8,691; parliamentary borough, 8,786. It sends two members to Parliament. Registered electors (1848), 721. Corporate revenue (1846-7), £1,242. Grantham is a remarkably neat and clean town, possessing an aspect of antiquity, which is increased by its ecclesiastical buildings, and the remains of monastic institutions. There are four principal streets, nearly parallel to each other, with smaller ones. The church is a fine specimen of the architecture of the 13th century, although from the style of its crypt, it is evident that it was erected upon the foundations of one of much greater antiquity. It has a handsome square tower at the west end, surmounted by an octangular spire, altogether 273 feet in height, which is often cited for the elegance of its proportions and ornaments. The interior decorations of this venerable structure are in perfect keeping with the exterior, and its costly monuments are of a highly interesting character, well deserving the attention of the traveller. Edward I. here erected a cross to the memory of Queen Eleanor, on St. Peter's Hill, near the south entrance to the town, and here her body lay in state in its progress to Westminster Abbey for interment. The remains of the religious houses are also worthy of notice. The grammar school, where Newton received his early education, has an annual revenue of £800, and exhibitions

collection of the works of Sir Joshua Reynolds; and amongst others, his much admired picture of the Nativity. The situation and aspect of Belvoir partly reesemble Windsor.

> Belvoir, art's master-piece and nature's pride,
> High in the regions of etherial air,
> Above the troubled atmosphere,
> Above the magazine of hail and snow,
> Above the place that meteors breed,
> Above the seat where lie the seed,
> Whence raging storms and tempest grow,
> That do infest the troubled world below.

The chief stronghold of the castle is an outwork defence, called Staunton Tower, the command of which is held by the family of that name, in the manor of Staunton, by tenure of castle-ground, by which they were anciently required to appear with soldiers for the defence of the castle. It has been the custom when any of the royal family have honoured Belvoir Castle with their presence, for the chief of the Staunton family to appear, and present the key of the stronghold to such distinguished person. Thus when the Prince Regent visited the Duke of Rutland in 1814, the golden key of Staunton was delivered to the illustrious guest, by the Rev. Dr. Staunton, by virtue of the tenure above described.

The building surrounds a quadrangular court, and assumes a majestic castellated appearance. The ancient gardens suspended, as it were, in terraces, afford a striking and irregular appearance. They are in a style well suited to the extent and magnificence of the castle, and consist principally of majestic rows of the taller trees on the declivity of the hills, with spacious walks beneath them. Below are the deeply-shaded plantations of yew and fir, and these bounded by more promiscuous groups and foreign wood, which connect the gardens with the neighbouring grounds; shrubs and flowers, which would be inconsistent with the grandeur of the scenery, are scattered only here and there in a few places as though by the hand of nature. Crabbe, the poet, was for some years chaplain at Belvoir Castle.

HOUGHAM. 3 m. N.W. of which, LONG PENINGTON. On the western side of the church is an entrenched eminence, the site of an ancient castle. The kings of Mercia are said to have had a palace here. 2 m. further, Staunton Hall, Rev. Dr. J. Staunton.

HOUGHAM STA.

CLAYPOLE. 3 m. w. at BALDERTON, New Hill, T. Godfrey, Esq.

CLAYPOLE STA.
Enter
Nottinghamshire.

NEWARK, a parliamentary and municipal borough, market-town and parish, county of Notts, on the Newark river, a navigable branch of the Trent. Area of parish, 2,080 A.; population of borough, 10,218. It sends two members to Parliament. Registered electors (1848), 1,016. Corporate revenue, £1,518 This ancient and interesting town formerly possessed a magnificent castle, erected by King Stephen, which was often the abode of royalty, and where King John died in 1216. It was dismantled by the Parliamentary army in the civil wars of the 17th century, and is now a very stately and picturesque ruin. The church is considered one of the finest parochial structures in England; its style, the florid Gothic, superbly ornamented in every part. It has a light and elegant stone tower, sustaining a lofty spire of remarkable beauty, forming a conspicuous object in the surrounding scenery. The town, which is approached from the north by a raised causeway on numerous arches, is well built, has a spacious market-place, a town hall—a handsome building, erected in 1805, at a cost of £17,000, containing the corporate offices, courts of law, and a public assembly room—a grammar school, founded 1529, and other charities, producing an annual revenue of £2,500, and several Dissenting chapels. Manufactures of sheetings and linen goods, with tile factories, foundries,

NEWARK STA.
Nottingham and
Newark Railway.

to Oxford and Cambridge. The other chief buildings are the guildhall, borough gaol, union workhouse, a neat theatre, and some Dissenting chapels. Grantham has a trade in malting, and exports corn, importing coals by means of a canal, which connects the town with the Trent. Independently of this direct London and York line, the Nottingham, Boston, and Lincoln Railway passes through the town. Market, Saturday.

Belton House, the seat of Earl Brownlow, was built by Sir John Brownlow, the third baronet, from the design of Sir Christopher Wren. It was commenced in 1685, and completed in 1689. The mansion presents four uniform elevations, originally surmounted by a balustrade and cupola; and the stone employed in its construction is of an excellent and durable quality. The apartments are well proportioned, and adorned with carvings by Grinlin Gibbons. William III. honoured the founder with a visit in 1695, after the death of his Queen, previously to which he had obtained permission to empale his lands, which he enclosed with a wall five miles in circumference. Sir John Brownlow, fifth baronet, who was created Viscount Tyrconnel, here formed gardens of great magnificence, which have been altered to the taste of the present age; and the grounds have received every embellishment that refined taste could suggest. Close to which is Syston Park, Sir John Thorold, Bart. 7 m. E. Haydar Lodge. 2 m. further, Culverthorpe Hall, John Archer Houblon, Esq. 2 m. N. of which is SLEAFORD, a market-town and parish, county of Lincoln. Population, 3,382. A castle appears to have been erected here at an early period, but of its history nothing is known, and of the building only some slight vestige remains. The town is particularly neat, well-paved, lighted, and supplied with water. A little to the west, South Raunceby, Anthony Peacock, Esq.

HOUGHAM STA.

2 m. S.E. at HONIGHTON, Willoughby House, Charles Allix, Esq. 1 m. N. of which, Sudbrooke House, Shelley Penny, Esq; Newton House, Benjamin Handley, Esq.

CLAYPOLE STA.
Enter
Nottinghamshire.

1 m. S.E. Stubton Hall, Sir Robert Heron, Bart. 3 m. further, Leadenham Hall, Colonel Reeve; Fulbeck, General Fane.

NEWARK STA.

Nottingham and
Newark Railway.

1 m. N.N.E. Winthorp Hall, G. Hodgkinson, Esq.; and 1 m. further, at LANGFORD, Langford Hall, Mrs. Haffenden. A little further, Collingham Hall. 2 m. E. Beaconsfield House, James Thorpe, Esq. 2 m. further, Beckingham Hall, C. Gery Milnes, Esq. 3½ m. N. on the Tuxford and Retford Road, Muskham Grange, J. Handley, Esq. The edifice, consisting of a centre and two wings, was partly erected at the end of the 17th century. The pleasure grounds, from which there are fine prospects, are well and agreeably laid out. Near which is Muskham House. This handsome residence was built in 1793, and consists of a centre of very fine elevation and two wings; the offices are very spacious, and the beauty of the grounds enhanced by the pleasing prospects they afford.

and considerable exports of corn, wool, meat, limestone and gypsum. The Nottingham, Boston, and Lincoln, as well as this railway, passes through the town. Market, Wednesday. 2 m. w. Kelham Hall, J. H. Manners Sutton, Esq., M.P. About 3 m. further, Upton Hall, H. Hawkes, Esq. 5 m. N.N.W. at CAUNTON, the Manor House, Samuel Hole, Esq.

1½ m. w. Ossington Hall, John Evelyn Denison, Esq., M.P.   CARLTON STA.

TUXFORD, a market-town and parish, county of Notts. Area, 3,000 A. ;   TUXFORD STA.
population, 1,079. Here is a free grammar school, a fair trade in hops, grown in the vicinity, and fairs for cattle, hops, &c., May 12th, and September 20th and 25th. Market, Monday. 2 m. w. Bevercote's Park.   Sheffield and Lin-
2 m. N. EAST MARKHAM. The church, dedicated to St. John the Baptist,   coln Branch.
is a large and ancient structure, with a lofty embattled tower, and contains a monument, erected to Judge Markham, in 1409. Tuxford Hall, Lady Elizabeth White.

4 m. s.w. Clumber Park, Duke of Newcastle. This magnificent seat   157¾ m. EAST
would require considerable space to give anything like a detail of its various   RETFORD STA.
beauties. The mansion has three splendid fronts—the one facing the lake is, perhaps, the handsomest, from the elegant Ionic colonnade in its centre, and when viewed from the lofty bridge which crosses the water in question, the front has a truly palatial appearance. The internal decorations, the proportions of the various state and other apartments, the collection of paintings, the furniture, articles of *virtu*, &c., are all in strict keeping with the character of the princely domain by which this mansion is surrounded. The park is eleven miles in circumference, and contains highly interesting and picturesque prospects, with venerable woods, from one of which, Clumber, the seat derives its name. It has been eloquently observed of this splendid mansion and estate, that " everything breathes the essence of life and the soul of magnificence." ½ m. s. HOARDSALL. 2 m. further, ELHESLEY. Apley Hill, Edward Parker, Esq. 2 m. N.W. Babworth Hall, The Hon. John Bridgeman Simpson ; Ranby Hall, C. C. Blaydes, Esq. ; Ranby House, R. F. S. Champion, Esq.

3 m. N.W. BLYTH. The Hall, Frederick H. Walker, Esq.   161¼ m. SUTTON
                                                                      STATION.

RANSKELL.   163¼ m. RANS-
                                                                      KELL STA.

SCROOBY. Here formerly stood a palace of the Archbishops of York, who   166 m. SCROOBY
are lords of the manor. Archbishop Savage (temp. Henry VII.), Cardinal   STATION.
Wolsey in the next reign, and Sandys in that of Queen Elizabeth, resided here occasionally. One of the daughters of Archbishop Sandys was buried   Enter Yorkshire.
here. The slight portion which remains of the palace has been converted into a farm-house. Bishopsfield, Fernley Fairfax, Esq.

BAWTRY, a market-town, in the parish of Blyth, counties of York and   167¼ m. BAWTRY
Notts, situate on the river Idle, which is navigable to this town for small   STATION.
craft. Population, 1,083. It is a small but well-built town, standing on the slope of an eminence ; but the marshes near the river are subject to inundations. Bawtry has a remarkably broad street, with several handsome

CARLTON STA.

7½ m. E.N.E. of Newark, CARLTON LE MOORLANDS, county of Lincoln. Area of parish, 2,610 A.; population, 331. There are several parishes of this name in this county, some within a few miles of each other. Carlton House, John Vere, Esq.

TUXFORD STA.

Gainsborough and Grimsby Br. ☞

3 m. N.E. by E. HEDBOROUGH. This was formerly the Gretna Green of Notts and the bordering counties, from the then rector, Mr. Sweetapple, being always ready to join in wedlock instanter all who applied to him for that happy purpose. 3 m. from which is THORNEY. Thorney Hall, Rev. Charles Nevile.

157¾ m. EAST RETFORD STA.

RETFORD, EAST, a parliamentary and municipal borough, market-town and parish, county of Notts, on the river Idle, which separates it from West Retford (a parish, same county, containing an area of 1,080 A., and a population of 618), and is here crossed by a bridge of five arches. Area of parish, 130 A.; population, 2,680. Population of parliamentary borough, 44,132, arising from the extension of the electoral franchise to the whole hundred of Bassetlaw, in consequence of the conviction of the borough of bribery in 1826. It sends two members to Parliament. Registered electors (1848), 2,665. Corporate revenue (1847), £9,894. The town is well-built, has a handsome Gothic church with a square tower, a free grammar school founded by Edward VI., annual revenue, £500; a fine town hall, a poor's hospital, union workhouse, news rooms, two branch banks and a small theatre. Market, Saturday. West Retford has an endowed hospital and other charities, with an annual revenue of £1,190. It is a suburb of East Retford, and with the exception of the church, contains nothing of note. 2 m. N.E. Grove Hall. The mansion was erected in the 16th century by the ancient family of Hercy, and with the exception of a new front of modern architecture, and internal arrangements more in keeping with the taste of the age, the old building is still entire. It is well situated on an eminence, in the centre of a well-wooded park, which affords many fine prospects over the surrounding country.

161½ m. SUTTON STATION.

SUTTON, or SUTTON CUM SOUND, county of Notts. Area of parish, 4,370 A.; population, 890.

163¼ m. RANS-KELL STA.

2 m. MATTERSEE. In the chancel of the village church is a curious carving, supposed to belong to the abbey, which was destroyed during the parliamentary war; the ruins may be seen about a mile from the village. It was found under the old pavement of the chancel, about fifty years ago, and represents St. Martin in the act of dividing his cloak with the beggar. The Hall, Benjamin Fearnley, Esq.

166 m. SCROOBY STATION.

Enter Yorkshire.

2 m. E. EVERTON. The church is an old embattled building, of the style of architecture of the 12th century, and contains a chancel separated from the nave by a finely-worked arch. About 1 m. N. Scaltworth, Captain Hotham.

167¼ m. BAWTRY STATION.

Gainsborough and Lincoln Br. ☞

1 m. N.N.E. AUSTERFIELD. A chapelry in the parish of Blyth, near which is FINNINGLY. The church, dedicated to St. Oswald, is a neat old building, consisting of a nave, north aisle, chancel, south porch, and square embattled tower, surrounded by crotchetted pinnacles at the angles. ¾ m. further N. Finningly Hall, John Harvey, Esq. The house is pleasantly

houses. Stone, timber, lead, and iron, are transported from this by the Idle to Hull and London. A small stream that runs through the yard of the 'Crown Inn' divides the counties of Notts and York. Near the town is a hospital for the poor, founded in the 14th century. Market, Thursday. Fairs, Whit-Thursday and November 23rd. Adjoining the town is the residence of the Dowager-Viscountess Galway. 2 m. w. HARWORTH. Serlby Hall, Viscount Galway, M.P.; Hesley Hall, C. S. Wright, Esq. 2 m. further, TICKHILL, where there is the remains of an ancient castle, and near which is Sandbeck, Earl of Scarborough.

3 m. N.W. Loversall Hall, Rev. A. Cook. | 170¾ m. ROSSING-TON STA.

DONCASTER, a municipal borough, is pleasantly situated, and one of the cleanest and best built towns in the kingdom. According to Camden the town was entirely destroyed by lightning about the year 759, at which period the castle, of which the founder and foundation are unknown, is supposed to have been burnt. The town is pleasantly situated on the bank of the river Don, and the surrounding scenery, especially on the western side, is exceedingly picturesque. It consists of several streets; the High Street, one mile in length, is remarkably handsome, and is considered the best for width and beauty on the road from London to Edinburgh. Christchurch is a noble cruciform structure, with a tower. 2 m. w. Cusworth, William Battie Wrightson, Esq., M.P., is beautifully situated upon an eminence in the centre of a fine park, and consists of a large quadrangular centre and two wings, of white limestone. It was built about the year 1740, by William Wrightson, Esq., but the wings were subsequently added to the building, under the direction of James Paine, the architect. The upper rooms command an extensive prospect over a fine sporting country, adorned with a great variety of gentlemen's seats, and the towers of York and Lincoln minsters, which are about forty miles distant. The park is skirted by very rich woods. It is watered by a lake, so contrived as to give it the appearance of a branch of the river Don, which is half a mile distant. The gardens are beautifully laid out. | 175½ m. DONCASTER STA.

ARKSEY. | 177¾ m. STOCK-BRIDGE STA.

ASKERN, a township in the parish of Campsall, West Riding of York. It is much resorted to by invalids for its sulphur baths. Area, 800 A. 1 m. further, Campsall, Bacon Frank, Esq. A very pretty estate. 2 m. further from which, Adwich Hall, Miss Simpson; Skellow Grange, G. Higgins, Esq.; Burgh Wallis, M. Tasburgh, Esq.; Owston Hall, P. D. Cooke, Esq. 4 m. N.W. from Burgh Wallis, Badgeworth Park, Joseph Scott, Esq. | 182¼ m. ASKERN STATION.

NORTON is a parish, in the township of Campsall. | 184¼ m. NORTON STATION.

WOMERSLEY, a parish in the West Riding, county of York. 1 m. w. of which, Stapleton Park, John Hope Barton, Esq. It stands in an extensive and beautiful park, watered by a stream that empties itself into the river Went, in the most fertile part of the county, bounded by an expanded range of distant hills, and is situated in the parish of Donington, in the wapentake of Osgoldcross. The mansion, built entirely of stone, was erected by Edward Lascelles, Esq., afterwards Lord Harewood. It is entered by a handsome Doric portico, and the centre of the principal front is ornamented with four Ionic columns, supporting a pediment. The entire suite of apartments on the entrance floor is of an elegant character, and the whole superbly decorated and furnished with refined taste. The chapel is also particularly neat. | 186¼ m. WOMERSLEY STA.

situated on a rising ground, in a fine sporting country. The village is in the county of Nottingham; but the mansion and part of the park are in Yorkshire. 1 m. E. NEWINGTON. 2 m. further, MISSAM. 5 m. further, MISTERTON. John Corringham, Esq. and James Sowthorpe, Esq. 3 m. N. of which is AXEY. 3 m. further, EBWORTH. This place was anciently the residence of the Howard family, who had here a castellated mansion, of which there are no remains, except the site, where within the last half century, were dug up some of the cannon belonging to the fortification.

170¾ m. ROSSINGTON STA.

ROSSINGTON, a parish, containing 2,930 A., with a population of 344, situated in the West Riding, county of York. Here is a bridge over the Torne. 2 m. N. Cantley Hall, John Walbanke Childers, Esq., M.P., is a large and elegant modern mansion, built by Childers Walbanke Childers, Esq., A.D. 1790. The trees and plantations are very luxuriant, and almost conceal the mansion from view; but it is a delightful spot, and the grounds are laid out with great taste.

175¼ m. DONCASTER STA.

1 m. S.W. Doncaster race-course, where the most celebrated races in the kingdom are held, which for some years have been increasing in splendour and attraction, and are attended by nearly all the families of rank in the north of England. These races were established in 1703; and in 1776, the famous St. Leger Stakes for three year olds were founded by Colonel St. Leger, and have since been run for annually in September, by the best horses in England. On the course is a magnificent grand stand, noblemen's stand, with every other convenience for the races, which directly and indirectly, contribute the chief resource of the inhabitants. 2 m. E. Wheatley Hall, Sir William B. Cooke, Bart. This fine mansion, which displays the architectural taste of the 17th century, was built by Sir H. Cooke, about the year 1680. It stands on the banks of the Don, in a low situation—our ancestors having preferred such positions; and when the river overflows the country round, presents a dreary aspect. Before the south front of the house is a beautiful lawn, ornamented with some of the finest oaks in the country. 2 m. further, Woodthorpe, — Parker, Esq. A handsome modern mansion, the plantations and pleasure-grounds laid out with great taste and judgment. 3 m. further, HATFIELD; and 2 m. further, THORNE.

177½ m. STOCK BRIDGE STA.

2 m. N.E. KIRKSANDAL.

182¼ m. ASKERN STATION.

8. m. E. THORNE, a market-town, West Riding, county of York, situated near the river Don, in a low, flat, and totally unpicturesque, but remarkably fertile tract of land. Vessels sufficiently large for the coasting trade are built at a place called Hangman's Hill, on the banks of the river, which is also a general landing-place for the merchandise of the town.

184¼ m. NORTON STATION.

1 m. E. FENWICK, at which is an ancient tower, called Fenwick Tower, the ancient seat of a family of that name, which has long been in ruins.

186¼ m. WOMERSLEY STA.

2 m. E. WHITLEY, a township, in the parish of Killington, county of York. 4 m. further, POLLINGTON; and 2 m. further, Cowick Park, Viscount Downe.

PONTEFRACT, a parliamentary and municipal borough, West Riding, county of York. See Yorkshire, Pontefract, and Goole Railway.

190¼ m. KNOT-TINGLEY STA.

Yorkshire, Pontefract, and Goole Branch.

Ledstone Park, late Michael A. Taylor, Esq. Close to which is Kippax Park, Thomas Davison Bland, Esq.

193¾ m. BURTON SALMON STA.

195¼ m. Milford Junction.

Leeds Branch.

SHERBURN. At this place the Archbishop of York formerly had a palace, of which there are some remains. Sherburn is remarkable for a particular species of plum, called the Winesour, which grows in the neighbourhood.

197¼ m. SHER-BURN STA.

1 m. w. Scarthingwell Hall, Lord Hawke.

199¼ m. CHURCH FENTON STA.

ULLESKELFE, a township, West Riding, county of York; and 2 m. w. Grimston, Lord Londesborough.

201¾ m. ULLES-KELFE STA.

3 m. N. BILBROOK. Thomas Lord Fairfax, the celebrated parliamentary general, who died in 1671, was interred in the church here.

202¾ m. BOLTON PERCY STA.

COPMANTHORPE, a chapelry in the parish of St. Mary, Bishopshill Junior. There is a small endowment for the education of children.

206¼ m. COP-MANTHORPE STA.

YORK, a city, parliamentary and municipal borough, and county of itself, capital of the county of York, is the second city of England in rank, but not in any other respect. It is situated in the centre of the county, at the junction of the three Ridings and Ainsty, on the Ouse, at the influx of the Foss, and at the meeting of railways from Berwick, London, and the central counties. Area of city, 2,720 A.; population, 28,242. The parliamentary borough comprises the whole or parts of thirty-six parishes, and some extra-parochial districts, and is nearly coincident with the municipal. It sends two members to Parliament. Registered electors (1848), 3,671; corporate revenue (1848), £7,404; gross revenue of archiepiscopal see (1843), £20,141. The charities in 1825 produced an aggregate revenue of upwards of £4,500. York is the Eboracum of the Romans, and from its reported resemblance to the Imperial City, was dignified with the title of "Altera Roma." Very few remains of the genius of that wonderful people are now extant in York—the principal are the arch in Micklegate Bar, the rectangular tower, and the south wall of the Minster Yard—these relics are highly prized by the antiquary. History proves that York was the residence of Hadrian, Severus, Constantius, Chlones, Constantine, and other Roman Emperors; and the funeral obsequies of Severus, who died there, A.D. 212, are said to have been performed at Silvers' Hill, west of the city. Under the Saxons it was successively the capital of the kingdoms of Northumberland and Deira. It suffered severely for its opposition to William of Normandy. In the civil wars of the 17th century it espoused the royal cause, but boldly opposed the fanatical and arbitrary proceedings of the bigoted James II.

210 m. YORK STA.

Harrowgate Branch.

The city, nearly three miles in circumference, is entered by four principal gates, or bars, and five posterns. Micklegate Bar is the handsomest of the gates, near to which is the portal of the priory of the Holy Trinity, which formerly occupied the whole space now called Trinity Gardens; and behind which is the site of an ancient building, supposed to have been a castle, afterwards converted into the prison of the Archbishop. The mound that

190¼ m. KNOT-
TINGLEY STA.

Yorkshire, Ponte-
fract, and Goole
Branch.

193¼ m. BURTON
SALMON STA.

195¼ m. Milford
Junction.

Hull and Selby
Branch.

197¼ m. SHER-
BURN STA.

199¼ m. CHURCH
FENTON STA.

201¼ m. ULLES-
KELFE STA.

202¼ m. BOLTON
PERCY STA.

206¼ m. COP-
MANTHORPE STA.

210 m. YORK STA.

York and Scarbo-
rough Branch.

York and Market
Weighton Br.

KNOTTINGLEY, a chapelry in the parish of Pontefract, in the West Riding, county of York, included in the parliamentary boundary of that borough. Close to Knottingley, at FERRYBRIDGE, Byrom Hall, Sir John William Ramsden, Bart.

BURTON SALMON, a township in the parish of Monkfriston. 1 m. N.W. of which is MONKFRISTON.

2 m. E. BIGGEN, a township, partly within the liberty of St. Peter's, York, and partly in the parish of Kirk Fenton. The plant easel (*Dipsacus falonum*), used in dressing woollen cloth, is said to have been first cultivated at this place.

1 M. E. CHURCH FENTON, or KIRK FENTON, county of York, West Riding. Area of parish, 4,410 A.

2 m. E. Nun-Appleton, Sir William Mordaunt Sturt Milner, Bart. This handsome mansion was built by Thomas Lord Fairfax, on the site of a priory of nuns, founded here by Adeliza de S. Quentin, from which circumstance it derived its name.

BOLTON PERCY, county of York. Area of parish, 7,320 A. The church is a magnificent edifice, erected in the early part of the 15th century, and contains some interesting monuments of the noble family of Fairfax, and some beautiful stained glass.

2 m. E. OSBALDWICK. The church, dedicated to St. Thomas, is endowed with £600 a-year royal bounty.

forms the area of this ruin corresponds with Clifford's Tower on the opposite side of the Ouse, and commands a beautiful view of the city, &c. York is divided into three parts by the rivers Foss and Ouse, the former of which is crossed by five bridges—the latter by one, on the eastern bank of which stands the castle, a splendid structure, built for the county prison, in 1701, on the site of the ancient fortress. In this building is also the Basilica, or New County Hall, an elegant structure of the Ionic order, built in 1777; but the pride of the city is the Minster, or Cathedral Church of St. Peter, which is the largest of its kind in England, chiefly built in the 13th and 14th centuries. It is 524½ feet in length, and 222 in breadth internally, with a great tower 234 feet high. Its magnificent west front is adorned with two towers 196 feet high, and it is richly adorned within. In 1829, Martin, a lunatic, set fire to this splendid pile, and it suffered also by an accidental fire in 1840, but these injuries have been perfectly repaired. Independently of the cathedral, we may cite amongst the ecclesiastical monuments of this ancient city, the churches of All Saints, the pavement of which is partly built of the ruins of the ancient Eboracum, All Hallows, St. Dennis, St. Margaret's, St. Lawrence, St. Michael-le-Belfry, and St. Martin's, and the ruined abbey of St. Mary, all of which merit the greatest attention. Of the other public buildings, we may name the Guildhall, a noble Gothic structure of the 15th century, the Mansion House, with an Ionic colonnade and a fine state-room, Chapter House, theatre, concert hall, and assembly rooms. The buildings of the Yorkshire Philosophical Society, subscription library of 17,000 volumes, museum, city gaol, banks, railway station, and several Dissenting chapels, all of which are deserving of notice. Outside of the city walls there are, independently of the Retreat, another institution, managed by the Society of Friends, about a mile distant, a county lunatic asylum, a county hospital, cavalry barracks, and Bishopsthorpe Palace, the residence of the Archbishop. The streets of York are generally broad and well-built, and in its centre is a broad open space, called Parliament Street, and many squares, well lighted. Round the walls of

the town is a beautiful promenade ; and in Peaseholme Green, a large area, wool and leather fairs are held. The whole city is excellently paved and lighted; and along the Ouse is a fine planted walk, with excellent baths. York is governed by a Lord Mayor (the only civic authority in England who is dignified with this rank, although the Mayor of London is generally, but erroneously, so styled), 12 aldermen, and 36 councillors. Courts of assize for the city and county are here held twice annually; and it has quarter

YORK
(continued).

Great North of England Railway.

The principal works on this line are the Dalton Cutting, near the Cowton Station, the Tees Embankment, Castle Hill Cutting, and the Northallerton Embankment. There are forty-two bridges over and under the railway, in about equal numbers, twenty-three culverts, and fourteen level highway and occupation crossings.

The principal bridges are those over the rivers Tees and Ouse. The former is a

Left of Railway from London.

2 m. w. Beningborough Hall, Hon. Payan Dawnay. 6 m. further, Allerton, Lord Stourton, is an elegant mansion, built by His late Royal Highness the Duke of York; it stands on a gently rising ground, and is surrounded by a park of about 400 a., presenting a variety of hill and dale, interspersed with groves of the most picturesque character. The land is extremely rich and fertile, and on a lofty eminence is an octagonal tower, with two spacious rooms, from which are seen the beautiful prospects presented by the variegated landscapes of the Park and the surrounding country. Here was formerly a Priory of Benedictines, founded by Richard Mauleverer, temp. Henry II. George IV. and the Duke of York resided here for some time in the years 1787 and 1789. Since the estate came into Lord Stourton's hands considerable improvements have been effected. *(215¾ m. SHIPTON STATION.)*

TOLLERTON, situated on a small branch of the River Nidd, which is supposed to have been formerly navigable, as in the year 1815 part of a ship was found beneath the foundation of a mill. *(219¾ m. TOLLERTON STA.)*

ALNE. The Hall, Edward Swainston Strangways, Esq. 5. m w. Myton Hall, Stapylton Stapylton, Esq. *(221¼ m. ALNE STATION.)*

2 m. w. BRAPERTON. *(223½ m. RASKELF STATION.)*

3 m. w. CUNDALL. A small parish. There is a school here, in which thirty children are educated from the proceeds of the parish poor lands. *(244½ m Pilmore Junction. Boroughbridge Branch.)*

3 m. w. Newby Park, G. Hudson, Esq., M.P. A neat and spacious mansion on the southern acclivity of Swailedale; the park is well stocked with deer. *(228¼ m. SESSAY STATION. Leeds and Thirsk Branch.)*

3 m. N.W. PICKHILL CUM ROCKSBY ; a pleasing village, situated on a rivulet, a branch of the river Swaile. At Pickhill was once a castle, and there are some fields still called the Roman Fields. The church is an ancient structure. 2 m. s.w. of which KIRKLINGTON, where there are several large entrenchments, supposed to have been thrown up by the Romans or Danes. 6 m. further w. MASHAM, pleasantly situated on a gentle eminence in a fertile district on the western bank of the river Ure. The houses are well built, and the air remarkably pure. It was anciently the residence of the baronial family of Scroope, to which belonged Henry Lord Scroope, Lord Treasurer, and Archbishop Scroope, both beheaded for *(232½ m. THIRSK STATION.)*

YORK (*continued*).	sessions, a court of pleas, and petty assizes twice a week. York has some manufactures, and a considerable import trade; but its prosperity is derived chiefly from its position as the northern metropolis. York communicates by various railways with most parts of England and Scotland. Markets, Tuesday, Thursday, and Saturday; fairs held every fortnight for horses and cattle, and other fairs annually; races are held about one mile from the city three times a-year.

Great North of England Railway.

handsome oblique structure, consisting of five large segmental arches, built of sandstone, from the design of Mr. Welch, surveyor for the county of Northumberland. The height from the surface of the water is about fifty feet. The bridge over the Ouse, at Nether Poppleton, is built principally of stone; the arches, three in number, of semi-elliptical form, and it stands thirty feet above the bed of the river.

Right of Railway from London.

215¾ m. SHIPTON STATION.	SHIPTON, a township; area, 1,840 A. 4 m. E. SUTTON ON THE FOREST. The celebrated Lawrence Sterne was vicar here, but removed to Coxwold after the parsonage house had been destroyed by fire. Sutton Hall, William Charles Harland, Esq.
219¼ m. TOLLERTON STA.	4 m. N.E. STILLINGTON. The Hall, Harry Croft, Esq. A neat mansion with pleasure-grounds on the west side of the Foss.
221¼ m. ALNE STATION.	3 m. N.E. EASINGWOLD, 2 m. from which is Bransby Hall, Francis Cholmeley, Esq.
223½ m. RASKELF STATION.	RASKELF. 2 m. E. THORENANBY.
224½ m. Pilmore Junction.	3 m. E. THORNTON HILL.
228¼ m. SESSAY STATION.	SESSAY. A long scattered village, with neat houses and gardens, containing 3,340 A.
232½ m. THIRSK STATION.	THIRSK. A parliamentary borough, town, parish, and township, county York, in the North Riding. Thirsk returns one member to Parliament. It is a polling-place for the North Riding. The town is situated on both banks of the Codbeck, an afflux of the Swaile, and contains an ancient church. It manufactures coarse linens and sacking. The markets here are for corn and fruit. 3 m. s. Thirkleby Hall, Lady Frankland Russell. 2 m. w. Woodend, Lord Greenock. 2 m. N.W. Thornton-le-Moor, Robert Hutton, Esq.; close to which is Brawith Hall, unoccupied.

high treason in the reign of Henry IV. 1½ m. s.w. Swinton Park, O. H. C. V. V. Harcourt, Esq.

SOUTH OTTERINGTON is a pleasant scattered village on the east side of the river Wiske. Otterington Hall, Mrs. Newton. 2 m. w. Scroby Hall, John Hutton, Esq.

237 m. OTTERINGTON STA.

4 m. w. NEWBY WISKE, William Rutson, Esq.; and SCRUTON. Scruton Hall, Henry Core, Esq. 1½ m. further Holtby Hall, Thomas Robson, Esq. 1 m. N.W. of which Enderby Hall, William Armitage Esq.; and 2 m. further Hornby Castle, the Duke of Leeds. It is a spacious structure, parts of which are of Gothic architecture, and others of the modern style. The apartments are grand, and superbly furnished, and the environs delightful. It stands on a fine elevation, commanding an extensive prospect over the valley in which Bedale is situated, and also over a large portion of the fertile country between Leeming Lane and the Western Moors, of which the lower eminences form a striking contrast to the rich plains below, and pleasingly vary the scenic beauties of the whole landscape. 2 m. further CATTERICK. Kiplin Park, Earl of Tyrconnel.

240¼ m. NORTH-ALLERTON STA.

↩ Bedale Br.

COWTON, EAST, North Riding, county York; area, 3,150 A. In the same parish are the townships of North and South Cowton. 2 m. w. Halnaby Hall, John Todd, Esq. 1 m. further MIDDLETON TYAS. Middleton Lodge, George Hartley, Esq.; West Hall, Major George Healey; East Hall, Mrs. Maria Morley; Kirkbank, John Carter, Esq.; a little to the north Kneeton Lodge, William Pybus, Esq.

247½ m. COWTON STATION.

Richmond Junc.

Enter Durham.

249¼ m. DALTON STATION.

CROFT, a parish, North Riding, county York; area, 7,060 A. Croft Hall, Colonel Clayton. 4 m. w. Stanwick Hall, Duke of Northumberland; Forcett Hall, Charles Mitchell, Esq. 1 m. s. of which is MELSONBY, where in a field near the rectory, are vestiges of a large building, supposed to be those of a monastery. 4 m. further w. Rokeby Park, J. B. S. and W. S. Morritt, Esqrs. The Hall is an elegant mansion, it stands on the site of an ancient manor-house, and has a gallery sixty-seven feet long, containing a profusion of curiosities, the productions of former times, and the admiration of the present age. The park is an angular area of the richest soil, and shaded by luxuriant woods, bounded by the Tees and Greta for about the space of one mile upwards in their confluence. The poetic genius of Scott has thrown a halo of imperishable celebrity around the romantic beauties of Rokeby, and imparted a national interest to its history.

251¾ m. CROFT STATION.

DARLINGTON; a market-town and parish, county Durham; area of parish, 7,610 A.; population, 11,877; population of town, 11,033. It is the place of election for the south division of the county, and a titular borough under the Bishop of Durham. The streets, diverging from a fine market-place, are neatly built, and well lighted. There is also a bridge of three arches, which crosses the Skerne, an afflux of the Tees. The church, which was formerly collegiate, dates from the twelfth century. Here is also a modern church, a blue-coat school, a grammar school, founded by Queen Elizabeth, with an annual revenue of upwards of £200, town hall, union workhouse, formerly the Bishop's Palace, and a mechanics' institute. Petty sessions and borough courts are held here. The trade of Darlington consists in manufactures of worsted and linen yarns, metal foundries, &c. It commu-

254½ m. DARLINGTON STA.

Darlington and Stockton ↩ Branch. ↪

237 m. OTTERING-
TON STA.

2 m. N.E. THORNTON-LE-BEANS. Thornton Lodge, Colonel Francis Bedingfield; Crosby Gate, Captain C. R. Dent.

240¼ m. NORTH-
ALLERTON STA.

NORTHALLERTON; a parliamentary borough, returning one member. It is supposed to have been a Roman station, subsequently a Saxon borough. At Cowton Moor, about three miles from the town, the celebrated battle of the Standard was fought in the year 1138, between the English and Scotch, in which the latter were defeated, with the loss of eleven thousand men. The spot is still called Standard Hill, and the holes into which the dead were thrown the Scots Pits. About 1174, Henry II. ordered the demolition of the Episcopal Palace, traces of which are still visible on the west side of the town. In 1318, the Scots plundered and burnt the town. During the civil war, Charles I., in one of his journeys to Scotland, lodged here in an old mansion called the Porch House. It stands in the beautiful vale of the Wiske, and consists chiefly of one spacious street, partially paved, and contains some good houses. 6 m. E. Harsley Hall, C. J. Maynard, Esq. 1 m. further E. Thimbleby Lodge, Robert Haines, jun., Esq. 1 m. further, Autley Hall, William Olivera, Esq.

247¼ m. COWTON
STATION.

Richmond Junc.

Enter Durham.

2 m. E. GREAT LINEETON. 2 m. N.W. SOCKBURN, county Durham. Sockburn Hall, a handsome Gothic mansion, Henry Collingwood Blackett, Esq.

249¼ m. DALTON
STATION.

DALTON ON TEES; a township in the parish of Croft, North Riding, county York. From hence a branch diverges to Richmond.

251¾ m. CROFT
STATION.

NEASHAM. The village consists of one street, extending some distance along the northern bank of the Tees, over which at this point there are a ferry and a ford. The latter is noted as the spot selected for the performance of a long-accustomed ceremony, in which, when the river is fordable, the Lord of Sockburn, or his agent, meets the Bishop of Durham on his first entering the county, presenting him with a falchion as an emblem of his temporal power, repeats as follows : " My Lord Bishop, I here present you with the falchion wherewith the champion Conyers slew the hound-dragon, or fiery serpent, which destroyed man, woman, and child, in memory of which the king then reigning gave him the Manor of Sockburn, to hold by this tenure, that upon the first entrance of every bishop into the county this falchion should be. presented." The Bishop, taking the falchion in his hand, immediately returns it, wishing the Lord of Sockburn health and long enjoyment of the manor. Neasham Hall, James Cookson, Esq. ; Neasham Abbey, Thomas Wilkinson, Esq. ; Pilmore, D. Laird, Esq.

254½ m. DARLING-
TON STA.

Darlington
and Stockton
Branch.

4 m. S.W. MIDDLETON. A small market-town, situated in a mining district. It has an ancient church, liberally endowed. The west side of the parish originally formed part of Teesdale, or Marwood Forest. A short distance from Middleton is Wynch Bridge. This fabric, made of wood, is suspended on two iron chains. Although it is sixty-three feet in length, and scarcely more than two feet wide, its height above the river (which falls in repeated cascades) is fifty feet. From the dashing of the waters beneath, and the tremulous motion of the bridge itself, considerable alarm and apprehension fills the bosom of the stranger in crossing it. Three miles from Wynch Bridge is High Force, or Force Fall, a sublime cataract, dashing its waters over a huge rock of black marble, seventy feet high. Above the fall the river is narrow, but here swelling into rage,

nicates by railway with Bishop Auckland and Stockton.   Market, Monday, with several annual fairs. 1¼ m. s.w.

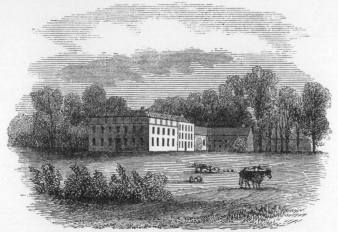

BLACKWELL GRANGE, WILLIAM ALLAN, ESQ.

¼ m. further, Blackwell Hall, Robert Henry Allan, Esq., F.S.A. J.P. This elegant seat is beautifully placed on the brow of a hill, rising over the river Tees, which forms an amphitheatre of three or four miles, hemmed in by rising wooded grounds.   ½ m. N.W. West Lodge.   4 m. further, Walworth Castle, John Harrison Aylmer, Esq.   4 m. W. Sellaby Hall, Jacob Maude, Esq.; Stub House, Thomas Harrison, Esq.

AYCLIFFE, a village of considerable antiquity.   Here, according to Saxon authority, a synod was held in the year 782, and again in 789.   1 m. s. of which is COTHAM MANDEVILLE.   Cotham Hall; Garth, John Trotter, Esq.

BRADBURY.   1½ m. N.E. Hardwick Hall, Hon. Mrs. Hamilton Russell. It is celebrated for the beauty of its pleasure-grounds, and the elegance of its buildings.   The mansion is an irregular edifice, erected by the late Mr. M. Russell, and the grounds beautifully ornamented.   In a pleasant meadow stands a temple, with an open colonnade, which is very splendidly fitted up. 2 m. N.W. Great Chilton, C. Mason, Esq.

FERRY HILL.   At an early period, the convent of Durham had a chapel here, with a court-house, swannery, and fish-pool.   There are still some remains of the swan-house.

SHINCLIFFE, a chapelry in the parish of St. Oswold, on the river Wear. ½ m. W. Shincliffe Hall, Robert Scott, Esq.   Sheltered by a beautiful amphitheatre of hanging woods.   This mansion is situated near the river Wear, and a rich expanse of meadows.

DURHAM, a city, parliamentary and municipal borough, and a celebrated episcopal see, capital of the county.   It sends two members to Parliament.   The appearance of this city from a distance is grand and imposing, from its romantic site, a rocky eminence of considerable height, almost encircled by the river Wear, which is here crossed by several bridges.

260 m. AYCLIFFE STATION.

Clarance, Hartlepool, and Weardale Branch.

264¼ m. BRADBURY STA.

267¼ m. FERRY HILL STA.

272 m. SHINCLIFFE STA.

274 m. SHERBURN STATION.

precipitates itself in an awful crash into a reservoir more than sixty feet deep.

> " Full swift it dashes on the rocky mounds,
> Where through a shapeless break the stream resounds,
> As high in air the bursting torrents flow,
> As deep recoiling surges foam below :
> Prone down the rock the whitening sheet descends,
> And viewless Echo's ear, astonish'd, rends.
> Far seen through rising mists, and ceaseless show'rs,
> The hoary cavern, wide surrounding, low'rs ;
> Still through the gap the struggling river toils,
> And still below the horrid cauldron boils."

The clouds of spray arising from the descending waters, assume, when enlightened by the beams of the sun, all the brilliant beauties of the rainbow. In winter it presents a very different, though not less interesting aspect. The projecting points of the rocks are then decorated with a boundless diversity of icy stalactites and curiously crystallized fringes, which form an endless variety of prisms that operate in the sun's rays like so many crystal lustres, decorating them in ten thousand directions in the most brilliant manner. The force and boiling of the waters has excavated several caverns in the solid marble, but of difficult access, except during severe frosts. The noise of the fall may be heard many miles round the country. At some distance below it, the rocks rise in square columns to the perpendicular height of 100 feet. Here the mineralogist and the botanist may wander with much satisfaction. Near this place was discovered the *Gentiana Verna,* though not previously known to exist in Great Britain.

260 m. AYCLIFFE STATION.	1 m. s. BRAPERTON. 1½ m. s.e. of which is NEWTON KELTON. 1¼ m. further N.E. GREAT STAINTON.
Clarance, Hartlepool, and Weardale Branch.	
264½ m. BRADBURY STA.	3½ m. s. Windleston Hall, Sir William Eden, Bart., whose ancestors were resident here in the time of Queen Elizabeth. The mansion is situated on a gentle ascent, with an eastern aspect.
267½ m. FERRY HILL STA. West Durham Branch.	¼ m. N. THRISLINGTON. ¾ m. further, CORNFORTH, near which is STOBCROSS, where a suicidal seducer was interred with a stake, or stop, through his body, and also the delfcote where the victim released herself from her mental pangs. The inhabitants still think the place haunted by her spirit in the form of a white dove. A little further, Coxhoe House, Anthony Wilkinson, Esq.
272 m. SHINCLIFFE STA.	WHITWELL. An extra-parochial liberty in the northern division of Easington Ward, county Durham.
274 m. SHERBURN STATION.	SHERBURN. A township and parish of Piddington, southern division of Easington Ward, close to which is Sherburn House, an extra-parochial liberty in the same ward. A hospital for lepers was founded here previously to 1181, by Hugh Pudsey, Bishop of Durham. In the reign of Henry VIII., the society consisted of a master, several priests, and sixty-

Durham is partly surrounded by the ancient city walls, beneath which, on one side, the slope of the hill is adorned with well-planted gardens and ornamented walks, descending to the edge of the river, while on the other the ground is rocky and precipitous. The noble castle, founded by William the Conqueror, which retains much of its original military aspect, though improved by recent alterations, is appropriated as a residence of the Bishop, as well as to the Ecclesiastical University, incorporated 1837. The cathedral, rising from the highest point of eminence on which the city is built, is one of the most superb edifices in the kingdom. It was founded in 1093, although not completed until nearly the end of the 13th century. Its architecture is principally of the Anglo-Norman character, although it exhibits the various beauties of the early English, or pointed style. It is 507 feet in length, including the western porch, by 200 feet in breadth, and has a central tower 214 feet high. It has a noble west front, with a Galilee chapel, and two richly ornamented towers 143 feet high. Within is the tomb of St. Cuthbert, and the chapel of the Venerable Bede. The see of Durham was one of the richest in the empire. It was founded in the 10th century, and in 1843 its gross income was £22,416, but under arrangements introduced by the Ecclesiastical Commissioners, the Bishop's income is fixed at £8,000 per annum.

½ m. w. Low Grange.

1½ m. w. Newton Hall.

2 m. w. Great Lumley.

1 m. w. Lambton Hall, The Earl of Durham, is situated on an elevated position, on the north bank of the Wear. It is a modern edifice, erected by Bononi. The library is a well-proportioned, quadrangular room, with a neat gallery around it. The grounds are agreeable, and the ride through a hanging wood, on the southern bank of the Wear, is very beautiful. A little further s.w. Lumley Castle, Earl of Scarborough, is majestically situated on fine elevated ground, bounded on the north by Lumley Beck, and rising on the south and west, from the river Wear, the east front being near the brow of a deep, well-wooded valley, through which the Beck winds towards the river. The mansion forms a quadrangle, with an area in the centre, projecting turrets at each angle, or observatories, of an octangular form, and which overhang the face of each square at the base, and are machiolated, for the purpose of annoying assailants; and they give to the general appearance of this stately mansion a most singular effect. The whole is composed of a yellow freestone. The front to the south is modern, and brought almost parallel with the tower, being 65 paces in length; and towards the east the castle retains its ancient form, and with the projecting gateway, commanded by turrets, has a most imposing aspect. The original fabric was constructed by Sir Robert Lumley, in the reign of Edward I.

1 m. n. Babuston. 2 m. n.w. Great Husworth. 5 m. w. Birtly, where there is a brine spring, from which salt is made.

275¼ m. Belmont Station.

◁ Durham Br.

276¾ m. Leamside Station.*

279 m. Fence-houses Sta.

281 m. Pain-shaw Sta.

Stanhope and Tyne Branch.

282 m. Washington Sta.

286¼ m. Bolden Station.

five lepers. It is yet in being, having been incorporated by Queen Elizabeth for a master and thirty brethren, and is still subject to the regulations then adopted. The Bishop of Durham appoints the master, who must be in holy orders, and of the degree of M.A. at least; the master nominates the brethren, who each receive a handsome yearly stipend, besides being comfortably clothed, lodged, and fed. At present this is one of the most richly endowed charitable foundations in the north of England. Its income amounts to several thousand pounds per annum. The hospital was enlarged in 1819, by fifteen additional lodging-houses for the accommodation of as many out-brethren, before which period there were only fifteen inmates. The building, to which is attached a chapel and apartments for the master, is of a quadrangular form, situated in an agreeable vale on the east side of Sherburn Water.

275¼ m. BELMONT STATION.	E. Belmont House, J. Pemberton, Esq. 2 m. E. Elmore House, G. Baker, Esq.
276¾ m. LEAMSIDE STATION.	S.E. PITTINGTON. Coal and limestone abound in this parish.
279 m. FENCE-HOUSES STA.	1 m. E. MORTON.
281 m. PAIN-SHAW STA.	PAINSHAW, a chapelry, county of Durham, in the parish of Houghton-le-Spring. Here are quarries of limestone and freestone. 4 m. N.W.

South Shields Branch. ☞

HIGH BARNES, ANTHONY ETTRICK, ESQ.

282 m. WASH-INGTON STA.	WASHINGTON. Area of parish, 5,130 A. The population are principally employed in the coal mines.
286½ m. BOLDEN STATION.	4 m. W. BOLDEN, lies in the Chester Ward, county of Durham. Area of parish, 4,760 A. The manor belongs to the Bishop of Durham, and
Brandon Ju. ☞	consists of two townships, East and West Bolden.

1 m. w. Usworth Place, Captain Shaw. 2 m. further, Usworth Hall, Mrs. Perith.

287¾ m. BROCK-
LEY WHINS STA.

1 m. s.w. Redhugh, George Hawkes, Esq. 1 m. further, Dunston Hill, Mrs. Carr; and 2 m. s. Ravensworth Castle. It is situated near the river Team, from which the ground rises considerably. The present mansion occupies part of the site of an ancient castle; two of the towers are built up in the offices, but the rest are partly in ruins, and covered with ivy. The origin of this fortress is supposed to be Danish. On the north and west the mansion is sheltered by a fine forest of oaks.

293 m. GATES-
HEAD STA.

Carlisle and New-
castle Rail.

Cross the Tyne.

Enter
Northumberland.

NEWCASTLE-UPON-TYNE, a parliamentary and municipal borough town, and river port, capital of the county of Northumberland, and a county of itself, is situated on the north bank of the Tyne, communicating with Gateshead by a bridge of nine arches. Area of town county, 2,000 A.; population of parliamentary borough, 69,430. It sends two members to Parliament. Registered electors (1848), 5,041. This very ancient and interesting town stands on steep declivities, rising from the vicinity of the river, and although, until within the last fifty years, it consisted principally of narrow streets and ill-built houses, it has now become one of the handsomest provincial towns in the kingdom. These great improvements owe their origin to the praiseworthy energy and enterprise of Mr. Grainger, a builder, and a native of the town; and it is said that their execution was effected at the cost of nearly £2,000,000 sterling. In our necessarily brief account of this place, it is almost impossible to do justice to the many noble and striking public edifices it contains, but we may cite the following as especially worthy of notice: The public market, containing an area of three acres; the new exchange, with its three beautiful Corinthian fronts; theatre, new music hall, the arcade, a Corinthian edifice, occupied by public offices, banks, &c.; the moot hall, or assize court for the county of Northumberland, on the model of the Temple of Theseus, at Athens; the guildhall and old exchange, mansion house, custom house, town gaol, police office, Pandon Dean Bridge, over a deep glen; the public baths, assembly rooms, racquet court, and large barracks. The above are the principal edifices, to which we may add the splendid column at the top of Grey Street, 136 feet high, supporting a statue of the late Earl Grey, by Bailey. Of the churches, we may name St. Nicholas, which has a steeple 201 feet high, St. Andrew's, St. John's,

297¾ m. NEWCAS-
TLE STA.

1 m. w. Elswick House, John Hinde Hodgson, Esq. 1 m. N.W. Evenham Hall. About 1½ m. further, Newbiggin House.

1 m. w. Gosforth House, Thomas Smith, Esq. The mansion, erected from the designs of Paine, is a handsome edifice, and the grounds beautifully disposed, being encompassed by a broad girdle of wood, the uniformity being broken by plantations and sheets of water. Low Gosford, George Fenwicke, Esq. 2 m. further w. Woolsington House, Matthew Bell, Esq. M.P. 2 m. N. Seaton Bourne House, Rev. R. H. Brandling. 2 m. w. Blagdon Park, Sir Matthew W. Ridley, Bart. 3 m. further, Kirkley Hall, Rev. John Savile Ogle. The mansion is a very handsome square building, with wings; the landscape to the east is extensive and good. 3 m. further, Belsay Castle, Sir Charles M. L. Monck, Bart., is one of the old border towers of Northumberland, which has always been maintained as a family residence, and is in a fine state of preservation. It is conjectured, from the style of the masonry, that it was built in the reign of King Richard II. The walls at the bottom of the castle are ten feet

302¾ m. KILLING-
WORTH STA.

306¾ m. CRAM-
LINGTON STA.

287¼ m. BROCK-LEY WHINS STA.	2 m. N.W. Hebburn Hall, C. Ellison, Esq.
293¾ m. GATES-HEAD STA.	GATESHEAD, a parliamentary and municipal borough and parish, county of Durham, on the south bank of the Tyne, opposite Newcastle, with which it communicates by a handsome bridge of nine arches. Area of parish, 3,320 A.; population, 19,505, employed in glass, iron, and coal works. It sends one member to Parliament. Registered electors (1848),
Cross the Tyne.	622; corporate revenue (1847), £1,298. It is the head of a poor-law union. It is a very dirty town, inhabited chiefly by artizans and pitmen.
Enter Northumberland.	The church is an ancient and handsome structure; and here is a hospital for poor brethren, refounded by James I.; revenue (1836), £525. Gateshead is connected by railway with Carlisle, South Shields, Sunderland, and Durham. GATESHEAD FELL, an adjoining parish, is famous for grindstones, which are exported to all parts of the globe.
297¼ m. NEWCAS-TLE STA.	and All Saints, with a spire 202 feet in height. There are also many other handsome chapels and places of worship for Dissenters of all denominations. Newcastle contains the following institutions: literary and philosophical, natural history, antiquarian, law, medical and botanical societies. It is the seat of one of the provincial medical schools of England, and has a trinity house, a royal grammar school, and many other places of education, a large infirmary, lunatic asylum, dispensary, lying-in hospital, and numerous other well-endowed charities. Quarter and petty sessions, mayor's sheriffs', and river courts, and the assizes and quarter sessions for Northumberland are held here. Corporate revenue (1848), £62,491; customs' revenue (1847), £483,760; registered shipping of port (1847), 314,700 tons. It communicates with all the northern ports of England by large steamers, and by railway with all parts of the kingdom. Newcastle is the principal centre of the English coal trade; within a radius of eight miles fifty coal pits are wrought; and in the year 1840, its trade in this article alone employed 1,327 vessels, manned by 13,548 sailors. The principal manufactures of this town are steam and other machinery, bottle and window-glass, iron wares, sheet lead, chemical products, leather, soap, ship and boat-building, rope and sail-making, malting, brewing, &c; and among the exports are metal from the Stanhope mine, bricks, tar, and grindstones. Newcastle derives its name from its ancient castle, founded by Robert of Normandy; and Leland tells us that in his time it was the best defended and strongest town in England. The wall of Hadrian passed through the site of the town, and some of its towers now remaining are used as halls of the corporate trades. The museum at Newcastle contains a splendid collection of Roman and other antiquities.
	1 m. s. Saltwell House, Charles Bulmer, Esq. 2 m. w. Jesmond, Richard B. Sanderson, Esq. A neat mansion, built by the present proprietor in the decorated or perpendicular style of architecture. Jesmond Dean, Joseph Hawkes, Esq.
302¼ m. KILLING-WORTH STA.	KILLINGWORTH, on Killingworth Moor. Newcastle races were held here until 1790, when it was enclosed for cultivation. 2 m. E. Earsden, Thomas Purvis, Esq.
306¾ m. CRAM-LINGTON STA.	CRAMLINGTON, a chapelry, in the parish of St. Andrew's, county of Northumberland. 1½ m. N. Hartford House, — Burdon, Esq. It is well situated on the wooded declivities of the Blyth, which in this neighbourhood affords very excellent landscapes. This manor paid fivepence one farthing as heriot to the abbots of St. Alban's. 3 m. further E. BLYTH, a sea-port town. Population, 1,921. The town is situated at the mouth of the river Blyth, where it empties itself into the German Ocean, and until late years consisted of a few irregular and narrow-formed streets. The port consists

thick, and the apartments vaulted. It was here that the cattle were secured at night against the incursions of the moss-troopers. Within is a deep well. The castle is a most interesting fabric, its strength and venerable appearance recalling vividly to the imagination the verses of yore, so powerfully described by the pen of the immortal Scott. Belsay has been the residence of the Middleton family from the earliest notice of the place in any existing record. In the reign of Edward III. it was forfeited by the rebellion of John de Middleton, but returned to the family in the 14th of Richard II., and has continued in it down to the present proprietor, who has assumed the name of Monck. The new family mansion stands at a short distance from the castle. The grounds are picturesque, and the situation extremely pleasant. 1½ m. N.W. of which, is Capheaton Castle, Sir John E. Swinburne, Bart. The present mansion was built by Robert Trollope, architect of the old exchange at Newcastle, and was constructed on the site, and from the materials of the ancient Castle of Swinburnes (mentioned by Leland, temp. Henry VIII.), and completed in 1668. Three of the fronts are in their original state, but considerable additions have been made to the house since that period. The apartments are spacious, the library being 56 feet long, and the house is well-sheltered by thriving woods and plantations; the walks, pleasure-grounds, and gardens, are extensive, and are ornamented with a noble sheet of water, containing an area of upwards of 80 acres. This property has been in the uninterrupted possession of the ancient family of Swinburne for nearly 600 years. Many Roman coins and vessels of silver have been discovered at this seat, some of which are in the present baronet's possession. 3 m. from which, are Denham Hall; North Denham Hall; Kirke Hall, Sir William Loraine, Bart.; Wallington Hall, Sir Walter Trevelyan, Bart. 2 m. N. of Belsay, is Bolam Hall, Lord Decies.

Cross River Blyth.

310¾ m. NETHER-TON STA.

MORPETH. A parish, and municipal borough town, in the county of Northumberland, on the Wansbeck, here crossed by three bridges. Area of parish, 7,600 A.; population, 4,237; population of parliamentary borough, 7,160; corporation revenue (1848), £1,195. It returns one member to Parliament. Registered electors (1848), 428. The town is surrounded by finely-wooded hills, and has a handsome town hall, and a grammar school, founded by Edward VI.: annual revenue, £220. Here is held one of the largest cattle markets in England, and among its institutions are several branch banks, mechanics' institute, and subscription library. The town was burnt down in 1215, by its inhabitants, to prevent its furnishing quarters to King John. 2½ m. w. Mitford Castle, Mrs. Osbaldeston Mitford, near which is the ruins of the ancient castle, which was burnt down in 1215, by King John and his ruters, a band of Flemish troops, when they so miserably wasted this country. 2 m. w. of which is Meldon Park, Isaac Cookson, Esq. 3 m. N.W. Netherwhitton House, Thornton Trevelyan, Esq. 1½ m. further, Rothley Park; near which is Rothley Castle, which from many points of view has the appearance of a seat of some ancient baron. It was built in the last century by Sir W. Blackett. 1 mile N.E. from Longwhitton is Stanton Park; close to which is Combe Hill.

313¼ m. MORPETH STATION.

LONGHURST. ½ m. w. Longhirst House, William Lawson, Esq.

317 m. LONG-HURST STA.

Cross Line Water.

3 m. w. Cawsay Park, W. W. Ogle, Esq. 2 m. further Todburn Park. 1 m. N. of which is Lindon, C. W. Bigge, Esq. 1 m. N. Weldon Hall; near which is Brinckbourne Priory, Hodgson Cadogan, Esq.

320¼ m. WID-DRINGTON STA.

ACKLINGTON, 1 m. N.W. Bank House. 1½ m. w. Acton House, John H. Hodgson, Esq. 1 m. further, Swarland House. 1 m. N. of which is Newton Hall, Henry Reyeley Mitford Esq. 9 m. w. ROTHBURY, a

325½ m. ACKLING-TON STA.

Cross the Coquet River.

Cross River Blyth.	principally in the exportation of coal. The yearly rent for anchorage here, at 4*d.* per ship, in 1346, was only 3*s.* 4*d.*; however during the siege of Newcastle, in 1644, the coal trade flourished greatly, but subsequently experienced great depression; it was again revived, and now furnishes occupation to nearly 100 vessels, of the aggregate burthen of upwards of 15,000 tons. The produce of the Beddington Iron Works, which are about three miles distant, are brought down the river Blyth for shipment for London. The harbour, which is free at all times from obstruction, is secure even during the most tempestuous weather. There is a dry dock, capable of receiving four vessels, and a branch custom house connected with the establishment at Newcastle. The circular stone lighthouse was built by Sir Matthew White Ridley, Bart., in 1788; and there is a beacon light, called the Basket Rock Light. Cowpen Hall, M. J. Sidney, Esq. To the north, between the Blyth and Wansbeck, is BEDLINGTON, a parish in Chester Ward. It was a royal franchise under the bishops of Durham, and enjoyed its own courts and officers, till it was stripped of those privileges by Henry VIII.; in all civil matters it is a member of the county of Durham. The monks of Durham, in their flight to Lindisfarne before the arms of the Conqueror, with the incorruptible body of St. Cuthbert, rested all night here. The ancient church enjoyed many privileges, and the purchasers of the lands after the Restoration, offered the King a large sum to confirm their rights for ninety-nine years; but instead of accepting it, he granted a commission of inquiry after all such purchases.
310¾ m. NETHER-TON STA.	
313½ m. MORPETH STATION.	1½ m. E. BOTHALL, where there are the ruins of a castle, the property of the Duke of Portland. The castle was built by Sir Robert Bertram, in the reign of Edward III., and is noted thus in the "Bothool Baronry" of 1576: "To this manor of Bothoole belongeth ane castell, great chaulmer, pailer, vij, bed-chaulmers, one galare, butterie, pantrie, lardenor, kitchinge, an court, called the Yethouse, wharin there is a prison, a porter-lodge, and a toure called Banke Toure, a gardine, a nurice chapel, and an towre, called Ogle's Towre, and pastrie, with many other prettie beauldings here not specificde, fair gardings and orchetts, wharin growes all kind of hearbes and flowres, and fine appiles, plumbes, peers, damselles, nuttes, cherries, to the black and reede, and also licories verie fyne, worth by the year, xxi." Of all these, only the gateway remains, and the outer walls, sadly shattered, and enclosing about two roods of land, scattered with fragments of buildings. The gateway is flanked on the north by two polygonal towers, fifty-three feet high, and on the south-west angle by a square turret, sixty feet high. The site of these ruins occupy a fine natural eminence in the midst of a deep valley, and washed on the south by the Wansbeck. The wood scene is picturesque. At a short distance east from the castle is the church, which contains a curious tomb in memory of the Ogles, made of alabaster.
317 m. LONG-HURST STA.	4 m. E. WOODHORN.
Cross Line Water.	
320¼ m. WID-DRINGTON STA.	1 m. N.E. WIDDRINGTON. A parochial chapelry, county Northumberland. Area, 4,510 A. Widdrington Castle, late Lord Bulkeley. 2 m. S.E. Cresswell House, Addison John Baker Cresswell, Esq.
325½ m. ACKLING-TON STA. Cross the Coquet River.	1½ m. E. HOGSTONE. 2 m. S.E. mouth of the river Coquet, which rises among the Cheviot Hills, pursues an eastward course by Hallington, Rothbury, and Felton, to Warkworth, immediately below which it falls into the sea.

market town and parish in thewestern division of Coquet Dale. On a brow of a hill on the south side of the river Coquet is Whitton Tower, formerly the seat of the Umfrayvills.

3 m. N.W. SHILBOTTLE. A parish in the eastern division of Coquet Dale Ward, county Northumberland. Coal of a superior quality is obtained here. 4 m. further EDLINGHAM, where there are the remains of an ancient castle built about the time of Henry II. It was the seat and manor of Sir Roger de Hastings, Knt., who bore a captain's commission in the expedition against the Moors in 1509. In the 10th of Elizabeth, it belonged to Thomas Swinburne, Esq., but heirs male failing in the reign of Charles I., it went by inheritance to the Swinburnes of Capheaton. The castle stands near the head of a narrow valley, and consists chiefly of one grey venerable tower.

About a mile before reaching Lisbury, the next station on the direct line, is a short one of 2½ miles to ALNWICK, which is situated on the irregular declivity of an eminence arising from the river Alne, over which at the north extremity of the town, is a neat stone bridge of three arches ; the streets are spacious, well paved, and lighted with gas ; the houses, chiefly built of stone, are modern, and many of them elegant. The history of the town is so connected with that of the castle, that we need not refer to it. Market-day, Saturday ; fairs, 12th of May, last Monday in July, first Tuesday in October, 28th of the same month, and the last Saturday before Christmas Day. Just through the town to the north-west is Hulne Abbey, the Duke of Northumberland. It stands in a woody and delightful solitude in Hulne Park. It was founded by Ralph Freeburn, a Northumberland gentleman, who had done good service in the holy wars in 1240. The outer walls and gateways are still entire, but the chapels, oratories, and offices are greatly dilapidated. The most perfect part of it is a noble tower, which was fitted up during the last century in the Gothic style. 4 m. from whence Eglingham Park, Robert Ogle, Esq. ; Roddam Hall, William Roddam, Esq. 3 m. w. Lemington Hall, John Allan Wickey, Esq. 1 m further, Broome Park, William Burrell, Esq. 1 m. further, Thrunton Craggs. 1 m. further, Callaly Castle, E. J. Clavering, Esq., formerly the seat of William de Callaly, who held it and Yetlington by drendage and other services of Henry III., from whom they descended soon after the death of Henry to an ancestor of the present possessor. The tower at the west end of this mansion has marks of high antiquity ; that in the east and the centre of the building are modern. The dining-room is 45 feet long and 25 feet high, elegantly stuccoed, and has a music gallery at each end. A range of high, rough hills, planted up their sides, and brown and craggy at their heads, sweep before the southern front at the distance of half a mile. Near Callaly is a conical hill, called Castle Hill, its top comprising about two acres, is girt by a high wall, and in the weakest place by a fosse seven yards deep, hewn out of the solid rock, and flanked on the outside with a wall. Down the western brow of the hill, about 100 paces, is another strong wall, its ruins measuring seven and a half yards at their base. The whole fortified area contains nearly six acres, and is difficult of access. There are several other ancient camps in this neighbourhood. Glanton Pike is also a conical exploratory hill; and near it, at Dear Street, beside Glanton Westfield, were found, in 1716, four "Restavens," one empty, the other containing each an urn filled with fine earth, charcoal, and human bones, bearing marks of fire; also near them two more urns of ordinary pottery. ¼ m. N. of Glanton Westfield, a "celt" of the old mixed brass, well preserved, was turned up. By the side of the highway, over Hedgley Moor, is a square stone pillar, called Percy Cross, embossed with the arms of Percy and Lacy, and set up in memory of Sir Ralph Percy, who was slain here by Lord Montacute in a severe skirmish, in 1463, before the battle of Hexham. Near which are Dancing Hall, and Collingwood House.

328¼ m. WARKWORTH STA.

Cross River Alne.

334½ m. ALNWICK STATION.

328¾ m. WARK-
WORTH STA.

Cross River Alne.

WARKWORTH. A parish and village, county Northumberland, on the Coquet, which nearly surrounds it; one mile from the North Sea, and here crossed by a stone bridge. Area of parish, 15,110 A. On the south bank of the Coquet, Warkworth Castle, Duke of Northumberland. It is in a very decayed state, but commands a splendid view. About one mile beyond, on the beautifully wooded bank of the Coquet, stands Warkworth Hermitage.

334¾ m. ALNWICK
STATION.

Alnwick Castle, the Duke of Northumberland. This splendid pile, the outer walls of which enclose an area of five acres, stands on an eminence on the south bank of the river Alne, which in its circuitous course washes the beautiful lawns that surround the castle. It is believed that Alnwick Castle was founded by the Romans, the foundations of the buildings, with Roman mouldings, having been discovered when a part of the keep was taken down for repairs. The fretwork round the arch leading to the inner court is evidently of Saxon architecture, but under the Flag Tower was a more ancient gateway, that had been walled up, directly fronting the present outward gateway into the town. The walls of the castle are flanked by sixteen massy towers. It has three courts or wards. The inner court is entered by a gateway of great antiquity, flanked by two octagonal towers,

ALNWICK CASTLE, DUKE OF NORTHUMBERLAND.

ornamented with armorial escutcheons; erected about 1350. From the inner court in the centre of the citadel is a staircase of singular form, expanding like a fan, the roof enriched with a series of one hundred and twenty shields, with the quarterings and alliances of the Percy family. The apartments are magnificent, both as to proportion and decoration. This castle underwent a memorable siege in 1093 from Malcolm III. of Scotland, who, with his eldest son, Prince Edward, were slain before its walls. This event was commemorated by a cross erected on the spot where the King fell, which was restored by the Duchess of Northumberland in 1771. In the year 1174, William III., King of Scotland, was taken prisoner here during a siege, which is also commemorated by a monument, with this inscription: "William the Lion, King of Scotland, besieging Alnwick Castle, was here taken prisoner, 1174."

1 m. N. RENINGTON. A chapelry in the parish of Hemblington, the southern division of Bamborough ward, county Northumberland. The living is a perpetual curacy, united with that of Rock, in the archdeaconry of Northumberland, and diocese of Durham, endowed with £400 benefactions, and £800 royal bounty. The chapel, dedicated to All Saints, is very ancient. Rock Castle, C. Bosanquet, Esq.

334¼ m. LONG HOUGHTON STA.

1½ m. w. Charlton Hall, John Cay, Esq.

339¾ m. CHRISTON BANK STA.

½ m. Ellingham Hall, Sir Edward Haggerstone, Bart. 6 m. further, Chillingham Castle, Earl of Tankerville. In Chillingham Park is a breed of wild cattle, the only one in the island. In Hepburn Wood are the remains of an ancient keep, a strong, vaulted building, similar to many others in the northern counties. 2 m. w. Lilburn Tower, Edward John Collingwood, Esq.

342¾ m. CHATHILL STATION.

SUCKER. A chapelry, parish Bamburgh, county Northumberland. 2 m. s.w. Twizell House, Prideaux John Selby, Esq. 5 m. further, New Hall. 2 m. further, WOOLLER. This place occupies the eastern declivity of the Cheviot Hills, and near it is the village of HEMBLEDON, celebrated for the memorable victory gained by Percy, Earl of Northumberland, in the reign of Henry IV., over a Scottish army of ten thousand men, under the Earl of Douglas. The engagement took place on a plain 1 m. N.w. of the town, where a stone pillar has been erected, commemorative of the event. At Wooller are Wooller Cottage, Mrs. Silvertop; Ewart Park, Sir Horace St. Paul, Bart.; Weetwood Hall, Rev. Leonard Shafto Orde. About 3 m. N.w. of Ewart Park is Flodden Field, celebrated for the victory gained over the Scots by the Earl of Surrey, 9th of February, 1513, the loss of the vanquished being twelve thousand men, including their King, James IV., and the flower of the nobility; that of the English only fifteen hundred. On the highest part of the Flodden Hill is a natural rock called the King's Chair, on account of James having made it his post of observation during the battle.

346 m. SUCKER STATION.

BELFORD. A market town and parish in the counties Northumberland and Durham. Area of parish, 9,380 A. The town, which is within two miles of the sea, is beautifully situated, and contains an extensive corn-market on Thursdays, and has a church, Dissenting chapels, and daily schools. Fairs, Tuesday before Whit-Sunday, and 23rd of August. 1 m. N.w. Middleton Hall, Stephen Fryer Gillum, Esq. 9 m. w. Earle Hall, Charles Selby, Esq.

348¼ m. BELFORD STATION.

Fenham Flats.

1 m. N.w. Haggerstone House, Sir Edward Blount, Bart. 2 m. further, Cheswick House, John Strangways Donaldson Selby, Esq. 3½ m. N.w. Barmoor Castle, Frank Sitwell, Esq. 3 m. further, Ford Castle, Marquis of Waterford. 1 m. N. of which Etal, Earl of Glasgow. 1½ m. w. Pallinsburn Hall, G. Askew, Esq.

355¼ m. BEAL STATION.

360¼ m. SCREMERSTON STA.

5 m. s.w. Norham Castle, John Hodgson Hinde, Esq. The castle stood on a high rock on the brink of the Tweed in 1121, but in 1138 the Scots, under King David, destroyed it. It was soon after rebuilt, particularly the great tower, which is still standing. In 1216 Alexander II., after investing it forty days with a mighty army, was obliged to raise the siege.

362½ m. TWEEDMOUTH STA.

Cross the Tweed.

334½ m. LONG HOUGHTON STA.	LONG HOUGHTON. A parish, county Northumberland. Area, 3,990 A. It has lead and coal mines. It is 3½ miles E.N.E. Alnwick. 1 m. N. Howick Castle, Earl Grey. This once ancient castle was taken down in 1787, when the present noble structure was commenced. It stands within a mile of the sea. Close to which is Cra'ster Tower, Thomas Wood Cra'ster, Esq.
339½ m. CHRISTON BANK STA.	2 m. E., on the sea coast, the ruins of Dunstonbrugh Castle, which was destroyed shortly after the battle of Hexham by Lords Wenlock and Hastings.
342¾ m. CHATHILL STATION.	CHATHILL. 3 m. N.E. BEADNELL, a chapelry in the parish of Bamburgh, county Northumberland. The village is pleasantly situated on the sea-shore, having a small harbour, and several vessels are employed in conveying lobsters, herrings, and other fish to London. Races were annually held here until 1826, when they were removed to Belford.
346 m. SUCKER STATION.	3 m. S.E. Bamburgh Castle. It stands upon a basalt rock of a triangular shape, accessible only to an enemy on the S.E., which is guarded by a deep, dry ditch, and a series of towers on the wall. Its crown is girt with walls and towers, which, on the land side, have been repaired; those on the E. are still ruinous. On a lofty point of the rock is a very ancient tower, which from its appearance challenges Saxon origin. The keep stands on the area of the rock, and is of that kind of building which prevailed at the Conquest. Within it is a draw-well, discovered in 1770, of the depth of one hundred and forty-five feet, cut through solid rock, of which seventy-five feet is whinstone. The remains of the chapel were found under a prodigious mass of land in 1773. The chancel is separated from the nave, and is thirty-six feet by twenty, and, after the Saxon fashion, semi-circular at the east end. The ancient font was discovered, and is preserved in the keep, and the altar has a passage round it. That it is one of the oldest castles in England may be inferred from the fact that Penda the Mercian besieged it in 672, and attempted to burn it. In 705 in was again besieged under Birthric, and nearly destroyed by the Danes in 993, but at the time of the Conquest was in good repair. It has subsequently undergone several sieges, but lost the greatest part of its beauty in a siege after the battle of Hexham. From that period it has suffered much by time and winds, but in 1757 it was repaired by Archdeacon Sharpe. Much since then has, however, been done, and it is matter of high gratification to see it now converted into apartments for the most wise and benevolent purposes.
348¼ m. BELFORD STATION.	EASINGTON, at which there is a church of very ancient structure, and fine architecture. 2 m. from the coast is Holy Island. Though situated in Northumberland, and only ten miles from Berwick-on-Tweed, it is a parish in Highlandshire, county Durham. In 941 it was invaded and plundered by Malcolm I., King of Scotland. In the great civil war it was a station and parliamentary garrison, and in 1715 it was seized by the adherents of the Pretender, who were, however, soon dislodged by detachments of the King's troops from Berwick.
Fenham Flats.	
355¼ m. BEAL STATION.	Haggerstone Castle, Lady Stanley; a modern house, built about sixty years since on the old Castle of Haggerstone. 1½ m. N. GOSWICK, a hamlet in the parish of Holy Island. This place, lying contiguous to a small bay of the North Sea, occupies the entrance to the main land between the sea and Holy Island.
360¼ m. SCRE-MERSTON STA.	
362½ m. TWEED-MOUTH STA.	TWEEDMOUTH, a parish and village, county Durham, opposite Berwick, on the right bank of the Tweed. It forms a handsome suburb to Berwick, joined to it by a stone bridge. Area, 4,520 A. It contains a Gothic church, iron foundry, and an extensive salmon fishery.
Cross the Tweed.	

North British Railway.

Left of Railway from London.	*Distance from London.*
BERWICK-ON-TWEED is a municipal and parliamentary borough, and sea-port town, county Northumberland, on the north bank of the Tweed, at its mouth. Area of parish, 5,120 A.; population of parish, 8,484; and of parliamentary borough, 12,578. It sends two members to Parliament. Registered electors (1846), 888; corporation revenue (1847), £11,364, arising from fisheries, lands, &c.; customs' revenue (1846), £15,728 14s.; registered shipping of port (1847), 4,584 tons. The aggregate burden of vessels entering and clearing out of the port has been for some years about 50,000 tons. The ancient town of Berwick is surrounded by fortifications, and, until the Reform Act, it was a free town, independent of both Scotland and England. It is now, however, an English county, for all purposes except Parliamentary elections. It is connected with Spittal and Tweedmouth, its suburbs, by a splendid old bridge of fifteen arches, erected temp. Charles I. There is also a remarkably fine bridge or viaduct over the river,	363¾ m. BERWICK STATION.
	369¾ m. BURN-MOUTH STA.
AYTON, county Berwick. A parish of Scotland, on the Ayr. Here are some traces of ancient camps.	371¼ m. AYTON STATION.
	⟨⟩ Dunse Br.
RESTON.	375¼ m. RESTON STATION.
	380¼ m. GRANT'S HOUSE STA.
OLD LAMSTORK, a maritime parish, counties Haddington and Berwick. Population, 604, of whom 138 are in the village, partly employed in the coal trade.	384¼ m. COCK-BURN'S-PATH STA.
STENTRID, a parish, county Haddington.	388¼ m. INNER-WICK STA.
DUNBAR, a royal, parliamentary, municipal borough, sea-port town, and parish, county Haddington, situated on an eminence at the mouth of the Frith of Forth. Population of parish, 4,471; population of town, 3,013; population of parliamentary borough, 2,978. In conjunction with North Berwick, Haddington, Lauder, and Jedburgh, it sends one member to Parliament. Registered electors (1848), 149; corporation revenue (1844), £1,662. Dunbar is well built, and possesses many good modern residences, and a new Gothic parish church, an ancient town hall, fine assembly rooms,	392¾ m. DUNBAR STATION.
LINTON, EAST, a village in the parish of Prestonkirk, county Haddington, situated on the river Tyne.	398¼ m. LINTON STATION.
	400¼ m. EAST FORTUNE STA.
HADDINGTON. A very ancient royal borough, its charter being dated 1624. King Alexander II. was born here, and the famous Reformer, John Knox, is believed to have been a native of this town.	404¼ m. DREM STATION.
	⟨⟩ Haddington Branch.
GLADSMUIR. The battle of Gladsmuir, better known as that of Prestonpans, was partly fought in this parish.	408¼ m. LONG NIDDRY STA.
TRANENT. A small town, county Haddington.	411¾ m. TRANENT STATION.

North British Railway.

Distance from London.

Right of Railway from London.

363¾ m. BERWICK STATION.

built for the North British Railway. The harbour of Berwick is sheltered by a pier of considerable extent. Among its principal structures we may cite a Gothic church of the 17th century, several Dissenting chapels, town hall, with an exchange and gaol attached, a governor's residence, pauper lunatic asylum, theatre, grammar and free schools, assembly rooms, public library, and infantry barracks. Manufactures of sail-cloth, cordage, and linen fabrics are here carried on, as well as a considerable iron foundry, in which steam-engine and mill machinery are made, and in the vicinity are several coal mines. Berwick has a good trade with Norway and the Baltic, from whence it imports timber, iron, stones, bones, hemp, cotton, and oil; and exports to London, &c., agricultural produce, coal, ale, wool, whiskey, and fish, particularly salmon—of which its fishery in the Tweed is still very productive. Races in July; markets, Wednesday and Saturday; fair, Friday in Trinity Week.

369¾ m. BURNMOUTH STA.

371¼ m. AYTON STATION.

HIGHMOUTH, a sea-port, where there is a good fishery, a fine bay, and an excellent harbour.

375¼ m. RESTON STATION.

380¼ m. GRANT'S HOUSE STA.

384¾ m. COCKBURN'S-PATH STA

COCKBURN'S-PATH, or COLBMAND'S-PATH, a parish of Scotland, county Berwick, in the vicinity of the North Sea. Here are remains of ancient forts, and Roman as well as Scottish antiquities. The district towards the south is very mountainous.

388¼ m. INNERWICK STA.

INNERWICK, or INVERWICK, county Haddington.

392¾ m. DUNBAR STATION.

several public libraries, docks for ship-building, iron foundries, and factories for sail-cloths, cordage, &c., and some breweries, distilleries, &c. The picturesque ruins of its celebrated castle have an imposing aspect at sea. The harbour is accessible to vessels of three hundred tons, although the entrance is rendered difficult by the rocks which abound here. Its imports are coal and foreign grain; exports, whiskey, corn, and fish, for London. Market, Tuesday.

398¼ m. LINTON STATION.

WHITEKIRK AND TYRMINGHAME, a united parish of Scotland. Population, 1,170. Near here are Whitekirk House, and Tyrminghame House.

400¾ m. EAST FORTUNE STA.

North Berwick Branch ☞

404¼ m. DREM STATION.

ABERLADY, a village on the Frith of Forth. At spring-tides vessels of seventy tons reach its small bay, which forms the port of Haddington.

408¼ m. LONG NIDDRY STA.

LONG NIDDRY, a village, county Haddington, remarkable only for its antiquity, and general aspect of decay.

411¾ TRANENT STATION.

Dalkeith Castle, the seat of the Duke of Buccleuch.	415¼ m. INVERESK STATION.
DUDDINGSTON. A parish, county Edinburgh, on the Frith of Forth, and comprising the borough of Portobello, and the villages Loppa and Duddingston, with a beautiful demesne of the Marquis of Abercorn. The church is Saxon, and beautifully situated on the borders of Doddington Lock, which skirts the base of Arthur's Seat. There is an ancient causeway between the village and Portobello.	418¾ m. PORTO-BELLO STA.
	421¾ m. EDIN-BURGH STA.

Peterborough, Boston, and Lincoln.

On this very important branch of the Great Northern Line, which traverses a perfectly level country, the works are confined principally to embankments, and the necessary bridges for passing the rivers, streams, and canals with which the district abounds, and to such works as were requisite for securing the proper foundations of the line in a wet and fenny country. The bridges between the Loop Junction (about three miles from Peterborough) and Gainsborough, number twenty-five, twelve of which carry roads over the railway, and thirteen by which the railway is carried over roads; to these may be added forty-three viaducts over rivers and streams, making a total of sixty-eight. All these works are constructed principally of timber. The most remarkable on the line are the Boston and Bardney Bridges, and the Longwood Viaduct. Boston Bridge is five hundred and seventy-two yards in length, crossing the river Witham; and the openings, including those on land, amount to seventy-eight, rising about thirty feet above the surface of the water.

Left of Railway from London.

Distance from London.

Great Northern Line.

2½ m. N.W. MARKET DEEPING, a market town, in the county of Lincoln. This county was the scene of many sanguinary conflicts at a very early date. Of the Anglo-Saxon kingdom of Mercia, this shire formed an important part, the northern portion being wrested from that kingdom by Edwin, of Northumbria. In 827, at Caistor, Egbert, King of Wessex, defeated Wiglaf, King of Mercia; and this part of the English territory being exposed by its locality to the incursions and ravages of the Danes, their sanguinary assaults was wreaked upon it with especial fury and violence. Early in the year 870 they destroyed the monastery of Bardney, and devastated the country all round with fire and sword. The latter end of the same year, Algar, Earl of Mercia, gave the Pagans battle, and routed them with great slaughter and the death of three of their kings. In 1174, Roger de Mowbray, an adherent of Prince Henry, in his rebellion against his father, Henry II., for a considerable time maintained an obstinate defence in the Isle of Axholme; and this isle, in the reign of Henry III., afforded a retreat to many of the disaffected nobles after the battle of Evesham. During the Civil War this county was the theatre of considerable military transactions. Grantham, Ancaster, Gainsborough, and Horncastle were, in 1643, respectively the scenes of slaughter; and in May, 1644, the Earl of Manchester stormed Lincoln, and captured its governor, Colonel Fane, with about 800 men. Market Deeping derives its name from the lowness of the land. The manor of Deeping was granted to the Abbey of Croyland in the time of the Saxons, and the grant confirmed by the King of Mercia in 860. Market-day, Thursday.

81¼ m. PEAKIRK, CROWLAND, AND DEEPING STA.

415¼ m. INVERESK STATION.	INVERESK, a village, and maritime parish, in the county of Edinburgh, in which is situated the town of Musselburgh.
418¾ m. PORTO-BELLO STA.	PORTOBELLO lies in a plain on the south shore of the Frith of Forth. It is a very fashionable watering-place for the inhabitants of Edinburgh, and has admirable hot, and other salt-water baths, assembly rooms, &c. It is a parliamentary and municipal borough, and sea-port town, in the county of Edinburgh. With Leith and Musselburgh it unites in returning one member to Parliament. Registered electors (1848), 238. Here is a branch bank, and amongst its factories may be cited glass, lead, mustard, and soap, with potteries and brickworks. The borough was founded in 1762, and is governed by a provost and two bailies.
421¾ m. EDIN-BURGH STA.	

Peterborough, Boston, and Lincoln.

Bardney Bridge, about one mile beyond the Bardney Station, is seven hundred and twenty-nine yards in length, with one hundred and three openings, one of which over the Witham, is of fifty-three feet span on the square, and one hundred on the skew, and twenty-two feet in height from the surface of the river. The line now runs by the side of the river nearly from Lincoln to Boston.

The Longwood Viaduct, near Fiskerton, is three hundred and seventy yards long, and has fifty-six openings, the height of the whole being only twelve feet. All other works upon this line beyond the usual character of railway construction, were rendered necessary by the natural formation of the soil, and the difficulties it presented for the formation of solid foundations: these were all admirably surmounted by the skill and talent of the engineer; but the *modus operandi* would be of no interest to the general or non-professional reader.

Distance from London.	### Right of Railway from London.
	Peterborough (see Great Northern).
81½ m. PEAKIRK, CROWLAND, AND DEEPING STA.	PEAKIRK, a parish, county Northampton; area, 630 A., situated on high ground, at the extremity of the fens of Lincoln. 5 m. N. from which is CROYLAND, or CROWLAND, a market-town, county Lincoln, with an area of 20,070 A. It is a place of great antiquity, as, during the Heptarchy, St. Guthlac, in the reign of Cenred, King of Mercia, took refuge in a hermitage there, and in 716, near the hermitage, Ethelbald founded a Benedictine monastery. This monastery was built upon an artificial foundation, on ground so rotten, "that a man mighte thruste a pole down-right thirty foote deepe." For—

> " Guthlake, the king, his bounty here doth bestow
> On an abbey faire, with much expense to reare,
> But seeing that the waterist fenne below
> These ground-works laid with stones unneath could beare;
> So quavring, softe, and moiste, the bases were.
> He caused piles made of good heart of oake,
> Pitch'd down to be with maine commanders stroke ;
> Then nine leagues off men sand in barges brought,
> Which once fast ramm'd by painfule workman's hand,
> Of rotten earth good solid ground was wrought,
> On which for aye such workes might fairly stande,
> And thus by his devise of new plantation,
> The church stands firme and hath a sure foundation."

This structure was destroyed by the Danes in 870, was rebuilt in 948, and, by an accidental fire, reduced to a heap of ruins in 1091; was again rebuilt in 1112, and, about the year 1150, again partially destroyed by fire;

There are several fairs held here annually, three of which are for the sale of wood only, and the others, seven or eight, for the sale of cattle. From this place to Croyland, and thence to Spalding, " Egelrick, Abbott of Croyland, afterwards Bishop of Durham, made for the ease of travailers through the middest of a vast forest, and of most deepe fennes, a sound causey of wood and sand, and called it after his owne name." The church, dedicated to St. Guthlac, is an ancient structure, containing many portions of its original Norman architecture. The town traces its origin to Richard de Rulos, chamberlain to William the Conqueror. 1½ m. s.w. is WEST DEEPING, in the county of Lincoln. The church is a handsome building of the early English style of architecture. 2 m. s. MAXEY, a parish, county Northampton. The church is a very ancient structure, principally in the Norman style. In this parish are nine bridges, adjoining each other, called Lolham Bridges, which were constructed by the Romans. 2 m. further s. HELPSTONE. In the centre of the village is a very ancient cross, date and origin unknown. The church has traces of the Norman, with insertions of the early English style of architecture. It is the birthplace of the peasant poet Clare.

1 m. s. NORTHBOROUGH. In the church, which is a fine specimen of the Norman style, is a monument, with other memorials to the family of Claypole, one of whom married a daughter of Oliver Cromwell, and was created a baronet in 1657. Their ancient mansion, a beautiful specimen of the decorative style, has been converted into a farm-house. A short distance from Northborough is Woodcroft Castle. Little of the ancient structure now remains.

ST. JAMES DEEPING, a parish, county Lincoln. Shortly after the Conquest, a lofty bank was raised to protect the land from the overflowing of the river Welland, and at one end of the bank is the above parish. *83¼ m. ST. JAMES DEEPING STA.*

LITTLEWORTH, a hamlet of Deeping. A neat church was erected here about the year 1844. *87½ m. LITTLEWORTH AND DEEPING FEN STATION.*

2 m. N. PINCHBECK, where are some considerable remains of an ancient mansion, which formerly bore the name of Pinchbeck Hall, the name of its owner, but having passed into the possession of the Otway family, is now called Otway Hall. It appears to have been originally a large building erected about the time of Henry VIII; it was moated round, and a few of the windows have square lights, with pointed heads; the chimneys are remarkably lofty, and the gable-ends have at the sides and ends many pinnacles, crowned with ornamental balls. In the gardens of this mansion were discovered, in the year 1742, a large brass commodus, on the reverse a woman sitting on a globe, with her right hand extended, and in her left a Victory. Since then several pipes of baked earth have been found here, The estate is the property of Thomas Buckworth, Esq. Pinchbeck House, Captain Browne. *93¾ m. SPALDING STATION.*

SURFLEET, county Lincoln. Area of parish, 3,730 A. Here is a large heronry, one of the few existing in this country. Surfleet House, Mrs. Esdaile. 2 m. N. Cressy House, — Smith, Esq.; close to which is Monk's Hall; a little further, QUADRING; and 1½ m. further, DONINGTON. *96¾ m. SURFLEET STATION.*

SUTTERTON. 1 m. W. WEGTOFT. 2 m. N.W. SWINESHEAD, at which there was an abbey for Cistercian monks, to which King John escaped after the loss of his baggage in crossing the Cross Keys Wash The ruins of the monastery have entirely disappeared, Swineshead Abbey, the seat of H. Ingram, Esq., having been erected by a portion of the materials. *100¼ m. ALGARKIRK STA.*

KIRTON, county Lincoln. Area of parish, 10,550 A. *103¼ m. KIRTON STATION.*

It is traditionally affirmed that large vessels could formerly sail up the river Witham from Boston to Lincoln, which report seems to be corroborated by the fragments of vessels that have frequently been found near its *107 m. BOSTON STATION.*

it was, however, soon restored, and flourished until the dissolution of monasteries, at which time its revenue was £1,217 5s. 11d. During the parliamentary war, it was occupied as a garrison, and, by those ruthless and fanatic emissaries, almost entirely demolished. The remains consist of the western piers, of the eastern portion in the Norman style, and of some of the nave and aisles of the old abbey church, the south piers and arches, and part of the clerosty, also the west front, highly enriched and ornamented with several statues of kings and abbots. The roof of that portion now used as the parish church is finely groined, the windows large, and decorated with elegant tracery. In the interior is a very ancient font, divided into compartments, a cylindrical stoup, some fine screen-work, and several curious ancient monuments. The first tuneable bells hung in England pealed their melody forth from this abbey. Numerous stone coffins, containing bones and various relics, have been dug up from the foundations of this pile, which are traceable to a considerable distance. In the centre of the town is a triangular stone bridge, built about the year 941, and may be regarded as an object of the greatest curiosity in Britain, if not in Europe. The bridge consists of three piers or abutments, whence spring three pointed arches, which unite their groins in the centre. The ascent is very steep, but it is used for foot-passengers only. The market has lately been re-established. The town, instead of being, as formerly, inaccessible, is now approached on all sides by excellent roads, and the drainage so efficient that it almost ceases to be classed with the fens.

83¼ m. ST. JAMES DEEPING STA.

1 m. E. Waldron Hall, now converted into a farm-house. The park and grounds have also been devoted to agricultural purposes.

87¾ m. LITTLE-WORTH AND DEEPING FEN STATION.

DEEPING FEN, part of which is extra-parochial, and part in the parish of Crowland.

93¾ m. SPALDING STATION.

SPALDING, a market-town, county Lincoln; a place of considerable antiquity, as, in the time of the Saxons, a cell was founded here by Therold de Buckenhale. In 1074, the manor of Spalding was given by Jno. Talbois, nephew of the Conqueror, to the abbey of St. Nicholas at Angers, and became an alien priory to that monastery. It subsequently was raised to an abbey, and so continued until the general suppression. A portion of the abbey buildings yet remains, part of which is converted into tenements, and the other is ruins. Many relics of antiquity have been discovered in the neighbourhood. The town is well built, paved, and lighted. The river Welland, which runs through the centre of the town, is navigable for small vessels. Ayscough Fee Hall, Maurice Johnson, Esq. 7 m. E. HOLBEACH. 4½ m. further, SUTTON ST. MARY'S.

96¾ m. SURFLEE? STATION.

FOSDYKE, a parish, county Lincoln. Between this place and Surfleet, and various directions in the immediate neighbourhood, are several Roman embankments.

100¼ m. ALGAR-KIRK STA.

ALGARKIRK is a parish in the county of Lincoln, parts Holland; area, 6,050 A. A curious statue in the churchyard is said to represent Algar, King of Mercia, who, with his gallant stewards, Bybuston and Leofrick, so valiantly opposed the incursions of the Danes, over whom near this place he obtained a decisive victory in 870, but paid for it by his life on the following day.

103¾ m. KIRTON STATION.

1 m. E. at FRAMPTON. Frampton Hall, Charles Keightley Tunnard, Esq.

107 m. BOSTON STATION.

BOSTON, a parliamentary and municipal borough, sea-port, and market-town, county of Lincoln, parts Kesteven, is situated on the river Witham, over which is a handsome iron bridge of one arch, 86 feet span and about

channel: at present, however, the river is navigable as far as Lincoln for small steam-boats. Its current before these improvements was so slow, that the mud accumulated in the channel, and consequently many serious inundations have from time to time taken place. By the roll of the "high fleet" of Edward III., Boston appears to have been then a considerable place, for it furnished a quota of 16 ships to the "maritime militia." Subsequent to that, the town gradually declined in the commercial scale, and about a century ago it sunk so low as nearly to lose the whole of its trade, owing to the navigation of the Witham being choked with silt. The barges, or flat vessels, which required only a small draught of water, could then reach the quays only at high spring-tides. But on cutting a new channel from the town to Dogdyke, an extent of 12 miles, the river was again rendered navigable. Formerly Boston had several religious houses, among which was St. Botolph's Priory, founded, according to Leland, by St. Botolph, in the time of the Saxons, whence the town derived both its origin and its name. Besides which, there was a priory near the sea, dedicated to St. Mary; four friaries of Austin, Black, Grey, and White Friars; and three colleges, dedicated to St. Mary, Corpus Christi, and St. Peter.

113¾ m. LANGRICK STA.

118 m. DOGDYKE STATION.

7 m. s.w. Haverholme Priory, The Earl of Winchilsea. This manor was given by Alexander, Bishop of Lincoln, to the Cistercian monks of Fountains Abbey, Yorkshire, in the year 1137, that they might build an abbey of that order, but after having made some progress in the same, they pretended not to like the situation, and therefore removed to Louth Park; the bishop then gave it to the Order of St. Gilbert, in whose hands it remained until the dissolution. Numerous additions were made to the old remains in 1788, corresponding with the improvements of the place. The house and grounds occupy an area of about 300 acres, fronting an island between two branches of the river Slea.

118¾ m. TATTERSHALL STA.

4 m. s.w. TIMBERLAND. 3 m. further, KIRBY GREEN. 1 m. N. of which, SCOPWICK. 1 m. further, at BLANKNEY, Blankney Hall, Charles Chaplin, Esq.

122¾ m. KIRKSTEAD STA.

6 m. w. DUNSTON. 3 m. further, on the heath, Dunston Pillar, at the top of which a lantern used to be placed to guide the traveller across the heath.

125¾ m. STIXWOLD STA.

4 m. s.w. Nocton Park, Earl of Ripon. The mansion is a very handsome erection, and consists of a body and two wings, with turretted angles, and cupolas at top, with an octangular cupola rising from the centre.

126¼ m. SOUTHREY STA.

4 m. s.w. POTTERHANWORTH.

128¾ m. BARDNEY STATION.

five miles from the sea. Area of parish, 5,220 A.; population, 12,942. It sends two members to Parliament; registered electors (1846), 1,083; corporate revenue (1846), £4,884; customs' revenue, £40,064; registered shipping of port (1847), 186 vessels—aggregate burden, 8,768 tons. It is a polling-place for the Kesteven division of the county. The town is divided by the river; it is well-built, paved, and lighted, but it suffers from the want of good water. The church of Boston, erected A.D. 1309, is an elegant, spacious, and highly interesting fabric, dedicated to St. Botolph, and is said to be the largest religious edifice without cross aisles in the kingdom, the tower, which forms a landmark visible for forty miles, is 281 feet in height, and has been compared with that of the cathedral of Antwerp; in beauty, however, there are few, if any, which surpass it. The interior of the church is richly ornamented, and the altar, which is of the Corinthian order, in oak, is adorned with a fine copy of Rubens' celebrated picture, "The taking down from the Cross," one of the greatest ornaments of the cathedral to which we have adverted. In the 14th and 15th centuries it was one of the most important commercial ports of the kingdom. It was the birthplace of the celebrated John Fox, the Martyrologist. Markets, Wednesday and Saturday; cattle fairs, May 4th and 5th, August 5th, and December 11th; horse fair, from 20th to 30th November.

East Lincolnshire Branch ☞

113¾ m. LAN-GRICK STA.

118 m. DOGDYKE STATION.

118¾ m. TATTER-SHALL STA.

TATTERSHALL, a neat market-town, county of Lincoln. Area of parish, 3,840 A. The church, which is cruciform, is one of the most spacious and elegant structures of the kind in the county. It was made collegiate A.D. 1438, by Ralph Lord Cromwell; but it has suffered great dilapidations from neglect and other causes. It formerly possessed very rich stained glass windows, and beautifully carved oak stalls, screen, &c. Many of the windows are now blocked up, and the rich decorations were destroyed by exposure to the air. Two beautiful brass figures of Lord and Lady Cromwell lie before the altar. Here are also the remains of Tattershall Castle, belonging to the Cromwell family. 5 m. E. NEW BOLINGBROKE. 2 m. N. Revesby Abbey, J. Banks Stanhope, Esq., near which is an encampment of the Broad Foss, measuring 300 feet by 100 feet.

6 m. N.W. Scrivelsby Court, Sir Henry Dymoke, Bart., the Hon. the Champion. This manor is held by baronry and grand sergeantry, namely, that at the coronation of the king he should attend well-armed, prepared to defend the right and title of the king and kingdom against all comers. 2 m. further, HORNCASTLE. Situated on the river Bane, which is navigable from its junction with the Witham. Here are some remains of Roman fortifications.

122½ m. KIRK-STEAD STA.

KIRKSTEAD, where there are the ruins of an old Cistercian abbey. Kirkstead Hall. About 2 m. from which stands Moor Tower, or Tower of Moor. It is a singular octangular building, with a winding staircase, no doubt used in former times as a watch-tower to Tattershall Castle.

125¾ m. STIX-WOLD STA.

STIXWOLD. 3 m. further, WOODHALL; beyond which, 3 m., HORN-CASTLE.

126¼ m. SOUTH-REY STA.

2 m. N.E. BUCKNALL. Tupholme Hall. 2 m. further, Gautby Hall, Robert Vyner, Esq.

128¾ m. BARDNEY STATION.

BARDNEY, is a parish of 3,490 A., parts of Lindsey, in the county of Lincoln. On a barrow here is a cross erected to the memory of Ethelred, King of Mercia, buried underneath. Bardney has a free school, with a revenue of £160 per annum. 5 m. N. WRAGBY (see Lincoln and Market Rasen Railway). Close to which is the ruins of Bardney Abbey.

AYINGTON.

133¾ m. FIVE-MILE HOUSE STA.

135½ m. WASH-INGBOROUGHSTA.

Nottingham and Newark Branch.

138 m. LINCOLN STATION.

1 m. S.E. Canwick Hall, Colonel Sibthorp, M.P. An elegant mansion, of modern style of architecture. 6 m. W. Doddington Hall, G. R. P. Jarvis, Esq.; close to which is The Jungle, Russell Collett, Esq. Owing to the marshy nature of the soil in the neighbourhood of Lincoln, an artificial trench, called the Foss Dyke, in the year 1211 was made, or materially altered by King Henry I., whereby vessels were enabled to be navigated from the Trent to Lincoln. The country being exceedingly flat, it became unnavigable from the increasing accumulation of mud, which rendered it useless for the purposes intended.

144 m. SAXILBY STATION.

2 m. S.W. Thorney Hall, Rev. Charles Neville, M.A.

148¼ m. MARTON STATION.

MARTON. The Roman Tile Bridge Lane passes through this parish, which is bounded on the left by the river Trent. Stow Park, John Landell, Esq. 1½ m. N. LITTLEBROUGH, where there is a church partly Roman.

151½ m. LEA STA.

LEA. Lea Hall, Sir Henry John Anderson, Bart.

155 m. GAINS-BOROUGH STA.

2 m. W. BECKINGHAM, with the hamlet of Sutton, is a village and parish, pleasantly situated on the east side of the river Witham, in the wapentake of Lovedon. The soil is mostly clay, and of good meadow quality. The church, dedicated to All Saints, is a handsome structure, in the early English style of architecture, consisting of a nave, chancel, north and south aisles, and a beautiful tower, surmounted with eight pinnacles, and containing six fine-toned bells. The church has recently been repaired and restored; the west arch opened, and a handsome stained glass window put in. On the north side of the church is a beautiful Norman doorway. In this parish the poor have a small portion of land let out to them in gardens. The Hall, C. G. Milnes, Esq., is surrounded by neatly laid-out pleasure-grounds. 3 m. further, GRINGLEY-ON-THE-HILL, anciently called Greenhaledge. Its very description calls it so, from its lofty situation on a hill overlooking the wide extent of Missencar. On this spot are several swelling mounds, which, were it not for their size, might be supposed artificial from their very bases. On these, however, have been thrown up three others. They are evidently the remains of Saxon or Danish work, and the part still called the Parks. It has been recorded to have belonged to a Saxon Lord.

Sheffield and East Retford Br.

BAUTRY STATION
(See
Great Northern).

Eastern Counties Railway.

The Eastern Counties Railway offers more advantages to the tourist in the shape of facilities for observing the landscape than almost any other line; for, from its construction on a nearly level surface, the traveller's view is not interrupted by long tunnels or interminable cuttings, but throughout the whole line he sees the country as well as from a coach road, and hence the alleged monotony of the district passed over is compensated for in one most essential particular.

It will at once be seen that the level nature of this district offered the greatest facilities for the construction of railways, and so early as 1836 Acts of Parliament were

133¾ m. FIVE-MILE HOUSE STA.	FISKERTON.
135½ m. WASHINGBOROUGH STA.	
Lincoln and Market Rasen Branch. ☞	
138 m. LINCOLN STATION.	LINCOLN. 2 m. N. Burton Hall, Earl of Warwick. 4 m. further, Hackthorn, Weston Cracroft, Esq. 2 m. further, Summer Castle; close to which is Glentworth, Earl of Scarborough.
144 m. SAXILBY STATION.	SAXILBY.
148¼ m. MARTON STATION.	1 m. E. STOWE. The church is a very ancient building, in the Norman style, with the upper part of the tower, west window, and other portions of a later date. Burton Hall, Earl of Warwick. The woods and park form a striking feature as seen from the cliff north of Lincoln.
151¼ m. LEA STA.	2 m. E. UPTON. 1 m. N. of which, HEAPHAM.
155 m. GAINSBOROUGH STA.	GAINSBOROUGH, an ancient market-town and parish, county of Lincoln, situated on the Trent—which is here crossed by an elegant bridge of three fine elliptical arches, opened in 1791—about 21 miles from its junction with the Humber. Such a national outlet on the eastern coast having been
Gainsborough and Grimsby Br. ☞	considered, in 1840 Gainsborough was constituted a sea-port, and now by means of canals connecting it with the Midland Counties, exports the manufactures of Manchester, Birmingham, and Sheffield. Area of parish, 7,210 A.; population, 7,860. The town, which consists principally of one long street running parallel with the river, is densely built, yet clean, well-paved, and lighted. Its church is a modern structure, although the tower is said to have been erected by the Knights Templars. The most curious ancient building it possesses, is called " John of Gaunt's Palace;" but upon what authority we know not. It contains three sides of a quadrangle, open to the south, and is chiefly composed of oak timber framing; its western exterior consists of a stack of huge brick chimneys; and at the north-east corner is an embattled tower. On the north side is a building that was formerly the chapel; the arches in the hall have niches, containing the figures of kings, warriors, &c.; and the whole building, though in a ruinous state, merits attention.
BAUTRY STATION (See Great Northern).	6 m. N.W. WALKRINGHAM. In the church of which there is a fine tomb. 2 m. N. Misterton, John Corringham, Esq. and John Lowthrop, Esq.

Eastern Counties Railway.

obtained for the formation of two distinct lines, one in a northerly direction, towards Cambridge, called the Northern and Eastern; and the other easterly, towards Colchester, called the Eastern Counties. The Colchester line was partially opened in 1839, and the Northern and Eastern to Broxbourne in 1840. It soon became apparent that it was the interest of both companies to unite; an Act was accordingly obtained, and in 1844 they amalgamated, preserving the distinctive title of the Eastern Counties Railways. In 1845 the Cambridge line had reached Bishop's Stortford, when it was extended to Brandon, and joined to the Norfolk Railway, which carried it on to Norwich. The

Colchester line had also been joined to another company, the Eastern Union, and in 1846 it reached Ipswich. Both these lines, however, had been constructed on a guage of five feet, differing from the national uniform guage of four feet eight inches and a half, and also from the Great Western's of seven feet. This error, which virtually excluded them from the general system of English railways, was quickly perceived, and the guage reduced to four feet eight inches and a half, that is, the rails were placed three inches and a half closer together, and all new carriages, locomotive engines, and rolling stock were constructed three inches narrower, and the old ones reduced by the same extent. This, of course, was accomplished at a considerable expense, but with no delay, for so perfect were the arrangements, that not a single accident, nor an hour's detention to the traffic, occurred. On the junction with the Norfolk Railway, the traffic thrown upon the Cambridge line was so overwhelming, that the Company really had not sufficient plant to carry on the business of the line, and some confusion and irregularity arose. Some early casualties have given the line a most discreditable notoriety, which engendered a sort of mania among the public for exaggerating every trivial irregularity into a most formidable and momentous occurrence, though, in many cases, incidents in every respect similar, and often far more alarming, on other lines, have scarcely been noticed. It will probably astonish many readers, even old Eastern Counties' travellers, to learn that from a Parliamentary Return dated February 6th, 1851, made to the Commissioners of Railways for the half year ending June 30th, 1850, though 1,537,868 passengers were conveyed over 1,185,628 miles of railway on the Eastern Counties line, not a single passenger was killed from causes depending upon the Company or its management. The same remark holds good during nearly the last five years, no passenger having been deprived of life, except by his own neglect or incaution, since July, 1846. There is no other railway in the kingdom of one quarter the length of the Eastern Counties that can say as much. This difficulty also was overcome, and there is now no railway in the world where more attention is paid to the comfort of the passenger than on the Eastern Counties. Whatever other faults may be found, this, at all events, must be admitted, that too great praise cannot be awarded to the officers and servants for their civility to travellers, and for their readiness to give any information required—items not always met with as readily as could be desired on the principal lines of railway in England.

This Company possesses 322 miles of territory, of which 228 miles are its own property. These different lines are distributed as follows :

LINES NOW OPEN FOR TRAFFIC.

		Miles.
London to Colchester	. . . . .	51¼
Stratford to Brandon	. . . . .	84½
Ely to Peterborough	. . . . .	28¼
March to Wisbeach .	. . . . .	8
Cambridge to St. Ives	. . . . .	12¼
	[Carried forward . .	184¼

Left of Railway from London.

Victoria Park. (See account of London, p. 12.)

STRATFORD-LE-BOW, county Middlesex; it is separated from Stratford, Essex, by the river Lea. Area of parish, 630 A.; population, 4,626. It is on the Roman highway, and has a very ancient church, and two free schools, one of which has an annual revenue of £500. Earl Cottage, Mrs. Anderson; Dorick Lodge, William Barnes, Esq.; Coborn Lodge, Henry Ford and William Gagen, Esqrs.; Tredegar House, Mrs. Gibson; Lambourne Cottage, James Oliver, Esq.; Coborn House, R. Sweeting, Esq.; Bow Lodge, E. H. Wulff.

Distance from London.

1 m. MILE END STATION.

2½ m. VICTORIA PARK AND BOW STATION.

Camden Town and Blackwall Railway.

3¾ m. STRATFORD STATION.

Enter Essex.

		Miles.
Brought forward	184¼
St. Ives to March	17¾
Broxbourne to Hertford	6
Stratford to North Woolwich	5
Maldon to Braintree	12
Edmonton to Enfield	3
	228

LINES WORKED BY THE COMPANY.

Brandon to Yarmouth	58
Wymondham to Fakenham	24
Reedham to Lowestoft	12
Chesterford to Newmarket	18
	118

The Company also supplies locomotive power and carriages to the Chesterford and Newmarket Company.

In the construction of these various lines the Company have spent a capital amounting to £12,998,207, raised by means of shares, and the work of the line is carried on by a staff numbering 2,933 officers and men, located at 103 stations, forming altogether one of the most important and influential corporations in the country.

On leaving the Bishopsgate Station, the line for a mile and a half runs on a viaduct of arches level with the tops of the adjoining houses, passing through a densely populated neighbourhood till we arrive at the Stratford works, comprising the locomotive engine and carriage factory, erected at a cost of about £100,000, and occupying, with its various yards, nearly twenty acres, the engine-room alone covering one acre and a quarter. The extent of the works here may be imagined from the fact that the operations of the line are carried on by 203 engines, 164 first-class, 154 second-class, and 164 third-class carriages, 241 horse-boxes, carriage-trucks, and luggage-vans, 2,151 goods-waggons, 679 sheep and cattle-waggons, 807 trucks, and 49 breaks, all of which require periodical repairs.

The only embankment of any importance is that of Wendon, which is 70 feet high, and the only tunnels are at a short distance from Wendon, where the line runs through two; the first 500 yards long, and the second 400. And here we may observe that the construction of these tunnels affords a striking instance of the perfection to which the art of engineering is now brought. One tunnel was begun at both ends, and so accurately were the works conducted, that the two borings met each other midway to within an inch.—(*Abridged, by permission, from the " Eastern Counties Railway and Illustrated Guide.")*

Distance from London.	
1 m. MILE END STATION.	**Right of Railway from London.**
2½ m. VICTORIA PARK AND BOW STATION.	Bow. (See Stratford.)
Camden Town and Blackwall ⊂⊃ Railway. ⊂⊃	
3¾ m. STRATFORD STATION.	STRATFORD, or STRATFORD LANGTHORNE, on the river Lea, crossed by an
Enter Essex.	ancient bridge in the parish of West Ham, county of Essex. Area, 5,160 A.; population, 12,738. It has a fine church, numerous chapels, distilleries,
Chelmsford and Colchester Line. ⊂⊃	chemical and print-works, flour-mills, &c. About ¼ m. s. WEST HAM. Forest Gate, C. R. Daines, Esq.; Ham House, Samuel Gurney, Esq.; West Ham Abbey, Richard Tebb, Esq.

This station takes its name from a neat iron bridge over the river Lea, on the Layton Road. 1 m. s.w. UPPER CLAPTON, which, with LOWER CLAPTON, forms a hamlet in the parish of HACKNEY, and extends from Hackney Church to Stamford Hill. The London Orphan Asylum, founded 1813, for the maintenance and education of destitute orphans, is a handsome building of light-coloured brick, with a lawn in front, and gardens behind, situated on a gentle elevation at Lower Clapton. The number of children in this institute generally exceeds three hundred. Summit Cottage, Richard Birkett, Esq.; Springfield House, Thomas Bros, Esq.; High Hill Ferry, J. Burch, Esq.; The Lodge, C. S. Butler, Esq.; Willow Cottage, J. R. Gibson, Esq.; Springhill House, J. Greatorex, Esq.; Springfield Cottage, W. C. Wright, Esq. 1½ m. N.W. STAMFORD HILL.

5¾ m. LEA BRIDGE STATION.

Cross the river Lea.

Re-enter Middlesex.

TOTTENHAM. The Yewes, James Dean, Esq.; Downhill House, John Lawford, Esq.; Whitehall, Charles Soames, Esq.

7¾ m. TOTTEN-HAM STA.

1 m. w. Bruce Castle. A modern building, on the site of an ancient castellated mansion, which was the residence of Robert Bruce (son of the King of Scotland), who died in 1303.

8¾ m. MARSH LANE STA.

¾ m. w. UPPER EDMONTON. Bush Hill, W. Brackenridge, Esq.; The Hyde, Mark Capper, Esq.; Bush Hill Park, Mrs. Currie; Trafalgar Cottage, C. J. Lloyd, Esq.; Rose Hall, William Lomas, Esq.

9¼ m. WATER LANE STA.

Enfield Junc.

¾ m. w. PONDER'S END. Eagle House, William Waller, Esq.; Durant's Harbour, William Maxwell, Esq.

11¾ m. PONDER'S END STA.

Enter Hertfordshire.

WALTHAM CROSS. A hamlet in Cheshunt parish; derives its name from one of those elegant stone crosses which the pious Edward I. erected in memory of his beloved and faithful consort Queen Eleanor, who died at Grantham, in Lincolnshire, in November 1291. Her heart was interred in Lincoln Cathedral, but her body was brought to London, and deposited in Westminster Abbey. At each of the places where it had been rested during this journey Edward afterwards erected a cross, of which only those at Geddington, Northampton, and Waltham now remain. 1 m. w. Theobald's Park, Sir Henry Meux, Bart. It was formerly the residence of the great Lord Burleigh, where, as his guest, Queen Elizabeth frequently resided, and held her Court in great magnificence; it was afterwards a favourite palace and hunting-seat of King James I., and the occasional residence of Charles I., who there received the petition from both Houses of Parliament in 1642, immediately before taking the field against them. A great portion of the palace was pulled down in 1650, and the materials sold to pay the army. Since then the seat has disappeared, and not a vestige of it remains. The present house, standing in a park of 205 acres, is a handsome brick mansion, built on an eminence at a short distance from the New River, which runs through the grounds, and a mile north-west from the site of the palace.

14¾ m. WALTHAM STATION.

CHESHUNT. Here is a college, a branch of the University of London, instituted by the Countess of Huntingdon, the students of which are provided with the means of procuring a first-rate education. Cheshunt Park, A. T. Russell, Esq.; Walnut-Tree House, William Stowburt, Esq.; Clock House, F. R. Crowder, Esq.; Cheshunt House, Sir G. B. Prescott, Bart., was formerly the residence of Cardinal Wolsey. It is a plain brick structure, which has undergone many alterations since the Cardinal's time.

16¼ m. CHES-HUNT STA.

BROXBOURNE, county of Herts. Area of parish, 4,580 a. The church, a very fine structure, has great claims to the notice of the traveller. Broxbourne Bury, George Jacob Bosanquet, Esq., is a spacious edifice, in the centre of a fine park. King James I. was here entertained by Sir Henry Cock, in his progress from Scotland. Wormley Bury, the seat of Earl Brownlow, is a substantial brick building, with a portico sustained on

19 m. BROX-BOURNE STA.

Hertford Br.

Re-enter Essex.

5¾ m. LEA BRIDGE STATION.	1½ m. N.W. WALTHAMSTOW. An ancient town, which, in the time of Edward the Confessor, belonged to Waltheof. Higham Hall, T. Capel, Esq.; Castle House, Robert Gore, Esq.; Buxton House, Robert Graham, Esq.; Church Hill, Captain Haviside; Shern Hall, Hon. Charles Maynard; Orford House, John Woodley, Esq. 2 m. further, WOODFORD. Oak Hill, John Bunce, Esq.; Mill Cottage, Edward Foster, Jun., Esq.; Woodford Bridge, Charles F. Kirkman, Esq.; Woodford Hall, William Morris, Esq. 2 m. further, CHIGWELL, an ancient village, formerly belonging to King Harold. Great West Hatch, Thomas Abbott, Esq.; Henault Hall, Walter Bearblock, Esq.; Woolston Hall, Robert Boodle, Esq.; Belmont House, James W. Bridges, Esq.; Manor House, E. Charrington, Esq.; West Hatch, C. J. Mills, Esq.
Cross the river Lea. Re-enter Middlesex.	
7¾ m. TOTTEN-HAM STA.	1 m. S.W. LOW LAYTON.
	1½ m. E. Claystreet, Charles Parkinson, Esq.; close to which is CHAPEL END.
8¾ m. MARSH LANE STA.	2⅓ m. E. Higham Hills, Mrs. Harman. The house is a square, brick building, with wings in both directions; the prospects are rich, diversified, and beautiful.
9½ m. WATER LANE STA.	2 m. N.E. CHINGFORD, on the border of Epping Forest, a short distance from which is a house termed Queen Elizabeth's Lodge, where the Courts of Forest Law are held.
11¾ m. PONDER'S END STA. Enter Hertfordshire.	2 m. N.E. Gillwell House, Gilpin Gosh, Esq.; close to which is HIGH BEACH. Beach Hill, Richard Arrabin, Esq.; High Beach, Sir G. Cockburn, Bart.; Maun House, Captain C. Sotheby.
14¾ m. WALTHAM STATION.	WALTHAM, WALTHAM ABBEY, or HOLY CROSS, a market-town, in the county of Essex, situated on the river Lea, surrounded by rich meadows. Area of parish, 11,870 A. It is a considerable town, in which are many excellent mansions, in the style of old manor-houses. A portion of the church presents the oldest specimen of Norman architecture in England, and is partly formed out of the remains of the famous abbey founded in the reign of King Canute. Here are the celebrated Government powder-mills, and at Enfield Lock, a distance of two miles, is a factory which supplies about 10,000 percussion muskets to the Government annually. Waltham has also corn and silk-mills, and a pin-factory, and the malting trade is here carried on. A. T. Tunnell, Esq.; Captain Harray Tullock; Sir William Wake, Bart., Lord of the Manor. Thrift Hall, John Soane, Esq. About 1 m. S. SEWARD'S STONE. Gillwell House, Thomas Husband, Esq. 2 m. S.S.E. beyond the Abbey is WARLEYS. 1 m. further, Copped Hall, H. J. Conyers, Esq. 2 m. E. of which is EPPING. Copersale Hall, Charles Appleton, Esq.; Thoydon Garnon, Richard Archer Houblon, Esq.; Park Hall, W. C. Marsh, Esq.; Hill Hall, Sir William Edward Bowyer Smijth, Bart.; The Grove, John C. Whiteman, Esq.
16¼ m. CHES-HUNT STA.	
19 m. BROX-BOURNE STA.	1½ m. S.E. NAZING. At the eastern extremity of the parish are vestiges of an ancient fortification, supposed to be British, called Ambers Bank. Nazing Bury, Edward Collins, Esq.; Nazing Park, George Palmer, Esq.
Re-enter Essex.	

four stone columns of the Composite order. The grounds, though not very extensive, are pleasing and well-disposed; and a sheet of water, across which is a Chinese bridge, adds considerably to the general effect.

ROYDON. Roydon Lodge, Mrs. M. Booth; Roydon Lea, J. Brown, Esq.; Mount Pleasant, Colonel Oates; Roydon Hamlet, J. Sibley, Esq. 1 m. N. Stanstead Abbots, Charles Booth, Esq.; Newland, Nathaniel Soames, Esq. | 22 m. ROYDON STATION.

¾ m. N. EASTWICK. 1 m. further, HUNSDON. Hunsdon Bury, Edward Calvert, Esq.; Briggins' Park, Charles Phelips, Esq. | 24¼ m. BURNT MILL STA.

½ m. N. Gilston Park, Bryse Pearse, Esq.

| 26¼ m HARLOW STATION.

SAWBRIDGEWORTH, county of Herts. Area of parish, 6,470 A. It is also called Sobridgeworth, and was the property of the noble family of Saye, in the reign of Edward IV., and long previously. Pishiobury, Rowland Alston, Esq. The mansion was built by Inigo Jones, but has undergone great alterations under the eminent architect, James Wyatt. It is approached by a serpentine avenue, stands in a fine park well-stocked with game, and is bounded on the south and east by the river Stort, which here divides the counties of Hertford and Essex. From its position on an eminence it commands an extensive view over the fertile district in which it is situated. 5 m. N.W. MUCH HADDAM. Here are the remains of a palace belonging to the Bishop of London, now occupied as the Hanwell Lunatic Asylum, containing about 40 inmates. Much Haddam, Lady Palmer; Winches, Mrs. Anthony.; Moore Place, Thomas S. Carter, Esq. | 28¼ m. SAW-BRIDGEWORTH STATION. Re-enter Hertfordshire.

BISHOP'S STORTFORD. A populous town and parish, county of Herts. Area, 3,080. It stands on an eminence, is watered by the river Stort, and consists of four streets. The church, a venerable Gothic edifice, stands at the western extremity of the town, and has a nave, chancel, and aisles, with a tower and spire, and several ancient monuments in the interior of the noble families who formerly resided in the vicinity. The other buildings consist of a town house, several Dissenting chapels, and two schools. It is a polling station for the county, and has a trade in corn and malt. Market, Thursday. Offord House, Colonel William Chamberlain; Tremhall Priory, Thomas W. Wall, Esq.; The Cottage, Francis Vandermulin, Esq. J.P. Albury Hall, the seat of John Calvert, Esq., was the residence of Sir Edward Atkins, Chief Baron of the Exchequer in 1686. 3 m. w. of which is HEMELLS. Sir J. Atty. The manor-house was built by Sir John Brograve, Attorney-General for the Duchy of Lancaster in the time of James I. The grounds are laid out with much taste, and display some beautiful land-scapes. 3½ m. N. BUNTINGFORD, a market-town, county of Herts. A fair and market, granted to Elizabeth de Bengo in the time of Edward III., first brought the town into notice. A chapel was built at this place in 1614 by voluntary subscription, and near it is an alms-house for four poor men, and as many women, founded and endowed in the year 1684 by Dr. Seth Ward, Bishop of Salisbury, who was a native of this town. Alnswick Hall, James Merchant, Esq.; Layston Villa, William Watts, Esq. | 32¼ m. BISHOP'S STORTFORD STA.

2 m. w. FARNHAM. Saving End, Mrs. M. Bush. | 35½ m. STANSTEAD STATION.

22 m. ROYDON
STATION.

1 m. s.e. GREAT PARNDON. Kingmore House, Frederick Houblon, Esq.

24¼ m. BURNT
MILL STA.

Little Parndon, Thomas Collins, Esq. 1 m. s. NETSWELL. One of the ancient parishes given by King Harold as an endowment to Waltham Abbey. Close to which is LATON. Marks' Hall, Rev. Joseph Arkwright, J.P.

26¼ m. HARLOW
STATION.

HARLOW, county of Essex. Area, 4,490 A. Harlow Bush Fair, which is held here September 9th, is one of the most celebrated for horses and cattle. Moor Hall, John Watlington Perry Watlington, Esq.; Hubbard Hall, C. F. and F. Simons, Esqrs. 5 m. s. NORTH WEALD. Woodside, J. Marsh, Esq.

28¼ m. SAW-
BRIDGEWORTH
STATION.

Re-enter
Hertfordshire.

Great Hyde Hall, Earl of Roden, is situated in the south-east part of the county, near the river Stort, in the hundred of Braughing. The park is a beautiful, though not an extensive one. From the mansion there is a fine display of beautiful scenery, and it is surrounded by productive meadow lands. The ·house is ancient, but the exterior has been modernized, and the interior is roomy and convenient. 2 m. E. Gladdens, Algernon Holtwhite, Esq. 2 m. further, HATFIELD BROAD OAKS. Matchings Barnes, Charles Appleton, Esq.; White House, George Paris, Esq.; Down Hall, J. T. Selwyn, Esq. From 5 to 10 m. s. and s.E. are the ROOTHINGS. Bird Hatch, Beetham Roothing, John Barnes, Esq.; Berners Roothing Hall, T. W. Bramston, Esq. and W. Robinson, Esq.; Gamish Hall, Martha Roothing, J. Charles Philips, Esq.; Maskell's Bury, White Roothing, Edward Paris, Esq.

32¼ m. BISHOP'S
STORTFORD STA.

1 m. Twyford House, George Frere, Esq. ½ m. further, Burchhanger Hall, Edward Jones, Esq. 2 m. E. at Takeley, Bassingbourne Hall, a large, handsome, modern edifice, situated on an eminence, with a very elegant front, and commands fine prospects. It derives its name from the ancient family of Bassingbourne, to whom it formerly belonged, some of whom lived here as early as the time of Henry III. Waltham Hall, Thomas Mumford, Esq.; Wearish Hall, Thomas Mumford, Esq.; Old House, Nicholas Patmore, Esq.; Sewers Hall, Captain W. Green Rubb. 4 m. further, Easton Lodge, Viscount Maynard. This venerable edifice stands on the west bank of the river Chelmer, opposite to Easton Magna. It has all the appearance of the early part of Queen Elizabeth's reign, and was probably erected by Sir Henry Maynard, whose son was secretary to the celebrated Lord Burleigh. It contains a fine armory, a handsome dining-room, which was formerly the chapel, the eastern window of which has six compartments of painted glass, displaying the principal events in the life of our Saviour. The grounds are extensive and pleasant, ornamented with canals, shrubberies, fine plantations, &c. Upon this estate, adjoining DUNMOW, coins of most of the Roman emperors have been discovered.

2 m. further, DUNMOW. Bigods, G. R. White, Esq.; Mark's Hill, Charles Barnard, Esq.; Langleys, John Livermore, Esq.; Clapton Hall, Charles Portway, Esq.; Upsall Park, William Portway, Esq.; 1½ m. s.w. Hallingbury Place, John Archer Houblon, Esq. A handsome and spacious red brick mansion, built at the commencement of the reign of George II. The ground plan is a parallelogram, and the angles are adorned with square towers, surmounted by cupola-formed roofs, terminating in vanes. It stands in a very extensive park, with ornamental grounds.

35½ m. STANSTEAD
STATION.

STANSTEAD MOUNT FISHET is one of the largest parishes in Essex, its circumference being computed at nearly forty miles. About ¼ m. from the

3 m. w. MANUDEN. Manuden Hall, Mrs. Patmore; Manuden House, | 37½ m. ELSENHAM STATION.
William Thomas, Esq.; Pinchpools, William Patmore, Esq. 3½ m. further,
THE PELHAMS. Pelham Hall, G. W. Hallam, Esq. 2 m. further, ORMEADE,
Captain Augustus Gould; Layston Villa, William Watts, Esq. 1½ m.
N.N.W. UGLEY. Of this place there is an old couplet,

> An Ugley church, and an Ugley steeple,
> An Ugley place, and an Ugley people.

Ugley Hall, Mr. J. L. Egerton; Bollington Hall, Edward Sandford, Esq.;
Quenden Hall, Mrs. Cranmer. 3 m. w. BURDEN, once the site of a small
priory of Augustine Canons. The learned Joseph Mead, M.A., was born
at Burden in 1736.

NEWPORT. At the north end of the village are slight remains of an hos- | 41¾ m. NEWPORT STATION.
pital, founded in the reign of King John by Richard de Newport. William
Nassau Bell, Esq.; David Shipper, Esq. 2 m. w. ARKESDEN. 4 m.
further, MEASDEN. John Perring, Esq. 2½ m. ANSTEY. Widdeal Hall,
C. H. Ellis, Esq. 1 m. further, CHIPPING. 1 m. N. of which Buckland.
Robert Sailboys, Esq.; William French, Esq.

Close to the line, WENDENS AMBO. 3 m. N.W. Loft's Hall, John Wilks, | 43½ m. AUDLEY END STA.
Esq. ½ m. s.w. LOWER CRISHALL. 1½ m. w. Cocken Hatch. It derived its
name from Cockenach, a Saxon, who possessed it before the Conquest. At the
dissolution, it passed with the Priory of Royston to Robert Chester, Esq.,
and became the principal seat of his family. The mansion is a singular
structure, but not inelegant, and it stands in a pleasant park. ½ m. w.
BARKWAY. Barkway Church contains various monuments and inscriptions,
together with many ancient slabs, formerly inlaid with brasses, scarcely any
of which are now remaining. Some fragments of a series of representations
of the creation in painted glass remain in the windows of the north
aisle, with arms, and other figures. A short distance from Barkway is
Newsells Park, Charles Drummond, Esq. Here, in a chalk-pit in Rockley
Wood, was found in the year 1743 a brass figure of Mars, with a brass
handle, and seven thin plates, having a figure of Vulcan engraved on two
of them, and on each of the others a Mars. On two of the latter were
also the following inscriptions:

MARTI
JOVIALI
TI CLAVIDOS PRIMOS
ATTU LIBER
V.S. L.M.
D. MARTI ALATOR
DVM CENSORINVS
GEMELLI FIL
V.S. L.M.

The word *alatorum* is supposed to relate to the Castra Alata of Ptolemy, | Enter Cambridgeshire.
and the plates to have been ornaments on a shrine of Mars about the time
of Dioclesian.

church is the mound of the keep of a castle, built about the time of the Conquest, William Fuller Maitland, J.P.

37½ m. ELSENHAM STATION. 1¼ m. E. Elsenham Hall, George Rush, Esq. A large red brick house, with battlements at top. The gardens are extensive, and beautifully laid out in flower-beds and shrubberies, surrounding a lake of between three and four acres.

2 m. N. Henham-on-the-Hill, William Canning, Esq. 2 m. E. of which, is BROXTED. Cherry Hall, William Dixon, Esq.; Broxted Hall, Thomas Leonard, Esq.; Church Hall, John White, Esq. 1½ m. S.E. TILTEY. Cold Harbour, Mr. Barnard; Tiltey Grange, J. Laurence, Esq. 3 m. E. LINDSELL. Lindsell Step, E. Halgar, Esq.; Tyers Hall, Thomas Smith, Esq. 3 m. N. of Tiltey is THACKSTEAD. Oram Hall, Captain E. Joddrell. 3 m. E. LITTLE AND GREAT BARDFIELD. Little Bardfield, William Phillips, Esq.; and William Spicer, Esq.; Great Lodge, John Brewster, Esq.; Park Hall, Thomas Pollett, Esq.; Claypit Hall, Mrs. B. Smith; Great Bardfield Hall, H. Smith, Esq.; South Lodge, Joseph Smith, Esq.; Park Gate, Mrs. R. Stebbing; Great Bardfield, John Walford, Esq., J.P.

41¼ m. NEWPORT STATION. ½ m. N. Shortgrove Hall, W. C. Smyth, Esq. It is a handsome mansion, with wings, occupying the summit of a pleasant eminence, and having in front the river Granta, flowing at the foot of a lawn, encompassed by plantations. Behind the house is a second lawn, with pleasure-grounds and canals, supplied with water from the river by an engine, invented by Dr. Desaquliers.

1 m. S.E. DEBDEN. Amberton Hall, R. Perry, Esq.; Mole Hall, Robert Perry, Esq.

43¼ m. AUDLEY END STA. About 1½ m. N. Audley End, Lord Braybroooke. The house originally consisted of two quadrangular courts; the rooms were large, but not sufficiently lofty. The gallery, which formed the eastern side of the inner court, 226 feet long, was pulled down in 1750, and previously to this three sides of the principal court had been destroyed by the bad taste of Sir John Vanburgh, who had been consulted as to the alterations. Notwithstanding these reductions, the mansion is still very extensive; the hall and saloon are noble apartments, and there are a variety of other good apartments, splendidly fitted up, with a collection of pictures and historical portraits of the most interesting character. The park and grounds are well wooded, and beautifully disposed. 1½ m. further, LITTLEBURY. Littlebury Green, E. Emson, Esq.; C. Ryder, Esq.

1¼ m. N.E. SAFFRON WALDEN. It is a municipal borough, market-town, and parish, county of Essex. Area of parish, 7,400 A.; population, 5,111. The town is well built, with a spacious market-place, a town hall, a grammar school, with an exhibition to Queen's College, Cambridge, several charities, and a considerable trade in grain and cattle. It derives its name from the saffron formerly raised in the vicinity. It is a polling-place for the county, and the head of a poor-law union. Walton Place, N. Cattlin, Esq.; Farmadine, Samuel Fiske, Esq. 4 m. E. RADWINTER. Radwinter Hall, John Davis, Esq.; New House, Mrs. M. Carter; Great Brockhold, Edward Emson, Esq.; Bendyshe Hall, H. Gibling, Esq. 1½ m. further, HEPSTEAD. Hepstead Hall, Mark Magger, Esq. About 1½ m. s. of which is SAMPFORD. Tynden Hall, Sir James McAdam; New Sampford Hall, General Sir William Cornwallis Eustace. 4 m. N.E. of Sampford is STEEPLE BUMPSTEAD. Moynes Park, G. W. Gent, Esq.; Bower Hall, William Henry Layton, Esq., J.P. An ancient and handsome edifice, for centuries the Enter Cambridgeshire. seat of the Bendyshe family, of whom Sir Thomas was a zealous and distinguished partizan of Charles I. The mansion is situated in a small park, with contiguous gardens. Claywall House, Mrs. French; Old Hall, Edward Fitch, Esq. 1½ m. E. BIRDBROOK. Burleigh House, Henry Sharpe, Esq.; Baythorne Hall, James Viall, Esq.

1 m. N.N.W. HICKESTON, where a Benedictine monastery was founded in the reign of Henry II., the revenue of which at the dissolution was valued at £80 1s. 10d. 1½ m. further, DUXFORD, where there are the remains of an ancient hospital, the chapel of which is now used as a barn. 2 m. w. TRIPLOW, celebrated as the place where Cromwell influenced the officers of the parliamentary army to commence the council of agitators.

5 m. W.N.W. FOULMIRE. 2 m. further, MELBOURNE. Melbourne Bury, John Edward Fordham, Esq.; Melbourne Lodge, Mrs. F. Hitch.

WHITTLESFORD. 3 m. N.W. NEWTON. 1 m. further, HARSTON. 1½ m. S.W. BARRINGTON. Lord Godolphin.

SHELFORD, GREAT and LITTLE, two adjacent parishes, county of Cambridge; the former contains an area of 1,900 A., the latter, 1,200 A.

CAMBRIDGE. A town of immense antiquity, supposed to have been the ancient Granta of the Romans, is a parliamentary and municipal borough, and market-town, capital of the county of Cambridge, the seat of one of the great English Universities, founded by Sigebert, King of East Anglia, in the 7th century. It is situated on both sides of the Cam, and contains an area (comprising 14 parishes, and extra-parochial districts of the University) of 3,470 A., with a population of 24,453, and 4,797 inhabited houses. The town itself is irregularly built, and consists principally of narrow streets, which have little to recommend them; nevertheless the public buildings of the town are handsome. The churches of St. Mary and Trinity are noble structures; while the circular church of St. Sepulchre, built after the Holy Sepulchre of Jerusalem, in the reign of Henry I., is a most interesting monument of antiquity. The shire and town halls, the general infirmary, the theatre, the gaol, in the interior of which are the remains of the ancient castle, the houses of industry and correction, founded by Hobson, the carrier, in the 17th century, the ancient grammar school, national school, numerous alms-houses and other charitable institutions would present considerable claims to the traveller's notice in any other locality; but the splendour of thirteen colleges and four halls of the richest architecture, of the most noble proportions, and some of them of most extraordinary design and execution, as even to puzzle the scientific of this knowing age as to the manner in which they were perfected, causes all the town and corporate buildings to be thrown into perfect obscurity. The colleges, according to their dates, are as follow: St. Peter's, or Peter-house, founded A.D. 1257; Clare Hall, 1326; Pembroke Hall, 1347; Caius, 1348; Trinity Hall, 1350; Corpus Christi, 1351; King's College, Queen's College, founded by Margaret of Anjou, 1446; Catherine Hall, 1475; Jesus College, 1496; Christ's College, 1505; St. John's College, 1511; Magdalen College, 1519; Trinity College, 1546; Emmanuel College, 1584; Sidney Sussex College, 1586; Downing College, 1800. Of these splendid collegiate halls and edifices, we may remark that Clare Hall

WATERBEACH. 2 m. N. Denny Abbey. In the year 1160 it was a cell to the monastery of Ely, which, in the following century, was occupied by the Knights Templars. In 1293 an abbey for Minoresses was founded here, which is now rented as a farm-house, and the refectory has been converted into a barn.

ELY, a city and episcopal see, capital of the Isle of Ely, county of Cambridge, situated on the river Ouse, here navigable. Area (comprising two parishes), 17,480 A.; population, 6,826. Ely is governed by a Custos

---

47½ m. CHESTER-FORD STA.

51 m. WHITTLES-FORD STA.

54½ m. SHELFORD STATION.

57¼ m. CAMBRIDGE STA.

Huntington and St. Ives Br.

Cross the Cam.

63 m. WATER-BEACH STA.

72¼ m. ELY STA.

Northampton and Peterborough Branch.

47½ m. CHESTER-
FORD STA.

CHESTERFORD, the Camboricum, or Buta Icenorum, of the Romans, county of Essex. The village lies on the Granta, and is remarkable for the quantities of coins, urns, and Roman antiquities found from time to time in the vicinity. In 1848 the remains of a Roman villa were discovered here. Area of parish, 3,030 A.; population, 917. A horse fair is held here

Newmarket
Branch ☞

July the 5th. LITTLE CHESTERFORD, an adjacent parish, in the same county, has an area of 1,260 A. Great Chesterford Vicarage, the Rev. Lord Charles A. Hervey; Great Chesterford Park, William Nash, Esq. LITTLE CHESTERFORD. Springwell, Charles Nichols, Esq. 4 m. N.E. of Chesterford, LINTON. 2 m. S.E. BARTLOE.

51 m. WHITTLES-
FORD STA.

½ m. N.E. PAMPISFORD. William P. Hammond, Esq. 1 m. N. SAW-STON. The Hall, Richard Huddleston, Esq.

54¼ m. SHELFORD
STATION.

Close to the line is STAPLEFORD. 2 m. N.E. Gog-Magog Hills, Lord Godolphin. On the hills, from which the mansion takes its name, is a triple intrenchment with two ditches, but whether British or Roman, is uncertain.

57½ m. CAM-
BRIDGE STA.

possesses a noble avenue of trees, beautiful gardens, and an elegant stone bridge across the Cam; Peter-house has a handsome chapel by Wren; Corpus Christi, distinguished for its noble buildings; Trinity Hall, a fine library; King's College possesses a chapel of surpassing beauty, the roof of which is almost a miraculous piece of architecture, and the like is not to be found in Europe; Queen's has lovely grounds; Trinity, the largest of all the colleges, and the most magnificent in the whole University, possesses buildings of the grandest and most imposing character. Independently of all these noble structures, the Senate House, public schools, observatory, the library, the University printing-office, and the Fitzwilliam Museum, are strikingly handsome edifices. In 1847 the total number of members on the boards was 6,638. Registered electors for the University, which sends two members to Parliament, amounted in 1849 to 2,780. Cambridge town also sends two members to Parliament. Registered electors in 1846, 1,834. The total revenue of the colleges amounted, in 1835, to £133,268; while the general income of the University is not suffered to exceed £5,500 per

Cross the Cam.

annum. The town is governed by a mayor, aldermen, and councillors; and the corporate revenue in 1847 amounted to £6,456. The executive government of the University is vested in the Chancellor (at present H.R.H. Prince Albert), Vice-Chancellor, High Steward, Commissary, Proctors, and other officers; but the internal government of each college is regulated by peculiar statutes; and the government of the colleges, as a confederation, lies with the senate, composed of two houses—the members being doctors or masters of arts. Cambridge was the birthplace of the good bishop, Jeremy Taylor, and of Cumberland, the poet. To give merely a list of the illustrious philosophers, statesmen, divines, senators, poets, warriors, and lawyers, who have been educated at this ancient and most distinguished seat of learning, would fill several volumes; it suffices to observe, that Newton and Bacon add the lustre of their names to the noble roll. 2 m. N.E. TEVERSHAM. 2 m. further, QUY CUM STOW. Quy Hall, Thomas Martin, Esq.

63 m. WATER-
BEACH STA.

3 m. S.E. Bottisham Hall, George Jenyns, Esq. 1 m. N.E. SWAFFHAM BULBECK; and 1 m. further, SWAFFHAM PRIORY. Swaffham Abbey, J. P. Allix, Esq. M.P.

72¼ m. ELY STA.
☞ Lynn and Ely
Branch.

The defence of the Isle of Ely forms one of the most striking events in the early history of England. Hareward, the last of the once celebrated order of Anglo-Saxon knights, and brother in arms of the patriots, Earls

Rotulorum, and is the only city in the kingdom which sends no representative to Parliament. The island, as well as the city, are supposed to derive their name from the quantities of eels which abound in this part of the country. The bishopric was founded in 1107, on the celebrated Abbey of Ely, which was erected by St. Etheldrida, the daughter of a Saxon king, about 673. In 870, it was destroyed by the Danes. The city itself is extremely ancient; and even the present houses bear all the appearance of antiquity. The cathedral was erected shortly after the commencement of the Norman dynasty, but was not completed until some time in the reign of Edward III. It presents almost every description of Saxon, Norman, and Gothic architecture; nevertheless, it has a grand and striking appearance. Its extreme length is 535 feet, by 190 feet in breadth in the transept. In the centre is an octagonal tower, and many interesting monuments attract the stranger's attention. Trinity Church, erected in the early part of the 14th century, is a truly superb structure. With the exception of the ecclesiastical buildings, the deanery, formerly the refectory of the old abbey, and a beautiful little chapel appertaining to the same, there are no buildings in the city worthy of particular attention.

79¼ m. MILDEN-HALL ROAD STA.

2 m. N. OCWOLD CUM WELTON. 2 m. further, FELTWELL ST. MARY. The church of St. Mary is a beautiful old edifice; its tower is superb and of stone, with various and appropriate sculpture surrounding it and the tower; in the interior are many ancient monuments, particularly one of brass inserted in the wall.

84¾ m. LAKEN-HEATH STA.

1 m. Ruins of Wheating St. Mary's Church. 1 m. further, Wheating All Saints. The Hall, John Angerstein, Esq.

Enter Norfolk.

4 m. N.N.E. Sinford House, Sir Richard Sutton Bart. 2 m. N.E. of which, is LANGFORD. Buckenham House, Lord Petre. 2 m. further, Cressingham, Robert Crowe, Esq. 2 m. E. Merton Hall, Lord Walsingham, an Elizabethan mansion, in the style of 1613,

88¼ m. BRANDON STATION.

1½ m. N. WALTON. 3 m. N. of Cressingham, is Ash Hill, Rev. B. Edwards.

THETFORD, a parliamentary and municipal borough and market-town, counties of Norfolk and Suffolk, was the ancient Sitomagus. From its proximity to the North Sea, it was frequently, during the Octarchy, desolated by the Danes, who having retained possession of the town for 50 years, totally destroyed it by fire in the 9th century. In 1004 it sustained a similar calamity from their King, Sweyn, who had invaded East Anglia; and in 1010 it became, for the third time, the scene of plunder and conflagration by these marauders, into whose hands it again fell after a signal victory which they had obtained over the Saxons. In the reign of Canute, Thetford much declined, but in that of Edward the Confessor, nearly regained its former prosperity. In the time of the Conqueror, the episcopal see of North Elmham was transferred here, and hence to Norwich, by Herbert de Losinga, in the following reign; but Henry VIII. made it the seat of a bishop suffragan to Norwich, which it continued during his reign. From the time of Athelstan to that of John, here was a mint, in which coins of Edward and Canute were struck. Thetford was also the temporary residence of Henry I., Henry II., Elizabeth, and James I. Elizabeth built a mansion, which is still called the King's House. It was once the capital of the kingdom of East Anglia, and the episcopal seat of the bishopric of Norfolk and Suffolk. We find also that as late as the 14th century, it possessed between twenty and thirty churches, monasteries, and other ecclesiastical institutions, the remains of which are visible in all parts of the town. It is situated on the rivers Thet and Little Ouse. Area of borough, including three parishes, 8,270 A. It sends two members to

95¼ m. THETFORD STATION.

Edwin and Morcar, and the successful foeman of William the Conqueror, endeavoured here to rescue from the deep the sinking fortunes of his race and country; and at last William, wearied out with the vain contest, condescended to treat with the only foeman left on British soil, and the only one whom he had ever failed to reduce. In the baronial wars of Henry III.'s reign, the isle was again doomed to become one of the chief scenes of civil strife and its attendant evils; but in the great contest between Charles and his Parliament, none of its towns sustained a siege, and no battles were fought. 6 m. S.E. SOHAM; a place of some note at a very early period. Abut 630 a monastery was founded here by St. Felix, first Bishop of East Anglia. This building, as well as the Bishop's palace, was destroyed by the Danish army in 870. Before the draining of the fens, here was a large lake or mere, over which was a dangerous passage by water to Ely; but was subsequently rendered more safe by the construction of a causeway through the marshes at the expense of the Bishop of Ely.

79¼ m. MILDEN-HALL ROAD STA.

8 m. S.E. MILDENHALL, a market-town and parish, county of Suffolk, situated on the river Larke, which travels along the north and south boundaries of the parish. Barton Hall, Sir H. E. Bunbury, Bart.; Barton Place, Captain W. T. Squire.

84½ m. LAKEN-HEATH STA.

2 m. S. LAKENHEATH. A large village, chiefly inhabited by farmers, and considered to contain more small holders of land than any village in the county; it comprises upwards of 10,500 acres, nearly 3,000 of which are open rabbit warren. Lakenheath Cottage, William Eagle, Esq.; Undley Hall, Thomas Waddelow, Esq.

Enter Norfolk.

88¼ m. BRANDON STATION.

BRANDON, a market-town, county of Suffolk, on the Little Ouse, or Brandon River, is celebrated for its warrens, which contribute greatly to the supply of rabbits to the London market; from here also formerly were obtained the best gun-flints, now in disuse. Brandon has a good church, a bridge over the Ouse, an endowed grammar school, almshouses, and other charities. Brandon Park, Henry Bliss, Esq.; Brandon Hall, E. M. Rogers, Esq.; North Court Lodge, Thomas Kenyon, Esq. 2 m. E. SANTON DOWN-HAM, Santon Downham Hall, Lord William Powlett.

95¾ m. THETFORD STATION.

1 m. E. Kilverstone Hall, John Wright, Esq. 3 m. further,

SHADWELL PARK, SIR ROBERT JACOB BUXTON, BART.

Parliament; registered electors (1848), 214; corporate revenue, at the same date, £853. The town is well built, though without any attention to symmetry; and independently of the churches—of which St. Peter's, or the "Black Church," from its being built of dark flint, is the principal, while St. Mary's, on the Suffolk side of the river, is a thatched fabric with a lofty square tower—it contains a guildhall, market-house, gaol, bridewell, theatre, and a cast-iron bridge across the Ouse. It possesses also a grammar school, almshouses and other charities. Thetford is a polling place for the western division of Norfolk, and the head of a poor-law union. Thetford Abbey, Thomas Featherstone, Esq. 1½ m. CROXTON. 4 m. further, WRETHAM. Wretham Hall, Wyrley Birch, Esq,; Forest Lodge, G. Wyrley Birch, Esq.

3½ m. N.W. Hockham Hall, H. S. Partridge, Esq. 3 m. N. Shropham Hall, H. D'Esterre Hemsworth, Esq.

| | 103¼ m. HARLING ROAD STA. |

2 m. N.E. Hargham Hall, Sir Thomas B. Beevor, Bart.

| | 106¼ m. ECCLES ROAD STA. |

ATTLEBOROUGH, supposed to have been a city, and the capital of the county in former times; is now a small market-town, in the county of Norfolk. Area of parish, 5,800 A. The church is a very spacious cruciform structure, and here are several places of worship for Dissenters, schools, and some charities. It has a Thursday market, a large market every other week, and several annual fairs. Attleburgh Hall, Sir William Bowyer Smijth, Bart.

| | 110 m. ATTLE-BOROUGH STA. |

| | Fakenham Branch. |

WYMONDHAM. A market-town and parish, county of Norfolk. Area of parish, 11,240 A. The most interesting edifice in this manufacturing town is the church, which formed part of an old monastery. The grammar school is well endowed, and has two exhibitions to Cambridge. The population is chiefly employed in manufactures of crapes and bombazines. Birfield Hall, Miss A. B. Borroughes; Silfield Hall, F. J. Skoulding, Esq. 3 m. N.W. Kimberley Hall, Lord Wodehouse, is a very handsome brick edifice, with offices detached, containing nobly-proportioned apartments, with a fine library. Its greatest beauty consists in the park, profusely adorned with a multitude of the most venerable oaks in the country, and bounded on the north and west sides by a pretty rivulet, which adds greatly to the beauty of the scenery. 3 m. N.E. from Wymondham, Hethersett Hall, A. J. and H. J. Back, Esqrs. 2 m. N. Melton Hall, Edward Lombe, Esq.

| | 115½ m. WYMOND-HAM STA. |

NORWICH. An episcopal city, parliamentary borough, and river port, capital of county of Norfolk, and county of itself, situated on the river Yare, here crossed by ten bridges. Area of city and county, 5,920 A.; population, 60,982. Norwich is bounded on the north and east by the river, and was formerly enclosed by fortifications, flanked with towers, and entered by twelve gates, the greater portion of which have been taken down. The city, which is irregularly built, except in the new quarters, is about five miles in circumference, and has a very large market-place. The cathedral, a splendid pile, was commenced in the 11th century, and not entirely finished until some hundreds of years after that epoch. It is 411 feet in length, by 191 feet in breadth, surmounted by the loftiest spire in England, except that of Salisbury. The bishop's palace, deanery, the cloisters, and the gates of St. Ethelred and St. Essingham, which connect the cathedral

| | 126 m. NORWICH STATION. |

A handsome mansion, in the Elizabethan style; the park richly wooded. In the grounds is St. Chad's Well, anciently much frequented by pilgrims on their route to the shrine of our Lady at Walsingham. ½ m. further, Rushforth Lodge, Rev. F. D. Panter, M.A. 2 m. E. Riddlesworth Hall, Thomas Thornhill, Esq. 2 m. s. Coney Weston Hall, Edward Bridgman, Esq.; Market Weston, John Thurston, Esq.; Euston Hall, Duke of Grafton. A large, commodious mansion, built of red brick. Near it is the river Ouse, over which is thrown a neat and substantial bridge. The estate of Euston is of very considerable extent, embracing a great number of villages and hamlets. On an elevated situation in the park stands a temple, built in the Grecian style of architecture, in 1746, and commanding an extensive prospect.

103¼ m. HARLING ROAD STA.

HARLING ROAD lies in the parish, and near the small market-town of HARLING, county of Norfolk. Area of parish, 2,990 A. Market, Tuesday. 1 m. s.w. Harling Hall, Lord Colborne; and 2 m. s. Garboldisham Hall, Thomas M. Montgomorie, Esq.

106¼ m. ECCLES ROAD STA.

½ s. Eccles Hall, late Sir James Flower, Bart., M.P. A very ancient house, said to have been a bishop's residence many years ago. 1 m. further, Quiddenhall, Earl Albemarle. 1 m. further, KENNINGHALL. The Grange, Nathaniel Cooke, Esq.

110 m. ATTLE-BOROUGH STA.

3 m. s. BUCKENHAM. St. Andrew's Hall, Sir Francis Baring, Bart. The house is not a large structure. The park is a very ancient enclosure, having belonged to the Black Canons of the Augustine Order in the reign of Henry II., and in the year 1242 King Henry III. issued his writ to those who held lands of Hugh de Albany, Earl of Arundel, that he should deliver to Robert de Tateshale two bucks, as the gift of the King, out of the said Hugh's park.

115½ m. WYMOND-HAM STA.

1 m. E. Stanfield Hall. About two years since, this mansion was the scene of a most terrific tragedy, in which the lives of its late owner, Mr. Jermy, and his only son, were sacrificed by the hand of their tenant, Rush, whose name will long be remembered as one of the most facinorous male-factors that ever disgraced the annals of crime. It is a structure of considerable antiquity, for although it has undergone great repairs and alterations in modern times, it is known to have been inhabited in the reign of Henry VIII. by a family named Flowerden, from whom it passed to Lord Cramond, and afterwards to the Prestons, from whom the late unfortunate owner derived the estate. The porch, the large mullioned windows, the clustered chimneys, with the spiral ornaments to the gables, give a correct idea of the architecture of the early period at which it was erected, while the interior contains every specimen of architecture, from the plain groined to the most florid style. The house is surrounded by a moat, and stands in the midst of a fine and well sheltered lawn on the highest ground in the county. 2 m. N. Ketteringham Hall, Sir John Peter Boileau, Bart.

Eastern Union Branch ☞
126 m. NORWICH STATION.

Brackendale Lodge, Mrs. A. B. Martindale. 2 m. s. BIXLEY. Bixley Hall, William Martin, Esq. The hall was erected by Sir Edward Ward, about the middle of the last century; it has three fronts, each containing three stories from the basement, and the attic windows are placed in the roof. The grounds are well wooded. The Lodge, George L. Coleman, Esq. 1 m. further, FRAMINGHAM EARL, J. B. L. Knight, Esq. 3 m. further, BROOKE. Brooke Lodge, George Holmes, Esq.; Brooke House, G. S. Kett, Esq. 3 m. further, WOODTON. Woodton Hall, Mrs. C. Gooch. 2 m. s.E. DITCHINGHAM. The Hall, John L. Bedingfeld, Esq.; Holly Hill Lodge, Mrs. E. Dowson; The Cottage, Mrs. Clara S. Foster; The Lodge, William Hartcup, Esq.; Ditchingham House, Mrs L. A. Margitson. A little further, BUNGAY, a market-town, county of Suffolk. The name is supposed to have been anciently Bongue, from the goodness of a ford over

with the city, are all fine buildings. Here are many churches: St. George, Colegate; St. Peter, Mancroft; St. Laurence and St. Saviour are peculiarly handsome structures, and many other churches have the peculiar round towers of the early Norman period. Here are also places of worship for almost every denomination of Dissenters, some of which are fine buildings; and many highly interesting remains of monastic and other ecclesiastical establishments, of which St. Andrew's Hall, now used for public meetings and civic festivities, was formerly a part of a Dominican convent. The castle stands on an eminence in the centre of the city, and consists of a quadrangular Norman keep, surrounded by three lines of walls, the river one, the "castle precinct," being laid out in public walks. The keep is now used as a prison, and on the castle-hill stand the new county gaol and the council hall. The other principal edifices of the city are the guildhall, the new city gaol, corn exchange, the great hospital, which has a revenue of about £7,000 per annum, the cavalry barracks, theatre, public library, and union workhouse. Of the educational and charitable establishments, we may cite the grammar school, the boys' and girls' hospital, with a revenue of £4,000 per annum, Doughty's hospital, Norfolk and Norwich General Hospital, and the blind asylum; and among the learned and literary societies are the Norfold and Norwich Literary Institute, art union, and a mechanics' institute. The worsted manufactures of this city owed their origin to the Flemings, who settled here in the reign of Henry I.; but Yorkshire has now the pre-eminence in this branch of trade, while Norwich bears the palm for shawls, crapes, gauzes, bandanas, and various kinds of silk, mohair, horsehair, sacking, and fringe fabrics. Here are also iron and brass foundries, mustard, snuff, oil, and corn mills, dyeing works, and breweries, a branch of the Bank of England, several private banks, and an insurance company. Corporation revenue (1847), £13,533. Mousehold House, General Sir R. J. Harvey. The mansion was erected in 1821 by the present owner on the left bank of the Yare, at its junction with the Wensum, on the rising ground at three-quarters of a mile distant from both rivers. It is surrounded by forty acres of wood, which forms a great ornament to the beautiful valley it overhangs. Near this site are the remains of St. Leonard's Monastery, which was afterwards the residence of the Earl of Surrey, when the Duke of Norfolk had his palace in Norwich.

2 m. s.w. Eaton Hall, Captain Morris.

2½ m. w. Earlham Hall, Joseph Gurney, Esq. 1 m. further, Coney Hall, Joseph Scott, Esq.

5 m. n.w. by w. Costessy Hall, Lord Stafford.

6 m. n.w. Taverham Hall, Nathaniel Micklethwait, Esq. 4 m. further, near ATTLEBRIDGE, Weston House, H. F. Custance, Esq.

2 m. n.n.w. CATTON, Captain H. F. Cubit; Rose Lodge, G. S. Everett, Esq. 4 m. further, Felthorpe Hall, Lady E. Fellowes. 3 m. n.w. of which Witchingham Hall, C. Kett Thompson, Esq. 3 m. further, n.n.w. Brandiston Hall, Captain C. J. Butcher. A little further, Booton Hall, Francis Parmeter, Esq., and Samuel Bircham, Esq. 1 m. from which Reepham Sall Hall, Sir R. P. Jodrell, Bart. 1½ m. n. Heydon Hall, W. E. Lytton Bulwer, Esq.

6 m. n. Haynford Hall, Rev. A. W. W. Keppel. 1 m. further, STRATTON. STRAWLESS. The Hall, Robert Marsham, Esq. A little further, at HEVINGHAM, Ripon Hall, Charles William Marsham, Esq. A little further, at MARSHAM, The Hall, Rev. C. Marsham; Bolwick Hall, John Warns, Esq. 2 m. further, AYLESHAM. Paradise, Mrs. B. Bulwer; Bushey Place, Thomas B. Cook, Esq. 1½ m. further, Blickling Hall, Dowager Lady Suffield; Blickling Lodge, John Thomas Mott, Esq. 2 m. further, Wolterton Hall, Earl of Orford. 2 m. further, Barningham Hall, John T. Mott, Esq.; and Hanworth, James Hunt Holly, Esq. 2 m. further, Fellbrigg Hall, William Howe Windham, Esq. 3 m. further, CROMER. Cromer Hall, Henry Baring, Esq.; Colne House, Mrs. N. Morri*

the river Waveney, by which the town and common is nearly surrounded, in the form of a horse-shoe, and by which a considerable trade is carried on in corn, malt, flour, and lime. Bigod, Earl of Norfolk, in the reign of Stephen, erected a castle here, which he was accustomed to boast of as impregnable, and is reported by Hollingshead to have made use of this expression:

> " Were I in my castle of Bungay,
> Upon the water of Waveney,
> I would not set a button by the King of Cockney."

On the accession of Henry II., however, this nobleman, who had invariably espoused Stephen's cause, was obliged to give a large sum of money and hostages to save this castle from destruction. Joining afterwards in the rebellion of Henry the Second's son against his father, he was deprived of the castle of Bungay, as well as Framlingham; but these and his other estates and honours were restored to his son and heir, whose posterity enjoyed them for several generations; but in the reign of Henry III. the castle was demolished. However, on the site, in the reign of Edward I. a mansion was erected, which Roger Bigod obtained permission to embattle. In 1688, a fire broke out in an uninhabited house, and the flames spread with such fearful devastation that, with the exception of one small street, the town was reduced to ashes, the records of the castle, and property of the estimated value of £30,000 were destroyed. The remains of the castle have been subsequently converted into cottages, and little more can now be traced of its former extent than some portions of the walls. Over the river Waveney, which here forms the line of boundary between the counties of Norfolk and Suffolk, is a handsome bridge. The streets are spacious and paved, the houses are in general modern, and the inhabitants are abundantly supplied with excellent water from springs which abound in the neighbourhood. In the market-place, situated on a gentle rising ground, and considered the handsomest in the county, are two crosses, in one of which fowls and butter are exposed for sale, and in the other corn and grain. The top of the former is adorned with a figure of Astræa, in lead, weighing 18 cwt. The theatre is a neat edifice, and the assembly rooms are handsomely fitted up. A botanical society has been instituted, also reading rooms. There are two churches; that of St. Mary, rebuilt in 1696, with flint and freestone, is a handsome and spacious structure, with a fine tower, and its pillars supporting the roof are remarkable for their lightness and elegance. It contains some interesting monuments. The other church, the Holy Trinity, is a small edifice with a round tower. There was formerly a church dedicated to St. Thomas, but of it there are no remains. In 1591 the Rev. Thomas Popeson annexed the vicarage of Ilkatshall to the mastership of the grammar school, and founded ten scholarships in Emmanuel College, Cambridge, but they have been subsequently reduced to four. The school also has an endowment of forty acres of land. Ten boys are provided for by this bequest. Near St. Mary's Church are some remains of a Benedictine nunnery, founded in the reign of Henry II. by Robert de Glanville and his lady, the Countess Gundreda, in honour of the Blessed Virgin and the Holy Cross, the revenue of which at the time of the dissolution was estimated at £62 2s. 1d. A few Roman coins, some seals and ancient tokens, have been found. Market-day, Thursday. The fairs are May 14th, and September 25th. Dukes Bridge House, Mrs. Barlee; Trinity Hall, Mrs. Dreyer; Trinity Cottage, Mrs. Ebbage; Olland's House, Mr. John Feltham; Rose Hall, John R. Webb, Esq.

1 m. s. Upland Grove, William Hartcup, Esq. 2½ m. s.w. Flixton Hall, Sir R. S. Adair, Bart. This is a noble structure, pleasantly situated near the Waveney. It was built about 1615, and originally surrounded by a moat, filled up some years ago. The style of the architecture has been denominated Inigo Jones's Gothic. The principal front faces the north.

4 m. N. Spixworth Park, John Longe, Esq.   The mansion is a fine   NORWICH
(continued).
specimen of the Elizabethan style of architecture, and has been in the
Longe family for the last two hundred years, and stands in a picturesque
park of one hundred and fifty acres.   3 m. further, Horstead Hall, Dowager
Lady Suffield; Horstead Lodge, John B. Wenn, Esq.; Mill House, Samuel
C. Cooke, Esq.   8 m. further, Gunton Hall, Richard Sanderson, Esq.

3 m. N.N.E. Beeston Hall, Nathaniel Micklethwait, Esq.   10 m. further,
Westwick Hall, J. Petre, Esq.   A little to the east, Westwick House,
Hon. William Rous.   2 m. further, NORTH WALSHAM.   2 m. N.N.E.
Witton Park, Hon. Captain E. T. Wodehouse.

3 m. N.E. Rackheath Hall, Sir Edward H. Stacey, Bart.   3 m. further
Wroxham Hall, S. Trafford, Esq.   1½ m. further, Salhouse Hall, Richard
Ward, Esq.   The hall stands on a richly wooded lawn, and is embellished
with a collection of works of art and *vertu*.   The estate is watered by the
river Bure in the beautiful neighbourhood of the Broads.   1½ m. further,
Overton Hall, H. N. Burrell, Esq., M.P.   A little further, Barton Hall,
T. E. Preston, Esq.

2 m. E. Burlingham, H. N. Burroughes, Esq. M.P.   132 m. BRUNDALL
STATION.

2 m. S. Ruins of Langley Abbey, founded in the year 1198.   1½ m.   134 m. BUCKEN-
HAM STA.
further, Langley Park, Rear-Admiral Sir William B. Proctor, Bart.   This
handsome seat was erected in 1740 by Sir W. B. Proctor, the first baronet.
The main building is in five divisions, adorned with a portico of the Doric
order.   Two wings are connected with the mansion by a semi-circular
sweep, presenting a noble carriage front; the whole is built in stone-   138 m. REEDHAM
STATION.
coloured brick.   The park possesses a pleasing variety of surface, with
extensive plantations.

YARMOUTH, or GREAT YARMOUTH.   A parliamentary and municipal   146 m. YAR-
MOUTH STA.
borough, sea-port town, and parish, county of Norfolk.   Area of parish,
1,270 A.; population, 24,086; area of parliamentary borough, including
GORLESTON, county of Suffolk, 3,940 A.; population, 27,500.   It sends two
members to Parliament.   Registered electors (1848), 1,960; corporation
revenue at the same period, £6,630; customs' revenue in 1846, £59,784.
Registered shipping in 1847, 689 vessels, aggregate burden, 47,321 tons.
Yarmouth is situated on a narrow slip of land, lying between the sea and the
river Yare, which is crossed by a drawbridge communicating with Little
Yarmouth, or South Town, and Gorleston.   In ancient times Yarmouth was
surrounded by a moat, and fortified by embattled walls, and is said to owe
its origin to the Anglo-Saxons.   Near Yarmouth, however, are the ruins of
Caister Castle, and the Roman station of Garianonum.   The town consists
of four principal streets, which run parallel to each other, intersected by a
number of alleys, or rows, which are said to amount to one hundred and
fifty-six, and so narrow that carts are constructed purposely to traverse them.
The ancient parish church of St. Nicholas is one of the largest in England;
it dates from shortly after the commencement of the Norman dynasty.
Here are also St. Peter's, a new structure in the Tudor style, and St.
George's, a handsome edifice, and the remains of religious houses suppressed
at the Reformation, as well as chapels and meeting-houses for almost every
denomination of sectarians.   The town hall, situated near the centre of the

NORWICH (*continued*).

The hall and staircase are grand, the apartments spacious. To the south was an open colonnade, now closed up, and made into separate rooms. The grounds in front are embellished with extensive plantations, which, together with the fine woods of the park, and the view of the river, produce a charming effect. 1½ m. s. of Bungay are the ruins of Mettingham Castle. The castle was of quadrangular form, and, from the present appearance of the gatehouse, and some parts of the walls still standing, must have been an edifice of considerable extent and strength. It was built by John de Norridge, who in the seventeenth year of Edward III. obtained permission to convert his house into a castle, in which he also founded a college or chantry, dedicated to God and the Blessed Virgin. The revenues of this house at the dissolution were valued at £202 7s. 5d. The shattered walls of this castle are now converted into a farm-house. Mettingham Castle, Rev. J. C. Sufford.

2 m. S.E. KIRBY BEATON. 1 m. further, BRAMERTON. The Hall, John Blake, Esq.

132 m. BRUNDALL STATION.

1 m. s. at SURLINGHAM, Leasingham House, Gibbs Murrell, Esq.

134 m. BUCKEN-HAM STA.

4 m. N.E. ACLE. A village, once a market-town. Richard II., in the 11th year of his reign, granted to the inhabitants freedom from all tolls, rents of shire and of hundreds, with other immunities.

138 m. REEDHAM STATION.

Lowestoft Branch ☞

146 m. YAR-MOUTH STA.

quay, is a fine building, and the other public buildings, consisting of the borough gaol, custom-house, the theatre, public warehouses, the suspension bridge over the North Water, and the Nelson column, are all worthy of inspection. The charities of Yarmouth are on a noble scale, and evince the philanthropy of the inhabitants. Among these we may cite Warren's general relief fund, a hospital for children, a grammar school, &c. The quay is one of the noblest in the kingdom, upwards of one mile in length. Here are ranges of handsome residences, and the harbour formed by the river is accessible to vessels of 200 tons. Here are also barracks for 1,000 men, a pier, and Victoria suburb, with several public gardens and prome-nades. Yarmouth exports agricultural produce, malt, and fish, particularly herrings, to the Mediterranean, the West Indies, &c. It is the principal seat of the herring fishery, in which it employs 250 vessels belonging to the port, and about 3,000 hands in the different departments. Yarmouth is much resorted to as a bathing-place by the residents of Norfolk and the adjoining counties, and it is specially remarkable for the surpassing beauty of its female population of every rank of life. Yarmouth is the most dangerous coast of England, and its roads have often been the scene of misfortune to the mariner. The sand-banks are, however, carefully marked out by a line of buoys and floating lights. In October 1827, during a dreadful storm, no less than from ten to twelve vessels were wrecked in these roads in one night.

London to Norwich.

There are no very considerable works on this line. The chief bridges are those over the Roding at Ilford, the Ingerbourne at Brentwood, the Wid a short distance from Chelmsford, the Blackwater past Kelvedon, the Colne near Mark's Tey Station, the

	Distance from London.

Left of Railway from London.

Distance from London.

From Shoreditch to Stratford (see page 110).

WANSTEAD. Holloway Down, Thomas Bartleet, Esq.; Blake Hall, John Brown, Esq.; Oak Hall, B. Cotten, Esq.; Park Gate, T. Q. Finnis, Esq.; Cam Hall, Richard Plaxton, Esq.; Little Black Hall, a very pretty place, having been built by the late Sir Thomas Nash, Deputy Chamberlain to the late George IV., John Ray, Esq.; Lake House, Thomas Wells, Esq.; Wood House, Money Wigram, Esq.　　　*5 m. FOREST GATE STATION.*

¾ m. N. Valentine House, Charles Halcombe, Esq. 3 m. N.E. Hainault Forest; on the Barking side of which stands the celebrated Fairlop Oak, of such great age, that the tradition of the country traces it half way up the Christian Era. About 50 years back the stem measured 36 feet in girth, the branches overspreading an area of 300 feet.　　　*7 m. ILFORD STA.*

ROMFORD, a market-town and parish, county of Essex. Area of parish, 3,340 A. Here is a very ancient church, an union workhouse, town hall, gaol, market-house, national school, almshouses, and large cavalry barracks. Markets, Tuesday and Wednesday. Gidea Hall, Mrs. Black; Hare Hall, John Braithwaite, Esq.; Dagnam Park, Sir Thomas Neave, Bart. 2 m. N. ATTERINGHAM-AT-BOWER. Round House, John Barnes, Esq.; The Grange, George D'Almaine, Esq.; Pergo Park, Robert Field, Esq.; Bower House, Edward Robinson, Esq.; Bedfords, John Rogers, Esq. 2 m. further, STAPLEFORD ABBOTS. Stapleford Hall, Charles Mollett, Esq.; Albyns, Raikes Currie, Esq., M.P.; Battles' Hall, George Fitch, Esq. 2 m. further, at FAYDON MOUNT, Hill Hall, Sir Wm. Bowyer Smijth, Bart. Hill Hall, which stands upon a commanding eminence, was built in the early part of the reign of Queen Elizabeth, by Sir Thomas Smythe, Secretary of State to Edward VI. and to Queen Elizabeth, the direct ancestor of its present possessor. The interior of the mansion, the hall, and the court, attract considerable attention, from their peculiar style of architecture, based upon the finest models of the Italian school of that age. The whole fabric was from the design of the learned founder himself, who is supposed to have arranged his plans with the celebrated John of Padua, during his travels in Italy. The building is quadrangular, the length of each front being 140 feet. The hall is 56 feet long by 30 feet wide, and 25 feet high. The suite of rooms on the east are handsome, and of good dimensions, being about 33 feet by 20 feet, and are adorned with some fine pictures by the great masters. The grounds are well disposed, and extensive.　　　*12 m. ROMFORD STATION.*

½ m. N.W. BRENTWOOD. A chapelry, formerly a market-town in the parish of South Weald, county of Essex. Area, 730 A. It has an old Gothic chapel, a free grammar school, founded in 1537, possessing an annual revenue of £1,452, an almshouse, and court-house, in which the assizes were formerly held. Fairs, July 11th, October 15th and 16th. 1½ m. W. SOUTH WEALD. Maskells, G. S. Collyer, Esq.; Langtons, Martin Harvey,　　　*17¾ m. BRENT-WOOD STA.*

London to Norwich.

Stour on the borders of Essex and Suffolk, the Gipping near Ipswich, the Waveney on entering Norfolk, and the Yare at Norwich. The only viaduct is that at Chelmsford, and the only tunnel that a short distance past Ipswich.

Distance from London.	Right of Railway from London.
From Shoreditch to Stratford (see page 110).	
5 m. FOREST GATE STATION.	½ m. E. LITTLE ILFORD. The church is a small, neat structure, and has some interesting tombs. North End, Charles Mann, Esq.
7 m. ILFORD STA.	ILFORD, or GREAT ILFORD, a ward and chapelry in the parish of Barking, county of Essex, with a village on the Roding, here crossed by a bridge. It has a hospital, founded in the reign of Henry II; a house of correction for the south division of Essex; and a modern church. The Rookery, Hon. and Rev. H. W. Bertie; Cranbrook Lodge, Miss Milles; Tyne Hall, Dr. Rees Price; Clements, J. S. Thompson, Esq. 1½ m. S. BARKING. Ripple Castle, Thomas Tyser, Esq.
12 m. ROMFORD STATION.	Averingwell Villa, William Colls, Esq.; Havering Well House, Mrs. Truston. 2 m. S.E. HORNCHURCH, Samuel Waddison, Esq. 1 m. further, UPMINSTER. Upminster Hall, Mrs. Branfill. Is curious for its antiquity. It was a mansion belonging to the abbots of Waltham; it is built with timber, and commands fine prospects over parts of the counties of Essex and Kent; the grounds are well wooded. Oak Hall, Joseph Lee, Esq.; adjoining which is CORBET'S TEY. Harwood Hall, Captain P. Z. Cox; Green Lanes, Thomas W. Towson, Esq.
	3 m. S. AVELEY. Bell House, Sir Thomas Lennard Lennard, Bart., is a spacious edifice, standing in a pleasant park, about three miles in circumference, and abounding with fine oaks and other trees. This mansion was built in the reign of Henry VIII., but was altered and greatly improved by the late Lord Dacre. The decorations are extremely neat, and made from his own designs. This manor possesses the peculiar privilege of excluding any person, however great in rank, from entering it in pursuit of game. 2 m. E. of which, STIFFORD. Ford Place, S. Francis, Esq.; Stifford Lodge, John Freeman, Esq.; Coppid Hall, Thos. Ingram, Esq.; Stifford Clays, Thos. Noakes, Esq. 1½ m. S. GRAYS. Grays Hall, W. T. Longbourn, Esq.; Belmont Castle, Richard Webb, Esq.
	4 m. S. RAINHAM. Berwick House, Major Crosse. 3 m. S.E. PURFLEET. West Thurrock, William Edward Hunt, Esq. 4 m. S.S.W. Dagenham Level. At this place, owing to the blowing of a small sluice in the Thames embankment, a very destructive breach was formed in the year 1707, which, through the rush of waters, overflowed upwards of a thousand acres of land, and carried nearly one hundred and twenty acres into the Thames.
17¾ m. BRENTWOOD STA.	½ m. S. Thorndon Hall, Lord Petre. It stands on an eminence, which rises at the end of an avenue, two miles long, leading from Brentwood to the north front of the building, three hundred feet in extent. The architecture is Italian, and consists of a large centre edifice, with two pavillions, connected by sweeping corridors, principally built with fine white brick. Upon the south front is a noble hexastyle portico, of the Corinthian order,

Esq.; Luptons, E. P. Ind, Esq.; South Weald Hall, Christopher Thomas Tower, Esq., is a handsome building, situated in a large park, in which is a prospect house, built in the style of an embattled tower, commanding an extensive view. The grounds are well wooded, and diversified with pleasant gardens. 3 m. N.W. KELVEDON HATCH. Brizes, Misses Dolbey; Kelvedon Hall, J. F. Wright, Esq., is a spacious building of red brick, with a centre, and two wings, situated in a beautiful and well timbered part of Essex, two miles from the market-town of Chipping Ongar, and five and a half miles from Brentwood. The oak flourishes with great vigour in this vicinity. The house is situated in the parish of Kelvedon Hatch, and was erected about a century ago, on the site of the old mansion. The Wright family have been established here upwards of three centuries. 3 m. further, CHIPPING ONGAR. A market-town and parish, county of Essex. It was anciently denominated Ongar ad Kaston, on account of its castle, and to distinguish it from High Ongar, a village in the vicinity. It was supposed to have been founded soon after the arrival of the Saxons in England. Richard de Lucy, Chief Justice of England under Henry II., built a castle on a high eminence at the east of the town, surrounded by a moat, of which there are some traces. The castle itself was destroyed in the time of Queen Elizabeth. Spains Hall, S. B. Brocket, Esq.; Marden Ash, H. Bullock, Esq., J.P.; Greensted Hall, William Gibson, Esq.; White House, B. B. Hurlock, Esq.; Ongar Park Hall, John Stallibrass, Esq. A little to the east, HIGH ONGAR. Wardens Hall, Samuel Lewis, Esq.; Nash Hall, J. Palmer, Esq.; Paslow Hall, T. D. Ridley, Esq.; Forest Hall, Rev. J. P. Stane, J.P.

INGATESTONE. A parish, formerly a market-town in Essex. This place was originally called Ingatestone, a name derived from the Saxon word Ingameddon. A roman military column stood here. There is a large fair for Scotch and Welsh cattle held on the 1st and 2nd December. Furze Hall, Henry Arundell, Esq.; The Hyde, John Disney, Esq.; White House, Charles Grant, Esq.; Bacons, William Havers, Esq.; Huskards, Gordon Kelly, Esq. 3 m. N.W. BLACKMORE. Home Cottage, Miss Crickitt; Jericho House, C. R. Vickerman, Esq. 2 m. further, NORTON MANDEVILLE. Chivers Hall, Thomas Stokes, Esq.: Spurriers, Horatio Kidd, Esq. ¾ m. N.E. MARGARETTING. Canterburys, Benjamin Bond, Esq.; Ivy Hill, P. Rogers, Esq.; Peacocks, George Straight, Esq. 2 m. N. Writtle Hall, V. Knox, Esq.; close to which is Copfold Hall. *(margin: 23¼ m. INGATE-STONE STA.)*

2 m. W. WRITTLE. Formerly a market-town, but long divested of its trade by the increased importance of Chelmsford. Here Morant and some other antiquaries have placed the CÆSARMAGUS of the Itinerary, but there is no evidence of its ever having been a Roman station. Near the village is a square plot of ground enclosed by a deep moat, supposed to have been the site of a palace, recorded in " Stow's Annals" to have been erected by King John about 1211. Some of the foundations were dug up between thirty and forty years ago. The church is an ancient and spacious building, consisting of a nave, chancel, and side aisles, with an embattled tower at the west end. Within the church are several elaborate monuments, and many inscriptions to the memory of respectable families who have resided in this parish, which is supposed to be the largest in the county, its circumference being estimated at fifty-two miles. Writtle Island, John Atwood, Esq.; Hon. Frederick Petre. 3 m. s.w. of which, at BOXWELL, is Skreens, T. W. Bramston, Esq., M.P. 2 m. N. BROOMFIELD. Brookland Mrs. Hills. 2 m. further, GREAT WALTHAM. Langleys, John J. Tuffnell, Esq., is a handsome building, standing on a pleasant eminence, bounded by the river Chelmer on the north, and by a small rivulet on the south. The park and grounds are judiciously laid out. *(margin: 29¼ m. CHELMS-FORD STA.)*

with a beautiful velvet lawn in front, and fine prospects extending over the fertile hills of Kent, on the opposite side of the Thames. The park is very extensive, well timbered, containing many fine views in its home scenery, and the neighbouring county, abounding in eminences, luxuriantly clothed with wood. The principal entrance to the house is by the north front, where a light and lofty staircase leads to the great hall, 40 feet square, and 32 feet in height; the roof of the hall being supported by 18 scagliola columns. The drawing-room is 38 feet by 26 feet; and the dining-room, 36 feet by 24 feet; the library, over the eastern corridor, is 95 feet long, by 20 feet wide, opening at the east end upon a gallery in the chapel, which occupies the eastern wing, and is 48 feet by 24 feet. The grand saloon is a magnificent apartment, 60 feet by 30 feet. Thorndon Hall contains a fine collection of pictures, and its late noble owner had the honour to receive George III. at this seat. At the south end of the park, EAST HORNDON. Herongate Lodge, Edwin James, Esq.; Park House, Mrs. A. Miles. 6 m. further, passing through DUNTON, BULPHAM, and THORNDON-ON-THE-HILL, is ORSETT. Orsett Hall, Mrs. J. Baker. 5 m. further, TILBURY FORT, which was built in the time of Henry VIII., and was the abode of Queen Elizabeth while she reviewed the English army collected to oppose the Spanish Armada.

23¼ m. INGATE-STONE STA.

3 m. s. BILLERICAY, Captain Ede; William Schneider, Esq.; T. J. Spitty, Esq. 1½ m. further, GREAT BURSTEAD, William Bulwer, Esq. A little to the left, LITTLE BURSTEAD, Captain Charles London. About 3 m. further, LANGDEN HILLS. The most considerable eminence in this part of the county, affords some fine and extremely extensive prospects over the river Loudon, the river Thames, the metropolis, and the hills of the coast of Kent as far as the Medway, the whole of which, in clear weather, are displayed to the view, and compose a scene of almost unequalled beauty. 3 m. E. of Billericay, RAMSDEN BELLHOUSE. Chithams, Thomas Gabbett, Esq.

29¼ m. CHELMS-FORD STA.

CHELMSFORD, a market-town and parish, the capital of the county of Essex, at the confluence of the rivers Chelmer and Cann, which are crossed here by two beautiful bridges of iron and stone. Area of parish, 1,750 A. The town is well built, and lighted; many of its houses have gardens extending to the rivers. The parish church, which has been lately rebuilt, is a fine structure in the decorated style. The other principal buildings are a handsome county hall, in which are the assize court, assembly rooms, and corn exchange; county gaol and house of correction, a grammar school, founded by Edward IV., with an annual revenue of nearly £500; a theatre, and a public conduit. Chelmsford is the seat of the assizes and local courts. It has no manufactures; but its retail trade and grain markets are extensive. Market-day, Friday; fairs, May and Nov. 12. ¼ m. s. Moulsham Hall, Sir H. B. P. Mildmay, Bart. A little further on the road to MALDON, Noakes' Place, George Clapham, Esq.; Great Baddow Hall, Mrs. Lacland; Baddow Court, Mrs. General Douglass; Baddow Lodge, Thomas Greenwood, Esq.; Baddow Place, Richard Crabb, Esq.; Vineyard, Mrs. L. Bullen; Grove Cottage, Mrs. Reynolds. 2 m. further, DANBURY. Danbury Place, John Round, Esq. M.P.; Riffhams, J. R. S. Phillips, Esq., J.P.; The Palace, Lord Bishop of Rochester; Wood Hill, Miss Hales. 2 m. further, WOODHAM. Mortimer Place, John Oxley Parker, Esq.

Witham House, W. H. Pattisson, Esq.   2 m. N. Rivenhall Place, P. M.   38¼ m. WITHAM STATION.
Smith, Esq.; Faulkbourn Hall, Jonathan Bullock, Esq., is a stately and
spacious mansion, erected at different periods. Part of it displays a tower-
gateway of curious architecture, and is said to have been erected by the   Braintree and Maldon Br.
Earl of Gloucester about the time of King Stephen or King Henry II.
The present family have made great improvements in the house and grounds,
the latter of which are very extensive, and agreeably disposed, several fine
springs of water adding greatly to their beauty. Here is supposed to be
the largest cedar tree in England.

3 m. W. at TERLING, The Hall, Lord Rayleigh. Was once appendant to
Ely Cathedral, but was granted to Ranulph Pevent by the Conqueror. The
Bishops of Norwich formerly had a palace and park here, and a chapel,
which possessed the privilege of sanctuary, and is recorded to have shel-
tered the great Hubert de Burgh from the indignation of King Henry III.
Henry VIII. had also a residence here, which he granted to Lord Audley,
from whom it passed into the family of Strutt. Berwick House, C. Gratton
Townshend, Esq.

½ m. N. Felix Hall, T. B. Western, Esq. The Hall is a neat modern building,   41¾ m. KELVEDON STATION.
standing in a small but pretty park. The interior of the house is elegantly
fitted up, and the gardens are laid out with much judgment. 2 m. further,
COGGESHALL. Marygolds, W. F. Hobbs, Esq.; Leeze House, Mrs.
Skingley; Mount House, Stephen Unwin, Esq. About 1 m. further,
Oldfield Grange, Osgood Hanbury, Esq. 1 m. further, Mark's Hall, W. P.
Honywood, Esq. The manor-house was partly rebuilt by Robert Honywood, Esq., of Charing in Kent, in 1605, who erected a handsome front,
over the porch of which are various quarterings of the family arms. It
stands on a rising ground near the church, in a pleasant park, which was
greatly improved by the late Titmus Honywood, Esq., M.P. for Kent, who
made it his principal residence. In the dining-room was a portrait of
Mrs. Mary Honywood, who died in 1620, in her ninety-third year, having
had sixteen children, one hundred and fourteen grandchildren, two hundred
and twenty-eight great-grandchildren, and nine great-great-grandchildren,
making three hundred and sixty-seven in all during her life.

2 m. N.E. FEARING. Fearingbury, Edward Catchpool, Esq.

MARK'S TEY. A small parish of 1,350 A. 3 m. N. WAKES COLNE. 1½ m.   46¾ m. MARK'S TEY STA.
N.W. from which is WHITE COLNE. Berwick Hall, John Beard, Esq.;
Countess Cross; F. Sewell, jun., Esq. About 1 m. S.W. EARLS COLNE.
Mark's Hall, Mrs. Honeywood Blake; Colne Priory, H. H. Carwardine,
Esq.; Colne House, Mrs. M. Gee; Marsh Hall, William F. Hobbs, Esq.;
Hay House, Oliver Johnson, Esq. 1 m. W. COLNE. Colne Park, Robert   Sudbury Br.
Hills, Esq.; Grove House, Thos. Sewell, Esq. 2 m. further, HALSTEAD.
Halstead Lodge, J. N. Brewster, Esq., J.P.; Stanstead Hall, Mrs. S.
Bridge; Letches, J. Cook, Esq.; Don John's, J. Houghton, Esq.; Sloe
House, P. S. F. Martin, Esq., J.P.; Claverings, John Nunn, Esq.; Parley-
Beans, Joseph Nunn, Esq.; Fitzjohns, R. B. Scale, Esq.; Boishall,
J. Sewell, Esq.; Hepworth, J. Smoothy, Esq.; Gladfin Hall, J. Woolmer,
Esq.; Starstyle, G. De Horne Vaizey, Esq. J.P.; Whitehall, J. Savill, Esq.
J.P.; Westwood House, Major Charles Rooke.

3½ m. N. GREAT HORKESLEY, Captain C. Rooke. 1 m. further, NAY-   51¼ m. COLCHES-TER STA.
LAND. A small parish on the river Stour (over which is a bridge of brick),
in a fertile valley, surrounded by hills, on the high road to Hadleigh.

1½ N.E. SPRINGFIELD. Mount Hill, A. R. Chalk, Esq.; Springfield Place, C. G. Parker, Esq.; Shrubland, Isaac Perry, Esq.; Old Lodge, John Seabrook, Esq. 1½ m. further, BOREHAM, R. G. Haslefoot, Esq., J.P.; Boreham House, Sir J. T. Tyrell, Bart., M.P.; Boreham, Rev. Sir Coventry Pane, Bart. 1 m. S.E. of which is TOFTS. Little Baddow, Hon. Miss Strutt.

WITHAM, a market-town and parish, county of Essex. Area of parish, 8,280 A. It is near the confluence of the Braine with the Blackwater, and has a church, almshouses, an endowed school and other charities, producing an annual revenue of nearly £250. Witham is said to be the site of the Roman station Canonium, and there are vestiges of a Danish camp in the neighbourhood. Witham, W. W. Luard, Esq., J.P.; The Grove, Rev. H. Du Cane, J.P. 2 m. E. Braxted Lodge, Captain Du Cane, R.N. It is a handsome mansion, pleasantly situated on a gentle eminence near the centre of a small park, commanding agreeable prospects of the surrounding country.

3 m. s.w. Hatfield Priory, Peter Wright, Esq.

KELVEDON, county of Essex, is an ancient place which belonged to Edward the Confessor, and consists of a street about a mile long, on the north bank of the river Blackwater. The church, dedicated to the Virgin Mary, was given by King Edward the Confessor to Westminster Abbey, and has a square brick tower with five bells. 1 m. E. INWORTH. 3 m. further, LAYER MARNEY. Layer Marney Hall, Quintin Dick, Esq., M.P., formerly the seat of the noble family of Marney, who flourished for many centuries as warriors and statesmen. It was originally a large quadrangular building, enclosing a spacious court, the chief entrance to which, a tower-gateway, still remains. This highly interesting relic of former grandeur, is built of brick, and consists of a lofty centre of two stories, flanked at each angle by an octagonal tower, rising from the ground to some height above the centre. Each of the octagonal towers contains eight floors, lighted by small pointed windows; the centre stories are lighted by two large square windows. The summit, chimneys, and divisions between the windows, are curiously ornamented with sculptured mouldings of various patterns. On the east and west sides of this gateway are considerable remains of the old mansion, now converted into a farm-house and offices. A most extensive prospect is obtained from the tower, which stands on high ground.

3 m. s.s.E. LITTLE BIRCH. Situated on the river Roman, over which there is a bridge, called Ichford. The church is now in ruins. Birch Hall, Charles Gray Round, Esq. A little further, GREAT BIRCH; and a little further, LAYER DELAHAY.

1½ m. s.E. COPFORD, at which there is a very ancient church of Saxon architecture, with a nave, south aisle, and chancel; the east end of which is semi-circular; the walls are very thick, and the pillars supporting the roof very massive. It has a wooden turret, containing three bells, and a shingle spire. There is a tradition that the shoe of a Danish prince was nailed on the door of this church. Copford Hall, Fiske Harrison, Esq., J.P. It is a handsome mansion, supposed to have been the residence of Bonner, Bishop of London, to which see the manor once belonged. The grounds are pleasant, and ornamented with several pieces of water. 1 m. further, Stanway Hall, Colonel Brewster.

½ m. s. COLCHESTER, the Camulodunum of the Romans, and one of their ancient stations, is a parliamentary and municipal borough, river port and town, county of Essex, situated on the Colne, over which there are here several bridges. Area of borough, comprising 16 parishes, 11,770 A. It is

It consists of several streets, in which are some good dwelling-houses. The inhabitants are supplied with water from springs. The adjoining eminences command a fine view of the harbour of Harwich and the surrounding country. The woollen manufacture flourished here for many years, but is now extinct. The river is navigable from Sudbury to Harwich, by which means a considerable quantity of corn and flour is conveyed to Mistley for London. The church, dedicated to St. James, is situated in the centre of the town, and is a fine structure of the Elizabethan style of architecture. In the interior is a good painting of our Saviour, and several ancient marble monuments, inlaid with brass. The living is endowed with £400 private benefactions, and £400 royal bounty, and in the patronage of the parishioners. The Independents have also a place of worship. The market has been discontinued, but a fair is held on the first Wednesday in October for horses, cattle, and toys. 4 miles E. of Nayland, LANGHAM. Langham Hall, Thomas Maude, Esq. 1 m. further, at STOKE, Tendring Hall, Sir J. R. Rowley, Bart.

ARDLEIGH. There are three places of this name, ARDLEIGH, ARDLEIGH WICK, and ARDLEIGH CROWN. Ardleigh Park, J. P. Osborne, Esq. 3 m. to the right, The Rookery, Thomas L'Estrange, Esq. | 55½ m. ARDLEIGH STATION.

2 m. N.W. EAST BERGHOLT. It was the birthplace of Constable the artist, in the neighbourhood of which most of his finest subjects are taken. Old Hall, Dowager-Countess Morton; Highlands, C. T. Oakes, Esq.; West Lodge, C. W. Halford, Esq. | 59 m. MANNINGTREE STA. Enter Suffolk.

BENTLEY. A small parish in the Hundred of Sandford. 2 m. w. CAPEL, Cooper Brooke, Esq. 1 m. further, GREAT WENHAM, John M. Syer, Esq. 2 m. N. COPDOCK. | 62½ m. BENTLEY JUNCTION STA. Hadleigh Br.

At and near Ipswich are the following seats: Orwell Place, Mrs. Barker; Stoke Park, Hon. Lyndsey Burrell; Birkfield Lodge, F. W. Campion, Esq. The Lodge is situated on the top of Stoke Hills, and commands a delightful view of the river Orwell to the extent of six miles. Red House, Rev. M. G. Edgar. An old mansion, built in the year 1688. Christ Church Park, W. C. Fonnereau, Esq.; Mount, T. S. Gowing, Esq.; Hill House, Mrs. Hamilton; Stoke Hall, Joseph Smyth, Esq.; Preston Lodge, Edward B. Venn, Esq., situated on the banks of the Orwell, remarkable for its fine wooded scenery. 2 m. w. The Chauntry, C. Lillingstone, Esq. 3 m. further HINTLESHAM. The Hall, J. A. Hardcastle, Esq., M.P. Hintlesham for a great length of time was the property of the Timperleys, but subsequently passed to the ancestors of the late proprietor. The mansion is in the Elizabethan style, and built of brick in the form of the letter H. It contains a choice collection of paintings by Vandyke, and other eminent masters. The park is pleasantly situated, and contains an area of 150 A. The church, which is an ancient fabric, is dedicated to St. Nicholas, and has a square tower. In the chancel are several monuments to the Timperley family, especially a tomb of blue marble, on which is the portraiture in brass of John Timperly, Esq., in complete armour, who died in 1400, and Margaret his wife, with a hound at her feet, and on which there is a Latin inscription. | 68 m. IPSWICH STATION.

a polling-place for the north division of the county, and sends two members to Parliament. Registered electors (1848), 1,235; corporate revenue (1847), £3,236; customs' revenue (1846), £14,220; registered shipping (1847), 9,447 tons. The town is built on an eminence, and was formerly surrounded by walls, portions of which still exist, as well as many antiquated buildings, and the remains of a castle of great strength, said to have been built by Edward the Elder, parts of which are now used as a prison and town library. Here are also interesting relics of an abbey, an ancient chapel, and a priory. The parish churches, of which there are twelve, are very ancient; and the town contains the following public edifices: a fine moot, or town hall, county house of correction, a general hospital, well-endowed poors' hospitals, an union workhouse, various money charities, savings' bank, several literary and scientific associations, custom house, large market-house, bonding ware-houses, and a neat theatre. The free grammar school has scholarships at Cambridge, and was presided over, in 1779, by Dr. Parr. Vessels of 150 tons approach the quay. The malting trade is here carried on; and it imports coal, timber, lime, oil cake, and manufactures and colonial produce; and exports corn and malt, and has thriving oyster fisheries. Many ancient Roman coins and other relics have been discovered in Colchester, and it was also a Saxon town of considerable note. Markets, Wednesday and Saturday. Fairs, Easter Tuesday, July 5th and 23rd, and October 20th. Olivers, T. J. Turner, Esq. 2 m. s. Berechurch Hall, Sir George Henry Smyth, Bart.

1 m. S.E. HYTHE. Hythe Hill, late Gen. Sir John Maclean. 3 m. WIVEN-HOE. Wivenhoe Park, J. G. Rebow, Esq.; Wivenhoe Hall, S. S. Brown, Esq. A little to the right is DONYLAND, P. Havens, Esq.; Donyland Lodge, Rev. J. Holroyd. 1½ m. below Wivenhoe, ALRESFORD. The Hall, W. W. Haw-kins, Esq. 4 m. further, ST. OSYTH. St. Osyth's Priory, W. S. Nassau. Esq.

55½ m. ARDLEIGH STATION. 2 m. s. YELMSTEAD. The Lodge, Charles Joscelyn, Esq. 2 m. further, BROMLEY. Bromley Lodge, Mrs. Bateman.

59 m. MANNING-TREE STA.

Enter Suffolk.

MANNINGTREE, a market-town, county of Essex, on the river Stour, which is here navigable. Area of parish, 30 A. s. of which is Mistley Park, J. T. Ambrose, Esq. 2 m. further, Bradfield, Captain Runnacles. 10 m. E. HARWICH.

62½ m. BENTLEY JUNCTION STA. 2 m. S.E. Tattingstone Place, T. B. Western, Esq. 2 m. further, HOL-BROOK. Holbrook Cottage, John Berners, Esq.; Woodlands, William Rodwell, Esq.

4 m. E. WOOLVERSTONE. The Hall, Archdeacon Hull.

68 m. IPSWICH STATION.

IPSWICH, a parliamentary and municipal borough, river port and town, capital of the county of Suffolk, situated on the river Orwell, which is here crossed by a handsome iron bridge, at the influx of the Gipping. Area of municipal borough, including the whole of eight, and parts of four other parishes, 1,720 A.; population, 19,824; area of parliamentary borough, comprising twelve parishes and parts of six others, 7,020 A.; population, 25,384. The borough sends two members to Parliament; registered electors (1848), 1,685; corporate revenue (1847), £5,085; customs' revenue (1846), £37,012; registered shipping (1847), 182 vessels, aggregate burden, 14,434 tons. The Orwell is navigable to the town for vessels of 200 tons burden. Ipswich was formerly environed by a ditch and ramparts, and had four entrance gates. It stands on a slope, sheltered by hills on the east and north. There is a town library, and grammar school founded by Cardinal Wolsey, who was a native of Ipswich, from a portion of the ancient Blackfriars monastery. Ipswich also possesses several minor endowed schools and charities, a Philological Society, and a mechanics' institute. It has manufactures, and exports considerable quantities of corn to London. The scenery of the river Orwell is deservedly praised by the tourist, its banks being beautifully planted, and the sea-view is magnificent. Ipswich was twice burnt by the Danes, A D. 991 and 1000, and some vestiges

BRAMFORD. Levetofts Hall, R. A. Wood, Esq.; The Grove, R. W. Mumford, Esq. ½ m. N.E. Bramford Hall, Sir Philip Broke, Bart. 1 m. S.S.W. SPROUGHTON. Boss Hall, C. Kersey, Esq.; Sproughton Hall, W. Woodgate, Esq.

70¾ m. BRAMFORD STATION.

1½ m. S.W. by W. LITTLE BLAKENHAM. William Haward, Esq.; Benjamin Morgan, Esq. About 10 m. further, CHELLESWORTH, Sir Henry Edmund Austin.

73 m. CLAYDEN STATION.

NEEDHAM, or MARKET NEEDHAM. A small market-town and chapelry, in the parish of Barking, county of Suffolk. 2 m. W. BATTISFORD, Edward Linwood, Esq. 2 m. further, LITTLE FINBOROUGH. 4 m. further, THORPE-MORIEUX.

76¾ m. NEEDHAM STATION.

STOWMARKET. A market-town and parish, county of Suffolk. Situated at the confluence of three rivulets, which form the river Gipping. Area of parish, 1,240 A. The Stowmarket Canal is navigable hence to Ipswich, and here are manufactures of tanned leather and iron, and a considerable trade is carried on in coal, malt, corn, and timber. Abbotts Hall, Mrs. A. S. Rush. 2 m. W. GREAT FINBOROUGH, Captain John Bussell; R. J. Bussell, Esq. ½ m. further, Bucks Hall, Robert A. Fuller, Esq.; Robert John Garner, Esq. About 3 m. further, RATTLESDEN, Captain W. Parker.

80 m. STOW-MARKET STA.

HAUGHLEY. Sorrells, Mrs. H. Jacob. 1 m. S.S.W. Tot Hill, James Ward, Esq. 1 m. further, ONE HOUSE. The Lodge, Mrs. Susan Page Wrench. 2 m. W. Plushwood, the Rev. Sir A. B. Henniker, Bart. 1 m. further, Haughley Park, Rev. H. W. Crawford.

82½ m. HAUGH-LEY STA.
Bury St.
Edmund's Br.

FINNINGHAM. The church is an ancient edifice, with a square tower and Gothic porch. It has a stone front, with beautifully carved cover, and the altar windows are of stained glass. Mrs. A. and E. Clayton. 1 m. W. WESTHORPE. 2½ m. N.W. of which is WALSHAM-ON-THE-WILLOWS, Captain Thos. H. Wilkinson. 3 m. further, STANTON ALL SAINTS, and STANTON ST. JOHN. Stanton Park, Mrs. S. Vautier.

86½ m. FINNING-HAM STA.

BOTESDALE. A chapelry, formerly a market-town, in the parish of Redgrave. The town consists of one long street, extending into the parishes of Rickenhall Superior, and Rickenhall Inferior. It has a chapel (from the titular saint of which the name of the town is derived), which is a neat structure, of the later style of English architecture, of which it exhibits some good specimens. In the interior are monuments to the memory of Sir Nicholas Bacon, and that celebrated lawyer and patriot, Lord Chief

91 m. MELLIS STATION.

are still extant of a castle erected here by William the Conqueror, as well as of some monastic institutions. 2 m. s.e. Berkwell Lodge, Henry Campbell, Esq. 2 m. s.w. Orwell Park, late Sir R. Harland, Bart.; close to which is Nacton, G. Tomline, Esq.

2 m. s. Worsted Hall, Lady Harland. 3 m. e. KESGRAVE. The Hall, Robert Newton Shaw, Esq. 3 m. further, MARTLESHAM. Beacon Hill House, E. S. Gooch, Esq.; about 3 m. n.e. of which is WOODBRIDGE. A thriving market-town on the banks of the river Deeben. Woodbridge Abbey, William Norton, Esq.; about 1½ m. w. of which is Bealings House, Major Edward Moore; Ufford Place, Francis Brooks, Esq. 1½ m. n.e MELTON. The Lodge, Richard Aplin, Esq.; Hill House, C. Sharpe, Esq.; Foxbury Hall, C. Walford, Esq. 3 m. n.w. Boulge Hall, J. Fitzgerald, Esq.

70¾ m. BRAMFORD STATION.

1½ m. n.e. WHITTON CUM THURLESTON. Whitton Cottage, S. Catt, Esq.; Thurleston Hall, Rev. E. Woolnough. 1 m. n. of which is AKENHAM. The Hall, Robert Baker Orford, Esq.; Walnut Tree, Stephen Heyward, Esq.; Rice Hall, R. Woodward, Esq.

73 m. CLAYDON STATION.

1 m. e. CLAYDON, Lieutenant-Colonel Kerby. 2 m. n. Shrubland Park, Sir W. Fowle Middleton, Bart. 2 m. further, HEMINGSTONE. The Hall, Richard Martin, Esq.; Charles Crow, Esq. 2 m. e. HENLEY. The Hall, Charles Steward, Esq. 1½ m. further, WITNESHAM. The Hall, Daniel Charles Meadows, Esq. Witnesham Hall is pleasantly situated, and is a very ancient structure. The Meadows' family have resided here since the time of Richard III. When it came into the present owner's possession, it was in a very dilapidated condition, but has since been restored and embellished in the Elizabethan style of architecture. Burghurst House, Rev. John Brewster Meadows.

76¾ m. NEEDHAM STATION.

1 m. n. THE CREETINGS. Creeting Lodge, B. Wilkinson, Esq. A delightfully situated and romantic dwelling, with ornamented pleasure-grounds. 4 m. e. GOSBECK. 6 m. n. of which is DEBENHAM, Samuel Dove, Esq.; Barrington Chevalier, Esq. 3 m. e. from Gosbeck, HELMINGHAM. The Hall, John Tollemache, Esq., M.P. 4 m. further, BRANDESDON. The Hall, Charles Austin, Esq., Q.C.

80 m. STOWMARKET STA.

4 m. e. STONEHAMS. STONEHAM ASPELL, William Taylor, Esq. EARL STONEHAM, Richard Dunningham, Esq. STONEHAM PARVA. The Cottage, Mrs. Welham. About 1½ m. n.e. STEWARTLAND, Charles R. Freeman, Esq.; Mill House, Miss Cross.

82½ m. HAUGHLEY STA.

1 m. e. OLD NEWTON, John George Hart, Esq. Close to which is GIPPING CHAPEL, a hamlet, which derives its name from its situation near the source of one of those springs which form the river Gipping. Gipping Hall, the seat of the ancient equestrian family of Tyrrell.

86¾ m. FINNINGHAM STA.

1½ m. e. WICKHAM SKEATH, Thomas Turner, Esq. 3 m. n.e. THORNHAM MAGNA. Thornham Hall, Lord Henniker.

4 m. e. THORNDON. Standwell Lodge, John Hayward, Esq.

91 m. MELLIS STATION.

3 m. e. YAXLEY. Yaxley Hall, Mrs. R. Leake. P. R. Welsh, Esq. 1½ m further, EYE. A parliamentary and municipal borough, market-town, and parish, county of Suffolk. Area, 4,320 A. It now sends but one member to Parliament, although the parliamentary borough extends over eleven parishes. Registered electors (1848), 330. The town is surrounded by a rivulet, from which circumstance it is said to derive its name of Eye, or Island. It consists principally of whitewashed and thatched houses of

Justice Holt, whose remains are deposited here. There is a free grammar school, founded and endowed in 1576 by Sir Nicholas Bacon. Botesdale Cottage, John Dyce, Esq.; Botesdale Lodge, Nathaniel Surtees, Esq. A little to the N., REDGRAVE. The Hall, G. St. Vincent Wilson, Esq.; Redgrave Cottage, E. P. Blake, Esq.

Enter Norfolk.

3 m. N.W. WORTHAM. Manor Hall, J. J. Tuck, Esq.

DISS. A small market-town. This place, formerly DUS, or DISE, was held a royal demesne in the reign of Henry I. The town is pleasantly situated near the river Waveney, by which it is separated on the south from the county of Suffolk, and consist of several well-built and paved streets. The principal manufactures are those of hemp and cloth. Market-day, Friday; fair, November 8th. Several distinguished characters have been born in this place. For instance: Ralph De Di Cito, Dean of St. Paul's in the reign of Henry II.; Walter of Diss, a Carmelite monk of Norwich, afterwards confessor to the Duke of Laucaster, and Acquetaine, King of Castile, and also to Constance, his Queen; and John Shelton, Poet Laureate to Henry VIII., and styled by Erasmus "the light and ornament of English scholars," was rector, and most probably a native of this place. 1 m. w. ROYDON. The Hall, Rev. Temple Frere. 3 m. further, SOUTH LOPHAM. The Grange, George Wharton, Esq. 2 m. N. of Diss, Wester-field House, Stephen Walter, Esq.

94½ m. DISS STA.

1 m. w. SHELFANGER. 1 m. north of which, WINFARTHING.

97 m. BURSTON STATION.

1½ m. N.W. FIBBENHAM. A village containing 3,120 A., the chief owner of which is J. Petre, Esq.

100 m. TIVET-SHALL STA.

1 m. FORNCETT. There are two Forncetts, St. Mary's and St. Peter's. In former times, the Knighted Court, as it was termed, was held here every three weeks. At this court all the great men who held their lands or tenements of the Norfolk honour were obliged to attend and commute for castle guard service for the castles' guard at Norwich.

103¾ m. FORN-CETT STA.

2 m. N.W. BRAKENASH. The Hall, Miss E. Burney.

106 m. FLORDEN STATION.

2 m. w. MULBARTON. The Lodge, Sir William Bellairs. 2 m. N. KESWICK. Old Hall, H Birkbeck, Esq.; New Hall, Hudson Gurney, Esq.

109 m. SWAINS-THORPE STA.

113¾ m. NORWICH STATION.
(See London and Yarmouth).

London and South=Western Railway.

The act for the incorporation of the London and Southampton Railway Company received the royal assent on the 25th of July, 1834; and various acts were subsequently passed, authorizing the company to raise sufficient capital to carry out their intentions, as it appears from the history of their proceedings, that the original estimate fell far short of the expenses actually incurred. The earth-works, cuttings, &c., were very heavy; the bridges, generally built of brick, numerous, averaging about two and a quarter per mile, although there is no particular bridge or viaduct throughout the line worthy of especial notice. There are but four tunnels, and two archways on the line, beyond Winchfield. Two of the tunnels are at Popham, one at Waller's Ark, and one at Lichfield. Those at Popham are each two hundred yards in length, twenty-five feet wide, and twenty-two feet high; the Waller's Ark tunnel is five hundred yards, and the Lichfield two hundred yards in length. The line from Vauxhall to Southampton was opened to the public throughout on the 11th of May, 1840, having cost, from the commencement of the undertaking, up to the 30th of June of the same year (without

a mean appearance, but its Gothic church is spacious, and it has a grammar school, with two exhibitions to Cambridge, a handsome guildhall, gaol, house of industry, almshouse, and a branch Bank of England. It formerly contained a castle, and eastward of the town are the ruins of a Benedictine monastery. Markets, Tuesday and Saturday.

Enter Norfolk.

94½ m. DISS STA. 1 m. s. PALGRAVE. St. John's Lodge, the Misses Harrison. 2 m. E. SCOLE. The Shrubbery, the Misses Lee ; Scole Lodge, Mrs. J. Whittaker. 1 m. further, OAKLEY. Oakley House, Mrs. B. Frank. 3 m. further, NEEDHAM. 1½ m. further, HARLESTON, once called Heroldveston, and Herofston, from a Danish leader named Herop, who came over to England with Canute, and probably settled at this place. It is situated about 1 mile from the river Waveney, over which there is a bridge. The manufacture of bombazine has been carried on of late years to a limited extent. Market, Wednesday. Sandy Hall, W. S. Holmes, Esq.

97 m. BURSTON STATION. BURSTON. 1 m. N.E. SHIMPLING. Shimpling Place, Duke of Grafton.

100 m. TIVET-SHALL STA. 1 m. E. TIVETSHALL. There are two villages of this name, St. Margaret and St. Mary's.

103½ m. FORN-CETT STA. 1½ m. E. LONG STRATTON. The Manor House, a handsome building in the Elizabethan style, the Rev. Ellis Burroughes. 1½ m. further, Boyland Hall, Frederick Irby, Esq. An Elizabethan mansion, built in 1571, and repaired in 1804 by its late owner, the Hon. Admiral Irby. The hall is situated in a valley, one mile north of Morningthorpe. This place formerly belonged to the Garneys' family, through whom it has descended to its present proprietor.

106 m. FLORDEN STATION. 3 m. E. SHOTTISHAMS, or Scenteshill, the village of Scots, or Portions. The landed property having been divided into twelve parts at the time of the Conquest, it now consists of two parishes, St. Mary and All Saints.

109 m. SWAINS-THORPE STA. 1 m. N.E. DUNSTON. A small parish on the river Tas, consisting of about 600 acres, principally the property of Robert K. Long, Esq., of Dunston Hall, Lord of the Manor.

113½ m. NORWICH STATION.

(See London and Yarmouth).

London and South-Western Railway.

reference to the Gosport and other branches), £2,054 5s. 5d. The Waterloo Station is admirably convenient, and is situated in the Waterloo Bridge Road, on the Surrey side of the Thames, within five minutes' walk of that great national monument, Waterloo Bridge, in the very centre of London.

The Nine Elms, or Vauxhall Station, the original terminus of this Company, being too far removed from the seat of commerce, and difficult of access, except by hackney or other conveyances, the directors, desirous to meet the public convenience, determined upon the metropolitan extension ; and erected that gigantic viaduct over the populous districts of Vauxhall and Lambeth, which was opened to the public on the 11th of July, 1848, and now connects the distant suburban station of Nine Elms with the Strand, the most central spot, and the greatest thoroughfare of the metropolis. Waterloo Station, beyond its great convenience in point of position, presents no remarkable feature as to architectural design or embellishment.

Left of Railway from London.

KENNINGTON. NORTH BRIXTON.

CLAPHAM COMMON, is situated in the parish of Clapham, county of Surrey, one of the most agreeable suburbs of London. The Common, which is its principal attraction, and contains about 200 acres, is prettily planted with trees and shrubs, and surrounded by handsome villa-residences, and beautiful gardens.

¾ m. S. MERTON. Is on the river Wandle, which is here crossed by a bridge. It has some handsome residences, not unlike the old manor-houses, a very ancient church, and some vestiges of a priory, which dates from the Conquest. A Parliament was held here in the reign of Henry III. In 1264 Robert De Merton, Bishop of Rochester, founded a college here, which was afterwards removed to Oxford, and called Merton College. Merton Grove, Alexander A. Park, Esq. Merton Cottage, William Adams, Esq.; Wandlebanks, Harry Pollard Ashby, Esq.; Long Lodge, Major James Colebrooke; Holmes Elms, Captain Thomas Hegar; Merton Rush, Miss Jenkinson; Spring House, J. H. D. Mandeville, Esq.; Dorset Hall, George Orme, Esq.; Cannons Hill, Richard Thornton, Esq.

1½ m. S. MALDON. Thomas Weeding, Esq.

1 m. S. TALWORTH. George Pugh, Esq. Worcester Park, Kensington Lewis, Esq. 2 m. S.S.W. HOOK. Gooseberry Hill, E. Jiggins, Esq. A little further, CHESSINGTON, near which, at Stoke Common, is Jessup's Well, celebrated for a mineral water of the same nature as that of Cheltenham. Its superior strength appears from the crystals retaining their figure and firmness for a year and a half after being formed, and it has been observed to have an extraordinary effect, probably owing to the steel it contains. Dr. Adee, an eminent physician at Guildford, in the early part of the last century, asserted that by a steady and cautious use of this water, some of his patients had been cured of scurvy.

1 m. S.W. ESHER. The scenery is highly interesting, being enriched with mansions and seats of the first order. Adjoining Esher, a priory and monastery was founded in the time of Edward II., on the site of which is Sandown House, James Nugent Daniel, Esq.; Esher Place, John William Spicer, Esq., is distinguished as having been the abode of Cardinal Wolsey. Claremont, built by Lord Clive, the conqueror of India, who, on setting out on his last voyage, gave directions to Brown the architect to pull down the mansion of the same name built by the Duke of Newcastle, and to build him a house, without regard to any expense. This he did to the satisfaction of his employer, at a charge of £100,000. It forms an oblong square of thirty-four yards by forty-four yards. The principal front has a flight of thirteen steps, which leads to the great entrance, under pediments supported

Distance from London.	**Right of Railway from London.**
2 m. VAUXHALL STATION	VAUXHALL GARDENS.
Windsor Line. ☞	
5 m. CLAPHAM COMMON STA.	BATTERSEA. It is principally occupied by market gardens, in which asparagus was first introduced, and is celebrated as containing above one quarter of the species of English plants. The church is dedicated to St. Mary, and forms an interesting object from the river. The windows over the altar are decorated with portraits of Henry VII., his grandmother, and Queen Elizabeth. The interior contains some interesting monuments, one of which is to the memory of Viscount Bolingbroke and his lady, and one to the memory of Edward Winter, an officer in the E.I.C.S., who is stated to have singly and unarmed killed a tiger, and on foot defeated forty Moors on horseback.
8 m. WIMBLEDON AND MERTON STATION.	WIMBLEDON is a very pretty picturesque village, in the county of Surrey, surrounded by the villas of the aristocracy, many of which are handsome structures. Its wild heath or common was once celebrated as the resort of duellists. Copshill, late Lord Cottenham; Wimbledon House, Mrs. Marryatt; Wimbledon Park, Duke of Somerset.
10½ m. MALDON STATION.	1 m. N. Coombe Wood, Samuel Smith, Esq.; Coombe Cottage, Edward Woodbridge, Esq.; Coombe Farm, Francis Garner, Esq.; Coombe Lodge, W. O. Hunt, Esq.
12 m. KINGSTON STATION.	KINGSTON NEW TOWN. A little further, SURBITON. Surbiton Hill House, Benjamin Hinds, Esq.; Surbiton Lodge, Captain Manderson, R.N.; Surbiton Cottage, Miss C. Massey; Gothic Cottage, John Smith, Esq.; West Field, Thomas Taylor, Esq. ½ m. further, KINGSTON-ON-THAMES, county of Surrey, a municipal borough town, containing 7,360 A. This is one of the most ancient and historical towns in England, built on the site of a Roman station, a fact which is satisfactorily attested by the numerous coins and other Roman antiquities from time to time discovered. Many of the Saxon kings were crowned, and Egbert held a great ecclesiastical council here in 838. The first parliamentary army assembled here in the civil wars; and this town also witnessed the last effort in favour of Charles I., when the Earl of Holland and others were taken prisoners, and beheaded. The town is prettily situated on the banks of the Thames, which is here crossed by a very elegant new stone bridge of five river arches. Seething Well, John Brown, Esq.; Fairfield, Thomas Chalk, Esq.; Woodbines, W. M. Christie, Esq.; Elmers, Mrs. A. Disney; Bury Lands, William F. White, Esq. A little to the E. Norbiton, Dowager Lady Liverpool; The Lodge, William Bulmore, Esq.; The Hall, Mrs. F. Jeyes.
Hampton Court Branch. ☞	
15 m. ESHER AND CLAREMONT STA.	1 m. N.E. THAMES DITTON, a neat village situated on the banks of the Thames, and much resorted to by the disciples of Isaac Walton. It was a favourite resort of the late Theodore Hook, and is supposed to be the spot where he played off the joke attributed to Daly in "Gilbert Gurney," of the Deputy-Assistant Surveyor of the Grand Junction Canal Company. Hon. Lady S. Fitzgerald; Weston Green House, General Sir John Lambert, Bart.; Boyle Farm, Sir Edward Sugden.
	½ m. N. Ember Court, Sir Charles Sullivan, Bart, long the residence of the Hon. E. Onslow, Speaker of the House of Commons, and his son, Earl Onslow. It is a commodious brick dwelling, covered with stucco, with a park of very considerable extent. About ½ m. further, EAST MOULSEY. Matham Manor House, Miss E. Bates; Elm Cottage, James Bland, Esq.; Bridge House, Thomas Flockton, Esq.; Walnut-Tree House, S. Kendal,

by Corinthian columns. The situation is well chosen for commanding views of the woods and plantations in the park. After Lord Clive's death in 1774, this estate was sold for not more than one-third what the house and alterations cost. Having passed through the hands of Viscount Galway, Earl Clanconnel, and Charles Rose Ellis, Esq., it was purchased for the Princess Charlotte and Prince Leopold, by whom it was offered to Louis Philippe as an asylum after his abdication of the French throne in 1848, and in which he resided until his death in August, 1850. West End Cottage, John Abbott, Esq.; Grove House, John L. Baker, Esq.; Moor Place, Right Hon. Lady Noel Byron; Esher Lodge, Thomas Chapman, Esq.; Stanza Cottage, Richard Cobbett, Esq.; Home House, John Duckett, Esq.; Melbourne Lodge, Major-General Sir Robert Gardiner, K.C.B.; Woodside, Samuel McDowall, Esq.; West End Lodge, Thomas Roberts, Esq.; Belvidere House, Thomas Stanborough, Esq.; Wolsey Grange, Thomas Vardon, Esq.; Holly Cottage, Mrs. Vesey.

HERSHAM. 1½ m. w. Burwood Park, Sir Richard Frederick, Bart., is an elegant mansion, built by the late Sir John Frederick, in a park containing 300 acres, without any road or footpath before the late enclosure, which added to it 150 acres more. Burwood Cottage, Henry Westcar, Esq.; Burwood Lodge, Thomas Terry, Esq.; Burhill Park, Colonel Kemeys-Tynte. 1 m. further, COBHAM. Cobham Park, Harvey Combe, Esq.; Cobham Lodge, Miss Molesworth; Paynes Hill, Mrs. Cooper; Hatchfield House, The Earl of Ellesmere. 17 m. WALTON AND HERSHAM STATION.

1½ m. s. BYFLEET. West Lodge, James Sparkes, Esq.; Byfleet Lodge, John Back, Esq.; Albany House, Mrs. Varden. 1 m. further, WISLEY. 1 m. further, Oakham Park, Right Hon. Stephen Lushington. 3 m. further, West Horsley Place, H. Currie, Esq., M.P. 19 m. WEYBRIDGE STATION.

EAST HORSLEY TOWER, EARL LOVELACE.

Esq.; Moulsey Park, James Todd, Esq. 1½ m. w. WEST MOULSEY. Grove Gottage, Right Hon. John W. Croker; Sutton Villa, Thomas Gunning, Esq.; Ivy Cottage, John G. Nicholls, Esq.; Mole Cottage, W. P. Palmer, Esq.

THE GRANGE, EDMUND LIONEL WELLES, ESQ.

The villa is charmingly situated between the village and the Mole. Its grounds are laid out with great taste and beauty, and being on a gravelly soil, is remarkably salubrious.

17 m. WALTON AND HERSHAM STATION. 1 m. N. WALTON HERSHAM. Walton-on-Thames, county of Surrey, is beautifully situated on the above river, which is crossed by a good bridge. It has a handsome church, with some fine monuments. Apps Court, Richard Sharpe, Esq. It was built on the site of an old mansion of Cardinal Wolsey's. Elm-Tree House, John Chapman, Esq.; Ashley Park, Sir Henry Fletcher, Bart.; Holly Grove, Captain John Shepherd; Mount Felix, Earl Tankerville; Manor House, Mrs. Colonel Taylor; Apps Court Cottage, Henry Tubbs, Esq.

19 m. WEYBRIDGE STATION.

Chertsey Br. ☞ WEYBRIDGE. The church, dedicated to St. Nicholas, contains some ancient and modern monuments, and among them one to the memory of the late Duchess of Kent, by Chantrey. On the green is a column thirty feet high, also erected to the memory of Her Royal Highness. Oatland, — Peppercorn, Esq., formerly the seat of the late Duke of York. This magnificent edifice was erected towards the end of the last century, the former building having been destroyed whilst the Duke was in Flanders. It stood near the middle of the park, on a noble terrace, from which the prospects are extensive and beautiful. Below the brow of the terrace was an artificial piece of water, made to appear as if Walton Bridge crossed it in the distance. On the side of the hill between the house and the kitchen garden rise some springs, which are formed into a small piece of water. By the side of it was a grotto, divided into three apartments, the sides and roof encrusted with petrifactions. One of the rooms was a bath, supplied by a small spring dripping through the rock. The park and grounds comprised about 3,000 A. Firsgrove, Sir J. Easthope, Bart.; White House, John Feetham, Esq.; Stanmore Villa, V. Flockton, Esq.; Holly House, J. H. Hardwick, Esq.

The mansion is Elizabethan, built of white flint and Caen-stone, and stands on the northern slope of the North Downs, and commands from the top of the tower a fine view over parts of Surrey, Middlesex, Herts, Bucks, Oxon, and Hants, including twenty-two churches, among which is St. Paul's, the race-stands of Epsom and Ascot, and the Roman camps at Farnham and St. George's Hill.

1½ m. s. WOKING. This is one of the royal demesnes of Edward the Confessor, and there was a royal palace at this place in the time of Henry VIII., who occasionally used it as a summer residence ; and it was here in September, 1551, that Wolsey received the letter from the Pope informing him of his elevation to the dignity of Cardinal. Sutton Place, A. Hicks, Esq.; Mrs. H. Wyndham. 2 m. further, SEND, Mrs. F. Boughton; Sendhurst Place, Hon. F. Scott, M.P.; Send Grove, George Rickards, Esq. 2 m. s.e. of Woking is RIPLEY. Ripley Court, Miss Harrison.

| | 25 m. WOKING STATION. |
| | ⬡ Guildford Br. |

FARNBOROUGH, George Morant, Esq.; The Hill, Dean of Chichester.

	33 m. FARN-BOROUGH STA.
	Guildford and Reading Railway.
	⬡ ☞
	37 m. FLEETPOND STATION.

WINCHFIELD. 1 m. further, Dogmersfield Park, Sir J. H. Mildmay, Bart. The mansion is a very extensive building, standing on an eminence in a park containing about 700 acres.

| | 40 m. WINCH-FIELD STA. |

1½ m. s.w. HODDHAM, the birthplace of the celebrated grammarian William Lilley. The Bury, Mrs. John Cole; Hatchwood House, Mrs. Thompson. 2 m. further SOUTH WARNBOROUGH, Thomas M. Wayne, Esq.

BASINGSTOKE is an ancient town, situated near to the canal bearing its name, and communicating with the rivers Thames and Wey, which, with the railway, facilitate a brisk trade in corn and malt. Area of parish, 3,970 A. Is has a church, built in the 16th century, a free school, with a revenue of £200 per annum, a blue-coat school, founded 1646, and several other charities, a market house, town hall, and a gaol. Shrubbery, Edward Cove, Esq.; Down Grange, Mrs. C. Terry; Winton House, F. C. G. Ritson, Esq.; Lawn Cottage, C. Simmonds, Esq. 1 m. s. Hackwood Park, Lord Bolton; still further, Herriard House, G. P. Jervoise, Esq. 2 m. further, BENTWORTH. Bentworth Hall, Charles Bush, Esq.; Binstead Hill, C. B. Coulthard, Esq. 2 m. further, ALTON. Willhall Cottage, Mrs. Abbott; Rose Cottage, Captain J. G. Duncan, R.N.; Anstey Hall, Misses Miller; Theddon Grange, John Wood, Esq. 1 m. s.w. CHAWTON. Chawton House, Edward Knight, Esq. 2 m. further, NEWTON VALANCE. Manor House, Henry Chawner, Esq.; Pelham House, Captain Lemprie, R.N. 1 m. s. EAST STISLEAD. Rotherfield Park, James Scott, Esq. 2 m. e. of Hackwood Park, UPTON GRAY, J. H. Mackay, Esq.

| | 48 m. BASING-STOKE STA. |

3 m. s.s.w. Farley House, Charles Bowyer, Esq. 3 m. further, PRESTON CANDOVER, Charles E. Rumbold, Esq., M.P.; North Hall, Francis J. Ellis, Esq.

2 m. s.w. CLIDDESDON. 1½ m. further, Kempsholt House, Edward W. Blunt, Esq.

1 m. e. Stratton Park, Sir F. T. Baring, Bart., M.P., formerly the property of the Duke of Bedford, and about the commencement of the present century a favourite hunting residence of the then Marquis of Tavistock, who pulled a large portion of the mansion down lest his successors should prefer it to Woburn. Since it passed into the family of the present proprietor, considerable improvements have been made in the

| | 58 m. ANDOVER ROAD STA. |

25 m. WOKING
STATION.

2½ m. N. Ottershaw Park, Richard Crawshay, Esq. A noble stone mansion, built by Sir Thomas Sewell, many years Master of the Rolls. Potters Park, George Wood, Esq.

3 m. N.W. CHOBHAM. Chobham Place, Sir Denis Le Marchant, Bart.; Grove House, William Keyton, Esq.; Westcroft House, Thomas Fielder, Esq.; Pankhurst, Richard Collier, Esq. 2 m. WOODLANDS, J. C. Tyler, Esq. 1 m. further, WINDLESHAM. Windlesham Hall, William Archer, Esq.; Windlesham House, the late Admiral Sir Edward Owen, G.C.B.

1 m. W. HORSELL. 3 m. further, BISLEY.

33 m. FARN-
BOROUGH STA.
Guildford and
Reading Railway.

1 m. N. FRIMLEY. Frimley House, John Tekell, Esq.; Windmill Hill, Lady Palmer; Hawley House, Henry Dumbleton, Esq.

37 m. FLEETPOND
STATION.

40 m. WINCH-
FIELD STA.

Basingstoke and
Reading Rail.

1 m. W. MATTINGLEY. 1 m. further, Strathfieldsaye, Duke of Wellington. North Hartley Row, Thomas Husband, Esq.; Belmont Cottage, Charles Gay, Esq.; West Green, Robert White, Esq. 2 m. further, EVERSLEIGH. Bramshill Park, Sir John Cope, Bart. Few places afford such an unmixed treat to visitors and lovers of old halls as the fine old house of Bramshill; Warbrook Cottage, Captain West.

48 m. BASING-
STOKE STA.

Near the station are the ruins of the ancient Chapel of the Holy Ghost, which owes its destruction to the ruthless hands of the Presbyterians during the civil wars of the 17th century. 1½ m. N. The Vine, William L. Wiggett Shute, Esq. This was formerly the seat of the celebrated Lord Sandys. The mansion is a long range of brick building, with wings. The grounds are extensive, and well wooded. A small stream of water crosses the lawn, that extends from the north front of the house. ½ m. further, Beaurepaire, Hon. P. Barrington. HECKFIELD, Right Hon Charles Shawe Lefevre. The house is situated on a hill, whence there is a fine view over a well-timbered country. 2 m. further, SILCHESTER. The Bangalow, Henry Newnham, Esq.

4 m. N.W. WOLVERTON. 1 m. s. of which is EWHURST. Manor House, W. J. Chaplin, Esq. A little further, Wolverton Park, Sir P. Pole, Bart. 2 m. W. of which is KING'S CLERE. Elm Grove, William Holding, Esq. 2 m. further W. SIDMONTON. Sidmonton House, William Kingsmill, Esq.

2 m. W. WORTING. Worting House, Mrs. P. Warren. A little further, Manydown, Rev. L. B. Wither. 2 m. further, DEAN. Oakley Hall, William Beach, Esq.; Dean House, Charles Harwood, Esq.

58 m. ANDOVER
ROAD STA.

4 m. N.W. WHITCHURCH. Close to which is Freefolk Priors, Melville Portal, Esq., M.P. A little to the left, Hertsborne Priors, Earl of Portsmouth. The mansion stands on elevated ground, commanding fine and extensive prospects. To the south and north it consists of a centre and two uniform wings, connected with the body of the house by colonnades. From the south, or principal front, the ground gradually slopes to a piece of water

house and grounds. 3 m. s. of which is NORTHINGTON. The Grange, Lord Ashburton. 2 m. further, ALRESFORD, or NEW ALRESFORD. It appears to have been a market and borough-town from time immemorial, and returned for some time one member to Parliament. The town was given by King Kenewalch to the church at Winchester. In 1220 the market, which had then decayed, was re-established by Bishop de Lucy. The town was destroyed by fire in 1690 and 1710, and since then has been nearly destroyed in a similar way. A noble piece of water, covering about 200 acres, to the south-west of the town, and which forms the head of the Itchen river, owes its origin to Bishop de Lucy, who, in the time of King John, completed it, and also made the river navigable to Winchester, and thence to South-ampton. In recompense for this vast and expensive work, the entire royalty of the river, from the head to the sea, and other privileges, were given to the Bishop and his successors. Close to which is OLD ALRESFORD. Lord Rodney; Earl of Guildford; Upton House, Colonel C. T. Onslow.

WINCHESTER, the Caer-Gwent of the Ancient Britons (one of their most important cities), afterwards a celebrated Roman station, is a city, parliamentary, and municipal borough, capital of the county of Hants, situated on the river Itchen, which is here crossed by a handsome stone bridge. Area of city and soke liberty, 2,250 A. It returns two members to Parliament. Registered electors (1847), 710. Winchester, which was the capital of England throughout all the Saxon, Danish, and early Norman dynasties, is well built, lighted, and paved, and contains many handsome mansions and modern ·residences, which, with its grand ecclesiatical structures, and ancient edifices in the by-streets, give it altogether a most venerable and interesting appearance. It was formerly enclosed by walls, no vestiges of which remain, and contained ninety churches, chapels, and monastic institutions, many of which were suppressed and destroyed at the Reformation. Winchester has now nine parish churches, the principal of which are St. Lawrence, the Mother Church, St. Swithin's, St. Michael's, a new structure, and St. Maurice, which was rebuilt in 1840. The south-east quarter of the city is almost exclusively occupied by the cathedral, which, according to the most learned antiquaries, was founded in the 2nd century. It is a vast structure, five hundred and forty-five feet in length, two hundred and eight feet broad at the transept, with a nave three hundred and fifty-one feet, and a choir one hundred and thirty six-feet in length, and a central tower one hundred and fifty feet high. Externally, the whole building is plain and heavy, with the exception of the west front, but the interior is magnificent. The ashes of many of the kings of Wessex, and the Saxon kings of England repose in carved chests over the choir, and William Rufus was here interred. The altar-piece, which represents the "Raising of Lazarus," is one of the best productions of West. Winchester College, founded by William of Wykeham, one of the most celebrated public schools in the kingdom, contains some fine buildings, and near it are the remains of the ancient Episcopal Palace, the City Cross, St. John's House, the barracks, formerly the palace of the sovereigns of England, who resided here from time to time until the death of Queen Anne; the assize hall, built on the site of the ancient castle, the guildhall, county gaol, house of correction, and county hospital, are all worthy of notice. Winchester has also a market-house, a theatre, and assembly rooms, many almshouses and other charities, mechanics' institute, public library, and savings' bank. There were formerly four entrance gates to the city, of which the west gate alone remains,. and in one of its chambers is still preserved the original Winchester bushel of King Edgar, and other Anglo-Saxon standards of measure. Near this gate is the public cemetery, which was laid out in

67 m. WINCHES-
TER STA.

which winds through the park, which is delightfully intersected, and abounds with wood and deer, particularly to the east of the house, where the beech and oak have obtained great size, and are extremely flourishing.

8 m. w. ANDOVER. A parliamentary and municipal borough, county of Hants, capital of division and hundred. Area of parish, 7,670 A.; area of borough, including the parish of Knights Enhan and Foxcott, 10,780 A. Andover returns two members to Parliament. Registered electors (1848), 243. It is a well-built and thriving town. Although its trade consists principally in the supply of the necessary articles of life to the neighbouring country, it possesses, however, a considerable silk factory. The church is a venerable Gothic structure, said to have been erected before the Norman Conquest. The town hall, a modern erection, a free school, hospital, and almshouses, are its principal public buildings. Andover is connected with Southampton by a canal. The Weyhill cattle fair is held in this neighbourhood. Market, Saturday. It has also horse, leather, and cheese fairs. Wood House, Charles Holdway, Esq.; Finckley, J. B. Mundey, Esq.; Red Rice House, Rev. Thomas Best; Abbotts Ann Rectory, Rev. Thomas Best. About 4 m. N. of Andover, HURSTBOURNE TARRANT. Prosperous House, Richard E. Bunney. Esq.; Ibthorpe House, Mrs. Mosdell. 3 m. w. Amport House, Marquis of Winchester.

2½ m. w. SPARSHOLT. The Dean, Charles Fielder, Esq.; Westley, James P. Fitt, Esq. 3 m. further, ASHLEY, W. L. P. T. Taunton, Esq. 1½ m. further, KING'S SOMBORNE. It was part of the ancient demesne belonging to the Crown previous to the Conquest, and Doomsday Book records it to have had two churches; but one of these most probably belonged to some dependent manor. John of Gaunt is said to have had a seat or palace here, and the tradition is supported by the appearance of a large mansion in ruins, in a vicinity abounding in yew-trees, which appear to have been assiduously cultivated about his age, for the use of archery. The surrounding grounds are laid out in a peculiar manner. In the church is an ancient tomb, with a mutilated effigy of either an ecclesiastic or a lady. The inscription, which appears to have been in the Saxon characters, is nearly defaced. The arch exhibits the trefoil ornament. Compton House, T. Edwards, Esq. 2 m. s. Shawford House, Sir H. B. P. St. John Mildmay, Bart. 1 m. N. LITTLE SOMBORNE. The Roman road passes through this village; and though the vestiges of it may not attract the incurious eye, sufficient remains for a considerable distance to engage the attention of the antiquary. Somborne Park, Sir F. H. Bathurst, Bart. 1 m. further, STOCKBRIDGE, a borough, market-town, and parish. It consists of one long street, which is intersected at the west end by the river Test. The streams are particularly favourable for trout fishing; and Stockbridge is much resorted to by the neighbouring gentry during the trout season. Parchment and glue are manufactured to a small extent. Robert, Earl of Gloucester, brother of the Empress Matilda, was taken prisoner in this town, on his flight from Winchester. It is said he took refuge in the church, after having effected the escape of the Empress, who was conveyed thence in funeral procession through the besieging army, under pretention of her being dead; but having arrived at a certain distance, she mounted a horse, and reached Gloucester in safety. Grosvenor Cottage, John Cunningham, Esq.; Houghton Lodge, Hon. A. Hallendale; North Maver Farm, John Payne, Esq. 2 m. N.W. of Stockbridge, Danebury Hill, on which is a circular entrenchment, enclosing an extensive area with high ramparts. The entrance is by a winding course protected by great banks, and very strong. The ditch on the east and north sides, where the ground is most abrupt and steep, is single; on the west and south-west, where the ground is more level, there is an outer work at a little distance. On the west and north-west of this camp are several barrows; one of them about a mile distance has the name of Canute's Barrow. 5 m. N.W. Quarley Mount, where there is another considerable camp occupying its summit,

1840, and here is an ancient obelisk, erected to commemorate the ravages of the plague in 1669. Winchester is the seat of the county assizes, and has quarter and petty sessions, a recorder's court, and a cheneery court of the bishop. It is also the place of election of members for the county. Henry III. was a native of this city. Henry VIII. entertained the Emperor Charles V., and Philip and Mary were married here in 1554. Sir Thomas Browne, Sir Henry Wotten, Collins, Otway, Hayley, Young, and the two Wartons were educated at Winchester school. Near Winchester, and included within the parliamentary borough, but at about one mile south of the city, stands the Hospital of St. Cross, founded in the reign of King Stephen. Its church is a remarkably ancient and beautiful edifice, and the venerable buildings attached to this rich monastic foundation are highly interesting. 3 m. N.E. Avington, Duke of Buckingham. 5 m. E. Tichborne Park, Sir Edward Doughty, Bart. 1 m. s. of which CHERITON. Cheriton Lodge, Mrs. M. Barrett; Hockley House, W. Taylor, Esq. 1 m. further S. BRAMDEAN. Bramdean Cottage, C. G. Oliver, Esq.; Woodcote House, Colonel William Cole. 2 m. further, WEST TISTEAD. 1½ m. further, Basing House, Joseph Martineau, Esq.

3 m. S.E. MORESTEAD. 1 m. further, OWSLEBURY. Rose Hill, Earl of Northesk; Marwell Hall, John Long, Esq.; Crab's Hall, James Trigg, Esq. 2 m. further, at UPHAM, Belmore House, William Ross, Esq. A little to the east of which is Preshaw House, Walter Long, Esq. 2 m. further E. WARNFORD. Warnford Park, E. R. Tunno, Esq.; Belmont Cottage, Richard King, Esq. 1 m. N.E. of which is WESTMEON, from whence, 1 m. E. at EASTMEON, Bourdeaux House, Captain Chawner; Berel House, John W. Drew, Esq.; Westbury House, Hon. Thomas William Gage; Langrish House, J. H. Waddington, Esq.

2 m. S. Twyford Lodge, John Thomas Waddington, Esq.; Twyford House, J. L. Dampier, Esq.

2 m. N. BISHOPSTOKE. Bambridge House, William Young, Esq.

74 m. BISHOP-STOKE STA.

1½ m. S.E. Fair Oak Park, William Bradshaw, Esq. 1½ m. s. Townhill Park, Edward Gaylor, Esq.; South Stoneham House, Miss L. Middleton.

Portsmouth and Salisbury Railway.

SOUTHAMPTON. A parliamentary and municipal borough, seaport town and county in the southern part of the county of Hants, occupying a peninsula between the mouths of the Test and Itchen rivers, at the head of the Southampton Water. Area of borough and county, 1,970 A.; population, 27,490. It returns two members to Parliament. Registered electors (1848), 2,258. The entrance to this beautiful town from the old London Road is by a magnificent avenue of trees, which lead by some very handsome terraces into its main, or High Street, upwards of a mile in length, above and below the Bar, or ancient gate, in the walls formerly enclosing the old town, parts of which still exist, and are in a good state of preservation. This is a very handsome street, with excellent shops, many of which are not inferior to those of the first-rate streets of London. The principal public edifices are the audit and custom houses, dock company's office, the assembly rooms, public baths, theatre, the cavalry barracks, and the town hall over the Bargate. Among the public institutions we may cite the free grammar school, founded by Edward VI., a hospital of Henry III.'s time, several almshouses, and other charities, a royal humane society, an infirmary, botanic garden, with a mechanics', and literary and polytechnic institutions. Here are also several churches, some of which are of considerable antiquity. Since the formation of the new docks at the east end of the town, Southampton has assumed a commercial importance suitable to its admirable natural position, and if a sufficient depth of water

80 m. SOUTHAMPTON STA.

and supposed to be the opposing camp to that of Danebury. On the south side the works are quadruple; the outer trenches are sixty paces asunder, and from the second to the third the space measures thirty-six paces. Various tumuli are scattered over the Downs in this vicinity.

3 m. s.w. Hursley Park, Sir William Heathcote, Bart. It is a substantial, spacious edifice, situated in a pleasant park. An ancestor of the present possessor purchased it from a descendant of Oliver Cromwell; and tradition states he made a vow, that because it had belonged to the Cromwells, "he would not let one stone or brick remain upon another, even to the foundations." In pulling down the old house, in one of the walls was found the dye of a seal, which, being very rusty, was supposed to be a Roman weight. When cleaned, however, it proved to be the seal of the Common-wealth of England, and the artist, Vertue, who saw it in the year 1760, considered it to be the identical seal which Oliver took from the Parliament.

74 m. BISHOP-STOKE STA.

Portsmouth and Salisbury Rail-way.

2 m. N.W. Cranbury Park, Thomas Chamberlayne, Esq.; Hampfield Park, James White, Esq. 1 m. s.w. Stoneham Park, John Willis Fleming, Esq.

80 m. SOUTHAMP-TON STA.

could be ensured at all times of the tide for ships of the heaviest burthen, we cannot doubt that it would speedily become the most flourishing seaport, and the safest harbour in the British dominions. The docks in question were opened in 1842, they contain an area of 208 A., and are capable of receiving steam-vessels of upwards of 700 tons burden. Southampton is the station for the West India, Mediterranean, and other mails, and it communicates by steam with all the southern ports of England, the Channel Islands, and Ireland, and by railway with the whole interior of the country. The port extends from near Portsmouth to Christchurch. In 1845, 707 ships of 150,826 tons burden entered, and 708 of 149,308 tons burden cleared out of the port, and in the same year British and Irish produce to the amount of £1,475,105 was exported. Registered shipping of port in the year 1847, 4,965 tons. Corporation revenue in 1847, £8,934. The mildness and salubrity of the air, the beauty of its position, the picturesque scenery of its environs, all combine to render Southampton one of the most delightful places of resort on this part of the coast of England: the Southampton Water covered with shipping, and the shores lined with beautiful parks and noble manions. There are annual races, and a regatta. Markets, Tuesday, Thursday, and Saturday. The station of the South-Western Railway at Southampton is a very neat elevation, replete with accommodation for the public.

Across the floating bridge, ITCHEN. Ridgway Castle, F. M. Lewin. Esq.; Highlands Cottage, Commodore John Lowry; Prospect Cottage, Richard Rosamond, Esq.; Fern Hill, Edward Westlake, Esq.; Oak Bank, Robert Wright, Esq. A little to the north of which is PEARTREE GREEN. Admiral Sir J. W. Loving. A little further, BITTERN. Bittern Grove, Alexander Hoyes, Esq.; Eastfield Lodge, George Parkhouse, Esq.; Brownlow Cottage, J. P. Hoare, Esq.; Bittern Lodge, H. Burgh, Esq.; Merry Oak, J. H. Forbes, Esq.; Manor House, Stuart Macnaghton, Esq.; Bittern Court, Captain J. Wigston. A little to the south of Itchen is WESTON. Barnfield, Mrs. P. Hulton; Weston Grove, John Trower, Esq. 1 m. further, Netley Castle, George Hunt, Esq.; and Netley Abbey, which stands on the declivity of a hill, rising gently from the water, and, except on a near approach, is secluded from observation by the beautiful woody scenery. The ruins have often furnished a theme for poetical description and moral precept. The lyre has been employed in mournful plainings over the fallen splendour of this foundation.

> "Now sunk, deserted, and with weeds o'ergrown,
> Yon prostrate walls their awful fate bewail;
> Low on the ground their topmost spires are thrown,
> Once friendly marks to guide the wandering sail.
> The ivy now, with rude luxuriance, bends
> Its tangled foliage through the cloister'd space;
> O'er the green window's mouldering height ascends,
> And fondly clasps it with a last embrace.
> While the self-planted oak, within confined,
> Auxiliar to the tempest's wild uproar,
> Its giant branches fluctuates to the wind,
> And rends the wall, whose aid it courts no more."

About 1 m. further, Netley Lodge, Rev. George Southouse. A little further, Sidney Lodge, Earl of Hardwicke. And still further, HAMBLEDON. Cams Cottage, W. H. Barkworth, Esq.; Bury Lodge, Thomas Butler, Esq.; Park House, John Foster, Esq.; West End, John Goldsmith, Esq.; White Dale, J. G. Higgins, Esq.; Fairfield Field, W. J. J. Higgins, Esq.; Ashling House, H. Jones, Esq.; Hamble Cliff, Mrs. W. Webber. *Itchen Viaduct.*

2 m. across Southampton Water, MARCHWOOD. Marchwood Lodge, F. K. Holloway, Esq.; Marchwood, John Lamprey, Esq.; Byhams House, Colonel Phipps. *82 m. BLECHYNDEN STA.*

½ m. s. ELING, called Edlingsdays in Doomsday Book. It appears from that record to have been a place of some consequence in the reign of Edward the Confessor. The manor was held by the tenure of providing half a day's entertainment for the King whenever he should pass that way. On sinking a well in this parish a few years ago, a quantity of fossil shells were discovered at the depth of thirty-six feet. Grove House, William Hallet, Esq.; Langley Cottage, F. C. Wilson, Esq. *85 m. REDBRIDGE STATION.* *Cross the Test.*

Soon after leaving Redbridge we enter the precincts of the New Forest, interesting not only in itself, but also from its historical associations. That this was a woody tract previous to its afforestation by the Conqueror may be inferred from its ancient name ITENE, or Y THENE. The forest, according to its earliest boundaries, included the whole of that part of Hampshire which lies between the Southampton river on the east, the British Channel on the south, and the river Avon on the west. In the reign of Charles II. the forest was limited to about 92,365 acres. The scenery of the New Forest affords as great a variety of beautiful landscape perhaps as can be met with in any part of England. Its woody scenes, its extended lawns, and vast sweeps of wild country unlimited by artificial boundaries, together with its river views and distant coasts, are all in a great degree magnificent. *88 m. LYNDHURST STA.*

1 m. N.W. Banneston Lodge, Mrs. Fitzhugh; Portwood Lodge, William Abbott, Esq.; Myrtle Cottage, Lieut.-Colonel Drummond; Portwood House, George Jones, Esq.; Rose Cottage, Mrs. M. Whitmore. Crossing Southampton Water, 2 m. s. HYTHE, a beautiful little hamlet in the New Forest Union, having many fine and extensive prospects from the adjoining eminence. Langdown House, Miss Tate. 1 m. S.E. FAWLEY. Fawley Cottage, Hon. Brownlow De Grey. Cadland Park, A. R. Drummond, Esq. The house is a plain, but commodious structure, standing on a gentle eminence, commanding the Southampton Water. The grounds, which include an area of about five miles in circumference, are tastefully laid out, and contain an abundance of old and venerable timber. A little further, Ashleet House, R. Hunter, Esq. Still further, Ower Cottage, Captain C. P. Copping. About 1 m. E. of Hoare, Calshot Castle, a small fort constructed by Henry VIII. as a safeguard to Southampton Water. It is constructed on a singular piece of land, which projects about half across the Southampton Water. It is but ill-adapted for defence, and at present of immaterial importance, except as a coast-guard station. A little to the w. on the sea-coast, Eaglehurst, Colonel B. Drummond. This fine mansion was formerly called Luttrell's Folly, having been erected by the Hon. Temple Luttrell. It occupies a very beautiful commanding eminence, which has been formed into a terrace, and extends a considerable way along the beach. The sea-view is remarkably interesting. 3 m. S.W. from Hythe is BOYLOW, where are the ruins of an ancient abbey, the outer walls, or a large part of which, still remain. It was erected by King John. It possessed the privilege of sanctuary, and afforded an asylum to Margaret of Anjou, wife of Henry VI., after the battle of Barnet, and to Perkin Warbeck, in the reign of Henry VII. Various immunities, amongst which is exemption from arrest for debt, are still attached to the manor. 2 m. S. Exbury House, John Royds, Esq.

Itchen Viaduct.

82 m. BLECHYN-DEN STA.

Milbrook Manor House, Charles Baker, Esq.; Summary House, B. C. Henderson, Esq.; Brookland Villa, Mrs. Admiral Jackson; Victoria Lodge, William Tetlow, Esq.

85 m. REDBRIDGE STATION.

REDBRIDGE. ¾ m. w. Testwood House, late Right Hon. W. S. Bourne; Little Testwood, Sir Henry Powlett, Bart. 1 m. further, NUTSHALLING. Rownham's House, Captain Colt; The Mount, Ralph Etwall, Esq.; Upton House, William Litchfield, Esq.; Lee House, George Rawlings, Esq. 2 m. N.W. Tadbury Mount, supposed to have been an ancient military station, and a royal hunting-seat. 1 m. further, HILL. Freemantle Park, Dowager Lady Hewitt; Hill House, Captain J. Wood, R.N.; Clifton Lodge, Captain J. Woodruffe, R.N.; Poulton House, W. S. Stanley, Esq.

Cross the Test.

88 m. LYNDHURST STA.

1 m. N.W. Northwood, Rev. Richard Pulteney. 1 m. further, LYNDHURST, a beautiful and picturesque village, situated in the centre of the New Forest, near (as tradition asserts) the spot where William Rufus was accidentally, or otherwise, slain by an arrow. Sir Walter Tyrrel, whose name for so many centuries has enjoyed the odium of this act, on his death-bed, and with his last words, utterly denied being in that part of the world at the period in question. The parish of Lyndhurst contains an area of 3,560 A. The Forest Courts are held here, and the King's House, the residence of the Lord Warden, is situated in this locality. A little to the w. Foxlease, James MacTaggart, Esq. A little to the w. Cuffnalls, Sir Edward Poore, Bart.; Holly Mount, J. P. Bulley, Esq.; Queen's House, Thomas White, Esq. 1 m. N. MINSTEAD. Castle Malwood, Major-General Robins; Minstead Lodge, William Robert Preston, Esq.; Manor House, Henry C. Compton, M.P. 1½ m. further, Bartley Lodge, Alexander Powell, Esq.; Bartley Manor House, William R. Preston, Esq. 2 m. further, BRAMSHAN. Bramshan House, T. D. Shute, Esq.; The Warrens, George Hare, Esq.

3 m. s.w. BEAULEAU. (See Southampton.)

91 m. BEAULEAU STATION.

1½ m. s. BALDREE. 2 m. further, LYMINGTON, pleasantly situated on the west bank of the river of the same name, which falls into the Soland Channel. Its excellent accommodation for sea-bathing have rendered it a favourite place of resort for invalids during the summer. N. Tweed Villa, General Gilbert; Hinchelsea, F. F. Lovell, Esq.; Mrs. H. Cox. w. Newton Park, W. A. Mackinnon, Esq., M.P. w. Bashley Lodge, John Bean, Esq.; Beacon Lodge, Hon. G. Berkeley; Rochliffe, Lady Carnac; Ashley Clinton, Lieutenant-Colonel Clinton; Barton, Mrs. Dent; Efford, Marchioness Hastings; Erney Wood, J. Hawkins, Esq.; Carringtons, R. Jennings, Esq.; Shooton Lodge, G. Marriott, Esq.; Ashley Arnewood, J. A. Roebuck, Esq., M.P.; Downton, Admiral Symonds; Newlands, F. R. West, Esq., M.P. E. Wolhampton, Rev. Sir George Burrard, Bart.; Worborne, Sir J. R. Carnac, Bart.; The Elms, R. H. Lewin; Pilewell, G. L. Peacocke, Esq.; Formosa, Captain Rooke, R.N.; East End, Joshua Wells, Esq. s. Fairfield, Mrs. Daniels; Woodside, W. W. Rooke, Esq.; Pennington House, Colonel Pringle Taylor, K.H.

2 m. s. HINTON. Hinton, Admiral Sir George J. Gervis, Bart.; Knee House, Colonel Cameron; Hubborn Lodge, Captain Hopkins. 3 m. further, CHRISTCHURCH. The most remarkable feature in this secluded town, which has very little trade, is its splendid old church, formerly collegiate, from which it derives its name. It was founded in the early Saxon period, but was rebuilt in the 11th century. It displays different styles of architecture, a finely carved altar-piece, and several handsome chapels. Near the town there are remains of a Roman encampment, and on a cliff named Hengistbury Hill, towards the sea, on the south-east of the town, are the ruins of an ancient castle. Market, Monday; fairs, Trinity Thursday, and October 17th. Sandhills, Hon. Sir George H. Rose; Purewell Cross, John Aldridge, Esq.; Hengistbury House, John Bayley, Esq.; Priory, Frederick Brander, Esq.; Jumpers, Charles Collins, Esq.; Stourfield, Captain W. Popham, R.N.; Wick House, John Sloman, Esq.

100 m. CHRIST-CHURCH STA.

RINGWOOD. A market-town and parish, county of Hants, situated on the Avon, chiefly employed in the manufacture of woollens and hosiery, and brewing ale for export. It is an ancient town, on the borders of the New Forest, but contains nothing remarkable to interest the traveller. Manor House, John Morant, Esq.; St. Ives, Charles Castleman, Esq. 2 m. s. Biston Park. 2 m. further, SOPLEY, William Tyce, Esq. 1½ m. w. HOLDEN-HURST, from which, 3 m. s.w. BOURNEMOUTH, Lady H. Hoare; BOSCOMBE, Major John Stevenson.

106 m. RINGWOOD STATION.

Cross the Avon.

1 m. s.e. CANFORD. A small village, pleasantly situated on the river Stour. The parish church is a picturesque and interesting structure, with a tower partly covered with ivy. In the interior are several monuments and brasses. Morley House, H. R. Willett, Esq.; Canford House, Sir J. J. Guest, Bart., M.P.; Knighton, W. R. Hayes, Esq. 1 m. E. of which is HAM PRESTON. Huddings House, E. Wright, Esq.; Long House, W. Biddell, Esq.

115 m. WIM-BORNE STA.

91 m. BEAULEAU STATION.

BROCKENHURST. A pleasing village of Saxon origin, of which date is the church. The arch over the doorway is ornamented with zigzag moulding. The font is a curious and very antique piece of workmanship, evidently constructed when total immersion was prevalent. Various tumuli are dispersed over the heath, south-west of the village. Some of them lie in the area of an entrenchment, and have a regular fosse and vallum, and are supposed to have been constructed about the time when the Britons, under Nantelsod, or Ambrosius, and the Saxons, under Cedric, were contending for empire. On removing the earth from a barrow, and digging below the surface of the natural land, a cell was perceived, about two feet square, evidently formed for the reception of an urn; and in another barrow an urn was found in a perfect state, composed of burnt clay, and containing ashes and small human bones in a state of calcination, mixed with an earth of the texture of peat. Brockenhurst House, John Morant, Esq. a handsome building, standing in a pleasant park, and commanding a very grand and picturesque view, in which both the foreground and distance are complete. Whatcombe House, in Brockenhurst Park, was three years the residence of Howard the philanthropist. New Park, Colonel W. Thornhill.

100 m. CHRIST-CHURCH STA.

1½ m. N.W. BURLEY-IN-THE-WOOD. Burley Park, George R. Farnall, Esq.; Burley Lawn, Lawrence Hill, Esq. 1¼ m. further, Post House, Mrs. Phillips. 4 m. N. Baldree Lodge. 3 m. further, CANTERTON, at which stood a celebrated oak-tree, said to be the very tree against which the arrow glanced that was shot by Tyrrell, and caused the death of William Rufus. This tree had become so decayed and mutilated about sixty years ago, that the then Lord Delawarr had a triangular stone erected, inscribed thus: "Here stood the oak-tree on which an arrow, shot by Sir W. Tyrrell at a stag, glanced and struck King William II., surnamed Rufus, on the breast, of which he instantly died, on the 2nd Aug. anno 1100. Anno 1745. That where an event so memorable had happened might not be hereafter unknown, this stone was set up by John Lord Delawarr, who had seen the tree growing in this place."

106 m. RINGWOOD STATION.

Cross the Avon.

2 m. N. ELLINGHAM. John Gabbatas, Esq.; Somerley, Earl Normanton. 1 m. further, HARBRIDGE. 2½ m. further, FORDINGBRIDGE, at which, at a place called God's Hill, is an ancient encampment, defended on one side by a double trench and ramparts, and secured on the other by the steepness of the hill, which is overgrown with oaks. Bemgate House. 1 m. further, at ROCKBOURNE, West Park, Captain Corry. 1 m. further, Breamore House, Sir Charles Hulse, Bart.; near which is Charlford, Samuel Whitchurch, Esq.; and Hale Park, Joseph Goff, Esq. 6 m. N.W. Orton Park. 3 m. further N. St. Giles Park, Earl Shaftesbury. 1 m. further, CRANBOURNE, a place of great antiquity and some importance in the Roman and Saxon times. On the Castle Hill, a little south of the village, is a circular fortification, with a well in its area, both supposed to be of Roman origin. The town is surrounded by a chase, as it has been from the earliest historical period. Alderholt Park, Jonathan Key, Esq.; Boveridge House, Richard Brouncker, Esq.; Cranbourne Lodge, John Tregonwell, Esq.

115 m. WIM-BORNE STA.

1 m. N.W. WIMBORNE. Wimborne Minster; Dean's Court, Rev. Sir James Hanham, Bart. ½ m. further, Stone Cottage, Captain J. G. Garland, R.N. 1 m. further, Kingston Hall, William J. Bankes, Esq.; Kingston Lacey, George Bankes, Esq., M.P. 6 m. further, BLANDFORD. This place derives its name from being situated near an ancient ford on the river Stour. It was nearly destroyed by an accidental fire, in 1579, but was soon after rebuilt. During the civil war, in the reign of Charles I., it was plundered by the parliamentary forces, and alternately possessed by each party in 1677 and 1713. It again suffered greatly from fire in 1731, and was entirely destroyed with the exception of forty houses. Bryanston

Poole Junction. This station stands about two miles from the town of 121 m. POOLE Poole, to which there is a short branch from the main line from South- JUNCTION STA. ampton to Dorchester, and as it extends no further, we shall here describe it. POOLE is a sea-port town, a parliamentary and municipal borough, and a county of itself, in the county of Dorset, situated on a peninsula, on the north side of Poole Harbour, which is an inlet in the English Channel, six miles in length, and four in breadth, having the Isle of Purbeck on the south. At the entrance of the harbour, a quarter of a mile across, is a shifting sand bar, with only fifteen feet of water at high tide, near to which are some large oyster beds. Here also the tide ebbs and flows twice in the twelve hours. The area of town, county, and parish, 170 A.; area of parlia- mentary borough, 6,040 A. It sends two members to Parliament; registered electors (1848), 522; corporate revenue (1847), £1,908; customs' revenue (1846), £8,856; registered shipping of port (1847), 13,715 tons. The town, which was formerly but a poor and mean place, has been much improved by the modern houses. The principal buildings are a new church, a chapel of ease, and Dissenting chapels, the guildhall, gaol, custom house, exchange, union workhouse, and library. Here are spacious quays, near to which vessels not drawing more than fourteen feet, can anchor. The trade is chiefly coasting, with exports of corn to London, and large quan- tities of Purbeck clay to the potteries in Staffordshire. Poole has also a considerable trade with our North American colonies. Holly Cottage, Captain J. Brine; Parkstone Villa, Hon. W. D. Damer.

WAREHAM, a parliamentary borough, county of Dorset, between the 126 m. WAREHAM Frome and Piddle, which are each crossed by a bridge, one mile from the STATION. mouths, in Poole Harbour. Area of municipal borough, 4,880 A.; popu- lation, 2,746; area of parliamentary borough, comprising Corfe Castle, Bere Regis, &c., 22,890 A.; population, 6,646. It sends one member to Parliament, with Corfe Castle; registered electors (1848), 424. The town, which is surrounded by an embankment, is regularly built, and the space between the rampart and the streets is occupied by garden grounds, the surplus produce of which is sent to Poole Here are also traces of ancient buildings. The church, a very fine old edifice, a free and other endowed schools and charities, almshouses, and the union workhouse, are the principal public buildings. Manufactures of straw plait, hosiery, and shirt-buttons, are here carried on, and immense quantities of pipe-clay is exported; but in consequence of the shallowness of the water, the harbour being accessible only to small craft, its trade has greatly declined. 1½ m. s.w. HOLME. Holme House, Major Edward Bridges. 3 m. s. CHURCH KNOWLE. 1 m. E. Corfe Castle, formerly a market-town, which owed its importance from a formidable castle erected by Edgar prior to the year 980, at the gate of which Edward the Martyr, when calling to visit his step-mother, Elfreda, was treacherously murdered. In the reign of Stephen the castle was taken by Baldwyn, Earl of Devonshire, who held it against the King. It was frequently the residence of King John, by whose orders twenty-two prisoners were starved to death in its dungeons. Richard III. was imprisoned here in 1327. During the parliamentary war it was assaulted by Sir Walter Erle and Sir Thomas Trenchard, but it was

House, Lord Portman; Langton House, J. J. Farquharson, Esq.; Littleton House, Mrs. W. Donaldson; Down House, Sir John W. Smith, Bart.; Charlton Marshall, Thomas H. Bastard, Esq. 2 m. N. Stourpaine, P. N. Bastard, Esq. 1 m. further, Hanford, H. K. Seymer, Esq., M.P.; Ranston House, Sir Edward De Baker Baker, Bart. 1 m. further, Iwerne, T. B. Bower, Esq.; Gussage All Saints, Miss Bower; Iwerne Cottage, Miss Williams. 4 m. N.E. from Blandford, Eastbury Park, Duke of Buckingham. 4 m. w. Turnworth House, W. P. Okedon, Esq.

3 m. w. CORFEMULLEN. Knowle House, W. C. Lambert, Esq.; Corfe House, Thomas Onslow, Esq.

121 m. POOLE JUNCTION STA. 1 m. N.W. LYTCHET MINSTER. The church, supposed to be dedicated to St. Mary, as one of the bells bears the inscription, is a modern structure, with the exception of the tower. There was formerly a priory, or minster in this place, from the ruins of which the church is built. In the church-yard there are two yew-trees, whose supposed age is 800 years. Lytchet Beacon, on Chronse Hill, commands an extensive view of Poole Harbour, Downsee, the Isle of Purbeck, and its neighbourhood.

Lytchet House, Sir Claude Scott, Bart.; Post Green House, H. House, Esq.; Manor House, W. R. Fryer, Esq.; Organ House, Thomas Cox, Esq. 2 m. further, LYTCHET TRAVERS. A scattered village, in which there is a church of ancient structure, in good repair, with a tower of four bells, and some good altar tombs. Manor House, H. D. Trenchard, Esq. This house stands on an elevated situation, in the midst of an extensive and picturesque lawn, or pleasure-ground, of park-like character and appearance, and is visible at a distance of several miles. It commands fine views of the surrounding country, with the Purbeck Hills in the extreme distance.

126 m. WAREHAM STATION. 4 m. N. BLOXWORTH. Bloxworth House, George Morant, Esq. 2 m. further,

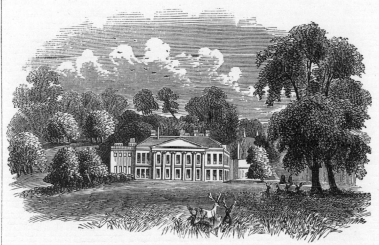

CHARLBOROUGH PARK, JOHN SAMUEL W. S. ERLEDRAX, ESQ.

heroically defended by Lady Bankes and her daughter: assisted only by her domestics, she endured a siege for six weeks, and sustained a loss of two men only, and preserved the castle for the King. In 1645 it was again besieged by the forces under Fairfax, when, owing to the treachery of an officer of the garrison, it was taken and demolished. The remains of this stupendous edifice are extremely interesting, and plainly indicate its former prodigious strength. Encombe House, Earl of Eldon. The house occupies the bottom of a very deep vale that opens to the British Channel. The situation is extremely fine, and a piece of water near the house is so happily managed as to have the appearance, from the windows, of forming part of the sea which terminates the view along the vale. The grounds are disposed with much taste, the plantations are extensive, and the mansion itself is a handsome building of Purbeck stone. Rempstone Hall, John H. Calcraft, Esq.

WOOL. Close to which are the ruins of Bendon Abbey. 2 m. s. COOMBE KINGS. 1 m. further, Lulworth Castle, Joseph Weld, Esq. It is a noble pile, situated on an eminence in the south-east corner of an extensive park, which occupies a circumference of nearly 4½ miles, surrounded by a stone wall upwards of 8¼ feet high. It commands a fine view of the sea from an opening in the hills, as well as an extensive prospect of the adjoining country. The castle is an exact cube of 80 feet, and has a Roman tower at each corner 30 feet in diameter, and rising 16 feet above the walls, which, as well as the towers, are embattled. The walls are 6 feet thick. The house has three stories, but the tower has four. In each front are three rows of four windows. In the towers are four rows of three each, exclusive of the offices. A little beyond the castle is the village of LULWORTH, where, at the top of a very high hill, is a fortification, consisting of three ramparts and ditches, including an area of about five acres. A little to the E. WEST TINEHAM. Tineham House, Thomas Bond, Esq.

1 m. N.E. MORETON. Moreton House, James Frampton, Esq.

2 m. N. TINKLETON. Cliffe House, Charles Porcher, Esq.

2 m. S.E. Carne House, Hon. Dawson Damer, M.P.; Sewell House, Mrs. Hawkins; and a little out of the direct road, ELLINGSTONE. 2 m. s. Ellingstone House, J. D. Bayley, Esq. On the road to Melcombe Regis, Melcombe House, Mrs. Lewis; Corfe Hill, Mrs. Balston; Uperay House, H. C. Gooding, Esq.; Nottingham House, Mrs. Stewart. MELCOMBE REGIS and WEYMOUTH. The towns of Melcombe Regis and Weymouth were united into one in the reign of Elizabeth, to terminate a long and prejudicial rivalry for the exclusive possession of the harbour, of which each place forms the opposite boundary. Weymouth was probably known to the Romans, as there are traces of a vicinal way from Maiden Castle to the via Iceniana, where the town of Melcombe Regis now stands. A grant was made by Athelstan, in 938, to the abbey of Melton, of "all that water within the shore of Waymouth, and half the stream of that Waymouth out at sea a saltem, &c," and it is noticed also at the Conquest. This port, in 1588, contributed six ships to oppose the Spanish Armada; and one of the enemy's vessels having been taken in the Channel, was brought into the harbour. In the reign of Edward I. Melcombe became the dowry of Queen Eleanor, on which account it obtained many valuable and extensive privileges; and in the reign of Edward III. it was a very important place. In

131 m. WOOL STATION.

136 m. MORETON STATION.

141 m. DORCHESTER STA.

The present mansion was rebuilt in the time of Charles I., the former mansion having been burnt by the King's forces of that date, the then proprietor, Sir Walter Erle, Knight, being a Parliamentarian, and a member of the Long Parliament, having sat for the borough of Wareham. He commanded the Parliamentary forces at the taking of Corfe Castle, which place was gallantly defended by the Lady Bankes. In one of the cellars is a principal beam brought from Corfe Castle at that date. The present mansion has been modernised by the late Richard Erle Drax Grosvenor, Esq., under the direction of Mr. Nash, and the present proprietor has made considerable additions, having built a picture-gallery, and formed an armory. In the pleasure-grounds there is a grotto, memorable for the meeting of certain patriotic gentlemen who assembled there in the year 1688 to arrange the expulsion of King James II., and the bringing over of King William III. On the borders of the park, and towering above the woods, is situated a very handsome Gothic tower, 120 feet in height, built by the present proprietor, who has also added much to the beautifying of the place by the enlargement of the park, which he was enabled to do by the formation of a new turnpike road from Wimborne to Dorchester, planned and completed through his instrumentality in the years 1841 and 1842.

131 m. WOOL STATION.

1 m. N. APPLETON, James C. Tyler, Esq. 3 m. further, BERE REGIS. The Hyde, Charles James Radclyffe, Esq. About 2 m. s.w. Witherbury Castle, an oblong, double-entrenched camp of about seven acres in extent. 2 m. N. from which is WINTERBORNE WHITCHURCH. Whatcomb House, Mrs. M. Mitchell. 1 m. further, MILTON ABBAS. Milton Abbey, Earl of Portarlington. The mansion occupies the site of an abbey, which was founded by King Athelstan. It was built from designs by Sir William Chambers, who intended it to assimilate in style with the beautiful collegiate church which nearly adjoins its southern front. The mansion, with its offices, form four sides of a quadrangle, and is cased with a fine white stone. There is on the south side of the abbey a venerable old room, once the refectory, called The Monks' Hall. It has a fine oak roof, painted and gilt, and a richly carved screen, with the date 1498 thereon.

136 m. MORETON STATION.

1½ m. s. WINFRITH NEWBURGH. About 2 m. further on the sea-coast are the arched rocks of Lulworth Cove.

141 m. DORCHESTER STA.

DORCHESTER, the capital of county of Dorset, was the Durnoraira of the Romans, the traces of whose ancient walls and other remains in the vicinity of the town, consisting of two strongly-entrenched stations, and the amphitheatre of Maumbury, considered to be the most perfect in the British empire, are particularly worthy the traveller's attention. Dorchester is a parliamentary and municipal borough, and is situated on the right bank of the river Frome. Area of borough, comprising three parishes, 1,870 A. It sends two members to Parliament. Registered electors (1848), 396; corporation revenue (1846), £259. It is one of the prettiest towns in England, being generally well built, with some particularly handsome structures, while the principal, or High Street, contains many excellent shops; added to this, the beautiful avenues which surround the upper parts of the town are delightful public walks, not unlike the boulevards which enclose the continental towns. Dorchester has three churches. That of St. Peter is a very ancient edifice, with monuments and stained glass windows worthy of particular notice. It contains also a fine town hall, and market-house, a county hospital, a county hall, gaol, and house of correction, large cavalry barracks, a theatre, banks, a grammar school, which has some exhibitions to the University, and several ancient charities. Dorchester,

the early part of the time of Edward IV. it was burnt by the French, and the inhabitants so greatly impoverished, that they petitioned the King for relief, which was granted by royal charter, and enjoyed until united with Weymouth. The air is so mild and pure, that it is much frequented in the summer. 1 m. s.w. on the road to Portland, Beefield Regis, Mrs. Buxton. About 4 m. s. PORTLAND. Portland Castle, Captain Manning; Pennsylvia Castle, Granville Penn, Esq. About 2 m. E. from Melcombe Regis, Southdown Cottage, John Sanders, Esq.; near which is Charlemont Lodge, Mrs. Kettle.

DORCHESTER *(continued)*.

London and South Coast Railway.

The Brighton Station is situated to the south of the South-Eastern Terminus, opposite the back buildings of St. Thomas's Hospital, and is altogether a distinct building from the Dover Station. It consists of a basement story, the centre of which recedes, having an octagonal advancing wing or tower at each end, between which is carried a wooden awning, or portico, supported by iron brackets, to protect the passengers from the rain while alighting from their carriages, &c. The booking office is a fine lofty room, but of irregular form, off which is a refreshment room, fitted up in the style of a handsome London coffee-house. The cloak room is in one of the wings to which we have adverted. There is no doubt that there are handsomer terminal stations than that which is devoted to this important railway, but it answers the purpose for which it was intended, as well as if it vied in splendour with the noble hall of the Euston Station. The passengers' arrival and departure platforms about seven hundred feet in length, are covered with a wooden roof, through which light is admitted by rough plate-glass, in sheets of eight feet long, and three feet six inches wide; and it may be justly observed that this, by far the most essential portion of a railway station, both as regards the convenience of the passengers, and the requisite space for the engines and carriages, covering nearly ten acres of ground, appears to be admirably constructed by the company's engineer, R. Jacomb Hood, M.I.C.E., who has evidently, and greatly to his credit, consulted the *utile*, rather than the *dulce*, which latter is only another word for extravagant outlay.

The works upon the first portion of this railway as far as Croydon are not of any great importance in point of constructive difficulty, as the line followed the general direction of the old canal, which was purchased by the Croydon Railway Company. The New Cross Cutting was the chief earth-work, the quantity of earth removed amounting to upwards of half a million cubic yards, a portion of which was applied to the formation of the embankment between New Cross and the Greenwich Junction. Between the London Station and Croydon there are eighteen bridges, independently of the viaduct adjoining the Greenwich Railway, and six large culverts, the chief of which are at New Cross and Sydenham. Six of the bridges over the railway are of novel design, and present a light and elegant appearance. That over the line at Forest Hill

DORCHESTER
(*continued*).

which is celebrated for its ale, has a large retail trade; and its fairs for sheep and lambs, pastured on the adjacent downs, held February 14th, July 6th, August 6th, and October 25th, are well and numerously attended. Markets, Wednesday and Saturday. 1 m. N.E. Stinsford House, Herbert Williams, Esq. ½ m. further, Kingston House, F. P. B. Martin, Esq. 3 m. further, FIDDLETOWN. Hilsington House, Earl of Orford. 2 m. further, DEWLISH. Dewlish House, John Walmsley, Esq. 2½ m. E. WEST STAFFORD. Frome House, John Floyer, Esq. 1 m. N.W. Woolveton House, J. Henning, Esq. 1 m. further, BRADFORD PEVERELL. Quatrebras Cottage, Captain J. J. Hamilton Burgoyne. 2 m. further, Frampton Court, Richard B. Sheridan, Esq., M.P. The house is large and commodious, built of Portland-stone, situated close to the river Frome, which runs through a finely-wooded park. It was built about 150 years ago, by Robert Browne, Esq., whose ancestors purchased the property from Sir Christopher Hatton in the reign of Queen Elizabeth. The house is built on the site of an old monastery, which was a cell to Caen in France.

4 m. N. GODMANSTONE, Joseph Goodenough, Esq. 3½ m. further, MINTERNE MAGNA. Minterne House, Edward St. Vincent Digby, Esq.

A little further, Ledling House, J. T. Tatchell, Esq. About 1 m. s.w. of Dorchester, Maiden Castle, one of the strongest and most extensive camps in England. It occupies the entire apex of a hill, and is supposed to have been the Castro de Stica, or summer station of the garrison at Dorchester. 3 m. further, Bridehead House, R. Williams, Esq.

London and South Coast Railway.

may be cited as an illustration. It consists of seven segmental arches; the central one over the railway is of thirty feet span, and twenty-seven feet six inches high, the abutment arches being each of twelve feet span, and of correspondent height to the soffits. The novelty consists in the main arch springing from the pier of the two adjoining arches on each side, instead of from its own, the spandrils above the haunches being left open.

The bridge at New Cross is constructed of cast-iron ribs, secured by wrought-iron ties, and has a very neat appearance. Here is the locomotive station of the Brighton and Dover Companies; the buildings are said to have cost upwards of £60,000. From Croydon to the terminus at Brighton, the earth-works, from the undulating surface of the country, assume a different character, amounting to no less than 6,861,683 cubic yards, being at the rate of 156,000 cubic yards per mile, exclusive of the tunnels.

The number of bridges over and under the railway from Croydon to Brighton amounts to ninety-nine, almost all of which are built of brick, with dressings of stone brought from the Heddon quarries, near Newcastle-upon-Tyne, the arches over the railway being all thirty feet span, and sixteen feet high. The principal tunnels are at Mersham, Balcombe, and Clayton Hill. Mersham Tunnel, one hundred and eighty feet in depth from the surface in the deepest part, is through chalk, which was raised to the surface of the ground by double horse-gins, one at the top of each, of twelve vertical shafts, from whence the skiffs were moved on small trucks by means of tramways. The length of this tunnel, one thousand eight hundred and twenty yards, will alone give an idea of the enormous labour expended upon its construction.

The Balcombe Tunnel, which is situated about thirty-four miles from London, is one thousand one hundred and twenty yards in length, and the difficulties attending its construction may be imagined from the report of Mr. Rastrick, who described the ground as very treacherous, requiring great caution on the part of the miners in working it, as "it swells and effloresces as soon as exposed to the air."

The Clayton Hill Tunnel, about forty-three miles from London, is a work of extraordinary magnitude, the very contemplation of which would have alarmed the architects and engineers of antiquity. It is two thousand two hundred and forty yards

in length, passing through the whole range of the South Down Hills in the direct line to Brighton.

The Patcham Tunnel, near Brighton, is insignificant when compared with those we have enumerated, as it is only four hundred and eighty yards in length.

The principal Embankments are those of Earl's Wood Common, about twenty-three miles from the London Bridge Station, and Vale Pool.

The largest Viaduct is over the Ouse Valley, just beyond the Balcombe Station, about thirty-five miles from London. It is one of the most magnificent undertakings of this

---

Left of Railway from London.	Distance from London.
	Enter Kent.
	Greenwich Railway.
	North Kent Branch.
The ground about here is in the occupation of market-gardeners, and from hence the Borough Market receives its principal supply of vegetables.	3 m. NEW CROSS STATION.
1 m. LEWISHAM. The name is a slight corruption of the Saxon, Lewis Ham, or dwelling among the meadows, and anciently written Levisham. Here was a Benedictine priory, subordinate to the abbey of St. Pilu, in Ghent, and most probably founded in the Saxon times, this manor having been given to King Elfruda, nephew to King Alfred. The village, which is situated on the river Ravensbourne, extends some distance along the Tunbridge Road, contains one principal street, and many pretty suburban residences. It is celebrated for its mineral springs. The waters, which are of mild cathartic quality, nearly resemble those of Epsom. Lewisham confers the inferior title of Viscount on the Earl of Dartmouth, who is Lord of the Manor, and who holds by his steward a Manorial Court once a year. Ravensbourne Park, Charles J. Blake, Esq.; Ivy Place, Charles Hicks, Esq.; Laurel Cottage, Hon. Spring Rice; The Limes, Edward Legh, Esq.	5¼ m. FOREST HILL STA.
SYDENHAM, a chapelry in the parish of Lewisham, in the county of Kent. It has a handsome church, an almshouse, &c. Perry Hill, William Skeat, Esq.; Sydenham Hill, Andrew J. C. Laurie, Esq; Brockley, W. H. Jackson, Esq.	6¼ m. SYDENHAM STATION.
	Enter Surrey.
1 m. E. BECKENHAM. A little further, Eden Farm, Earl Auckland. 2 m. further, BROMLEY. The Palace, Bishop of Rochester. It is a plain brick building, rebuilt in 1777. In the garden there is a chalybeate spring, called Blaise's Well. Plaistow Lodge, Robert Boyd, Esq.; Bromley House, Colonel Tweedy; Strawfield Lodge, Mrs. S. Meynell; Bromley Lodge, W. Potts, Esq. A little further, WIDMORE. Sundridge Park, Samuel Scott, Esq. This mansion stands on a hilly spot, and the famous architects, Repton, Nash, and Wyatt, have each bestowed a share of their skill upon the construction of this house. The principal front is adorned with three porticos—one in the centre and one at each end, the centre one being circular, supported by six columns, and surmounted by a dome; the other two have each four columns supporting a pediment. They are all of the	7¼ m. ANERLEY STATION.

nature that has ever been constructed in this country. It consists of thirty-seven arches, each of thirty feet span, and about sixty feet in height, and one hundred feet in its greatest height from the surface of the water to the parapet, its whole length being four hundred and sixty-two yards. When viewed from the circumjacent country, it is a beautifully picturesque object, while from the train the traveller cannot fail to admire the extensive prospect which opens to his view at this interesting part of the line.

The Brighton Terminus, although not remarkable for architectural adornment, is a very commodious and convenient station.

Distance from London. Enter Kent.	𝕽𝖎𝖌𝖍𝖙 𝖔𝖋 𝕽𝖆𝖎𝖑𝖜𝖆𝖞 𝖋𝖗𝖔𝖒 𝕷𝖔𝖓𝖉𝖔𝖓.
3 m. NEW CROSS STATION.	NEW CROSS, is a hamlet in the parish of St. Paul, Deptford, in the counties of Kent and Surrey, which owes its principal increase to the establishment of the station in this locality, although long known to the traveller by reason of its turnpike.
5½ m. FOREST HILL STA.	FOREST HILL. This precise spot has been ushered into notoriety solely by the establishment of the railway station; but the scenery by which it and other places similarly situated are surrounded, serves to show how much that is beautiful was hidden from our sight before the country was intersected by railways.
	1½ m. N.W. DULWICH. At which is Godcliffe College, founded in 1619, by Edward Alleyne, Esq. The building is chiefly in the Elizabethan style, and occupies two-thirds of a quadrangle, of which the chapel constitutes one. The east wing was rebuilt in 1740, of red brick, ornamented with stone, and contains a school room, and apartments for the fellows. The opposite wing comprises the library, and apartments for scholars. The altar-piece in the chapel is ornamented with a fine picture of the Ascension, presented to the college by Mr. Hall; and in front of the chancel is a black marble slab, covering the tomb of the founder, who was buried in the chapel. An extensive collection of pictures was bequeathed to the college by Sir Francis Bourghers in 1811, for the reception of which a handsome gallery has been erected at the south end of the college. Visitors are admitted by tickets, which can be procured from the principal printsellers in London.
6¼ m. SYDENHAM STATION.	1½ m. W. NORWOOD. This village derives its name from an adjacent wood, which borders on a common formerly well known as the haunts of gipsies. Its elevated situation, the beauty of the surrounding scenery, and the salubrity of the atmosphere, have of late years caused the erection of many elegant seats in the vicinity. The Beulah Spa, a spring discovered in 1827, is held in some estimation. Hill Lodge, B. D. Colvin, Esq.; The Oaks, John Howe, Esq.; Biggins Wood, Hugh Bowdich, Esq. 2 m. further, STREATHAM. Streatham Park, George Phillipps, Esq.
Enter Surrey.	
7¼ m. ANERLEY STATION.	ANERLEY, county of Surrey, is remarkable for the beauty of its scenery, and the good accommodation afforded at the pretty inn and grounds, built and laid out since the formation of this line. It is a favourite place of resort during the summer season.
	2 m. W. Norbury Park, A. K. Barclay, Esq. The mansion was built by the late William Lock, Esq., on a new site, having pulled down the greater part of the old building, which stood in a low situation, reserving only the north end for his farm. It stands on a hill, commanding beautiful and extensive prospects, and is justly considered one of the handsomest houses in the county of Surrey. The architecture is striking, though not perfectly regular, and the walls of the principal rooms are painted by the

Corinthian order, and of perfect dimensions. At CHISLEHURST, Camden House, T. Bownar, Esq., the residence of the historian Camden when he compiled his annals of Queen Elizabeth. Frognals, Viscount Sydney; Pheasant Grove, Lord Wynford; Chislehurst, Right Hon. Sir H. Jenner Fust; Chesnut House, J. Bland, Esq.

8½ m. NORWOOD STATION.

1 m. E. ADDISCOMBE. Addiscombe House, a handsome edifice, said to have been built by Sir John Vanburgh, and the walls and ceilings painted by Sir James Thornhill. In the 16th century it was possessed by the Heron family; and in later times it was successively occupied by Lord Chancellor Talbot (who died here), Lord Grantham, and the Earl of Liverpool. Addiscombe, the military college of the Honourable East India Company, Major-General Pasley. 3 m. further, HAYES. Hayes Place, formerly the seat of the Earl of Chatham, and the birthplace of his son, William Pitt. 2 m. further, FARNBOROUGH. Locksbottom, General Williams. At Epwood Hill, in this parish, are the remains of an immense elliptic encampment. Roman bricks and coins have been found here, and hence it is supposed to have been the Roman station of Noveo Magnus, once the capital of the Belgio-British tribe of the Ribrosi. 2 m. N.E. ORPINGTON. The Priory, William Berens, Esq.; Mayfield House, Joseph Jackson, Esq. About 3 m. S.E. Lullingstone Castle, Sir P. H. Dyke, Bart. The castle, stands in a park 1½ miles long containing 1,800 acres. Nearly adjoining the south-east side of Lullingstone Park, and close to the Darent, stood Shoreham Castle, by some improperly called Lullingstone Castle. The demesne is now a farm. The farm-house appears to have been constructed of the materials of the fortress, which was in ruins in Leland's time. Phillpott says this castle, if not built by, was certainly very anciently in the possession of the family of Aldham, one of which resided in this place in the time of Henry III. About 2 m. S.E. of Hayes is KESTON, Captain C. Bates. 1 m. S.E. of Farnborough, Sir John W. Lubbock, Bart. 2 m. further, HALSTEAD, J. P. Atkins, Esq. 2 m. E. SHOREHAM. 3 m. S.E. ADDINGTON. Addington Place, Archbishop of Canterbury, is a handsome modern building, standing nearly in the centre of a well-wooded park. It was commenced in 1772 by Alderman Trevothick, who had purchased the estate for £35,000, and was subsequently sold by his nephew, to form the palace of the Archbishop of Canterbury, instead of rebuilding the old one at Croydon. The mansion is nearly square, and its centre, slightly projecting, is surmounted by a pediment.

10½ m. CROYDON STATION.

2 m. N.E. SANDERSTEAD. Selsdon Park, George R. Smith, Esq., was chiefly built from the designs of its proprietor, and the construction of this very handsome mansion exhibits a choice selection from our ancient architecture. The centre is occupied by a very light cloister of five arches, the spandrils of lancet-pointed open work, springing from buttresses, the interstices of which are filled with light tracery of stone. This arcade is terminated by two small turrets, rising above the embattled parapet, which surmounts the whole. The house stands on a hill, and commands most beautiful prospects. A little further, SALMONS. Garstone House, M. J. Langdale, Esq. 2 m. further, Marden Park, Colonel Sir W. R. Clayton, Bart. The house is a handsome quadrangular building, on a rising ground near the church. The extensive pleasure-grounds are agreeably diversified, and embellished with two fine sheets of water.

14½ m. STOAT'S NEST STA.

celebrated artist Barret with views of the Cumberland and Westmoreland lakes and mountains. The park is extensive, agreeably diversified, and embellished with the richest plantations. The walnut-trees are here most abundant, and about a century ago Norbury Park was said to possess no fewer that 50,000. In some years £600 worth of walnuts have been gathered in this park ; and, to show the uncertain produce of this tree, in other years they have not yielded a bushel.

8½ m. NORWOOD STATION.

Epsom Br. ☞

10½ m. CROYDON STATION.

2 m. N.W. NORWOOD. (See Sydenham.)

CROYDON, a market-town, county of Surrey. Area of parish, 940 A. ; population, 16,712. It is a very old town, built on the site of the ancient Noviomagus, and alternately with Guildford the seat of the county assizes. It has also a county court and petty sessions, and is the place of election of members for East Surrey. The town is well built, and continually increasing, the situation being salubrious, and its communication with the metropolis so rapid. Its principal public buildings are the town hall, poultry market-house, gaol, union workhouse, and its various places of worship. The church is a spacious structure, in which are the tombs of several archbishops of Canterbury, whose archiepiscopal palace is in the vicinity of the town. Independently of the Trinity Hospital for forty poor persons, with a revenue of £2,000 per annum, there are some alms-houses, and other charities, producing £500 per annum, and several public schools, including Archbishop Tennison's for thirty children, and one belonging to the Society of Friends. Croydon has a considerable trade in corn for the London markets. Market, Saturday ; fairs, July 6th, and October 2nd, 3rd, and 4th. Near the town are some barracks. Waddon, Joseph Lanfear, Esq. ; Seldson House, G. R. Smith, Esq. ; Oakfield Lodge, R. Sterry, Esq. ; Birdhurst Lodge, J. W. Sutherland, Esq. 1½ m. w. BEDINGTON. Bedington Park, Charles Hallowell Carew, Esq. The present mansion was built in 1709. It formerly consisted of three sides of a square, but the interior of the north wing having been burnt soon afterwards, it was never restored. The centre is a large and lofty hall, with a noble Gothic roof of wood. The great door has a curious ancient lock, very richly wrought, a shield with the arms of England, which moves in a grove, concealing the key-hole. The old mansion was built in the 16th century, by Sir Francis Carew, who expended vast sums of money in laying out the gardens and grounds, and is said to have first planted the orange-tree in England. In August, 1599, Queen Elizabeth passed three days here on a visit to Sir Francis. The orangery at Bedington was long famous. In 1691 it was described as above 200 feet in length, most of the trees being 13 feet high, and that in the previous year the gardener had gathered from them 10,000 oranges. Bedington House, Sir Henry Bridges.

14½ m. STOAT'S NEST STA.

2 m. w. WOODMANSTERNE. 2½ m. further, BANSTEAD. Nork Park, Dowager Lady Arden ; Burgh House, Earl of Egmont ; Banstead Park, Mrs. E. Spencer. 2 m. N. from WOODMANSTERNE, The Oaks, Earl of Derby, considered one of the most delightful spots in England, was originally a small edifice built by a society of sporting men called "The Hunters' Club," for the convenience of the Epsom race meetings. The mansion was greatly enlarged by the late Earl of Derby, who purchased it of General Burgoyne, and the grounds improved with beautiful plantations, made out of a part of the common, which was enclosed for that purpose, nearly three miles in circumference. The lawn is remarkable for the beauty of its turf, and here is a singular beech-tree, the boughs of which have grown into one another.

5 m. E. Sheneoaks, Rev. E. F. Baynard. It is a handsome villa residence, situated on a romantic situation amongst the hills and woods.
7 m. s.s.e. by E. Titsey Place, William Leveson Gower, Esq.

1½ m. N.N.E. NUTFIELD.   This place is noted for producing fuller's
earth, superior to any other of England. In 1755 a quantity of brass Roman
coins, of the Lower Empire, were found in this parish in an earthen vessel.
Nutfield Park, Daniel B. Meek, Esq.; Hall Land, Miss S. M. Fuller;
Pilcher House, Thomas Hoof, Esq.; Pendell Court, John Perkins, Esq.
1 m. further, Mertsham House, Sir W. G. H. Jolliffe, Bart.

3 m E. BLETCHINGLEY. Previous to the Reform Bill, a borough, returning two members to Parliament.   It once possessed a castle, supposed
to have been built by Richard de Tonbridge.   In the reign of Henry III.,
his descendant, Gilbert, surnamed the Red, having joined the disaffected
barons, and commanded a division of their forces at the battle of Lewes, in
1264, his conduct, though his party proved victorious, occasioned the
demolition of this fortress; for the King's forces, then in garrison at Tonbridge Castle, hearing of his defeat, sallied out on the Londoners, who had
been dispersed in the beginning of the engagement, and were collecting
their shattered remains at Croydon, and destroyed Bletchingley Castle in
their way. This castle stood at the western extremity of the town on a
bold brow of a hill, but now only the foundations are to be found. 2 m. further, GODSTONE. Rook's-Nest Park, Charles Turner, Esq. A handsome
mansion, situated near the foot of the chalk hills, in the centre of 240 acres
of land, of which 140 are laid out as a park. It was formerly a part of the
priory of Tandridge, and was long the residence of Sir Henry Strackey,
Bart., Master of the Household to George III. 1 m. further, TANDRIDGE.
Tandridge Hall, John Pearson, Esq.; Tandridge Court, the seat of the
Pepys' family; Southlands, Mrs. Trowers; The Priory, Captain R.
Wellbank.

2 m. s.e. BURSTOW. Burstow Lodge, Mrs. M. A. Sanders. 3 m.
further, Fellbridge House, a handsome mansion, at the southern
extremity of the parish of Godstone, on the borders of Sussex, was erected
by the late James Evelyn, Esq., on the site of a former house, called Heath
Hatch. It stands in a park, bounded on the south by Fellbridge Water, a
small stream which here divides the counties of Surrey and Sussex.

6 m. E. EAST GRINSTEAD, George Covey, Esq. The ruins of Brambletye
House, a castellated mansion in the Italian style, of the time of James I.,
are situated about a mile south of the town. Brookhurst, F. Capes,
Esq.; Kidbrooke Park, Lord Colchester; Ashdown House, Augustus E.
Fuller, Esq., M.P.

2 m. E. Wakehurst Place, Sir Alexander E. Cockburn, M.P. 5 m. further,
Pippingford Park, John Mortimer, Esq. 2 m. N.E. of which, HARTFIELD.
Hartwell House, Sir Thomas Bradfield, Bart.; Hollywyche House, General
F. Maitland; Sandhurst, Richard Price, Esq.; Holtye House, Robert
Whatley, Esq. 3 m. E. WITHYHAM. Buckhurst Park, Earl Delawarr;
Penns' Rocks, Stephen Beeching, Esq.; Highfield Park, R. Price, Esq.

1½ m. N.N.E. LINDFIELD. Oat Hall, John Bent, Esq.; New House,
Alexander Graham, Esq.; Buckshalls, Charles Jolland, Esq.; Beadleshill,
Stephen Lowdell, Esq.; Gravely, Thomas Scutt, Esq. 4 m. s.e. FLETCHING.
Danehurst, Colonel Francis John Davies; Woodgate, Warburton Davies,

20¾ m. REIGATE
STATION.

◁ Dover Rail-
way.

25½ m. HORLEY
STATION.

Enter Sussex.

29¼ m. THREE
BRIDGES' STA.

33¾ m. BALCOMBE
STATION.

37¾ m. HAY-
WARD'S HEATH
STATION.

Hastings
◁ Line.

Dorking and
Reading Br. ☞

3 m. s. CHIPSTEAD. Hooley Cottage, H. Butler, Esq.; Shabden Park, Mrs. A. Little; Pirbright, John Pape, Esq.

20¾ m. REIGATE
STATION.

2 m. w. REIGATE. A parliamentary borough and market-town, county of Surrey, situated on a branch of the river Mole. Area of parish, 5,900 A.; population, 4,584; population of parliamentary borough, 4,415. It sends one member to Parliament. Registered electors (1848), 198. It is a well-built town, with many superior residences. The church contains several handsome monuments, and it has a grammar and national schools, a town hall, market-house, and clock tower. Reigate is the head of a poor-law union, and amongst its curiosities may be named the foundations of an ancient castle, with a cave, in which it is said the barons held meetings to settle the articles of Magna Charter. The neighbourhood of Reigate is remarkable for the beauty of its scenery, and the sand of the county, used in glass-making, together with fuller's earth, produce some trade to the inhabitants. Market, Tuesday. Linkfield Lodge, Thomas Burt, Esq.; Great Dood House, Mrs. D. Hume; Heath House, Henry Lainson, Esq.; Springfield House, Samuel Relf, Esq.; Reigate Lodge, Thomas Smith, Esq.; Priory Park, Earl Somers, a modern mansion, in beautiful grounds, standing at the southern extremity of the town of Reigate, on the site of a religious house founded by William de Warren, Earl of Surrey, whose chief seat was Reigate Castle, not a portion of which now remains. In the centre of the area in which the old castle stood is the entrance to a cave, which is supposed to have served as a depôt for treasures and military stores, and a place of safe custody for prisoners. It is 235 feet in length, one room being 123 feet long, 13 feet wide, and 11 feet high to the crown of the arch, in one part of which is a crypt, nearly 50 yards long, with a stone seat which extended the whole length of the room on both sides. Park Cottage, W. Williams, Esq.; Deville House, William Yatman, Esq.

2 m. N. GATTON. Gatton Park, Countess of Warwick, for many years the residence of Sir Mark Wood, Bart., who was the owner of both Upper and Lower Gatton, stands in the centre of an extensive park, in which is also situated the parish church. In the piping times of the rotten borough system, it is recorded that the elections for Gatton were conducted in the servants' hall of this mansion, Sir Mark's butler acting as returning officer. Gatton (Upper), John Currie, Esq., is a handsome mansion, standing on the hill next to Chipstead, surrounded by a park of about 100 acres.

25½ m. HORLEY
STATION.

Enter Sussex.

HORLEY. The church is a fine edifice, and here are the traces of a considerable castle. Horley Lodge, George Birch, Esq.; Kennersley Park, John Clark, Esq.

29¼ m. THREE
BRIDGES' STA.

Horsham Br. ☞

1 m. w. CRAWLEY. Oakfield, William Brown, Esq.; Ifield, Mrs. Lewin; Crabbett Park, H. Dawes, Esq.; Broadfield, — Briggs, Esq.; Buckingham Hill, Rev. S. B. Piggott. 1 m. N.W. HIGHFIELD. The church, dedicated to St. Margaret, contains statues of a knight and his lady recumbent.

33¾ m. BALCOMBE
STATION.

BALCOMBE. A parish in the rape of Lewes, county of Sussex. Area, 6,050 A. The only remarkable feature of this locality is the tunnel to which we have adverted in our account of this railway. Benjamin F. Robinson, Esq. 2 m. further, Hill House, Lord William de Blackhear.

37¼ m. HAY-
WARD'S HEATH
STATION.

2 m. w. CUCKFIELD. The parish church contains some monuments by Bacon, Flaxman and Westmacott, and a very beautiful stained window, by Ward, has lately been placed in the church by Thomas Waller, Esq., of London. The adjacent paving of the floor has been covered with tiling

Esq.; Searles, Sir Thomas M. Wilson, Bart, The mansion stands rather low, in a park of between 500 and 600 acres, the entrance to which is under a large Gothic arch, shaded by stately trees. The gardens alone contain upwards of 100 acres. 2 m. further, MARESFIELD. Forest Lodge, Lady Campbell; Marshalls, Arthur Le Blance, Esq.; Maresfield Park, Sir John Shelley, Bart.; Twyford, Robert Trotter, Esq. J.P.; Nutley Court House, George Wilson, Esq. About 2 m. s. UCKFIELD. It is situated on the river Ouse, through the aid of which it carries on a considerable trade with Lewes. Uckfield House, Mrs. S. Kelly; The Rocks, R. S. Streatfield, Esq.; Buxted Park, Earl of Liverpool.

5 m. E. CHAILEY. The Hooke, Robert W. Blencowe, Esq.; Ades, James Ingram, Esq. 2 m. further, ISFIELD, Newick Lodge, John Day, Esq.

41½ m. BURGESS HILL STA.

1 m. E. CAYMOORE, William Cheeseman, Esq. 1 m. further, DITCHLING. Here, on the Downs, is Ditchling Beacon, 864 feet high. There are also remains of an ancient British camp. Knevington, J. B. Cripps, Esq.

43½ m. HASSOCKS GATE STA.

Lewes Line.

BRIGHTON, or BRIGHTELMSTONE. Supposed to have been a Roman station, is said to have derived its name from Brichtelm, a son of Cissa, the first King of Sussex. In the middle of the last century it was but an insignificant fishing village; it is now a parliamentary borough, sea-port town, and parish, and one of the most fashionable watering-places in England. Many of its streets, squares, crescents, &c., vie in point of elegance and architectural taste with the most aristocratic parts of the metropolis, while its shops display every article of fashion and luxury that can be found in the grand emporiums of Regent Street, and other great thoroughfares of London. It owes its origin as a place of resort, and its magnificence as a splendid city (in all but the name), to the long-continued favour of George IV., who, when Prince of Wales, erected the oriental palace or pavilion which, with its gardens, occupies so conspicuous a portion of the valley in which it is situated. Brighton is sheltered on the north and north-east by the South Downs, and extends along the sea-shore for nearly three miles, the frontage to the ocean being defended by a high sea wall, which forms a beautiful promenade. Area of parish, 1,980 A. It is difficult to give a very accurate estimation of its population, as it is subject to continual fluctuation; but in 1841 it amounted to 46,730, while the ascertained population of the parliamentary borough was 48,567. It

50¾ m. BRIGHTON STATION.

Brighton to Portsmouth.

The line from Brighton passes through Shoreham, Worthing, Littlehampton, Bognor, Chichester, Emsworth, and Havant, to Portsmouth. The level nature of the country has dispensed with the necessity for any of those gigantic works which ornament and beautify most of the districts which are traversed by railways; but great credit is due to Mr. John Urpeth Rastrick, the Company's engineer up to 1846, for the construction of the timber viaduct at Shoreham, the great drawbridge at Arundel, and the swing-bridge

of an ancient pattern by the same gentleman. Oaklands, Hon. E. Curzon; Bolnore House, Misses Dealtry; Mill Hall, Edward Ludlow, Esq.; Borde Hill, Captain William Preston, R.N.; Staplefield Place, Sir John Shaw; Cuckfield Place, Rev. John Sergison. The house was erected in the latter part of the 16th century, in a picturesque situation, surrounded by a park. The approach is by a spacious gravel walk to the gate-house, which opens into a court leading to the principal entrance of the mansion. 6 m. further, COWFOLD. Avisford, Sir John William Anson, Bart. 2 m. further, WEST GRINSTEAD. Knep Castle, Sir Charles M. Burrell, Bart. The castle was built about fifty years ago, and named after an ancient castle, some small remains of which are still to be seen on the high road leading to Horsham.

41½ m. BURGESS HILL STA.

Close to the Station, Clayton Priory, Lieutenant-Colonel Charles W. Elwood.

43½ m. HASSOCKS GATE STA.

2 m. w. HURST, or HURST PIERPOINT. Hampton Lodge, Richard Weekes, Esq.; Danny Park, W. J. Campion, Esq.; Pakyns Manor, Nathaniel Borrer, Esq. 4 m. further, SHERMANBURY. Shermanbury Place, Stephen Challen, Esq.

2 m. s.w. Newtimber Place, Lady Gordon.

50¾ m. BRIGHTON STATION.

returns two members to Parliament. Registered electors (1846), 2,766. It is governed by a constable, and twelve headboroughs. Petty sessions are held weekly, and a daily court of county magistrates is held in the town hall. Its principal structures are the suspension chain-pier, an elegant work of art, extending 1,014 feet into the open sea, the church of St. Peter, which possesses an ancient Norman font, numerous other churches and chapels for all denominations of sectarians, the town hall (a noble building), county hospital, assembly rooms, theatre, baths, and perhaps some of the handsomest and best hotels in the kingdom. There are no less than 158 daily schools, many almshouses, infirmaries, and other charities, and amongst its learned establishments we may cite the Sussex Literary and Scientific Institution. With the exception of the fisheries, which employ about 150 boats, chiefly for the London markets, Brighton has only a retail trade for the supply of its inhabitants and visitors, but its Thursday market is admirably furnished with all the luxuries of the table. Brighton communicates with France by a regular line of steam packets between its port and that of Dieppe, and with Hastings and Portsmouth by different branches of this railway. Annual races are held here in August. Fairs, Holy Thursday, and September 4th.

Brighton to Portsmouth.

near Portsmouth. These, with the exception of a short tunnel at Windmill Hill, Brighton, about two hundred yards in length, the very beautiful brick viaduct over the London Road, at the entrance to Brighton, and a large terminal station at Portsmouth, the two latter works designed and carried out by R. Jacomb Hood, Esq., C.E., are all the works we can enumerate on the line from Brighton to Portsmouth.

Left of Railway from Brighton.

HOVE. It is a pretty little watering-place, has a fine old church, and possesses many good houses.

HOVE STATION.

SOUTHWICK STATION.

KINGSTON, or KINGSTON-ON-LEA.

56 m. KINGSTON STATION.

SHOREHAM, a parliamentary borough, sea-port town and parish, in the county of Sussex. Area of parish 170 A.; population, 1,998; area of parliamentary borough, including a considerable part of the rape of Bramber, 27,980. It returns two members to Parliament. Registered electors (1847), 1,921; customs' revenue, £25,182; registered ships, 8,962 tons. It is an old and ill-built town; it has however, like most parishes in this county, a very fine old church, a market-house, and a noble suspension bridge over the Adur, the piers of which are surmounted by the supporters of the Duke of Norfolk. The harbour which is formed by the mouth of this river is a very indifferent one. Ship-building, and the import of corn, coal, and Irish provisions, with exports of timber, &c., form the chief trade of this place. Markets, Saturday and Monday. Charles II. made his escape from Shoreham to Fes Camp after the battle of Worcester.

56¼ m. SHOREHAM SLATION.

LANCING. Stands immediately on the sea-coast, and although frequented during the bathing season it has a dull and desolate aspect.

LANCING STA.

¼ m. s. WORTHING. A celebrated watering-place and chapelry, in the parish of Broadwater, county of Sussex, situated on the English Channel. Population, 4,702. The rapid rise of this place from an obscure village within the memory of man, is said to be due to the patronage bestowed upon it by George III. The air is exceedingly mild, and the sands along the shore form a delightful promenade of several miles. The inns are excellent, and the modern buildings towards the village of Broadwater display considerable taste and elegance. The parish of Broadwater has an area of 2,240 A., with a population, including Worthing, 5,345. Its church is of Saxon origin, and is a remarkably picturesque and interesting edifice. Here are cattle fairs, June 22nd and October 30th.

61¼ m. WORTHING STATION.

GORING, a small parish, in the rape of Arundel. Courtland, William Olliver, Esq.

64 m. GORING STATION.

1 m. s. KINGSTON. 1 m. s.w. RUSTINGTON. Greenfold, Captain Edward Penfold.

66¼ m. ANGMER-ING STA.

1½ m. s. LITTLE HAMPTON. Is a small harbour, much frequented for sea-bathing. It is situated at the mouth of the river Arun, which has its source in St. Leonard's Forest, whence it flows for a few miles by Horsham, thence turns due south, having received the water of the Rother, which rises from the north-west part of the county, and joins it near the village of Stopham. Its course becomes very serpentine as it flows through a rich tract of marshes by the town of Arundel to the sea at Hampton. This river is celebrated for its mullets, which, in the summer season, are seen in shoals as far as Arundel, and it abounds in eels and other fish.

68¼ m. ARUNDEL AND LITTLE HAMPTON STA.

Cross the river Arundel.

Distance from London.	**Right of Railway from Brighton.**
HOVE STATION.	N. BLATCHINGTON. ANGLETON.
SOUTHWICK STATION.	SOUTHWICK has a very ancient and interesting church.
56 m. KINGSTON STATION.	Kingston House, William Gorringe, Esq.
56½ m. SHOREHAM STATION.	1 m. N.E. OLD SHOREHAM, formerly a town of some importance, situated near the mouth of the Adur, is mentioned in our ancient history as the spot where Ella, the first King of the South Saxons, made good his second landing on his return from Germany with the reinforcements which enabled him to accomplish the conquest of this province. The church, great part of which lies in ruins, is a fabric of very early date. The arches are large, in the Saxon style, and adorned with the zigzag ornaments. On the south side is a remarkable door-way, the columns nearly buried in the ground, with foliage to the capitals, supporting an arch, having in the architrave three distinct parts ; the first contains a sort of triglyphs, the second diagonals, and the third pateræ. Buckingham House, Harry Bridger, Esq. ; Erringham House ; Thomas Elane, Esq.; Highden, Sir H. D. Goring, Bart.; Combs, John Hampton, Esq. ; Cysbury, Hugh Penfold, Esq. ; Finden Place, W. W. Richardson, Esq. ; Rowdell, Major Sandham.
LANCING STA.	1½ m. N. COOMBS. ½ m. further, BOTOLPHS. A little further, STEYNING, anciently a place of much note. King Ethelwald, father of Alfred the Great, and St. Cuthman, are buried here.
61¼ m. WORTHING STATION.	1 m. E. DONNINGTON. A little further, SOMPTING. 4 m. further, Weston Park, The Reverend Goring. This place gave birth to three brothers, sons of Sir Thomas Shirley, who attained to considerable eminence. Sir Anthony Shirley, the second son, becoming known to Robert Earl of Essex, in 1596 embarked on a voyage of adventure to Africa and the West Indies. He took the Island of Jamaica, but being deserted by his ships, was obliged to return to England. Sir Robert, the third son, entered into the service of Persia, and performed such eminent services against the Turks, that the Sultan gave him a relation of his own in marriage. Sir Thomas, the eldest son, undertook several sea voyages to foreign parts, to the great honour of his nation, but small enriching of himself.
	3 m. N.W. FINDON. Findon Place, William W. Richardson, Esq. ; Muntham House, Thomas Fitzgerald, Esq.
64 m. GORING STATION.	1½ m. N. Goring Castle, Captain Sir George B. Pechell, Bart.; Goring Hall, David Lyon, Esq. A little further, Patching, Sir Richard Hunter, Bart. ; Mitchell Grove, John Forth, Esq.
66¼ m. ANGMER-ING STA.	ANGMERING. Ham House, W. K. Gratwicke, Esq.
68½ m. ARUNDEL AND LITTLE HAMPTON STA.	ARUNDEL. A municipal and parliamentary borough, market-town and parish, county of Sussex, situated on the river Arun. It is a well-built town, and has a thriving trade in corn and timber, the river being deep enough to permit vessels of 200 tons to approach the town. Arundel Castle, Duke of Norfolk. This noble pile, one of the grandest palaces in the kingdom, enjoys a twofold celebrity—in its great antiquity, and its peculiar privilege of conferring the title of Earl on its possessor.
Cross the river Arundel.	

> " Since William rose, and Harold fell
> There have been Counts of Arunde
> And Earls old Arundel shall have
> While rivers flow and forests wave."

½ m. s.w. FORD. 1 m. further, CLIMPING.

70¼ m. FORD STATION.

½ m. s. YAPTON, C. H. Gibbins, Esq.; J. P. Holloway, Esq. 2 m further, MIDDLETON. The village, which, as the name implies, formerly stood in the centre of the parish, is now on the sea-shore. The church is entirely swallowed up by the sea.

71½ m. YAPTON STATION.

2½ m. s. BOGNOR, formerly called Hothampton, is a market-town and chapelry, on the south coast, in the parish of Berested, in the county of Sussex, and a well-frequented bathing-place during the season. Population, 2,190. This was a favourite spot of the Princess Charlotte, who here founded a school, and from a small fishing village, has become a very considerable town, containing good terraces and pleasant residences overlooking the sea, several places of worship, and a good market. The coast here is rocky and dangerous. Markets, Thursday and Saturday. Manor House, Dr. and Lady Mary Arnold; Aldwick Place, John Cabbell, Esq.; Beach House, Sir John Chetwode, Bart., M.P.; Felpham House, John Dale, Esq.; Aldwick Pavilion, Captain Dixie, R.N.; Chapel House, Mrs. Admiral Jackson; The Lodge, Lord George Lennox; Bersted Lodge, Earl of Mayo; Aldwick Lodge, Captain Money, R.N.; Dome House, Admiral Schomberg; Sudley Cottage, Christopher Teesdale, Esq.; The Pavilion, Charles Walters, Esq.

74½ m. BOGNOR STATION.

1 m. s. MERSTON.

77 m. DRAYTON STATION.

Chichester Harbour, about two miles from the city, is formed out of a creek, or inlet, in the English Channel, the entrance to which is both narrow and dangerous, and can only be entered at a certain time of the tide. In this creek are situated Hayling and Thorney Islands. At low water it forms a vast area of many thousands of acres of mud, the effluvia from which in the summer season is far from conducive to health, and renders this part of the country from Chichester to the vicinity of Portsmouth very insalubrious.

79¼ m. CHICHESTER STA.

6 m. s. SELSEA. It is an island, or more properly, peninsula, being a considerable flat tract of land which runs far into the sea, so as to be surrounded at high-water on all sides but the west. There is a ferry a little below Sidlesham, and a good road at low water, with a small bridge across the narrow stream. This place is remarkable as having been originally an episcopal see. After its removal to Chichester, the Bishop continued to have a mansion and park here, no traces of which are now left; but at the beginning of Elizabeth's reign, by virtue of an act empowering the Queen to take into her hands certain of the temporal possessions of any see that should become vacant, making compensation for the same with parsonages impropriate and tithes, Selsea, with seven other manors, was separated from the estates belonging to the bishops. The church is situated at the north-east corner of the peninsula, nearly two miles from the village. It is an ancient building, and appears to have once been larger than at present. At the west are some ruins, which are said to have formed part of a tower begun some years ago, but the design was relinquished. In the middle aisle are several ancient coffin-shaped stones, two of which have crosses or pilgrims' staves upon them. Near the churchyard are the marks of some

2 m. N. Bignor Park, John H. Hawkins, Esq. A little further, Coates Castle, John James King. 2 m. E. Stopham House, George Barttelott, Esq. N. Tottington, William Stubbs, Esq.

70¼ m. FORD STATION.

71½ m. YAPTON STATION.

1 m. N. WALBERTON. Walberton House, Richard Prime, Esq., M.P.; Avisford, Lady Elizabeth Reynell; Hill House, P. Cobbett, Esq.; Hill Cottage, John Halliday, Esq. 1½ m. further, EARTHAM, the Hon. Mrs. Huskisson; Charles Bailey, Esq. 1½ m. E. Dale Park, John A. Smith, Esq., M.P. 3 m. further, Lavington House, Bishop of Oxford. It is beautifully situated under the steepest and highest range of the South Downs, which are here clothed with magnificent woods. It commands an extensive view over a rich and variegated country, and, with its extensive woods, forms one of the most beautiful seats in this county.

74¼ m. BOGNOR STATION.

4 m. N. Petworth Road. 1 m. further, Burton Park, E. Bainbridge, Esq., is a very handsome edifice. which was commenced in the year 1740, from designs by Leoni, after the old mansion of the reign of Queen Elizabeth was partly destroyed by fire. The principal front is 173 feet long, and very imposing in its appearance. In the centre is a small Doric doorway, over which are balustrades, and a large circular-headed window. The pediment which crowns this division bears in its tympan the arms of the Biddulph family. The whole front is in five divisions, upon a rusticated basement, with a bold blocked cornice surmounting the principal story, upon which is the drawing-room and the saloon. The situation of this mansion is one of great beauty, in the midst of a large park, picturesquely diversified, and intersected by a succession of small lakes falling into each other. There are beautiful views of the Downs, from the verge of which is a fine prospect of the sea. 3 m. further, New Grove House, unoccupied. ¼ m. further, PETWORTH. Petworth House, Colonel Wyndham. 1 m. N.E. Hillyears, Mrs. L. Ladbrooke. 8 m. N. Shillinglee Park, Earl of Winterton. 4 m. N.W. Lodsworth House, H. Hollish, Esq.; and Blackdown House, James Henry, Esq.; Pitshill, Mitford, Esq.

77 m. DRAYTON STATION.

1 m. N. HAMPNETT.

79¼ m. CHICHESTER STA.

CHICHESTER is a city and county of itself, a parliamentary and municipal borough, capital of the county of Sussex. Area of city liberty, 1,680 A.; population, 8,512; population of parliamentary borough, 8,084. It sends two members to Parliament. Registered electors (1848), 789. Chichester is surrounded by Roman walls, which are now formed into public promenades, and planted with trees. Many Roman coins, and other antiquities, have been discovered in the city and suburbs, and it is supposed to have been the Regnum of that people. It was partially destroyed A.D. 491 by the East Saxons, under Ella, but rebuilt by his son Cissa (from whom it derives its name), and was constituted by him the capital of the kingdom of Sussex, and so continued until its conquest by the West Saxons. Without pretending to magnificence beyond its ecclesiastical buildings, Chichester is a clean, and neatly-built cruciform city, well drained, paved and lighted. The market and council houses, corn exchange, gaol, infirmary, the guildhall (part of an ancient priory within an enclosure), the hospital of St. Mary, almshouses, grammar school with a revenue of £1,300 per annum, blue-coat, Lancasterian, national, and other schools, with the mechanics' institute, and the literary and philosophical society, are its principal public buildings. In the centre of the city, from whence diverge the four streets of which it is composed, stands its beautiful octagonal cross, erected in 1478. The cathedral is a plain structure in comparison with the general character of such buildings in this country, but it is nevertheless a most interesting fabric. It was built in the 13th and 14th centuries, and is 410 feet in length, and 227 feet in extreme breadth, having a noble spire 300 feet high. Although the interior is plain, the choir is very richly and elaborately adorned, and, amongst other curiosities, are the

place of defence thrown up in a semicircular form. Here also was the
first monastery founded in this county, the charter of which was given by
Adelwalch, King of Sussex, and included the whole peninsula, with part of
the hundred of Manwode. This monastery for canons regular was dedicated
to St. Peter, and was erected on the south-east side, and contiguous to the
spot where the parish church now stands. The remains of this building,
and the adjoining city, according to Camden, " are visible at low water,
the sea having here encroached considerably upon the land." About a
mile and half out at sea there are several places having rocks, or the ruins
of buildings under water. The best anchoring off the island is, to this day,
called the Park, and the rocks between the islands and the shoals farther
out, bear the name of The Streets, where a tomb-stone, with an inscription,
is said to have been a few years since picked up by some fishermen.

1 m. s. BOSHAM, situated on the north of Chichester Harbour, was
formerly a place of considerable merchandise, but Chichester has since
absorbed the whole of the trade of this and other small mercantile towns.

82¼ m. BOSHAM
STATION.

Enter Hampshire.

EMSWORTH. One of the most beautiful, if not the most beautiful little
town on the south coast. It is situated in Hampshire, just on the borders
of Sussex, on an arm of the same inlet which forms Chichester Harbour. It
was formerly a small fishing hamlet, but from its favourable situation has
become a populous and thriving town. It is neatly built, and contains a
church, in the Norman style of architecture, with two towers at the west
end, and surrounded with octagonal turrets, terminating in low spires. It
has several vessels employed in the coasting trade, and a considerable
number of boats in the oyster fishery, for which it has long been celebrated.
Highland Cottage, William Baynes, Esq.; Verletta, Major John Temple.
1 m. s. Thorney Island.

86¼ m. EMSWORTH
STATION.

HAVANT, a market-town, county of Hants, consists of one long street, in
the centre of which stands its venerable cruciform church, and square stone
tower. From Havant there is a communication by bridge with Hayling
Island, and in the vicinity is the pretty village of Warblington, with its
picturesque church, and the lofty ivied tower of its ruined castle. Shaw-
field Lodge, G. A. Shaw, Esq. 2 m. s. NORTH HAYLING. 2 m. further,
SOUTH HAYLING. Gothic Cottage, Miss M. Brereton; Lennox Lodge,
Rev. Frederick Leicester; Clarence Cottage, Richard Meade, Esq.; Manor
House, William Padwick, Esq.

88 m. HAVANT
STATION.

portraits of all the sovereigns of England, with many other historical subjects, and some ancient and other monuments, which are beautiful specimens of statuary, two or three of which are by Flaxman. The Bishop's palace and gardens, the cloisters, and other ecclesiastical buildings, are on the south side of the cathedral, within an enclosure. The annual revenue of the see, which extends almost entirely over the county, is about £6,000. There are eight parishes in the city, but the modern church of St. Peter, a handsome structure, is the only one worthy of especial notice. Markets, Wednesday and Saturday; fairs for cattle and horses, May 4th, Whit Monday, October 10th and 20th. In the vicinity of the city are some barracks, and Kingley Bottom, on the south-east of Chichester, is said to have been the burial-place of the South Saxon kings. Collins and Hayley, the poets, were natives of this place. Nyton, Charles P. Peckham, Esq.; The Palace, Bishop of Chichester. 3 m. N. Goodwood, Duke of Richmond. Few situations present greater advantages of a local nature for an extensive mansion than are found at this splendid place. The scenery around is most beautiful, embracing a view of the Channel, the Isle of Wight, and Chichester spire. The house, situated in a spacious park, is grand and extensive. The carriage-front extends 166 feet, and is ornamented with two circular turrets of white flint, with hemispherical roofs. The entrance is formed by a portico two stories high, consisting of the Doric and Ionic orders, with a bold block cornice, and surmounted by a balustrade. From either turret there is a front of 106 feet towards the east and south, which stands upon an angle of 45°. The whole building is composed of square flint stones of the neatest masonry. Over the entrance in the garden front there is a pediment, and on this side of the house are some fine cork-trees. 1 m. N.N.E. Molecombe House, Earl of March, M.P. A little further WESTDEAN. Charlton, Rev. G. H. Woods; Chilgrove, L. Woods, Esq. 1 m. N. of SINGLETON, Grove House, Colonel G. Wyndham. 4 m. further, MIDHURST. Cowdray Lodge, Earl of Egmont; Heathfield, T. A. Davis, Esq.

82¼ m. BOSHAM STATION.

2 m. S. Stoke House, Sir H. Seymour, Bart., M.P. Stoke House was for many years the residence of Lord George Lennox, grandfather of the Duke of Richmond. On the south acclivity of Stoke Downs are two large mounds, supposed to have been erected over the bodies of the sea-kings whom the men of Chichester encountered and slew in the year 900.

Enter Hampshire.

Berkeley Lodge, Henry Collins, Esq.; Stone Wall, John Pannell, Esq. A little to the N. FUNTINGTON. Oakwood, John Baring, Esq.; Densworth House, B. Winter, Esq.

86¼ m. EMSWORTH STATION.

2 m. N. Stanstead Park, 3 m. further, SOUTH HARTING. Uxholt Park, Frederick Bullock, Esq.; Down Park, Henry Wilmer, Esq.; Up Park, Sir W. Fetherstonhaugh, Bart. In the 17th century this park was the residence of Ford Gray, Esq., who pulled down the old house, and erected the present magnificent seat. It was purchased in 1796 by Sir Matthew Fetherstonhaugh for nineteen thousand pounds, the wood and park being computed to be worth all the money.

88 m. HAVANT STATION.

½ m. N. Leigh Park, Sir George Thomas Staunton, Bart., M.P. 4 m. N.W. Idsworth House, Rev. Sir J. C. Jervoise, Bart. 3 m. further, BURITON. Manor House, K. Fielder, Esq.; Old Ditcham, John Chase, Esq.; Ditcham Park, Earl of Limerick; Nurstead House, Colonel Hugonin. 2 m. further, PETERSFIELD. Though only a chapelry to Buriton, is a market-town and borough of considerable antiquity. Its first charter of incorporation was granted by Queen Elizabeth, who empowered the inhabitants to return two members to Parliament. Two returns had, however, been previously made, one in the 35th of Edward I., the other in the time of Edward VI. Near the church is an equestrian statue of William III.,

Fareham Br.

PORTSMOUTH. This principal naval station of England is a parliamentary and municipal borough, and sea-port town, in the hundred of Portsdown, the county of Hants, situated at the south-west extremity of Portsea Island, at the entrance of its noble harbour. Area of parish, 110 A.; population, 9,354; area of borough, including the town and parish of Portsea, 5,090 A; population, 53,027. It sends two members to Parliament; registered electors (1848), 2,189, and is a polling-place for the south division of the county. The town is enclosed by bastioned ramparts, faced with masonry, surrounded by deep trenches and extensive outworks, and entered by four gates, with drawbridges, &c., forming in every respect a perfect fortress. In the main, or High Street, which is generally well built, is the governor's house, and several excellent hotels; and amongst the principal buildings we may enumerate the church, a spacious structure, with a cupola, several Dissenting chapels, the new market-house, town hall, and gaol, the garrison, marine and other barracks, the theatre, assembly and ball-rooms, new almshouses, Philosophical Society's rooms, &c. The by-streets generally are mean and ill-built, and in that which leads to the Point are many low public-houses for the accommodation of sailors and boatmen. At the Point is the station of the floating-bridge, which connects Portsmouth with the opposite town of Gosport. The ramparts round the town are well planted with trees, and form an agreeable promenade, from which the views of Spithead, the Isle of Wight, Southsea (now a fashionable watering-place), its castle, and Cumberland Fort, with the continual movement of Britain's bulwarks to and from the harbour, are truly picturesque and beautiful. Portsea, which is a

95¼ m. PORTS-
MOUTH STA.

South=Eastern Railway.

The new Terminus of the South-Eastern Railway at London Bridge has lately been opened. It occupies the central portion of the main building. The elevation is in the Italian style, and consists of three stories, terminating with an ornamental cornice, and surmounted by a clock, set in a frame of cement decorations. Around the station is a covered way, on iron columns, which is glazed to the extent of the pathway in order to give light to the rooms on the ground floor; and a portion of the covering extends beyond the pathway, as a further protection to the passengers against rain in setting down.

The departure and arrival platforms have a wooden roof, between seven hundred and eight hundred feet in length, and nearly one hundred feet span. A considerable portion of the covering is of rough plate glass, in sheets eight feet long, and three feet six inches wide, the spaces between the plates being plastered and panelled.

On the left-hand side of the approach to the station is a covered passage, similar to the Lowther Arcade in the Strand, with shops, and a large refreshment-room in the centre of the thoroughfare which fronts the terminus. This building, which is nearly two hundred feet in length, has its basement in Tooley Street, whence it rises about sixty feet, divided into three stories, the upper elevation forming the arcade on a level with the railway, the lower part in Tooley Street forming a range of ordinary shops. The Arcade is also finished with a bold cornice, and its western extremity surmounted by a clock similar to the one over the centre of the main building.

This Company, as far as Reigate, use the same line as that to Brighton. From Reigate the South-Eastern diverges to the left through a deep cutting in a sand hill, and soon reaches Bletchingly Tunnel, one thousand and eighty yards in length. Near Tunbridge is the central station, covering twelve acres of land. The cutting of the Tunbridge Wells Tunnel is through a very remarkable strata, which may be called a geological phenomena. It shows, first, a bed of sandy brown clay, passing into a dark blue clay, divided by sand and ironstone. Near a spring there is a thin land of limestone containing fossils. Passing through the tunnel, alternate beds of clay and sandstone

standing on a lofty pedestal, and inscribed to his memory by a William Jolliffe, of considerable importance in the annals of the borough. Broadsbush, William Askew, Esq.; Borough House, Mrs. Eames.

95¼ m. PORTS-
MOUTH STA.

suburb of Portsmouth, and is only separated from it by the Mill-Dam Creek, is also enclosed within an additional line of fortifications. Here is the grand naval dock-yard, with its splendid wet and dry docks, basins, warehouses, iron and copper mills, block and rope houses, anchor forges, with all conveniences for the construction and outfit of ships of war. The yard contains also the residence of the Port Admiral, the Royal Naval College, and a chapel, and building docks for war-steamers are in course of construction at the north-east of the yard. The Gun-Wharf, or Arsenal, with its large artillery and ammunition stores, and the quays bordering on the harbour stand between the dock-yard and Portsmouth. At Landport, also a suburb within the borough, are the Tipner and Hilsea barracks. Portsea has a free grammar school, a mechanics' institution, St. Paul's Academy, female penitentiary, a general hospital, and savings' bank. Steam packets ply several times a day between Portsmouth and the Isle of Wight; and there is a regular communication also by steamers with Southampton, Plymouth, Dublin, and Havre. Portsmouth Harbour is only 220 yards wide at its entrance, but within it the whole navy of Britain may ride in safety. It is about four miles long, and in one place extends to a width of nearly five, but is much narrower in general. The trade of Portsmouth consists chiefly in imports of coal, cattle, corn, sheep, and provisions from Ireland, with wine and timber from abroad. Registered shipping, 213 vessels of 14,682 tons; customs' revenue (1848), £60,577; corporate revenue (1848), £2,395. Markets, Tuesday, Thursday, and Saturday.

South=Eastern Railway.

appear, followed by a seam of white marl on black clay, approaching to lignite. At the forty-second mile more black vegetable clay rests upon sandstone, quarried for buildings. The strata here changes from an angular to a dome-like appearance, when they abruptly end at what geologists call "a fault." The sand rocks are gone, and their places filled with clay. The depth, the contortions of the strata, and various colours of sand and clay, make this perhaps the most interesting of all railway cuttings.

The situation of the Tunbridge Wells Station is remarkable, being constructed in the centre of the natural basin in which the town is built, and is approached each way by tunnels; in fact, the station may be said to be situated in the centre of a tunnel, which in the low ground approaches so near the surface as to allow the station being made.

At Ashford are the workshops of the Company. These consist of the large engine-shed, two hundred and eight feet long, by sixty-four feet wide. The total length of the workshop is three hundred and ninety-six feet. The engine repairing shop is two hundred and fifty four feet long, by forty-five feet wide; the large crane, capable of lifting twenty tons, traverses over this part. The machine-shop, or turnery, is one hundred and forty-two feet long, by forty-five feet wide. Over the engine-house, which adjoins this part of the building, is a tank holding 54,700 gallons of water. The tender-shop is seventy-two feet long, by forty-five feet wide. The smiths' shop is one hundred and seventy-four feet long, by forty-five feet wide, and contains twenty fires. The wheel-hooping and boiler-shop is one hundred and forty-two feet long, by sixty feet wide; it contains the furnaces for bending, and a hydraulic press for stretching the tires, besides several smiths' fires. The whole of these buildings are twenty-eight feet high. The length of the carriage and truck-house is six hundred and forty-five feet, capable of holding fifty carriages and eighty trucks. The store-room is two hundred and sixteen feet long, by forty feet wide, and is a perfect model of neatness. Here is deposited every article which can by any possibility be required, from things the most unwieldy and huge in bulk, to the

most diminutive screw, and the whole arranged with the precision, elegance, order, and symmetry, which distinguishes a British man-of-war

At Saltwood is a Tunnel nine hundred and fifty-two yards long.

Although not exactly within the scope of our work, we may be allowed here to refer to the advantages derived by travellers to the continent from the exertions of this Company to render the harbour of Folkestone available at all tides. That terrible shingle, which has so long baffled the exertions of infant science, and even now, at Dover, braves the exertions of the British Government, has, at Folkestone, at length yielded to the natural lights of scientific experience, under the tutelary genius of commercial enterprise.

Folkestone Viaduct, which spans the little river Foord, is supported by nineteen arches of uniform span, each of thirty feet. The height from the lowest point is one hundred feet, and the total length seven hundred and fifty-eight feet. The pressure is calculated to be one thousand two hundred pounds to the square foot.

The engineering features of the line between Folkestone and Dover are most remarkable. The line is alternately through chalk rock and on artificial embankments washed by the sea, and embraces the Martello Tower Tunnel, six hundred and thirty-six yards; and the Abbott's Cliff Tunnel, one thousand nine hundred and thirty-seven yards. Those interested in such works should first ride in an open third class carriage between the two points, and then walk on the summit of the cliffs along the pathway on the edge. The blasting of the Roundown Cliff on the 26th of January, 1843, was a feat which attracted learned men, geologists, and crowds of spectators. Sir John Herschel was its historian, and his account may be read in the "Athenæum" for 1843, p. 111. The cliff rose three hundred and seventy-five feet above the level of the sea, and was the highest point of the ridge. Upwards of nineteen thousand pounds of gunpowder were used on this occasion. The explosion was almost noiseless—a low murmur, lasting hardly more than half a second. In ten seconds, four hundred thousand cubic yards were thrown down four hundred feet, and distributed over eighteen acres, at an average depth of fourteen feet, and in many parts from thirty to fifty feet. There

---

Left of Railway from London.

Mertsham House, Sir W. G. H. Jolliffe, Bart. 1 m. s. NUTFIELD (see page 164.)

2 m. N. GODSTONE, a pretty village, county of Surrey, surrounded by elegant mansions, is chiefly remarkable for its sandstone quarries. Area of parish, 6,600 A.; population, 1,896. 1 m. E. Rook's-Nest Park, C. H. Turner, Esq. 1 m. further, Tandridge Hall, John Pearson, Esq.; Tandridge Court, the seat of the Pepys' family; Southland, Mrs. Trowers; The Priory, Captain Welbank. 2 m. N.E. of Godstone, OXTED. Oxted Court, Richard Dartnall, Esq.; Barrow Green House, C. L. H. Master, Esq.; Perrisfield House, Charles M'Niven, Esq.

EDENBRIDGE takes its name from its situation on the banks of the river Eden, one of the heads of the Medway, which crosses the village. 5 m. N. WESTERHAM. Squeries, Charles Warde, Esq. ½ m. E. Hill Park, David Baillie, Esq., is an elegant spacious edifice, in the Italian style, and has a most classic appearance, standing in a recess. The chimney-piece in the dining-room is very superb and ancient. The park is of great beauty. On its western extremity its principal feature is a winding valley, surrounded on each side by considerable hills, sometimes precipitous, and at other times forming a broad slope to the edge of the lake below, now and then studded with majestic oaks. A stream of pellucid water travels along the bottom of the valley, and in its progress expands itself into a lake of several acres. In the wood, and immediately in front of the dining-room windows, the brook falls over a rock 30 feet in depth into a dark pool below. The house is backed to the west by a bold eminence, covered with fine oaks; on the south by a beautiful wood, animated by the cascade; and on the east and north are open sweeps, which are gradually lost in the horizon, or in the surrounding

---

Distance from London.

LONDON BRIDGE STATION.

19 m. to Mertsham.

21 m. Reigate Ju.

27 m. GODSTONE STATION.

32 m. EDENBRIDGE STA.

was no smoke, but dust curled out at the borders of the vast rolling and undulating mass. There was scarcely any tremor. Not a single fragment flew out as a projectile in any direction, and altogether the whole phenomenon was totally unlike anything which, according to ordinary ideas could be supposed to arise from the action of gunpowder. Nothing, concludes Sir John, can place in a more signal light the exactness of calculation which (basing itself on a remarkably simple rule,) could enable the eminent engineer (Mr. Cubitt), by whom the whole arrangements are understood to have been made, so completely to task to its utmost every pound of powder employed, as to exhaust its whole effect in useful work, leaving no superfluous power to be wasted in the production of useless uproar or mischievous dispersion, and thus saving at a blow not less than £7,000 to the South-Eastern Company.

The two parallel tunnels excavated through the centre of Shakspeare's celebrated cliff are each thirty feet high, twelve feet wide, and one thousand three hundred and ninety-three yards long, of a Gothic form, and securely arched with brickwork, except where the extreme hardness of the chalk does not require such support. Seven shafts are sunk from the surface to the tunnels, and the same number of outlets to the face of the cliff, through which the excavated chalk was, during the progress of the work, carried to the sea. The viaduct that leads from the terminus to the tunnel is a ponderous piece of workmanship. It is formed of heavy beams of timber securely framed and bolted together, and might not be improperly called a "Giant's Causeway." The sea-wall beyond the Shakspeare Tunnel is one of the most gigantic works of the railway, being upwards of three-quarters of a mile in length, from sixty to seventy feet in height, and about twenty-five feet in thickness at the foundation. It is composed entirely of the shingle or beach, formed into a compact body with lime burnt from the chalk thrown down to form the slantings of the cliffs. These slantings are marvellous, and the works between Dover and Folkestone are of the most stupendous character, and are probably unequalled by anything of the kind in the kingdom.

Distance from London.	
LONDON BRIDGE STATION.	**Right of Railway from London.**
19 m. to Mertsham.	½ m. w. GATTON. Gatton Park, Countess of Warwick.
21 m. Reigate Ju.	
27 m. GODSTONE STATION.	3½ m. S.E. LINGFIELD, where are the remains of Starborough Castle, built by Sir Richard de Cobham, in the time of Henry III. During the civil war in the time of Charles I. this place was garrisoned by the Parliament. It appears to have had a round tower and a dome at each corner, a drawbridge, and a court in the centre. 3 m. S. EAST GRINSTEAD.
32 m. EDENBRIDGE STA.	2 m. S.E. HEVER. Hever Castle, E. W. M. Waldo, Esq. The castle is a very fine and venerable remain, surrounded by a moat, crossed by a drawbridge, and supplied by the river Eden. The entrance gateway, which consists of a centre, flanked by round towers, is embattled and strongly macheolated, and is also defended by a portcullis. The inner buildings form a quadrangle, enclosing a court. The hall still retains vestiges of its ancient splendour. It was once the property of Sir J. Boleyn, grandfather of Anne Boleyn. The Boleyns made this their principal residence; and here, during the halcyon days of courtship, the stern and inflexible tyrant Henry, who, without a relenting pang, could consign that beauty to the scaffold which he had raised to his bed, is said to have spent some of his happiest days. Tradition states that when on a visit to the castle with his attendants, he used to wind his bugle-horn when he had reached the top of the hill to which its towers were visible, in order to give notice of his approach. On the decease of Sir Thomas Boleyn, Earl of Wiltshire and Ormond, and father to the unfortunate Anne, Henry seized this estate as in

country. In the wood, among the old forest trees, is a beech of the prodigious girth of 28 feet. This place formerly belonged to, and was the favourite retreat of Arthur Lord Hillsborough, who changed its ancient name of Valons to Hill Park. Dunsdale Lodge, C. Newton, Esq. A little further, Brasted Park, Edward Turton, Esq.; Combe Bank, Lord Templemore; Montreal, Viscount Holmesdale; Chevening, Earl Stanhope.

4 m. N. Bellevue, Colonel H. Austen. A little further, Kippington, Colonel Thomas Austen; close to which is SEVENOAKS, a market-town and parish, partly above and partly below the great ridge of sand-hills which runs across this county, and divide the upland from the weald. Knole Park, Earl Amherst. Knole has been a remarkable mansion from the period of the Conquest. It stands in an extensive and beautiful park. The principal entrance is through a great tower-portal, leading into the first or outer quadrangle. On a grass-plot on each side are models of ancient statues, the 'Gladiator,' and 'Venus,' and 'Orta Mari.' There is an entrance from this court through a large tower in the centre of the building to the inner quadrangle, which has a portico in front, supported by eight Ionic columns. Over this is an open gallery, with a balustrade. Some of the water-spouts bear the date of 1605, and others 1607. The great hall is 74 feet 10 inches long, 27 feet broad, and 26 feet 8 inches high. At one end there is a richly-carved screen, supporting a grand music gallery, on which are the arms of Thomas Earl of Dorset, and those of his Countess. In the chimney are a very curious pair of ancient dogs of elaborate workmanship. The hall, which is adorned with several family portraits, has at one end the daïs, or raised floor, according to ancient custom, for the principal table of the noble possessor of the mansion, while other tables are placed lengthways down the hall, for tenants and domestics of the family. The windows are of stained glass. The Holbein Gallery contains an extensive collection of portraits, and is 88 feet long. The apartments contain a rare and large collection of curious, tapestry, cabinets, state beds, &c. They exhibit a perfect idea of the style of decoration of the time of James I. St. Julians, Right Hon. J. C. Herries, M.P.; Bradbourne; H. Hughes, Esq.; Beachmont, William Lambard, Esq.; Park Villa, Lady Nelthorpe; Under River, Francis Woodgate, Esq. A little to the north, Chipstead, Henry Newton, Esq.; Sir Richard Rycroft; Chipstead Place, Frederick Perkins, Esq. 2 m. N.E. of Sevenoaks, is SEAL. The Wilderness, Marquis Camden; The Grove, Sir Alexander Crichton, Bart; Seal Chart, Lord Monson.

37 m. PENSHURST STATION.

TUNBRIDGE is an ancient market-town, situated on the river Medway, county of Kent. Here are no less than five branches of the above-named river—one called the Tun—each of which is crossed by a stone bridge. The church, town hall, market-house, some chapels, and the union work-house, are its principal public edifices. It has a grammar school, with sixteen exhibitions of £100 each at the Universities, several minor exhibitions, a fellowship and a scholarship at Oxford, and a revenue of £700 for payment of masters' salaries. The ruins of Tunbridge Castle, built shortly after the Conquest, are strikingly picturesque. Its ancient court is now a beautiful garden, and a modern residence has been erected within the old castle walls, which are extant. Here are also the remains of a priory. Tunbridge has a considerable manufactory of toys and turned ware. Market, Friday. Colebrook Park, Benjamin Smith, Esq. 4 m. N. SHIPBORNE, Dowager-Viscountess Torrington; Sir John Jervis; Fairlawn, Miss M. E. Yates.

41 m. TUNBRIDGE STATION.

right of his late wife, and afterwards enlarged it by purchases from others of her family. The next possessor was Anne of Cleves, who, after her divorce, had this and other adjoining manors settled on her for life. She made Hever Castle her general place of residence, and died here in the 4th of Philip and Mary.

37 m. PENSHURST STATION. Red Leaf, William Wells, Esq.; and 1 m. s. Penshurst Castle, Lord de Lisle and Dudley. This ancient, historical, and interesting mansion, which stands at the south-east corner of the park, is a large irregular building, containing many spacious and noble apartments, in which the architecture of the different ages to which they belong are easily traced. In Hasted and Harris's "Histories of Kent" are some views of the house as it was in days of yore. Even now it presents a truly venerable aspect, and gives an admirable idea of the splendour and magnificence in which our ancestors resided in their baronial halls. The principal entrance is through an ancient gateway, over which is the following inscription:

> "THE GREAT RELIGIOUS AND RENOWNED
> PRINCE EDWARD THE SIXT, KINGE OF
> ENGLAND, FRANCE, AND IRELANDE, GAVE
> THIS HOUSE OF PONCESTER, WITH THE MAUNORS,
> LANDES, AND APPURTENAYNCES THER
> UNTO BELONGINGE VNTO HIS TRUSTYE
> AND WELBELOVED SERVANT SYR
> WILLIAM SYDNEY, KNIGHT BANNERET."

The front quadrangle is of great architectural beauty. The hall, a noble room, with a fine timber roof, and the chapel, are striking objects. In the inner quadrangle are the kitchen, buttery, and other domestic offices; and the old family dinner-bell, set in a wooden frame, serving as a memorial of baronial festivity, still remains in the centre of the yard. The park, of about 400 acres, is beautifully diversified with hills, woods, and lawns, and well planted with large oak, beech, and chesnut-trees. The gardens are extensive, and laid out in terraces. In some lofty beech-trees on a hilly part of the estate is the ancient heronry. The south side of the park is watered by the Medway, and a tree is still pointed out, said to be the celebrated oak called the "Bear's Oak," which was planted at the birth of the gallant and accomplished Sir Philip Sydney. It measures 27 feet in circumference, and is celebrated in some lines by Waller the poet, as well as by Ben Jonson in his "Forest." Penshurst Castle is open to the public every Monday and Saturday.

1 m. further, PENSHURST, county of Kent. Was formerly the residence of the Saxon kings of Kent, and the birthplace of that flower of chivalry Sir Philip Sydney, and of the no less celebrated patriot Algernon. Area of parish, 4,630 A.; population, 1,470. Fair, July 1st. The Grove, Mrs. Allnutt; New House, Thomas Hillman, Esq. 1 m. further, South Park, Viscount Hardinge. 2 m. S.E. ASHURST.

41 m. TUNBRIDGE STATION. Tunbridge Wells Branch. 1 m. s. Mabledon Park, John Deacon, Esq.; Tunbridge Castle, T. E. West, Esq. 4 m. w. Tunbridge Wells, to which there is a branch from the Tunbridge Station.

TUNBRIDGE WELLS, a market-town in the counties of Kent and Surrey, celebrated for its medicinal waters. It is prettily situated in a valley, surrounded by three hills, called Mounts Ephraim, Pleasant, and Sion, on which are numerous villas, and capital hotels. The town contains a pump room, baths, ball rooms, libraries, theatre, parade, market-house, church, a handsome chapel of ease, and several Dissenting places of worship, numerous schools, library, and two medical institutions. In the vicinity of the wells, in a sequestered spot, are some curious rocks, which have a very picturesque appearance. 2 m. further, FRANT. Shernfold, Hon. P. Ashburnham; Ely Grange, Mrs. H. Hebden; Saxonbury Lodge,

The principal part of this mansion is supposed to have been erected about the latter end of the 17th century, but great additions have since been made to the building. It is a large, substantial and convenient edifice, situated in a finely-wooded park. Fairlawn, — Ridgway, Esq. It formerly belonged to the Vane family, of whom was Harry Lord Vane, whose wife was the heroine of Smollett's "Lady of Quality." Oxenhoath, Sir W. R. P. Geary, Bart.

3 m. N.E. Hadlow. Green Trees, Thomas Kibble, Esq.; Hadlow Castle, W. B. May, Esq.; North Frith, Sir Jasper Atkinson.

4 m. N. East Peckham. Riding Hall, William Cooke, Esq. A little further, Mereworth Castle, Baroness Le Despencer. Though called a castle, it has not the least pretension to that appellation, except having been built on the site of an old and embattled mansion, and being surrounded by the old moat.

46 m. PADDOCKS WOOD STA.

4 m. N. Linton Place, Earl Cornwallis. This mansion has been greatly improved by the present noble owner, whose alterations and improvements have been ably executed by the Messrs. Cubitt. The house is situated on an eminence, from the summit of which there is an extensive view over the Weald of Kent. Two avenues of trees contribute greatly to the improvement of the landscape. The mansion displays a fine Corinthian portico and two wings.

51 m. MARDEN STATION.

4 m. N. Chart Sutton, James Russell Howe, Esq. Sutton Vallance, Charles Hoare, Esq. At this place are the ruins of Sutton Castle, which though not extensive, are very picturesque. The crumbling walls of what appears to have been the keep are finely mantled with ivy, and partly grown over with brushwood. All the upper part is destroyed.

53 m. STAPLE-HURST STA.

Headcorn. 2 m. E. East Sutton Place, Sir Edmund Filmer, Bart. 2 m. further, Leeds Castle, Charles Wykeham Martin, Esq., M.P. It forms a very imposing feature in the central division of this county. It is surrounded by a very broad moat, and the entrance to the west is approached by a bridge of two stone arches, communicating with a strong gateway with portcullis. The inner gate opens into a spacious court, containing two ranges of embattled buildings, in which are the principal apartments. The park contains some fine timber, and variety of ground.

56 m. HEADCORN STATION.

2 m. N.N.E. at Pluckley, Surrenden, Sir Edward Dering, Bart. It was erected by Sir Edward Dering on the site of the old original manor-house, and is described by Philipot, in his "History of Kent," to be as "eminent for its magnificence and beauty, as for its contrivance and curiosity." It is situated on the brow of a hill, in the midst of rich pasture and noble woods, and commands picturesque and varied prospects. In the time of the Commonwealth, the learned Sir Edward Dering suffered much in the cause of royalty; but having previously adhered to the Commonwealth, for his inconsistent conduct, his estate was confiscated, and his house four times plundered by the parliamentary soldiers. 2 m. further, Chartfarver. Calehill Park, Edward Darell, Esq. 4 m. further, Otterden Park, Charles Wheler, Esq. 1 m. further, at Charing, G. E. Sayers, Esq.

62 m. PLUCKLEY STATION.

Ashford, a market town, county of Kent. It has one principal street, of great length, well-paved and lighted. The church, which was formerly collegiate, is a spacious and venerable edifice, and contains some remarkably interesting and noble monuments. It has also a grammar school, which was founded, in 1638, by one of the ancient Kentish family of Knatchbull. Market, Thursday. Fairs, for cattle, horses and wool, August 2nd, September 9th, October 12th and 24th. Ashford House, Viscount Strangford. 3 m. w. Hothfield Park, Sir Tufton, Bart.

67 m. ASHFORD STATION.

Ramsgate Br.

Thomas Marling, Esq.; Knowle House, Samuel Newington, Esq.; Eridge Castle, Earl of Abergavenny. The house, a regular building in the castellated style, is embattled and flanked with round towers, but without any mixture of ancient architecture in either doors, windows, or other parts., It stands on a bold eminence, in a park containing about 2,000 acres. 2 m. w. of Tunbride Wells, SPELDHURST. Broomhill Bank, Colonel Armytage; Burrswood, and Broome Hill, David Salomons, Esq., Alderman of London.

46 m. PADDOCKS WOOD STA.

6 m. s.w. LAMBERHURST. Bayham Abbey, Marquis of Camden; Scotney Castle, Edward Hussey, Esq. The old mansion is of very ancient date; it was castellated in the time of Edward III. or Richard II., having been for many years the property of the Barons de Scoteni, the first of whom,

Maidstone Br. ☞

Lambert (temp. Henry II.), may possibly have given his name to the adjoining village of Lamberhurst (anct. Lambert's Hurst, or Wood). It passed into the family of Archbishop Chicheley, thence to the Darells, and finally to the ancestors of the present owner. The present house was built in 1837.

51 m. MARDEN STATION.

5 m. s. at GOUDHURST, Bedgebury Park, Viscount Beresford; Finch Oaks, Richard Springetts, Esq.; Twisden, Robert Springetts, Esq.; Midwells, Miss Cornwallis; Brandford House, Mrs. T. C. Roberts; Pleasant Place, George Hindes, Esq.; Paynetts, S. Stringer, Esq.; Taywell, Giles Miller, Esq.; Taywell House, James D. Warre, Esq.

53 m. STAPLE-HURST STA.

1 m. s. STAPLEHURST, G. J. Ottaway, Esq.; Lodden House, Mrs. Usborne. 2 m. s.e. FRITTENDEN. 2 m. further, the ruins of Sissinghurst Castle. This ancient mansion, which occupied a secluded situation near a branch of the Rother, having been long uninhabited, was, during the late wars, made use of as a French prison, and from this circumstance acquired the name of Sissinghurst Castle. 3 m. further, BENENDEN. Hemsted Place, Thomas L. Hodges, Esq.

56 m. HEADCORN STATION.

4 m. s. BIDDENDEN. 4 m. further, TENTERDEN. This place was one of the first in which the woollen manufacture was established in the reign of Edward III. It became a scene of early opposition to the Church of Rome prior to the Reformation, when in the time of Archbishop Warham 48 inhabitants of its town and neighbourhood were publicly accused of heresy, and five of them condemned to be burned. It possesses all the privileges of the Cinque Ports, and confers the title of Baron on the Abbott family.

62 m. PLUCKLEY STATION.

4 m. s. HIGH HALDEN.

2 m. s.e. BETHERSDEN, Charles Scriber, Esq.; George Witherden, Esq. Bethersden was formerly much celebrated for its marble quarries, and though they are now but little used, the marble obtained here was at one time in considerable request for chimney-pieces, &c. It is of the grey terbonated kind, and bears a good polish. From its similarity to the Peskworth marble, it is frequently confounded with that, and called by the same name. In the parish church are several brasses of the Lovelaces, and among the sepulchral monuments is one to Sir George Chute, Bart., and several for the family of Witherden.

67 m. ASHFORD STATION.

2 m. s. KINGSNORTH. 3 m. further, ORLESTON. 2 m. beyond, KENARD-INGTON. Here are remains of ancient entrenchments, chiefly consisting of breast-work, and artificial mounts, and below them, in the marsh, are other

Hastings Br. ☞

remains, which seem to have been connected with the former by a narrow ridge, or causeway.

1 m. s.e. Sandling Park, William Deedes, Esq., M.P.   1 m. further, 75 m. weston-hanger and hythe sta. HYTHE, a parliamentary and municipal borough, a market-town, and one of the cinque ports, county of Kent.   It lies in a valley towards the east end of Romney Marsh, upwards of half a mile from the sea.   Its once famous harbour has been entirely choked up with shingle, and on the beach, which stands many feet higher than the town, are several martello towers.   The principal public edifices are the county hall, borough gaol, branch bank, theatre, library, and its beautiful old church, which is cruciform, in the early English style of architecture; and under its remarkably beautiful chancel, is a crypt full of human bones.   Here is a very ancient hospital, of which the chief is styled Prior, with an annual revenue of £275, and another with £189 per annum.   Hythe is frequented for sea-bathing.   Market, Thursday. Richard Strangeways, Esq.; Thomas T. Hodges, Esq., M.P.; Bellevue, E. C. Hughes, Esq.   3 m. e. SANDGATE.   Cheriton, R. Brockman, Esq.

2 m. n. HAWKINGE.   5 m. further, DENTON.   Denton Court, Sir John 83 m. folke-stone sta. W. E. Bridges, Bart.   It is built in the Elizabethan style, and contains spacious apartments.   This fine place was for a long time inhabited by the Rev. William Robinson; and in the year 1766, the poet Gray was for some days the guest of this gentleman, who in one of his letters, says: " My residence was at Denton, eight miles east of Canterbury, in a little quiet valley on the skirt of Barham Downs."   Dane Hill, Lady Montefiore.   A little further, Broome Park, Sir H. C. Oxenden, Bart., is situated in the same valley as Denton.   The house is a respectable building, of the time of Charles I., and was erected by Basil Diswell, Esq.

DOVER.   A parliamentary and municipal borough, cinque port, and 88 m. dover station. market-town, county of Kent.   Area of borough, 320 a.   It sends two members to Parliament.   Registered electors (1847), 2,060; corporation revenue (same date), £5,049 7s.; registered shipping (same date), 109 vessels; aggregate burden, 4,249 tons; customs' revenue (1846), £23,590 14s.   The town, properly so called, is irregularly built on the banks of the Pent, immediately under a high cliff, on the top of which is situated the citadel, and other important military works, ascended from its principal street (Snargate) by a double spiral stone staircase of beautiful construction.   There are also various other minor streets and lanes.   Its principal edifices are three parish churches, several Dissenting chapels, the town hall, gaol, workhouse, theatre, museum, baths, assembly rooms, military hospital, the Maison Dieu (a structure of great antiquity), custom house, docks, bonding warehouses, and several excellent hotels. For some years past Dover has assumed much importance as a fashionable watering-place, and to meet its increasing popularity many handsome residences and terraces have been built on the old rope-walk, commencing near the inner basin of the harbour, and extending along the shore as far as " Smith's Folly," under the Castle Cliff, forming altogether a beautiful promenade.   The Castle, one of the most picturesque objects on the English coast, is a fortress of great strength and antiquity, occupying 35 acres.   There are conflicting opinions as to its origin; but it is quite certain that some early portions of the edifice are Roman, and others Saxon. Its spacious keep is a splendid specimen of this style of building, while the Roman and Saxon towers here and there invest the whole area with an interest to the antiquary and historian, which few other spots can surpass.   Indepen-

75 m. WESTON-
HANGER AND
HYTHE STA.

2 m. N. Monks Orton Park.

2 m. E. Beachborough, E. D. Brockman, Esq., M.P. The house is situated amongst most romantic grounds, with conical hills rising in front, clothed with smooth sheep pasture. On one of the hills is an octagonal summer-house, commanding a very extensive view of the coast and across the Channel to France. 3 m. N.E. SIBTON, — Honeywood, Esq. 2 m. further, ACRISE. Acrise Court, Thomas Papillon, Esq. This seat was built by Thomas Papillon, Esq., a merchant of eminence in London, in the time of Charles II. The present proprietor has expended considerable sums in improving the house and opening the grounds, which formerly enclosed many pleasing views of hills and valley.

83 m. FOLKE-
STONE STA.

FOLKESTONE. A parliamentary and municipal borough, market-town, and sea-port, and member of the cinque port town of Dover. It lies in a hollow between two high cliffs, which are connected by a viaduct of this railway. A few years ago it was one of the most straggling and miserable-looking towns in England, but it has lately risen into importance to the detriment of Dover, in consequence of its superior position with regard to the passage between its port and Boulogne, and many handsome villas and several hotels have been erected for the accommodation of visitors, who are also attracted to this spot by the fine sands and the bold and beautiful scenery by which the town is surrounded. It is most irregularly built, but it has a handsome market-house, built by the Earl of Radnor, an endowed school, and other charities, a gaol, library, and capital baths. It has also a pier, battery, and a harbour, which has been greatly improved of late, as vessels drawing from 10 to 12 feet can now enter it at high water. The church is a very ancient edifice. With Hythe, &c., it sends one member to Parliament. Folkestone has a great traffic with Boulogne, but the population derives its chief support from its fisheries. Market, Thursday. Folkestone is the birthplace of the celebrated Harvey, who discovered the circulation of the blood. Broadmead, J. S. Banks, Esq.; The Ford, James Kelcey, Esq.; Ivy Cottage, John White, Esq.

88 m. DOVER
STATION.

dently of these curious remains of antiquity, the bomb-proof magazine, the extensive barracks for thousands of soldiers, the magnificent views from its ramparts are well worthy of inspection, and combine to render Dover Castle, and the military works which extend along the neighbouring height, a still formidable defence against any attempted invasion of this portion of our shores. Dover harbour, though difficult of access, owing to a movable bar of shingle, has undergone great improvements of late, and consists of three basins—the outer one enclosed between two piers 150 feet apart. The harbour of refuge in progress of formation in the bay, has met with some obstruction, owing to the recent storms, which did considerable injury to the tackle, &c., used in its construction; but when completed, it will be a source of considerable advantage to the town, as well as security to the shipping interest. Steam packets ply regularly between this port and France and Belgium, from which countries it imports large quantities of fruit, eggs, vegetables, &c. Dover has an excellent coasting trade and fishery. The borough is governed by a mayor, aldermen, and councillors, and is the seat of quarter sessions, a board for licensing pilots, and a Court of the Constable of the Cinque Ports. Markets, Wednesday and Saturday. Fair, November 23rd.

5 m. N.N.W. Waldershare, Earl of Guildford. This mansion was built by Sir Henry Furness, upon a large scale, after a design said to be by Inigo Jones. He also enclosed a spacious park, and planted it with long avenues. The park is well stocked with deer. It was enlarged some years ago; and on digging the ground a great many Roman utensils of different coloured earths were discovered. 4 m. N.E. Oxney, Richard Roffey, Esq.

Ashford to Margate.

2 m. w. Eastwell Park, Earl of Winchilsea and Nottingham. The mansion is a large edifice, without extraordinary ornament, standing in an extensive park, well furnished with deer, and rendered interesting by a bold equality of ground, some part being so elevated that both the seas may be plainly seen, namely, that of the buoy of the Nore towards the north, and the other on the south over Romney Marsh towards the coast of France. This hill is clothed with fine woods, through which eight avenues of walks, called the Star Walks, branch off in opposite directions from an octagon plain. On the top of the hill nearly adjoining the park, on the south, is Eastwell church, a small edifice, dedicated to St. Mary, and divided into two parts by pointed arches, supported on octagonal colonnades. Eastwell church contains several fine monuments of the Finches: and on the north side of the chancel is an ancient tomb, said to belong to Richard Planta-genet, whom tradition asserts to have been a natural son of Richard III., and whose burial is thus recorded in the register of Eastwell, under date 1550: " Rychard Plantagenet was buried the 22ijth day of December. Anno di supra." It is observable that a similar mark to that prefixed to the name of Plantagenet occurs before every subsequent entry in the old register, where the person was of *noble blood;* but whatever may be the truth of the tradition, the tomb itself seems of an earlier date; it had been inlaid with brasses, which are now gone. Of this Richard a very curious account has been left by the late Dr. Thomas Brett, of Spring Grove, which was subsequently published in Peck's " Desiderata Curiosa," vol. II. lib. III. p. 13.

CHILHAM, county of Kent. The ruins of its ancient castle and its fine old church are worthy of especial notice. Chilham Castle, J. B. Wildman, Esq. The mansion was erected by Sir Dudley Digges, Knight, Master of the Rolls in the reign of Charles I., as appears by an inscription over the principal entrance :

> " THE LORD IS MY HOUSE OF DEFENCE, AND MY CASTLE.
> " DUDLEY DIGGES.   MARY KEMPE."

The situation is commanding and beautiful, rising with a gentle ascent on the north side of the river Stour. Upon the extreme verge of the hill, which rises very abruptly on the side next the river, stands the keep of the ancient castle of Chilham; and it is related, that when Sir Dudley Digges erected the present mansion, which is very near the castle, he discovered in digging the foundation several traces of building, apparently of Roman construction, and fragments of armour, coins, arms, &c., and other evidences to justify the supposition of its having been a Roman station, and a day's march from where Julius Cæsar first landed in Britain. The keep is apparently of Anglo-Norman construction, and is the only portion of the castle remaining. Its principal feature is an octagonal tower of about 40 feet diameter in extent, and about 25 feet within the walls, being about 8 feet in thickness. The ground-floor of the tower is now used as a brewhouse. It is about 30 feet high, having over it what is supposed to

Ashford to Margate.

Right of Railway from Ashford.

72 m. WYE STA.

½ m. E. WYE. A village situated on the river Stour, in the county of Kent, which is here crossed by a five-arched bridge. Wye in former times was a market-town of some little importance. Spring Grove, Charles Jennings, Esq.

1 m. N.

River Stour.

OLANTIGH, J. S. W. SAWBRIDGE ERLE DRAX, ESQ., M.P.

76 m. CHILHAM STATION.

2 m. N.E. CHARTHAM. On Chartham Downs, which extend along the south side of the road between Ashford and Canterbury, are a vast number of barrows of different sizes scattered over the ground, which in the ancient deeds of the adjoining estates is described by the name of "Danes Banks." Several of these have been opened at different times, and the remains of bodies, both male and female, with various articles of trinkets, &c., found in them. It is supposed by early writers that this is the spot where Cæsar first encountered the Britons, and that the fortress which stood south-west of the barrows was that to which they retired. On the contiguous plain to the south, called Swaddling Downs, are three or four lines of entrenchments which cross the whole line from east to west, and on the road under Denge Wood eastward from Julliberrie's grave is another small entrenchment. The manor of Chartham was given to the priory of Christ Church, by Duke Elfrid, in the year 871, towards the clothing of the monks, who had a church here. In the time of Edward I. they had also a vineyard here, and in that of his successor the prior had confirmation of the liberty of free warren in this manor. After the dissolution, Henry VIII. granted it to the dean and chapter of Canterbury, to whom it still belongs. The priors of Christ Church had a residence here, and it was probably to this house that Archbishop Winchelsea retired when suffering under the displeasure of Edward I. Prior Goldsten, about the year 1500, repaired and rebuilt certain portions which had fallen to decay, and in 1572 a large chapel connected with the house was taken

have been the principal state-chamber, panelled with oak. The roof of the tower, which is ascended by the great staircase, is covered with lead, and affords a splendid view of the country. Chilham Castle has belonged to some of the most celebrated warriors and noblemen whose actions have graced the pages of history, but the records are too long for insertion here. A little to the s. GODMERSHAM, William Baldock, Esq.; Godmersham Park, Edward Knight, Esq.

1 m. N.W. Old Lees, William Hillyard, Esq.

2½ m. further, at SELLING, Belmont, Lord Harris; Leveland, Thomas Dodd, Esq.; Harefield, Charles Neame, Esq.; Court Lodge, John Neame, Esq.; Luton House, Miss C. Neame. A little further, SHELDWICH. Lord's House, Charles Dupin, Esq.; Lees Court, Lord Sondes. This splendid mansion was erected by Sir George Sondes, K.B., temp. Charles I. from a design by Inigo Jones, upon the site of the old mansion of Lees Court. The front is adorned with fourteen Grecian-Ionic pilasters, which divide the windows. Above the ground-floor the building is raised one story, and covered with a cottage roof, supported by brackets; it is altogether a very stately edifice, surrounded by beautiful grounds. 1 m. N. of Selling, at BOUGHTON, Boughton House, John P. Lade, Esq.; Brenley House, Edward Jarman, Esq.; Groves, Colonel Percy. ½ m. further, on the road to Faversham, Nash Court. 2½ m. w. of which, is FAVERSHAM, a place of considerable note. In 930 a wittanegemot was held here by Athelstan. King Stephen and his Queen Matilda were interred here, at the abbey built by him for monks. At the dissolution of the monasteries, the body of King Stephen was thrown into the river, and his leaden coffin broken up. James II. was arrested here in 1688, when attempting to escape. Preston House, Mrs. F. Barnes. A little to the w. of Faversham, is OSPRINGE. Ospringe Park, General Sir Thomas Montresor; Oaks, Edward Toker, Esq.; Syndale House, John Hyde, Esq.; The Mount, General G. Gosselin; White Hill, Mrs. B. Foord.

CANTERBURY, a city, borough, and county of itself, and the metropolitan see of England, is situated on the river Stour, in the county of Kent. Area, including fourteen parishes, 3,240 A.; population (1841), 15,435; inhabited houses, 2,769. It returns two members to Parliament; registered electors (1848), 1,924; corporate revenue (1843), £3,204. This venerable city is replete with historical associations. At the period of the Roman invasion it was a settlement of the Britons, and a place of great religious note, and the Romans fixed upon it as one of their principal stations. Historians, and the venerable chroniclers who sought truth, without reference to its application to particular arguments, assert that Christianity was introduced here in the 2nd century, upwards of 400 years before the arrival of St. Augustin, the first priest who ever preached the doctrines, and introduced the discipline of the Romish Church into England, but not without great opposition on the part of the British clergy, who are said to have derived their knowledge of Christian doctrines from the Bible, and the preaching of St. Paul. Canterbury afterwards became the capital of the Saxon kingdom of Kent, by the name of Caer Cant, whence is derived the Latin Cantuaria, and Canterbury. The archbishopric was founded A.D. 597; and amongst the archbishops—of whom there have been 93 up to the present time—we may cite as the most famous, St. Augustin, St. Dunstan, Lanfranc, Anselm, Becket, Cardinal Pole, Cranmer, Abbot, Laud, Tillotson, and Howley. The city of Canterbury is situated in a vale, and has four principal streets, branching from a centre at right angles, extending as far as the ancient city walls, beyond which are considerable suburbs. No city in England, and scarcely any in the north of Europe, abounds in such rich and magnificent ecclesiastical monuments. The cathedral was erected in the 12th, 13th, and 14th centuries, on the

81 m. CANTER-
BURY STA.

down. The seat of the priors is now called the Deanery, having been the residence of the deans of Canterbury for several years immediately preceding the Commonwealth. The church dedicated to St. Mary is a spacious edifice, built in the form of a cross (without aisles), with an embattled tower at the west end. The chancel has a light and elegant appearance. The windows are large and filled with painted glass. Among the more remarkable sepulchral memorials is a large slab in the chancel, inlaid with brass of a knight as large as life, crossed-legged, in mail armour, with a surcoat above a shield on his left arm, a lion at his heels, and a long sword hanging pendent from a very rich girdle. It is intended to perpetuate the memory of Sir Robert Septrand, who was with Richard I. at the siege of Acon. Mystole, Sir John Fagg, Bart. The Faggs resided here in the time of Charles II., and the present mansion was built in the time of Queen Elizabeth. It is a moderate sized house, pleasantly situated in a small park. Not far distant from this house, in 1668, in digging a well, at the depth of nineteen feet the workmen turned up a parcel of strange and monstrous bones, some whole, some broken, together with four teeth of an unusual size, perfect and sound, but in a manner petrified and turned into stone, each tooth weighing about half a pound.

81 m. CANTER-
BURY STA.

site (as it has been said) of the first Christian church in England. It is built in the form of a double cross, with a central and two western towers, the whole comprising every feature of Christian architecture. The choir is the finest in England; and in the chapel of the Holy Trinity is the tomb of Thomas à Becket, around which the pavement is worn into hollows by the knees of the pilgrims worshipping at his shrine. In the recent reparations of this edifice discoveries were made, which induced the authorities to remove the old carvings, when highly-elaborated stone stalls were brought to light, and the original character of the building restored, rendering this cathedral the most uniform and splendid of British ecclesiastical structures. Amongst the highly-interesting monuments on this sacred spot, that of the Black Prince is well worthy of inspection. His effigy in black marble, as perfect and as shining as at the period of its erection, reposes at full length on a stone tomb. Attached to the cathedral are the chapter-house, cloisters, and a most splendid library; while under the cathedral is a spacious crypt, which has been used as a French Protestant church ever since the reign of Elizabeth. Amongst the numerous ecclesiastical buildings and antiquities belonging to this city, we may name the parish churches, some of which are very ancient, an ancient gateway, the ruins of St. Augustin's Abbey, and the remains of a huge Norman castle, the Old 'Chequers Inn,' the resort of the pilgrims, and the Donjon, or Dane John Field, now beautifully planted and laid out as a public promenade. Canterbury possesses many educational institutions, with a grammar school founded by Henry VIII., for 50 pupils, having several exhibitions and scholarships at Cambridge. Amongst its hospitals and charitable foundations, we may cite that which owes its origin to Archbishop Lanfranc, for poor brethren, with an annual revenue of £411;

Jesus Hospital, founded 1595, revenue, £584; and another with a revenue of upwards of £300. Of the public edifices of the city, the ancient guildhall is the most curious. There are also an infirmary, a sessions house, gaol, house of correction, large barracks, exchange, workhouse, theatre, ball-room, museum, library, and a philosophical institution. The trade of Canterbury consists chiefly in exports of hops and agricultural produce. There are however some woollen mills in the neighbourhood, and the city is famous for its brawn. It is the seat of quarter sessions, and petty sessions are held every Thursday. The Archbishop of Canterbury is "Primate of all

---

From Canterbury there is a short branch to WHITSTABLE, which is partly in the parish of Seasalter, and partly in the parish of Whitstable, lying near the entrance of the East Swale, opposite to the Isle of Sheppy. On the shore by Taggerton, are several copper-houses, where considerable quantities of copperas, or green vitriol, are manufactured. Whitstable Bay is frequented by a considerable number of colliers, from which Canterbury and the surrounding places are supplied with coal. Many boats are employed in the fisheries, Whitstable being a royalty of fishery, or oyster dredging, appendant to the manor; and for the due regulation of the trade, a court is held annually in February. Great quantities of Roman pottery have been found in dredging for oysters round a rock, now called the Pudding Pan, which is supposed by some to have been the island of Kaunoss Op Tommanæ, though now covered with the sea. Court Lees, William Hyder, Esq.; Swalecliffe; W. F. Hilton, Esq. On the coast, about 4 m. E. of Whitstable, is HERNE BAY, a watering-place of very modern origin, having sprung into existence in a few years. It is much frequented for the purpose of bathing, and enjoying the healthy and bracing air. One of the most prominent objects in the town is a very handsome clock-house, or tower, erected on the parade at the sole expense of Mrs. Thwaites, which serves at the same time as an excellent land-mark for mariners.

4 m. N. HERNE. Broomfield House, William Cutforth, Esq.; Hunters' Fostall, Lieutenant W. G. Goddard. 2 m. further, HERNE BAY.

4. m. N. The Reculvers. That this was the site, not only of a large military station, but of a town in the time of the Romans, appears from the many cisterns, vaults, and foundations of buildings which have been discovered at various times by the fall of the cliff, and from the great number of Roman and British coins, pottery, &c., found here.

2 m. N. BURCHINGTON. Quex Park, J. P. Powell, Esq. Here King William is stated to have taken up his abode till the wind was favourable for his embarking to Holland.

CANTERBURY
(continued).

England," and the first peer of the realm next to the royal family. It is his privilege to crown the sovereigns of England; and he has the power to confer degrees in divinity, law, and physic. His diocese comprises 258 parishes, independently of 100 parishes in other sees, called "peculiars," over which his jurisdiction extends. Net revenue of Archbishopric (1843), £20,969; revenue of chapter, consisting of a dean, twelve prebends, six preachers, six minor canons, &c. (1831), £15,982. Markets, Wednesday and Saturday. Its fair begins October 10th, and lasts upwards of a week. Canterbury races are held at Barham Downs, in the vicinity of the city.

---

4 m. s.e. PATRICKSBOURNE. Bifrons, Dowager Marchioness Conyngham. A little further, Bourne Place, Lord Londesborough; Knackington House, Lord Sondes. A little further, BISHOPSBOURNE, Captain H. H. Douglas; Charles Oxenden, Esq. 4 m. e. LITTLEBOURNE, Lee Howletts, George Gipps, Esq.; Lee Priory, Captain Frederick D. Swanne. This beautiful residence is situated in a most delightful neighbourhood. The manor was anciently called Legh, and was the seat of a family which derived its name from the estate. The house was originally built in the reign of James I., and was improved and altered to its present state by Thomas Barrett, Esq., in 1782, under the superintendence of the late James Wyatt, Esq., the architect. The entrance to the grounds is through a lofty gateway, between two octagonal embattled towers. The principal front of the mansion is on the north, where the centre forms a square embattled tower, with pinnacles on the angles, and octagonal turrets at the extremities. In the west front is a large mullioned window, above which rises the large octagonal tower containing the library. It is surrounded by a singularly beautiful ornamented parapet, selected from the best models of antiquity, terminating in a well-proportioned spire, conspicuous in the distance above the mass of foliage which envelopes the mansion. This beautiful seat was left to its late possessor, Thomas Brydges, by his uncle, Thos. Burrett, Esq., and here Sir Egerton Brydges, who resided with his son, established his celebrated printing-press, at which he reprinted many of the rarest tracts of antiquity, with poems and original works of his own. 2 m. further, Dane Court, E. B. Rice, Esq. 1 m. further, Goodnestone Park, Sir B. W. Bridges, Bart. The mansion, environed by a mass of the richest foliage, is a plain brick edifice, spacious and commodious, without any ornamental decoration on the *façade*, except a large pediment over the centre of the building; but the internal arrangements are excellent, affording every requisite accommodation. The park, upwards of 200 acres in extent, is beautifully diversified, with extensive lawns of varied surface, whose gentle undulations are bounded by eminences covered with wood. On an elevated spot in the park is a pavilion which commands a beautiful view of the surrounding mansions and churches, and the adjacent country.

84 m. STURRY
AND HERNE BAY
STATION.

STURRY. A parish in the county of Kent, on the Stour, which is here crossed by a handsome bridge. Near the church are the ruins of Sturry Court, formerly in the possession of the Strangford family. This is the nearest station to Moles Hill, Alfred De Lanney, Esq.

88 m. GROVE
FERRY STA.

4 m. s. WINGHAM. During a long period Wingham belonged to the see of Canterbury. The archbishops had a palace here, in which Edward I. was entertained by Archbishop Winchelsea, Edward II. by Archbishop Walter Reynolds, and Edward III., with many nobles, by Archbishop Meerphan.

93 m. MINSTER
STATION.
Sandwich and
Deal Branch.

MINSTER. A parish in the county of Kent. The church, the most remarkable feature in this historical spot, was built on the site of the Saxon nunnery of St. Mildred, founded as early as 640, and is a noble

⤙⥁ Margate Br.

101 m. MARGATE
STATION.

MARGATE. A sea-port, market-town, and watering-place, county of Kent, on the North Sea, about three miles w.n.w. of the North Foreland. Its principal edifices are its churches, town hall, market house, assembly rooms, theatre, public library, schools, almshouses, infirmary, baths, bazaars, and hotels. It has long been a favourite place of resort for the holiday people during the bathing season, the communication with London by steamers, as well as railway, being both cheap and expeditious, while nothing is wanting on the part of the caterers for the public taste to render its amusements agreeable to the visitors. The harbour is formed by a curved stone pier, with a lighthouse. Depth of water from 8 to 13 feet at high, and dry at low tide. Margate has some trade, and a fishery.

Minster to Deal.

Left of Railway from Minster.

Distance from London.
MINSTER STA.

98 m. SANDWICH
STATION.

SANDWICH. A parliamentary and municipal borough, cinque port, and market-town, on the river Stour, about two miles from its mouth in Pegwell Bay. This venerable town was formerly the outport of the metropolis, and having risen into great commercial importance upon the decline of Richborough, the ancient Rhutupium, towards the 6th century, it has in its turn ceded to the more happy positions of other ports; and, notwithstanding its trifling exports of agricultural produce, malt, bark, leather, ashes, and wool, and its import of coal, principally for the consumption of the town and its vicinity, it is now a place of very little importance, and although the railway may effect great improvement in its trade, it is impossible that it can recover itself as a sea-port, owing to the natural impediments to its navigation. The town, which is very nearly surrounded by ancient fortifications, is large, irregularly built, and exceedingly dull. It contains three parish churches. That of St. Clement's is a fine specimen of the early Norman architecture, with a massive tower. The other principal edifices are the guildhall, gaol, hospital, and Dissenting places of worship. It has a free grammar school, with several scholarships in Lincoln College, Oxford, and the alternate nomination to four in Caius College, Cambridge. Some of the houses are curious for their antiquity. The borough sends two members to Parliament. Registered electors (1848), 943. About two miles from the town lies Richborough, which was destroyed by the Danes in the 11th century. Here are the vestiges of a castle, and the traces of the ancient Roman station, Rhutupium.

structure. Ebbsfleet in this parish was the landing-place of Hengist and Horsa, as well as of St. Augustin, the first Romish priest who ever visited the shores of Britain, although Christianity had been established in England upwards of 500 years previous to that period.

97 m. RAMSGATE STATION.

RAMSGATE. This celebrated watering-place and sea-port town is situated in the Isle of Thanet, in the county of Kent. The town occupies portions of two cliffs, and the gorge or valley between them, in which is the commercial or trading part, leading to its beautiful, if not most useful and convenient harbour. The houses, terraces, crescents, &c. are handsome, and the town is well lighted, paved, and supplied with water. Its principal edifices are the modern Gothic church, custom house, market house, assembly rooms, baths, barracks, libraries, &c. The harbour is one of the handsomest in England, and contains the largest artificial haven; its construction was commenced by Smeaton in 1750 and completed by Rennie. The piers extend nearly 2,000 feet into the sea enclosing an inner basin, with wet and dry docks, storehouses, &c., and its entrance is guarded by batteries and a lighthouse. The cost of construction was enormous, and far beyond the amount of service that can ever be derived from it, as it is sometimes difficult of access, and only fit for the reception of vessels of small burden at any time. Ramsgate is a member of the ruined cinque port of Sandwich, and has a considerable import and coasting trade. Customs' revenue (with Margate) in 1848, £10,044; registered shipping, 7,144 tons. Markets, Wednesday and Saturday. Cliffe House, Sir W. Curtis, Bart.; East Cliffe Lodge, Sir Moses Montefiore, Bart.; Dandelion, Mrs. E. Rammell; Shottindane, Mrs. G. Jolly.

Minster to Deal.

Distance from London.

MINSTER STA.

Right of Railway from Minster.

98 m. SANDWICH STATION.

4 m. w. STAPLE. Grove Park. 1 m. further, Dane Court, E. R. Rice, Esq., M.P.

2 m. s.w. EASTRY. Eastry was an ancient demesne of the Saxon kings, who are said to have had a palace here, in which, according to the chroniclers Thom and Malt of Westminster, the two cousins of Egbert, King of Kent, were murdered by the courtier Thunor, and afterwards buried in the hall under the royal throne. The church is a spacious edifice, and consists of a nave, chancel, and aisles, with a large and strong tower at the west end, the entrance to which opens under a semicircular arch. Brookstreet House, Mrs. Mary Boteler; Updown House, Sir John Bayley, Bart.; Eastry Court, William Bridger, Esq.; Walton, Thomas Castle, Esq.; Statenbro', Henry Elve, Esq.; Harnden, H. W. Harvey, Esq.; Statenbro' House, George Sayer, Esq. About 2 m. further, Knowlton Park, Captain Hugh Daeth; and a little further, at NONNINGTON, St. Alban's Court, William O. Hammond, Esq.; Fredville, John P. Plumptre, Esq.

DEAL, a municipal and parliamentary borough, and market-town, county of Kent, situated near the south extremity of the Downs, opposite the Goodwin Sands. Although the town is nominally divided into Upper, Middle, and Lower Deal, the first-named is entirely detached, lying at the distance of half a mile from the town, and consists chiefly of detached houses, amongst which are several handsome residences, and the parish church, a spacious edifice, but without any peculiar claims to the notice of the traveller. Middle and Lower Deal consist principally of one long street, stretching along the shore for a great distance; Lower Deal forming the chief residences of the hardy and courageous boatmen, to whose daring and humanity the shipwrecked mariner so often owes the preservation of his life. The houses in Middle Deal are well built. The principal edifices of the town are the castle, court house, gaol, custom house, naval store house, and the new public rooms, with library and baths. Deal Castle was built by Henry VIII., and is coeval, and of precisely similar construction with those of Sandown and Walmer, which stand at the north and south extremities of the town. The ornamental changes which have been effected, from time to time, in these castles, are due to the taste of the different Lords Warden of the cinque ports, and the Captains of Deal Castle, of whom the late Lord Carrington held the latter appointment for many years, and greatly improved its appearance. Sandown, which retains its primitive, fortlike, and forbidding aspect, was the prison of the regicide, Colonel Hutchinson. The inhabitants of Deal are chiefly connected with maritime traffic; and during the war, the supply of slops	102 m. DEAL STA.

Brighton to Newhaven.

	Distance from Brighton.
### Left of Railway from Brighton.	
Stanmer Park, Earl of Chichester. This mansion, which stands nearly in the centre of a fine park, whose undulating surface is varied by thick masses of rich foliage, forming a pleasing contrast to the downs by which it is surrounded, was built by Henry Pelham, Esq., about 1724. The building is uniform, and is approached by a road which sweeps round a lawn of rich verdure. The house is composed of two stories, the east or principal front of the mansion being surmounted by a pediment, the entrance being ornamented with a portico. The gardens and shrubberies are laid out with great taste and judgment.	4 m. FALMER STATION.
See Hayward's Heath and Hastings Line.	8 m. LEWES STA.
	Hastings ◁ Line.
2 m. E. SEAFORD, a cinque port. The river Ouse, the estuary of which formerly constituted its harbour, now empties itself into the sea at Newhaven. Seaford was originally a member of the port of Hastings, but was made a port of itself by charter of Henry VIII.	15 m. NEWHAVEN STATION.

102 m. DEAL STA.

from this town to the ships lying in the Downs, was a source of great profit. Markets, Tuesday and Saturday; fairs, April 5th, and October 12th. WALMER, an adjoining village, assumes a very different aspect, and has some pretty marine villas and handsome residences. The beauty of the scenery towards the castle, and in the vicinity of the village, has induced many fashionables to resort to this spot during the bathing season. The church, partly of Roman architecture, stands on rising ground near the shore. Deal Castle, Marquis of Dalhousie ; Sholden Lodge, Edward Banks, Esq. ; Oxney Court, William Banks, Esq.; Northbourne Court, Mrs. Hannam. 1 m. s. Walmer Castle, Duke of Wellington. Walmer Castle stands close to the sea-shore and commands a beautiful view of the Downs and coast of France. This fortress is appropriated to the Lord Warden of the cinque ports. Here the late Mr. Pitt, who held that office, frequently spent some of the summer months.

2 m. s.w. RIPPLE. In this parish is an oblong entrenchment called Dane Pits, comprehending about half an acre of ground, and having various small eminences in it. At a short distance north from Ripple Church is another ancient camp, supposed to have been thrown up by Cæsar on his march to Barham Downs. Ripple Court, John Baker Sladen, Esq., J.P.

Brighton to Newhaven.

Distance from Brighton.

Right of Railway from Brighton.

4 m. FALMER STATION.

FALMER, a small parish in the rape of Lewes. 3 m. s. of which is OVINGDEAN. In this parish, not far from the church, is an ancient farm-house recently modernised, in which Charles II. sought refuge, and was entertained for a few days prior to his escape to the continent, which he effected in a small vessel from Shoreham. 1 m. s.e. of Ovingdean is ROTTINGDEAN, near which the cliffs are peculiarly grand, those called the Free Charles or Cheorles are the highest on the Sussex coast, rising about 500 feet above the sea.

8 m. LEWES STA.

15 m. NEWHAVEN STATION.

NEWHAVEN, a small sea-port, situated at the mouth of the Ouse on the English Channel. It is a neatly-built town, has a church, a fort, a drawbridge across the Ouse, and a fair harbour. Its trade consists in exports of corn, &c., and imports of coal and timber. Customs' revenue (1846), £13,480; shipping, 1,187 tons.

The Great Western Railway.

The scientific world has admitted that this noble line is one of the grandest achievements of the engineering art, on which the name of Brunel is indelibly stamped, from London to the Land's End. It is not, however, our intention to enter into a history of the Company, the difficulties it had to encounter in its parliamentary progress, the millions invested in the accomplishment of the main line and its tributary branches, nor to expiate upon the gigantic establishments called into being by the system of locomotion over which the Company so admirably presides; we merely undertake to point the traveller's attention to the wonders of nature and art, as they almost vie with each other on his rapid flight from the metropolis to the western coasts of Britain, and, above all, to those stupendous works which the hand of science, undaunted by the aspect of those solid rocks, which even the Egyptians and Romans would have regarded as impenetrable barriers, has achieved by the union of genius and labour, by penetrating into the very bowels of the earth, and overcoming the stubborn obstructions opposed to man's project by nature's original structure. We shall abstain, too, from any mention of the gradients, levels, earthworks, and other technical details which can only interest the scientific and professional reader, and confine ourselves exclusively to a brief description of the visible, and at times, from the darkness, almost invisible, though well-appreciated works which, to the end of time, will mark the power and perfection of science, commencing with the tunnels. Of these wonderful works, the Box Tunnel between Bath and Chippenham is the most stupendous. It is upwards of three thousand one hundred and twenty-three yards, or rather more than one mile and three-quarters in length, cut through the solid stone, the surface of the country at the eastern entrance of the tunnel being sixty-nine feet six inches above the level of the rail, and at the western entrance sixty-four feet. Air and some light are admitted into this monster tunnel by means of eleven shafts, varying from ninety-four to two hundred and ninety-three feet in depth. Between Box and Bristol are seven other tunnels, the first of which, commencing at the Bristol end, is nine hundred and ninety feet long, thirty feet wide, and thirty-five feet high at each entrance. The west front, or entrance, is in the Roman style of architecture, and presents a very pleasing and bold outline. The next, No. 2, or the Ivy-Mantled Tunnel, is four hundred and seventy-five feet in length, and its greatest depth from the surface of the land is ninety-nine feet six inches. The western face represents the entrance to an old ivy-mantled castle, and is so pleasing an object that it has long been considered one of the principal attractions of the neighbourhood.

The Brislington Tunnel (No. 3) is three thousand one hundred and forty-eight feet in length, and one hundred and sixteen feet six inches from the surface of the ground to the rails.

Left of Railway from London.

EALING. A parish, county of Middlesex, one part of which is called GREAT, and the other LITTLE EALING. From its situation near the western part of the metropolis, it has become a favourite residence, and contains several handsome villas and seats. Among the learned persons who are buried in Ealing churchyard may be mentioned Old Mixon, the dramatist; Serjeant Maynard, an eminent lawyer; John Horne Tooke, author of "Diversions of Purley;" and the celebrated Mrs. Trimmer. Grove House, James Gardner, Esq.; Dane Cottage, John Graham, Esq.; Heathfield Villa, Thos. Harvey, Esq.; Ealing Park, William Lawrence, Esq. The gardens of Ealing Park are laid out in a most costly and beautiful style, and are famed for the prize exotics they produce. Stafford House, Mrs. Nunn; Ealing Grove, Robert Slark, Esq.; Gore House, George Smith, Esq.; Sutherland House, Captain Augustus W. Wetherall, R.N.

Distance from London.

Thames Junction Railway.

5½ m. EALING STATION.

The Great Western Railway.

The Saltford Tunnel (No. 4) is five hundred feet in length.

The Twiverton Tunnel (No. 5), arched throughout, is seven hundred and sixty-seven feet six inches in length, the entrances are of castellated Gothic architecture, with a retaining wall in connection with the tunnel one thousand one hundred and twenty feet long, and forty-nine feet high.

Independently of the above, there is a short tunnel through Middle Hill, west of the Box Tunnel, and an archway east of Brislington Tunnel one hundred and eleven feet long, thirty feet wide, and thirty feet high.

Among the principal bridges, that of the Wharncliffe Viaduct, which carries the railway over the valley of the Brent at Hanwell, is the grandest effort of architectural science and ingenuity of this description which the line can boast. It consists of eight semi-elliptical arches, each of seventy feet span. The whole length of the structure is eight hundred and eighty-six feet, the height from the foundation to the top of the parapet eighty-one feet, and the width between the parapets thirty feet. The design is remarkably elegant, and this viaduct is considered one of the finest features in the whole undertaking, while its picturesque appearance on the landscape, and the extensive views of the surrounding country, obtained from its summit, rivets the traveller's attention. The bridge, which crosses the Thames at Maidenhead, is a wonderful work of art. It consists of ten arches, two across the river, each of the extraordinary span (for brickwork) of one hundred and twenty-eight feet, the remaining eight being land arches of different spans, varying from twenty-one to twenty-eight feet.

The Bath Viaduct, upwards of three hundred and six feet in length, consists of sixty-five segmental arches, varying in span from nineteen feet and a half to twenty feet and a half. The design, in perfect keeping with the architecture of the city of Bath, is both chaste and elegant.

Near to this viaduct is the bridge across the river Avon, constructed of wooden framing, resting on stone piers. It consists of two openings, each of eighty-nine feet, and rising sixteen feet nine inches; the height from the surface of the water to the rails thirty-six feet. The Twiverton Viaduct is two hundred and forty-five feet long, and consists of nine arches, seven of fifteen feet, and two of twenty-four feet span each, and fourteen feet six inches high.

All the bridges over the railway, many of which have considerable pretensions to architectural beauty, have a general clear width of thirty feet between the parapets.

The London Terminus is situated at Paddington. As to the passenger portion of the station, whatever may be the ultimate intentions of the directors, it at present consists of three or four of the dry arches under the Harrow Road, fitted up for the accommodation of passengers, but without any attempt at architectural display.

Distance from London. Thames Junction Railway. 5½ m. EALING STATION.	**Right of Railway from London.** 1½ m. N.W. Castle Bere, Thomas Hunt, Esq. Castle Bere Lodge, for many years the residence of the late Duke of Kent. A little before reaching Ealing we pass through ACTON. There are few historical events connected with this place, and those entirely relate to the civil war of the 17th century. Shortly previous to the battle of Brentford, which was fought in November, 1642, the Earl of Essex (Lord General) and the Earl of Warwick fixed their head-quarters at Acton. On Cromwell's triumphant return to London after the battle of Worcester, he was met in this village by the Council of State, the principal members of the House of Commons, and the Lord Mayor, &c., of the city of London.

HANWELL, county of Middlesex, has a population of 1,469, within an area of 1,160 A. The county lunatic asylum, which in situated in this parish, is a fine building, with extensive grounds, and is conducted in a manner which reflects great credit upon the county; the average number of inmates is 800. The railway viaduct is a noble piece of architecture, and Hanwell can also boast an artesian well 290 feet in depth. The church was rebuilt in 1782, and in the vaults underneath lie the remains of Jonas Hanway, founder of the Marine Society. Holly Lodge, Thomas Jones, Esq.; The Briars, John Kennedy, Esq.; Heath House, Thomas Reed, Esq.; Rose Cottage, William Smith, Esq.

7¼ m. HANWELL STATION.

Southall Green, Benjamin Armstrong, Esq. 1 m. s. NORWOOD, Colonel Phipps; Norwood Green, Miss Thackthwaite. ¾ m. further, HESTON. Alfred Cottage, William Ashby, Esq.; The Cottage, Mrs. McArthur. 1 m. E. at White Green, Osterley Park, Earl of Jersey. This celebrated mansion was commenced by Sir Thomas Gresham, to whom the City of London is indebted for its Royal Exchange, and here Queen Elizabeth was entertained by Sir Thomas with all the magnificence which wealth and loyalty could suggest. In 1760 the ancient structure was taken down, and the present mansion built on the site. Osterley is of a quadrangular form, 140 feet in length from east to west, and 117 feet from north to south. The ground plan of the former house is nearly preserved in the present edifice. At each corner of the original building stood a square turret, which are retained as vestiges of the original fabric, but have been newly cased. In the east are twelve columns, composed of the Ionic order, supporting a richly ornamented angular pediment. The entrance is by a spacious flight of stone steps, and the building finished at top in every direction with a stone balustrade. The gardens are very extensive, and formerly contained a valuable collection of rare birds, representations of upwards of one hundred of which are given in a volume called "The Osterley Menagerie," published in 1794, by William Hayes of Southall, at present the property of our publisher.

9 m. SOUTHALL STATION.

WEST DRAYTON. A large irregular village, separated by the river Colne from the neighbouring county of Buckingham. The Paget family erected a spacious mansion in this parish, which was taken down by the Earl of Uxbridge in 1750. This mansion stood near the church, and two fine avenues of trees still denote the former stately character of its approaches. The site of the mansion is at present occupied by a market-garden. Manor House, Rev. Robert L. de Burgh. A commodious dwelling, a short distance from the church, formerly the property of Lord Boston. Burroughs, Miss M. Arabin. An old and spacious brick mansion, which obtains its name from having belonged to Sir Thomas Burgh, who was Esquire to the body of Edward IV. This is a residence of the dull, secluded character favourable to traditional story; many a marvellous tale is accordingly told respecting its hall, its chambers, and the pensive shaded walks of the attached grounds. Among these stories it may be mentioned as the most remarkable, that not a few rustic neighbours believe the mansion of Burroughs to have been an occasional residence of Oliver Cromwell, and that the body of the Protector was privately conveyed to this place when threatened with disgraceful exposure, and was re-buried beneath the pavement of the hall.

13 m. WEST DRAYTON STA.

Enter Buckinghamshire.

Drayton Hall, Peter Pole, Esq. 1 m. s. HARMONDSWORTH, E. Mills, Esq.; The Hall, Henry Smith, Esq. 2 m. w. COLNBROOK. A chapelry, partly in Middlesex, and partly in Buckinghamshire. This place, which is of great antiquity, and is supposed to have been the station Ad Pontes of Antoninus, derives its name from the river Colne, by which it is separated from Middlesex, and is intersected by several branches of that river, over each of which is a small bridge. Why this river is called the Colne may be considered one of the wonders of topographical orthography. The Colne is a small brook having its rise at Loudon Colney in Hertfordshire, which

7¼ m. HANWELL STATION.	N. Hanwell Park, Thomas Turner, Esq. The mansion is not large, but situated in pleasant grounds, and commands a delightful view over the valley of the Brent. Hanwell church is situated close to the mansion, and there is the following curious entry in the register of Hanwell parish:

                                            daughter

"Thomas, son of Thomas Messenger, and Elizabeth his wife, was born and baptized October 24th, 1731." In the margin is the following note: "By the midwife at the font called a boy, and named by the godfather Thomas, but proved a girl." 1½ m. N. GREENFORD. (See North-Western.)

9 m. SOUTHALL STATION.	1 m. N. SOUTHALL. Although only a village in the parish of Hayes, county of Middlesex, it has a weekly market on Thursday for the sale of cattle, inferior to none in the county. Southall Park, Lady Ellis.

3 m. N.W. HAYES, a small parish, county of Middlesex. Manor House, Rev. C. Hale. Some interest is thrown over the ancient annals of this parish, from the circumstance of the Manor House having been occasionally occupied as a residence by the Archbishop of Canterbury in 1095. A difference occurring between Ansolme, then archbishop, and William Rufus, the archbishop was commanded to reside there for more easy communication with the King at Windsor. During this compulsory residence at Hayes, the archbishop was attended by the majority of the English prelates, who unavailingly solicited his submission to the terms of the monarch. After some time, however, a transient reconciliation took place between these two great parties. Whitehall, Mrs. Collenge; Hayes Park, Colonel Joseph Grant. The park, though of moderate extent, attracts considerable notice, as the appendages of wood and water are beautifully diversified.

13 m. WEST DRAYTON STA.	About 1 m. N.E. Cowley Grove, Thomas Williams, Esq. 1 m. N.N.E. HILLINGDON, Hon. Count F. de Salis; Hillingdon House, R. H. Cox, Esq.; Hillingdon Lodge, Thomas H. Bent, Esq.; Herenden Heath, C. Rutter, Esq.; Hillingdon End, R. C. Walford, Esq. 1 m. further, LITTLE HIL-LINGDON, Charles Mill, Esq. 1 m. further, UXBRIDGE. It has little to
Enter Buckinghamshire.	recommend it beyond its corn market, which is the largest in England, its numerous flour mills, malt works, and a brickfield. It is on the verge of the county, and in the parish of Hillingdon. It communicates with London by the Grand Junction Canal and Branch. The 'Crown Inn' was formerly known as the "Treaty House," from its having been the place where the Commissioners of Charles I. and the Parliament met in 1644; and in the neighbourhood are the remains of a camp, attributed to the Britons. Mill House, William Currie, Esq.; Dawley Lodge, Countess de Salis; Montagu House, Daniel Rutter, Esq.; Huntsmore Park, C. T. Tower, Esq.; Belmont, Richard Fell, Esq. A spacious brick mansion, built in the early part of the last century, which was long the residence of Mr. Harris, joint patentee of Covent Garden Theatre.

1½ m. N.E. of Uxbridge is ICHENHAM. Swankley Park, T. T. Clark, Esq. It is a curious old family mansion, built by Sir Edmund Wright, 1638. It was afterwards the property of Sir James Harington, one of the judges of Charles I., the celebrated author of "Oceana," and subsequently it became the residence of Sir Robert Vyner, the facetious Lord Mayor of London who entertained Charles II. at Guildhall. This mansion, which is a square, substantial building, with two wings slightly projecting, is composed of brick, with stone groins, window casings, and finishings. In the upper story is a scroll of stone-work pediments. The grounds, though rather flat, are agreeably wooded with venerable timber, and adorned with plantations and evergreens. A branch of the Colne passes through the grounds in front of the house. 1 m. further, RUISLIP.

empties itself into a much larger stream, the Ver, running through St. Albans, the ancient Verulam which confers the title of Earl on the Grimstone family. The Gade and the Cess also join the Ver, and yet the little brook Colne not only swallows up these three streams, either of which has six times its bulk of water, but gives its own name to the whole from St. Albans, five miles above its junction with the Ver, to Staines where it falls into the Thames. Lieutenant R. Cordner. 1½ m. s.w. by w. Richings Park, General Sir Thomas Willshire, Bart. This mansion, formerly the residence of the Right Hon. John Sullivan, is situated on the low grounds near Colnbrook. The ground and gardens are well disposed. Richings Lodge, J. G. Murdock, Esq.

LANGLEY MARSH, or ST. MARY'S, county of Buckingham. The parish has an area of 3,820 A. Langley Park, Robert Harvey, Esq.; Horsemore Green, John Russell, Esq., and Samuel Goldney, Esq.; South End Manor House, Mrs. Alexander. 1 m. s. Ditton Park, Lady Montagu. It is a handsome mansion, erected in the early part of this century by Lord Montagu, the former mansion having been destroyed by fire in 1812. The park is flat, partaking of the character of all the land bordering the Thames on the Middlesex and Buckinghamshire sides of the river, but it contains some fine timber. The house and pleasure-grounds are surrounded by a moat. 16 m. LANGLEY STATION.

SLOUGH. Although in the immediate vicinity of numerous wonders of nature and art, this spot has no remarkable feature beyond the station, if we except the observatory erected by the late Sir William Herschel, on the roof of the house in which he resided for many years of his life. Slough Wellington Villa, William Abbot, Esq.; Finefield, William Beauchamp, Esq.; Belle Vue, William Bonsey, Esq.; Preston Cottage, Mrs. Du Bois; Sussex House, Thomas Gould, Esq. 18 m. SLOUGH STATION.

Windsor Br.

Just after passing the Slough Station is a short branch to Windsor and Eton. 1 m. distant is Eton College, founded by Henry VI. This royal and justly celebrated place of learning has sent forth into the world a larger amount of learned men, of illustrious senators, statesmen, and warriors, than all the other public schools of the empire. The college consists of two quadrangles, one appropriated to the school and the lodgings of the masters and scholars of the foundation (between seventy and eighty), the other contains the apartments of the provosts and fellows. The library is one of the finest in Europe, containing some very valuable drawings, paintings, and Oriental manuscripts. Under the presidency of Dr. Hawtree, the present learned and worthy head-master, the number of pupils—sons of the nobility and eminent gentry of the British empire—has greatly increased, amounting in some years to nearly eight hundred. The chapel, in which the cathedral service is performed by the choir of the Royal Chapel of St. George's, Windsor, is of exquisite architectural beauty, and is similar in the disposition of its parts to that of King's College, Cambridge, which owes its foundation to the same royal benefactor. In the neighbourhood of the Slough Station are the seats of many of the nobility and gentry. Dorley Court, Lady Palmer. In the neighbourhood, Salt Hill, famous as the place of rendezvous of the Etonians during the ancient Montem, and no less celebrated for possessing two of the most delightful inns on the Western Road, 'Botham' and the 'Castle.'

1 m. N. from Uxbridge, DENHAM. G. G. Wandesford Piggott, Esq. 2 m. further, HAREFIELD. Harefield Place, C. N. Newdigate, Esq.; Brakespeare, J. A. Partridge, Esq. 3 m. further, RICKMANSWORTH. 2 m. N.W. from Denham, CHALFONT ST. PETER. Hill House, Mrs. Acton; Orch Hill, William Blount, Esq.; Chalfont Park, John Nembhard Hibbert, Esq.; Fernacre Lodge, William Jones, Esq.; Milton Green, John Marshall Marr, Esq.; Bulstrode Park, Colonel Reid, M.P.; Elm Cottage, Miss Hibbert. 2 m. further, CHALFONT ST. GILES. Misbourne House, Anthony Davis, Esq.; The Vache, Thomas N. Allan, Esq.; Stonedean, George Du Pré Kaledon, Esq.; Nightingale House, John Mair, Esq.; The Grove, George Priestley, Esq.

1½ m. S.W. from West Drayton, IVER. Iver Lodge, John Boswell, Esq.; Delaford Park, Charles Clowes, Esq.; Heath Lodge, J. A. Edwardes, Esq.; Broadmoor, R. Ellis, Esq.; Iver Grove, T. H. England, Esq.; Belle Villa, William Goodman, Esq.; Lee Cottage, William Haw, Esq.; Sandstone Castle, H. P. Loddington, Esq.; Mansfield House, William Medley, Esq.; Iver Elms, Mrs. Snook; Thorney House, William Trumper, Esq.; The Hill, Arthur Warner, Esq.; Dromenagh Lodge, H. G. Warley, Esq.

16 m. LANGLEY STATION.

1 m. N. Langley Marish, M. Swabey, Esq. This mansion is a fine square stone building, with a pediment on its principal front. The apartments are finely proportioned, and it is surrounded by a park abounding with fine timber, and enlivened by a piece of water which runs along the south front of the house, at the foot of a sloping lawn, ornamented with clumps of trees and woodland scenery. Windsor Castle and its distant forest are seen in the background. This house was built by the Duke of Marlborough in 1740, who planted an extensive enclosure with firs, now called the "Black Park," from the dark hue of its trees. In the centre of this almost impenetrable forest, for such it appears now from the self-sown trees which have sprung up in all directions, is a fine lake.

18 m. SLOUGH STATION.

1¼ m. N. the village of STOKE POGES. Its church and its rural and picturesque churchyard have been immortalised by the elegy of the poet whose ashes, together with those of his mother, repose under its sod. Sussex Cottage, Captain Ibbotson; Buckingham Villa, Mrs. Stafford; Stoke Place, General Vyse. The pleasure-grounds, which contain a sheet of water in front, are tastefully laid out. Stoke Farm, Dowager-Countess Sefton; Stoke Park, G. J. Penn, Esq. This is one of the most charming and magnificent residences in this part of the country. The house was built in 1789, but has since undergone considerable alterations. The entrance front is formed by a colonnade consisting of ten Doric columns, and approached by a flight of steps leading to the Marble Hall. The south front, one hundred and ninety-six feet in length, has also a colonnade, consisting of twelve fluted columns of the Doric order. Above this ascends a projecting portico of four Ionic columns, sustaining an ornamental pediment. The park commands some very fine views, particularly one to the south, over a large sheet of water towards Windsor Castle. Bayliss House, William Butts, Esq. A little further E. Burnham House, George Grote, Esq.; Burnham Grove, Sir Hugh Hoare, Bart.; Britwell House, William Miller, Esq. 6 m. w. BEACONSFIELD. Area, 3,710 A. It derives its name from its position on an eminence, where beacon-fires were lighted in olden times, and consists of four streets, which assume the form of a cross. In the church, a neat structure, repose the ashes of the celebrated Edmund Burke, and there is a monument to the famous poet Waller, who was lord of the manor, in the churchyard. It has a weekly market on Wednesdays; and fairs, 13th February and Holy Thursday. Hall Cottage, Mrs. Hall; Hall-Barn Park, John Hargreaves, Esq. 1 m. N. Wilton Park, James Du Pre, Esq. An elegant mansion, built of Portland-stone, situated in a finely wooded park of about 250 acres.

SLOUGH
(continued).

WINDSOR. A town in Berkshire, situated on the right bank of the Thames. Is connected with Eton by three arched iron bridges, with granite piers. It sends two members to Parliament, and has a weekly market for the supply of provisions. The houses are well built in general, and amongst them are some good substantial, and even elegant residences. The most distinguished building is the Castle, one of the finest castellated palatial residences in Europe. It has been said that England is deficient in royal palaces, but we doubt that any foreign power can boast a rival to Windsor. Nature and art have combined to endow it with a truly majestic grandeur. The Home and Great Parks are remarkable for their venerable trees and beautiful scenery. The Castle, Her Majesty and H.R.H. Prince

WINDSOR CASTLE.

Albert, was founded by William the Conqueror, and improved by Henry I., who added many new buildings, and surrounded it with a wall. Henry II. held a Parliament here in 1170, and King John found shelter within its walls during the wars of the Barons. Edwards I. and II. resided here to enjoy the beauties of its position, and Edward III., or Edward of Windsor, so called from its being his birthplace, afterwards destroyed the old fabric, and built a new one, under the superintendence of the famous William of Wickham, Archbishop of Canterbury, whose pride at the achievement of so glorious a building, induced him to place a stone in front of one of the towers, with the following inscription :

"THIS MADE WICKHAM,"

at which the King, who took the whole merit to himself, was greatly

22¼ MAIDEN-
HEAD STA.

1 m. s. of Maidenhead, BRAY. A parish in the hundred of Bray, county of Berks, comprising the divisions of Bray Touchen, Water Oakley, and a part of the town of Maidenhead. The present town of Bray is supposed to occupy the site of the Roman station Bibracte, as Camden states that this place was occupied by the Bibroci who submitted to Cæsar, and obtained his protection, and with it a secure possession of one of the most beautiful spots in the county. Philippa, the Queen of Edward III., had rents assigned to her from this and the adjoining manor of Cookham. Bray now forms part of the royal demesne, being included within the liberty of

incensed, and but for the happy manner in which the Archbishop translated his meaning, as being the making of himself, would have brought him into disgrace. During the wars of the Roses, the castle was suffered to go to decay. Edward IV. afterwards repaired it, and made additions, which were enlarged by Henrys VII. and VIII., as well as by Queen Elizabeth. During the civil war it suffered, but was restored to its ancient splendour by Charles II., and remained in that state until it underwent an entire restoration under his late Majesty George IV., a monarch whose refined taste for the arts is best attested by the magnificence of this exquisite palace. The lofty position of the castle, its splendid terrace, 1,870 feet in length, faced with a rampart of stone overlooking the transparent waters of the Thames as it meanders in its serpentine course through verdant meadows, and the parks and pleasure-grounds of the neighbouring gentry,—in fact, the whole prospect from the terrace over many counties is so enchanting, that it is difficult to pronounce whether art or nature has contributed most to charm the senses. The Home, or Little Park, well stocked with deer, is four miles in circumference, and completely enclosed by a high brick wall. The apartments are all on a truly royal scale of grandeur. St. George's Hall is magnificent, but we have not space to enumerate its beauties. The Round Tower or governor's residence, is the highest building on the castle walls. From the top there is an uninterrupted view over eleven counties: Middlesex, Essex, Hertford, Bucks, Oxford, Wilts, Hants, Surrey, Sussex, Kent, and Bedford. There are two courts. In the upper there is a fine equestrian statue of Charles II., and in the lower the beautiful chapel of St. George, with the residences of the dean and canons, and the Poor Knights of Windsor are situate. The picture gallery, and all the other beauties of this noble castle, must be visited to be appreciated. The wishes of the public have been kindly and condescendingly considered by Her Most Gracious Majesty, all, except the absolutely private apartments of the Royal Family, being open to public inspection. St. George's Chapel, built by Edward III., was enlarged and beautified in the reign of King Henry VII., from designs by and under the personal superintendence of the celebrated Sir Reginald Bray, Speaker of the House of Commons, and for some years Prime Minister to that monarch. Many of our sovereigns are interred in the vaults of this royal chapel, and the banners and ensigns of all the eminent and valiant Knights of the Garter, from the earliest institution of that noble order to the present time, ornament the stalls in the choir. The Great Park comprises 3,800 acres, and Windsor Forest is fifty-six miles in circumference. Frogmore, Duchess of Kent. A little to the right of Windsor is CLEWER. Clewer Villa, Captain Thomas Bulkeley; Manor House, Edward Foster, Esq.; St. Leonard's Hill, Captain W. B. Harcourt; Forest Hill, W. F. Riley, Esq.; Leen Cottage, Mrs. Sydenham; Clewer Lodge, Hon. H. Ashley. 4 m. s.w. from Windsor, WINKFIELD. Martins Wen, Lady M. Berkeley; Spring Cottage, Richard Boore, Esq.; Ascot Place, Miss Ferrard; Baston Lodge, George Hardy, Esq.; Grove Lodge, Lady King; Winkfield Park, W. B. Martin, Esq. About 2 m. further, Ascot Race Course.

½ m. N.W. MAIDENHEAD, county of Berks, is a municipal borough and town, situate on the right bank of the Thames, in the parishes of Bray and Cookham. It communicates with the opposite county of Bucks by means of a handsome stone bridge of seven arches, and by a viaduct erected by the Railway Company. It has an endowed school and several charities, and a weekly market on Wednesday. Folly Hill, Edward Barlow, Esq.; Kidwell, Robert Cranwell, Esq.; Sun Cottage, Mrs. A. Hobbs; Maidenhead Bridge, J. Jeffries, Esq. 2 m further, Boyne Hill, Elizabethan Cottage, George Morrell, Esq. 2½ m. N. of Maidenhead is COOKHAM, Dowager

Windsor Forest, but retains some peculiar privileges, among which may be included an exemption from tolls in the adjacent market-towns. A custom prevails in this place, agreeably to which, in default of male heirs, lands are not divided among females of the same degree of kindred, but descend only to the eldest. The church is dedicated to St. Michael, and is an ancient structure, composed of various materials, and exhibiting a mixture of almost every style of architecture. Bray is celebrated from the memorable conduct of a vicar, whose name was Symon Symonds, and who possessed the benefice in the reign of Henry VIII., and the three succeeding monarchs. This man was twice a Protestant, and thrice a Papist, and when reproached for the unsteadiness of his principles (if principles they can be called), which could thus suffer him unhesitatingly to espouse any form of religion, and permit him to veer with every change of administration, replied that "he had always governed himself by what he thought a very laudable principle, which was, never on any terms to part with his vicarage, but live and die Vicar of Bray." He died in the forty-first year of Queen Elizabeth. The principal charitable institution is a hospital called Jesus Hospital, founded in 1627 by William Goddard, Esq., for forty poor persons (six of whom must be free of the Fishmongers' Company, under whose governorship it is placed), who, in addition to their place of residence, are allowed eight shillings a month. Over the door of the almshouse is a statue of the founder, which the tasteless veneration of the inhabitants induces them to keep finely whitewashed. Bray Vicarage, Rev. William Levett; Bray Wick Lodge, John Hibbert, Esq. A neat edifice, on a gentle eminence, commanding pleasing views of a richly cultivated district, interspersed with meadow-land, stretching as far as Windsor, washed by the waters of the Thames. The views of Cliefden, Taplow, and Hedsor, with their luxurious woods, with Windsor Castle and Forest in the distance, are highly picturesque. Braywick Grove, J. J. Coney, Esq.; Common Hill, Mrs. E. Law.

4½ m. s.w. WHITE WALTHAM.

HEYWOOD LODGE, CHARLES SAWYER, ESQ.

Lady Young; Formosa House, John G. Bergman, Esq.; White Place, Mrs. G. Leycestor. About 3 m. N.W. GREAT MARLOW. Harleyford House, Colonel Sir R. W. Clayton Bart.; Thames Bank, T. S. Cocks, Esq.; Dyer Cottage, Robert Collins, Esq.; Townshend Cottage, Robert Hammond, Esq.; Manor House, R. Hampden, Esq., M.P.; Westhorpe House, Sir George Edmund Nugent, Bart.; Beech Lodge, Frederick Parker, Esq.; Spinfield House, James Simpson, Esq.; The Deanery, Wadham Wyndham, Esq. 4 m. N.W. BISHAM. Bisham Abbey, George Henry Vansittart, Esq. It is a very ancient edifice, supposed to have been erected by William Montacute, Earl of Salisbury, in 1333, for canons regular of the order of St. Augustin. The Abbey has undergone many alterations and repairs at different periods. It was frequently visited by King Henry VIII., and Queen Elizabeth resided here for some time. A state apartment, of noble dimensions, yet retains the name of the Queen's Council Chamber. The church is close to the Thames. 1½ m. S.W. HURLEY. Hall Place, Sir Gilbert East Clayton East, Bart.

4 m. N. HIGH WYCOMBE. Wycombe Abbey, Lord Carrington; Newland Cottage, John Furness, Esq.; Castle Hill, John Neal, Esq.; Brook Lodge, John Pain, Esq.; Terriers House, Robert Wingrove, Esq. 2 m. N.W. by W. WEST WYCOMBBE. West Wycombe Park, Sir J. D. H. Dashwood King, Bart.; Plumer Hill House, Charles Venables, Esq.; Plumer Cottage, John Verey, Esq.

½ m. N. TAPLOW. Taplow Hill, R. M. Bird, Esq.; Springfield Cottage, Hon. Edward Fitzmaurice; Berry Hill, Hon. John Knox; Woburn Common, William Langfield, Esq.; Ely Banke House, Miss Payne; Taplow Hill Cottage, Harry Tyer, Esq.; The Elms, Mrs. Venables; Taplow House, Earl of Orkney, the ancient seat of the Marchioness of Thomond. In the park is an oak said to have been planted by Queen Elizabeth. Taplow Lodge, Miss Tunno, was once the property of the celebrated Sir John Lade, Bart. Taplow contains many other beautiful seats and villas. About 2 m. Cliefdon House, Marquis of Stafford, was built by George Villiers, second Duke of Buckingham, and went by marriage to the late Earl of Orkney. This stately mansion, with the exception of the wings, was destroyed by fire in 1795. The estate was sold by auction in 1819, and Sir George Warrender became the purchaser of the principal lots, comprising the wings of the old mansion, the grounds, &c., which are not to be surpassed in beauty by any in the country. They rise boldly from the Thames, and command the most lovely and extensive views. Dropmore House, Lady Grenville, was purchased by the late Lord Grenville of the learned Dr. Friend. Hedsor Lodge, Lord Boston, near Cliefden, stands in a lofty situation. The declivities of the hills towards the west are steep, and on the south, near the Thames, is a chalky precipice, whence the ground rises boldly to the summit, on which the mansion, a very elegant structure, appears conspicuous. The views from this spot are delightful. Down Place, three miles from Maidenhead, in Bucks, is a very elegant villa, from which the views of Windsor Castle and Forest are unequalled.

Nethercliff Lodge, Mrs. S. Taylor; Shottesbrooke House, A. Vansittart, Esq., is a substantial brick house, covered with stucco, and surmounted by an embattled parapet. This very ancient manor was long the property of the Trussel family, one of whom, Sir William, who founded a small religious house here, no traces of which now remain, is supposed to have been the last speaker of *both* Houses of Parliament in the reign of Edward III.

1½ m. s. HURST. A very extensive parish, containing four liberties. It has an almshouse, founded in 1682 by William Barker, Esq., for eight single persons, who each receive sixpence a-day, and a gown once in two years. The church is a very fine Gothic structure, and consists of a nave, and very ancient chancel, which separates it from the church by ornamental and elaborately carved oak, surmounted by the royal arms, and Prince of Wales' plume. It has two arched ceilings, supported in the centre by four large and beautiful Gothic arches, resting on columns of the same order; the present pulpit is chaste, in carved oak, in keeping with the rest. There are many curious ancient monuments. About 2 m. s.e. Billingbear Park, Le Marchant Thomas, Esq. 1 m. further E. BINFIELD. Forest Lodge, William Batty, Esq.; Manor House, George Augustus Bruxner, Esq.; Pope's Lodge, G. Fitzgerald, Esq.; Park Cottage, Miss Hopkins; Marchfield House, Captain H. and Lady Harriet Mitchell; Pope's Wood Villa, Mrs. Stevens; Binfield Place, W. Chute, Esq.; Grove House, Alfred Caswell, Esq.; Jacob's Court, Captain J. W. Hall; Binfield Grove, Richard Lowndes, Esq.; Binfield Villa, William Stevens, Esq.; Paradise Cottage, Captain C. M. Wright, R.N. It was at this village that Pope resided whilst he was composing his poem of "Windsor Forest;" and there existed until lately, even if it does not now, a tree on which "HERE POPE SUNG" are inscribed in capital letters, and it would appear the poet had these still haunts before him when he wrote these lines:

> "There interspers'd in lawns and op'ning glades,
> Thin trees arise, that shun each other's shades;
> Here in full light the russet plains extend,
> There wrapt in clouds the blueish hills ascend.
> E'en the wild heath displays her purple dyes,
> And 'midst the desert fruitful fields arise,
> That crown'd with tufted trees and springing corn,
> Like verdant isles, the sable waste adorn."

READING lays claim to very high antiquity: it was inhabited by the Saxons before the incursions of the Danes, and formerly possessed two castles. It is a municipal borough and market-town, the capital of the county of Berks, and is situated on the river Kennet, close to its junction with the Thames. It consists of three parishes, with a population of 18,499, comprised within an area of 2,080 a., and returns two members to Parliament, chosen by about 1,300 electors. Its main streets, well paved, and lighted with gas, are spacious, and contain many handsome residences. Several bridges cross the various branches of the Kennet, which passes through the town. Of the public edifices, charities, endowments, and institutions, we may cite three old churches, a grammar school, founded in the reign of Henry VII., of which the celebrated Dr. Valpy was formerly head master, a blue-coat school, founded in 1646 for forty-seven boys, which enjoys a revenue of £1,000 per annum, a county hospital, a county gaol and house of correction, a borough gaol, formerly the priory, a town hall,

30¼ m. TWYFORD STATION.

Guildford and Reigate Br.

35¾ m. READING STATION.

Basingstoke Branch.

TWYFORD is a chapelry in the counties of Berks and Wilts. 1½ m. s.w. Bulmershe Court, J. Wheble, Esq. 3 m. n.w. Shiplake House, J. Phillimore, LL.D. 1½ m.n. WARGRAVE. 3 m. further, HENLEY-ON-THAMES, supposed by some antiquarians to have been a town of the Ancient Britons, by others the Roman station Caleva. Leland mentions the discovery of gold, silver, and brass coins of the Romans at this place, but no notice of the town occurs in history until after the Norman Conquest. In 1643 the parliamentary forces were quartered here when they were attacked by the royalists, who entered the town, but were dispersed by the firing of the cannon down Duke Street, which did much execution. In the following year the inhabitants sustained considerable damage from the wanton conduct of King Henry's soldiers, who plundered most of the houses. The town is beautifully situated at the foot of the Chiltern Hundreds, on the banks of the Thames, which is crosssd by a stone bridge. The key-stone on the face of each arch is adorned with a sculptured mask, from the chisel of the Hon. Mrs. Damer. Grove House, Benjamin Ferry, Esq. ½ m. N. of Henley, Fawley Court, W. P. Freeman, Esq. During the civil wars the King's troops committed great havoc here, and nearly destroyed the beautiful mansion which then existed, with the title-deeds, and other valuable property of the Whitelock family. The present manor-house was built by Colonel Freeman, in 1684, from designs by Sir Christopher Wren. It is a spacious and handsome edifice, with four regular fronts. The apartments are of fine proportions, and elegantly finished; and in the grounds are disposed several antique statues of great value, which considerably augment the beauty of this truly delightful locality.

1½ m. N.W. Henley Park, J. W. Birch, Esq. 3 m. further, Stonor Park, Lord Camoys. 4 m. further, Wormesley Park, near which is Ibstone Park, Philip Wroughton, Esq. 3 m. w. WATLINGTON. Watlington Park, T. S. Carter, Esq. A little to the north, Sherborne Castle, Earl of Macclesfield. 3 m. w. from Stonor Park, SWINCOMBE. Swincombe, Rev. C. R. Keene.

1½ m. N.W. from Henley, Badgemore, Charles Lane, Esq. A substantial red brick mansion, built by Jenkins, the clerk of the works to Sir Christopher Wren in the building of St. Paul's; and the brickwork shows the skill used in the selection of the materials. It has good gardens and pleasure-grounds. A marble temple at the extremity has views of the Thames, cut through vistas in the woods, quite unique in their kind. 1 m. further, Gray's Court, Misses Stapleton.

CAVERSHAM. The church, dedicated to St. Peter, is of different styles of architecture. The lower division of the steeple being Norman, while some of the windows on the south side are of the date of Henry I.; those on the north front, three mullions, showing the style of Richard II.; and the continuation of the aisle to the east, is of the style of Henry IV. In this church is preserved a proclamation of King James, appointing certain days for persons afflicted with the king's evil to receive the royal touch. The canons of Notely, county of Bucks, had a cell here, and some remains of the chapel may still be seen near the bridge. In this chapel was a famous relic, which is said an angel with one wing brought to Caversham, viz., the spear-head which pierced our Saviour on the Cross. Caversham House, Mrs. S. Brown; Thames Villa, Captain Thomas Gill, R.N.; Rue Hill, Mrs. M. A. Pocock; Cane End, W. S. Vanderstegen, Esq.; Priory, Charles May Worthington, Esq.; Trevor Cottage, Cheyne Wright, Esq.; The Grove, Wilson Yates, Esq.; Laurel Lodge, John L. Young, Esq.; The

library, a news-room, museum, mechanics' institute, several learned societies, a theatre, baths, and the interesting ruins of a magnificent abbey, founded by Henry I. The Forbery, a handsome public walk, was formerly a part of the Abbey Close. Several Parliaments were holden in Reading Abbey in the time of the Plantagenets and during the civil wars. One of its churches, St. Laurence, suffered greatly from the troops of the Parliament. St. Mary's, the most ancient church of the town, is greatly admired for its tesselated tower. Reading is a polling-place for the county, is the head of a poor-law union, and has two weekly markets, on Wednesday and Saturday. Its principal manufactures are silks and velvets. It is also a very extensive mart for corn, malt, cheese, timber, and wool, and possesses large flour-mills, breweries, and iron foundries. It has various means of transit by the Thames, and the Kennet and Avon Canal, which connects it with Bristol, while a branch of the South-Eastern Railway causes its easy communication with Guildford, Dorking, and Reigate. Reading was the birthplace of Archbishop Laud in 1573. 1 m. s.w. Prospect Hill, William Stephens, Esq. 1 m. further, Calcot Park, Colonel John Blagrave. The mansion was built on the site of an old one in 1755, and much improved by the present proprietor in the year 1830. Calcot Lodge, Major John Smith.

4 m. s. SHINFIELD. Hartley Court, Hon. Captain G. C. A. Agar; Shinfield Lodge, Mrs. Babington; Shinfield House, Rev. George Hulme; Manor House, Colonel William Dunn; Grazeley Lodge, Mrs. Farmer; Trunkwell House, Henry Greenway, Esq.; Three Mile Cross, Miss M. R. Mitford; Highlands, William Merry, Esq.; Good Rest Lodge, Sir Jasper Nicholls. A little to the N. ARBORFIELD. Arborfield Hall, Sir John Conroy, Bart.; The Cottage, Edward Conroy, Esq.

PANGBOUBNE. A small village, celebrated as one of the best places for angling on the Thames.　41¼ m. PANG-BOURNE STA.

West End Lodge, Sir James Fellowes, Bart.; Shooter's Hill, Captain Henley; Lower Bowde, E. W. Peele, Esq.

About 2 m. further, BRADFIELD. Bradfield Hall, Rev. John Connop; Bradfield Place, The Misses Le Mesurier.

1½ m. s. TIDMARSH. Tidmarsh House, John Hopkins, Esq.

1½ m. s.w. Delabere Court, Henry Rudd, Esq. 1 m. s.e.

PURLEY HALL, FREDERICK WILDER, ESQ.

Hill, G. H. Montagu, Esq.; John Stephens, Esq. In the year 1803 a mineral spring was discovered here; the water is saturated in the highest degree with iron, held in solution by the carbonic acid of gas. From a gallon of water 32 grains of solid contents have been obtained, the greater part of which seem to be oxide of iron. 1 m. further, SHIPLAKE. Crowsley Park, Henry Baskerville, Esq. The house is a brick building, with ornamental parapet and square embattled towers. The park contains about 160 acres, is well stocked with deer, and enriched with some noble oaks. Holmewood Park, Hon. Mrs. Stonor.

1½ m. N.W. MAPLE DURHAM, a small village on the borders of the river Thames. In the neighbourhood of Maple Durham the hills are ranged in soft and beautiful variety along the margin of the Thames, and indeed this division of the county is altogether picturesque. Through the thick woods which now only crown the top of the elevations, and now beetle down even to their base, are cut walks prolific of captivating prospects. Maple Durham House, M. Blount, Esq. It is a large and venerable mansion of the Elizabethan age. The house is situated on an extensive lawn; in front is a noble avenue of elms, more than a mile in length. During the civil war Sir Charles Blount fortified Maple Durham in aid of the royal cause, under the superintendence of Sir Arthur Aston, Governor of Reading, and the situation of the place rendered it most important; it was courageously defended when exposed to the assault, but at length compelled to submit. During the attack several of the parliamentarian soldiers were much hurt by the bursting of their own petard.

41¼ m PANG- BOURNE STA.

N. Just across the Thames, WHITCHURCH; near which, at a place called Collins's End, there is a small public-house, once honoured with the presence of King Charles I. While Charles was suffered to remain at Caversham Lodge, he rode this way under the escort of a troop of horse. Bowls were then a fashionable amusement, and this inn possessed a bowling-green, occasionally resorted to by the neighbouring gentry, in which sport the King joined, forgetting for a time his sorrows. Hardwick House, Henry Philip Powys, Esq., a handsome and ancient, but not large mansion, on the border of the river. Coombe Lodge, built by the present proprietor's grandfather, Samuel Gardiner, Esq., during the latter part of the last century. The mansion is constructed of stone-coloured bricks, with portico and wings on either side, all in the Grecian style of architecture. It is situated on the slope of a hill, backed with beech woods and fir plantations. The south park, which commences from the south front of the house, descends in a graceful slope to the river Thames, which runs for some distance through the estate. The house and woods have a very beautiful appearance from the Berkshire side of the river, or the railway, about half a mile from the Pangbourne Station. The next station, Goring, is likewise on the estate; and the line passes through the lands belonging to S. Gardiner, Esq., till reaching the village of Southstake, about one and a half mile beyond. 3 m. N. Woodcot House, Adam Duff, Esq. The Chiltern Hills stretch from Gathampton, a little village about a mile north-west of Whitchurch, in the north-east direction as far as Watlington. This tract, which contains 64,788 acres, is chalk, in some places very white and pure, in others imperfect, which is covered at various depths with a clayey loam, generally

1 m. south of which,

SULHAM HOUSE, REV. JOHN WILDER.

Sulham House, which has lately been rebuilt by the present owner, was erected by Nicholas Wilder, Esq., of Nunbridge House, in the reign of Henry VII. Purley Hall was subsequently purchased of H. Hawes, Esq., by the Rev. Dr. Wilder, Rector of Sulham. Purley Park, Rev. Dr. Thomas Dowler; Purley Lodge, R. W. Ramsay, Esq.

2 m. N.N.W. BASELDON. White House, James Elton, Esq.; Basildon Park, James Morrison, Esq. This splendid mansion is constructed entirely of stone, and stands in a park about three miles in circumference.

GORING. J. W. Raughton, Esq., J.P.; and A. Duff, Esq., J.P. Cross the Thames to STREATLEY, Streatley House, W. H. Stone, Esq. 2 m. further, ALDWORTH. 2 m. further, COMPTON. Roden House, Francis Crowdy, Esq. 2 m. N.W. by w. is EAST ILSLEY. Ilsley Hall, Mrs. Williams; Fiddler's Green, Mr. W. Gegg.

2 m. w. ASTON TIRROLD, remarkable for the exuberance of its cherry and apple orchards. 2 m. further, BLEWBERRY. A field between Blewberry and Aston is thought to have been the scene of a severe conflict between the Saxons under Ethelred and his brother Alfred, and the Danes, in which the latter were defeated with great slaughter. Many human skeletons and military weapons were found near the spot in 1804, in making a new turnpike-road. In the parish are two ancient roads, one a Roman, and the other British, also an encampment of great extent, on Blewburton Hill. Loughborough Hill, the loftiest eminence in this county, has been crowned by an ancient work, apparently constructed for the purposes of warfare. About 1 m. N. of Aston Tirrold is SOUTH MORETON, a little to the N. of which is NORTH MORETON.

Cross the Thames.

Enter
Oxfordshire.

44¼ m. GORING
STATION.

47½ m. WALLING-
FORD ROAD
STATION.

Cross the Thames.
Re-enter
Berkshire.

sound and dry, containing a considerable quantity of flints, mostly brown, rough, and honeycombed, some to perforation. Many of these flints have also a sparry incrustation, and the best soils are most often covered with them. The hills vary in height. High Down is 820 feet; Ipstone Heath, 720 feet. The Stewardship of the Chiltern Hundreds is an honorary government office, accepted by members who desire to vacate their seat in the House of Commons. If Oxfordshire in its central division lose in a great measure that inequality of surface so prolific in beauty, it can boast of its forests and woods fraught with national benefit, and displaying at every rude turn a captivating though circumscribed grandeur of prospect. On the north (and particularly on the western part of that district), stone fences supply the place of the thick-set hedges, decorated with a profusion of wild flowers which form the boundary of other enclosures, and the eye is often fatigued by a rude and frigid monotony of scene. But the rivers which flow through the country are the chief sources of its beauty. These, gliding through almost every district, call forth luxuriant vegetation in a thousand smiling meadows, and regale the traveller with a continual and enchanting change of prospect, whether they stretch over fertile champaign or break from woody interstice.

Cross the Thames

Enter Oxfordshire.

44¼ m. GORING. STATION.

A little to the north is a medicinal water, called Springwell, which was in high repute in the early part of the last century for the cure of cutaneous diseases. It had its day of celebrity, and is now disregarded. The country people have sagaciously discovered the cause of its efficacy. When the water cured, it was dispensed gratuitously, the proprietor then demanded a fee from the patients, and its usefulness immediately disappeared.

47½ m. WALLING-FORD ROAD STATION.

Close to the station is CHOLSEY. Winterbrooke, Mrs. Kirby. 3 m. N. WALLINGFORD. The town of Wallingford, county of Berks, claims great antiquity and historic celebrity. It is situate on the banks of the Thames, which is here crossed by a stone bridge of nineteen arches, with four draw-bridges. By the river side are traces of an old castle, which sustained a siege in the reign of King Stephen; it was demolished in 1653. The town was formerly surrounded by a wall, and boasted twelve churches, only three of which now exist. It was once a place of importance, and is again recovering its commercial position, having a considerable trade in malt, corn, and flour. It is a parliamentary and municipal borough town and parish, and sends one member to the House of Commons. Area of parliamentary borough, with some adjoining parishes in the county of Oxford, 7,780 A. Number of electors (1848), 398. Its public buildings are not remarkable, but it has several schools and almshouses. 1 m. N. Howberry,

Cross the Thames.

Re-enter Berkshire.

W. S. Blackstone, Esq., M.P.; Chalmore Cottage, William Allnatt, Esq.; Winterbrooke, Captain Bond; St. John's House, William Shaw Clarke, Esq.; Castle Priory, Thomas Duffield, Esq.; Bridge House, Mark Morrell, Esq.; The Retreat, Robert Morrell, Esq. Crossing the Thames a little to the south, Newnham Murren, John Sanders, Esq; William Lorvey, Esq.

3 m. N.E. Brightwell Park, William Francis Lowndes Stone, Esq. BRIGHTWELL SALOME. Brightwell House, Sir Samuel Hancock.

DIDCOT. A small village, county of Berks. 2 m. s.w. HARWELL. Rowstock, Robert Hopkins, Esq.

53 m. DIDCOT STATION.

1 m. s. Milton Hill, J. S. Bowles, Esq.

56¼ m. STEVAN-TON STA.

2 m. s. WANTAGE. A parish, county of Berks, situated in the Vale of the White Horse, on a branch of the Ock, and of the Wilts and Berks Canal. It is celebrated as an ancient seat of royalty, and the birthplace of Alfred the Great, A.D. 849; and in commemoration of the one thousandth anniversary, a festival was held there on the 25th of October, 1849. Area of parish, 7,530 A. It has a brisk trade in corn and malt, and has some manufactures of sacking, twine, and coarse cloths. The church, which is cruciform, is a very handsome structure, and the town possesses almshouses, and several other charities. The surrounding country was formerly the patrimony of the West Saxon Kings. Market-day, Saturday. Stirlings, Henry Hayward, Esq.; Grove Cottage, Mrs. Taylor. 2 m. E. of which EAST LOCKINGE. Betterton House, Rev John Ferdinando Collins; Charlton House, Rev. W. Hayward.

60 m. WANTAGE ROAD STA.

2 m. s.w. SPARSHOLT. Sparsholt House, Rev. John Nelson. Close to which is KINGSTON LISLE, E. Martin Atkyns, Esq. A little south of this village is a very singular stone, called the Blowing Stone, being a large perforated sarsden, brought from the adjoining hills, which on being strongly blown through, emits a sound which can be heard for a distance of near four miles.

63¾ m. FARRING-DON ROAD STA.

1½ m. s. EAST CHALLOW. Challow Hall, F. F. Bullock, Esq. 1½ m. LETCOMBE REGIS. Little Benhams, Thomas Goodlake, Esq.; Benhams Manor House, Mrs. Hawkins. 1½ m. further, LETCOMBE BASSETT. A parish in the hundred of KINTBURY EAGLE, county of Berks. The church is dedicated to All Saints, and the living is a rectory in the arch-deaconry of Berks and diocese of Salisbury, rated in the King's Books at £15 0s. 2½d.; and in the patronage of the president and fellows of Corpus Christi College, Oxford. There is also a Dissenting place of worship. Dean Swift, during his residence at the rectory, in 1714, wrote his pamphlet, entitled "Free Thoughts on the Present State of Affairs;" but it was not printed until 1741. The ancient Iknield Street crosses the Vale of the White Horse in this parish. The white horse was formed by the direction of Alfred the Great, in commemoration and as a trophy of the signal victory which he obtained over the Danes at Ashdown in this neighbourhood, in the year 871. The horse is portrayed in a gallopping position on the upper part of a hill, where its steep situation and barren soil furnish a complete security against the inroads of the plough, the stagnation of waters, or the grazing of cattle. Its dimen-sions occupy about an acre of ground, and its shape is determined by hollow lines which are trenches cut in the white chalk between two and three feet deep, and about ten broad. The head, neck, body, and tail are composed of one line varying in width, and one line or trench has also been made for each of the legs. The chalk in the hollowed spaces being of a brighter colour than the turf that surrounds it, catches the sun's rays, and renders the whole figure visible at several miles' distance. Though the situation of the horse preserves it from all danger of being obliterated, yet the peasants of the surrounding country have a custom of assembling at stated periods for the purpose of clearing it of weeds. The holders of land in the neighbourhood of the White Horse were, by the conditions of tenure, obliged to cleanse and repair it. The obliga-

53 m. DIDCOT
STATION.
Oxford and
Banbury Br. ☞
56¾ m. STEVAN-
TON STA.
60 m. WANTAGE
ROAD STA.

1½ m. N. APPLEFORD, Jesse King, Esq. 1 m. w. of which SUTTON COURTNEY. The Abbey, Rev. John Gregson; Sutton Wick, W. Musson, Esq. 1½ m. E. LITTLE WITTENHAM, W. Hayward, Esq.

1 m. N.E. MILTON. Milton House, John B. Barrett, Esq.

1¼ m. N.N.E. EAST HANNEY. 2 m. further, GARFORD. 2 m. N.W. of which is KINGSTON BAGPUZE. Kingston House, Mrs. Blandy. The manor of Bagpuze was at an early period in the baronial family of Summery. A part of this estate seems to have been subdivided, and to have formed two distinct manors, which, from the families by whom they were afterwards possessed, acquired the name of Kingston Ferrars, and Kingston Largveile. A third manor retaining the name of Kingston Bagpuze, was for many years in the family of Kingston. The manors became afterwards the property of the Blandys. The manor-house is a modern brick mansion, The parish church was rebuilt early in the present century. It is a small, neat structure, and contains a few monuments of the Blandys, which were carefully preserved when the old church was pulled down. 4 m. further, WITNEY. 4 m. N.W. Cherberry Camp. Its width at the widest part is 310 paces, in the narrowest, 211. It is surrounded by a triple vallum.

63¾ m. FARRING-
DON ROAD STA.

6 m. N.W. FARRINGDON. It is situated about two miles from the Isis, on the west side of Farringdon Hill, where stands the church, a large and ancient edifice, displaying various styles of architecture. It was built in the form of a cross, with a double transept. In the organ gallery are several niches, some of which contain carved busts of heads of religious orders. Part of the spire was destroyed during the civil wars. The church contains several fine monuments, including that of its unknown founder. Robert, Earl of Gloucester erected a castle here, but King Stephen levelled it to the earth, and the site was granted by King John in 1202 for a Cistercian abbey, the possessions of which at the dissolution of monastic institutions were granted by Edward VI. to Thomas, Lord Seymour, after whose attainder they were bestowed by Queen Mary upon Sir F. Englefield. Farringdon Hill, an eminence rising gradually from the Vale of the White Horse, is surmounted by a grove, which commands most extensive views over parts of Oxfordshire, Gloucester, and Wilts. Near Farringdon is a Danish camp, two hundred yards in diameter, with a ditch twenty yards wide. It was on the adjoining flat that Alfred obtained his twelfth victory. Human bones are frequently discovered in the swampy ground one mile south of the hill. The town of Farringdon is neatly built, and very clean, has a town hall, some charities, and a weekly market on Tuesday. It is the head of a poor-law union, and a polling place for the county. Area of parish, 6,910 A.; population, 3,593. Farringdon House, Daniel Bennett, Esq. This elegant mansion was built by the late Henry James Pye, Esq., the Laureate. It stands in a small park on the north side of the town, the view of which is excluded by lofty elms and some judiciously disposed plantations. The grounds are agreeable from their inequality of surface. During the civil wars the ancient mansion was garrisoned for Charles I., and was one of the last places that surrendered, its defenders having repulsed a large party of the Parliament's forces but a short time before the reduction of Oxford. This attack was attended by a singular circumstance: Sir Robert Pye, the owner of the house, who had married Anne, eldest daughter of Hampden, and was a colonel in the parliamentary army, being himself the person who headed the assailants. About 1 m. E. of Farringdon, Wadley House, Thomas Mills Goodlake, Esq.

2 m. N. STANFORD. 2 m. further, PUSEY. Pusey House, P. Pusey, Esq. 1½ m. N.W. BUCKLAND. Buckland, Sir Robert Throckmorton, Bart. The

tion is now void as the frequent changes which the property has undergone, and the endeavours of the purchasers on each transfer to avoid restrictions, have contributed to cancel every record that could make it binding. The peasantry therefore preserve the memory of its existence, and celebrate it with a rustic festival and various games. The horse, though simple in its design, may hereafter vie with the pyramids for duration, and perhaps exist when those shall be no more.

3 m. s.w. ASHBURY. In this parish is an encampment, called Alfred's Camp, near to which are two barrows. Here are also some tumuli and a cromlech, called Weyland Smith, with which a tradition introduced by Sir Walter Scott in his romance of "Kenilworth" is connected. 3 m. further, Ashdown Park, Earl of Craven. | 71¼ m. SHRIVEN-HAM STA.

7 m. s. AULDBOURNE. A name compounded of the Saxon term Hauld (hold), and Bourne (a brook). It anciently gave a name to a royal chase, granted by Henry VIII. to Edward Seymour, Duke of Somerset, which for a long period served as a rabbit-warren, but is now enclosed and cultivated. Previous to the battle of Newbury, in the reign of Charles I., a sharp skirmish took place here between the Parliamentary and the Royalists troops. The southern part of the vicarage house is supposed to be the remains of a hunting seat which belonged to John of Gaunt, Duke of Lancaster. Near a farm-house, called Percy's Lodge, are vestiges of an ancient bridge and encampment. | Enter Wiltshire.

1 m. s.e. SWINDON. A market-town and parish, county of Wilts. A very neat and well-built town, situate on an eminence, commanding a good prospect over the adjoining counties of Berks and Gloucester. It has no particular trade, but has a lively and cheerful appearance in consequence of the many persons of independent fortune who have chosen it as a residence. The public buildings are magnificent. It has a free school, and a weekly market on Monday for corn and provisions, and a cattle, or great market, as it is called, every alternate Monday. It has also five annual fairs, and the petty sessions for the Swindon division of the hundred are held here. There are some good stone quarries in the neighbourhood. The Lawn, Ambrose Goddard, Esq. 1½ m. s. WROUGHTON. Wroughton House, H. J. Lovell, Esq.; Elcombe, Edward Budd, Esq.; Elcombe Hall, Mrs. Pavey; Salthrop Lodge, John Simpson, Esq. A little further, Burderop, J. J. Calley, Esq. 3 m. further, OGBOURN ST. GEORGE. Manor House, Samuel Canning, Esq. A little further, OGBOURN ST. ANDREW. Rochley House, Edward Jones, Esq. About 2 m. further, MARLBOROUGH. Tottenham Park, Marquis of Aylesbury; Savenake Forest, Earl Bruce; Stitchcomb House, Henry Woodman, Esq.; Wye House, Stephen Brown, Esq. | 77 m. SWINDON JUNCTION STA.

3 m. s. Manor House, Horatio N. Goddard, Esq. About 1 m. further, BROADHINTON. 1 m. further, WINTERBOURNE BASSETT. 1 m. further, BARWICK BASSETT. 1 m. further, WINTERBOURNE MONCKTON. 1 m. further, AVEBURY. Manor House, Mrs. Kemm. Avebury has particular claims on | 82¾ m. WOOTTON BASSET STA.

mansion was built in 1757 by Sir Robert Throckmorton, Bart., from the designs, and under the superintendence of John Wood, Esq., of Bath. The dining-room, library, and chapel are handsome rooms; the ceiling of the library, painted by Cepriani, is greatly admired. The pleasure-grounds are laid out with great taste. The manor has been in the family of the present proprietor since 1545. Carswell House, T. H. Southby, Esq.; Newton Villa, W. W. Wintle, Esq. 3 m. further, Bampton-in-the-Bush, F. Whitaker, Esq., J.P.

71¼ m. SHRIVEN-HAM STA.

SHRIVENHAM, a parish, county of Berks. It has an area of 8,430 A. With the exception of the church, which is a handsome Gothic structure, there is nothing remarkable at this place. Beckett House, Viscount Barrington. The house was built by the present Viscount, in 1831, from designs of the Hon. Thomas Liddell, and under his superintendence. The remains of a large house were pulled down in 1816, part of which had been burnt down during the civil wars. 4 m. N. HIGHWORTH. 1. m. w. Annisley Hall, Captain Johnson, R.N.; Lushill House, John Archur, Esq. 2½ m. N.E. of which, is Coleshill House, Earl of Radnor. It was built from the designs of Inigo Jones, in 1650, and still remains as one of the most perfect specimens of that architect's style. Its elevation is simple, yet imposing; and its plan that of a perfect quadrangle, with rusticated groins, divided into a basement and two principal stories. The doorway in the centre is ascended by a flight of steps, and surmounted by an elliptical pediment. The windows have bold carvings, with architrave and cornice, and its high sloping roof terminates with dropping eaves and blocked cornice, having dormer windows finished with pediments; a balustrade and gazebo crown the whole. The interior is finished in the same style, with bold projecting mouldings and ornamented ceilings. The grounds abound with pleasing scenery, and are diversified by that irregularity of surface which renders landscape picturesque and beautiful. The river Cole meanders through the vale which skirts the western side of the park, and the town of Highworth in the distance forms an agreeable object. 1 m. w. Warneford Place, Lady W. Warneford. 1 m. N.W. Stanton Fitzwarren, Rev. J. C. A. Trenchard; Kingsdown House, D. Archer, Esq. 2 m. N. Buscot Park, Pryse Loveden, Esq. 2 m. N.W. LECHLADE. Manor House, George Milward, Esq. 3 m. w. FAIRFORD. Fairford Park, J. R. Parker, Esq.

Enter Wiltshire.

77 m. SWINDON JUNCTION STA.

Cheltenham Union. ☞

Lydiard Tregoze, Viscount Bolingbroke. It is a fine mansion, surmounted by a pediment. The grounds are extensive, and contain many beautiful clumps of trees, among which are numerous venerable oaks, the park being also ornamented with a handsome sheet of water. Lydiard Park, C. O. Wombwell, Esq.; Marsh Cottage, Captain B. Horsell; Midge Hall, Cornelius Bradford, Esq. A little to the N. LYDIARD MILLICENT. Lydiard House, Rev. H. T. Streeten. A little further, PURTON. Bentham, William James Sadler, Esq.

2 m. N. LITTLE BLUNSDEN, J. J. Calley, Esq. On Blunsden Castle Hill is a large circular entrenched work, which is generally supposed to have been a Roman encampment, and that has been rendered extremely probable by the circumstance of the Roman road passing close under the hill.

82¾ m. WOOTTON BASSET STA.

WOOTTON BASSET, an ancient borough, county of Wilts, which from the reign of Henry VI. until the passing of the Reform Bill sent two members to Parliament. It has a weekly market on Tuesday, and six annual fairs. The houses, although built of brick, are mostly covered with thatch, and lie

the attention of the antiquary, for at this place are the ruins of the most gigantic and most interesting of our British monuments, and yet perhaps less known than many objects of a similar nature; for though it may be classed with Stonehenge, Stanton Drew, Long Meg and her Daughters, and various other monuments of the kind, and surpasses all in the number and magnitude of its upright stones, its vallum and foss, and its collateral appendages, it has failed to attract the same degree of attention and notoriety which attaches to many of the others. This is to be accounted for by the relative situations; for while Stonehenge, being placed on a commanding and conspicuous spot near a prosperous city has had many essays and volumes published respecting it, Avebury, being a village, obscured by trees, hedges, and houses, is so little seen as a whole, that, with the exception of Dr. Stukeley's folio volume, there has been very little published about it. In its original state, this great temple must have presented a singular and impressive appearance. The whole is surrounded by a broad ditch and lofty vallum; within the enclosure was a series of upright stones, consisting of one hundred in number, placed at a distance of twenty-seven feet from each other, and mostly measuring from fifteen to seventeen feet in height, and about forty feet in circumference. Within the area of this circle, the diameter of which was about one thousand four hundred feet, were two double circles, each consisting of two concentrix circles, and comprising the same number of stones. In the interior of the south concentrix was an upright stone of larger size than any other, as it measured more than twenty feet in height, and within the northern were three stones, placed perpendicularly, and having a large flat one for an impost, which appears originally to have measured seventeen feet by thirty-five feet. There were two entrances into the grand circle, formed by rows of upright stones. On the north side of that leading towards Birkhampton was another group of three stones, two of which still remain, and are verbally denominated the Devil's Quoits. 1½ m. s. of Avebury is KENNET, noted for the peculiar excellence of its ale.

CHIPPENHAM. A parliamentary and municipal borough town and parish, county of Wilts, situated on the Avon, which is crossed by a fine bridge of twenty-two arches. It formerly had some manufactures of silk and woollens. Its retail trade is still brisk, and its markets well attended. It consists principally of one street, in the centre of which is the town hall, and has a large and ancient church, a portion of which dates from the 12th century. Area of parish, 9,100 A. It has a union workhouse, a literary institution, and several charities. Chippenham returns two members to Parliament. Market-day, Saturday. Fairs, May 17th, June 22nd, October 29th, and December 11th. Corporation revenue in 1846—7, £271 15s. Monkton House, F. M. Esmeade, Esq.; Ivy House, Mrs. Humphries; Avon Cottage, G. J. Whitmarsh, Esq. 4 m. s.e. Bowood Park, Marquis of Lansdowne, stands in a fine park, which is diversified in natural features, and richly adorned with plantations. Within the boundaries of the park there are no less than nine beautiful valleys, in the broadest of which is a noble lake, and on an elevated piece of ground above is the mansion, which is of three distinct features, having been built at various periods; the edifice, therefore, presents an irregular mass. The chief front was built from the designs of the Adams', in the modern Italian villa style; a large wing, in imitation of a wing of Dioclesian's palace, three hundred feet in extent, was subsequently added, and forms the southern side of two quadrangular courts, which are surrounded by domestic offices.

2 m. E. CALNE. Highway Manor House, the property of Henry Augustus Tonge, Esq.; Highlands, William Waite, Esq.; Springfield, William Gundry, Esq.; Castle Field, Captain J. Stanton, E.I.C.S.; Chilvester Lodge, Captain Warren, R.N. A little to the s. Blackland, William Tanner, Esq.

93¾ m. CHIPPEN-HAM STA.

Trowbridge Branch.

principally in one street, in the centre of which are the shambles, market-house, and town hall. Formerly this place had a considerable trade in broad-cloths. The church is a very ancient structure, but contains nothing of interest. There are two free schools for twelve boys and twelve girls. Area of parish, 4,830 A. Greenhill House, Richard Parsons, Esq.

3 m. m. N.W. BRINKWORTH. Box Bush House, Robert Stratton, Esq. 3 m. further, SOMERFORD. 3 m. further, MALMESBURY. A castle, called Ingleburne, existed here before the middle of the 7th century; and about 642, Maleduff, an Irish monk, erected a monastery from the names of its founders, styled Maeldelmesbyrigg, which has gradually been altered to the modern appellation of Malmesbury. It was splendidly endowed, and its revenue at the dissolution amounted to £803 17s. 7d. A part only of the nave remains, which has long been used as the parish church. A town soon rose round the abbey; and notwithstanding it was burnt by the Danes in the reign of Alfred the Great, it became a place of much import-ance. In the reign of Henry I. a strong castle was built, which suffered much under the invasion of Prince Henry, afterwards Henry II. During the civil war, in the reign of Charles I., the town was besieged and captured by Sir William Waller; it was afterwards retaken by the Royalists, who could not however long retain it, and the parliamentary troops kept possession until June, 1646. Burton Hill House, John Cockerill, Esq.; Melbourne, Henry Gale, Esq.; Cole Park, Peter A. Lovell, Esq. A little to the N. Charlton Park, The Earl of Suffolk and Berkshire. The house is a large magnificent freestone structure, in the form of an oblong square, with four dissimilar fronts, of which the centre one is designed by Inigo Jones.

2 m. w. DAUNTSEY. Manor House, Ven. Archdeacon Fenwick.

93¾ m. CHIPPEN-HAM STA.

1 m. N.N.E. LANGLEY BURRELL, George Fisher, Esq. 1½ m. N. DRAYCOT CERNE. Draycot Park, Viscount Wellesley. The house is a large, irregular structure, and has an extensive park, with pleasure-grounds attached to it. Contiguous to the house is the church, a very curious and interesting fabric. 2 m. further w. Stanton St. Quinton Park. N. Huish Park, Thomas Clutterbuck, Esq. 1½ further, KINGTON ST. MICHAEL. The church was erected, as tradition reports, by Michael, Abbot of Glaston-bury, in the reign of Henry III., but the style indicates it to be of earlier date. It consists of a nave, chancel, and two side aisles, with a tower at the west end, which little more than a century ago was, according to Aubrey, surmounted by a spire. The north doorway has a semi-circular arch, with zigzag mouldings, and has a crowned head (supposed to be that of King Ethelred, whose seat this was) cut in bold relief over the key-stone. Three of the arches dividing the nave from the aisles are also circular, as is that which separates it from the chancel. The other arches are in the early pointed style, and so are all the windows, except those of the tower, which are rounded. In some of the windows are fragments of stained glass, exhibiting mutilated representations of male and female figures, coats of arms, &c. Aubrey states that the south window, in his time, contained full-length portraits of King Ethelred and his Queen. In the church are several ancient monuments. Kington House, Nathan Atherton, Esq. 5 m. N.W. Castle Combe House, George Poulett Scrope, Esq., M.P. In a picturesque valley, on the banks of a rapid stream. Within the park, are the ruins of the old castle of Combe, the ancient seat of a barony, but dismantled since the time of Henry II. The family of Scrope have resided here since the reign of Richard II., whose chancellor was Sir Richard Scrope.

s. are Monk's Park, Thomas Dowell, Esq.; Nestor Park, J. B. Fuller, Esq.; Jaggard's House, Captain Cochrane. 2 m. E. Notton House, Sir John W. Awdry. 98¾ m. CORSHAM STATION.

3 m. S.W. LACOCK. Lacock Abbey, William Henry Fox Talbot, Esq. One of the most perfect and picturesque remains of a monastic institution in the kingdom, is situated in a level and fertile part of the county, adorned with venerable trees, and the meandering river Avon. The ancient buildings of the nunnery are preserved with great care, and yet the residence is replete with modern comforts. The abbey was founded by Ela, Countess of Salisbury, in 1233. At the dissolution the abbey was granted to Sir Henry Sherrington, Knight, who converted the ancient buildings into a residence, preserving with religious veneration any portion of the old fabric. The carriage front, the principal compartment of the edifice, is flanked by octagonal turrets, crowned with cupolas, similar to the buildings of the period of Henry VIII., and the roof partially concealed by an ornamented open parapet. The principal entrance is by a double flight of steps. On the left is a range of buildings, having two pointed windows, with buttress and battlements, and beyond a high gable-roofed building. On the right angle is a large octangular tower, ornamented with balustrades, and a staircase turret crowned with a cupola. On the garden front is a large tower, with a curious old gabled building, having a twisted ornamental chimney, and on the east side are the remains of the chapter house, vestry, and old kitchen. The ancient cloister, a remarkable feature in the edifice, extends round three sides of the quadrangle; on the fourth are the hall and cellars. Several parts of the mansion bear a modern character in their construction. Lackham House, Captain Frederick William Rooke. A large stone mansion, situated in a large fertile park. Ragbridge Cottage, Miss Ridler. A little further, Bowden Park, Egerton Harman, Esq. The house was built from designs of Sir Jeffrey Wyatville, the celebrated architect, by the late Bernard Dickenson, Esq. Its principal front towards the west has a semi-circular portico, with Ionic columns. It stands on the brow of a steep hill, commanding extensive prospects. The grounds are beautifully disposed, with plantations and luxuriant woods. At the eastern extremity of the park is a handsome lodge, from the design of the same architect. A little further, Spye Park, John Baynton Starky, Esq. The house stands on lofty ground, near the south-west extremity of the park, and commands a fine distant prospect. This was once one of the best-timbered estates in the county, but many of the venerable trees were felled some years ago. The mansion is an old structure, with a modern front. It was the residence of the witty and profligate Earl of Rochester, the friend of Charles II., of whom Lord Orford observed: "He was a man whom the Muses loved to inspire, but were ashamed to avow."

Box, county of Wilts, is a parish comprising an area of 4,150 A. It has an endowed school, with a revenue of £50 per annum. The most remarkable feature of this place is the tunnel excavated by the Great Western Railway Company at Box Hill in this parish, which passes through a freestone formation a distance of one mile and three-quarters. Many Roman antiquities have been discovered in the neighbourhood. Shailors House, William A. Bruce, Esq.; Newtown House, Henry Holworthy, Esq.; Middle Hill Spa, Mrs. Lewis; Middle Hill Villa, Mrs. Neate; Alcombe Lodge, Henry Ricketts, Esq.; Ashley Grove, John J. Rogers, Esq. 101¾ m. BOX STA.
Box Hill Tunnel

3 m. S.S.W. Monckton Farleigh House, Wade Browne, Esq. The present manor-house is built on the site of an old monastery of Clueniac monks. Bishop Jewel died in the priory, and the pulpit in which he preached is still in the parish church. Enter Somersetshire.
Cross the Avon.

1 m. S. Prior Park, Roman Catholic College. This stately mansion, entirely built of Bath-stone, stands about four hundred feet above the city. It consists of a front pavilion and wings, forming altogether a line of building 106¾ m. BATH STATION.

98¼ m. CORSHAM
STATION.

CORSHAM, a parish, county of Wilts, containing an area of 6,710 A. It has two annual cattle fairs, March 7th and September 4th. Its charitable institutions produced a revenue of £237 in 1836. Its parsonage-house was formerly a priory. Corsham Court, the splendid seat of Lord Methuen, which contains a most valuable collection of pictures by the old masters, and is one of the finest mansions in the county.

1½ m. N.W. PICKWICK. Haatham Park, J. A. Case, Esq. The house was principally built by Lady James, the friend and correspondent of Sterne, who greatly embellished the park and gardens. Pockridge House, J. Edridge, Esq. SLAUGHTERFORD. A village situated near Biddlestone, on the Box Brook, and bears in its name the memory of some great slaughter, as tradition reports of the Danes. Whitaker, in his "Life of St. Neot," contends that it was the scene of the battle of Ethandum; but various opinions are entertained as to the accuracy of this statement. A short distance from Slaughterford, near the Fosse Road, is a large wood, called Bury Wood, within which are the remains of a large encampment, reputed to be of Danish construction, and supposed to have been the fortress to which the Danes retreated after their defeat. This entrenchment is stated to consist of a double ditch and vallum, enclosing an area of eighteen acres, and having two entrances. In this vicinity is the village of COLNE, which was almost totally destroyed by fire in 1770. Near Slaughterford is BIDDESTONE, or BIDSTON, a parish of considerable extent, and comprises a district which was formerly divided into two parishes. In the church is a monument to the memory of Edmund Smith, M.A., who was a poet of some repute, and died in 1709.

101¾ m. BOX STA.

Box Hill Tunnel.

3 m. N. MARSHFIELD. In this parish are some entrenchments, supposed to have been raised by the Britons or Saxons about 599, when the battle of Dyrham took place in this neighbourhood. Leland mentions the existence of a nunnery also, but there are no vestiges of it. In the vicinity, at a place called the Rocks, are three stones, which mark the limits of the counties of Somerset, Gloucester, and Wilts.

Enter
Somersetshire.

Cross the Avon.

106¾ m. BATH
STATION.

BATH a city, and parliamentary and municipal borough, the capital of the county of Somerset, is situated on the Avon, here crossed by seven bridges, two stone, two iron, and three suspension. It was known to the

extending one hundred and thirty feet. The style is Corinthian, surmounted
by a fine balustrade. From the centre front a fine portico projects, supported by six large and elegant columns. Fielding, who laid the scene of
the early years of "Tom Jones" at this place, has given a picture of the
beautiful situation of the mansion, whose former occupier, Mr. Allan, is the
"Allworthy" of his novel. Making allowance for the fancies of an author
in an imaginary river, sea, distant island, and ruined abbey, the description
is tolerably correct; at least many of its most agreeable features are real.
It was here that Pope passed some of the happiest days of his life in the
society of its founder, Mr. Allan, to whom also he introduced his friend
Warburton, and was thus the founder of his fortune. 1 m. further,
Midford Castle, Charles John Conolly, Esq. The castle is situated on
the brow of a hill, which descends to the village of Midford on the old
Warminster Road. This structure stands on a bold projection, surrounded
with elegant terrace plantations, which command at different points several
picturesque views of the vale and surrounding hills. It was erected about
seventy years ago by Disney Roebuck, Esq., on a most curious plan, which
combines the interior convenience of modern architecture with the dignity
and grandeur of the ancient. It was purchased by Charles Conolly, Esq., of
Tatchbury Mount, Hampshire, the great-grandfather of the present proprietor,
and to his excellent taste and judgment both the castle and enclosures
round it are greatly indebted for their present beauty and elegance. Besides
other improvements, he furnished the principal apartments with many
valuable paintings of celebrated masters, and other curiosities. Attached
to the castle is a chaste Gothic chapel, the interior of which is ornamented
with several curious specimens of ancient Christian sculpture. On the
north-east of the pleasure wood stands a very picturesque building, called
The Priory, which serves as an ornament to the plantations, and to unfold
the view of a beautiful glen, and several cascades, all of his formation.
1 m. further, Hinton Charter House. It is an extensive freestone
building, of two fronts. East front, ninety feet in length, and the south
fifty-three feet. About 1 m. further, at NORTON ST. PHILIP, the Duke of
Monmouth defeated the Royal forces under Lord Faversham and the Duke
of Grafton. A little to the east, the ruins of Farley Castle, a place of very
great antiquity, having for many years been in the possession of the Saxon
forces. Farley Castle, J. T. Houlton, Esq., attached to which is the old
chapel of the castle, which is nearly perfect, and the curious monuments in
it are in tolerable preservation. This building consists of a nave fifty-six
feet in length, and twenty feet in breadth, and a chantry on the north side
twenty feet in length, and fourteen feet in breadth. The estate consists of
two manors in a ring fence, and comprises a park well stocked with deer,
well wooded, and agreeably diversified with hill and dale. 1 m. further,
Chatley House, Thomas Meade, Esq. A little further, BECKINGTON; and
a little to the left, Seymour's Court, H. Shepherd, Esq.; and a little to the
right, Orchardleigh, the seat of the Champneys. 2 m. further s. FROME.
East Hill, Rev. E. Edghill. 3 m. w. of Frome, Mells Park, — Horner,
Esq.; Keyford House, William Sheppard, Esq. 1 m. s. Marston House,
Earl of Cork. 1½ m. further, Longleate, Marquis of Bath. The mansion
is a superb, uniform, magnificent structure, standing on a lawn near a
branch of the river Frome. It is in the form of a parallelogram, two
hundred and twenty feet long, and one hundred and eighty feet deep. It
is built of freestone, and ornamented with pilasters of the Doric, Ionic, and
Corinthian orders. The surrounding park within the plantations is about
fifteen miles in circumference. 2 m. E. from which is WARMINSTER.

5 m. s.w. Camerton Park, John Jarrett, Esq. A little further, Wood-
borough, William Savage Wait, Esq. 1 m. s. WRITLINGTON. 1 m. s.e.
of which is Ammerdown, Colonel Joliffe. Near which is Kingswell, Captain
Scobell, R.N. The architecture of the house is Grecian, and was built
by Captain Scobell about ten years ago. It stands on an elevated slope,

Romans by the name of Aquæ Solis, and its first baths were erected in the reign of the Emperor Claudius. Its charter, granted by Richard I., was confirmed by Henry III., and considerably extended by George III. The position of this city is most imposing: it is enclosed by an amphitheatre of hills, on the western declivity of which its finest buildings extend in a succession of terraces. The houses, being mostly built of white free-stone, with great attention to architectural beauty, Bath has acquired the just reputation of being the handsomest provincial city in the three kingdoms. Amongst its public buildings we may cite the Abbey Church, in the latest Gothic style, two hundred and ten feet in length, with a tower one hundred and seventy feet in height. This fabric was the church of the venerable monastery to which it was attached. St. Michael's, St. James's, the freemasons' lodge, assembly and concert rooms, a splendid theatre, subscription club-house, the guildhall, the gaol, several well-endowed hospitals, and the bath-houses. The hot springs, to which this city owes its name and its celebrity, are saline and chalybeate, at a temperature of from 90° to 117° Fahr.; they rise on the bank of the Avon, and supply five establishments—the King's, Queen's, Cross, Hot, and Abbey baths. The first four belong to the corporation, and, notwithstanding the decline of the city's celebrity, yield a revenue of about £1,500. The Great Pump Room at the King's Bath is eighty-five feet in length, forty-eight feet in breadth, and thirty-four feet in height, and contains a marble statue of the famous Beau Nash, the master of the ceremonies, to whom Bath owed much of its prosperity. The Abbey Baths are private property, belonging to the Earl Manvers. They are furnished in a very superior style, and are frequented only by the most wealthy sojourners. Bath possesses a grammar school, founded by Edward VI., to the mastership of which is attached the rectory of Charlcombe; and a blue-coat and national schools. Among its charitable institutions we may cite Partis's College, for thirty decayed gentlewomen, and the hospital of St. John the Baptist, with a revenue of £11,395. Among its learned establishments, we may mention the Bath and West of England Society, a literary and philosophical institution, a public subscription library, a mechanics' institute, and a Roman Catholic collegiate establishment. Bath was once famous for its manufacture of coarse woollens, termed "Bath Coating," but it has greatly declined. The area of the borough is 980 A.; population, 52,346; registered electors (1843), 2,941. It sends two members to Parliament. The corporation revenue (1847), was £21,345, and its expenditure, £19,928. Markets, Wednesday and Saturday; fairs, February 14th and July 10th. Bath, with Wells, form a bishopric, comprising within its diocese all the county of Somerset, except a part of Bristol; but the Bishop's palace and the cathedral are at Wells. Among the promenade and public walks of Bath, Victoria Park and Sidney Gardens are delightful resorts; and at Lansdown, a short distance from the city, races are held, at which there are two meetings in the spring, and a week after Ascot. 3 m. N.W. Aston Lodge, Robert Bush, Esq.; Tracy Park, Sir Alexander Hood, Bart.; Hamswell House, Robert Whittington, Esq. 3½ m. N. COLD ASTON. 2 m. further, Dyrham Park, George Wm. Blathwayt, Esq. Dyrham is celebrated for a battle fought between the Britons and Saxons, in the year 599; and an encampment on Hinton Hill is pointed out as the Saxon camp, including twenty acres. Dyrham Park is a very handsome mansion, the principal front being 130 feet in length. The park contains nearly 500 acres. 2 m. further, Dodington Park, C. W. Codrington, Esq. On the brow of the hill, at LITTLE SODBURY, are the remains of a very strong camp, in the form of an oblong square, extending from north to south about 300 yards, and from east to west 200 yards. The north-west side is defended by a precipitous declivity, the other three by double ditches and ramparts. This is the last of a series of five camps on the points of the Cotswold Hills, from Painswick to Little Sodbury. The whole are supposed to have been formed or occupied by the Romans.

amidst higher hills, and has a rich and extensive view over the surrounding country. 9 m. s.w. from Writlington is Wells, and about 7 m. s.s.w. Shepton Mallett. Between these two, Dinder House, James C. Somerville, Esq.

108¼ m. TWERTON STA.

Twerton. 2 m. w. Newton Park, W. H. P. Gore-Langton, Esq., M P. The pleasure-grounds were laid out by Messrs. Brown and Repton. The Norman barons of St. Loe had a castle near the site of the modern house. The fine old keep or tower, and a handsome archway, the former entrance to the castle, still remain. King John is said to have been confined there.

111½ m. SALTFORD STA.

3 m. s.w. Houndstreet Park, Edward William Popham, Esq. Close to which is Publow. 2 m. further, Stowey House, Right Hon. H. Labouchere, M.P. 5 m. e. Stone Easton Park, Sir J. S. Hippisley, Bart.

113¼ m. KEYNSHAM STA.

Cross the Avon.

Keynsham. A market-town and parish, county of Somerset, on the banks of the Avon, which is crossed by a good stone bridge of fifteen arches. The town, which is built on a rocky eminence, consists chiefly of one street. The church is a handsome Gothic structure, with a lofty tower, and possesses many ancient monuments, particularly one in honour of Sir Thomas Bridges. It has a union workhouse, and some small woollen and linen manufactures. Area of parish, 3,330 a. Market-day, Thursday. At this place the railway emerges from a tunnel 1,012 yards in length.

118 m. BRISTOL STATION.

Bristol and Exeter Rail.

Bristol. A sea-port, city, and county of itself, so constituted by Edward III., although properly speaking it lies in the counties of Somerset and Gloucester. It was a place of eminence in the time of the Anglo-Saxons, but its origin is uncertain, although it is ascertained to have been fortified as early as the 3rd century. In the time of the Normans it possessed a castle, built by the Earl of Glo'ster, son of Henry I. Under Henry VIII. it was erected into a bishopric, which has lately been united with that of Gloucester. During the riots of 1831 the episcopal palace and many of the other buildings were destroyed. It is situate on the Avon, at its confluence with the Frome, eight miles south-east of its *embouchure* in the Bristol Channel. The area of the borough, including the district added by the Municipal Act, is 9,870 a., and it extends over several hills and intermediate valleys. The Old City between the Avon and the Frome is ill-built, and further south the buildings are of an inferior character, but the squares, new streets, and modern residences all around are very handsome, especially on the north and west, in the latter of which lies Clifton, which is within the city liberty. Bristol is well paved, lighted, and drained, and the supply of water abundant. It contains many public edifices of great beauty, with nineteen churches of the Established religion, of which the most interesting are those of St. Mary Redcliff, completed in 1376, and considered one of the finest in England, St. James's, formerly collegiate, St. Stephen's, built about 1470, St. Mark's, now the chapel of the mayor, and the Temple Church. The Cathedral is a beautiful structure, founded in the time of King Stephen. It has a tower one hundred and forty feet high, ornamented with four pinnacles. This building contains many Gothic beauties. It is adorned with painted windows, and possesses several elegant monuments, particularly one to Mrs. Draper, the Eliza of Sterne. Its gateway is one of the most splendid remnants of Gothic architecture extant. The other principal buildings are the exchange, built in the Corinthian style, erected at a cost of £50,000, and used as a corn market, the commerce rooms, the guildhall, built in the reign of Richard II., the new council hall, gaol, and bridewell; the Bristol institution and the infirmary, which possesses fine libraries and museums, and receive annually about 7,500 patients, the general hospital, the Victoria rooms, the office of the Bristol Steam Navigation Company, with a hall used for concerts, &c., the baths and pump-room at Clifton, a handsome

108¼ m. TWER-
TON STA.

2 m. N.W. by W. Kelston Park, Joseph Neeld, Esq. 3 m. N. Ashton Court, the late Sir John Smyth, Bart.

111¼ m. SALT-
FORD STA.

SALTFORD. 2 m. N. BILTON. The church, dedicated to St. Mary, is a large and handsome edifice, with a finely ornamented tower, partly in the Norman and partly in the early English style of architecture. The river Avon flows along the south border of the parish.

113¼ m. KEYN-
SHAM STA.

Cross the Avon.

118 m. BRISTOL
STATION.

Gloucester
and Birmingham
Rail. ☞

theatre, and numerous fine bridges. About a mile from the city is the celebrated Bristol hot well, said to be a specific for scorbutic and other diseases. Of the numerous schools and charities in this city we may cite a few: the grammar school, founded in 1532, has several small exhibitions, and two fellowships of £30 each at St. John's College, Oxford. Queen Elizabeth's Hospital educates one hundred boys, and has a revenue of £5,000. In 1841 there were nearly six hundred schools in the city, educating twenty-one thousand eight hundred and sixty-four pupils, of which twelve were endowed. There are also numerous almshouses, and other charities, estimated at £23,000, besides £12,000 and £15,000 voluntary annual contributions. Bristol has a new proprietary college belonging to the Baptists, a school of medicine, a public library of thirty thousand volumes, also distinct law and medical libraries, and a mechanics' institution. It was long esteemed the second city of the empire, but other ports have carried away much of its commerce. It has still large iron and brass foundries, copper, tin, zinc, and glass-works, chemical and colour-works, sugar refineries and distilleries, and considerable manufactures of pins, shot, china, earthenware, soap, leather, tobacco, cottons, hats, and floor-cloths, with huge establishments for ship-building. The Avon, though narrow, is deep enough at Bristol for the largest ships, and at the commencement of the present century its course was turned at a cost of £700,000, leaving the old channel to form a harbour, furnished with locks and quays six thousand feet in length. At Ringroad, in the mouth of the river, ships of large burthen and first-class steamers load and discharge. Bristol still retains a large share of the West India trade, and imports all colonial produce, as well as wool, turpentine, hemp, timber, wine, and brandy from North and South America, the Baltic, and France. Its exports are its manufactured goods to foreign ports, and colonial produce to Ireland. Value of exports, in 1845, £216,778. In the same year four hundred and thirty-two British and foreign ships, aggregate burden, 97,764 tons, entered, and two hundred and forty-three, burden, 69,000 tons, cleared out of the port. Customs' revenue (1846), £911,314 13s.; registered shipping (1847), two hundred and ninety-five vessels, aggregate burden, 38,914 tons. It has a chamber of commerce, and several mercantile corporate bodies, with six banks. The regular steam communication with the United States was first established at Bristol, where

the 'Great Britain' steamer was built. The government of the city is by a   BRISTOL
mayor, sixteen aldermen, and forty councillors; and the corporation has   *(continued)*.
jurisdiction over the Avon from four miles above the city down to the sea,
and along the channel to Clevedon, and the right to license pilots to
numerous ports in the Bristol Channel. Corporation revenue (1843),
£49,176; in 1847, £48,473; expenditure, £53,000. Markets, daily, that
on Thursday for cattle. Fairs for horses, leather, &c., March the 1st, and
September the 1st. The spring assizes for civil causes, quarter sessions,
sheriff's, and other courts, are held here. Bristol belongs to the Clifton and
Bedminster poor-law union. It sends two members to Parliament, and the
registered electors in 1846 amounted to 11,032. Bristol claims to be the
birthplace of Sebastian Cabot, Chatterton, Southey, and Bayley the
celebrated sculptor.

Bristol to Exeter.

Although this railway does not display the same amount of engineering wonder and
difficulties as many others, on which the tunnels, viaducts, cuttings, and embankments
are of such a gigantic nature as to give of themselves a character to the line, it must be
confessed that few, if any, present greater natural beauties, the country which it traverses
being highly picturesque, and offering the most pleasing and romantic prospects to the
traveller's notice. About a mile from Bristol the line branches off from the Great
Western on the right, and before it reaches the first station passes through a tunnel
about three hundred feet in length. From Yatton there is a short branch of four miles to
the village of Clevedon, which is situated on the Bristol Channel. From this station to
the Banwell Station there is nothing in the construction of the line which is worthy of
especial notice, except the neat bridge across the river Yeo; but the country is
remarkable for its beauty, the romantic nature of its scenery being greatly increased by
the Mendip Hills on the left, while on the right there is an uninterrupted view of the sea,

---

Left of Railway from Bristol.	*Distance from London.*
3 m. N.N.E. BARROW GURNEY, is situated on the same ridge of hills as Clevedon. The summit of one which overlooks the village, is distinguished by an old Roman encampment, called Cadbury Castle. The camp is of oval form, and surrounded by a large double rampart, composed of loose limestone, the produce of the spot on which it is placed. Barrow Court, Montague Gore, Esq, 2 m. s. Winford House; Butcomb Court.	126¼ m. NAILSEA STATION.
¼ m. S. YATTON. On Canterbury Hill, in the vicinity are vestiges of an ancient fortification. In 1782 thirteen human bodies, some of them fresh, and of unusual size, and a stone coffin, were discovered in a limestone quarry, about 2½ feet below the surface of the earth. 4 m. S.E. Paradise House. Close to which is Mendip Lodge, Benjamin Somers, Esq. It commands fine views over the Welsh mountains. Langford Court, Henry Addington, Esq. 1 m. further, Blagdon Rectory, Rev. G. G. Waite; Blagdon Manor House, H. Seymour, Esq. On the summit of Blagdon is the highest spot on the Mendips. From this place, on a clear day, nearly two hundred miles in circumference can be seen. There are also Roman and British encampments in the neighbourhood.	130¼ m. YATTON STATION. Cross the Yeo.

BRISTOL (*continued*).	CLIFTON is a watering-place and parish. It comprises elegant terraces and crescents, built on the sides and summit of a precipitous limestone hill, commands fine views, and is separated from a similar cliff by a deep chasm, through which flows the navigable Avon. Its celebrated hot baths have a temperature of 73° Fahr. Many of the wealthy inhabitants of Bristol permanently reside here. Races are held annually in April. In the neighbourhood of Bristol, in Gloucestershire, are Redland Court, James E. Baillie, Esq.; Redland, Charles Ludlow Walker, Esq.; Stoke House, Sneed Park, Daniel H. Collins, Esq.; Henly House, Kingsweston Park, P. W. S. Miles, Esq., M.P.; Leigh Court, W. Miles, Esq.; Henbury, Edward Sampson, Esq.; Over Park, Knowle Park, Colonel Master; Stoke Park, Oldbury Court. Near Bristol, in Somersetshire, are Ashton Court, the late Sir John Smyth, Bart.

Bristol to Exeter.

almost as far as Bridgewater. At Hutton is another short branch on the right to the pretty watering-place of Weston-super-Mare. From this spot we notice nothing more in the engineering department, except the bridges over the rivers Axe and Brew, until after quitting Bridgewater. Crossing the river Parret by a neat bridge, the prospect becomes highly interesting, the river Tone running on the left of the line for upwards of seven miles through the valley, presenting occasional spots of most romantic scenery. Passing the Taunton and Wellington Stations, about four miles from the latter, the line enters a tunnel upwards of half a mile in length, and emerges through a deep cutting into the valley of the river Culme. Beyond is the Tiverton Station, from which there is a branch line of about seven miles to the ancient town of Tiverton. From Collumpton Station the line still wends its way through the valley of the Culme, until its arrival at the Exeter Terminus, a distance altogether from Bristol of about seventy-six miles.

Distance from London.	Right of Railway from Bristol.
126¼ m. NAILSEA STATION.	NAILSEA, a parish, county of Somerset, celebrated for its manufacture of crown glass. It has also very extensive coal-works. 2½ m. N.E. by E. Belmont House.
	2 m. N.E. Charlton House.
	2 m. N. CLAPTON-IN-GORDANO, Naish House.
	3 m. N.W. at WALTON-IN-GORDANO, Walton Castle, the ancient seat of the lords of the manor, stands on the summit of the Clevedon Ridge, and commands a fine and extensive prospect. It is embattled round, and adorned with a small turret at each angle. The keep, or citadel, is octangular, and has a small turret of semicircular shape on the south-east side. The floor and roof are now fallen in, and a great part of the walls are going fast to decay.
130¼ m. YATTON STATION. Clevedon Br. ☞ Cross the Yeo.	From this station there is a short branch, about four miles, to Clevedon, a spot much resorted to by the inhabitants of Bristol for the purpose of sea-bathing. Clevedon Court, Sir Charles Elton, Bart. On one of the rocks in the neighbourhood of this village, with great boldness and grandness to an immense height, was formerly a tower, called Wakes' Tower, which has long been demolished; and in this place, in the year 1738, a summer-house was built by M. Elton, Esq., which has since gone to ruins. The mansion house of Clevedon is situated on the south of the village, on the slope of a hill. It is a noble old building, erected at different periods.

BANWELL. A monastery was founded here by one of the early Saxon kings, to the abbacy of which Alfred the Great appointed Hassan, his subsequent biographer. It was entirely demolished in the Danish irruptions, and, although restored, never recovered its former splendour, having fallen into decay several years before the general suppression of monasteries. About the year 1820 two caverns in the rock, one denominated the Bone, and the other the Stalactite, were discovered here. The former, when first observed, contained several waggon-loads of bones; the latter exhibited some fine specimens of transparent stalactites. The Caves, Rev. James Thomas Law.

133¾ m. BANWELL STATION.

6 m. S.E. AXBRIDGE. An ancient borough and market-town. The Axe drainage, effected about forty years ago, improved so much the value of property in this parish, that land worth only 2s. 6d. per acre is now rented at £5. 4 m. further, Stoke Lodge. 3 m. further, WELLS. The town is small, but handsome, from its numerous ecclesiastical buildings. The Cathedral is of the time of Edward III. Its interior is highly decorated, and contains the tomb of Ina, King of Essex. The other principal buildings are the episcopal palace of the Bishop of Bath and Wells, the chapter house, deanery, St. Cuthbert's parish church, &c. Cardinal Wolsey and Archbishop Laud were bishops of this diocese. 1 m. further, Dinder House, J. C. Somerville, Esq. 3 m. further, SHEPTON MALLETT.

136¾ m. WESTON-SUPER-MARE STATION.

Cross the river Axe.

Cross the river Brew.

11 m. S.E. GLASTONBURY, once so famous for its monastic institutions. There is a branch line in progress which is intended to pass close to it. This ancient municipal borough and market-town contains an area of 7,216 A. It consists of two parishes, and two streets, crossing each other at right angles, the ancient market cross, once so admired, but now so decayed, standing at the point of intersection. Of its once splendid abbey, which with its dependencies covered sixty acres, and with the abbey lands produced an income of £40,000 per annum, nothing remains but the ruins of the church, St. John's Chapel, and the Abbot's Kitchen. Many other interesting monuments of Glastonbury's halcyon days of ecclesiastical power are still extant, such as 'St. George's Inn,' formerly the abbey hospitium, the abbey house, the tribunal, the great gate-house, now also an inn, the Hospital of St. John, founded in 1246, the two ancient parish churches, and St. Michael's Tor, a most interesting tower on a hill near the town. The church and monastery appertaining to it were destroyed by an earthquake in 1271. The abbey was founded in 605, on the site of a British church, said to owe its origin to St. Joseph of Arimathea, whose " miraculous thorn," which constantly blossomed on Christmas Day, and the shrine of St. Dunstan, one of its abbots, attracted multitudes of the faithful in the Middle Ages. At this venerable and long venerated place many kings, nobles, and prelates were interred, amongst whom was the illustrious Arthur, whose remains were discovered some centuries back, under the front of the high altar of the abbey church. At the dissolution of monastic institutions, the last Abbot of Glastonbury refusing to surrender the abbey to Henry VIII., was, with two of his monks, drawn on a hurdle to the Tor, and there hanged. 2 m. w. from Glastonbury, Sharpham Park, Lord Cavan. Here Fielding the novelist was born in 1717. 2 m. N.W. Splash House, and 3 m. s. Butleigh Court, Dean of Windsor; and 1 m. further, Bartram House. Knowle Hall, Mrs. Dakin.

145¼ m. HIGH-BRIDGE STA.

11 m. S.E. SOMERTON. A small market-town and borough. The town was at one time the residence of royalty. Ina, and several other West-Saxon monarchs held their courts here, and by them it was called " The Pleasant Place." John, King of France, was confined after his removal from Hertford in the castle of Somerton, of which only a part of the town wall and a round tower remain, but in a very ruinous condition. Somerton was at one time occupied by the Romans, and strongly fortified. In the year 877 it was plundered and laid waste by the Danes, but subsequently rebuilt, and became an important place, both for possession and the strength

151¾ m. BRIDGE-WATER STA.

133¾ m. BANWELL STATION.	1½ m. w. WALL, where there are vestiges of a Roman camp. 1 m. further, KEWSTOKE. A priory of Augustine canons was founded in 1210 by William de Courtnay, and dissolved in 1534, when its revenue was valued at £110 18s. 4¼d. The remains of the monastic building is now converted into a farm-house, and the chapel and refectory into a barn. 2 m. N.W. WICK ST. LAWRENCE. 2 m. N. KINGSTON SEYMOUR. The Manor House, erected in the reign of Edward IV., though it has undergone many alterations, is still remarkable for its antiquity.

Weston-super-Mare Branch.

136¾ m. WESTON-SUPER MARE STATION.	From this Station there is a short line of about 1½ m. to WESTON-SUPER-MARE, a maritime town and parish, which, from an unsightly village, has recently risen into a favourite watering-place. It has all the appliances of good sands, bathing establishments, neat villa residences, and a fine view of the opposite coast of Wales.

Cross the river Axe.

Cross the river Brew.

145¼ m. HIGH-BRIDGE STA.	HIGHBRIDGE, on the Brew, which rises on the western borders of Wiltshire, not far from the town of Bruton, past which it flows nearly in a south-westerly direction—some miles lower, however, it assumes a north-westerly course, and passes at a short distance south-westward of Glastonbury to the Bristol Channel, near the mouth of the Parret. From the vicinity of Glastonbury the course of this river is entirely through the marshes; it is navigable up to Highbridge, a distance of two miles from its mouth.

1½ m. N.W. BURNHAM, situated near the mouth of the Parret, which rises at South Parret in Dorsetshire, and then entering this county, flows nearly northward by Crewkerne to Langport, where it is joined on the east by the small river Yeo, and assumes a north-easterly direction to Bridgewater, having nearly midway between these towns received the waters of the Tine from the west, forming the harbour of Bridgewater; it thenceforward pursues a very devious course, for the most part in a northerly direction, and finally falls into Bridgewater Bay at Sterk Point. The navigable part of its course commences at Langport, whence to Sterk Point is a distance of about twenty miles. Burnham church, dedicated to St. Andrew in 1316, is a spacious edifice, with a lofty plain tower, that serves as a landmark. It contains the fine altar-piece designed by Inigo Jones for the chapel of the intended palace of Charles II., at Whitehall, and afterwards placed in Westminster Abbey; by the Dean and Chapter of which it was presented to Dr. King, of Rochester, and for many years incumbent of this parish, who erected it in the church at his own expense. It is of white marble, and is executed in the Grecian style, the principal objects are three boys holding a Bible, two children in a kneeling attitude, one pouring incense on the altar from a thuribulum, and the other bearing a paten, with two angels in the act of reverence, inclining toward the altar as supporters.

151¼ m. BRIDGE-WATER STA.	BRIDGEWATER, county of Somerset, on both sides of the river Parret, which is crossed by a stone bridge. The tide rises at this place six feet at a time, the "boar," as it is termed, being frequent on the rivers of the Channel, particularly the Severn. Bridgewater is a parliamentary and municipal borough, and a port, situated about seven miles from the mouth of the river in the Bristol Channel. The parish, which comprises almost the whole borough, contains 3,530 A., with a population of 10,436. It is a neat town, clean, and well supplied with water from a cistern under the town hall. It was incorporated as a borough by King John, who here

of its fortress. The scenery around Somerton is peculiarly beautiful. The church is very ancient, and in the south wall of the belfry is an effigy of " Edithe in portraiture of stone." Somerton Eardley, William Pinney, Esq., M.P. 4 m. s.e. ILVERCHESTER, or ILCHESTER. A very ancient town. It was the Cair-Pensavelcoit of the Britons, the Ischalis of Ptolomy, and the Gifelcestre of the Saxons. The Romans also fortified the town, vestiges of which are still visible. There was formerly a castle here, and in the ruins was found a staff, with a head of brass, having statues of two kings, a queen, and an angel, with the following lines in old French round the bottom:

JESU DE DRU ERIE,
NEME DUN ET MIE.

At the Friary House (some remains of which are visible) Roger Bacon was born, in the year 1214. He was unfortunately surrounded by bigotry and intolerance ; nevertheless his researches and discoveries will command respect to the latest era of human science. Ilchester was also the birth-place of Mrs. Elizabeth Rowe, the celebrated authoress.

9 m. s.e. LANGPORT. Once a royal burgh, and certain privileges are still enjoyed by the inhabitants. In, or about 1312, a hospital was founded for poor lepers. Near this place is MICHELNEY, or GREAT ISLAND. Here a Benedictine abbey was founded by King Athelstan, and its ruins have been converted into a barn. Of the ancient edifice may yet be seen part of the kitchen, some painted glass, and several stone staircases and pointed arches. Hill House, Mrs. Stuckey ; Herds Hill, Thomas W. Baggelote, Esq.

TAUNTON, one of the principal towns in the county of Somerset, and a parliamentary borough, is situated on the river Tone, and contains a population of 12,306, within an area of 2,730 a. A castle was built here for a royal residence by Ina, King of the West Saxons, about the year 700, in which he held his first great council. This castle was afterwards demolished by his Queen, Ethelburga, after expelling Eidbright, King of the West Saxons, who had seized it. The town and manor are supposed to have been granted to the church of Winchester in the following reign, and another castle is said to have been built on the site of the first by the Bishop of Winchester in the reign of William the Conqueror. At this period Taunton had a mint, some of the coins bearing the Conqueror's effigy being still in existence. In the reign of Henry VII., in 1497, Perkin Warbeck siezed the town and castle, which he quickly abandoned on the approach of the King's troops. In 1645 it again participated in civil war, being celebrated for the long siege it sustained, and the defence it made under Colonel (afterwards the renowned Admiral) Blake, who held it for the Parliament against 10,000 troops under Lord Goring, until relieved by Fairfax. Taunton was again implicated in rebellious proceedings by its connection with James, Duke of Monmouth, who was proclaimed King on the Cornhill of this town June 21st, 1685, many of whose followers, after his defeat at Sedgmoor, were inhumanly put to death on the same spot by the brutal Kirke, without any form of trial, besides those who were condemned by the merciless Judge Jeffreys at the bloody assize which he held here in the following September. This very ancient town is well built, the streets are wide and open, while most of the houses have small gardens in front. Its two churches are dedicated to St. James and St. Mary. The latter is a splendid specimen of the florid Gothic, and its lofty tower is said to be of truly magnificent workmanship. The interior, roof, &c., deserve inspection, and its organ is the finest in the country. It

163 m. TAUNTON STATION.

erected a castle, and it was one of the first towns seized by the barons, temp. Henry III. It was in this town also that the unfortunate Duke of Monmouth was proclaimed King, and lodged some time in the castle previously to his defeat at Weston Moor, 3 m. distant; and it is also celebrated as the principal scene of Judge Jeffrey's butcheries, assisted by Colonel Kirke, after the battle, when nearly all the prisoners (1,500) were, as it is said, executed. The town is irregularly built, but the streets are well paved. The church, which is very ancient and has the loftiest spire in the county, is considered a very fine specimen of Gothic architecture, and possesses an altar-piece of exquisite beauty, *said to be* by Guido, the subject of which is "The Descent from the Cross." Bridgewater has a grammar school and other endowments, an almshouse, infirmary, town hall and market-house, with a dome and Ionic portico, union workhouse, gaol, court-house, and three banks, most of which are creditable buildings in point of architecture. The entrance of its harbour is difficult, but the quay is accessible to vessels of 200 tons. It is connected with Taunton by means of its canal. The borough returns two members to Parliament, and the registered electors in 1846 were 529. It is also a polling place for West Somerset. Bridgewater was the birthplace of the celebrated Admiral Blake, A.D. 1594. Markets, Tuesday and Saturday, and four fairs—second Thursday in Lent, June 24th, October 2nd and 3rd, and December 28th. 4 m. N.N.W. Hill House, R. E. Evered, Esq.

3 m. N.W. Cannington Park, Brymore House, Hon. P. P. Bouverie, formerly the seat of the renowned John Pym; but nothing remains of the old mansion except the porch. 3 m. further, Fairfield House, Sir P. P. F. P. Acland, Bart. A little further, KILNCOURT. Alfoxton House, Langley St. Albyn, Esq.

3 m. w. Enmore Castle, William Trevelyan; Halsewell House, Colonel Kemeys Tynte; Barford House, Earl of Cavan. 2 m. further, at NORTH PETHERTON, Shovel House, C. Chapman, Esq.

163 m. TAUNTON STATION.

1 m. w. Norton Manor, Charles Noel Welman, Esq., recently built in the Tudor style, with extensive terraces, on the slope of a wooded hill. Belmont Lodge, J. E. Marshall, Esq.; Wheatley, Captain Barbor; Sandhill Park, Sir J. Hesketh Lethbridge, Bart. The mansion was built in 1720, since which it has undergone many alterations and improvements, two wings having been added to the building in 1815. The character of the edifice is Doric, with a portico supported by eight handsome columns at the entrance, and a bay in the eastern front corresponding with the same. The park is one of the most beautifully wooded in the county, commanding magnificent views of the vale, bounded by the Quantock Hills on the north-east, and the Blackdown Hills on the south. A little to the north of which, Cothelstone House, Edward Jeffries Esdaile, Esq. This mansion, which was erected some years ago by the present proprietor, is built of white sandstone from a quarry on the estate, and is a correct and fine specimen of the Grecian-Ionic architecture. The principal front has coupled pilasters supporting a regular entablature throughout, the centre being broken by two columns, which with the capitals, cornice, mouldings, &c., are taken from the Temple of Minerva Polias, at Athens. Cothelstone is most beautifully situated, and commands magnificent prospects over the Vale of Taunton and the Browndown and Blackdown Hills. Bagborough House, F. Popham, Esq. 4 m. further, Hartrow, Bickham Escott, Esq. 4 m. further, Nettlecombe Court, Sir Walter C. Trevelyan, Bart. 4 m. N. of which is WATCHET, and 2 m. N. Cleave Abbey. 3 m. N.W. of which DUNSTER. Dunster Castle, John F. Luttrell, Esq. It is situated on a steep hill at the southern extremity of the principal street; it is surrounded by beautiful parks embellished with trees, and affording pasture to a great number of sheep and deer; the view from it is delightful, varied, and extensive. The original castle was built prior to the Norman Conquest.

has some very fair public buildings, chapels, and excellent institutions, hospitals, almshouses, grammar and other schools, and charities. It still manufactures a few silks and woollens; and its trade, which consists principally in exports of agricultural and dairy produce, is carried on by means of the Bridgewater Canal. It returns two members to Parliament. The registered electors in 1848 numbered 1,016. Weekly markets, Wednesday and Saturday.

1 m. s. Wilton House, William Kinglake, Esq.; Eastshell House; John Wybart, Esq. 1 m. further, Orchard House. A little further, Amber House, John Gould, Esq.; Poundsford Park, Thomas Thompson, Esq.; Poundsford Lodge, C. J. Helyar, Esq.; Barton Grange, F. W. Newton, Esq.; Norton Manor, C. N. Welman, Esq.; Mounsell Court, General Sir J. Slade, Bart.; Linkford House, J. A. Allen, Esq. 3 m. s. Henlaide House, Mrs. Anderton. A little further, Hatch Court, William Oakes, Esq.; Hatch Villa, W. P. Collins, Esq. A little further, Crocombe Court, Mrs. Carew. 4 m. further, ILMINSTER, near which are Jordans House, William Speke, Esq.; Dillington House, J. Lee Lee, Esq. This mansion, which is supposed to have been erected in the time of Elizabeth, or her successor, is situated in a fertile vale, surrounded by a park, and beautifully diversified scenery. It is a handsome, gabled, stone edifice, its form being that of the letter E. In the centre of the principal front is an embattled porch, with a large mullioned window of painted glass on each side, giving light to the hall and apartments. The rear of the house is sheltered by a gently rising bank, which greatly contributes to the beauty of the situation. Barington Court, John Lee Lee, Esq. 3 m. further, at CREWKERNE, Hinton St. George, Earl Poulett. This mansion is supposed to have been erected by Sir Amias Poulett in the 15th century, and it certainly bears the characteristic features of the age in which he lived. The south front displays an extensive range of buildings in the castellated style, which has recently been improved. The principal carriage entrance is on the west side. At the end of the approach stands a finely-proportioned tower, and under a Gothic arch is the entrance to the grand hall, or saloon, which for elegance of construction is almost unequalled. This magnificent room leads to a noble suite of apartments. The body of the edifice is chiefly of stone, and is partially surmounted by a pierced parapet. The gardens attached to the mansion are highly cultivated, and the park, which is well timbered, commands fine prospects over the greater part of the county. 3 m. s. Crickett St. Thomas, Lord Bridport. 3 m. s.w. CHARD.

WELLINGTON, county of Somerset, is a market-town and parish, containing a population of 5,595, within an area of 4,830 A. The town is well built, and consists of four streets, the principal one, in the centre of which stands the market-house, being very spacious. The church is a large and handsome Gothic structure, with an elegant embattled tower at the west end, one hundred feet high. In its south chapel is a splendid monument to the memory of the learned Chief Justice Sir John Popham, who had also served the office of Speaker of the House of Commons, and was a native of this place, as well as its most munificent patron. His mansion here was garrisoned for the Parliament, and besieged by the Royalists, by whom it was destroyed. An hospital for twelve infirm persons, founded by him, is still in existence. Wellington has a union workhouse, several chapels, some woollen mills, and a celebrated manufacture of earthenware. This town has the honour to give the titles of Viscount, Earl, Marquis, and Duke to the hero of Waterloo, which glorious victory is commemorated by an obelisk 120 feet high, erected on a lofty hill three miles south of the town. E. Drakes Place, Mrs. Thomas; Heatherton Park, Alexander Adair,

2 m. w n.w. of Dunster is MINEHEAD, and 8 m. further being also 35 m. from Bridgewater,

ASHLEY COMBE, EARL OF LOVELACE.

This place, resembling a convent in the Apennines, stands 200 feet above the sea, on a terrace erected on the slopes of the bold wooded hills of North Somerset, which rise abruptly for 1,500 feet from the water's edge. The house commands a view northwards of Swansea Bay and the Welsh mountains of Carmarthenshire, and eastward up the Bristol Channel of above 30 miles. Owing to the mildness of the temperature, many of the shrubs and trees belonging to the southern climates endure the winters here, and grow with great vigour and beauty, especially the pine tribe.

½ m. N. Olridge House, Captain Maher. It is an ancient manor-house, situated in the centre of an extensive orchard and gardens, close to the river Tone. 1 m. N. Pyrland Hall, R. M. King, Esq. 1 m. further, Hester-combe, Miss Warre. 2 m. further, Tetton House, J. D. Acland, Esq. 1 m. further, Fine Court.

3 m. N.E. Walford, R. King Meade King, Esq. The grounds are finely timbered, and the range of the Quantock Hills immediately behind afford some of the most picturesque views in the county. Monkton House, E. W. Rundell, Esq.

1 m. N. Nynehead Court, E. A. Sanford, Esq. 2 m. N.W. Shipley Park. 1 m. further, Spring Grove, J. Spurway, Esq.; Court House, A. Glass, Esq. MILVERTON, a very ancient market-town, situated in a richly wooded country, well cultivated and very populous. 3 m. S.S.W. WYVELL LIS-COMBE, called by the Saxons Whitefield Liscombe, is encompassed on every side, with the exception of a small opening towards Taunton, by lofty hills, whose summits are encircled by beautiful woods. At the time of the Romans this was a place of some importance, as appears from the remains of an encampment, or large Castreme, on a hill about a mile from the town, still called the Castle. The summit of this hill contains about five acres, and vestiges of fortifications and foundations of buildings have often been dis-covered near its surface; in the year 1711 numerous Roman coins were found.

North of Wellington are London House, J. Walrond, Esq.; Tone Dale, Henry Fox, Esq.; Swallowfield, Mrs. Jackson; Fox Dove, Charles Fox, Esq.; Binden House, H. G. Moysey, Esq.; Wellesley House, H. G. Smith, Esq.

Esq. The mansion house, built by the late Sir Thomas Gunston, Knight, has been greatly enlarged and improved by the present possessor. Though standing on an eminence, and commanding extensive views of the vale, *Enter Devonshire.* it is so encircled with stately timber that only a partial view of it can be obtained from the railway, and that not of the principal front, which looks upon the range of the Blackdown Hills.

1 m. E. Bridwell House, John Were Clarke, Esq. The mansion is a *179 m. TIVERTON* handsome modern building, situated on a fine sloping lawn, bounded by a *JUNCTION STA.* fine sheet of water and some fine overhanging trees. The grounds are diversified, well stocked with timber, and display many pleasing prospects. 2 m. further, HEMYOCK, an extensive parish bordering on Somersetshire. It formerly contained a castle, which had two round towers at the entrance, with a portcullis, and was enclosed with an entrenchment. In the time of the civil wars it was garrisoned against Charles I., and is believed to have been demolished soon after the Restoration. It is thought Hemyock Castle was built on Roman foundations, as the hills in this neighbourhood abound with iron pits, and quantities of wood and iron scoria are found in this and the neighbouring parish. 1 m. s. The ruins of Dewkswell Abbey; a little further, Walford Lodge. The house is delightfully situated on the south side of a high range of hills. Fine hanging woods and young plantations decorate the declivities. The mansion was built about the beginning of the present century, and the prospects from it and the surrounding hills embrace much beautiful scenery, including the city of Exeter, the towns of Honiton and Ottery, the courses of the Exe, Otter, and other streams. South-west from the house, at a short distance, is a large entrenchment called Hembury Fort, supposed to have been the Roman station, Moridunum, or the site of a Roman camp. Roman coins and antiquities have been found in the immediate neighbourhood.

5 m. S.E. Hembury Grange, Edward Simco Drew, Esq.; Hembury Fort *181¼ m. COLLUMP-* House, William Porter, Esq. 4 m. further, HONITON. Honiton has been *TON STA.* noted for the valuable quality of its lace, some kinds of which were sold for more than five guineas per yard, being made of thread imported from the Netherlands, and rivalling in beauty and excellence Brussels lace. In the vicinity of the town are quarries, producing a peculiar quality of stone, used for making whet-stones for scythes, the trade in which is by no means inconsiderable. 3 m. further, AXMINSTER. 3 m. further, RHODE HILL, Hon. Admiral Sir John Talbot, K.C.B. 2 m. further, LYME REGIS. In the neighbourhood of Lyme Regis, Weare Cliff, Robert Ray, Esq.; Penhay House, John Ames, Esq.; Monckton Wild, Rev. R. S. Hutchings; Wootton House, F. Drew, Esq.; Ford Abbey, — Mialls, Esq.; Sadboro' House, Colonel Bragge; Fairfield, John Hill, Esq.; Somerhill House, P. Risden, Esq. Fern Hill, C. Bowden, Esq.; Hay, B. Clewett, Esq.

Enter Devonshire.

179 m. TIVERTON JUNCTION STA.

Tiverton Br. ☞

TIVERTON. From this station is a line to Tiverton, in the county of Devon, a parliamentary and municipal borough town, on both sides of the rivers Exe and Loman. It is of great antiquity, delightfully situated on the slope of a hill, and contains four principal streets, in a triangular form, enclosing an area of gardens, in the centre of which is a fine bowling-green. The borough contains a population of 10,040, within an area of 16,790 A. The principal buildings are the castle, the church, and the free grammar school. The castle, from its remains, appears to have been a place of great strength, and in the reigns of King Stephen and Charles I. it was often the scene of military operations. The church is considered the finest in the whole county, with the exception only of Exeter Cathedral. Its tower is 116 feet in height. The view from the churchyard over the river Exe in its serpentine course, the fertile plain of pasture ground on its banks, the buildings of Westex, and beyond all the rising hills; the ruins of the castle, surrounded by venerable trees, appearing on the right, and Exe Bridge on the left, baffles all description: it must be seen to be appreciated. The grammar school, founded by a private gentleman, Peter Blundell, is a noble building, cased with Purbeck-stone. Tiverton possesses also other grammar and endowed schools, almshouses and charities, a town hall, theatre, market-house, corn market, assembly and reading rooms. Many of its inhabitants are employed in the manufacture of lace, and some in woollens. A navigable canal connects it with the Tone, Taunton, &c. It sends two members to Parliament, and the number of its registered electors in 1848 amounted to 442. Tiverton has suffered much at different periods from fire and pestilential diseases. Collipriest House; Rembarton Court; Tiverton Court; Ashley Court; Hensley House; Calverleigh Court, Joseph Charles Nagle, Esq. 3 m. N. BAMPTON. The town is pleasantly situated in a vale, watered by the river Exe. A chalybeate spring, strongly impregnated with iron, rises near the town. The site of an ancient castle, erected in 1336 by a member of the family of Coburn, is still discernible. John de Bampton, a Carmelite, and the first who read Aristotle publicly at Cambridge, was a native of this town. 4 m. s.w. of Tiverton is Creweyshays House. 4 m. further, SOUTH MOLTON. Castle Hill, Earl Fortescue; Cochrane House; Little Bray House, — King, Esq.; Court Hall, Lord Poltimore.

181½ m. COLLUMP-TON STA.

COLLUMPTON. A market-town and parish, county of Devon, built on a small elevation gradually declining towards the river Culm. The parish contains an area of 5,790 A. The town, which suffered greatly by fire in 1839, is tolerably well built; it has many antique houses, some slated and others thatched, and its church, dedicated to the Virgin Mary, originally collegiate, is a curious and venerable structure, consisting of three aisles, containing an area of 4,621 feet, with an elegant roof of gilt carved work, highly ornamented with seraphim, &c. At the south side of the church is another separate aisle, built by John Lane, a clothier of the town (temp. Henry VIII.), and called after him, "Lane's aisle." The tower is a remarkable piece of architecture, 100 feet high, ornamented with lions, eagles, &c. Collumpton is a polling-place for the north division of the county; has county sessions, and a large serge factory. Market, Saturday; fairs, 1st Monday in May and November.

2 m. s.w. Killerton Park, Sir Thomas Dyke Acland, Bart., M.P. The mansion is a splendid edifice, and its situation under an eminence, clothed with the most luxuriant trees, is most happy. The park by which it is encircled contains some noble timber, and is well stocked with deer and game of every description, and in many situations the most delightful prospects over the vale are obtained.

EXETER is a city of great antiquity, and has for centuries been con- sidered as a place of importance; it is the capital of the county of Devon, a municipal and parliamentary borough, a river-port, a bishopric, and a county in itself. It is situate upon the river Exe, which is here crossed by a handsome stone bridge. It is about three miles in circumference, the area of the city, which includes nineteen parishes, being 1,800 a., with a population of 31,312—the population of the whole borough being 37,231. It has two main streets, each nearly two miles in length, and crossing at right angles. Many handsome modern squares and terraces are intermixed with antique narrow streets, and there are two fine market places, and several suburbs containing numerous elegant villas. Its venerable cathe- dral, which was commenced in the 13th century, is a noble specimen of ancient English architecture, the beauties of which we cannot attempt to describe in a work of this limited nature. The episcopal palace was built in the reign of Edward IV., and there are fifteen churches within and four without the city walls, many of which have claims upon the traveller's attention. In the north-east front of the city are the ruins of the castle of Rougemont, once a strong fortress and of great extent; it was formerly the residence of the West Saxon Kings. Independently of the interest these ruins inspire with the lovers of antiquity, the views from the ramparts over the proverbially picturesque scenery of this part of Devonshire are most enchanting. When the castle was erected is unknown, but it was either rebuilt or repaired by William the Conqueror. In the castle-yard stands the county sessions house. The principal public buildings of the city are the grammar school (founded 1633), a modern county hospital, lunatic, blind, deaf and dumb asylums, female penitentiary, infirmary and work- house, a county and city gaol and bridewell, large cavalry and artillery barracks, ancient guildhall, containing some interesting portraits, a theatre, circus, baths, ball-room, park, promenade, several fountains, a public library, museum, athenæum, mechanics', and scientific and literary institu- tions, about six banks, custom house, bonding warehouse and cloth halls. There are many other well-endowed schools and ancient hospitals. Exeter has also five weekly newspapers, and there are still some manufactures of serges, paper, &c., large breweries and iron foundries; but its trade has declined notwithstanding the improvement of its port by the formation of a floating basin, and the deepening of the Anchorship Canal to Topsham, by which vessels of 300 tons may now approach the city. Markets, Wednesday, Friday, and Saturday—Friday being the largest for corn and wool in the west of England. Races in August. Corporate revenue (1847), £8,195; corpo- rate debt (two-thirds of which was incurred by the ship canal), £150,000. Exeter sends two members to Parliament, and has done so since 1286. Registered electors in 1847, 3,798; it is also the place of election for the south division of the county. Exeter was erected into a bishopric in 1050, by Edward the Confessor: it comprises four archdeaneries and 640 benefices, including nearly the whole of Cornwall and Devon. The episcopal revenue in 1831 was £2,700; the revenue of dean and chapter, inclusive of twenty- four prebendaries, about £10,000.

4 m. N. Stoke House, E. A. Sanders, Esq.

4 m. N.N.E. Poltimore House, Lord Poltimore.

5 m. N.E. BLUE HAYS. 6 m. N.E. by E. TAYSBEAR. A little further, Rockbear House. 4 m. further, OTTERY ST. MARY.

4 m. E. Bishop's Court, John Garrett, Esq. Close to which is Winslade

185¼ m. HELE STATION.	2½ m. W. BRADNINCH, which formerly sent two members to Parliament, is now almost in ruins. Its church is an ancient Gothic structure, dedicated to St. Denys.

1½ m. N. Pynes, Sir Stafford Northcote, Bart. 5 m. further, ESCOMBE and CADBURY. 5 m. N.W. Downes, J. W. Buller, Esq. 4 m. W. Fulford House, B. Fulford, Esq. Although this venerable mansion has undergone many alterations, it still retains most of its original architectural character. It stands on a gentle eminence near a noble sheet of water, and consists of a quadrangle, with a large entrance gateway, from whence there is also a door leading to a neat chapel. Over the gateway are sculptured the arms of the Fulford family. This house was garrisoned for King Charles during the civil wars, and suffered greatly; but was afterwards thoroughly repaired by Colonel Francis Fulford. In this mansion is the portrait of King Charles, by Vandyke, presented to Sir Francis Fulford, Knt., by the King, as a testimony of his royal approbation. The park abounds with every description of forest tree, beautiful plantations, and that undulating surface which creates so great a charm in landscape, whilst the scenery in the vicinity and the views of the distant country are extremely delightful. Close to which is Creedy House, Col. Sir H. F. Davy, Bart. This elegant mansion has two fine fronts, and is delightfully situated in an extensive park, surrounded by a high wall. It was here that the learned Sir Humphrey Davy, Bart., resided. A little to the south CREDITON, a borough, market-town and parish in Devon. In the reign of Edward I. this place sent members to a Parliament held at Carlisle, and in 1316 Bishop Stapleton obtained for it the grant of a market and two annual fairs. Towards the end of the 16th century the opponents of the Reformation assembled their forces at Crediton, but were compelled to withdraw by Sir Peter Carew, who was sent against them with a superior force. In 1644 Charles I. reviewed his troops in this town, which was subsequently possessed by the army under Sir Thomas Fairfax. Crediton is pleasantly situated in a vale, on the banks of the river Creedy, and within ¾ of a mile of the river Exe, with which this river unites near Exeter. 2 m. Coombe, John Sallifant, Esq.; Stockleigh Court, J. P. Bellew, Esq. 12 m. further, CHULMLEIGH. 1¼ m. s. of Chulmleigh, Edgersford House.

4 m. further, KING'S NIMPTON. Broome House, D. G. Pearce, Esq.; New Place, Sir P. P. F. P. Acland, Bart. 10 m. further, BARNSTAPLE. This place, a Saxon borough in the reign of Athelstan, was formerly a port of considerable trade, and a principal depôt for wool, from which circumstance it seems to have derived its name. In 1588 it furnished three ships to assist Queen Elizabeth in her expedition against the Spanish Armada, and during the civil war in the time of Charles I. it was the scene of several conflicts between the rival troops. It is pleasantly situated in a fertile vale, sheltered by a range of hills, on the east side of the river Taw, over which there is a bridge of sixteen arches. Upcott, J. W. Harding, Esq.; Bremsworthy House, S. May, Esq.; Towstock Court, Sir Bourchier Palk Wrey; Fremington House, W. A. Yeo, Esq.; Kingdoms; Youlston, Sir Arthur Chichester, Bart.; Arlington Court, Sir John Palmer Bruce Chichester, Bart.; Inkledon Castle. 8 m. N. of Barnstaple, ILFRACOMBE.

8 m. w. at TAPHOUSE. Fulford House, B. Fulford, Esq. 5 m. further, Twidge House. 8 m. further, OAKHAMPTON. Is an ancient town situated in a recluse valley surrounded by hills. At the time of the Domesday Survey it was held by Baldwin de Brioniis, a Norman, whose exertions for the Conqueror were rewarded by the office of Hereditary Sheriff of Devon; he built a castle here which he made his principal residence. The ruins of this castle are situated about one mile south-west of the town, on a high

House, Henry Porter, Esq.   2 m. further, Farringdon House.   It is a
spacious and commodious mansion, the grounds pleasant, and the plantations
particularly flourishing.   The view from Windmill Hill, at a short distance
from the house, supposed to be the site of a Roman entrenchment, is
beautiful and extensive.   From the reign of Richard I. until the beginning
of the 16th century this estate belonged to the family of Farringdon, the
last of whom committed suicide through sorrow at the loss of his wife.
5 m. further, HARPFORD.   3 m. s.e. from which is SIDMOUTH.   11 m.
further, COLYTON.   3 m. w. of which is Wiscombe Park.   3 m. s.e. North
Brea House ; Wear House, Sir J. T. B. Duckworth, Bart., M.P. ;
The Retreat, A. H. Hamblin, Esq.   A little further, TOPSHAM.
1 m. Elford House, Colonel Lee.   1 m. further, on the east bank of the
Exe, Nutwell Court, Sir T. T. F. E. Drake, Bart.   1 m. further, Courtlands,
J. Spicer, Esq.   7 m. e. from Topsham is Bicton Lodge, Lady Rolle.
This elegant mansion, for many years the seat of the late venerable Lord
Rolle, is a spacious building, with beautiful gardens, standing in a fine
park, plentifully stocked with oak and beech trees, and abounding in deer
and every description of game.

*EXETER
(continued).*

Exeter to Plymouth.

It is scarcely possible to picture to one's mind a more beautiful country than that which is
traversed by the South Devon Railway in its short journey of fifty-three miles from
Exeter to Plymouth.   It is true that this line, like the preceding line from Bristol to
Exeter, does not present to the eye of the traveller those colossal works which attest the
skill and science of the engineer, and are so conspicuous on the Great Western and other
lines ; but the natural beauties of hills and valleys, magnificent sea-views—the railroad
absolutely skirting the ocean for many miles after leaving Exeter—the splendid seats with
which the county is studded, and the venerable towns and primitive villages passed in
rapid succession, each vying with the other in all that constitutes the picturesque and the
beautiful, these lovely scenes more than compensate for the absence of stupendous
viaducts, or the dark and dismal tunnels which pierce the bowels of the earth.   After
leaving the Exeter Terminus, the line crosses the river Exe by a handsome bridge, and
continues its course along the right bank to Starcross, a little beyond which it skirts the

Left of Railway from Exeter.

*Distance from
London.*

2 m. E. crossing the river Exe, EXMOUTH.   It derives its name from its
proximity to the mouth of the river Exe, and is one of the most frequented
watering-places in Devon, its rise having being very rapid, as little more
than a century back it was a small hamlet inhabited by fishermen.   One of
the Judges on circuit received great benefit from its waters about the
period named, which first brought Exmouth into repute.   It is furnished
with every accommodation necessary for a watering-place.   The town is well
sheltered from the north-east and south-east winds by lofty hills which rise close
behind.   There are many good houses and an excellent assembly room, &c.
The walks are delightfully pleasant, and command splendid views.   The
tourist is presented with a magnificent view of about twenty miles (from
a hill called Chapel Hill), extending along the coast from Exeter to Berry
Head.   This line is broken by several hills that gradually ascend from the
coast on the opposite side of the river, which is interspersed with splendid
wood and foliage.   Behind these hills spring up bold towering headlands,
woody summits, and rocks so formed as to constitute a complete landscape.
EAST BUDLEIGH.   A parish in the hundred of East Budleigh in the county
of Devon.   The antiquity of the place is evinced by its having given name

202 m. STARCROSS
STATION.

EXETER
(*continued*).

mass of rock which rises from the verdant meadows of the valley, and is skirted on one side by the western branch of the river. The extensive area which they include, the solidity of their structure, and the advantages of situation, prove that this fortress before it was dismantled must have been strong and important. A lofty keep rises magnificently from a large conoidal elevation, which is opposed on the other side of the stream by a deep wooded bank. The river meanders through the intervening meadows, and laves with its waters the roots of the ruined walls. The whole of the surrounding scenery is exceedingly pleasing, the acclivities being covered with fine woods which, in combination with the mouldering turrets and ivy-clad ruins of the castle, form some very picturesque views. The church like the castle is situated on an eminence at some distance from the town, and from the opposite heights makes a fine landscape. The old chapel in the market-place was founded originally as a chantry. Oakhampton Park; Oaklands, Albany B. Savile, Esq. s.w. Peamore, Samuel K. Kekewich, Esq. 2 m. s.w. Shillenford Abbey. Near which is Haldon House, Sir Lawrence V. Palk, Bart.: Kenbury House. A little further, Trayhill House, J. H. Ley, Esq.

Exeter to Plymouth.

sea by Dawlish, &c., until it arrives at Teignmouth, whence it continues its course along the north bank of the Teign, which it crosses just before arriving at Newton Bushel, one mile beyond which station a branch line diverges to Torquay, a distance of five miles. After crossing the river Dart, by a well-constructed bridge, it reaches Totness, from whence, verging westward, it approaches the mountainous district of Dartmoor Forest, in which many distant eminences rise from 1,500 to nearly 2,000 feet above the level of the sea. Between the Brent and Kingsbridge Road Station, the railway is carried over the river Avon by a good bridge, and across the Erme beyond the Ivy Bridge Station, by a fine viaduct. Two other rivers, the Yelme and the Plym, are crossed by well-constructed and handsome bridges before arriving at Plymouth. It is almost an idle compliment to state that the works upon this line, although partaking chiefly of the ordinary routine of railway construction, have been, not only most efficiently, but admirably performed.

Distance from London.

Right of Railway from Exeter.

202 m. STARCROSS STATION.

STARCROSS, a small sea-port town, in the parish of Kenton, situated on the west side of the river Exe, and much frequented as a watering-place. On an eminence in the neighbourhood is a conspicuous landmark, erected in 1773, by Lord Courtenay, consisting of a lofty triangular tower, with an hexagonal turret rising from each corner. 2 m. N. Powderham Castle, Lord Courtenay. The castle is situated on the banks of the river Exe, which, at high water, is one mile and a half broad, and about three miles from its confluence with the Bristol Channel. The views from the house are extensive, picturesque, and beautiful, with an uninterrupted prospect of the ocean to the west. The mansion, although of vast antiquity, has been altered in its external appearance since 1752, up to which period its embattled towers, frowning turrets, its draw-bridges and portcullis, still retained the formidable aspect of the ancient fortress. It is however still a castellated building, but of the modern style, and the interior contains many noble apartments. The grounds of Powderham are very extensive, the park well stocked with deer, the shrubberies, plantations, lawns, pleasure-grounds, are all on scale of grandeur and magnificence, the domain lying within a circumference of about ten miles. On an eminence in the park is

to the hundred. A market was formerly held on *Sunday* and afterwards on Monday, but is now wholly discontinued. There is an annual fair held on Easter Tuesday. Budleigh Salterton in this parish is rising into repute as a watering-place; hot and cold baths have been built, and there is good accommodation provided for visitors. There are some remains of an ancient chapel dedicated to St. James. The church is a small structure. At Poer Hayes, formerly a mansion, now a farm-house, the celebrated Sir Walter Raleigh was born about the year 1552.

On Dawlish Beach are neatly-built baths, library, reading room, billiard and assembly rooms. An annual regatta is generally celebrated in August. The towering cliffs which overhang the sea, give an air of grandeur to the scenery which is finely contrasted with the rich fertility of the vale and the luxuriant foliage of the wood-crowned heights. 1 m. N.N.E. MOUNT PLEASANT.

206 m. DAWLISH STATION.

TEIGNMOUTH, a maritime town, occupying a site on both sides of the river Teign at its mouth in the English Channel, in the county of Devon. The two parishes of East and West Teignmouth contain an area of 1,280 A. and a population of 4,459; and are connected by a bridge of many arches, one of which opens or swings so as to admit vessels of between 350 and 400 tons to pass into the river. The climate of Teignmouth is so mild that geraniums, myrtles, &c. grow in the open air. Teignmouth, which is now one of the most fashionable bathing-places on the western coast, is a place of great antiquity: it was burnt by the Danes, and again nearly destroyed during the early part of the 18th century when the French landed and set fire to the town. The situation is beautiful, and the scenery very picturesque. The sea views are magnificent, while it is sheltered on the east and north-east by a range of hills, at the base of which stands the pretty village of Shaddon, which forms a suburb to West Teignmouth. The cliffs have a singular deep-red colour, which contrasts strangely with the occasional patches of verdure. The Den and other public gardens are beautifully planted, and nothing in fact is wanting to render it agreeable to the visitors who frequent this delightful spot. The principal buildings are the new octangular church of West Teignmouth, besides other places of worship, spacious assembly rooms, a theatre, and the bathing establishment. Here is also a dockyard, in which small ships of war have been occasionally launched, and a quay from which considerable quantities of pipe-clay and granite are exported. Coal and provisions are its chief imports. Market, Saturday.

209 m. TEIGN-MOUTH STA.

2 m. E. HACCOMBE, a demesne long inherited by the Carew family. It enjoys some extraordinary privileges—it is not included in any hundred; no officer, civil or military, has right to take cognizance of any proceedings in this parish; and by a royal grant from the crown it was exempt from all duties and taxes, in consequence of some noble service done by an ancestor of the Carews. It is the smallest parish in England as to the number of dwellings, which are two only—the mansion-house and the parsonage.

214 m. NEWTON STATION.

4 m. E. TORQUAY, a market-town and chapelry, situated in a cove of Torbay, in the county of Devon. Population, 4,085. This favourite watering-place is so sheltered by heights, the climate so temperate, and the scenery so picturesque and beautiful, that it affords a pleasant retreat for invalids and persons of delicate health. The town consists principally of ranges of terraces, built in a superior manner, on the slopes of the hill down to the quay, interspersed with elegant villas, admirable hotels, with library, assembly, and news' rooms, mechanics' and other institutes, capital schools, a bank, and all necessary bathing establishments. The harbour is good, and Torquay has some timber trade, a share in the Newfoundland fishery, excellent markets, and steam communication with Portsmouth and Ply-

219 m. TORQUAY STATION.

the Belvidere Tower, built in 1773, which commands the most delightful prospects in this most beautiful part of England. 2 m. w. Mamhead, Sir Robert William Newman, Bart. The mansion was commenced by Sir Peter Ball, Knight, an eminent loyalist, in 1680, and was finished by his son. It subsequently came into the possession of the first Earl of Lisburne, who greatly improved the estate. In front of the house, the smooth verdure of the lawn is relieved by groups of trees and shrubs judiciously disposed, while towards Haldown Hill, the most beautiful plantations of firs and forest trees are crowned at the top of the hill, called Mamhead Point, by an obelisk of Portland stone, 100 feet high. The views of the surrounding country are most beautiful from this spot.

206 m. DAWLISH STATION. DAWLISH, a village on the British Channel, county of Devon. Area of parish, 4,710 A. It is much resorted to for sea-bathing, its scenery and climate are delightful, and it has a fine beach. 1 m. w. Luscombe House, Charles Hoare, Esq.

209 m. TEIGN- MOUTH STA. ½ m. Eastcliffe House, G. S. Curtis, Esq. ½ m. further, Brookfield House, — Winstanley Esq. 2 m. N.W. Lindridge. The present mansion, spacious as it is, is but a very fragment of the enormous pile originally standing on this site, which is said to have covered an acre of ground. The present edifice is formed out of the central part of the old mansion, and contains many noble apartments, amongst which is one fitted up as a ball-room, in 1673, and preserved untouched from that period. The panels are of burnished gold, the gilding having cost £500. The grounds are sweetly picturesque and finely wooded—oak, beech, chestnut, elm, plane, and walnut flourishing so luxuriantly, as to be the theme of admiration throughout the county. 4 m. further, at CHUDLEIGH, Ugbrooke House, Lord Clifford. This is considered one of the most enchanting spots in the county, the grounds containing every object which constitutes beautiful scenery—woods, lakes, rocks, cataracts, lawns, and inequalities of surface; while the noble park, plentifully stocked with deer and game of every sort, abounds with elm, oak, chestnut, and ash, of the most luxuriant growth; and with the home, or pleasure-grounds, occupies an area of eight miles in circumference. The mansion is built in the quadrangular form, having two fronts, and four towers furnished with battlements, and rough-coated. The internal accommodation is most complete, the rooms being generally spacious and numerous, and the state apartments of noble dimensions. The library and chapel form an additional wing, which communicates with the main building by a large room and a lofty gallery. 3 m. N.W. from Chudleigh, Canonteign, Viscount Exmouth.

214 m. NEWTON STATION. NEWTON, or NEWTON-ABBOT, with NEWTON-BUSHEL, form a market-town in the parish of Woolborough, in the county of Devon, on the river Teign. 2 m. N.W. Stover Lodge, Duke of Somerset. 2 m. s.w. Hogwell House, P. J. Taylor, Esq.

219 m. TORQUAY STATION. 6 m. w. ASHBURTON, a parliamentary borough, market-town, and parish, county of Devon, was anciently called Aiseburtone. It was made a town by charter of Edward III., in 1328, being noted for the mines of tin and copper which then abounded in the neighbourhood. In the parliamentary war, having been previously occupied by the royal troops under Lord Wentworth, it was taken by the parliamentary troops under General Fairfax on his march westward, in January, 1654. The town is surrounded by hills, and consists principally of one long street. It is well supplied with water, the river Yeo running through the town, and the river Dart within 1½ miles. The manufacture of serge for the East India Company is carried on to a great extent, the annual returns being said to exceed £100,000.

mouth. A portion of the ancient abbey is now used as a Roman Catholic chapel. Chelston, Sir John Louis, Bart.; Fuze Park, Mrs. Grundy. Torbay, an inlet of the English Channel, is one of the most picturesque bays on the Devonshire coast, and lies between the headlands of Bob's Nose and Berry Head. Latitude of the last-named 50° 24′ north; longitude, 3° 28′ west. The cliffs by which the bay is environed abound in fine marble quarries, and contain some highly curious caverns. On the west lie Brixham and Paington; and during the prevalence of the westerly winds the bay is crowded with shipping. It was at this place that the Prince of Orange landed in 1688. Torbay has important fisheries.

TOTNESS, a parliamentary and municipal borough, market-town and parish, situated on the river Dart, in the county of Devon, opposite Bridgetown, with which it is connected by a bridge. Area of borough, which comprises the parish of Totness and the manor of Bridgetown, 1,411 A.; population, 4,240. It sends two members to Parliament; registered electors (1848), 378. Totness is a town of remote antiquity, and consists principally of one long street, in which some of the houses are ornamented with piazzas, while the upper stories project considerably over the lower. The castle, the keep of which is still in tolerable preservation, is a large circular turreted building, standing on an immense artificial mound. The church is a fine edifice, and its handsome tower is adorned with pinnacles. Bridgetown, which may be regarded as its suburb, contains more modern erections. Here are several places of worship, an endowed grammar and blue-coat schools, a guildhall, council house, theatre, assembly rooms, &c. The situation of Totness is highly picturesque, and the scenery in the vicinity most pleasing. Corporation revenue (1848), £438. 1 m. N.E. Gatcombe Park, Captain B. Williams; Park Hill, John Harris, Esq. A little further, Bury House, Thomas M. Moore, Esq.; Loventor, Sir George Baker, Bart. 1 m. S.E. by E. Weston House, George Farwell, Esq. 4 m. further, Whatton Court, Henry Studdy, Esq.; Sandridge, Lord Cranstoun; Greenaway House, Colonel Carlyon. S.W. Magonett, R. P. Hulme, Esq.; Sharpham, Richard Durant, Esq.; Ashprinkton House, Major Northcutt. 2 m. s.

222¾ m. TOTNESS STATION.

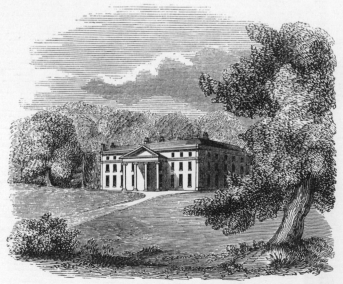

FOLLATON HOUSE, GEORGE S. CARY, ESQ.

The mines of tin and copper are still worked, as also some very fine quarries of slate. The church, dedicated to St. Andrew, was formerly collegiate, It is a venerable and spacious cruciform structure, in the later style of English architecture, built in the form of a cross, and having a handsome tower ninety feet high terminated by a small spire. In the chancel are several stalls; and in one part is a memorial stating that in 1754 the representatives of the borough "chose to express their thanks to their constituents by purchasing an estate for educating the boys of the borough." Adjoining the church is an ancient chapel or chantry, now used as a grammar school. 3 m. N.W. Buckland Court, E. R. P. Bastard, Esq.

222¾ m. TOTNESS STATION.

1 m. N. Dartington Hall, A. Champernowne, Esq. This was a place of some importance at the time of the Norman Conquest, as William gave it to William de Falaise. In the reign of Richard II. it was escheated to the Crown, and about a century afterwards it came into the possession of an ancestor of the present proprietor. The hall is a building, or rather mass of buildings, of considerable antiquity, of as early a date as the commencement of the 15th century. It stands on an elevated spot, and commands fine views of the beautiful vale of Totness and other distant places. The walls are of black marble, and strongly built. The hall, or apartments now used, appear to be nothing more than offices to the originally superb structure. From the remains of walls, it is evident it comprised a double quadrangle. Opposite the present edifice are the remains of an immense range of building, supported by an arched front, and the foundations of several walls have been discovered at various times. The ancient mansion was approached by a flight of steps from five doorways projecting from the front. In the present mansion is a fine apartment, called the Great Hall, 70 feet in length, and 40 feet wide. The roof is of oak, curiously framed. and the chimney-piece 14 feet high. The outside is embattled and strengthened by buttresses. There are a collection of paintings by the first masters. The Vineyard, Rev. Richard Champernowne.

N.W. Wensland, Charles Weller, Esq.; Broomborough, James T. P. Phillips, Esq.; Fristford, E. W. W. Pendarves, Esq. BERRY. Pomeroy Castle. The ruins of this magnificent fortress are situated on a rocky eminence, at the base of which flows a beautiful brook, and, combined with the general scenery of the district, forms one of the most picturesque objects in the whole county. The castle was erected by one of the noble family of Pomeroy, shortly after the Conquest; and his progeny resided here until the reign of Edward VI., when the estate was sold to Edward Seymour, Duke of Somerset, in which family it has remained ever since. The principal remains are, the great gate, the walls of the south front, the north wing of the court, or quadrangle, some apartments on the west side, and two turrets beautifully mantled with ivy. BUCKFASTLEIGH, a village. An abbey was founded here by Ethelwardus, in the reign of Henry I., and vestiges of it are still to be seen. Many of the houses in the village, with a large manufactory, were built with materials from the ruins of the abbey, and a modern Gothic mansion has been erected on part of its site. Prior to the dissolution a weekly market was held—the market-house is still standing. The church is situated on an eminence northward from the village, and comprises a nave, chancel, transepts, and a tower, and two small chapels on the north and south sides. Within the limits of the parish are vestiges of an encampment.

At Tor Abbey and Follaton Park reside the descendants of the historic family of Cary, the parent stem of the Lords Hunsdon and Falkland—the former nearly related to Queen Elizabeth, and the latter rendered illustrious by the cavalier Lord Falkland, "the generous and the just." Dundridge House, the property of J. Parrett, Esq., unoccupied; Sandwell House, Mrs. Bennett; Bowders House, William D. Adams, Esq. The mansion cannot be seen from the railroad, but some of the plantations are visible at the hill overlooking Totness. In the approach from the lodge to the house there is a beautiful and extensive view over the surrounding country, bounded by the high hills of Dartmoor. 4 m. s.w. DARTMOUTH, a parliamentary and municipal borough and sea-port, most picturesquely built on a steep acclivity, forming a succession of terraces often connected by stairs. The Government dockyard and quay project into the river. It is defended at its entrance by a strong castle and battlement. It sends one member to Parliament, and gives the title of Earl to the Legge family.

BRENT, or SOUTH BRENT, on the river Avon, in the county of Devon. Area of parish, 10,180 A.; about seven miles from Ashburton. The church of South Brent contains some very ancient and curiously-carved seats. 1 m. s. Black Hall, James Cornish, Esq.

229¼ m. BRENT STATION.

Kingsbridge Road. 3 m. L. MODBURY. 6 m. S.E. KINGSBRIDGE.

231¾ m. KINGS-BRIDGE ROAD STATION.

IVY BRIDGE derives its name from the bridge covered with ivy, which here crosses the river Eune. It is a village and chapelry in the county of Devon, lying in several parishes. 2 m. s. Fleet House, John C. Bulteel, Esq.

235 m. IVY BRIDGE STA.

PLYMPTON, or PLYMPTON ST. MARY, in the county of Devon. Area of parish, 11,200 A. ½ m. s. lies PLYMPTON MAURICE, or EARL'S PLYMPTON, a market and stannary town, and a municipal borough by prescription. Area of parish, 170 A.; population, 933. It was formerly a place of some importance, but is now decayed. The town is ancient and irregularly built. The guildhall, an antique building, contains a portrait of Sir Joshua Reynolds, who was a native of the place, painted by himself; an endowed school, and the ruins of a castle. Market, Saturday. 1½ m. w. Saltram House, Earl of Morley; Chaddlewood, Mrs. Symons. 2 m. s. Kitley, E. R. P. Bastard, Esq. Situated near the estuary of the Yealm, formerly the seat of the Pollexfen family. Edmund Pollexfen, a distinguished lawyer, died in 1710 without male issue; and his daughter married William Bastard of Gerston, whose descendants have ever since resided at Kitley. The present house was built by the late E. P. Bastard, Esq., M.P. for South Devon, from the designs of Mr. Repton.

241¾ m. PLYMP-TON STA.

PLYMOUTH, a parliamentary and municipal borough, sea-port town, and naval station, situated on the east side of a peninsula between the rivers Plym and Tamar, at the head of Plymouth Sound, in the hundred of Roborough, in the county of Devon. The borough comprises the parish of Stoke Damerel, and contains a population of 36,527, and with the adjacent borough of Devonport the united area consists of 2,300 A., and a population of 80,059. Plymouth sends two members to Parliament; registered electors (1848), 2,231. The town is irregularly built and laid out, but the buildings have a fine substantial appearance. The citadel, a fine bastioned fortress, stands on the top of a cliff in the Hoe, an open space between the town and the Sound, and contains fine barracks and the residence of the governor; and in this vicinity are several handsome modern streets. The chief buildings of the town are the guildhall, new market-place, gaol, the

246¾ m. PLY-MOUTH STA.

229¼ m. BRENT STATION.

1½ m. N.W. SHARPTAWE, in Dartmoor Forest. This forest was originally made by King John, and its boundary set out by perambulation in the reign of Edward III. From its higher parts innumerable streams descend, spreading beauty and fertility through a considerable portion of the country. Its surface is also diversified by vast masses of granite, which spring up at various parts, and are distinguished by the name of Taws, and may be seen at the distance of many miles. It was at one of these, at Crochem Taw, that the Stannary Parliaments of this county held their meetings.

231¾ m. KINGS-BRIDGE ROAD STATION.

2 m. N.W. HARFORD.

235 m. IVY BRIDGE STA.

2 m. N.W. COMWOOD, a parish in the hundred of Ermington. The church, dedicated to St. Michael, contains three stone stalls. The ground is hilly, with several small streams encompassing the parish; the river Yealm running through it, and the Orme separating it from the parish of Harford, one mile from the Stake.

241¼ m. PLYMP-TON STA.

1 m. N. Boringdon Park, Earl of Morley. The house was built about the end of the 14th century; and although it has been much altered and diminished, it still contains a fine old hall and other good rooms. It has been occupied as a farm-house. Close to the house is a deer park, of about 500 acres, which includes a variety of fine and picturesque scenery. At the beginning of the last century, Lady Cotham removed her residence from Boringdon to Sotham. 1½ m. w. Elfordleigh, R. W. Langmeade, Esq. 1 m. further, Little Efford, G. W. Soltau, Esq. It stands on an elevated position, and commands one of the most beautiful and varied views in the neighbourhood, in which the Laira, and the seat of the Earl of Morley, form prominent features. 1 m. N.W. Newnham Park, George Strode, Esq.

246¾ m. PLY-MOUTH STA.

DEVONPORT formed a part of Plymouth, and was called by that name until 1824, when it received its present name, an event which was commemorated by a fine Doric column, erected on a height. The town stands on an eminence, and is enclosed by ramparts, and defended by several batteries. The naval dockyard, which is similar to that at Portsmouth, occupies 96 acres. The buildings are nearly all of granite and limestone, and have a noble appearance. The residence of the Port Admiral, theatre, assembly rooms, chapels of ease, barracks, and military hospitals, are the principal public buildings. It sends two members to Parliament. Registered electors (1848), 2,161; population, 43,532; corporate revenue (1846-7), £1,873; expenditure, £1,420. Markets, Tuesday, Thursday, and Saturday. 1 m. N. Manudon, Mrs. Walrond. About 1 m. further, is Compton Hall, George Baughton Kingdon, Esq. 1 m. further, Maristow, Sir R.

PLYMOUTH (*continued*).

hospitals, freemasons' hall, theatre, Athenæum, library, the Royal Union baths, barracks, and the Royal Hotel, a first-rate establishment. Plymouth has four parochial churches, of which St. Andrew's is spacious and contains some interesting monuments, and has an embattled tower; there are also several places of worship for Dissenters of different denominations. Amongst its educational, learned, and scientific institutions, Plymouth boasts the following: a grammar and other schools, the Natural History Society of Devon and Cornwall, theological, law, medical, and public libraries, a mechanics' institute, a branch of the Bank of England, and several other banking institutions, and various well-endowed charities, producing an annual revenue of about £2,300. Of the government buildings we may cite the observatory, the royal naval and military hospitals at Stonehouse, the victualling office at Devil's Point, the gun-wharf, and the military prison—all these are solid stone structures. Plymouth Harbour consists of the Hamoaze (the mouth of the Tamar opposite Devonport) and the Catwater (the mouth of the Plym at the east of Plymouth), on which are situated Hoo, Oreton, and Turnchapel with their several wet and dry docks for merchant-ship building. The Sound also forms a noble harbour for ships of war by reason of the Breakwater built across it, a stupendous structure, and a noble work of art, composed of granite and marble, 1,700 yards in length and sixteen yards in width at the top, on the western point of which is a lighthouse. On the east coast of the Sound lies Borriland Bay, and at the west are Cawsand Bay and Mount Edgecumbe, and in it are several islands, the principal of which, Mount Batten, has a strong fortification opposite the Hoo. The trade of Plymouth with London, Newcastle, Bristol, &c. is very extensive. Its imports consists chiefly of West India and colonial produce, and timber from North America and the Baltic; and it has sugar refineries, a celebrated distillery famous for its gin, soap, starch, and glass works, manufactures of sailcloth, &c., and considerable pilchard and other fisheries. Its registered shipping amounts to 394 vessels, of the aggregate burden of 34,808 tons, and the customs' revenue amounted in 1847 to £108,055. Corporation revenue (1848), £14,154. Markets, Monday, Thursday, and Saturday.

Lewes and Hastings Railway.

Left of Railway from Hayward's Heath.

Distance from London.

38 m. HAYWARD'S HEATH STA.

1 m. N. BARCOMBE. Barcombe Place, George Grantham, Esq.; Beechland, W. H. Blaauw, Esq.; Newick Park, J. H. Slater, Esq.

47¼ m. COOKSBRIDGE STA.

4 m. N. PLATCHET PLACE. A little to the north, Malding Deanery, — Green, Esq.; Hamsey Place, — Whitfield, Esq.; Horstead Place, J. Barchard, Esq. 3 m. further, UCKFIELD.

50 m. LEWES STATION.

2 m. E. Glyndebourne, Sir James Langham, Bart. The mansion is a noble pile of buildings of the age of Queen Elizabeth, the front exhibiting numerous bay windows and other rich ornaments of antiquity. The terrace commands a fine view of the surrounding country. The church is in the Grecian style and of modern date. It is built of flint and faced with stone, having a spacious portico. The large east window is richly adorned with scriptural and other paintings.

PLYMOUTH
(continued).

Lopes, Bart. A little further, Buckland Abbey, Sir T. T. F. E. Drake, Bart., is situated on the eastern banks of the Tay, and was formerly a monastery of Cistercians, founded in 1278, by Amicia, wife of Baldwin de Rivers, Earl of Devon. Modern alterations have nearly obliterated the monastic character of this edifice, but its ancient features are traceable in various portions of the building. In the church of Buckland is a fine monument to Lord Heathfield, the illustrious defender of Gibraltar, to whom this estate belonged, who died July 6th, 1790. Roebury House, Sir R. Lopes, Bart.; Bickham House, J. H. Gill, Esq.; Pound, Sir A. Buller; Woodtown, — Cornish, Esq.; Walreddon, — Courtenay, Esq.; Sortridge, — Spry, Esq.; Halewall House, — Scobell, Esq.; Grenofen, Miss Carpenter. 2 m. further, TAVISTOCK, a parliamentary borough, town and parish, county of Devon, situated on the Tavy, here crossed by three bridges. The town is well built. It has a church, situated on the site of an ancient abbey, Dissenting chapels, guildhall, &c. Sir F. Drake was born here, in 1545, and the poet, W. Brown, 1590. Tavistock gives the title of Marquis to the Duke of Bedford, who has much property in the neighbourhood. 1 m. E. Mount Tavy, Mrs. Carpenter; Park Wood, — Bridgman, Esq. ½ m. further, Hazelden, — Hitchins, Esq. 1 m. w. Manor House, Duke of Bedford. 1 m. further, Killworthy and Hurdwick, Duke of Bedford. 6 m. further, Endsleigh Cottage, Duke of Bedford.

1 m. s.w. across the mouth of the harbour, Mount Edgecumbe, Earl Mount Edgecumbe.

6 m. s.w. Stoketon House. 2 m. N.W. of which is Pentillie Castle, J. T. Coryton, Esq. 2 m. further, Cote Hill, Earl Mount Edgecumbe. A little further, Harewood, Sir T. Trelawny, Bart.

Lewes and Hastings Railway.

Distance from
London.

38 m. HAYWARD'S
HEATH STA.

47¼ m. COOKS-
BRIDGE STA.

50 m. LEWES
STATION.

Right of Railway from Hayward's Heath.

Combe Place, Sir H. Shiffner, Bart.

LEWES, a parliamentary borough in the county of Sussex, situated on the river Ouse, which is here navigable from Newhaven and crossed by a stone bridge. The town, which is built on the site of the Roman station Mutuantonis, contains a grammar school, a county hall (a very noble building), county gaol, house of correction, theatre, and banks. Lewes boasts of one of the oldest almshouses in England, founded by Gundeda, fourth daughter of William the Conqueror. The borough sends two members to Parliament; registered electors (1848), 844; is a polling place for the eastern division of the county, and the head of a poor-law union. It carries on a considerable trade with London by Newhaven in corn, malt, cattle, wool, &c., and large sheep fairs are held here in September and October. Henry III. was here defeated by the Barons, A.D. 1264, and confined in the castle. Priory House, W. C. Mabbot, Esq.; Manor House, W. C. Verrall, Esq.

Glynde House, Lord Dacre.   2 m. N.E. Loughton, Sir Thomas Downman.

53 m. GLYNDE STATION.

1½ m. N.E. HARLINGTON, and 2 m. N. CHALVINGTON.

57¾ m. BERWICK STATION.

From hence there is a short branch to HAILSHAM. The only object worthy of notice is the church dedicated to St. Mary, nothing is known respecting its foundation; but we find it mentioned as early as the time of Edward III., it is a handsome edifice consisting of a nave and two aisles, paved with tiles. The tower is ornamented with a pinnacle at each corner and a vane in the middle. Major C. H. Sinnock. 6 m. N. HEATHFIELD, Captain J. T. Fuller; Heathfield Park, Sir Charles Richard Blunt, Bart.

61⅓ m. POLEGATE STATION.

⊲ Polegate Br.

3 m. N. HURSTMONCEUX. Hurstmonceux Park, William D. Gillon, Esq. Near the south edge of Hurstmonceux Park are the ruins of the castle, one of the oldest brick buildings in the kingdom. A little further, Windmill Hill, H. B. Curteis, Esq.

65 m. PEVENSEY STATION.

BEXHILL, a parish in the rape of Hastings, county of Sussex, remarkable for its various chalybeate springs.

72 m. BEXHILL STATION.

N.W. ORE. Cogurst Hall, M. Brisco, Esq., M.P.; Beauport, Sir C. M. Lamb, Bart.; Doune Lodge, William L. Shadwell, Esq.; Stoare Place, Dowager Lady Elphinstone; Ivy House, Mrs. H. Harkness; Mount Pleasant, H. E. Wyatt, Esq.; Valebrooke, Colonel Elliot; Ridge Cottage, Mrs. Whistler. A little further, Crowhurst Place, George Gatty, Esq. 1½ m. further, BATTLE. Heming Fold, George Duke, Esq. Ferme Ornée, beautifully surrounded by and adjoining the neighbouring parks, having Beauport, the seat of Sir Charles M. Lamb, Bart., on the east, the estates of Battle Abbey on the west, and Crowhurst Place, belonging to — Papillon, Esq., and the residence of George Gatty, Esq., on the south. Battle Abbey, Sir Godfrey V. Webster, Bart. The remains of this ancient and highly historical structure were converted into a mansion house by the descendants of Sir Anthony Browne, who purchased the estate of the grantee, soon after the dissolution of monasteries. Much of the old abbey had however been destroyed, and the materials sold. The grand entrance is composed of a large square Gothic building, embattled at the top with a fine octagonal tower at each corner: this is supposed to be part of the original building, at all events it is of very ancient date. The front of the gateway faces the town, and is adorned with a series of arches and neat pilasters. The remains of the abbey occupy nearly three sides of a large quadrangle, and it is supposed that the fourth was taken down when the opposite side was converted into a modern habitation, in order to open the view. The side of the square occupied at the present time by the dwelling-house has undergone the greatest alterations. The remaining side opposite to the gateway consists of two low parallel walls, which once supported a suite of chambers, and terminated in handsome turrets: this was part of another gate. On the outside of the house appear nine elegant arches, which are the only remains of the old abbey church, and in all probability belonged to the inside of a cloister. The other ruins consist of a great hall, or refectory, standing contiguous to the church; but the most beautiful part of the remains is a detached building, used as a barn. It has twelve windows on one side, and six on the other. Under the hall is a curious vaulted building, in the Gothic style, formed by crypts of freestone, divided by elegant pillars and springing arches. With the exception of a heavy modern roof, this may be considered the most ancient part of the abbey. This celebrated abbey was built in performance of William the Conqueror's vow, to found a monastery in honour of St. Martin, if victory crowned his

74¼ m. HASTINGS STATION.

53 m. GLYNDE STATION.	1 m. S.E. Firle Place, Viscount Gage.
57¾ m. BERWICK STATION.	BERWICK, a small village consisting of a few straggling houses. Berwick Court. 2 m. s. Little Hinton, Thomas Cutt, Esq.
61¼ m. POLEGATE STATION.	1 m. s. FOLKINGTON. Folkington Place, Thomas Sheppard, Esq., M.P.; Ratton, Thomas Freeman, Esq. 2 m. further, EASTBOURNE, which is also reached by a short branch from Polegate. Eastbourne possesses a theatre, ball-room, library, chalybeate spring, and a good beach for bathing. Within
Eastbourne Branch.	three miles of this place is Beachy Head, the highest headland on this part of the English coast, which rises 564 feet above the level of the sea, and has a lighthouse on its summit. Compton Place, Hon. Mrs. Cavendish; South-Field Lodge, Sir William Domville, Bart.; Rose Cottage, Robert Johnson, Esq.; Lark Field, C. W. Rowden, Esq.
	3 m. s.w. Friston Place.
65 m. PEVENSEY STATION.	PEVENSEY. It is reckoned among the sea-ports ravaged by Godwin, Earl of Kent, in the time of Edward the Confessor; it is also celebrated as the place where William the Conqueror landed with his invading army. On the east side of the town are the ruins of Pevensey Castle, supposed to have been constructed out of the remains of some Roman fortress.
72 m. BEXHILL STATION.	
74¼ m. HASTINGS STATION.	HASTINGS and ST. LEONARD'S. Hastings is a parliamentary and municipal borough, and one of the cinque port towns, situated on the English Channel at the east termination of this Railway; it is however connected by branches of the South-Eastern Railway with Dover, Tunbridge, &c., &c. It returns two members to Parliament. Registered electors (1848), 899; corporation revenue (1847), £1,939. The town, which consists of two principal streets, is built at the base of the cliffs which nearly surround it. On the marine parade, Pelham Crescent and the squares and terraces are very handsome residences. There are two ancient parish churches, and a new church which is a very elegant structure, a grammar school, founded 1618, a town hall, gaol, custom house, union workhouse, assembly rooms, baths, libraries, and capital hotels. Here is also a fort, and on the summit of the cliff the extensive and most picturesque ruins of the castle in which the Conqueror took up his abode prior to the fatal battle of Hastings. In the time of Queen Elizabeth the harbour was destroyed, and with it the extensive trade it then carried on; it has now no pretensions to commerce, beyond its fisheries and boat building, but it is one of the most favourite bathing-places on this part of the coast. Markets, Wednesday and Saturday. Manor House, Earl Waldegrave; Alton House, P. F. Robertson, Esq.; Hastings Lodge, Frederick North, Esq.; Bohemia House, W. Brisco, Esq. A little to the west, ST. LEONARD'S, a very beautiful new town commenced about fifteen years ago. The buildings are handsome, the new church displays great architectural taste, and it is altogether a most agreeable watering-place. Alligria, Robert Holland, Esq., M.P.; North Lodge, Thomas Wood, Esq.; Park Cottage, William H. James, Esq. 1 m. E. FAIRLIGHT. Fairlight Place, R. Batley, Esq.; Fairlight Lodge, P. Martineau, Esq. A little further, Bromham, Dowager Lady Ashburnham; Gesling Lodge, Arthur Louis, Esq.; Gesling Cottage, G. G. Monk, Esq. 2 m. further, ICKLESHAM. New Place, Henry Farncomb, Esq. 2 m. beyond which is WINCHELSEA, one of the cinque ports, a town of great antiquity, having been granted by Edward the Confessor to the monks of Fescamp, in Normandy. In 1006 the Conqueror landed here; and 1188, Henry II. In 1250 three hundred houses were destroyed by the sea, and a new town built a little further inland. It was stormed by Prince Edward, in 1266, and in 1287 the whole town was entirely swallowed up by the sea. In 1360 it was pillaged by the French; and in 1380 by the Spaniards. Henry VIII. built the castle of Camber, the ruins of which are

arms with success. 2 m. w. of Battle, is Ashburnham Place, Earl of Ashburnham. This noble mansion stands in the midst of an extensive park, abounding in fine timber, and well stocked with deer. The edifice was rebuilt under the superintendence of George Dance, Esq., R.A. The principal front is divided in seven compartments, separated by hexagonal turret-formed buttresses, and these, being carried above the building, supply the place of pinnacles. The centre, with its two side sections, is surmounted by a parapet with quatrefoil piercings. The intermediate spaces between the buttresses are filled with handsome labelled windows. The grand portico, a beautiful piece of architecture, projects so as to afford a convenient sheltered carriage-way. From the centre of a fine terrace a flight of steps leads to the park and canal, both of which are appropriately adorned and embellished. At and near Battle, are Vine Hall, T. Smith, Esq; Oaklands, H. Sharpe, Esq.; Marley, Frederick Webster, Esq. 4 m. N.W. Rose Hill Park, Augustus E. Fuller, Esq., M.P.; Rose Green, Don Miguel; and 6 m. N. Iridge Place, Sir S. B. Peckham Micklethwaite, Bart.

𝕻𝖆𝖉𝖉𝖔𝖈𝖐 𝖂𝖔𝖔𝖉 𝖙𝖔 𝕸𝖆𝖎𝖉𝖘𝖙𝖔𝖓𝖊.

𝕷𝖊𝖋𝖙 𝖔𝖋 𝕽𝖆𝖎𝖑𝖜𝖆𝖞 𝖋𝖗𝖔𝖒 𝕻𝖆𝖉𝖉𝖔𝖈𝖐 𝖂𝖔𝖔𝖉.

Distance from Paddock Wood.

2 m. N.W. EAST PECKHAM. Riding Hall, William Cooke, Esq.; Merewith Castle, Baroness Le Despencer.

3 m. YALDING STATION.

WATERINGBURY, a pretty village, situated in the most fertile part of the county of Kent, in the midst of gardens and hop-grounds. In former times it was a market-town. 5 m. N.W. Addington Park, Hon. Colonel John W. Stratford. 3 m. N. MALLING. St. Leonard's House, J. Savage, Esq.; Clare House, Alfred Wigan, Esq. A little further, at LARKFIELD, Bradbourne Park, Captain John Twisden. 1 m. w. of which, at LEYBOURNE, Leybourne Grange, Sir J. Hawley, Bart.

5 m. WATERINGBURY STA.

8 m. EAST FARLEIGH STA.

1 m. w. Barham Court, formerly called Teston Hall, Right Hon. Thomas Pemberton Leigh. This elegant and commodious residence consists of a centre and two wings; a small portico adorns the centre, having on each side two windows. The grounds are varied and beautiful, and a neat conservatory is on the right of the mansion. During the civil wars of the 17th century this house was plundered and demolished, and its owner, Sir Philip Botelor, grievously persecuted for his loyalty. He was afterwards slain at the head of the regiment he had raised in defence of the King. In the reign of William the Conqueror this mansion belonged to Odo, Bishop of Bayeux. 8 m. N.W. Preston Hall. 1 m. N.W. Boxley House, Viscount Marsham; Boxley Abbey, Lady Maria Finch; Brocklyn House, Edward Burton, Esq.; Sandling, C. Tracey, Esq.

10 m. MAIDSTONE STATION.

1 m. E. Vinters, James Whatman, Esq. The park is undulating and finely timbered, particularly with elm and oak, some of the elms measuring twenty-four feet in circumference at three feet from the ground. The old house was very much altered in 1582, and a great part of the present house is of that date. In 1783 Mr. Whatman rebuilt a great portion, and enlarged the park, throwing into it a very beautiful secluded valley of half a mile in length. The house contains a valuable and extensive library, and some pictures.

<table>
<tr><td>HASTINGS
(continued).</td><td>still standing. In the time of Queen Elizabeth it had attained its greatest splendour; but towards the end of her reign, the calamity of a returning sea began to be felt, the channel was at first choked, and by insensible degrees the whole coast was deserted. The population declined apace— the houses and churches fell to ruin, and desolation spread over the whole compass of the hill on which it stood, so that the town, once containing a space of two miles in circumference, is now shrunk into a small compass, and contains only a population of 627 souls. The Fryers, Richard Styleman, Esq. 2 m. N.E. of Winchelsea, is RYE, also one of the cinque ports. George I. once landed in the town, having taken refuge in the harbour from a storm. Leasham House, E. B. Curteis, Esq.; Springfield, Jeremiah Smith, Esq.; Conduit Hill, E. N. Dawes Esq.</td></tr>
</table>

Paddock Wood to Maidstone.

Distance from Paddock Wood.	### Right of Railway from Paddock Wood.
3 m. YALDING STATION.	1 m. E. YALDING. This place has been several times afflicted with the plague, particularly in 1510, 1603-4, 1609, and 1666. The contagion appears to have been introduced by taking children down from London. A little further, Jennings Hunton, John Savage, Esq.
5 m. WATERING-BURY STA.	½ m. S.E. WEST FARLEIGH, Sir Henry Fitzherbert, Bart.; Bowhill, Richard Whitehead, Esq. The following extracts, from an agreement between the vicar and his parishioners, in the 33rd year of Elizabeth, are curious: The communicant, first time, pays 1*d*., afterwards, 2*d*.; baptizing a child, 4*d*.; marriage, 1*s*. 6*d*., and 4*d*. to the clerk; burying a man or woman, 8*d*.; child, 4*d*.; herb garden, 1*d*.; grain, one-tenth as in all other things.
8 m. EAST FAR-LEIGH STA.	EAST FARLEIGH.
10 m. MAIDSTONE STATION.	MAIDSTONE, a parliamentary and municipal borough, and market-town, county of Kent, situated on the river Medway, which is here crossed by a bridge of five arches. It sends two members to Parliament. Registered electors (1848), 1,556. It is an assize town, and the principal place of election for West Kent. In the time of the Britons it was a considerable city, the various interesting ecclesiastical buildings it now possesses proves its importance in the middle ages. Its spacious church, known as "The Pilgrims' Chapel," has been splendidly restored, and may be regarded as one of the most ancient parish churches in the kingdom. Here are also the remains of a priory, part of which is used as a school, an ancient palace, formerly belonging to the Archbishop of Canterbury, and many very ancient and curious houses, and a market-cross. Amongst its public edifices, we may enumerate the town and county halls, county lunatic asylum, county gaol, house of correction, union workhouse, large barracks, county assembly and concert rooms, theatre, library, philosophical society, mechanics' institute, and the banks. Amongst its educational and charitable institutions, are a proprietary, and a grammar and other endowed schools, and numerous almshouses. The position of Maidstone, in the "Vale of Kent," is beautiful, the land is most fertile, and produces the best hops in the whole county. It was here that the hop-vine was first planted upon its introduction into England, in the 16th century. Vessels of sixty tons come up to the town, by which means the stone of the neighbouring quarries is exported. There are several extensive paper mills in the vicinity of the town, which is continually increasing in commercial importance and prosperity. During the civil wars of the 17th century, Maidstone stood two attacks from the parliamentary forces. Market, Thursday. The Mote, Earl of Romney. 6 m. S.E. Hollingbourne House, B. D. Duppa, Esq.

London and Greenwich Railway.

The advantages of selecting a convenient metropolitan terminus is fully shown in the case of this line. Had this line terminated even a quarter of a mile south of its present site, the whole of the south and south-eastward lines would assuredly have been carried to independent termini. The line leaving the London Terminus in the borough, runs along the side of Tooley Street to the right of St. John's Church, Horsleydown; thence crosses the Nichirigu and Grange Roads, and continues to the right of St. James's New Church, then slightly curving crosses Blue-Anchor Road, Corbett's Lane, and the

	Distance from London.
## Left of Railway from London.	LONDON BRIDGE STATION.
DEPTFORD, a parliamentary borough which, with Greenwich and Woolwich, sends two members to Parliament (see Greenwich), and a naval port, situated on the Thames at the junction of the Ravensbourne. Area of its two parishes, 1,060 A.; population, 23,165. It is a very populous but mean and dirty place. Independently of its two churches it possesses a well-endowed charity school, two very ancient hospitals for decayed pilots	DEPTFORD STA.
GREENWICH, a parliamentary borough and market-town, in the county of Kent. Area of parish, 2,030 A.; population, 29,755; population of parliamentary borough (including Deptford and Woolwich), 72,748. Returns two members to Parliament; registered electors (1848), 3,928. This town, which has undergone vast improvements within the last twenty years, has an European reputation from the magnificence of its hospital for decayed seamen, erected on the site of the ancient palace of the Sovereigns of England, the Placentia of the Tudors and the Stuarts, which is said to have been erected from the designs and under the superintendence of Sir Reginald Bray, Speaker of the House of Commons, who greatly assisted in the construction of Henry VII.'s beautiful chapel at Westminster, and St. George's Chapel at Windsor (see Manning's "Lives of the Speakers"). This noble pile, certainly the finest palatial structure in the kingdom, was commenced in the reign of Charles II., granted by William III. as an asylum for decayed or disabled seamen of the royal navy, and completed, by the aid of parliamentary grants, from designs and under the personal but gratuitous superintendence of Sir Christopher Wren. It consists of four noble quadrangles, between Greenwich Park and the Thames, having a river frontage or terrace 865 feet in length, bounded by a noble iron palisade extending throughout its entire length, which forms one side of the great square; the buildings on the other two sides are surmounted by domes of beautiful proportions. At the head of the square is the older portion of the palace, built by Inigo Jones. The hospital contains dormitories and dining-halls for 2,700 pensioners, independently of those who live outside the hospital; a beautiful chapel, ornamented with carved work, and one of West's best pictures—the Shipwreck of St. Paul; a spacious hall 106 feet in height by 56 in breadth, decorated with portraits of our great naval heroes, representations of celebrated engagements, the coat worn by the great and gallant Nelson when he received his death wound, his sword and other relics of the hero	3¾ m. GREENWICH STATION.

London and Greenwich Railway.

Surrey Canal, from whence it reaches Deptford, and from thence London Street, Greenwich; the whole distance being three miles and three-quarters. The entire distance is on a viaduct, consisting of eight hundred and seventy-eight arches of eighteen feet span. The whole width is twenty-six feet and the height twenty feet; the arches are eighteen inches and the piers five feet in thickness. Spanning the river Ravensbourne is a balance-bridge, which requires the force of eight men to raise it, when necessary, to allow masted vessels to pass above the bridge.

Distance from London.	
LONDON BRIDGE STATION.	
DEPTFORD STA.	and their widows, belonging to the Trinity House, and a naval arsenal, victualling office, and dockyards, founded by Henry VIII., which cover an area of upwards of 30 acres. The population is chiefly employed in the Government establishments, and in the private ship-building yards, which are numerous in this locality.
3¾ m. GREENWICH STATION.	of Trafalgar, the statue of the hero of Acre, &c., forming altogether a gallery of great historical and national interest. For the better support of this noble institution, the estates of the unfortunate Earl of Derwentwater, forfeited for his loyalty to the house of Stuart in 1715, were granted to it for ever, which, with other parliamentary grants and aids vested in commissioners for the management of its estates, &c., now amounts to an annual revenue of nearly £140,000, the expenditure being £134,233 per annum. Near the hospital is a naval school for the sons of officers and seamen. Greenwich Church is a very fine stone edifice; and of the various charities of the town we may cite Trinity Hospital, founded by the Earl of Northampton in 1613, and Queen Elizabeth's College, founded by the learned antiquary Sergeant William Lambard in 1558—the former producing an annual revenue of £2,270, and the latter about £700—with various well-endowed schools. The hotels of Greenwich are of a very superior order, and much frequented during the summer season for white-bait and other delicacies. Greenwich Park, one of the most favourite resorts of Cockneyism, and the scene of the most roysterous merriment during the Easter and Whitsuntide fairs, which attract thousands from the metropolis, was originally a portion of Blackheath, and was emparked by the good Duke Humphrey of Gloucester, who was Protector during the minority of Henry VI. It contains about 200 acres of land beautifully wooded, and numerous herds of deer. The hill in Greenwich Park upon which the Observatory stands rises 160 feet above the river. This building owes its origin to Charles II. who founded it in 1674; it is the residence of the astronomer royal, and the longitudes in all British charts are reckoned from this locality. Latitude 51° 28′ 6″ north, longitude 0° 0′. Of the original Palace of Greenwich, or as it was when repaired and partly rebuilt in the reign of Henry VII., not one stone remains; but for many centuries it was a favourite royal residence, and the birthplace of the bluff Hal and his daughters Mary and Elizabeth: here also Edward VI. died.

The North Kent Railway.

The London Terminus of this short but very picturesque line of railway between the metropolis and Rochester, or more correctly speaking of its suburb, Strood, a distance of thirty-one miles, consists of two narrow passages through the north side of the building of the South-Eastern Terminus, opposite Tooley Street, which serve the purposes of booking-offices for the first and the second and third classes. The platform for the departure and arrival of passengers is similar to that of the Greenwich Railway, to which it adjoins, and from which it is separated only by a wooden fence between the arched columns which support the roofs of the three stations, Dover—North Kent, and Greenwich, all which belong to the South-Eastern Company. Passing over the densely-populated neighbourhood of Rotherhithe, &c., by the old and well-known Greenwich viaduct, during which the traveller breathes nothing but sulphur and ammonia from the myriads of chimney pots just below the level of the line, at a distance of about a mile from the station, the eye is regaled with a view of the Surrey Hills as the train branches off to the right upon its own viaduct, which passes over low grounds and market-gardens, and is continued by an embankment and cuttings as far as the New Cross Station, from which point the country assumes a perfectly different aspect. Over the embankment of about thirty feet in depth at and near New Cross, are several well-constructed bridges of one and three arches, of a light and elegant appearance; and here and there are bridges for foot-passengers, composed of wood supported by lofty brick piers.

At the Lewisham Station, which is on the slope of an eminence, the scene is particularly cheerful, beautiful green meadows rising abruptly to the summit of the hill on the left, with here and there some remarkably pretty cottage residences and handsome gardens, and the common with its green turf intersected by various cross roads, and studded with country inns and houses on the low ground or valley to the right. The country from this to the Blackheath Station is exceedingly pretty. At Blackheath the heavy work of this line commences, and continues scarcely without intermission until the line enters the open country at the Plumstead Marshes. Deep cuttings, lined with brickwork, lead for a considerable distance to the entrance of the long, dark, dismal, and dreary tunnel, upwards of a mile in length, which crosses an entire angle of Blackheath, from which the train emerges near to Charlton and thence proceeds onward to the next station, within a stone's throw of Woolwich Dockyard. From this spot it passes onwards again through short tunnels and under numerous bridges, which indeed abound on this line, and through lofty retaining walls till it reaches the Woolwich Arsenal Station, and then has a run of some miles on a slight embankment through Plumstead Marshes; the view here being bounded on the left by the Thames, and the Essex Coast, the rising ground of Plumstead with its red-towered Church, and Abbey Wood lying on the right. Beyond the Abbey Wood Station to the right are the beautiful woods of Belvidere, and immediately on the left of the line the picturesque and venerable Church of Erith with its primitive spire. From the Erith Station to Dartford are occasional views of the river and its shipping, interrupted by a succession of short tunnels, bridges, cuttings, and embankments, and, indeed, along the whole line the engineering works sufficiently attest the great amount of labour which must have been expended in its construction. At the Dartford Station is a long viaduct which crosses the river Darent, and carries the line over that marshy locality. Here is a fine view of the town of Dartford on the

Left of Railway from London.

1 m. N. in Greenwich Park, Ranger's Lodge, Earl of Aberdeen. James I. often resided at Greenwich. His Queen, Anne of Denmark, added to the buildings, and laid the foundation of the house, now the Ranger's Park Lodge.

Distance from London.

4 m. NEW CROSS STATION.

5 m. LEWISHAM STATION.

The North Kent Railway.

right, and on the left beneath is a pretty lake-like pond, studded with little islands, and on its banks a neat residence near the large mill. Objects of considerable picturesqueness which attract the traveller's attention before reaching the Greenhithe Station, are the old sandpits, which are traversed by this line. They contain an area of many acres, the cuttings being of great depth, and it must have been the work of ages to have fashioned them to their present form. On their summits trees are growing to the very edges of the cliffs, and here and there are summer-houses in the same perilous position, while the bottoms of the pits are laid out and cultivated with vegetables. Through the openings that occasionally intervene, and in emerging from some of the short tunnels, the most lovely and diversified prospects now present themselves to the traveller's view. The wide reaches of the noble Thames, with the smoke of innumerable steamers gracefully curling in the air, contrasted with the snowy whiteness of the sails of the homeward bound merchantmen, all in motion, adds the greatest vivacity to the scene, which is bounded by the distant hills of Essex, while on the right is that undulating surface of richly-cultivated land for which the county and Kentish farming are peculiarly celebrated. At Northfleet another beautiful view presents itself, heightened by the picturesque appearance of Huggins's College, with its quadrangular range of buildings, and its elegant spire. From this station an almost continuous cutting, of great depth in many places, and crossed by a series of handsome bridges, leads to Gravesend. In the modern erections in this town, which have been necessitated by recent fires of great magnitude, there is a general improvement in the style of building, which has not been lost sight of by the Directors of the North Kent Railway, who appear by the taste they have here displayed to have emulated the public spirit of the inhabitants.

The Gravesend Station consists of two very pretty elevations of light-coloured brick, with stone dressings, the one on the left for the down train, that on the right of the line for the up train. Although both have considerable architectural pretensions, that for the up train is a much more imposing building than the other, and consists of a centre, with two slightly-projecting small wings, the space between which is filled up by a portico and entablature, supported by four handsome columns, and two pilasters against the wing walls, of fine stone. The Booking-office and Waiting-room is a well-proportioned apartment, with a large bay window in the centre, overlooking the line. Handsome glazed sheds cover each side line of way, which are sustained by iron columns, and the roofs supported by ornamental iron girders, the centre line of rail being open. From the station the cutting is continued, with occasional retaining walls, and numerous bridges over the line, until its junction with the Rochester Railway at Milton, near Gravesend, which follows the line of the old canal, and enters the town of Strood just after emerging from a tunnel upwards of a mile in length. This tunnel, which was executed by the Thames and Medway Canal Company many years ago, is the only work upon the line the merit of which does not belong exclusively to the Railway Company. We cannot close this brief account of the North Kent Railway without expressing our admiration and astonishment at the persevering ingenuity and the scientific manner in which the natural difficulties of this country have been overcome by the skill of the engineer. His selection of the line was bold and hardy, but the manner in which it has been accomplished is highly creditable to him.

Distance from London.	Right of Railway from London.
4 m. NEW CROSS STATION.	
5 m. LEWISHAM STATION.	s. LEWISHAM. The Limes, Edward Legh, Esq. This house and lands was formerly the favourite resort of the late Rev. John Wesley. Ravensbourne Park, Charles J. Blake, Esq.; Ivy Place, Charles Hicks, Esq.; Laurel Cottage, Mrs. Spring Rice.

BLACKHEATH. A large common in the lathe of Sutton-at-Hone, chiefly   6 m. BLACK-
in the parish of Greenwich, county of Kent, adjoining Greenwich Park,   HEATH STA.
which originally formed a part of the heath. Upon and around this
beautiful spot are many handsome villas and residences, and on, and in the
immediate vicinity, are two chapels of ease, and Morden College, with an
annual revenue of £5,000, founded by Sir J. Morden in 1695, for decayed
merchants, consisting of 30 brethren above 50 years of age, and a chaplain.
This spot has figured considerably in history, particularly as the scene of
the early insurrectionary movements of Wat Tyler and Jack Cade. The
heath is traversed by the Roman Watling Street, and, independently of its
curious caves, many sepulchres and relics of the middle ages have here
been discovered. From several points of the heath, near Greenwich, there
are beautiful views of the river and the metropolis. It is a favourite resort
of the holiday people from London, who frequent its annual fairs, held May
the 12th and October the 11th.

9 m. CHARLTON
STATION.

Woolwich Arsenal. This is the largest arsenal in England, occupying   9 m. WOOLWICH
upwards of 100 acres, and containing 24,000 pieces of ordnance, inde-   DOCKYARD.
pendently of other warlike stores, for both army and navy, with a royal   10 m. WOOLWICH
laboratory. In the arsenal is a foundry capable of melting from seventeen ARSENAL.
to eighteen tons of brass metal at one time; and connected with this
department is a splendid description of machinery for boring and turning
brass or iron guns, working in circular or horizontal directions with the
greatest correctness. In the extensive range of buildings near the wharf
are outfittings and every appendage for 10,000 horses for artillery service,
kept ready for immediate use. It is also the head-quarters of the Royal
Corp of Horse and Foot Artillery, Engineers, and the Sappers and Miners,
for whose accommodation here are substantial and excellent barracks.
Here are also barracks for the Marines and other troops, and a military
academy for engineering and artillery. The observatory and model
departments are situated on the parade, a fine piece of ground at the south
end of the town. Woolwich, in conjunction with Deptford and Greenwich,
sends two members to Parliament; and the county magistrates sit here in
petty sessions monthly.

To the left of the line are Plumstead Marshes, which were first enclosed   12 m. ABBEY
in the reign of Edward I., by the monks of Lessons' Abbey, from which   WOOD STA.
frequent communications were issued by the Crown for repairing the banks

6 m. BLACK-
HEATH STA.

Lee Manor House, The Right Hon. F. T. Baring, M.P.; Lee House, William J. Stuart, Esq. 2 m. s.w. ELTHAM. Cold Harbour, Lieut. Bedford, R.N.; Elmstead House, Edward Major, Esq.; Park Place, Mrs. L. Whitbread. A little further, Mottingham Court Lodge, Jos. Carter, Esq.;

FAIRY HALL, JOHN FRITH, ESQ.,

now in the occupation of James Hartley, Esq. It is a red brick mansion, pleasantly situated in a small park, in the rural hamlet of Mottingham, on the road to Chislehurst. The house was originally built by Henry Earl Bathurst, who resided here when High Chancellor of England.

9 m. CHARLTON
STATION.

CHARLTON. Charlton Manor House, Sir T. M. Wilson, Bart., a splendid mansion in the Elizabethan style. The church is also a fine edifice. Horn Fair, so called in honour of that saint, is held here on St. Luke's day.

9 m. WOOLWICH
DOCKYARD.
10 m. WOOLWICH
ARSENAL.

WOOLWICH. The town is situated on the Thames, county of Kent, but nearly separated from the river by the royal dockyard, the most ancient establishment of the kind in the British dominions. Some of the finest ships in the service were formerly built in this yard, amongst which we may cite the unlucky 'Royal George,' lost at Spithead, the 'Nelson,' 'Trafalgar,' &c.; but owing to the shallowness of the river, ships of a smaller draught, and principally steamers, are now constructed here. The dockyard has undergone great improvement of late years, and some fine new docks have been added to it. The town is irregularly built, and not the cleanest in the world; it possesses two churches, the old one placed conspicuously on a hill immediately over the town, several chapels and Dissenting places of worship, numerous schools, and a theatre. Area of parish, 840 A.; population, 25,785, mostly employed in the Government establishments. 1½ m. s. SHOOTER's HILL. Wood Lodge, J. A. Hooper, Esq.; Shrewsbury House, Captain Hornby, R.N.; The Shrubbery, Anthony Strother, Esq.; The Grove, H. A. Soames, Esq.; Bloomfield House, Captain F. Warde; Sevendroog, A. Turner, Esq. At this place is a tower erected to commemorate the reduction of Sevendroog, a strong fort near Bombay, in the year 1756.

12 m. ABBEY
WOOD STA.

PLUMSTEAD. Bramblebury House, Mrs. Dickinson; The Mount, Sir Edward Perrott, Bart.; Gloucester Lodge, William H. Power, Esq.; Manor House, John Russell, Esq. 4 m. s. BEXLEY. Lamb Abbey,

and breaches. Through insufficient attention, however, upwards of 2,000 acres were inundated in the time of Henry VIII., and were not wholly recovered until the reign of James I. It is here that the reviews of the artillery take place.

ERITH, a beautifully situated village, on the banks of the Thames, about two miles and a half from Crayford. Its ancient and primitive-looking church, nearly covered with ivy, with its slender steeple, backed by the ornamental timber of Belvidere Park, render this, particularly when viewed from the river, one of the prettiest and most picturesque spots between London and the Nore. Woodland Cottage, Mrs. Chamberlayne; Yewtree Cottage, William Crafton, Esq.; Veranda Cottage, James Page, Esq.

14 m. ERITH STA.

Edward III. held a tournament at Dartford, on his return from France, in 1331. The most remarkable historical event, however, connected with this manor, was the insurrection under Wat Tyler, in the reign of Richard II., which was as singular in its origin as in its termination. The insolence of the tax-gatherer so incensed the people of this shire, that they rose in arms, making Tyler their Captain. The King having refused a personal interview, they marched to London and siezed the Tower. At length Richard consented to a conference, and repaired to Smithfield, where he was met by Tyler, on horseback, who made such unreasonable demands, and insisted on them with such rudeness, even lifting up his sword in a menacing manner, that Walworth, Lord Mayor of London, with one blow of his sword laid Tyler dead at his feet.

17 m. DARTFORD STATION.

GREENHITHE, a hamlet, in the parish of Swanscombe, county of Kent, situated on the banks of the Thames. Many of its population, which exceeds 1,000, are employed in the chalk and lime works in the vicinity. The hamlet consists of a main street, with a pier in the Thames for the convenience of steam-boat passengers. Ingress, James Harmer, Esq. The house is beautifully situated in a park, the lawn reaching the Thames, and is entirely built of stones taken from Old London Bridge.

20 m. GREEN-HITHE STA.

NORTHFLEET, on the banks of the Thames, county of Kent. Area of parish, 3,980 A.; population, 3,621. The village is on a chalk cliff, rising to a considerable height above the river, and has a venerable church, with some curious brasses of great antiquity, some interesting monuments, and a massive tower. Near Northfleet is Huggins's College, a noble institution for decayed gentlemen and gentlewomen, in which the comforts of the inmates have received as much attentive consideration from its beneficent founder, as the architectural beauty of this Samaritan palace. The building is a very conspicuous object in the surrounding scenery, and the Christian kindness which prompted a single individual to found and endow such an institution, must ever be registered in the archives of the heart. Wombwell Hall, John Blenchley, Esq., Oldbury Cottage, Samuel Gould, Esq.; Rosherville Gardens, J. Rosher, Esq.; Brook Vale, William Hubble, Esq.; New House, Frederick Kelly, Esq.

22 m. NORTH-FLEET STA.

GRAVESEND, a municipal borough, river port, market-town and parish, on the banks of the Thames, county of Kent. The recent terrible conflagrations (two dreadful fires having occurred within a few years), though

24 m. GRAVESEND STATION.

N. Malcolm, Esq.; The Hollies, Thomas Lewen, Esq.; Penn Hill, William King, Esq. About 1 m. s. THE CRAYS. Pauls Cray Hill, James Chapman, Esq.; Frognalls, Viscount Sydney; The Rookery, General Samuel Crawford; Kivington, J. Berens, Esq.

14 m. ERITH STA. 1 m. N.E. BELVIDERE. Sir Culling Eardley, Bart. The house occupies a very beautiful situation about one mile from the river Thames. From the continued passage of shipping the view is uncommonly animated —not a sail can navigate the river but must pass in full view of the building, whilst the romantic situation of the mansion from the river excites the admiration of every passer-by.

1 m. w Holly Hill House, Mark Boyd, Esq.

1 m. s. Lessness Heath, Thomas Gilbert, Esq. A little further, CRAYFORD, Mrs. S. Barnes; May Place, John F. Burnett, Esq.

17 m. DARTFORD STATION. DARTFORD is situated near to the ancient market-town and parish of Dartford, in the lathe of Sutton, in the county of Kent, formerly a royal residence, to which purpose its ancient nunnery, founded in 1335, was converted at the period of the Reformation, and some remains of which now exist. Dartford lies in a valley, on the river Darent, which is navigable from the Thames, and over which is an ancient bridge. The church is a venerable structure at the foot of the hill, on the old Dover road, and the town contains a market-house, a county bridewell, union workhouse, grammar and charity schools, branch bank, almshouses founded in the reign of Henry VI., and other charities. It is the seat of the lathe sessions and a county court. Dartford has extensive gunpowder, paper, oil, and flour mills, with a factory for steam engines, and carries on a considerable trade with London by the Darent and Thames. Market, Saturday. West Hill House, E. Hall, Esq.; Bowman's Lodge, Mrs. King; Waterside, John Hall, Esq.; Low Field, Henry Mungeam, Esq.; Powder Mills, C. Pigou, Esq. 1½ m. s. WILMINGTON, Mount Pleasant, Major-General Monteith; Oakfield Lodge, Josiah Rolls, Esq.; Summerhill House, Mrs. E. Russell; Church-hill House, Mrs. Tasker.

20 m. GREENHITHE STA. A little to the s. SWANSCOMBE, Lieutenant Frederick Bedford, R.N.; Cross, Benjamin Ranyard, Esq. This place is celebrated from being considered the spot where the Conqueror, on his march was impeded by the men of Kent till he consented to grant them a full confirmation of all their ancient laws and privileges. Whether this story is true or not is uncertain, but that the Kentish men did preserve their privileges is a remarkable and indisputable fact, and these were as frequently insisted upon before the Justices Itinerant, in the reigns of Henry III. and his successor, Edward, and as frequently acknowledged and confirmed.

22 m. NORTHFLEET STA. 2 m. s. SOUTHFLEET. Was so named from its situation near Northfleet, and from its standing on a fleet or broad expanse of water, which anciently flowed up the Thames to this parish. This spot, it is said, was chosen by the Danes as a wintering place for their navy; and this seems to be proved by the fact of anchors having been dug up from part of the marsh, a considerable distance from the river; and if we consider the position of this valley and the size of the ships then used, this tradition is not improbable. Cadbury House, Francis Andrews, Esq.; North End, William Armstrong, Esq.; Southfleet House, Z. Piggott, Esq.; Betsome House, Thomas Tilden, Esq.

24 m. GRAVESEND STATION. 1 m. E. MILTON. Fort House, William Alexander Coombe, Esq.; The Grove, John Humpage, Esq.; Clarence Cottage, Joseph Mabbott, Esq.

calamitous, no doubt, to the uninsured owners of property, will have the effect of adding greatly to the beauty of the old part of the town, which has been nearly destroyed. The upper town is open, well built, and lighted, containing terraces, handsome rows of houses, new streets, and detached villas, commencing from the Old London Road, and extending to the top of Windmill Hill, from whence the most extensive and beautiful prospects are enjoyed. Inland, over a fertile and picturesque country, studded with ancient seats, while here and there the lovely villages of Kent, with their venerable embattled church towers, like distant castles, add imaginary grandeur to the scene. Seaward, all is motion, from the humble fishing-smack to the proud Indiaman; from the gay, green, mastless and matchless steamboats of the Diamond and Star Packet Companies, to the leviathan Scotch, Irish, and foreign steamers, which at every instant are heralding forth their approach from the dangers of the sea into the calm waters of Father Thames by huge masses of black smoke, which rise in graceful curls into the clear blue sky of the horizon. A constant succession of such scenes is presented to the visitor of Gravesend's famous hill, surpassing in beauty, if not in grandeur, the forests of masts collected in the port of London. The principal edifices of the town are the churches and chapels, market house, town hall, a battery, custom house, free school, some handsome endowed almshouses, theatre, bazaars, libraries, baths, concert room, and the new river piers, both of which are elegant constructions, forming most agreeable promenades, while the public gardens on the east, near the new pier, extending to the shore, are laid out with great taste, and are much frequented in the season. On the Essex shore, opposite to the town (to which there is a ferry), stands Tilbury Fort, a large brick fortress, erected by Henry VIII., and surrounded by a moat, which, from the marshy nature of the ground, may be completely laid under water. On the west, between Northfleet and Gravesend, lies Rosherville, famous for its garden, formed out of an old and extensive chalk-pit, in which there is every species of amusement for the public, consisting of dancing, singing, instrumental music, &c., concluding with a display of fireworks. Here is also a new and elegant river pier. In the reign of Richard II. the town of Gravesend was burnt by the French. Milton, next Gravesend, is a pretty village, with a handsome church. Markets, Wednesday and Saturday. Parrock Hall, Thomas Colyer, Esq.; Cliffe Cottage, Henry Ditchburn, Esq.; Parrock House, William Harvey, Esq.; Millers Cottage, Thomas Goddard, Esq.; Clifton House, Miss Penn; Ruckland Villa, Charles Spencer, Esq.; Parrock Cottage, Edward Tickner, Esq.

1½ m. N. HIGHAM. Hermitage, Mrs. M. A. Bentley; Brick House, Mrs. M. A. Street; Oakley, George Lake, Esq.   28 m. HIGHAM STATION.

STROOD, or STROUD. The terminus of this railway is situated on the west bank of the Medway, county of Kent. It is a long, straggling village, a suburb of Rochester, within its jurisdiction, and with which city it communicates by the bridge, to which we shall refer in our account of that city. Area of parish, 1,340 A.; population, 2,881.   31 m. STROOD, ROCHESTER, AND CHATHAM STA.

ROCHESTER, a city, parliamentary and municipal borough, and river port, county of Kent. Area, with Chatham, 6,150 A.; population of parish, 4,908; population of parliamentary borough, 11,943. It sends two members to Parliament. Registered electors (1848), 1,277; corporation revenue (1848), £4,300; customs' revenue (1848), £16,922; registered shipping, 17,625 tons. It is situated on a bend of the Medway, and communicates with Strood by an ancient and very handsome bridge of eleven arches, built in the reign of King John. Rochester contains many antique houses, and its principal street is long, narrow, and winding. The cathedral was chiefly built by Gundulph, the first Bishop after the Conquest, and is one of the best specimens of Norman and early English architecture. Its length is 383 feet.

2 m. s. HIGHFIELD COURT. 2 m. further, MILLPHAM. Camer House, William M. Smith, Esq. About 1 m. S.E. of Highfield is COBHAM. In the chancel of the church, which is very spacious and has lancet windows, there is a series of brasses in memory of the Cobhams, which are considered unrivalled for their richness, antiquity, and high preservation. Twelve of these are inlaid on grave-stones which measure 12 feet long by 8 feet broad, and are arranged in two rows in front of the altar. Wood House, John Braithwaite, Esq.; Cobham Hall, Earl of Darnley. The various dates at which this mansion had been constructed during several centuries, together with some alterations of a modern style, rendered it a building by no means handsome or agreeable in effect, until the late Earl, without destroying any portion of the original edifice, rendered it more uniform in appearance and improved its general aspect. At the end of the magnificent picture gallery, which occupies a portion of the principal floor of the north wing, is an apartment in which Queen Elizabeth is reported to have slept in one of her progresses through Kent, and in the centre of the ancient ceiling are still preserved her arms and the date, 1599. The apartments are truly grand and splendidly ornamented. The collection of pictures is very fine. The grounds and plantations have been arranged with great taste. The deer park and woods are very extensive, and many of the old oaks and Spanish chestnuts are of enormous girth and size. The avenue leading to the village of Cobham, consisting of four rows of lofty old limes, is one of the finest specimens of the old style of ornamental planting. The drives through the park are most perfectly picturesque, and the adjoining wood displaying the rich forest scenery and the varied prospects of the rivers Thames and Medway, render this place perfectly grand and beautiful.

28 m. HIGHAM STATION.

31 m. STROOD, ROCHESTER, AND CHATHAM STA.

1½ m. s. SHORNE. Court Lodge, T. C. Barratt, Esq. 1½ m. S.E. MERSTON. Gads Hill, J. W. Thomas, Esq.

The parish church of St. Nicholas is also a very venerable building; and the following are the principal public edifices—Town hall, a handsome brick edifice, built in 1687; custom house, theatre, baths, assembly rooms, two forts, the grammar school, founded 1542, with six exhibitions to the Universities; free mathematical school, with an annual revenue of £650; St. Catherine's Hospital, for poor women, founded in 1815; Watts' ditto, for the nightly entertainment of six poor travellers, revenue (1837) £2,503; Hayward's House of Industry; and other charities. Of the antiquities of this city we may cite numerous remains of ancient walls, gateways, and monastic structures; and on a rock rising from the river are the picturesque ruins of a Norman castle built by the architect of the cathedral, Bishop Gundulph, presenting to the eye of the traveller for many miles around the majestic keep of this noble and once powerful fortress. Coal is imported in large quantities for the supply of the city and country, and hops are its principal export; vessels of heavy burden come up to the bridge. Market, Friday. Next to Canterbury the bishopric is the oldest, but it is one of the smallest and poorest in England.

CHATHAM is a continuation of Rochester, and consists of one long, irregularly-built street, well paved and lighted, but remarkable in itself for little beyond its shops, which are well supplied. It is a parliamentary borough, and sends one member to Parliament. Registered electors, 893; population of parish, 15,411; population of parliamentary borough, 17,093. The heights around the town are crowned by strong forts, and its dockyard is inferior only to that of Portsmouth. It was founded in the reign of Queen Elizabeth, and occupies above 90 acres. It contains five tide docks, and six building slips for ships of the largest size, saw mills, forges, machinery works, roperies, an armory, officers' and artificers' quarters, a chapel, &c. The military and naval establishments are separated from the town by a line of fortifications, and comprise large infantry, marine, engineer, and artillery barracks, a school for engineering, and a noble marine hospital. Opposite the dockyard are moored the hulks for the convicts who work in the dockyard. BROMPTON, a military suburb of Chatham, is neatly and handsomely built. The parish church of Chatham is almost entirely modern, but a small portion of the old Norman structure is embodied in it. Bishop Gundulph's Hospital, founded in 1078, with an annual revenue of £3,000, a seaman's hospital, a proprietary school, a literary institution, and a museum, are the chief public buildings. The inhabitants of Chatham are chiefly engaged in the Government works, or in the necessary trades for the supply of those employed in the dockyard, and other establishments. Market, Saturday. Fairs, May 15th and October 20th. Races in August. In 1667, Admiral de Ruyter sailed up the Medway and burnt several vessels and stores, notwithstanding the forts. 11 m. S.E. SITTINGBOURNE, at and near which are Bedgar House, George Cobb, Esq.; Glover House, J. D. Dyke, Esq.; Rodmersham, Richard Demme, Esq.; Afton Court, Edw. Homewood, Esq.; Borden Cottage, J. G.

London to Epsom.

Left of Railway from London.

	Distance from London.
London to Croydon (see Brighton Line).	
½ m. S. Barrows Hedges. 1½ m. further, The Oaks, Earl of Derby. 1 m. S.E. LITTLE WOODCOTE.	13 m. CARSHALTON STA.
5 m. S. BANSTEAD. (See Brighton Line.)	14¾ m. SUTTON STATION.
	15¾ m. CHEAM STATION.
5 m. S.E. Nork Park, Dowager Lady Arden. The mansion was built by Christopher Buckle, who died in 1759.	17¼ m. EWELL STATION.
½ m. S.E. Woodcote, Baron de Tessier. 1 m. further, The Race Course. There are three race weeks at Epsom, the dates of which are regulated by Easter: one the beginning of April, the Derby the week preceding Whit Sunday, and the other in October; if, however, Easter should fall in March the Derby week is postponed a fortnight. The Derby stakes, which amount to the largest sum of any run for on any course in the kingdom, come off on the Wednesday, and the Oaks on Friday, and generally collect 100,000	18½ m. EPSOM STATION.

STROOD (*continued*).

Gifford, Esq.; Morrice Court, William Gascoigne, Esq.; Sharstead Court, E. B. Faunce, Esq.; Rodmersham Lodge, William Lushington, Esq.; Bobbing's Court, Thomas Knight, Esq.; Tunstall House, William Murton, Esq.; Trotts Hall, William K. Packman, Esq.; Bobbing Place, V. Simpson, Esq.; Marston House, J. M. Tracey, Esq.; Woodstock Park, Edward Twopenny, Esq.; Milstead Manor House, Sir John Maxwell Tylden;

GORE COURT, FRANCIS BRADLEY DYNE, ESQ.

London to Epsom.

Right of Railway from London.

London to Croydon (see Brighton Line).

13 m. CARSHALTON STA.

CARSHALTON, a parish, county of Surrey, has some claims to antiquity, and was formerly a market-town. It contains several handsome villas, and some mills that are worked by a beautiful stream of water, which, running through the village, adds greatly to its picturesque appearance. 1 m. N.E. Bedington Park, C. H. Carew, Esq.

14¾ m. SUTTON STATION.

SUTTON. The Manor House, Francis Gosling, Esq.

15¾ m. CHEAM STATION.

CHEAM. Lower Cheam, Sir E. Antrobus, Bart. 1 m. w. Nonsuch Park, W. F. G. Farmer, Esq.

17¼ m. EWELL STATION.

EWELL. The Rectory, Rev. Sir L. Glyn, Bart.; Garbrand Hall, Henry Batson, Esq.; Ewell Castle, James Gadesden, Esq.; Ewell Grove, Sir John R. Reid, Bart.

18½ m. EPSOM STATION.

EPSOM, a large and remarkably pleasant village on the road from London to Dorking; towards the close of the 17th century a place of fashionable resort on account of its mineral waters, the spring, situated on the common, being the first of the kind discovered in England. About 1640, the fame of these waters had spread into France, Holland, Germany, and other countries, from which were prepared salts sold at 5s. per ounce, and the demand was greater than the supply. In 1609, a ball-room

(Continued from page 258)

visitors. 1½ m. further, Tadworth Court, Mrs. Hudson, a handsome old Dutch house, built in the year of the Revolution. It has a fine old hall and superb stair-case, and when built was considered inferior to none in size and beauty in the county.

    2 m. s.w. Ashstead Park, Honourable F. G. Howard. 2 m. further, LEATHERHEAD. Randall's Park, Nathaniel Bland, Esq.; Elm Bank, Mrs. Clarke; Vale Lodge, Thomas Dickens, Esq.

EPSOM
(continued).

(Continued from page 259)

EPSOM
(continued).

was erected, and such was the course of visitors that neither Bath nor Tunbridge exceeded in splendour. About the beginning of the last century these waters gradually lost their reputation, through the knavery of an apothecary, who started in opposition a pump-room. At present the well is preserved, but few visitors resort to it. The principal source of the wealth of Epsom is derived from the races. Horton Place, John Trotter, Esq., M.P.; Horton Lodge, Henry Willis, Esq.; The Cedars, William Everest, Esq.; Abele Grove, Peter Hunter, Esq.; Pitt Place, Richard D. Neave, Esq.; The Elms, James Pierson, Esq.; Durdans, Sir G. J. Heathcote, Bart.

COMPLETE INDEX

for

VOLUME I

'All routes from London'

and

VOLUME II

'Provincial routes'